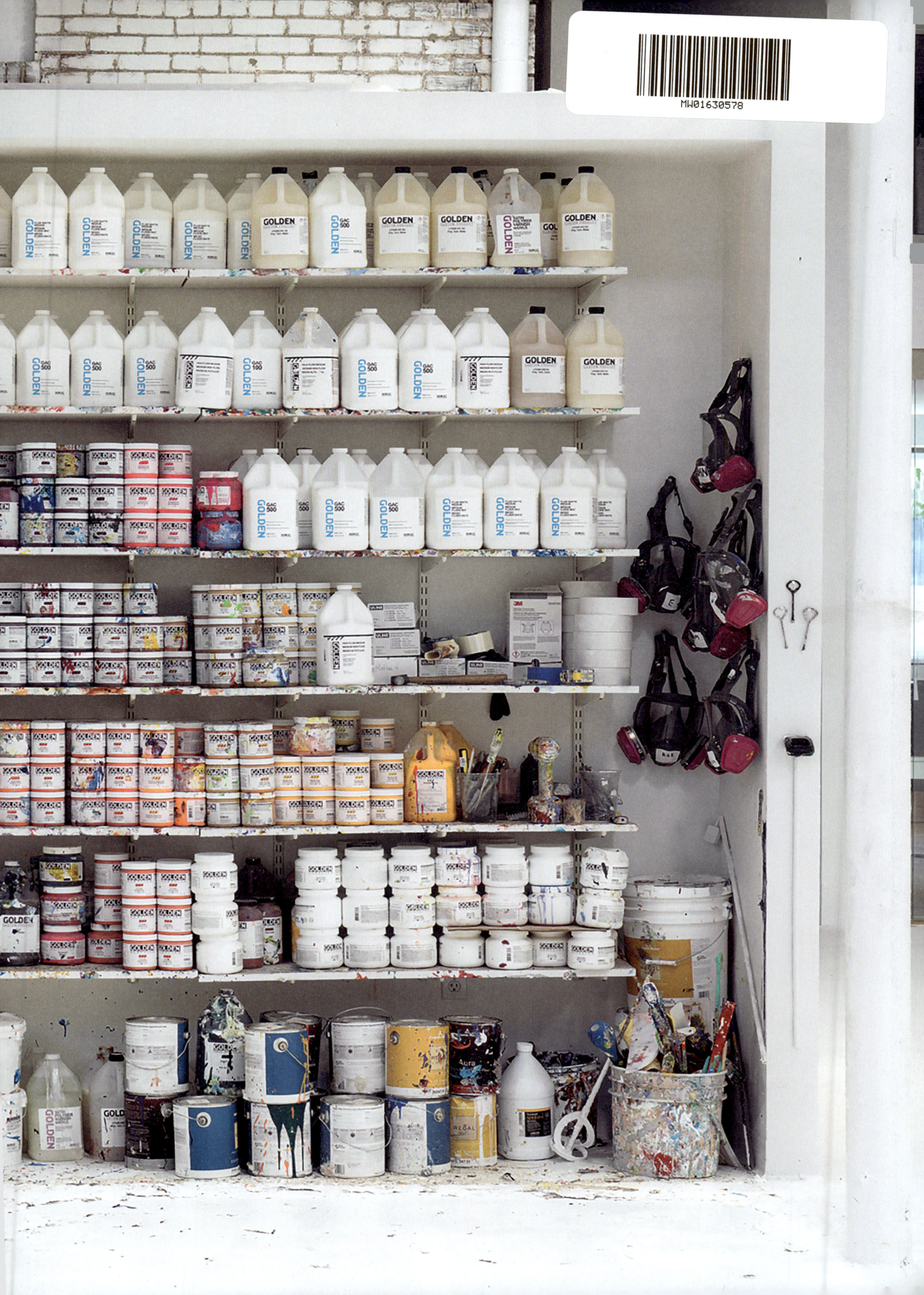
GOLDEN
GAC 500
GAC 100

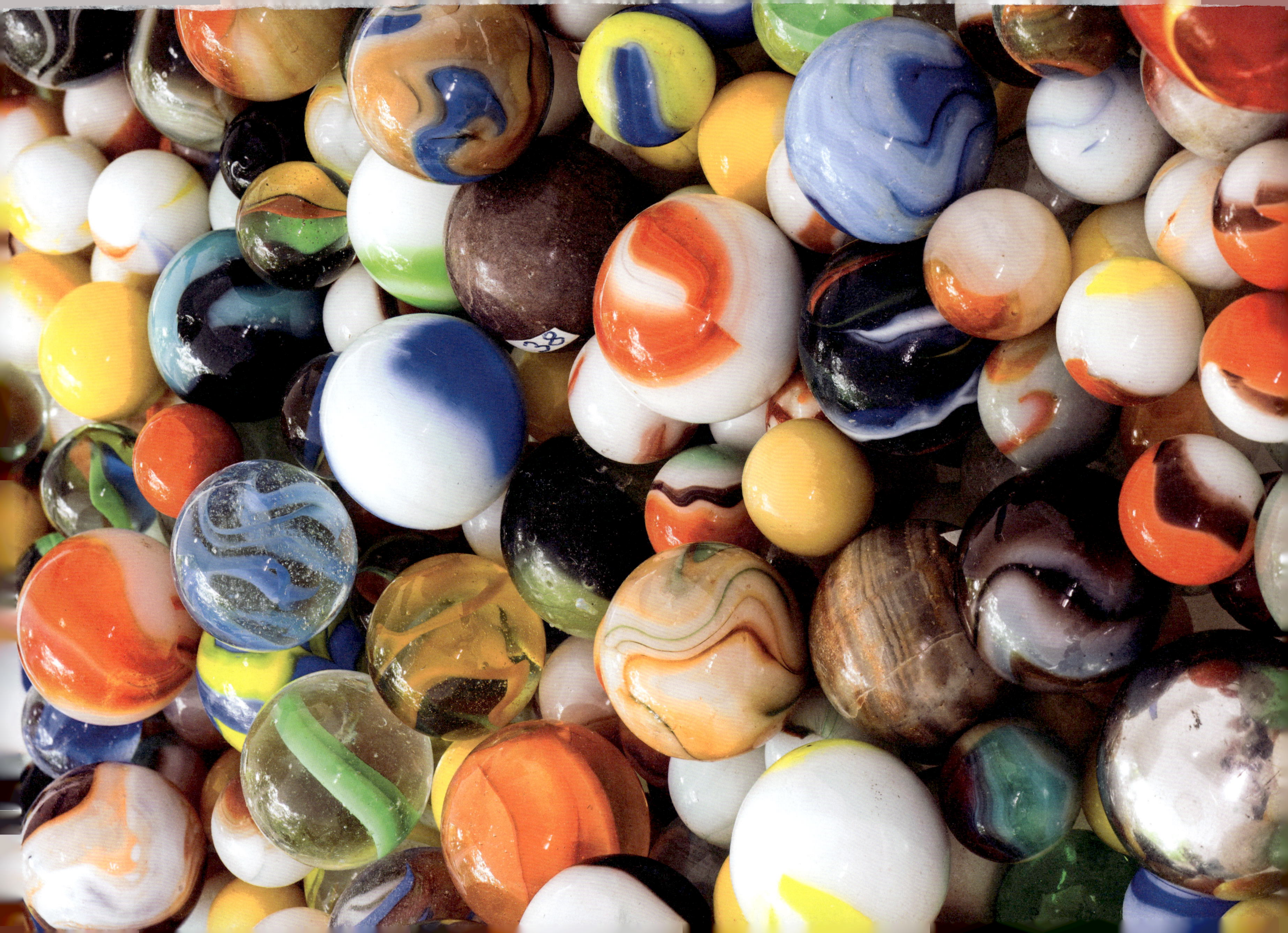
38

SAM GILLIAM

Texts by Ishmael Reed, Mary Schmidt Campbell, Sam Gilliam and Andria Hickey

SAM GILLIAM

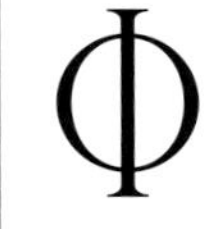

TABLE OF CONTENTS

7 GILLIAM'S RAINBOW
Ishmael Reed

12 SAM GILLIAM: A LIFE
Mary Schmidt Campbell

56 THE TRANSFORMATION OF NATURE THROUGH NATURE
Sam Gilliam

258 SAM GILLIAM: A DANCE OF ENDURANCE CHRONOLOGY 1933–2022
Andria Hickey

296 LIST OF WORKS
303 AUTHOR BIOGRAPHIES
CREDITS AND ACKNOWLEDGEMENTS

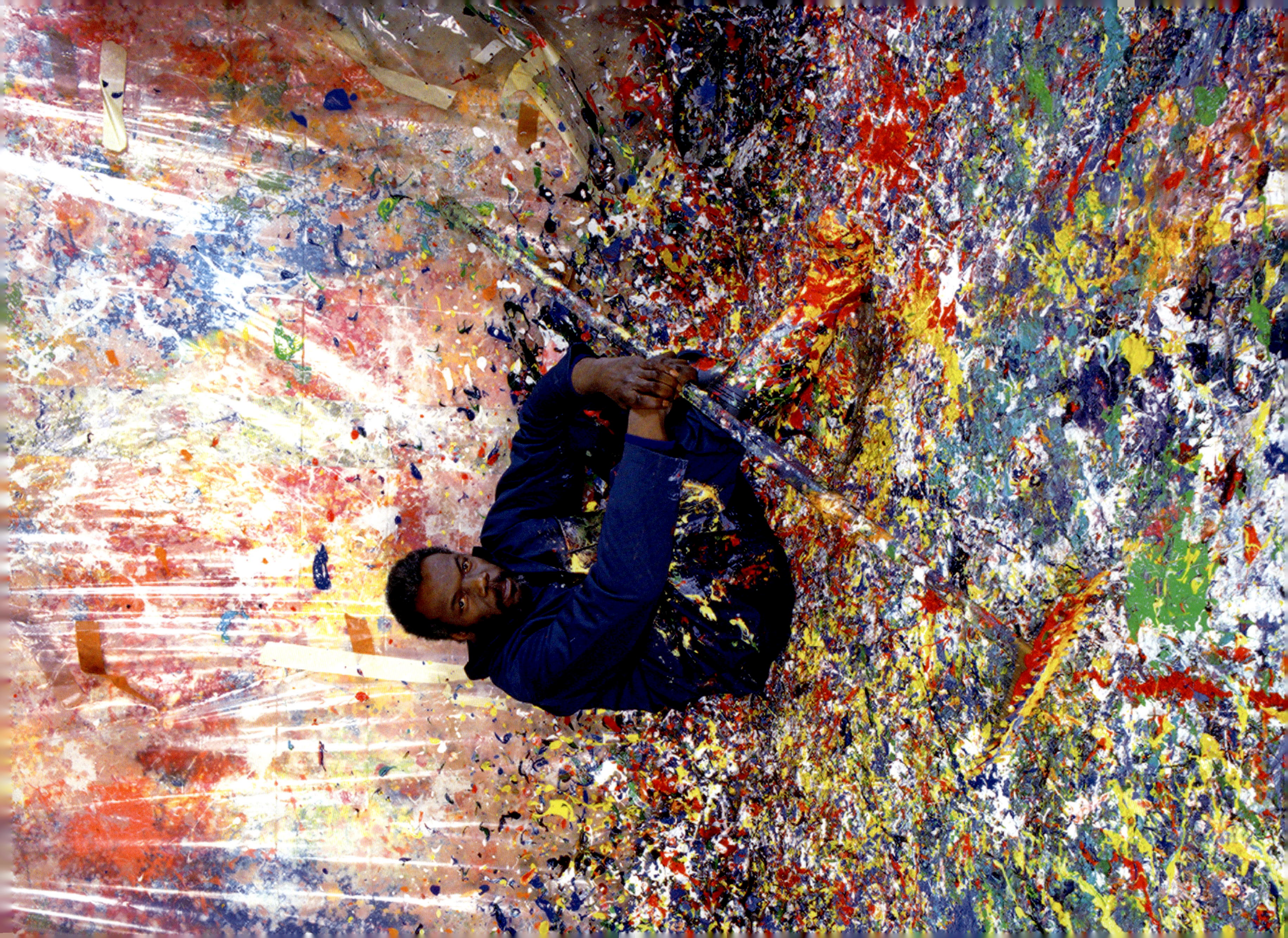

Sam Gilliam in his U Street studio, Washington, D.C., 1990

GILLIAM'S RAINBOW

Ishmael Reed

Sam Gilliam's art was about

Freedom, his paintings are

Not stationary but crawl across

The floor like roaming caterpillars

Museums could not pin them down

Like John Coltrane, whose horn

Wore out every chord in "Bye, Bye Black Bird,"

Gilliam got everything

One could possibly get out of

Cotton building on a tradition that reached

Back to coded quilts and

The Diné blankets that Noland

Copied.

The colors cascade like Niagara Falls lit at night.

The cloth draped like tapestries, or they're

Shaped as though they are about to be

Airborne, flying back to Africa.

His hues could be Frisco cool

Or Tupelo hot

Startled by the lack of a rainbow

That usually followed the rain

The people went searching for it.

They found it in Sam's studio

And that was OK.

—I HOPE THEY
FEEL THE
ENERGY AND
JOY OF LIFE
THAT COMES

OUT OF THE PAINTING. I PAINT WHAT IT'S LIKE TO BE <u>ALIVE</u>.

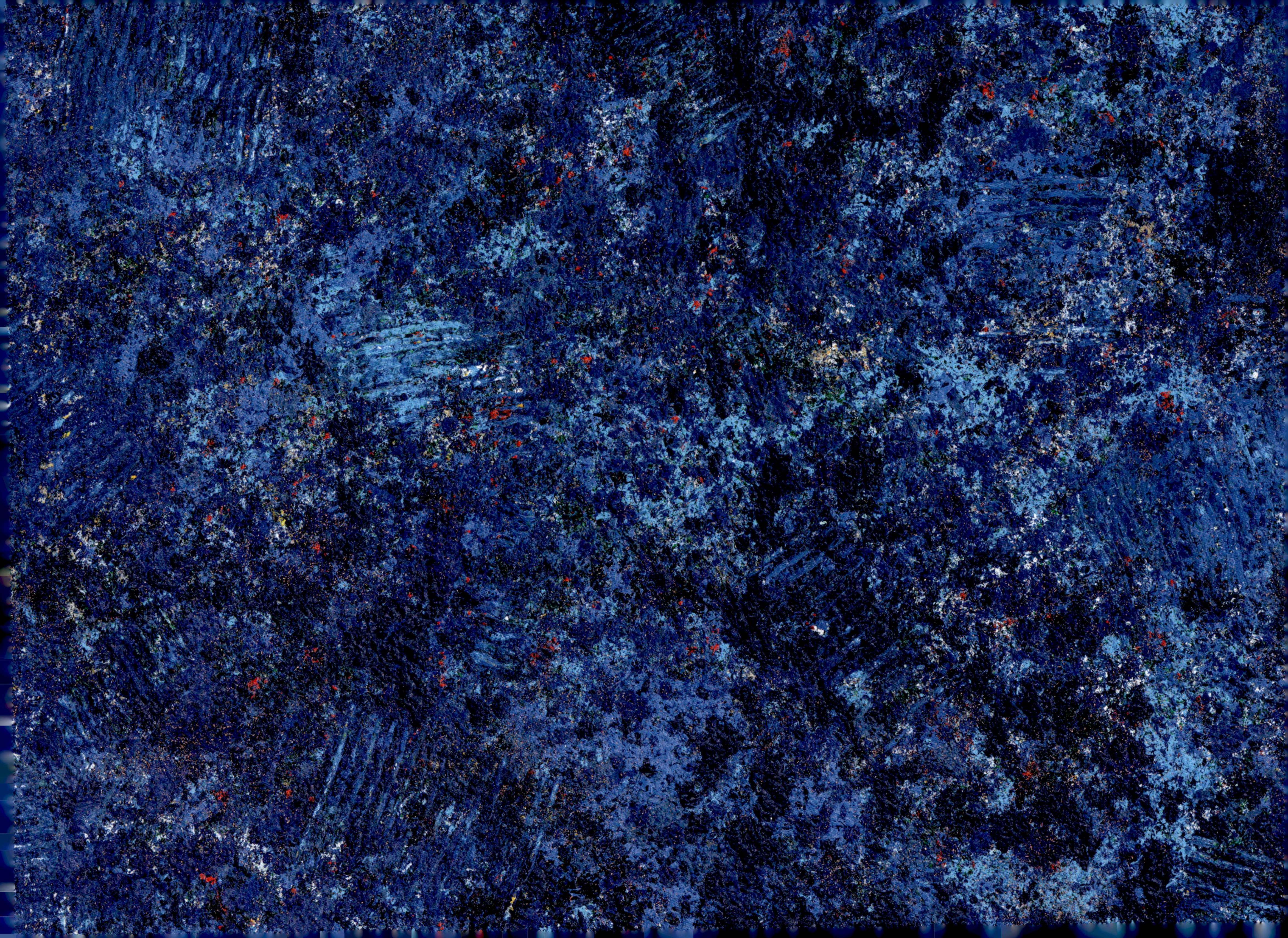

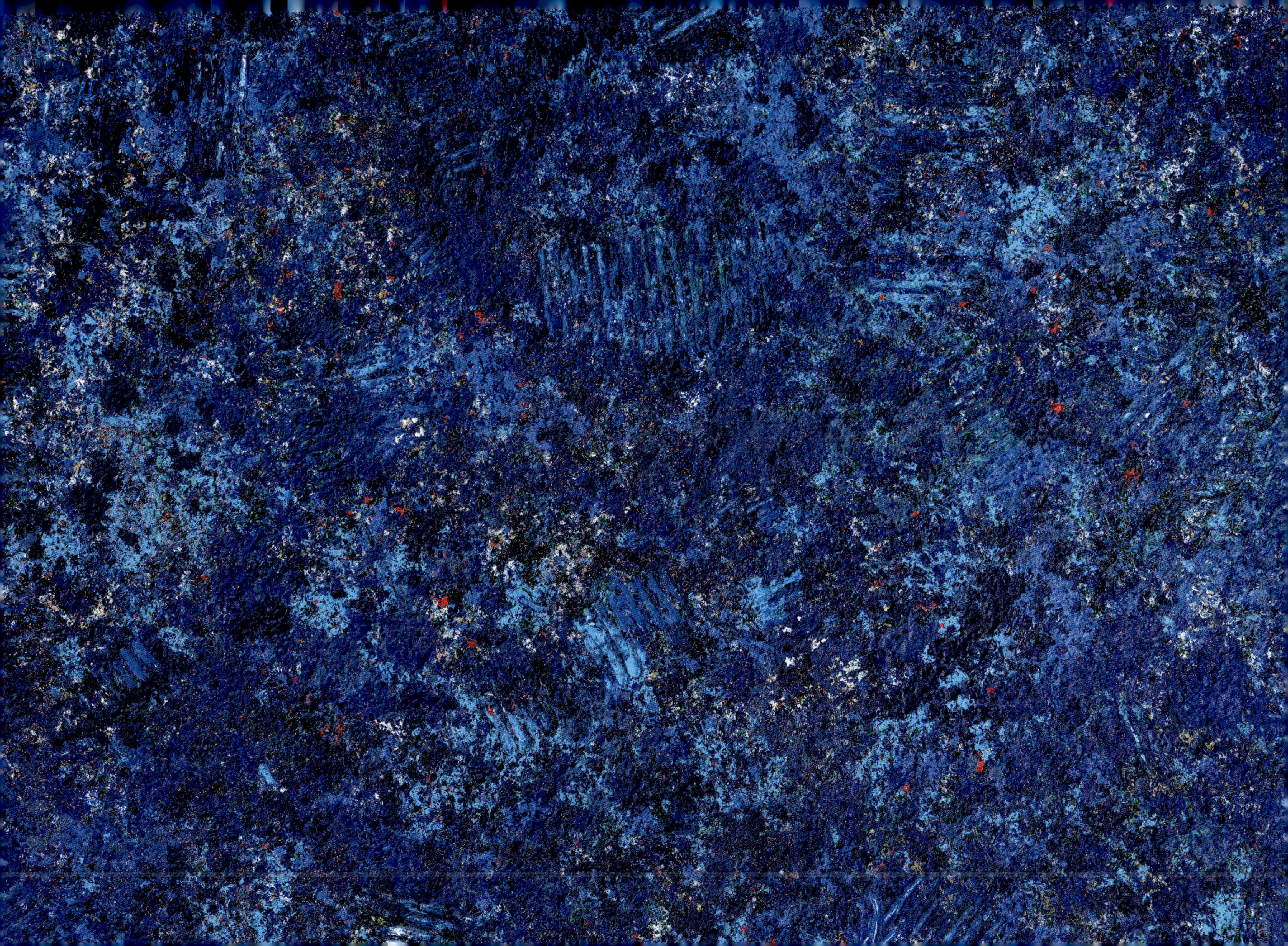

SAM GILLIAM: A LIFE

Mary Schmidt Campbell

In his later years, still at work in his studio, Sam Gilliam often referred to himself as 'Big Dog'.[1] Even as his health was failing, and his tall, athletic frame grew frail, Big Dog worked almost to the end, maintaining his characteristic air of supreme self-confidence. Gilliam's death on 25 June 2022 marked the end of a revolutionary, over six-decade artistic career and left in its wake studio bins filled with scores of works in progress. Ten years earlier, the maverick dealer David Kordansky had set off a resurgent interest in Gilliam's work, when he invited the artist to join his eponymous Los Angeles gallery.[2] An exhibition of Gilliam's hard-edge abstract paintings in 2013, curated by the artist Rashid Johnson, astutely reminded the public of Gilliam's historic artistic debut in the early 1960s, as an important member of the Washington Color School. Kordansky followed that show with one that focused on the period from 1967 to 1973, a time when Gilliam definitively demonstrated that his early affiliation with Color School artists was just the beginning. In the space of those years, Gilliam launched a rapid-fire series of innovations in painting that Johnson perceptively labelled 'serial manumissions', gaining Gilliam critical recognition as a singularly unique and original talent. A major solo exhibition, mounted in 2018 at Kunstmuseum Basel, Switzerland, titled 'The Music of Color. Sam Gilliam 1967–1973' included an expansive selection of works from this period, as well as an annotated chronology that demonstrated Gilliam's capacity for experimentation.[3] The display of the depth and breadth of his disruptive reinvention of painting ignited a firestorm of interest in Gilliam's work worldwide, critically and commercially.

In response to the resurgence of attention, the octogenarian announced, with his characteristic swagger, 'I'm just getting started'.[4] His words could not have been truer. Kordansky judiciously reintroduced Gilliam to the founder and owner of New York's prestigious Pace Gallery, Arne Glimcher. Of the same generation, Glimcher and Gilliam immediately bonded and in 2019, Pace Gallery became Gilliam's first gallery representation in the city. The Pace Gallery exhibition, 'Sam Gilliam: Existed Existing', containing all new work, debuted at the end of 2020.[5] Not even the onset of the global COVID-19 pandemic in early 2020 could interrupt the pace of Gilliam's artistic output in the last two years of his life. The works in that show were a revelation, possessed of a daring and bravado as fresh as anything he had created as a young artist. Gilliam, in the months before the show, was undaunted by calls to 'shelter in place'. To produce works for the Pace Gallery exhibition, he followed a strict routine. His wife, Annie Gawlak, would drive him to his studio every day, where, aided in the spring of 2020 by a new team of studio assistants, led by artist Jenn DePalma, Gilliam would enter carrying armfuls of books, albums, bottles full of marbles, anything that inspired him. He and his team donned HAZMAT

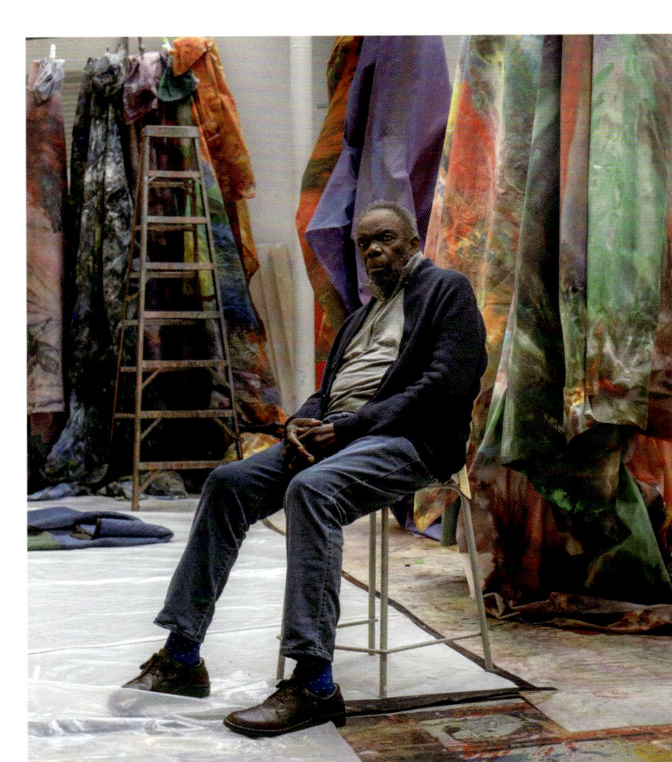

Sam Gilliam in his studio in Washington, D.C, 2018

suits, double masks, and scrubbed and sanitized every inch of the studio every day so that Gilliam could work non-stop.[6] Spreading entire rolls of canvas on the floor, he resumed his 'serial manumissions' with renewed energy. Gawlak estimates that in the last two years of his life, he produced more than one hundred new works.

The opening of the Pace Gallery show, delayed to the end of 2020, was yet another success in a series of late-in-life exhibitions that added to the narrative of a remarkable career. One of those shows was suggested to Gilliam by Oliver Shultz, Chief Curator at Pace Gallery, New York.[7] He invited Gilliam to reunite with sculptor Melvin Edwards, and Gilliam responded enthusiastically, suggesting that painter William T. Williams also be included. Edwards and Williams were two artists with whom Gilliam had forged one of his most important life-long relationships and the 'three amigos', as Gilliam called the trio, had a history of joint exhibitions that stretched over decades. They discovered one another in 1969 at the Studio Museum in Harlem's exhibition, 'X to the Fourth Power' (more about that later), organized by Williams, where they exhibited together with the painter Steven Kelsey. Shultz chose the title, 'Epistrophy', for its relevance to jazz – a title taken from a jazz composition by pianist Thelonious Monk and drummer Kenny Clarke – as well as for its meaning in poetry. *Epistrophe*, a refrain or repetition, suggested the recurrent coming together the artists enjoyed over the course of their careers. Programming that accompanied the exhibition included a music and spoken-word event presented by the scholar Brent Hayes Edwards.[8] The show opened in April 2022 at Pace Gallery, a few months before Gilliam's death.

One of the last major tributes to Gilliam was in his hometown of Washington, D.C., at the Hirshhorn Museum and Sculpture Garden. 'Full Circle' displayed earlier work by Gilliam in the museum's permanent collection in concert with an exciting selection of new paintings. In addition to the American celebrations, literally dozens of solo and group shows worldwide in his final years paid homage to various aspects of the artist's prolific output.

Gilliam would have claimed all these late-in-life tributes as his rightful legacy. Gawlak once observed, 'there are twelve Sam Gilliams and Sam enjoyed being each and every one of them', even, one might add, when they contradicted each other.[9] His unshakeable self-confidence was incubated in the heart of the Jim Crow south and mid-west, inside the cocoon of a large, supportive family, his first artistic community, and continued with an education that affirmed his artistic talent from elementary to graduate school. He entered the world as an artist in the late 1950s, slender, tall (6 foot 2), dark-skinned and regal in his bearing, striding into any setting with an air of assured belonging. In his lifetime, he was a part of many worlds. He was as comfortable in the classroom of the predominantly Black McKinley Technical High School in Washington, D.C., teaching teenagers what it meant to be an artist, as he was in the galleries of the Museum of Modern Art (MoMA), displaying his large-Drape paintings. He counted Washington, D.C. artist Rockne Krebs and master printmaker Lou Stovall as artistic partners. He travelled easily around the world, crossing cultural boundaries and could engage a collaborative team of German craftspeople to assist in the fabrication of a major installation as effectively as he managed a team of assistants in his studio. His mentors included the scholar James A. Porter, renowned historian of African American art and chair of the art department at Howard University (Porter counselled him to teach High School as a means of making a living while he painted), as well as Washington Color School painter Thomas Downing or museum directors Walter Hopps at the Corcoran Gallery of Art in Washington, D.C. and Peter Morrin at the Speed Art Museum in Louisville (on whose board he sat for several years). Though some members of the Black Arts Movement and other Black nationalists chided him for adopting abstraction, charging that abstract art was irrelevant to the realities and struggles of Black people, Gilliam was steadfast in his aesthetic stand. Proud to be affiliated with the Washington Color School painters as a young man, he exhibited with them regularly, just as he regularly exhibited his work in exhibitions featuring Black artists exclusively.

The evolution of the multiple Gilliams, and the artist's ability to stand inside of the clash and disruption of the contradictions, is a story that proceeds along multiple paths with detours, U-turns and occasional rest stops. To look at his life's work at any given point in his career, is to feel the push and pull of dynamic forces in motion. It is also to experience his firm grasp of the history of his medium, the history of his people, his generosity of spirit and occasionally his outrage, his whimsy, his mischievousness and, at times, his sorrow. Gilliam's work often radiates exhilaration, manifest most often in the audacity of his artistic gestures and breathtaking expressions of beauty. What he has left behind is a body of work created in a language unmistakably his own. In so doing, he mastered an astonishing range of media, materials, spaces, working processes, themes and art-historical precedents to carve out his own singular canonical presence in the history of modern art. This book charts Gilliam's path forward, the geographies he traversed, the clashes and contradictions he encountered along the way, and the work that challenges us to experience the world with our imaginations fully charged.[10]

Gilliam came of age at a turbulent time in our country. The demands for basic civil liberties of Civil Rights and Black nationalist movements in the United States were growing ever more urgent. At the same time, across the continent of Africa, one nation after another was declaring its independence from decades of European colonialism and cultural hegemony. As a young Black person in the United States, during this era, I remember feeling a sense of infinite possibility and a rapidly expanding sense of freedom to choose a life – in my case, as an art historian – never before chosen in my family. To a young Black artist like Gilliam, freedom meant fierce independence. He chose abstraction as his artistic language and like any number of other Black artists who also worked in an abstract idiom during that era –

Williams and Edwards, as mentioned earlier, and Jack Whitten, Al Loving, Howardena Pindell, Barbara Chase-Riboud, Richard Hunt – stood firm against his critics.

This essay is comprised of two sections. The first looks at Gilliam's roots, his childhood in the South during the Great Depression, his upbringing within the embrace of his family, his education as an artist in Louisville and early years in Washington, D.C. From 1962, Washington was his lifelong home. Washington is where he and his first wife, Dorothy Butler Gilliam, raised three talented daughters – Stephanie, Melissa, and Leah Franklin – and where he gained national and international art-world acclaim. Washington is where he would spend the last forty years of his life with his widow: artist, art dealer and thought partner, Gawlak.

The velocity of Gilliam's early development is rare for young artists, let alone a young Black artist in the United States. Gilliam quickly dropped figurative abstraction and moved to non-objective abstraction in his first year in the capital, gaining recognition as a serious modernist painter in the process. His experiments with paint applied directly to unprimed canvas in a hard-edge style were inspired by the works of other Washington Color School painters, especially Kenneth Noland and Morris Louis. As Gilliam began to innovate with stretched and unstretched canvas, he pushed boldly past the boundaries of the Color School and followed instead his own distinctive artistic impulses. Five years after his arrival in D.C., he enjoyed a solo exhibition at The Phillips Collection, one of the country's oldest museums devoted to modernism. By the end of the 1960s, his signature Drape paintings catapulted him to national recognition. Inclusion in the 1972 Venice Biennale raised his visibility in the global art world. From there, Gilliam's stature continued to grow as he moved with assurance from one major innovation to another, creating new possibilities for modernist painting. He was like an explorer, always searching out new territory, clearing the terrain for others to follow in whatever he discovered, but never lingering too long himself. The phrase that Johnson invented, 'serial manumissions', is particularly apt. It literally means freedom from prior servitude. Gilliam's work always seemed to be liberating itself from any interpretation or set of expectations that would confine him or make him predictable.

The second section focuses on the multiple ways in which Gilliam engaged his artistic language. In one of his many recorded interviews, he observed, 'sometimes I comment to myself; sometimes I comment to an audience'.[11] He was constantly placing his work in conversation with himself. In a 1986 Commencement speech, delivered to young art students at Memphis School of Art, he references the thoughts of the early twentieth-century American artist Robert Henri, who in the slim 1923 volume *The Art Spirit*, counsels young artists to think about the work they create as treasures they accumulate over time. Drawing on this advice, Gilliam advised the young artists to think of those works as being stored in a knapsack that, from time to time, they can reach back to plunder.[12] He spent a lifetime plundering his own work, re-discovering and re-working themes, materials, media and processes. An ardent student, he studied other artists from other eras; but he also studied himself. Watercolour was an early and life-long inspiration, the movement of colour on paper enabling him to surrender control of the motion of paint.

Shedding the stretcher and draping stained, brushed, daubed and soaked canvas is an approach that he discovered early in his career and one that lends itself to a wide range of expressions. He experimented further by adding new media to his vocabulary. His interest in printmaking sent him to printmaking shops all over the United States. His partnership with Washington, D.C. artist and master printmaker Lou Stovall and Stovall's Studio Workshop, Inc. thrived over his lifetime, the two producing a collaborative publication.[13] He exercised dominion over the malleability of canvas by draping, folding, shaping the fabric into tondos, cowls and tents in ways that injected new energy into painting. He called attention to the versatility of surface by using paint thin enough to see the weave of the material, or thick and encrusted with layer upon layer that he would rake, scrub, paint over, erase and paint again, sometimes adding bits and pieces of collaged elements, everything from fragments of canvas to the debris in his studio. His artistic heroes were always hovering close: Barnett Newman, Kazimir Malevich, Georges Braque, Joan Miró, Romare Bearden, Renaissance painters (Tintoretto in particular), Constructivists, avant-garde jazz musicians, the poet Pablo Neruda, writer Ralph Ellison and sculptor Thaddeus Mosley. Just as he plundered the knapsack of his past work, he plundered the treasure trove of worlds past. Colour was always dominant and, as his work matured, scale became an essential component. Scale, the way his work enters space, changes the space it occupies, sets the tone and pace of the way we, the spectators, must respond in space becomes a critical component of much of Gilliam's work. Though non-representational, his painting finds ways to relate itself to the human body, to architecture, to the natural world.

Commenting to an audience was important as well. There is no doubt that Gilliam's innovations altered the dialogue around painting, but they also opened up a dialogue between artist and spectator. The humanity of that dialogue, his impulse to engage, perplex or play is important to his legacy. Gilliam's sense of engagement appealed especially to other artists, and he has influenced not only visual artists like Johnson, Mark Bradford or Julie Mehretu, but musicians like Jason Moran, writer Ishmael Reed and scholar/poet Fred Moten, among many others. His work is often a conversation, not always comforting, but a conversation nonetheless. His decision to take on monumental public commissions suggests the extent to which he relished public engagement and understood the power of art to create a sense of place and community. Making connections began with his earliest community, his family and the environments of Tupelo and Louisville. By the end of his life, as he himself said, he was as close to those early communities that shaped him as he would ever be.

PART I: BECOMING SAM GILLIAM FROM TUPELO TO WASHINGTON, D.C.

The older you get the more you think about what your beginning was like. So that I think the South has a lot of influence in my work.[14]

Sam Gilliam Jr. was the seventh of Estery and Sam Gilliam, Sr.'s eight children. He was born in Tupelo, Mississippi, on 30 November 1933, to parents who respected creative handiwork. His father, who worked on the railroad, was also a carpenter and his mother was a seamstress and homemaker. Gilliam displayed his creative talent early on, drawing pictures in the dirt or assembling toys constructed from wood and flattened bottle tops. His mother encouraged him by providing sheets of paper and cardboard that he filled with images of the horses he saw all around him – horse-drawn milk carts, ice carriages, junk haulers. 'I became an artist in Mississippi', he would report to Kenneth Young, the interviewer for the 1984 oral history at the Archives of American Art (AAA).[15] He especially admired his multi-talented father, whom he remembers as always at work, fastidiously constructing things and assuming the multiple roles not only of carpenter but 'a farmer, a baseball pitcher, a deacon, a janitor'. Gilliam has said of his father, 'He is who I became'.[16] Along with his parents, his seven siblings, each creative in his or her own right, five sisters and two brothers – Isabella, Essie, Lizzie, Clenteria, Lillie, Clarence and Calvin – were the bedrock of Gilliam's childhood. Though the adult Gilliam would rebel against participating in organized religion, his family was anchored in the church. Attendance was mandatory. He recalls one of his church elders, an 'auntie' paying him for one of his drawings, reinforcing the value of his artistic gifts. At home, he benefited from the discipline of sitting around the dining room table with all his siblings every night to listen to each recite his or her lessons.[17]

The family's move to the more progressive, though still segregated, city of Louisville in 1941 only strengthened the young artist's self-assurance.[18] Gilliam had high praise for his Central High School teachers. In the 1984 AAA interview, he notes that because 'Central was a segregated school, in a very segregated world, persons felt extra responsible to build you through your dreams and to literally send you where you really wanted to go'. He goes on to observe, 'your studies were like your wings'.[19] He entered the Hite Art Institute at a newly integrated University of Louisville in 1951, joining a growing number of Black students around the country who were choosing professional training in the arts. The Cooper Union for the Advancement of Science and Art, Pratt Institute in New York, the School of the Art Institute of Chicago, and the Master of Fine Arts (MFA) program at Yale were among a few art schools noteworthy for producing leading Black American artists in the late 1950s and early 1960s.[20]

In addition to being integrated, the University of Louisville was progressive in other ways. German expatriate artists, champions of European modernism, escaping the persecution of the Nazi government during World War II, had emigrated to the United States. Several found their way to the University of Louisville. Justus Bier, a German Jewish scholar, chaired the Fine Arts Department. He was joined by German artists Ulfert Wilke and Charles Crodel. Wilke, a German expressionist, was affiliated with leading Abstract Expressionists such as Ad Reinhardt, Mark Rothko, Robert Motherwell and David Smith.[21] Gilliam once told an interviewer that his European professors were more involved with Black culture than his American professors.[22] He worked as a studio assistant to Wilke, with the job of running the slide projector in Wilke's classes – an assignment that allowed the young artist to see a range of artistic styles from different eras and cultures. He also developed a liking for his teacher's art collection, which consisted of German woodcut prints, African sculpture and watercolours by Paul Klee, whose work would influence Gilliam's early forays into non-objective abstraction. Gilliam revelled in this environment that was rapidly expanding his horizons.

After graduation, having been a member of the Reserve Officer Training Corp (ROTC), he went on to serve in the United States Army for two years.[23] Service became yet another opportunity to expand his cultural horizons. While stationed in Yokohama, Japan, he recalls his introduction to Kabuki theatre, visiting a show of Yves Klein in Tokyo that made a deep impression, and seeing a Pablo Picasso show in a Yokohama gallery. He remembers, too: 'the ritual, climbing mountains, Japanese songs … Within the cultural element of Buddhism, the stillness, etc … you begin to understand the meaning of time … And from that I started making a lot of watercolors'.[24] An anecdote from that period is telling. When he accompanied a group of Japanese people on a hike up a nearby mountain they happily taught their tall companion Japanese folk songs. On the way down, Gilliam reciprocated by teaching them something quintessentially American, the Bunny Hop, a rock and roll dance of the 1950s, which they cheerfully performed on their way home.[25] After his honourable discharge, he returned to begin graduate studies.

Gilliam's return to the University of Louisville reunited him with a circle of supportive teachers and artists. He would complete his thesis under the direction of Crodel, a visiting professor from the Bayerische Akademie der Schönen Künste (Bavarian Academy of Fine Arts).[26] Three years of graduate school gave him the opportunity to continue studying European modernists of the late nineteenth and early twentieth centuries – Matisse, Mondrian, Braque, Cézanne, German Expressionists and Picasso. His teachers also introduced him to California figurative painters, favourites of both Crodel and Wilke. These Bay Area artists, Nathan Oliveira, David Park, Richard Diebenkorn and Elmer Bischoff, defiantly brought the figure back into abstract painting. If only briefly, their work influenced Gilliam's early paintings. Jazz blossomed as another major influence during his graduate-school years. A patron of Louisville's vibrant jazz scene, he often engaged other artists in spirited conversations about music and art in general. Gilliam favoured the musicians who were breaking with the melodic compositions and dance-friendly rhythms of earlier jazz. His heroes were Miles Davis, Ornette Colman, John Coltrane and Thelonious Monk. He loved the compositional complexity, the daring of the musicians to challenge tradition and the joyful unpredictability of improvisation.

As a graduate student, Gilliam was an ardent social and political activist. He co-founded the Gallery Enterprises art collective (1957–61), which included artists like Bob Thompson. They gathered regularly to discuss the relationship between art and politics. As a graduate student, he was a member of the executive council of the Louisville branch of the National Association for the Advancement of Colored People (NAACP). In that role, he advised a youth group, assisting in the organization of sit-ins, protests and other acts of civil disobedience. His years in undergraduate and graduate school were fraught with change and danger. The 1954 Brown vs. Board of Education Supreme Court ruling set the stage for dismantling separatism in American life, legitimized by Jim Crow laws. Heroic acts of activism, like those of Dr. Martin Luther King, Jr. and Rosa Parks in the Montgomery bus boycott, were front and centre in the media: the buses of freedom riders heading south to register voters, attacked and set aflame by law enforcement; college students beaten while asking for service at segregated lunch counters; governors who called out the National Guard to halt the integration of public schools; church bombings and assassinations of activists appeared regularly in the news. By the end of his graduate-school career, however, Gilliam decided emphatically that political activism was not for him as a means of igniting change. The historic March on Washington, which he attended together with his then wife Dorothy in 1963, shortly after he moved to D.C., was probably one of his last traditional 'activist' gestures. Gilliam would go on to create his own expressions of independence and resistance in the face of the status quo.

Washington, D.C. became Gilliam's Paris, as he would say.[27] He came to the city in 1962, the year that he and Dorothy Butler, a talented young journalist, married in Louisville. Butler, whom Gilliam had met as an undergraduate and courted over the course of seven years, had finished a Master's degree in journalism from Columbia University in 1961. The *Washington Post* offered her a job that same year, as a general assignment reporter, making her the first Black woman to work at the renowned newspaper. Gilliam had been briefly employed as a dining-car porter in the summer of 1961. The two would become a formidable Washington celebrity couple. Dorothy was a rising star in the world of journalism and, soon after his arrival, Gilliam would become a rising star in the art world.

When he first arrived in Washington, Gilliam was working in a figurative abstract style that emulated the Bay Area figurative painters admired by his graduate-school professors. The Washington Color School painters, however, had ascended to the ranks of the avant-garde of American modernism. Gilliam's early friendship with a leading Color School painter would be transformative. Thomas Downing, who had studied with Noland in the 1950s and shared a studio with Color School artist Howard Mehring, visited Gilliam's 1963 solo exhibition at Adams-Morgan Gallery. Downing was not at all interested in the dark, muddy abstract figurative paintings on display, reminiscent of the work of artists like Oliveira and Park. The older artist was attracted, instead, among the several watercolours in the show, to the one abstract Klee-inspired work, the only non-objective work on view.

Downing invited the young artist to his studio and introduced him to his work – canvases filled with carefully balanced geometries of circles and grids that became Downing's signature style. He also introduced Gilliam to the work of other Washington Color School artists – his studio mate, Mehring, along with the work of Paul Reed, Gene Davis and the two stars of the movement, Noland and Louis. Louis, who was teaching at Howard University at the time, died the year Gilliam arrived in D.C., before they were able to meet, and Noland had moved to New York City.[28] Gilliam felt an immediate kinship with the work of these painters and came to know them, except for Louis, personally. (Years later, he would meet Noland on a visit to his Vermont studio, establishing a relationship with the older artist). A year after his first solo show, Gilliam's 1964 exhibition at the Adams-Morgan Gallery displayed the fruits of his study: a selection of hard-edge paintings that displayed his embrace and mastery of the Color School ethos. Ever the diligent student, Gilliam continued to study Washington Color School artists closely, and on trips to New York, often with Downing, their precursors, Color Field artists, such as Hans Hofmann, Mark Rothko, Barnett Newman (a particular favourite), Ad Reinhardt and Helen Frankenthaler.

Stephanie Jessica, the Gilliams's first daughter, was born in 1963, and the family would continue to grow rapidly over the next few years. Gilliam held on to his teaching job at McKinley Technical High School for his first five years in the capital city. He often took his students on field trips to local museums and galleries, one of his favourites being the Barnett-Aden Gallery. Barnett-Aden was founded in 1943 by Howard faculty member James V. Herring and his student Alonzo J. Aden, a curator, briefly, at the Howard University Art Gallery. Filled with renowned European artists, and American artists, Black and white, Barnett-Aden allowed Gilliam to introduce his students at the predominantly Black school to Black masters such as Henry Ossawa Tanner, Romare Bearden, Jacob Lawrence and Washington, D.C. artist and former schoolteacher, Alma Thomas, as well as examples of work by Picasso, Chagall and Matisse. Even as Gilliam's star was rapidly rising as an up-and-coming painter, he was still grounded in the day-to-day realities of the lives of his students and the demands of a growing family.[29]

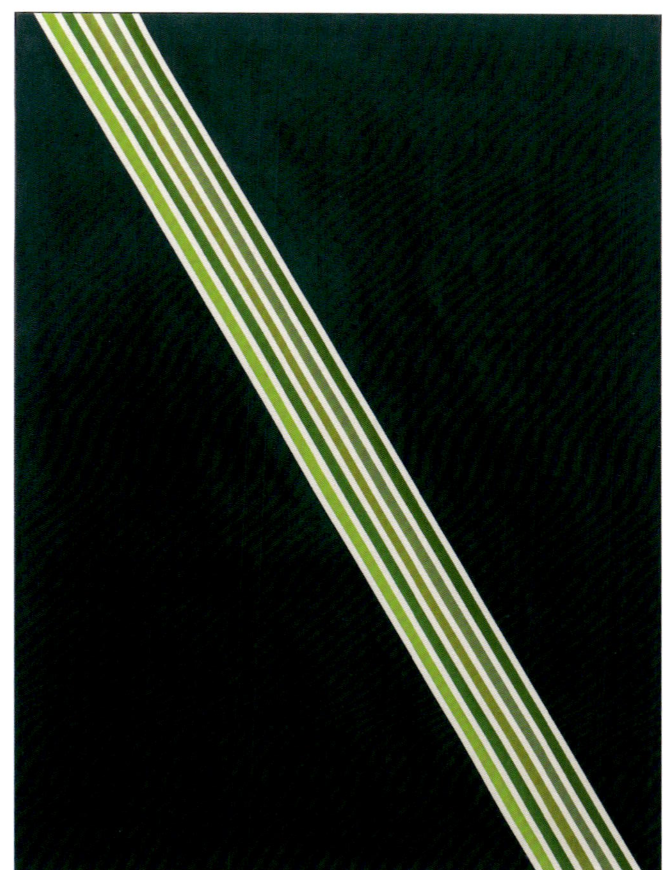

Stems, 1965

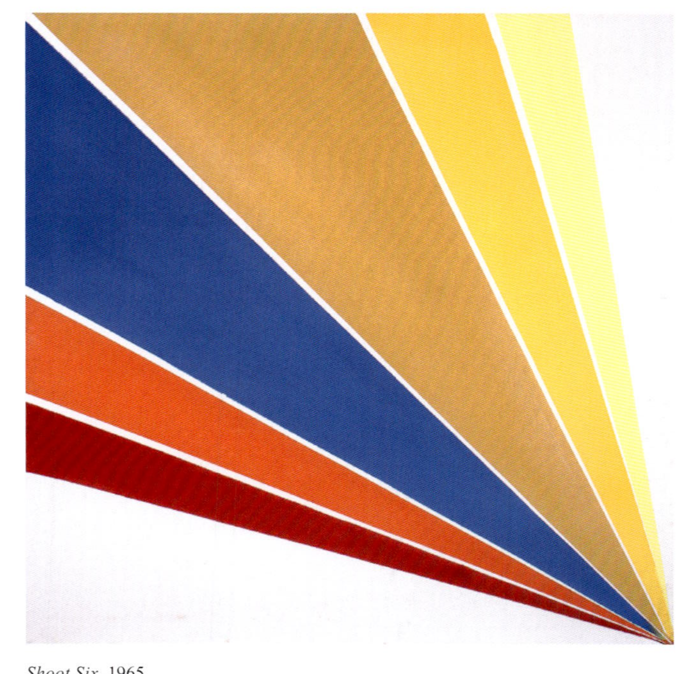

Shoot Six, 1965

In those early years in Washington, D.C., inspired by the artists Downing had introduced to him, Gilliam meticulously copied what he understood as the working process of Color School painters. Control was critical and he started each canvas with a compositional sketch, then, making use of masking tape, he marked boundaries so that the result came out according to plan. Like his Color School colleagues, he applied paint thinned enough to see the weave of an unprimed, unstretched canvas. Planning, measuring, taping and applying thinned paint produced highly controlled surfaces. Frankenthaler, a Color Field artist whose paintings were a departure from the expressive explosiveness of Abstract Expressionism, influenced the Washington artists with her canvases stained with paint thinned with turpentine. Color School artists, as Gilliam would learn, used Magna acrylic paint, a specific brand developed by Leonard Bocur, mixed with water-tension breaker, to thin the paint and, at the same time, retain chromatic intensity. The intense thinned colour focused the eye on the surface of the canvas, as did the elimination of external subject-matter references, a striking contrast to the paintings of an earlier generation of abstractionists. 'Post-painterly abstraction' was the term the critic Clement Greenberg invented that included the accomplishments of the Washington, D.C. artists. Greenberg made use of the terminology in the exhibition catalogue for a landmark 1964 exhibition, 'Post-Painterly Abstraction' at the Los Angeles County Museum of Art (LACMA). The phrase distinguished an earlier generation of New York-based, gestural painters like Jackson Pollock, Willem De Kooning and Franz Kline from the work of painters who concentrated on the formal elements that underscored the flat surface of the picture plane and eschewed any references to a world outside of the painting.

Gilliam's early Washington Color School paintings earned him only a tepid critical response. His embrace of the Color School mode of working and aesthetic did earn him, however, a spot in Greenberg's 1964 exhibition at LACMA and inclusion in group exhibitions with other Color School artists. Despite the lack of critical acclaim, Gilliam's hard-edge paintings found support from local Washington, D.C. galleries. Nesta Dorrance, director of the Jefferson Place Gallery, mounted a 1965 solo show of Gilliam's newest Color School canvases. Disappointingly, only one was sold. Many decades later, on the occasion of a major 2005 retrospective at the Corcoran Gallery of Art, curated by Gilliam scholar Jonathan Binstock, Gilliam decided that those early hard-edge paintings were not only old, but old-fashioned. In his mind they did not reflect his individual contribution to abstract painting. He and Binstock concluded that the show should begin with what Gilliam uniquely contributed to modernist painting. Thinking the hard-edge paintings were too derivative, they omitted them.[30] Years after the retrospective, however, Gilliam would be taken aback by an unexpected reawakened interest in these early paintings, an interest sparked by the intervention of gallerist Kordansky and painter Johnson, a new generation of admirers. Both were inspired by Gilliam's early work. Both recognized in those early hard-edge paintings a point of departure from which the radicalism of future innovations could be calibrated.

Almost fifty years after his hard-edge paintings debuted in Washington, D.C., Johnson's curatorial selection for the 2013 show commands us to see the distinctiveness of Gilliam's contribution to the Color School ethos in these early paintings. Looking at the calm, deliberate yet self-assured surfaces of these early abstractions makes the velocity of the so-called, 'serial manumissions' that followed even more remarkable.[31] Johnson's curatorial skill calls attention to Gilliam's early mastery of colour. The artist created hard-edge canvases that were, at times, subtle balances of tone or stark contrasts of saturated colour. To re-examine the paintings from that period is to see that Gilliam made an enormous leap in one year from the dark muddy palette of a work like his 1963 figurative abstractions to the carefully modulated tones and lucidity of these early Color School paintings. Perhaps critics found these hard-edge paintings too reminiscent of works by Louis or Noland. There is similarity, no doubt, between Louis's *Hot Half* (1962), with its band of stripes across the canvas, and Gilliam's painting, *Long Green* (1965, p. 61), also with stripes that burst from the corner of a monochromatic field. There is an emphatic definitiveness, however, in Gilliam's work, not present in Louis's more lyrical painting. Another attribute of Gilliam that was highlighted in the 2013 show is the presence of a coiled energy in some of the canvases. Razor-sharp stripes, tilting in a precarious balance or exploding from the corners of the canvas to the outer expanses, are a prelude to the energy, coiled or released, of his later work. *Helles* (1965, p. 58), a work much-reproduced in art-historical surveys and texts, and the pulsating vibrancy of *Theme of Five I* (1965, right) or *Shoot Six* (1965, p. 17), are examples of canvases that demonstrate his particular talent in controlling colour, movement and the dynamic forces that reside in his best work.

A lack of critical or commercial success in response to these early abstractions did not dampen Gilliam's sense of adventurousness. He continued working, experimenting and pushing boundaries, even as he welcomed his second daughter, Melissa Lynn, in 1965. By 1966, he had removed the masking tape while the paint was still wet, letting the canvases dry overnight, the weight of the heavy folds, and the crumpling and pleating, dictating the flow of the paint. The striations that resulted the next morning, when he allowed the paint to run through the creases of the canvas, earned them the title 'slice paintings' (*Green Slice*, 1967, top right). Gilliam's surrender to the flow of the paint calls to mind past advice from his teacher, Wilke, who admonished him 'to respect the liquid medium itself' and 'let it happen, you know, let it be paint. Don't let it be so precious'.[32] Allowing accidents to enter the controlled surfaces was liberating. Between the years 1966 and 1967, Gilliam's experiments, pouring paint on unstretched canvas, eventually stretching the canvas on bevelled and chamfered edges, won him recognition as an inventive artist who was

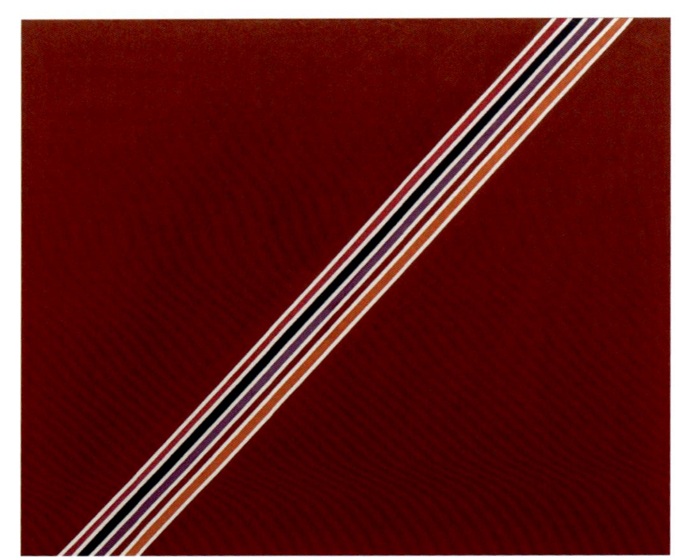

Theme of Five I, 1965

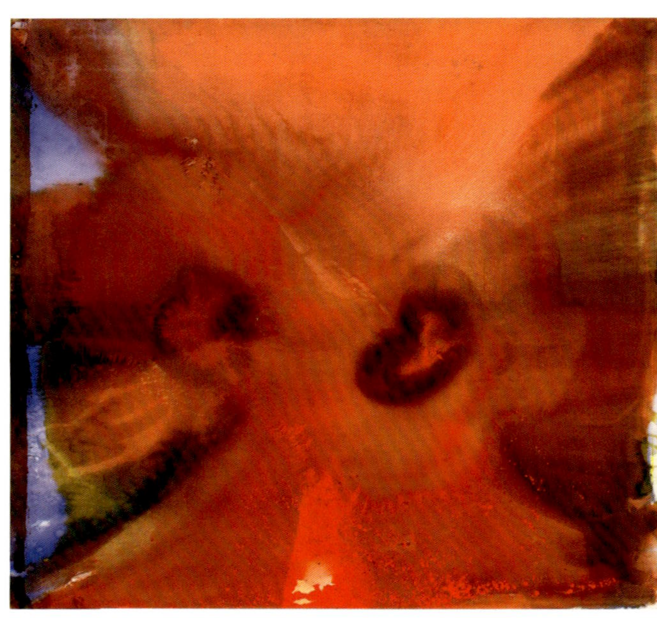

Red Petals, 1967

willing to challenge himself and to incorporate practices he learned. Bevelling and chamfering are carpenter's techniques, the means by which a skilled carpenter transitions from one flat surface to the next, as his father, Sam, Sr. was able to do. Gilliam, keeping his roots close, freed the surface of the canvas from lying flat against the wall.[33]

Discovering the canvas as a site of experimentation was a breakthrough for Gilliam. Marjorie Phillips, the Director of the Phillips Collection, wife of and co-founder with Duncan Phillips, saw Gilliam's work at the Jefferson Place Gallery. She considered him an artist of great promise, and during the summer of 1966, offered him a solo exhibition. Gilliam had been in Washington, D.C. for five years, at the time of the Phillips Collection show. Phillips curated the exhibition, her selection earning Gilliam national attention overnight. One of the works included in the exhibition, which the museum would acquire for its permanent collection, was *Red Petals* (p. 18), a 1967 painting that was searing in its expressive power. A large work, measuring 88 by 93 inches, *Red Petals* epitomized Gilliam's mastery of his newly discovered technique: colour poured onto unprimed and unstretched folded canvas, left to dry overnight. In Gilliam's words: '*Petals* is when I first really felt that I was getting somewhere on my own, beginning to see and unfold … And not imitate all the paintings I had seen in Washington.[34] The impact was riveting. Writing about this piece in 1982 as a young curator, I had this to say: 'intense bleeding red stains and dark, almost black blue, brushed at the outskirts, define the image of an oversized flower. Like Van Gogh's tortuous yellow bouquet, *Red Petals* appropriates colour and the natural worlds for the artist's own symbolic purposes. Red, a colour of unsettling emotional power, becomes even more visceral set against the dark blue-black vortex of colour at the painting's center'.[35]

Included also in the Phillips Collection show were watercolours, a medium that, as both Downing and his teacher Wilke recognized, freed Gilliam to yield control of the paint, and unlocked his willingness to let the movement of the paint suggest new directions. The results of his experimentations dramatically opposed the restraint of the hard-edge paintings. There is an unabashed invitation for the viewer to feel something emotional in a canvas like *Red Petals* – a stark contrast to the more precise, carefully planned hard-edge canvases. He would prove himself masterful at both approaches to his art, as always, standing comfortably in the contradiction between radical control and liberating improvisation.

Change in Gilliam's art was accompanied by changes to his family as well. Leah, his third and youngest daughter, was born in 1967. Dorothy Gilliam, who took a leave from her *Washington Post* position while their three children were very young, referred to this period as 'intense'.[36] Space and the need for more of it, as the family grew, was urgent. Fortuitously, recognition of Gilliam's artistic prowess was on the rise in time for a decision on the part

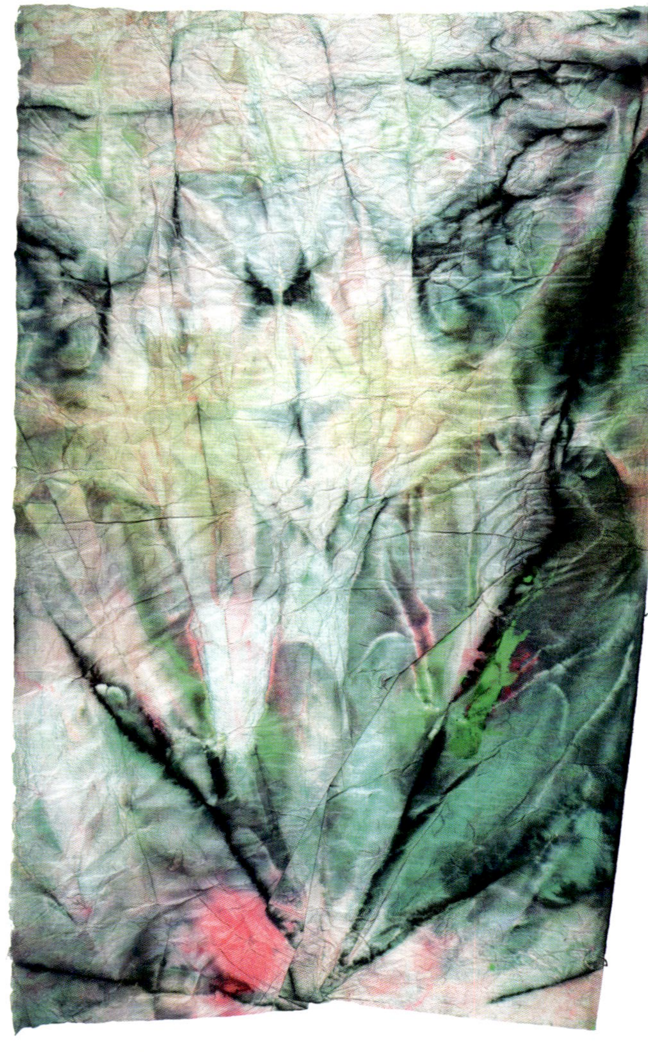

Green Slice, 1967

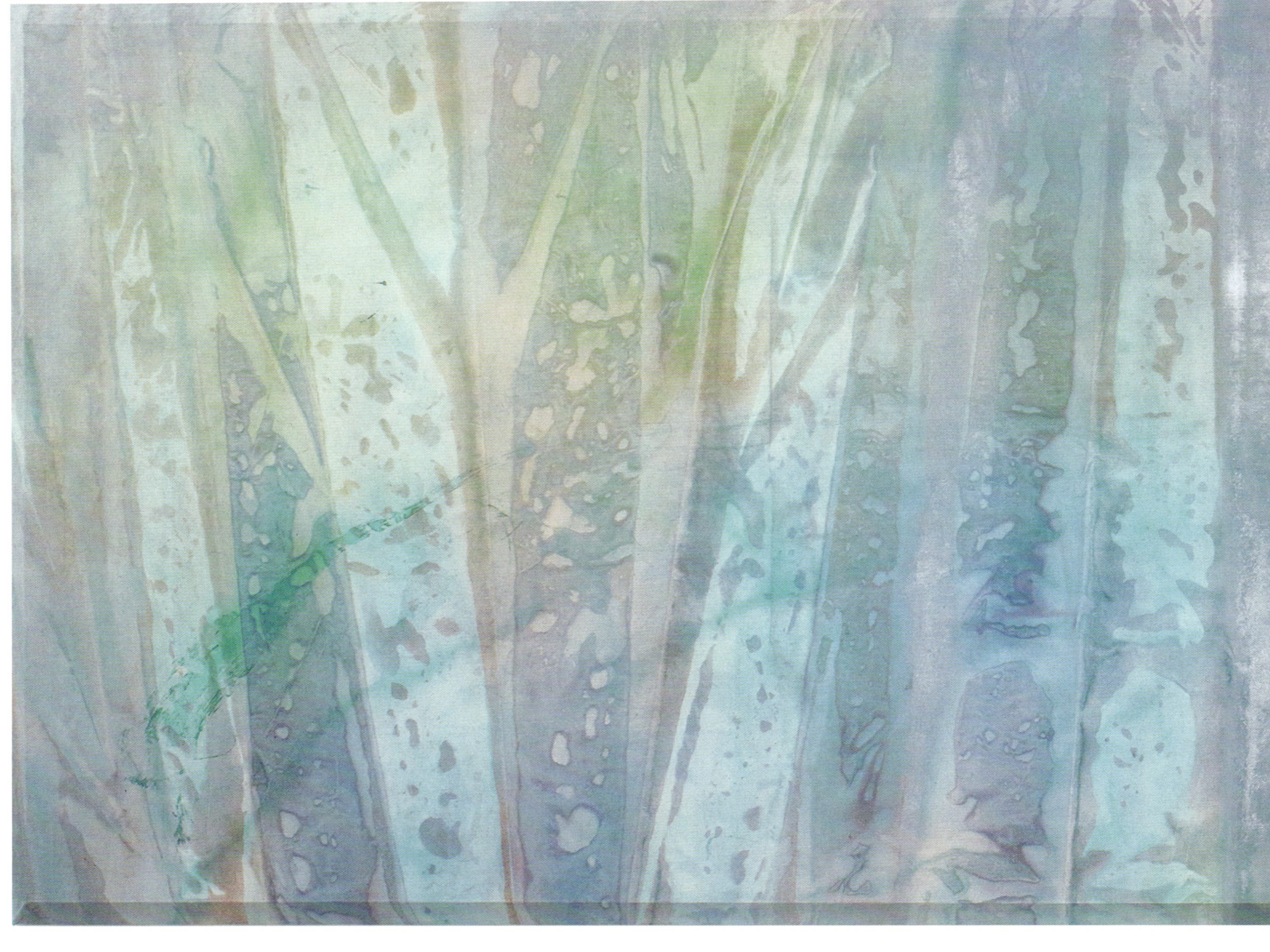

Green April, 1969

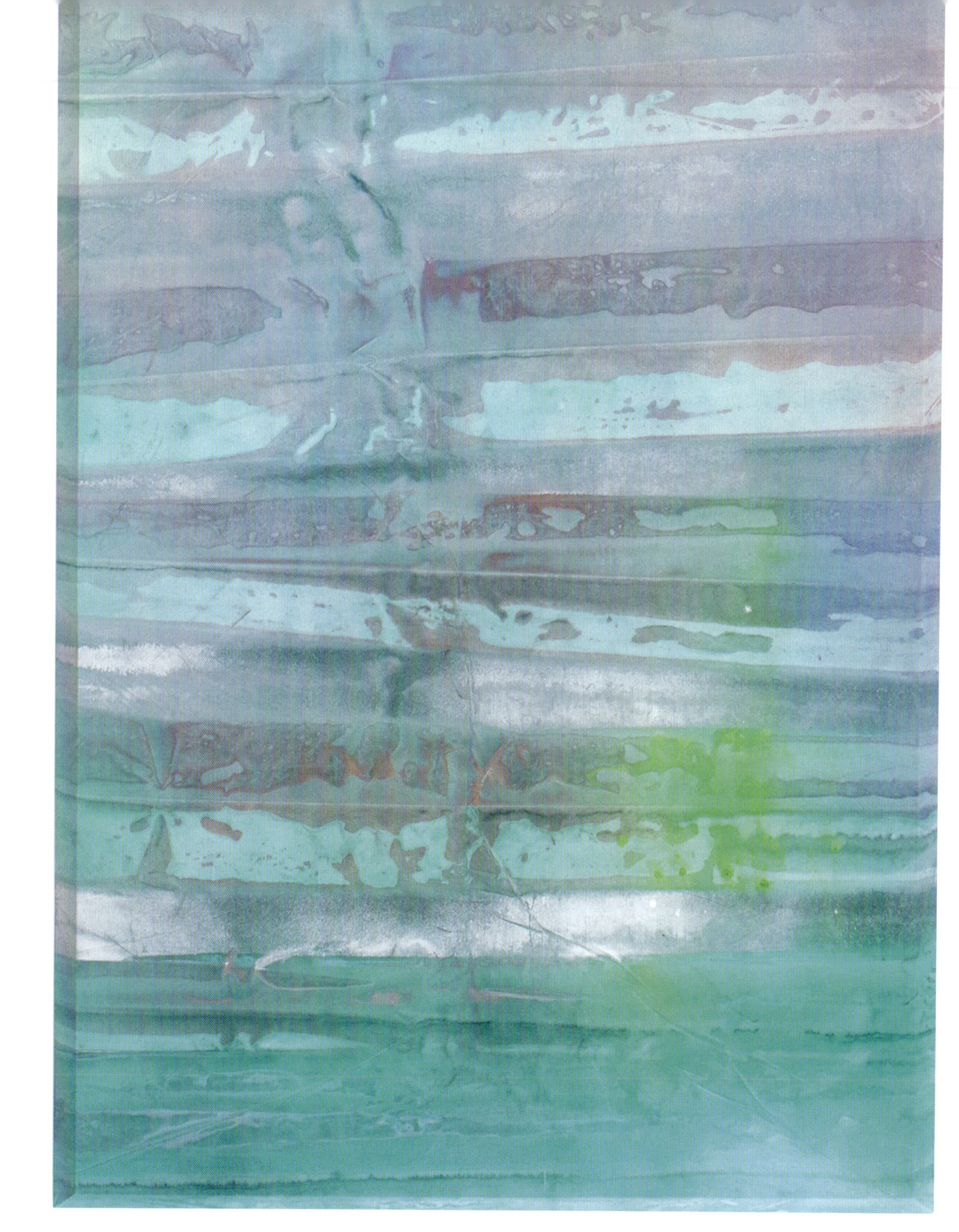

of the National Endowment for the Arts (NEA) that began providing individual artist's grants. Gilliam was among the first to receive an NEA individual artist's award. That grant and one from Walter Hopps, whose impact on Gilliam's life will be recounted later, came at a critical moment. The money afforded his family the luxury of making a down payment on a three-storey home in the Mount Pleasant area of Washington, D.C. with a studio, and the ability to quit his full-time job as a high-school teacher.

That Lamont Street house was where he and Dorothy would raise their three remarkable daughters. By all accounts, the house, located in a racially and economically mixed neighbourhood, was a community in and of itself. With Gilliam, a rising art star, and Dorothy Gilliam, one of Washington, D.C.'s leading Black journalists, who would eventually return to *the Post* full-time, their home was filled with discussions of art and the comings and goings of leading members of D.C.'s creative, intellectual and political circles. Their daughters recalled the excitement of living in a household where they would come home from school and find the front porch painted a different colour or a household filled with interesting people and lively conversations. Collectibles of all sorts were visible everywhere: marbles, large and small, toy banks, fabric, art books and, of course, artworks – Gilliam's, and the work of other artists whom he admired.

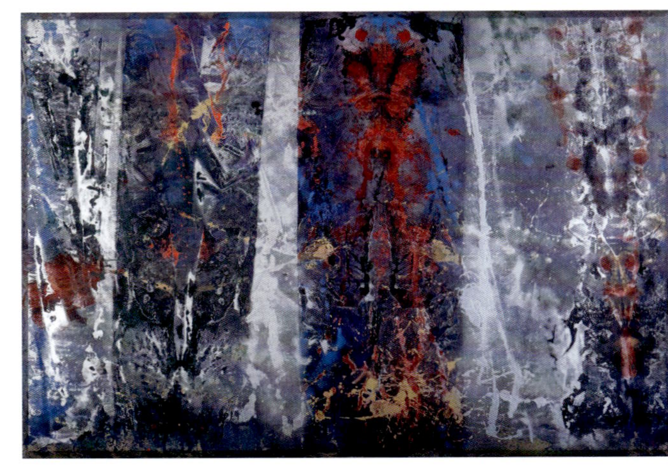

Restore, 1968

1967–1973: AN ERA OF EXPERIMENTATION, INNOVATION AND DISCOVERY

In the last decade of Gilliam's life, as noted earlier, two exhibitions celebrated the period from 1967 to 1973 as high points in his artistic evolution. David Kordansky Gallery mounted, 'Sam Gilliam: Green April' in 2016. Two years later, the Kunstmuseum Basel, Switzerland, staged a major retrospective, 'The Music of Color. Sam Gilliam 1967–1973', co-curated by Binstock and museum director Josef Helfenstein, that included an expansive selection of works from this period. What both shows have in common is an acknowledgement that this time was not only intensely generative for Gilliam – with the introduction of the Drape paintings he reinvented painting in general and rejuvenated abstract painting in particular – but it was a time of immense social and political churn globally. Personally, Gilliam was enjoying near unanimous applause for his first solo museum show at The Phillips Collection. He would meet Walter Hopps, who would become a major influence in his life. Hopps was a legendary arts impresario, visionary, museum director and curator, who had arrived in Washington, D.C. from Pasadena in 1966 to assume a fellowship at the Washington Institute for Policy Studies. Hopps quickly assumed the role of executive director of the Washington Gallery of Modern Art and oversaw its merger with the Corcoran Gallery of Art. He then served as the highly influential director of the Corcoran Gallery of Art from 1969 to 1972.

One of Hopps's most important contributions to Washington, D.C. was artists' studio space. He established a network of studios for working artists around the city in different disciplines. Gilliam and Krebs were the recipients of one of the space grants that Hopps managed to corral. Through the grant's largess, the two artists were able to establish a studio from which they could run workshops at 1737 Johnson Avenue, NW. The idea was not only to use the network of studios that Hopps was establishing for the work of the artists assigned to them, but to open the studios up to other artists, a responsibility that Gilliam took very seriously. His studio space quickly gained a reputation for being hospitable to aspiring artists, an openness that benefitted gifted artists like Houston Conwill, then a student at Howard University, whom Gilliam took under his wing by hiring him as an assistant.[37] When Hopps became the new director of the Corcoran Gallery of Art, he invited both Gilliam and Krebs, along with the artist Ed McGowin, to create works specifically for a 1969 group show, urging the three artists to think ambitiously.

Hopps's invitation came at an auspicious time. Gilliam's solo show at the Phillips Collection had received enthusiastic reviews and his experimentation was becoming bolder. Scale, along with colour, had captured Gilliam's attention, influenced by a show entitled 'Scale' at the Corcoran, featuring the works of Newman, Tony Smith and Ronald Bladen. Gilliam used the occasion of his first New York exhibition at the Byron Gallery in 1968, a year after the Phillips Collection exhibition, to experiment with scale. He hung a piece measuring 9 by 30 feet, entitled, *Sock it To Me* (1968), and exhibited *Restore* (1968, left), a luminous bevelled-edge painting measuring 9 by 12 feet. *Sock it to Me* (1968), which took its title from a line in Aretha Franklin's popular song, *Respect*, and a refrain used in a popular American television comedy show, also made use of his technique of bevelled edges, in this case, inverted. The gargantuan size taxed the gallery walls with its weight. Gilliam was left to solve the problem of mounting a large, heavy painting on his own. Finding novel solutions to the problems that his paintings posed became an integral part of his practice. As Jenelle Porter reports in her essay for the catalogue *Sam Gilliam: Green April*, in trying to hang one of these oversized canvases, Gilliam dropped a corner of the canvas. The way the canvas folded, freed from the wall, was one of the inspirations for the idea that draping could be a potent part of his visual vocabulary.[38]

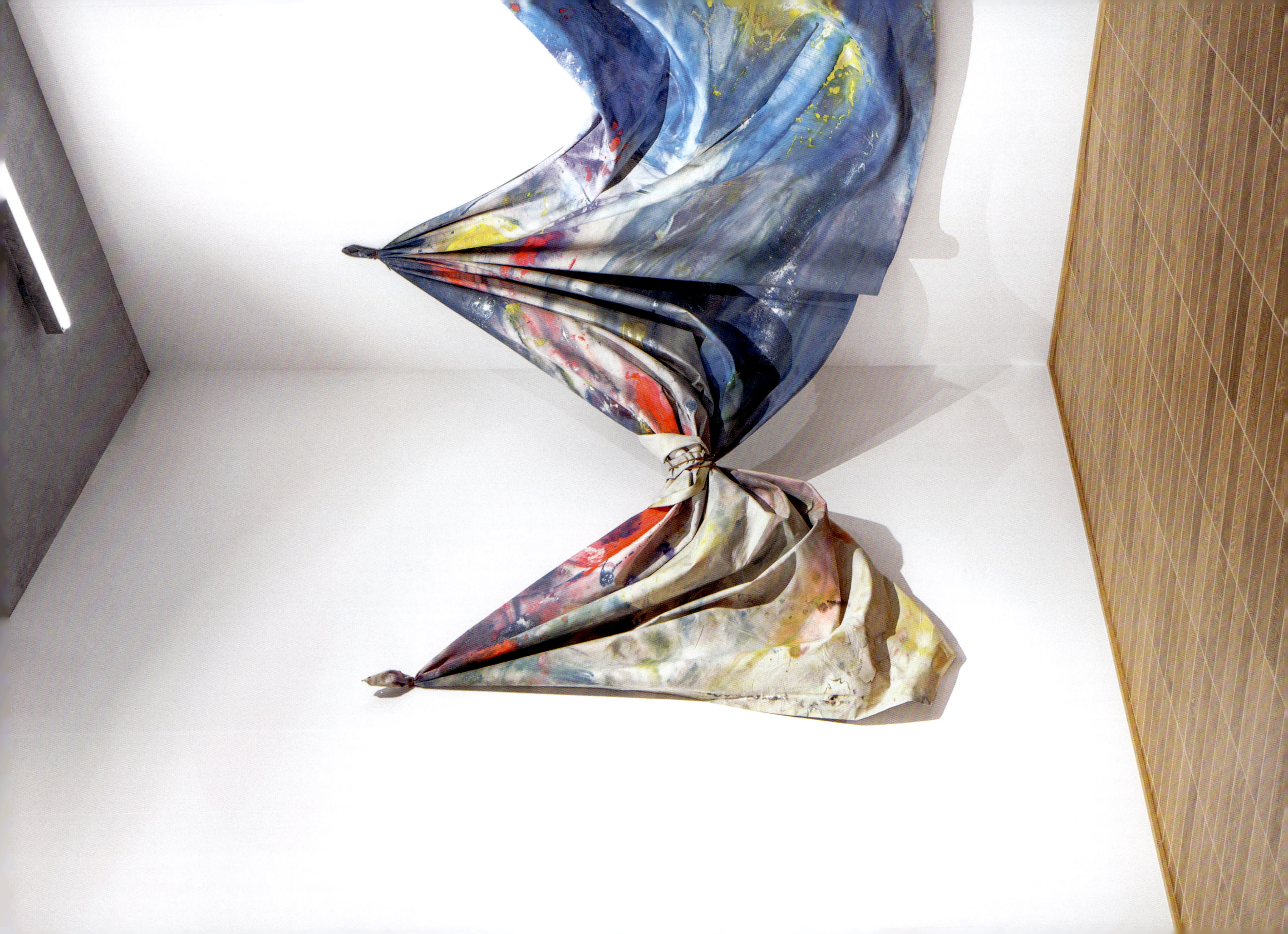

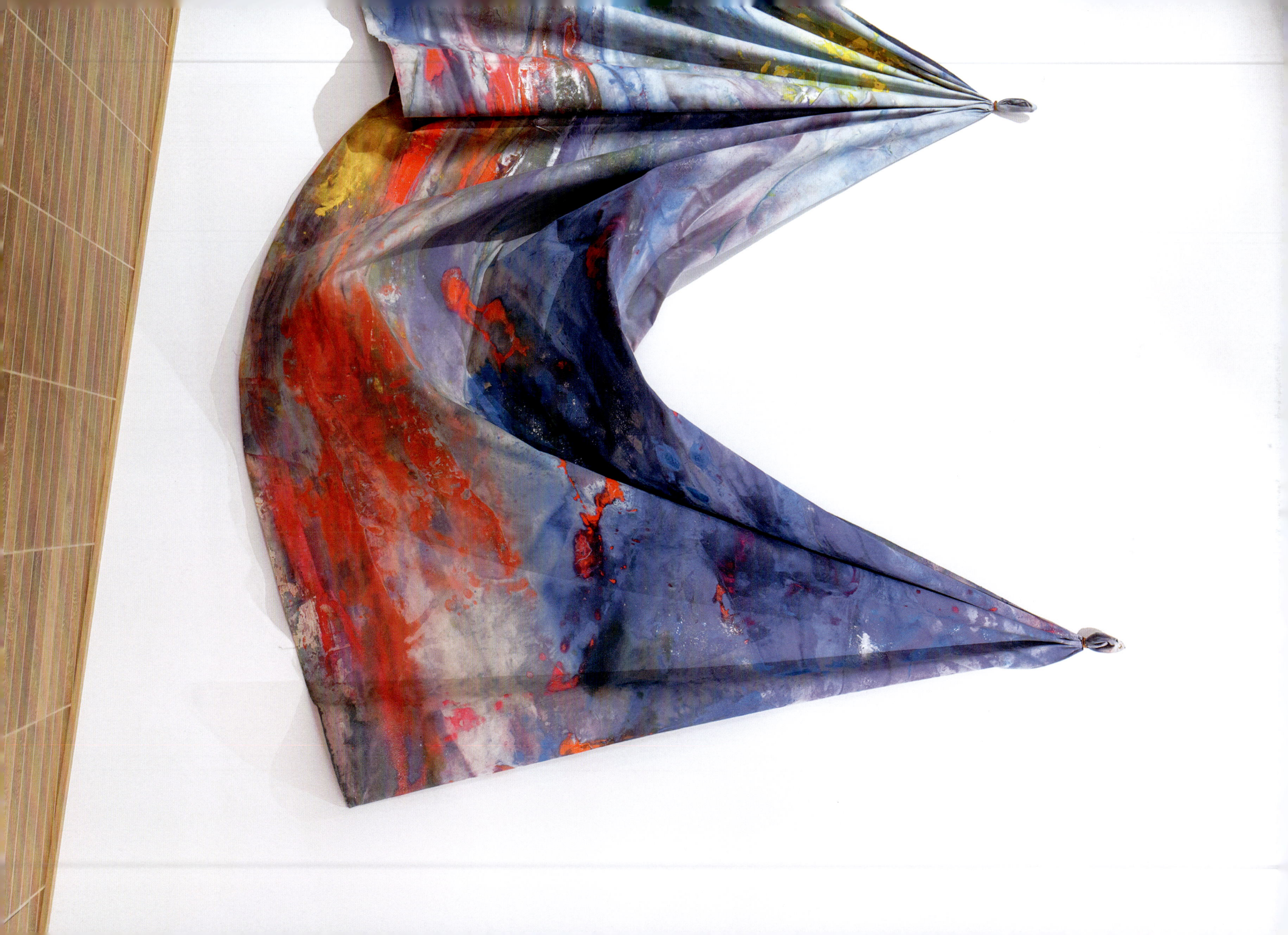

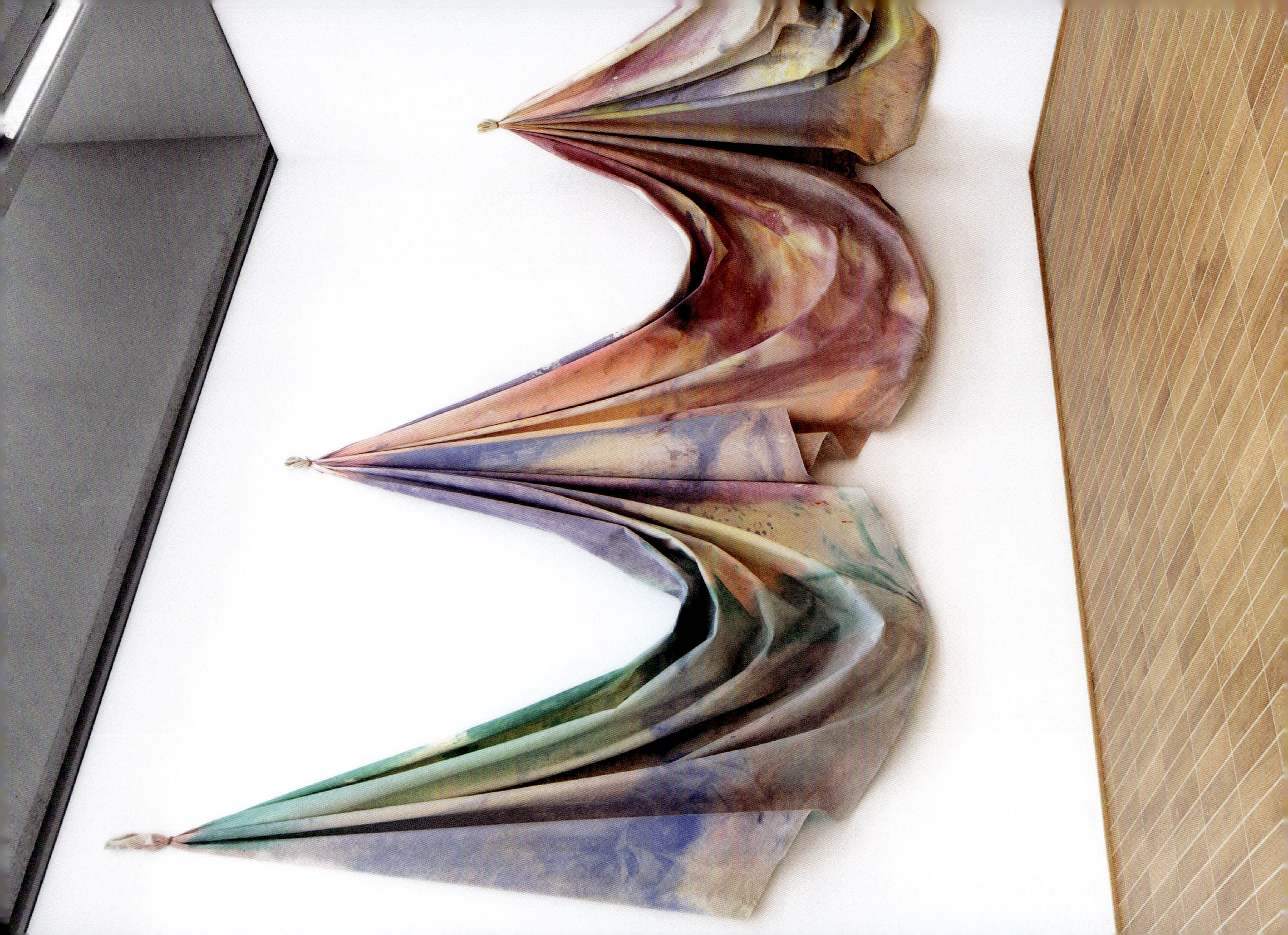

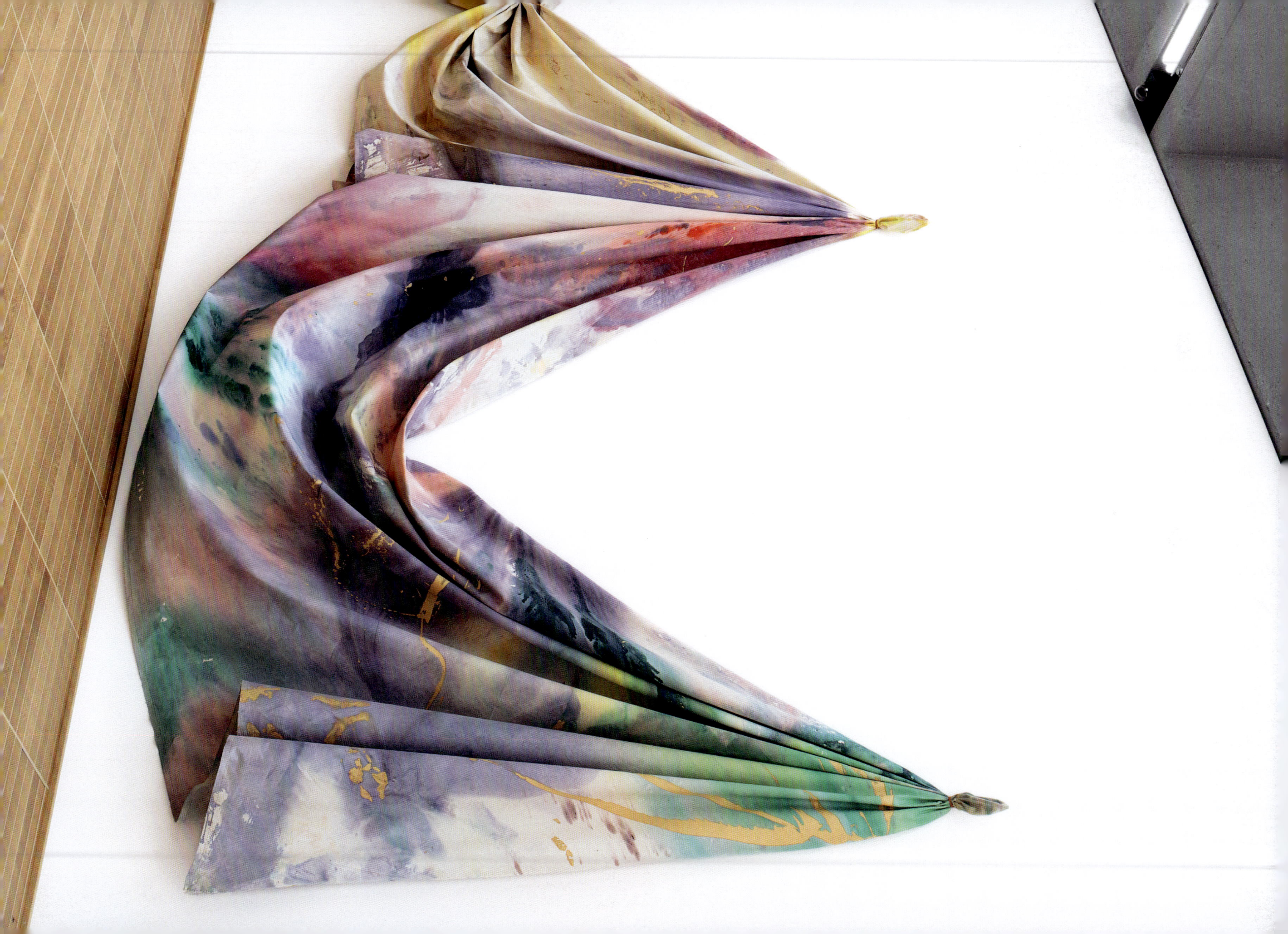

1968: A PIVOTAL YEAR

The year 1968 was one of revelation and determination... Something was in the air and it was in that spirit that I did the Drape paintings.[39]

The pivotal year of 1968 saw Gilliam painting on canvas drawn taut against the bevelled edges of a stretcher, such as the painting *Rouge* (1968), shown in the 2017 Kordansky Gallery show. *Rouge* is a particularly expressive example of his method of pouring, daubing, staining and letting the paint dry of its own accord. Even as Gilliam was still producing works on bevelled-edge stretchers, he was experimenting with draping. His earliest drapes have an improvisational playfulness balanced by the care with which he was experimenting with instruments and tools that allowed him to manage and control the flow of the canvas's fabric. *Swing Sketch* (1968, below right). *Swing Sketch* is an example of the improvisatory staining and pouring that is a stark contrast to the way in which the artist has very deliberately folded and hung the fabric from three points on the wall. Yet another example is the even more jubilant, *Niagra* (1968, pp. 24–25), a work that demonstrates Gilliam's growing ambition with draping in the way that it traverses a corner connecting two walls. Pieces like these were a prelude for his most ambitious work to date.

Not only was 1968 a landmark year in Gilliam's formal evolution, but it was also a milestone year in the wider world. Gilliam, a disavowed activist, found himself in his studio with Krebs, his studio mate, on the eve of the 1968 assassination of Civil Rights leader Dr. Martin Luther King, Jr. He and Krebs watched their beloved city, seized by grief and rage, unravel. So troubled was Gilliam by what he was witnessing that he implored Dorothy to take their three daughters to stay with friends outside of Washington, D.C., while he and Krebs watched the city explode right outside of their door.[40] There is no definitive proof of cause and effect, on the one hand, between the events of the late 1960s and 1970s and, on the other hand, Gilliam's art of that period. What is clear is that paroxysms of rage seized dozens of urban centres in the United States with civil insurrections from the mid-1960s to the early 1970s. King's death was followed that summer by the assassination of Senator Robert Kennedy, five years after his brother's death. Riots disrupted the Democratic National Convention during the summer of 1968, and student protests wracked campuses from Berkeley to Mexico City to Paris. Gilliam's work from 1968 to 1973 may not have been 'caused' by these events. The audacity and beauty of these paintings, coupled with their expressiveness is nonetheless undeniable. Undeniable, too, is his invented lyrical vocabulary during this period, which he set to music, creating works that were symphonic in their impact.

'Baroque' is the term that Gilliam has used to describe the voluminous folds of the monumental *Baroque Cascade*

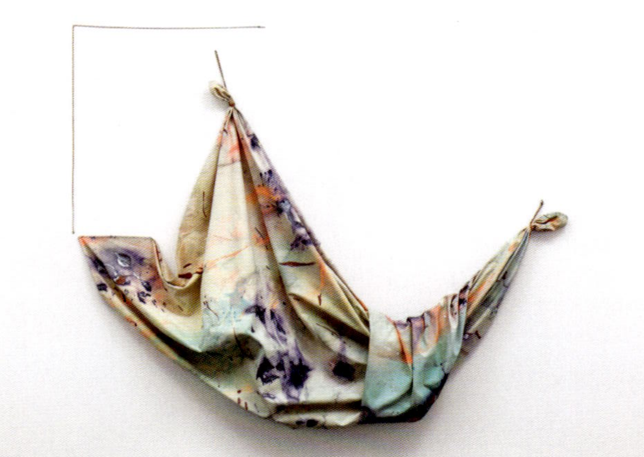

Above: *Swing Sketch*, 1968
Right: *Dakar I*, 1969

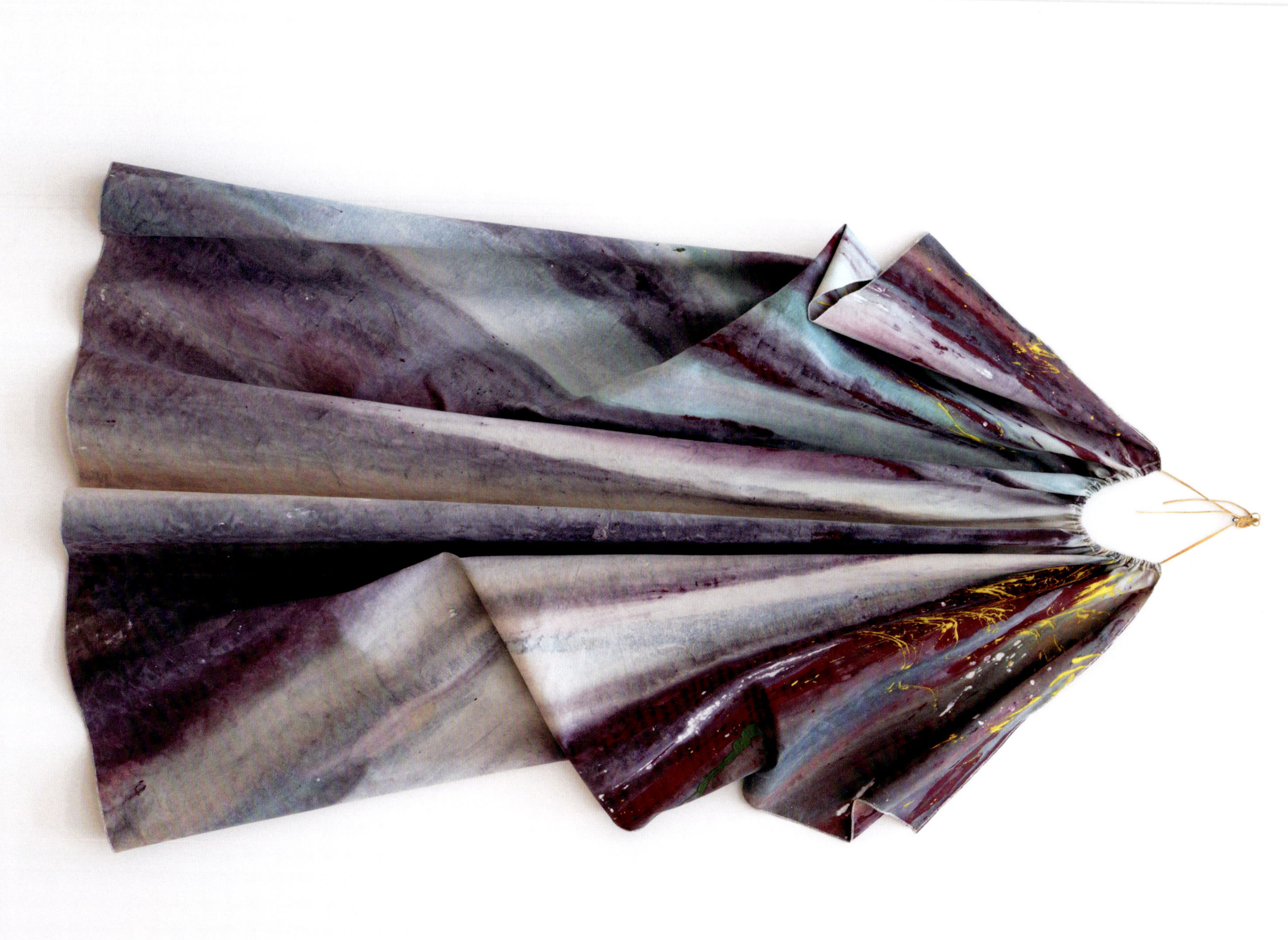

(1969), the largest of the Drape paintings exhibited at the Corcoran Gallery of Art in 1969. Gilliam found inspiration for the work in past traditions of painting, even as the piece propelled abstract painting into the future. He cited visits to the National Gallery of Art as inspiration, where he had looked at paintings by Baroque artists like Canaletto, but also Renaissance artists like Ghiberti and Michelangelo.[41] Inspirational, too, was the natural world, and, on other occasions, he has cited Albert Bierstadt and Thomas Cole, in particular paintings of Niagara Falls, as sources. In an interview with Barbara Rose, Gilliam listed the French painters he met in the 1960s in Paris who painted, *sans chassis*, as yet another influence. The intrusion of the accidental, of course, was another revelation.

Others have seen inspiration in the performance of everyday life. MacArthur award winner Fred Moten, in an essay for the Pace Gallery 2020 exhibition catalogue, *Sam Gilliam: Existed Existing* sees in the idiom of monumental draping a poetically rendered statement about Black women's work that opens into a symbol of infinite horizons. Moten writes of 'his building and tenting and billowing of tint; his folding and sculpting of shade. Having seen through an open window the secret of women hanging laundry, he set sail on quilted, common winds, in long drawn-out circumnavigation'.[42] Gilliam himself, in an interview with Binstock published in the 'The Music of Color' exhibition catalogue, suggests the role of memory.[43] He recalls a childhood inspiration, one of his sisters' cat's cradles, or more currently, the hang of shower curtains from an armature during a bathroom renovation in his home.

The largest of the three drapes, *Baroque Cascade*, which measures 150 feet in length, hung above the heads of visitors who stood on the ground floor of the Corcoran Gallery of Art's two-storey, 42-foot-high classical atrium.[44] It must have been humbling for visitors to look up at the massive canvas, stained and folded, swooping across the space above their heads. As Hopps points out, viewers from the second-floor balconies had a closer, eye-level view of the folds and luscious colours of the stained canvas. *Light Depth* (1969, pp. 26–27), 10 by 75 feet, like the earlier *Niagara*, spanned the juncture of two walls in one gallery. A smaller work, *Carousel Form II* (1969), which landed on the cover of the September/October edition of *Art in America*, was hung in the atrium space. To say that Gilliam's Drape paintings excited the art world with their audacity and daring is an understatement.[45] In 2019, Dia Beacon presented an installation of Gilliam's work entitled *Double Merge* (pp. 100–01) with the date of 1968–2019. The over fifty-year span was explained by the fact that Gilliam literally decided to merge two Drape paintings, each titled *Carousel II*, completed in the 1960s. Along with *Double Merge*, also exhibited at Dia, is *Spread* (1973, pp. 106–07), an example of his bevelled-edge paintings. Co-owned by Dia and the Museum of Fine Arts, Houston, the installation called attention to the daring of his formal discoveries in the period between 1967 and 1973, and his willingness to continuously dig into his knapsack to reconsider and re-think from the past.[46]

There is no question that the 1969 Corcoran Gallery of Art show was a landmark moment. Yet, months earlier, in June of the same year, Gilliam made another decisive move that would impact the rest of his career. He joined three artists for a group show at a venue that could not have been more antithetical to the grand galleries of the Corcoran Gallery of Art. In a 10,000 square foot loft over a liquor store and a Kentucky Fried Chicken in central Harlem that also housed artists in residence, he forged a lifetime alliance. Abstract painter William T. Williams, fresh out of Yale Graduate school, visited the Byron Gallery during the run of Gilliam's solo show. He was immediately taken with the monumental paintings on display. 'There was a light coming out of them and a color palette that was broader than anything I had ever seen', he recalled.[47] As noted earlier, Williams invited Gilliam to participate in a group exhibition that he was organizing for a new Harlem arts organization, the Studio Museum in Harlem. The show's title, 'X to the Fourth Power', suggested a mathematics equation, underscoring its commitment to an abstract vocabulary. In addition to the celebration of abstraction, Williams's interracial exhibition was intended to emphasize the Studio Museum in Harlem as a space of mutual artistic respect, irrespective of race. In addition to himself, Williams's plan was to include sculptor Melvin Edwards, a Black artist, painter Steven Kelsey, a white artist, whom Williams knew from art school and, hopefully, Gilliam. Gilliam agreed, and the show opened just a few months before the Corcoran Gallery of Art show.

Scale, as well as abstraction, dominated 'X to the Fourth Power' as a unifying attribute. Williams's canvases of overlapping slats of bold colour measured 12 by 7 feet; Edwards's draped metal chain, a hundred yards long, and Gilliam's massive Drape canvases asserted themselves in the loft space, along with Kelsey's abstractions. Critical response from *The New York Times* critic James R. Mellow characterized the art on display as 'art in an age of risk'.[48] This risk, according to Mellow, is the igniting of divided loyalties in a Black community that he presumed preferred representational or more politically motivated art. A bond was forged, nonetheless, between Gilliam and two of the artists, Edwards and Williams. They had much in common with Gilliam. Both were born in the south; both were as avidly committed to abstraction as Gilliam; both were athletic and devotees of jazz; and both were Black. Edwards worked primarily in metal, his solid football-player frame well-suited to the hands-on labour of the welding studio. Williams was a painter, who had already contributed any number of progressive ideas to the nascent Studio Museum in Harlem, including its now renowned artist-in-residence programme.

Both were also deeply engaged in their communities, but in ways dramatically different from Gilliam. Williams and Edwards had been actively involved with the organization Smokehouse Associates, and from 1968–71 would execute eight community projects in public parks and spaces throughout Harlem.[49] Demonstrating their entrepreneurial prowess, with two other artists, Billy Rose and Guy Garcia, they established partnerships between the city of New York and private funders. Narrative representational murals had become popular with Black Arts Movement groups like AfriCOBRA. Smokehouse Associates, by contrast, aimed to re-envision the environment with bold abstractions that changed the tone and tenor of the space, energizing it, in Edward's words, with the suggestion of the power of the imagination. Their connection was immediate and within the space of the next six years alone, they would exhibit together three more times.

Gilliam's innovations came at a time of both stylistic and institutional pluralism. Stylistically, Pop art, Conceptual art, Minimalism, performance art, installation and environmental art, along with street art and graffiti, loosened the prescriptive grip of some of the art world's authoritarian critical dictates. Institutionally, museums and galleries, previously homogenous, interrupted, if only briefly, the status quo to reconsider whom they exhibited and how they presented the artists they chose to show. Perhaps even more importantly, the number of alternative spaces was growing as well, expanding audiences for the arts and for who got to display their work in New York. In addition to the Studio Museum in Harlem, founded in the pivotal year of 1968, Howardena Pindell's feminist space, A.I.R. Gallery, Linda Goode Bryant's Just Above Midtown, and Joe Overstreet and Corinne Jennings's Kenkeleba House brought a new vitality to the art scene and a more diverse selection of artists. Additionally, a collective like Kamoinge Workshop, the downtown space in the Clock Tower, Creative Time, or the re-purposed school building that provided artists with working and exhibition space, P.S. 1 (now part of MoMA), or El Museo Del Barrio in East Harlem or in the South Bronx, The Bronx Museum and Fashion Moda and other so-called alternative spaces (some of which went on to become full-fledged museums) attracted growing numbers of diverse artists, patrons, collectors, scholars and curators. Art historian, critic and curator Barbara Rose, in a cover story for the September–October 1970 *Art in America*, with one of Gilliam's Drape paintings on the cover, announced that 'American culture desperately needed an infusion of new energy and creativity'.[50] Her verdict was that Black artists were uniquely positioned to provide that energy.

Whether they were celebrated as the cutting edge of American modernism or emblematic of a blossoming of Black art, Gilliam's abstractions were welcomed in a range of spaces, reflecting the growing cultural pluralism of the art world and his relationship to its diversity. The Howard University Art Gallery is one example. It was at this show that Conwill, along with his future wife, Kinshasha Holman Conwill, who would become a leading arts administrator in New York and Washington, D.C., would come to know Gilliam.[51] A year later, Gilliam's Drape paintings were showcased in a solo display at one of the country's mainstream New York museums, 'Projects', at the Museum of Modern Art in 1971. His groundbreaking works that redefined painting were displayed the same year that MoMA mounted retrospectives – for the first time in its history – of the work of two Black artists at the same time: collage artist, Bearden and sculptor, Richard Hunt.[52] Even as he was showing at MoMA, Gilliam accepted an invitation from artist/curator Peter Bradley to exhibit in the 'DeLuxe Show' displayed at the DeLuxe, an abandoned movie theatre in Houston's Fifth ward. Organized by Greenberg and sponsored by the Menil Collection, a major Houston cultural institution, the show assembled an interracial group of abstract painters and sculptors and exhibited them in the heart of the inner city in an effort to attract a more inclusive audience. By the end of the decade, a painting by Gilliam was included in Rose's exhibition at the New York University's Grey Art Gallery, 'American Painting: The Eighties', a show designed, in her estimation, to represent the best American painters of the decade.

During the 1970s, Gilliam's international stature rose as well. He had met Darthea Speyer during a trip to Europe and she became his Parisian dealer for the next twenty years. Speyer's gallery exhibited not only Gilliam, but Bearden, Beauford Delaney, Thomas and other leading Black artists. In 1972, Hopps included Gilliam as one of six artists whom he chose for the US Pavilion at the 36th Venice Biennale, only the second time a Black artist had shown at the international art exposition.[53] Glimcher remembers vividly the impact of Gilliam's work: 'no one could forget the 75-foot piece that Sam made for the American Pavilion at the Venice Biennale in 1972. It stole the show … and made a profound impression on everyone who saw it'.[54] From the late 1960s forward, Gilliam had truly become a very big dog.

The period of 1967 to 1973 was not only one of radical formal growth, but also a time when Gilliam produced a number of series and individual works of incomparable feeling and depth. An example is a series of paintings that have been referred to as his 'Cowl' paintings. They are so named because the stained, draped folds hang like a cloak, reminiscent of a religious vestment. Just over life-size, the works are usually about 8 feet in length. He frequently displayed them by hanging them from a hook on the wall so that they look like a coat someone has shed and hung up. The gathered top of the drape suggests a hood, while the fall of the drape evokes shoulders and a body that could bear the weight of the cloth. One of the more successful pieces in the series, *Dakar I* (1969, p. 29) refers to the 1966 First World Festival of Negro Arts (Premier Festival Mondial des arts nègres) in Dakar, Senegal, hosted by the poet and first president of Senegal, Léopold Sédar Senghor.[55] Gilliam was one of ten visual artists who was invited to send work. The event was designed to celebrate the unity of the African diaspora through leading Black poets, playwrights, musicians and visual artists. *Dakar I* marks that historic gathering.

Gilliam's masterpiece 'Cowl' painting was an ensemble that he made in the mid-1970s when he constructed an homage to the great Paul Robeson, renowned thespian, bass-baritone and political activist. The story is particularly revealing for what it says about the way Gilliam sometimes matched his formal discoveries to personal circumstances. Dorothy Gilliam had decided to write a biography of the radical Black activist and artist, who, like King, challenged the social and political status quo in the United States. To help her mother get permission from the Robeson family, Melissa, their middle child, who at the time was about ten years old, wrote to the family, championing her mother's request to write the book and assuring the Robesons that her mother was a good speller![56] Gilliam joined the family effort, his tribute being three monumental 'Cowl' paintings that debuted in 1975, during the 34th Biennial of Contemporary American Painting at the Corcoran Gallery of Art. Instead of hanging from a hook on the wall, the three drapes consumed an entire gallery, rigged in such a way that each of the three 'garments' appear to hang from the ceiling, as if waiting for some larger-than-life presence to inhabit them. Evoking the sacredness of the original 'Cowl' paintings, Gilliam adds the audacity of scale, making the works occupy the space in such a way that visitors must yield to and be directed by their presence. There is no political position stated in these paintings, yet, as installation photographs attest, the three draped cowls, hanging regally from the ceiling, convey a sense of majesty and power. Reviewers showered the piece with praise when it debuted.[57]

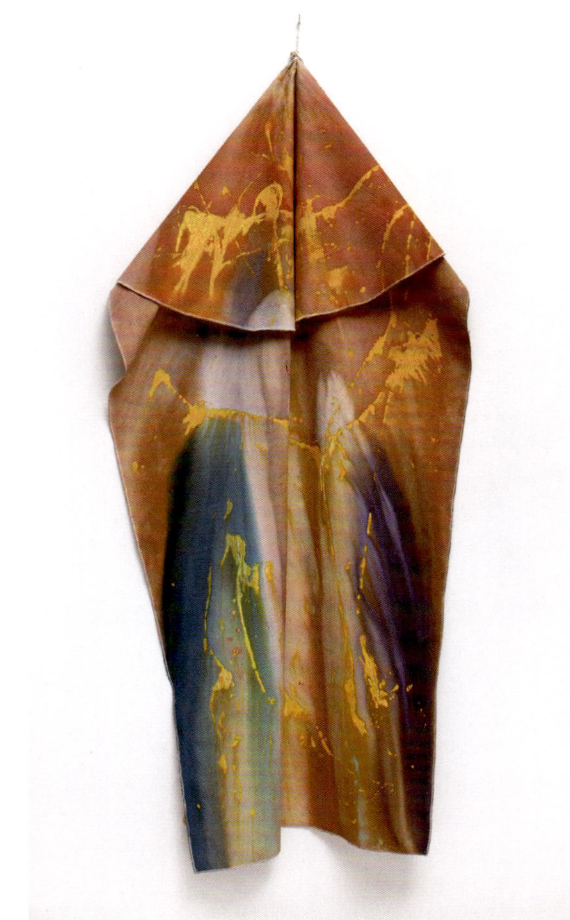

Simmering, 1970

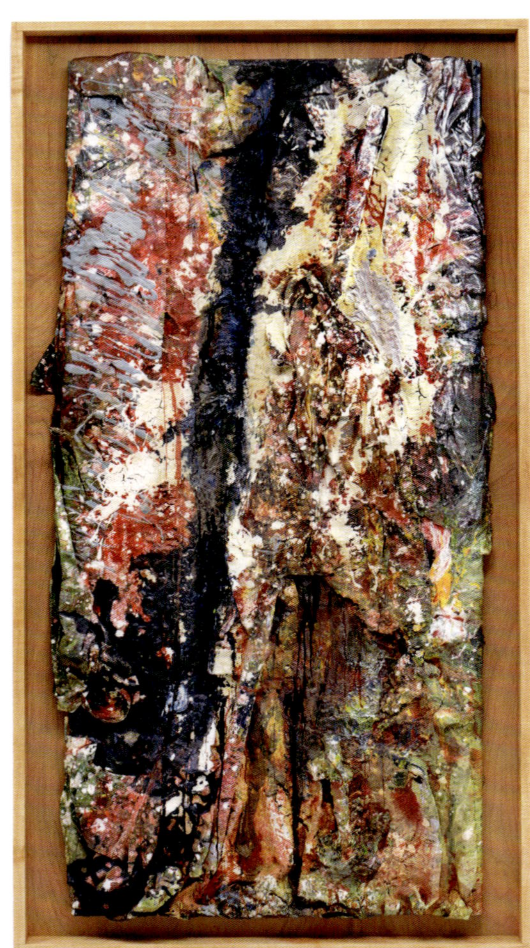

Composed (formerly Dark As I Am), 1968–74

Another and perhaps starker example of anatomical reference is the much-debated construction, *Dark as I Am*, which began in 1968, in Gilliam's studio and emerged for public exhibition in 1973 with a new title, *Composed (formerly Dark as I Am)* (1968–74, below left).[58] Gilliam worked on the piece during the entire time it was resident in his studio. Critics have often remarked on its resemblance to Robert Rauschenberg's assemblages, but Rauschenberg made use of found objects. In contrast, Gilliam deliberately chose intensely personal objects to include. Photographs of the installation reveal a piece that looks as though someone has opened the artist's private closet to reveal the personal objects that make up his daily life: a knapsack with a leather strap that would cross a chest; a denim jacket that, in the way it hangs, evokes the shoulder and torso that bore the weight of jacket and bag; boots crusted with layers of paint suggesting the feet (large ones) that wore them and the weight of standing; a trowel conjuring images of the artist's hands. Over the years, Gilliam applied layers of paint so thick and hard and dark that in the photos of the assemblage, the piece looks as though it were cast in bronze. He has chosen to underscore his physicality in his choice of title, as well. Dark skinned and unmistakably a Black man, he names the piece first *Dark as I Am*. Later changing the title, when the work emerges from his studio, to *Composed (formerly Dark as I Am)*, he suggests that he is what he composes and creates.

Dark as I Am, the piece that resided in his studio for many years, introspective and autobiographical, and the 'Cowl' paintings linger over yet another series from this period, 'Jail Jungle'. Like the 'Cowl' paintings, the works that make up the Jail Jungle series reference outerwear, a cloak providing protection from the elements. Overlaid on the draped canvases is an accumulation of objects. Gilliam, once again, inserts not just found objects, but objects evocative of an explicit narrative of incarceration. Unlike the personal references of *Dark as I Am*, which suggest the private and intimate, the autobiographical, the content of the 'Jail Jungle' series turns outward, made of up what the artist has observed. He has encased the drapes in boxes and placed the fabric under glass, confronting the viewer with a bracingly candid empiricism. Unlike in much of Gilliam's work, glass separates the viewer from the painting.

Throughout his career, Gilliam has created works that are uncanny in the way in which they evoke a person or a relationship. Perhaps the most famous is his 1969 painting, *April 4* (1969, pp. 108–09) a tribute to Dr. Martin Luther King, Jr. on the one-year anniversary of his death. Gilliam would paint a series of six or seven canvases on this theme. *Red April* (1970) is another example of a painting that made use of his formal innovation to reflect the state of his city and, with the evocation of the wounded in the stains and drips of colour, is elegiac in its tribute to King. Another example is a painting that memorializes an experience of his youngest child, Leah Franklin. As Leah remembers, they were in middle school, wrestling with a school assignment. Their task was to 'create a work of art in the manner of an artist you admire'. Leah chose Renoir, but was struggling with the assignment. Gilliam noticed the difficulty they were having and gave them a set of watercolours and words of encouragement that allowed them to work through an impasse. *Leah's Renoir* (1979, pp. 36–37) was the piece he created to celebrate their breakthrough.[59] Binstock notes the sheer physical labor that went into making the piece, the raking, mopping, construction of collage pieces, the layering of the paint on the surface as well as the size convey the work of creativity. The piece is one of the largest paintings on a stretcher that Gilliam made.[60] Under the dense surface, layered with dark blue, almost black paint, bright sparks of colour pierce the surface like electric bolts, commemorating struggle and discovery. The painting, a masterpiece that now resides in the permanent collection of the Metropolitan Museum of Art, is one of those moments in Gilliam's oeuvre when abstraction speaks intimately. His tribute to his youngest child is a powerful example of the artist commenting both to himself and to his audience. His capacity to do both is particularly evident in the public commissions he would take on starting in the mid-1970s and continuing to the end of his career. The changes he provoked in his practice, working processes and material is worth examining closely.

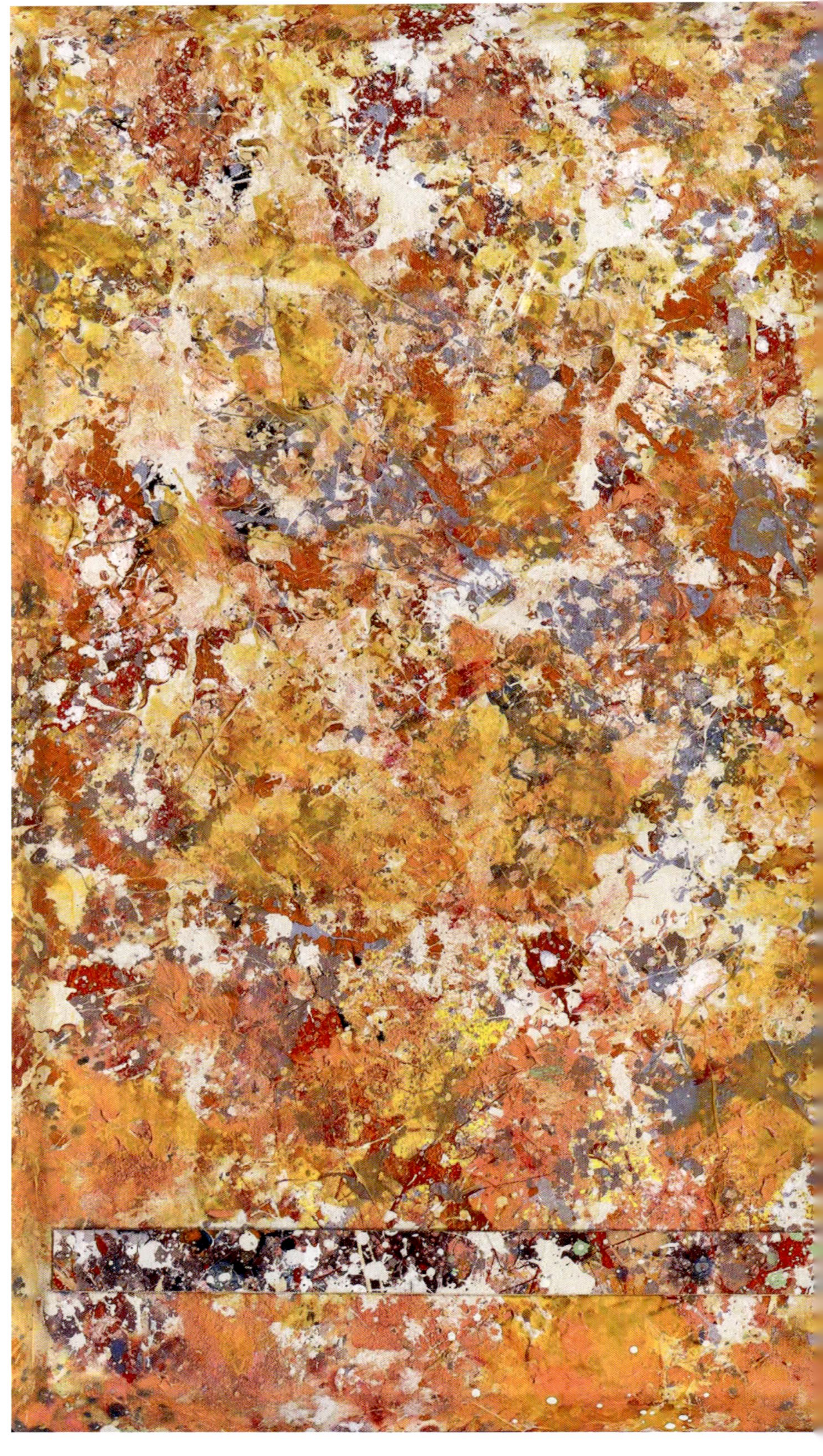

Toward a Red, 1975

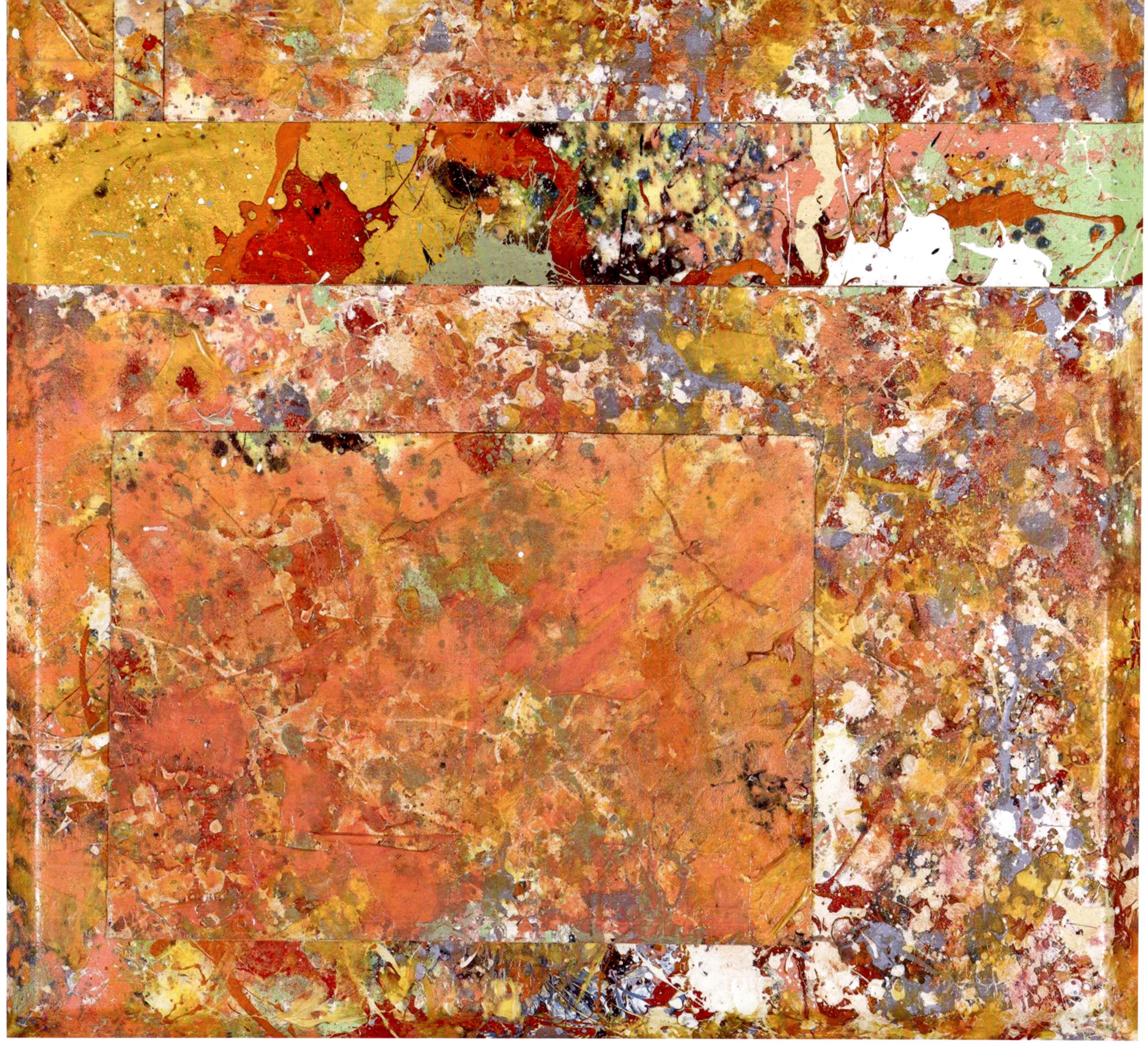

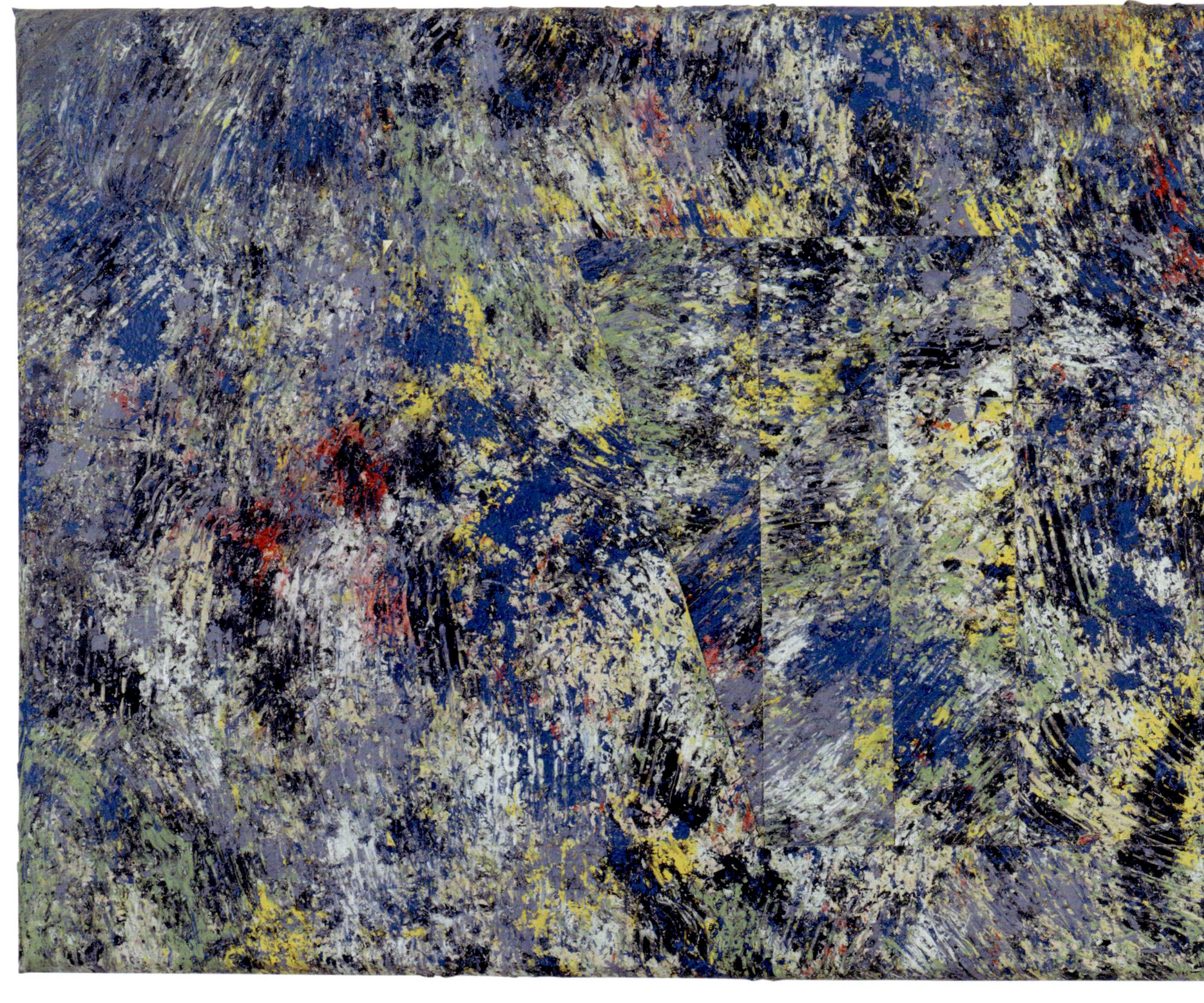

Leah's Renoir, 1979

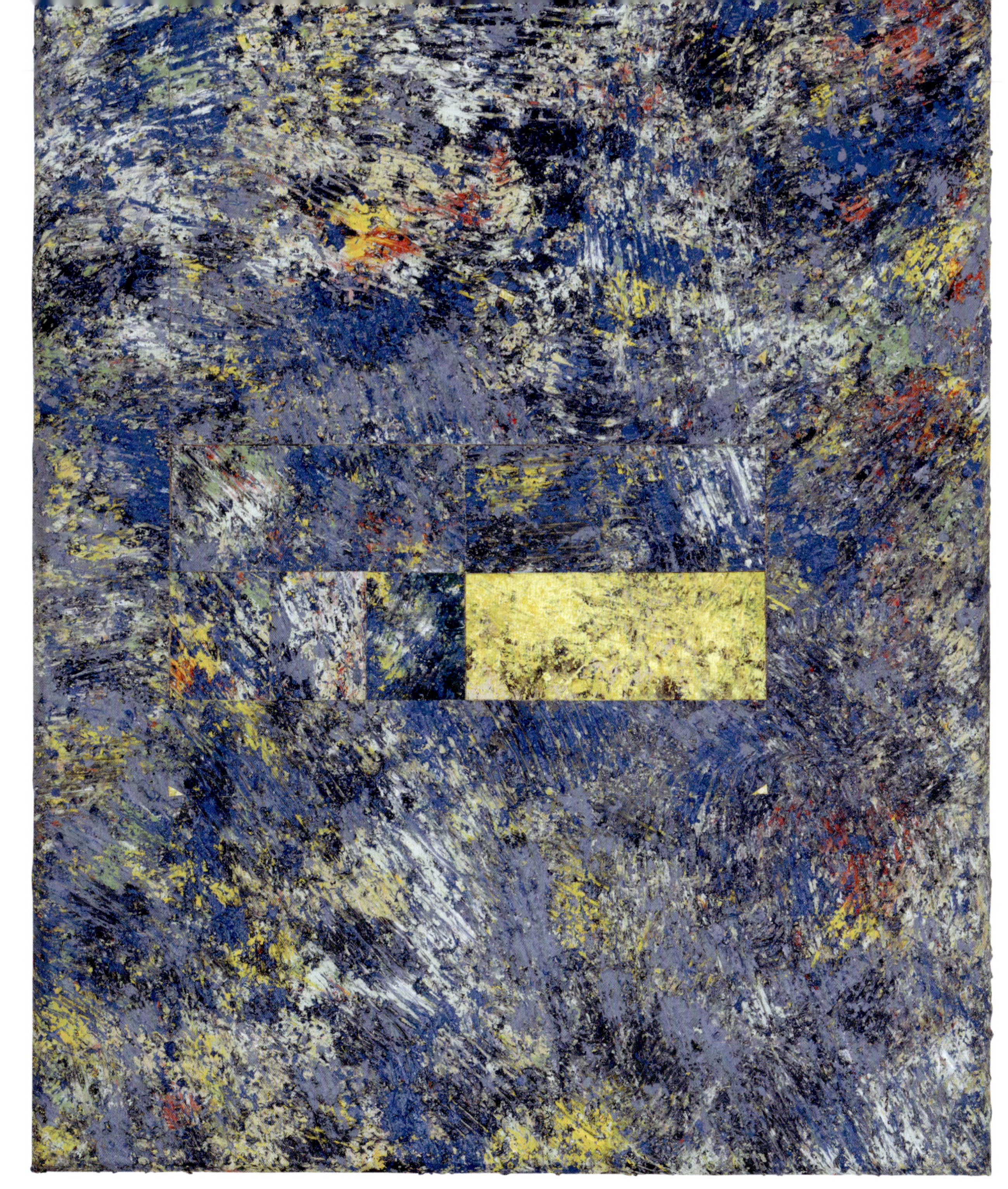

The Philadelphia Museum of Art (PMA) is a majestic structure. Whenever I walk down Spring Garden Street, I spot the museum as I cross the bridge over the Schuylkill River. The river divides my scrappy inner-city, West Philadelphia neighbourhood from the elegant Center City hill, atop which the museum resides. In the 1970s, buoyed by a new federal program, 'Art, and Architecture', sponsored by the United States General Services Administration (GSA), the museum commissioned a series of artists to create public works. Their intention was to connect the museum, which stood remotely on a hill, to the vitality of the city below. Gilliam's studio mate Krebs received a commission and Gilliam would quickly discover that accepting and eventually competing for public commissions was a way to make a living. When the call from the PMA came, he made several visits to Philadelphia.[61] He noted a bronze sculpture of Neptune that stood outside of the museum and a series of bronze rings that encircled the museum's façade, a reference to the rings that according to Greek mythology were used to tie seahorses to Neptune's temple. In 1975 with the help of sail makers, Gilliam created six pieces – two were 30 by 90 feet and four were 30 by 60 feet – and named the piece *Seahorses* (1975, pp. 40–41). The six works billowed gracefully and playfully with the wind, echoing the shape and movement of seahorses. No longer confined by interior space, Gilliam found the exterior space liberating. Even huger than his inaugural display of Drape paintings at the Corcoran Gallery of Art, the project consumed 16,800 square feet of material and 250 gallons of paint. Vast though it may have been, the contrast between the brightly stained canvas and soft, graceful folds, against the unyielding surface of the monumental museum had a cheerfulness that belied the museum's solemn exterior. Wind and rain savaged the drapes and caused Gilliam to re-install them twice. Each time, he invented a new way to strengthen the cords and pulleys, until he had a reasonably secure way to keep his sea animals gracefully dancing along the museum's surface.

This early commission benefitted from work completed a few years earlier. In his 1971 painting, *Rondo* (p. 133) he had shaped the draped folds into a tondo and hung it on the wall. A commission from the San Francisco Museum of Modern Art, two years before the Philadelphia Museum of Art commission, produced *Autumn Surf* (1973). Hung from a twenty-foot ceiling, the piece, as presented in photographs, consumed its interior space as if it were an oversized interior tent or shelter. Gilliam's use of polypropylene, a synthetic fabric used for sail boats, instead of cotton duck, gave him experience in working with the material in advance of the Philadelphia commission. Gilliam also had to invent a system of cords, lines and pulleys that, together with wooden beams, could hoist the material and, at the same time, underscore the idea of the process of construction. *Autumn Surf* was mounted and remounted at several galleries and museums across the country, at times renamed *Niagara* or *Niagara Extended* (also the title of a 1968 draped painting). Composing the piece in response to the different interior spaces of the museums lent an air of intrigue and unpredictability to Gilliam's work.

From *Autumn Surf* and *Seahorses*, Gilliam moved to a major public project with his 1977 environmental installation, *Custom Road Slide* (pp. 134–35) at Artpark in Lewiston, New York, which he installed on the shale cliffs near Niagara Falls. The space was nature itself, in all its volatile and unpredictable manifestations. Stephanie, his oldest child, was the first to accompany him and serve as his assistant, Melissa followed later. The experience contributed to Stephanie's decision to become an architect. She was moved by 'the way the spaces we occupy influence the way we feel' (she later switched professions to film and television production design). They both remember the thrill of working outdoors in an environment that refused to remain stable. Of this piece, in a letter to Hugh Davies, Gilliam noted, 'the initial phase was performed rather than constructed, in that lengths of cloth and fabric hung over the cliff and were destroyed by a series of storms until they lay like ordinary objects on a slope of shale thirty feel below'.[62] Environmental art is the name that the era bestowed on works of art built to exist as part of the landscape. No stranger to the outdoors, Gilliam was excited by the fickle conditions of a cliff-side site. Whatever they constructed during the day, the wind and unstable terrain near Niagara Falls would alter the next day, setting up a whole new set of challenges. Process, working, constructing, altering and responding to change were all welcomed by an artist whose practice thrived on those attributes.

Gilliam continued to develop his facility with public installations as he worked on complicated temporary installations. Intense planning and design, for example, was evident in his working process for one of his most stunning temporary installations, *Of Fireflies and Ferris Wheels*, which was displayed from 3 May–22 June 1987 (p. 137). Not strictly speaking a public commission, the work, however, had a set of complex, intensively collaborative production requirements. The documentation of its staging, released several years after the video was shot, provides a close look at the types of problems posed by works executed in public places. The short, YouTube video that documents its composition reveals Gilliam's willingness to explore ever-more daring solutions.[63] The site for the piece was the eleventh-century monastery that now houses the chapel gallery of the Kunstmuseum Kloster Unser Lieben Frauen, in Magdeburg, Germany. Here, memory was Gilliam's inspiration. He recalls an outing when he took his YMCA students on a Ferris wheel ride. Looking down from the heights, he noted that the sun reflecting on the water in a river below made the water look like ribbons. He remembers thinking to himself, 'I wish I could paint that'. His opportunity to capture this memory came with the commission in Magdeburg. Gilliam would comment that the work of art and the working processes became their own theatre. Part of the labor involved was incorporating an ambitious print-making procedure into the finished piece. He used hundred-yard lengths of paper that he fed through a web-press-like device. To see the finished product, Gilliam and his small army of assistants had to unroll the long sheets of printed fabric on a frozen lake. Onto the printed sheets, Gilliam then applied splashes, brushes and pools of paint. His ability to master such a complex printmaking process is no accident. Beginning with his partnership with Stovall, Gilliam, as noted earlier, had visited print workshops all over the United States and Europe. The expertise he accumulated paid off. Using a total of a thousand yards of polypropylene, Gilliam harnessed the energy of a team of printmakers and painter's assistants to create the playfulness of a remembered childhood, by festooning the ceiling of the chapel. What is particularly revealing in the video of the Magdeburg installation is the way in which he corrals the collaborative team to create a work that has a single authorial voice – a task that he faced with all of his public work, temporary and permanent.

Success with early temporary public works such as *Seahorses*, and *Custom Road Slide* brought a stream of opportunities for Gilliam to work on more permanent public commissions. These started with *Triple Variants* in 1979 for the Richard Russell Federal Building, Atlanta, and continued throughout his career with at least one installed posthumously. His installations took him all over the United States as well as to Chile, Korea and Germany, and introduced new ways of thinking about planning and organizing a team of collaborators. Public work required formal planning and design, often working with architects or engineers and construction crews on the installation. Gilliam was able to immerse himself in these, sometimes complex problems and still explore the 'serial manumissions' of his own work. *Triple Variants*, his first engagement, made Gilliam quickly realize that the accidental and serendipitous might work for an environmental piece, but a permanent installation required more planning. He engaged a young architect's assistant, Steven Spurlock, who would produce a total of eight maquettes for successful and unsuccessful commissions. Spurlock worked in a loft above Gilliam's studio and with Stephen Freitch, Gilliam's assistant, helped visualize the work the artist had conceived for various commissions, each one posing a unique set of problems.

Of the many public commissions that Gilliam completed, two works deserve special mention: *Sculpture with a "D"*, (1983, pp. 276–77) for the Davis Square subway station in Cambridge Massachusetts, and *Yet Do I Marvel (Countee Cullen)* (2016, p. 42) for the lobby of the National Museum of African American History and Culture in Washington, D.C. *Sculpture with a "D"* was 15' 7" by 44' 10", an assemblage of geometric metal panels, some monochromatic, some bearing stained stripes – a bold statement on how public art could alter the environment. As Gilliam would quickly learn when making the work for the Massachusetts Transportation Authority, transit stations pose a challenge for public artwork. The audience for art in a subway or light-rail station is transient, often distracted and consumed with the urgency of getting from one place to the next. As John Anderson notes: 'public art, almost by necessity, requires scale. It's in the open, away from a studio, gallery, home. It competes with buildings, passersby, car horns, landscape … it is expected to be there tomorrow, next month, and oftentimes next decade, requiring material that will withstand the elements: wind, rain, snow, ice and harsh sunlight'.[64] Gilliam understood these requirements. Aluminium replaced canvas as his material of choice and he enlisted the expertise of Spurlock and Freitch to create the necessary armature, a complicated metal grid that, on the one hand, would hold Gilliam's dense metal structure and, on the other hand, attach to the smooth concrete retaining wall. Nothing of the complicated installation is evident. The piece is an unexpected splash of excitement in an otherwise bland environment, its decorative metal D hanging playfully on the bottom of the piece as a delightful piece of whimsy.

Gilliam's bold constructions were often called on to fill the walls of libraries, schools and cultural institutions. One widely heralded event was the opening of the National Museum of African American History and Culture in 2016. After years of determined effort, the new museum marked an acknowledgement of the monumental cultural contributions that the ancestors of the formerly enslaved in the United States made to American culture. Gilliam's five panels for the lobby evoked the city itself. He enjoyed a life-long fascination with the visual heraldry of Washington, D.C., a global city filled with embassies, each waving its national flag, with many memorials and monuments. The seat of American government, it emanates a sense of ceremony and ritual. In an interview with the artist, Peter Halley, Gilliam commented, 'Washington is a tremendous town of emblems. The American Flag, or really all sorts of flags are displayed everywhere. Many of the flags of nations were displayed in a building that was semicircular near the State Department. There would be flags on staffs the width of an entire window. Visually and literally, I think that was really a source painting'.[65]

Each of the five panels is like a flag that lays claim to a newly discovered territory, the hard-fought acknowledgement of the effort to lay claim to the value of African American history and culture to the American narrative. This heraldic work, a formal masterpiece, also resonates musically with the building's design elements, echoing the overlapping slats that architects, Sir David Adjaye, J. Max Bond Jr. and Philip Freelon chose for the lobby's ceiling. The dimensions are monumental: with an overall dimension of 96 x 258 by 4 ½ inches. Overlaid on the strict architectonic structure is the lyrical title, *Yet Do I Marvel*, taken from a line in Countee Cullen's 1925 poem: 'Yet do I marvel at this curious thing: To make a poet black and bid him sing!' (see pp. 287–288) This work continues Gilliam's ongoing celebration of Black cultural heroes in literature,

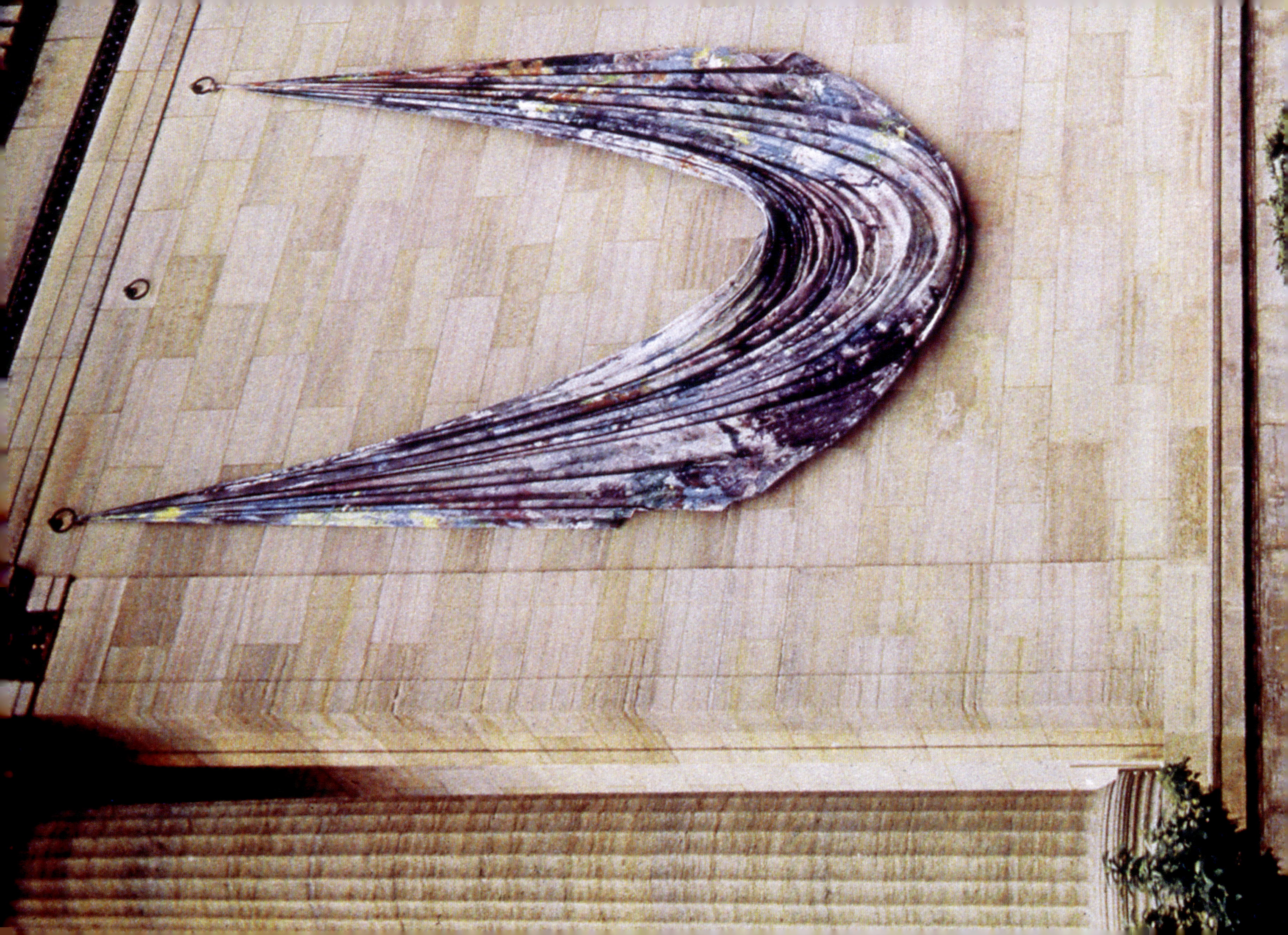

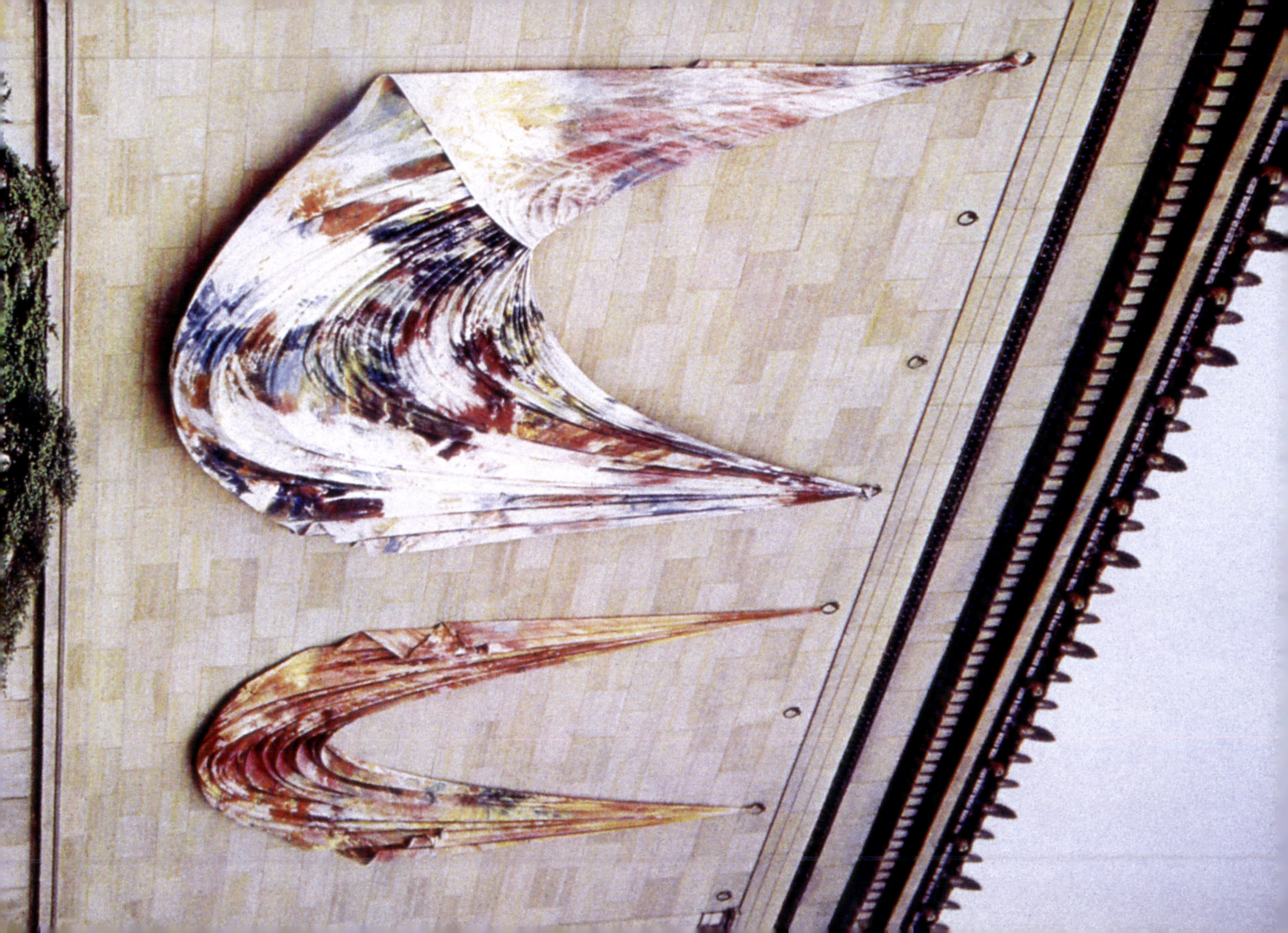

poetry and music and harkens back to his personal history. In its straight lines and saturated surfaces, the monumental piece looks back to Gilliam's hard-edge abstractions, and forward to his re-working of those earlier works. An example of the latter is *Homage to the Square* (2016–17, below right), a set of four squares, each 60 x 60 x 3 ⅜, and a carefully calibrated balance of colour and geometry that looks like a bigger, bolder version of Gilliam's earlier hard-edge paintings.

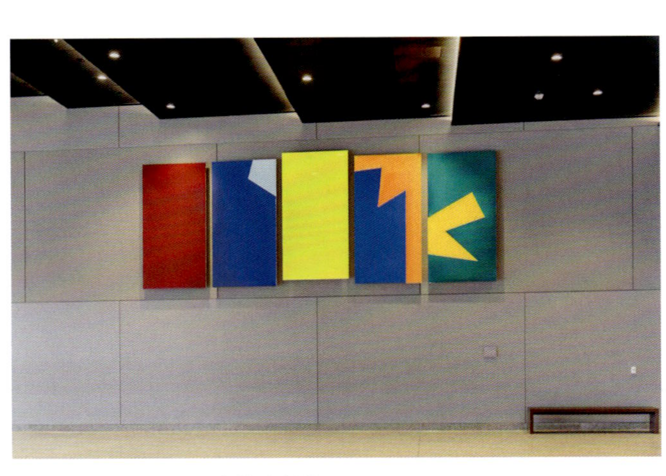

Yet Do I Marvel (Countee Cullen), 2016

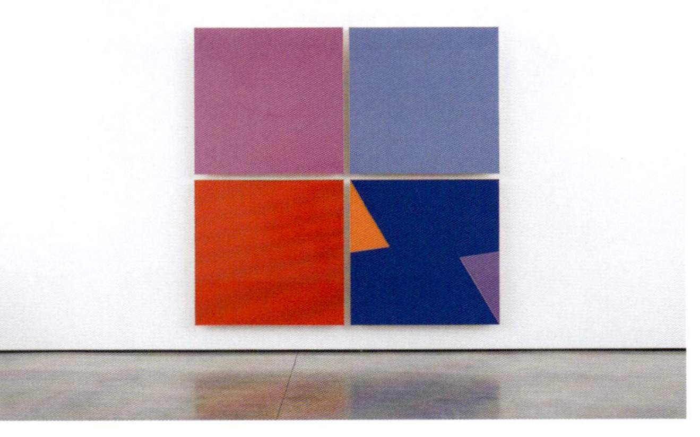

Homage to the Square, 2016–17

RED AND BLACK TO "D"

As Gilliam moved from the 1970s to the 1980s, he not only returned to painting on canvases that he stretched, but he also re-emphasized a cornerstone of his painting: colour. Always a dominant formal element, colour was a subject in and of itself with the emergence first of white paintings, then red, followed by black as dominant colours. Malevich was a predecessor for both his white and black paintings and his white on white painting, an invitation to see infinite variety in the seeming uniformity of white. Gilliam also seems to be inviting the viewer to pause and see what resides below the surface of a seemingly bland, undifferentiated surface: a dappled and stained canvas. Raking, scrubbing, building up layers of paint and erasing them only to re-build surfaces, Gilliam produced a palette of bright colours below the encrusted white surface that emerges on close inspection.

Decades after the initial white paintings, Gilliam returned to white as a dominant colour in 2021 in the exhibition, 'Moving West Again', one of several mounted by David Kordansky Gallery in the last decade of his life. A video, filmed on the occasion of the exhibition captures Gilliam's expression of the multiple ways of experiencing the paintings. In one observation, he notes the physicality of seeing the paintings in the interior space of a gallery: 'it's like an essay, with the various presentations, the look, the way that it interacts with you visually and your body presently. And the way that the light, or the atmosphere, the space within the gallery creates a kind of content as you move around it. The presence of the painting in a sense being very simple. White melds with the wall, and the whiteness makes it less visible, but sort of pleasant, sort of Zen-like'.[66]

Jason Moran, who wrote the essay for the catalogue, *Moving West Again*, recalls that in his interview with Gilliam, the artist referred to the surface of these paintings as building 'a callus'. Moran, himself refers to the layers of paint as 'sediment' and labels the taut, bevel-edged canvas as 'skin', and the frame or stretcher a 'gourd'.[67] Moran's references to the natural world give the sense that he is talking about the paintings as if they were a living thing. This was not an uncommon response from those who fell in love with Gilliam's work. Gawlak remembers one of his collectors referring to the beating heart inside of Gilliam's painting. Moran describes the way in which the artist has caught the light with 'tin shot, aluminium, wax pellets, and copper', and, as noted earlier by Williams, 'there was a light coming from the work'. As he did his entire life, Gilliam allowed himself the luxury of taking a sudden U-turn to renew and rework a style from deep inside the knapsack of his past work.

Gilliam's foray into white paintings was followed by an investigation of red and black surfaces. An outstanding example is the 1975 painting, *Toward a Red* (pp. 34–35), which incorporated collaged pieces of canvas, creating a dense surface to the painting. The black paintings, the third in the trio of colours, also possibly influenced by Malevich, takes on an ironic meaning, based on recent art-historical scholarship. Scholar and curator Adrienne Edwards makes note of a recently discovered inscription that Malevich appended to his 1913/1915 painting, *Black Square*. In his own hand, referencing an earlier French artist, Alphonse Allais, Malevich has written in French: 'negroes battling in a cave'.[68] Given that this discovery was not made until 2015, Gilliam had no knowledge of this 'fugitive reference' when admiring the work of this early abstractionist. Its belated discovery, nonetheless, counsels caution around what might be hidden, submerged, beneath layers of paint.

Around this time, Gilliam also worked with shaped canvases, using a single colour and the addition of collage. This exploration catapulted him in new directions, as he let go of the immensely successful drapes that brought national attention. I met Gilliam at a milestone moment during his exploration of the colours red and black, when we collaborated on his solo exhibition 'Red and Black to "D"' at the Studio Museum in Harlem in 1982. In preparation for the show, Gilliam sent me the following narrative:

The 'Red/Black' [underline his] is a series of single paintings made to exist within architectural spaces through the process of installation.

The first series of works was exhibited in a show entitled 'Installations: Antonokos, Gilliam, Krebs' at the Middendorf-Lane Gallery in the Summer of 1981. As the title implies, the show had to do with the process of installations. This was a small series of the paintings and filled the downstairs spaces.

The next enlarged version of the show contained fifteen paintings and was shown at the Nexus Gallery in Atlanta in the Fall of that year.

The final exhibition of these works occurred at the Miami-Dade Public Library in February 1982.

These works are formalized in the studio and gain their concept through the process of installation in any given space. The works are installed vertically or horizontally from all corners and centers – no two installations are ever the same.[69]

'Red and Black to "D"' opened on 16 November 1982, and ran until 27 February 1983. By the time the show was mounted, the museum had moved from its loft space, where Gilliam first exhibited in 1969, to a 60,000 square foot building on west 125th street, Harlem's main commercial corridor. The institution was well on its way to becoming a fully accredited fine arts museum, one of the many pluralistic grass-roots organizations that sank their roots and ignited a permanent diversification of the American art world. Gilliam's exhibition was an important show of support for the museum from an A-list artist. Attracting critics from major publications, collectors and other museum professionals, Gilliam's celebrity also provided young curators and scholars like me, as well as the late Deirdre Bibby and a young Kellie Jones, now a MacArthur award-winning scholar, with the opportunity to engage an artist of national and international stature. Jones researched and compiled the excellent chronology for the catalogue and later wrote a landmark publication for an assessment of Black abstract artists, previously cited, *Black Artists and Abstraction 1964–1980*. Chromatic focus, the use of collaged elements and shaped canvases introduced to Gilliam's art during the fiercely experimental decade of the 1970s, gave the exhibition an unusual focus and intensity. Whereas the Red and Black paintings were intense, the D paintings were more playful. Full of colour, smaller than the red or black paintings, they bore metal D shapes protruding from the bright surfaces. 'Red and Black to "D"' was a breathtaking exhibition in the double-height galleries of the new Max Bond designed space. A viewer could stand in the atrium and look down on the paintings or in the gallery below, with its 17-foot ceilings, and be surrounded by them. The viewer experienced the space as dictated by the paintings' impact: their scale, the pulsating, almost living density of colour and the assertiveness of the surfaces filled with paint, rhoplex, and slices of canvas and paper. Together, mass, colour and scale combined to create the sense that each painting was a 'bas-relief', as I wrote in the catalogue essay forty years ago.[70]

Titles of the paintings in 'Red and Black to "D"' bore references either to nature or to art, ancient and modern.[71] Several titles referenced *Tholos*, taken from the Greek meaning a circular structure, often a tomb. Another title, *Cartouche* (1981, pp. 140–41) references an Egyptian tablet filled with hieroglyphics. The painting *Lion's Rock Arc* (1981, pp. 146–47) is perhaps an evocation of Lion Rock in Sigiriya, an archaeological site in Sri Lanka. With its dense layering, the painting evokes the act of digging that comes with disinterring the cultural footprint of civilizations long gone. In a more contemporary vein, one of the 'D' paintings, *To Miró – to Birds*, is a tribute to the modern artist, one of his European artistic forebears, and to nature. *Elm* in its verticality, resembles a tree, and *Raven*, both black paintings, are evocative of nature, as well. Winning critical praise, Gilliam's work, even as late as the 1980s, still faced resistance from at least one local resident who visited during the run of the show. A young mother brought her three children to the museum and, after touring the galleries, demanded to see the director. When I appeared, she chided me for not displaying work that taught her children Black history and heritage. I am not sure that I was convincing, but I tried to assure her that she was witnessing the evolution of that cultural heritage right before her eyes.

'Red and Black to "D"' marked yet another new phase for Gilliam. After twenty years of marriage, raising three daughters, managing two high-powered careers and often hectic schedules, he and Dorothy Gilliam separated in 1982.[72] In the following years, Gilliam would forge a forty-year relationship with Gawlak, an artist in her own right and one-time director of Washington, D.C.'s Middendorf Gallery. Fully immersed in the ins and outs of the art world, she became Gilliam's trusted thought partner and most ardent cheerleader.

The Studio Museum's solo exhibition of Gilliam's work would be his last in New York, until 1989, when he returned to the city for an exhibition at the Barbara Fendrick Gallery in Soho. For that show, Gilliam layered the surface of his playful 'D' paintings with acrylic paint, mixed with gel, until the surface had the texture of ceramic, raked and ploughed. Often, he would cut the canvas into different shapes so that the painting resembled an assemblage. He then attached loops of heavily painted metal that burst from and contrasted with the geometric shapes of the canvas. John Beardsley, who wrote a brief commentary for the exhibition brochure, notes the way in which Gilliam has 'started to pun' on this hybrid mixture of painting and sculpture.

SAM GILLIAM AND RALPH ELLISON

As Gilliam entered the 1990s, with his national and international artistic reputation well established and his daughters all grown, a colleague recalls that the years had done nothing to mellow his confident swagger. He could still be seen tooling around Washington, D.C. in his Porsche, with his leather jacket and sunglasses, as always, assured in the direction he was headed.[73] Yet Gilliam still had no New York gallery, a circumstance that kept his work on the periphery of the commercial art market, even while he enjoyed critical success. To be on the periphery meant to keep hustling, keep moving from one project to the next, and to keep the wheels of his artistic production turning. The advantage of his situation was that he still maintained the right to sell works from his studio. In the years after I left the Studio Museum, I approached him about acquiring a painting.

Like many Gilliam collectors before us, my husband and I made a trip to his studio. Being inside of the studio felt like being inside of Gilliam's head, witnessing ideas as they took shape, undergoing revisions, additions, subtractions, or complete reconceptualizations. Because it would take us three years to pay for the painting, the one we chose underwent many changes. As our 19 April 1989 signed purchase agreement attests, the original title was *Painted Fingers*, dated 1986, its dimensions 110 x 114 x 8 inches, acrylic on canvas, and acrylic and enamel on aluminium. Shortly before delivery, Gilliam sent us a Polaroid. The piece we were now getting was a newly constructed work entitled *The Superior Soprano I*, dated 1990, acrylic on sculpted canvas, its dimensions 89 x 51 x 24 inches.[74] In his elegant penmanship, Gilliam sent along a note attached to a typewritten text:

This narrative explains the title of the painting:

From 'Going to the Territory' by Ralph Ellison

In the essay, 'The Little Man at Chehaw Station' [underline his], *Ellison reveals how he learned, while a student at Tuskegee to perform for an audience who was not there but might take the appearance of The Little Man at Chehaw Station. The little man sits behind a pot-bellied stove and wears a homburg hat. Such a person is universally conversive about the arts and could cause the artist to lose his abstract pretention and become classical or familial.*

This lesson of the Little Man at Chehaw Station was revealed to Ellison as a music student who used the form of lip sync rather than the classical form in a performance. It was a long time before Ellison felt that he met the little man in the homburg hat.

That time came when he was carrying a petition and he appeared before a door at the basement of a tenement

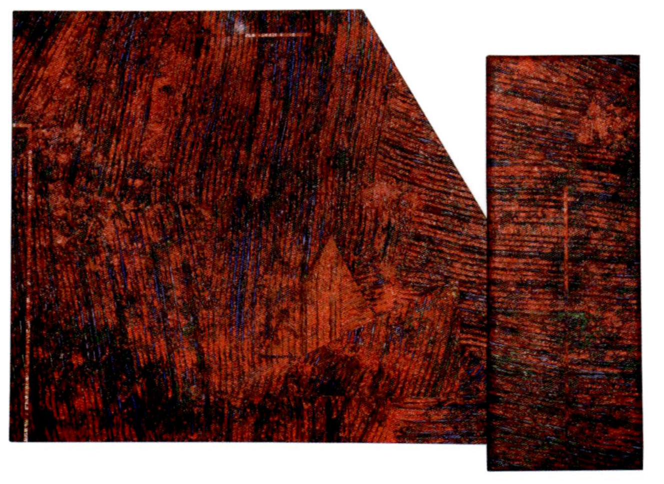

Master Builder Piece, 1981

building where he heard such a noise. The individuals inside were like heavyweights who appeared to be fighting in a very cautious way. Upon opening the door, he found four large men, coal men, who were discussing loudly, before a window ... casting its yellow light ... and ... seated around a circular dining room table where there was a hald [sic]- full pint of whiskey. They were shouting: she is ... she is not ... she is the superior soprano at the Metropolitan.[75] *Ellison who had by this time decided to write rather than perform, knew that he was meeting the Little Man at Chehaw Station.*

This narrative supports the recent works and with bringing before the audience the general spiritual appeal of Amazing Grace to the humerous [sic] appeal that suggests always do your best for the audience, because you never know where you'll find the Little Man.

Accompanying the piece as well was a detailed plan for its installation, in case it had to be moved and re-installed, which indeed it did. The installation plans are an example of the way in which Gilliam had grown increasingly comfortable with detailed plans for the installation of complex works, in this case a sculpted painting. Formally, *The Superior Soprano* resembled the paintings exhibited in the Fendrick Gallery exhibition. There are examples reproduced in the brochure that accompanied the exhibitions. One that forecast *The Superior Soprano* is the piece illustrated in the brochure entitled *Waking Up* (1989). With the title of the piece and reference to Ellison's essay, Gilliam added new meaning to our greatly revised and renamed piece, a personal message directed to us: excellence and its appreciation can be anywhere, not confined only to the cultural community or the art world, but resident in the most unexpected places.

POST-BLACK: ART IN THE 21ST CENTURY

By the turn of the twenty-first century, the art world that Gilliam had entered as a young man had changed in many ways. One measure of that change was an exhibition mounted in 2001 by the Studio Museum in Harlem's Director and Chief Curator, Thelma Golden, with curatorial assistance from Christine Kim, entitled 'Freestyle'. Underscoring the need to cast off labels that confined artists, 'Freestyle' reintroduced the term 'Post-Black',[76] popularized by Golden and artist Glenn Ligon, into the lexicon of art-historical discourse, asserting that a new generation of artists considered discussions of race irrelevant.[77] Whatever one may have thought of the term, it did usher in a shift in both the value of the work of Black artists in the art market and the flourishing of several Black scholars whose work was re-thinking the history of American art. Several books explicitly dealt with Black artists who had chosen abstraction as their artistic idiom. Jones, currently Professor in Art history and Archaeology and the Institute for Research in African American Studies at Columbia University as mentioned, authored the lead essay for the 2006 Studio Museum of Harlem exhibition catalogue, *Black Artists and Abstraction 1964–1980: Energy/Experimentation*. British art historian, Kobena Mercer, formerly Professor of History of Art and African American Studies at Yale and now Charles Stevenson Chair in Art History and the Humanities at Bard College, edited and contributed to a collection of two important volumes, *Cosmopolitan Modernisms* in 2005 and *Discrepant Abstraction* in 2006, both of which set Black American abstractionists within a global and mostly non-western context. A year later, Darby English, the Carl Darling Buck Professor of Art History at the University of Chicago and formerly Consulting Curator at MoMA, presented the complexities of visual representation using a case study for each of five Black artists – Kara Walker, Fred Wilson, Isaac Julien, Glenn Ligon and William Pope. L – represented in *How to See a Work of Art in Total Darkness*. More recently Courtney J. Martin, director of the Yale Center for British Art commissioned by collectors, Pamela Joyner and Fred Giuffrida, compiled and contributed to a collection of art historians to trace Black abstract artists over four generations for the publication, *Four Generations: The Joyner Giuffrida Collection of Abstract Art*.[78] Though Gilliam was included in only two of these studies, each widened the context within which his art could be viewed, which was a significant change from the world he entered as an artist fifty years earlier.

As the lens of the American art-historical narrative was opening, the broader perspective served as a backdrop to a major retrospective of Gilliam's work that Binstock curated at the Corcoran Gallery of Art in 2005. Binstock's selection made it abundantly clear that Gilliam was a major innovator. Accompanied by a comprehensive essay on his work, based, in part, on Binstock's dissertation research, 'Sam Gilliam: A Retrospective' was a major addition to the canon of Black American art. For two years, the show travelled with stops at the Speed Art Museum in Gilliam's hometown of Louisville, where he is still a local hero, then to the Telfair Museum of Art in the coastal town of Savannah, Georgia. The tour ended at the Contemporary Art Museum in Houston. All were excellent museums, but none (save for Houston, perhaps) resided in a major art market. Gilliam, once again, was undeterred. In the years following the retrospective, he seemed to regain new energy, fresh ideas and a surge in his already ferocious productivity. This surge coincided with an auspicious visit from a set of admirers. The result is an encore every bit as exhilarating as the main show.

WHAT TOOK YOU SO LONG?

During a late-night conversation with Johnson, Kordansky discovered that, like him, his friend not only admired but revered Gilliam. Gilliam's work had been a seminal influence on Johnson's evolution as an abstract painter during his years at the Art Institute of Chicago and an inspiration during Kordansky's tenure as an art student at the California Institute of the Arts.[79] Five years after the Corcoran Gallery of Art retrospective ended, the two friends travelled east to Washington, D.C., accompanied by Mike Homer, a partner and senior director at David Kordansky Gallery, to make a pilgrimage to Gilliam's studio. Touring the studio, the trio 'discovered' a stash of hard-edge paintings from the 1960s. Johnson was struck by the rigour of the paintings and how fiercely they defied the expectations of Black artists during that era. The group was jubilant, as if they were raiding the treasure trove of the artist's knapsack. Surprised by the jubilation the group evinced at the sight of the paintings, tears of joy came to Gilliam's eyes, and he asked the trio, 'what took you so long?' Kordansky began representing Gilliam in 2012 and invited Johnson to curate a show mounted the next year that would become a major reassessment of Gilliam's early work and a reintroduction of his artistic journey to a younger generation of artists and to an entirely new generation of collectors, critics and patrons.

Kordansky followed the exhibition of Gilliam's hard-edge paintings with a series of solo shows that were the equivalent of a slow-motion retrospective, allowing viewers to get a focused close-up of Gilliam's work. He followed 'Sam Gilliam: Hard Edge Paintings 1963–1966' with the 2016 exhibition 'Sam Gilliam: Green April', which concentrated, as noted earlier, on Gilliam's early radical innovations form 1967–73, a period that covered some of his most dramatic breakthroughs and put Gilliam on the international art map. Complementing the 2016 show, three years later was a look at Gilliam's watercolours from about the same period, titled 'Sam Gilliam. Starting: Works on Paper 1967–1970'. This opportunity to look back through these several carefully curated exhibitions, some accompanied by serious publications, also provided an opportunity to continue expanding Gilliam's audience. In 2018, a major retrospective of the critical 1967–73 period at the Kunstmuseum Basel provided an in-depth penetrating examination of these years, supported by a major publication.

Gilliam's exhibition in Basel, followed by Kordansky's introduction of the artist to Glimcher, fuelled even more interest in Gilliam's work. Glimcher's Pace Gallery, the hub of which resides in New York, has satellite sites all over the world. Like Kordansky, he made the requisite pilgrimage to Washington, D.C. to visit the octogenarian in his studio. For any number of reasons, Gilliam had maintained his independence and never signed with a New York gallery. Getting him to change at this point in his career was a challenge.

In the months before Glimcher formally invited Gilliam to join Pace Gallery, he made several trips to Washington, D.C. with plans for his new Chelsea gallery, and on one occasion showed them to Gilliam, excitedly describing the new gallery space. Gilliam showed no emotion during the presentation. When Glimcher had finished, the artist was silent. Finally, he asked, 'are you asking me a question?'.[80] The question, of course, was whether Gilliam would break his life-long resistance to a New York gallery and show in this dramatic new space. His answer, as we know, was yes. Pace Gallery, New York, along with Kordansky's Los Angeles-based gallery, acted as an accelerant for new work.

'Sam Gilliam: Existed Existing', delayed for a few months, because of COVID-19 shutdowns, opened at the end of 2020. Even for those who knew Gilliam's work well, the exhibition presented several brand-new directions executed by the eighty-six-year-old artist. Brightly dyed pyramidal structures (Gilliam referred to them as three-dimensional paintings) of dyed wood and metal resonated with the multiple geographies of Gilliam's influences: Constructivism, Ancient Sudanese and African architecture, the sculptures of Smith, the memory of his father's carpentry skills. On the wall hung circular structures, bas-reliefs, with their smooth dyed surfaces allowing the texture of the wood to emerge as if it were its own brushstroke. Accompanying the sculptures were large squares (some as big as 6 feet) of richly saturated monochromatic watercolours on various types of Japanese paper, representing Gilliam's endless experimentation with the medium. So saturated were the watercolours that their surfaces, as Glimcher noted, looked like the skins of something living. Gilliam, in fact, could name the bark of the three trees that supplied each sheet of paper.[81] Completing the show was a selection of densely layered large stretched canvases, some measuring 20 feet wide. Their thick white or black surfaces bristled with the labour of his raking, pouring and sprinkling with sawdust left over from the wooden pyramids. Heroic in size, many celebrated Gilliam's heroes – John Lewis, Nikki Giovanni, Serena Williams, Beyoncé and Althea – jutting out from the walls with Gilliam's signature bevelled-edge stretchers.

On the heels of the successful Pace Gallery exhibition came David Kordansky Gallery's 'Moving West Again'. In preparation for his catalogue essay, musician/composer Moran reverently visited Gilliam in his studio. Gilliam was there with his friend Bennie Johnson. By Johnson's account, the conversation between Moran and Gilliam lasted over four hours.[82] Moran would go on to write a brilliant essay for the 2021 exhibition catalogue for 'Moving West Again'. There is no better text on the ineluctable bond between Gilliam's painting and jazz. Of his many observations on Gilliam's work, Moran likens his radical compositional adventurousness to the explorations of Ornette Coleman and his need for 'stone presence'.[83] Coleman, a saxophonist whom Gilliam admired, avoided the strictures of the marketplace, which, in Coleman's case, was commercial recording studios. Instead of being beholden to a record label, he and his quartet would occupy a Soho loft, awarding themselves the freedom to explore until they found the 'sweet spot'. Gilliam's studio and his resistance to affiliating with a New York gallery until late in life was his equivalent to Coleman's liberated space. Creative liberty was essential for Gilliam, and the accomplishments of the musicians he admired represented that liberty.

As the end neared, 'Epistrophy', the show that Shultz curated, enabled jazz and a friendship to re-assert their importance in Gilliam's life. For me, the show that reconvened Gilliam, Edwards and Williams, was a requiem, a moving reminder of their connection to each other, and the mix of artistic kinship and communal alliance that had been a steady constant, a refrain, throughout careers of dramatic shifts and changes. This longstanding triumvirate underscored a set of common bonds: the deliberate choice of abstraction as their principle artistic vocabulary, their defiance of complaints about the irrelevance of abstraction to a Black reality, the sheer joy and pleasure they took in each other's company, so evident in the video that documents their last meeting, just months before Gilliam's death. Edwards has said that the relationship started out like one of Gilliam's off the stretcher canvases – unpredictable, exciting and ultimately fulfilling.[84] Like their relationship, the works that Gilliam chose to display in 'Epistrophy' highlight his never-ending inventiveness. Stained canvases draped over sawhorses like work clothes after a hard day's labour, mixed with hanging drapes, stark contrasts to the lean constructivist works he had exhibited at Pace Gallery two years earlier. Right to the end, he continued to remind us that there are at least twelve Sam Gilliams.

CODA

During the fall of 2022, I visited Gawlak in their home. Her devotion to and love of everything Gilliam are evident in every word she speaks. She walked me through each room of their home that borders Rock Creek Park. Rock Creek is a dense forest of trees interlaced with trails and changing vistas, a respite from an insistently urban environment. Gilliam enjoyed an unobstructed view of the park as he sat at his desk that faced the floor-to-ceiling windows opening out onto the dense foliage. On his desk, just as he left it, sits a red plastic toy truck, a head shot of Gilliam on the driver's side pasted to the windshield next to a headshot of his young neighbour, a little girl of about ten, who idolized him and his work, on the passenger side. The child inside, who delighted in Ferris wheels and fireflies and mischievousness never left him. On the white walls of his studio and throughout the orderly, austere home are paintings, prints and drawings of some of his artistic heroes – Jacob Lawrence, Glenn Ligon, Rashid Johnson, Julie Mehretu – and of course, his own work. Pieces of brightly coloured furniture, constructions of Gilliam's, introduce sudden bursts of colour that warm and animate the room. He is present everywhere. The force field of his energy still vibrates with the high energy of his final years. When Gawlak drives me to his studio, tended by his current studio manager, Jenn DePalma, who so ably led the team of assistants that fuelled his productivity, Gilliam is present at every turn – in the turntable and stack of vinyl records, the bins filled with works in progress, cans of paint stacked neatly like library books, his notes, tools and materials – all of it ready and waiting for Big Dog to walk into the room.

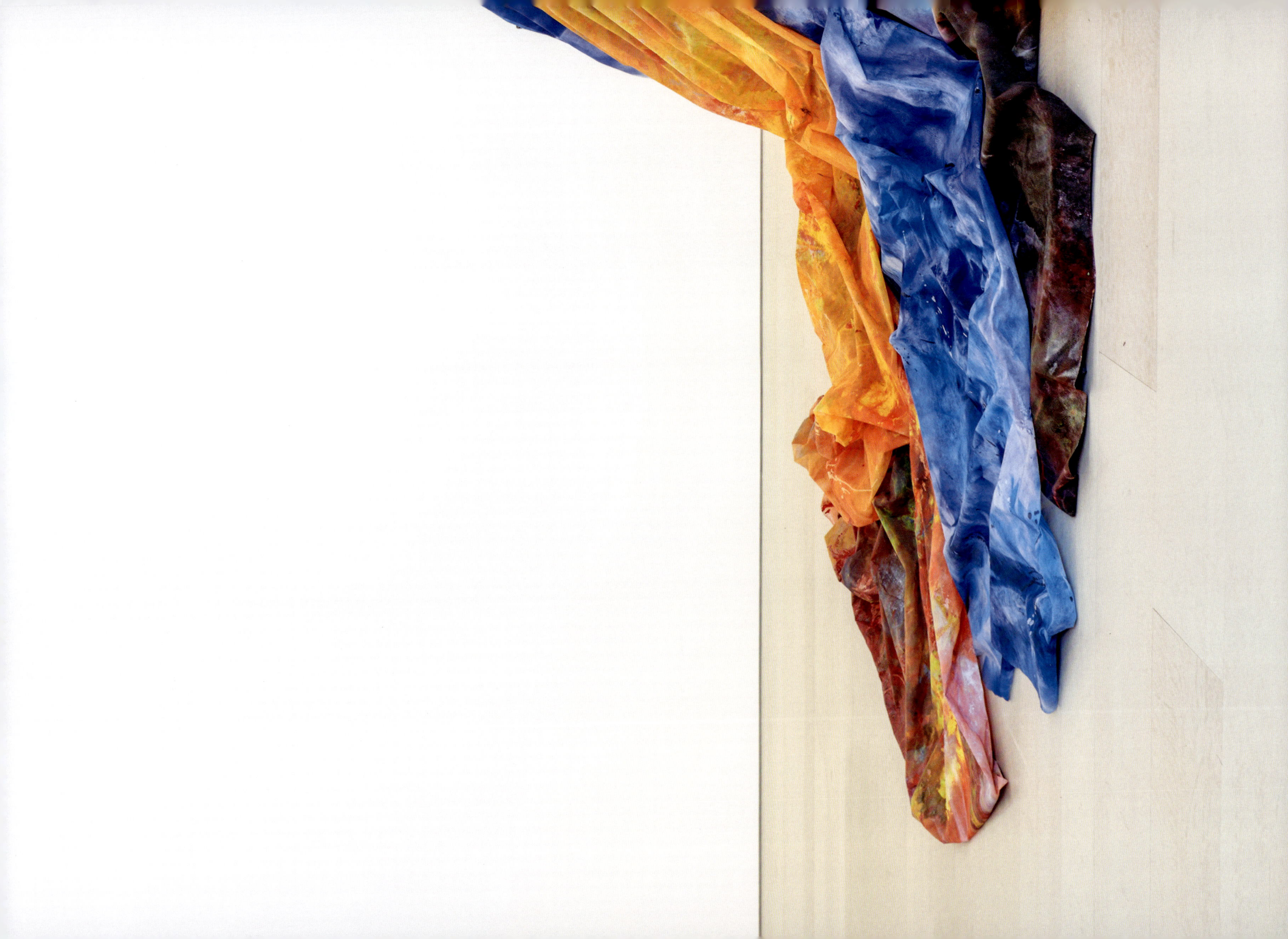

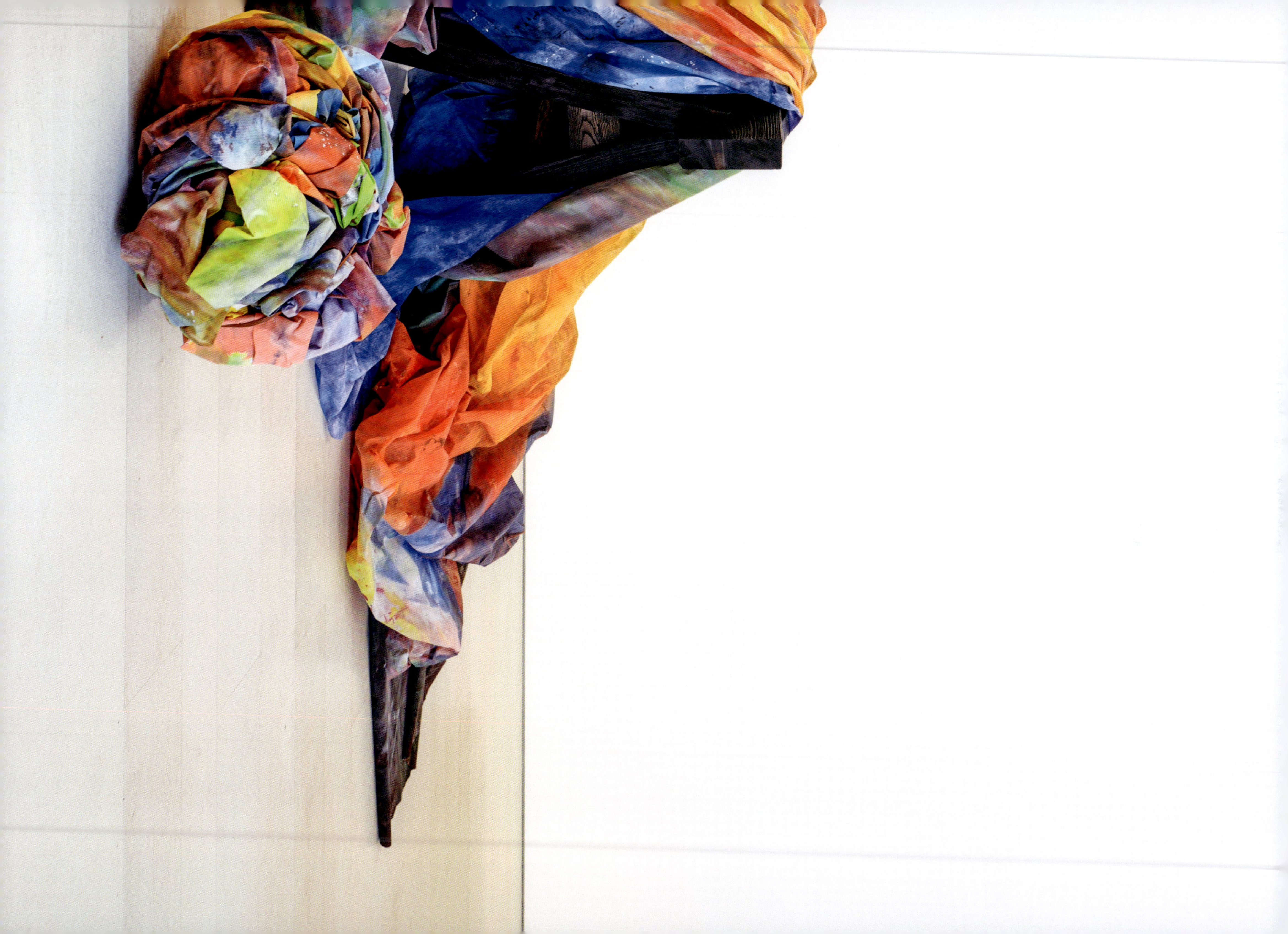

ENDNOTES

1 Telephone interview with Annie Gawlak, Sam Gilliam's widow, 15 September 2022. Gawlak graciously offered details of Gilliam's final years in his studio, insights into their 40 years together as well as anecdotes from his early life.

2 Telephone interview with David Kordansly, 13 October 2022. Kordansky signed Gilliam in 2012. A full list of Gilliam's solo exhibitions at the Kordansky Gallery can found at https://www.davidkordanskygallery.com.artist.sam-gilliam.

3 Jonathan Binstock and Josef Helfenstein, *The Music of Color. Sam Gilliam 1967–1973* at Kunstmuseum Basel, 9 June–30 September 2018, pp. 181–187.

4 Sam Gilliam in conversation with Jennifer Samet, 'Beer with a Painter: Sam Gilliam', 19 March 2016. https://hyperallergic.com/284543/beer-with-a-painter-sam-gilliam/

5 The catalogue of the exhibition includes important texts by Glimcher, Fred Moten, Courtney J. Martin and an interview of Gilliam with Hans Ulrich Obrist, *Sam Gilliam: Existed Existing*, New York: Pace Gallery, 6 November–19 December 2020.

6 Gawlak provided a photograph of Gilliam in his studio dressed in a HazMat suit and a detailed description of the working conditions of Gilliam and his staff led by Jenn DePalma in an email dated 4 February 2023.

7 Shultz relayed the genesis of the exhibition, 'Epistrophy', to Michele Robecchi, Phaidon Press, in an email dated 2 June 2023.

8 Edwards authored the book, *Epistrophies: Jazz and the Literary Imagination*, Cambridge: Harvard University Press, 2017. A video of the program of spoken word, music and song can be found at https://www.pacegallery.com/artists/sam-gilliam/ 27 May 2022.

9 Gawlak, in an email to the author, 19 October 2022, quoted a curator from the Metropolitan Museum of Art, New York.

10 For details of the first twenty years of Sam's life in Washington, D.C., I am especially grateful for the groundbreaking work of Jonathan Binstock. His dissertation, *Sam Gilliam: The Making of a Career 1962–1973* (Ph.D. diss., University of Michigan, Ann Arbor, 2000) and the exhibition catalogue, Jonathan Binstock, *Sam Gilliam: A Retrospective*, Washington, D.C.: Corcoran Gallery of Art, 2005 are comprehensive. Telephone interviews with Gilliam's family provided details of the Gilliams's family life from 1962–1982: Stephanie Gilliam, 14 October 2022; Melissa Gilliam, M.D., MPH, 16 September 2022; and Leah Franklin, 22 October 2022 and Dorothy Gilliam, 31 October 2022. Dorothy Gilliam's autobiography, *Trailblazer: A Pioneering Journalist's Fight to Make the Media Look More Like America*, (Nashville, New York: Center Street, 2019) contains a chapter on her life with Gilliam, 'Being Mrs. Sam Gilliam, 1962–1982', pp. 121–152, which she stated candidly in the interview, Gilliam did not like.

11 Conversation moderated by Ruth Fine with Sam Gilliam, Melvin Edwards, William T. Williams, National Gallery of Art, Washington, D.C., https://www.nga.gov/audio-video/edwards-gilliam-williams.html.

12 Gilliam, 'The Transformation of Nature through Nature', (1986) in Kristine Stiles and Peter Selz, eds. *Theories and Documents of Contemporary Art: A Sourcebook of Artists' Writings* (Berkeley: University of California Press, 1996, revised and expanded in 2012), p. 727–729. See also pp. 56–57 of this volume.

13 *In the Spirit of Collaboration: Sam Gilliam and Lou Stovall*, Miami: Griots' Gallery, 10 June–30 September 2017. My thanks to Lou Stovall's widow, Di Stovall, who provided a number of publications on which Stovall and Gilliam collaborated.

14 Gilliam interview with Don Ball, *NEA Arts Magazine*, Issue 2001, no. 4, arts.gov article.

15 Gilliam interview with Kenneth Young in the Archives of American Art, 18 September 1984.

16 Hans Ulrich Obrist, 'A Conversation with Sam Gilliam', 1 December 2019, Washington, D.C. & June 16, 2020, Skype, in the exhibition catalogue, *Sam Gilliam: Existed Existing*, p. 37.

17 Telephone interview, Dorothy Gilliam.

18 Binstock references in *Sam Gilliam: A Retrospective*, the observation made by scholar, Judith Wilson in her Ph.D. dissertation. See Wilson, *Garden of Music: The Search for Creative Community in the Art and Life of Bob Thompson (1937–1966)*, (Ph.D. diss., Yale University, New Haven, 1995).

19 Sam Gilliam, Oral History Interview, Archives of American Art, 1984.

20 Kellie Jones makes this observation in her essay for the exhibition, *Energy/Experimentation: Black Artists and Abstraction 1964–1980*, New York: Studio Museum in Harlem, 6 April–2 July 2006, 15.

21 Peter Morrin provides insights into Gilliam's teachers at University of Louisville in 'A Remembrance: Sam Gilliam', delivered at the 18 September 2022 memorial at the Speed Art Museum, Louisville, Kentucky. See https/undermain.art/visual-arts/a-remembrance-sam-gilliam/

22 Samet, 'Beer with a Painter', *Hyperallergic*.

23 Obrist, 41.

24 Ibid.

25 Telephone Interview, Gawlak.

26 Gilliam's thesis was titled, 'A Study of Different uses of Solid Forms in Painting'.

27 Gilliam interview with Paul Davis, Curator of Collections, Menil Collection, Houston, https:/m.youtube.com/watch?v=Kmu4QXECi0g.

28 In his dissertation, Binstock includes a full discussion of the pre-eminent role of Howard University in the Washington cultural scene of the 1960s.

29 Dorothy Gilliam recounts Gilliam's hospitalization for anxiety and depression, after becoming agitated and depressed during a visit to Louisville, Christmas, 1963. Years later another incident on a plane in 1976 attracted public attention. *Traiblazer*, pp. 132, 148.

30 Gilliam and Binstock discuss why they did not include the hard-edge paintings in the 2005 Corcoran Gallery of Art retrospective. See Binstock and Helfenstein, *The Music of Color*, p. 19.

31 Installation photographs of the 2013 exhibition can be found at https://www.davidkordanskygallery.com/artist/sam-gilliam/

32 Morrin.

33 Rick Powell (moderator), Jonathan Binstock, Valerie Cassel Oliver, Lisa Farrington, Kellie Jones, Luke Stewart, '(In Person) Coming Full Circle: Conversations about Sam Gilliam', Hirshhorn Museum and Sculpture Garden, YouTube, 22 September 2022. Valerie Oliver Cassel used the phrase 'keeping his roots close', when discussing the way in which Gilliam often introduced into his work cultural references from his early life.

34 See text at https://www.phillipscollection.org/collection/red petals.

35 Mary Schmidt Campbell, *Red and Black to "D": Paintings by Sam Gilliam*, New York: Studio Museum in Harlem, 1982, p. 5.

36 Telephone interview, Dorothy Gilliam.

37 Telephone interview with Kinshasha Holman Conwill, Conwill's widow, 31 October 2022. What was striking about the relationship, according to Kinshasha Conwill, was Gilliam's generosity towards the younger artist.

38 Jenelle Porter, 'Composed', *Sam Gilliam*, Los Angeles: David Kordansky Gallery, 2017, p. 25.

39 Gilliam quoted in Larne Abse Gogarty, '"Something in the Air:" Aesthetic Optimism and Sam Gilliam's Drapes', *The Music of Color*, p. 157.

40 Dorothy Gilliam interview.

41 *The Music of Color,* p. 24.

42 Fred Moten, 'The Circle with a Whole in the Middle', *Sam Gilliam: Existed Existing*. Moten's essay situates Gilliam's art at the nexus of the work of major intellectuals of the African Diaspora as well as vernacular expressions of Black culture, poetry, jazz and the 'whorl', as he puts it, of Gilliam's words.

43 Binstock, *The Music of Color,* p. 21.

44 Walter Hopps, 'Remembering a Revelation', *Sam Gilliam: A Retrospective*, xvi.

45 Carousel Form II landed on the cover of *Art in America*, September–October 1970.

46 See Jasmine Weber, 'Basking in Sam Gilliam's Endless Iterations', *Hyperallergic*, 29 November 2019, https://hyperallergic.com/529762/basking-sam-gilliam-endless-iterations/

47 Telephone Interview with William T. Williams, 5 February 2023

48 James Mellow, 'The Black Artist, The Black Community, The White Art World', *The New York Times*, 29 June 1969.

49 For a comprehensive overview of major installations and impact of the Smokehouse Associates, see, Eric Booker, ed. *Smokehouse Associates*, contributions by Charles Davis, Ashley James, and James Trainor, New Haven: Yale University Press, Distributed for the Studio Museum in Harlem, 2022. See also, Darby English, 'A Year in the Life of Color', *Social Experiments in Modernism*, Chicago: University of Chicago Press, 2016, p. 197.

50 Barbara Rose, 'Black Art in America', *Art in America*, September–October 1970, p. 55.

51 Telephone Interview with Kinshasha Conwill. Conwill noted that although the Howard University Art Gallery was known at that time as a champion of the Black Arts Movement, Jeff Donaldson and Gilliam were good friends. Donaldson was chair of the art department at Howard and a founder and prominent member of Afri-Cobra, a group of artists who embraced the BAM. Their friendship is an example of Gilliam standing firmly inside of his contradictions.

52 MoMA mounted a solo exhibition of the work of the Black, self-taught sculptor, William Edmundson, 20 October–1 December 1937. There had not been a solo show of a Black artist since that time.

53 Gilliam is often cited as the first Black artist to represent the United States at the American pavilion of the biennale; however, Katherine Kuh, curator of the Art Institute of Chicago, included Jacob Lawrence and Norman Lewis in her exhibit curated for the 28th Venice Biennale in 1956.

54 'Arne Glimcher Recounts His Friendship with Sam Gilliam', 27 June 2022, https://www.pacegallery.com

55 For an account of the festival see David Murphy, ed., *The First World Festival of Negro Arts,* Dakar 1966, Liverpool: Liverpool University Press, 2016.

56 Campbell, *Red and Black to "D"*, p. 10.

57 '…The best painting [Gilliam's] ever made'. Benjamin Forgey, 'Corcoran Show is Mostly Big', *Washington Star*, 21 February 1975, quoted in Binstock, *Sam Gilliam: A Retrospective*, p. 104.

58 Jenelle Porter discusses the transition of the privately assembled *Dark As I am, 1968–1973* to the publicly displayed *Composed (Formerly Dark As I Am)*, 1968–74, pp. 22–30.

59 My thanks to Leah Franklin for sharing the details of the genesis of the painting during a telephone interview, 22 October 2022.

60 Binstock, *Sam Gilliam: A Retrospective*, p. 118.

61 John Anderson, 'The Public Artworks of Rockne Krebs & Sam Gilliam', https://jefferson placegallery.com/public-artworks-krebs-gilliam. Anderson provides an account of Gilliam's introduction to the Philadelphia Art Museum commission. See also Binstock, 'Protean Sam Gilliam', *Sam Gilliam: A Retrospective*, pp. 102–104.

62 Binstock, pp. 113–118. My thanks to Stephanie Gilliam and Dr. Melissa Gilliam for sharing details of the experience, working with their father in separate telephone interviews.

63 Video filmed by Linda Lewett, ARTtvLLc, hhttps://www.youtube.com/@LindaLewettARTtvLLc, 26 March 2007.

64 Anderson, https://jefferson placegallery.com/public-artworks-krebs-gilliam-exhibition/

65 Gilliam in conversation with Peter Halley, *Sam Gilliam: Green April* exhibition Catalogue, Los Angeles: David Kordansky Gallery, 2017, p. 85.

66 See video at https://www.davidkordanskygallery.com/exhibitions/samgilliam/

67 Jason Moran, 'Looking For a Moment', *Sam Gilliam: Moving West Again*, Los Angeles: David Kordansky Gallery, 2021, p. 49.

68 'Russia Discovers Two Secret Paintings under Avant-Garde masterpiece', *The Guardian*, 13 November 2015 https://www.theguardian.cm/world/2015/nov/13russia-malevich-black-square-hidden-paintings. Adrienne Edwards cites the reference in 'Sam Gilliam: The Theater of Life', *Beauty Born of Struggle: The Art of Black Washington*, ed. Jeffrey Stewart, New Haven: Yale University Press and National Gallery of Art, 2023.

69 Undated type-written narrative, errors included, as it was sent to the author in 1982.

70 Campbell, *Red and Black to "D"*, p. 10.

71 *Red and Black to "D"*, 29 for a complete list of the titles.

72 The importance of family, despite marital differences is evident in the accomplishments of their three daughters: Stephanie Jessica Gilliam is current ly production designer for the popular television show, 'Chicago Meds;' Melissa Lynn Gilliam, MD, MPH is currently Executive Vice President Provost of the Ohio State University, Columbus; Leah Franklin is Senior Strategy and Design Officer, Lambent Foundation, New York.

73 Telephone interview with Gilliam's friend, Bennie F. Johnson, 13 June 2023.

74 Both the title and the dimensions are recorded on the detailed instructions for the installation of the work and illustrated here.

75 Undated text as Gilliam typed and sent it to the author.

76 Art historian and Yale faculty member Robert Farris Thompson (1932–2021) is acknowledged as the first writer to use the term 'Post-Black' in 1991. See Robert Farris Thompson, 'Afro-Modernism', *Artforum*, September 1991, pp. 91–94.

77 Christine Kim and Franklin Sirmans, eds. *Freestyle*, New York, Studio Museum in Harlem, 2001.

78 Telephone interview with David Kordansky, 13 October 2022 and telephone interview with Rashid Johnson, 28 November 2022. Both Kordansky and Johnson spoke of the 'radicality' (to use Johnson's word), of Gilliam's innovations and the way in which they traversed performance, architecture, constructivism, sculpture as well as painting. Kordansky and Johnson both shared details of the visit to Gilliam's studio that resulted in Kordansky signing Gilliam and Johnson curating the 2013 exhibition of a selection of the early hard-edge paintings.

79 Glimcher, 'Arne Glimcher Recounts His Friendship with Sam Gilliam', ibid.

80 Courtney J. Martin, 'Imagine the Show on the First Day', *Sam Gilliam: Existed Existing*, New York: Pace Gallery, p. 121.

81 Johnson, Ibid.

82 Moran provides a full discussion of the environment that Coleman required for compositional freedom. See 'Looking for Moment', *Moving West Again*, p. 51.

83 Melissa Gilliam, Ibid.

84 When I learned of news of Gilliam's death, Melvin Edwards was the first person I called. During our long telephone conversation, among many insights, he offered the comparison between Gilliam's disruption of traditional painting and the lifelong friendship among the three artists.

—I'D CALL
MYSELF A
MIRROR, A
MIRROR THAT
<u>REFLECTS</u>,
<u>BORROWS</u>, AND
<u>STEALS</u> FROM

DIFFERENT ART
MOVEMENTS,
REORIENTING
THEM IN
ORDER TO
SQUEEZE OUT
NEW LIFE.

THE TRANSFORMATION OF NATURE THROUGH NATURE

Sam Gilliam

Commencement speech given at the Memphis School of Art, May 1986.

Graduates, Mr. President, teachers, proud parents, and other guests: Ever since I was asked by Bob [Riseling] to address this illustrious group, I have been filled with a certain sense of pride and anxiety. One, I have finally made it to Tennessee, and, secondly, there is nothing more responsible than speaking to a group of artists who are about to embark on their maiden voyage in a great occupation. I have sat in many audiences where one has bemoaned the artist. Thus, I have come to praise the role he plays as a transformer of nature. I have also come to challenge the process of that transformation to greater heights.

Robert Henri, in his book *The Art Spirit*, a collection of lessons and orations given to his students, encouraged them to "keep your old work. You did it. There are virtues and there are faults in it. You can learn more from yourself than you can from anyone else." I have always used this quotation for my students and particularly for the group of students I have taught the past two years in a seminar course on survival. I like its meaning in that it proposes that the work that you have done is a treasure chest that should be savored. The work that you have done is much like a knapsack of your anticipated belongings. The work that you have done is also a crystal and when held up to the sun will radiate the aspirations of the whole of society whom it is your intention to serve.

Let's look at the artist in this way. They tell me that once upon a time in a very mythical land that was filled with small huts there existed a huge volcano. It had an amazing fire that came from within it. This was such a great fire that it kept the valley warm, lighted, and always with pleasant weather. What was not known was that behind the volcano was a team of little people armed with bellows and logs fanning the fire and making it blaze higher. These little people formed a long lineage. I will name only a few: Rembrandt, Leonardo, Monet, Van Gogh, Eva Hesse, Cézanne, Pollock, Avery, and many others. And now you have been called to join that team. For the illusions, the spaces, the forms that you create will keep your fellow persons warm, lighted, and always in good weather.

I am reminded of a statement that was made to my class when we graduated from the University of Louisville in the 1960s. We had been blessed by having a very great teacher who had taught at the Bavarian Academy in Germany. Unfortunately, he had been captured and placed in a concentration camp as an artist during World War I. He mentioned to us how he had run and hidden in order to keep his life. He also mentioned how in appreciation to whatever being that kept him alive, he drew every day while on the run. He said his reasons for drawing were to keep his memories of life alive. He pointed out that even when captured and placed in prison, he made art in his head to keep his sanity. And how upon repatriation, he afforded himself a trip around the world, mostly to check out if things were still the same and when he was assured that things were, he went back to making his art. However, this time he resumed his art with things from Japan, India, Greece, etcetera, in a crazy quilt way. He also said that one of the things that entered his work was the figure of a Centaur and that this symbolized for him the mythical aspect of being the artist. Hence, among Greece, Italy, India there stands the mighty Centaur. The most special thing that I remember from this period of my life was that he suggested, "keep on working. For in the work you not only see, but you also help others to see."

He said during this time he had one complaint. That in Munich where he had taught, he had taught many students who had great talent. However, when he visited them, many had gone on to become teachers of art. And, of course, they readily showed him the work of their students. And when he asked for their own work, they said they had stopped. This, young graduates, shocked the old man and hurt him. He said, "you, by stopping your art, have erased the Centaur from the work. You have allowed the fire to go out. An artist must stay an artist. For without the artist in him, he cannot see and others cannot see through him".

It is said that at this time in 1986 there is a lull in art, that the thing that was sought in post-WWII years by many immigrants coming here has been lost. It is said that even the sense of this land as honored by the Hudson River School is lost from American art. What has come to replace this great inheritance is known as rampant commercialism and production. It is suggested that there is not a transcendence between the public and the art, that only a special group counts. It sounds like Sodom and Gomorrah reigns in this mythical land with the gigantic volcano.

Many of us have come to recognize the absence of the Centaur, the lowering of the light. But do we recognize, more specifically, the possibility of losing the nature of humanity in this way? Do we realize that there is a need for the artist to act as an artist? Where does this come from?

I guess the most immediate answer is contained in something I have already expressed earlier in this speech. That is of the professor who even though on the run, made drawings, who even though imprisoned, kept art alive in his head and who upon release went around the world to make sure that the world was still there, who created the mighty Centaur as a symbol of himself, as an artist to remind himself that the artist was still there.

Picasso in his series about the artist and the model keeps himself there. Rembrandt in his self-portrait keeps his presence in art. My teacher chided his students for not keeping themselves present as artists before their students. Now, I challenge you that the most important thing you must do is to keep the artist present in you, keep the artist present in your work, to use the artist in you to secure you on the nights when you have to run and hide, to keep the artist in your presence and mind in times when you are hostage to situations, difficulties, like bad grades, and keep the artist in you even though you cannot work as an artist. You are coming aboard the Grand Armada. You have first watch. The nature of nature is your quest. It is the only way that the valley can be warm. It is the only way that the valley can be lighted and it is the only way that the valley can have good weather.

I have not been around the world as my teacher had, but I have found a clever way to climb aboard the Grand Armada and to experience the world. It is something I figured out in 1962 when I first came to Washington.

I realized that in any day I had four hours I could go to the National Gallery and walk the entire gallery which extends some two blocks and look at paintings, allowing trails of man's existence to crisscross and interface in various beautiful rhythms. In four hours one can see all of the paintings in the National Gallery. I remember that one: "in order to see a painting, one must be a painting." Thus, having remembered this, I know that the nature of man as defined by art is in me. Secondly, in many hours alone in a studio I have often thought about such trips ...

Thus, I want to say to you, as the artist, you are nature. I must say that you as the artist must always make new work. You as the artist must keep the Centaur present. You as the artist must keep the fire blazing.

It is the hope of the world. More importantly, it is the hope of America; it is the hope of Tennessee. It is the hope of each individual that we are immediate to.

We are, as was Georgia O'Keeffe, or as are Louise Nevelson, Frank Stella, and many among you, avatars, all of whom, including you, have chosen to transform the sense of nature through yourselves for others.

Let me end as I have begun. "Keep your old work. You did it. There are virtues and there are faults in it for you to study. You can learn more from yourself than you can from anyone else."

Represent the Centaur. Stock the volcano. Good luck. God bless you all.

Hello and goodbye to you all.

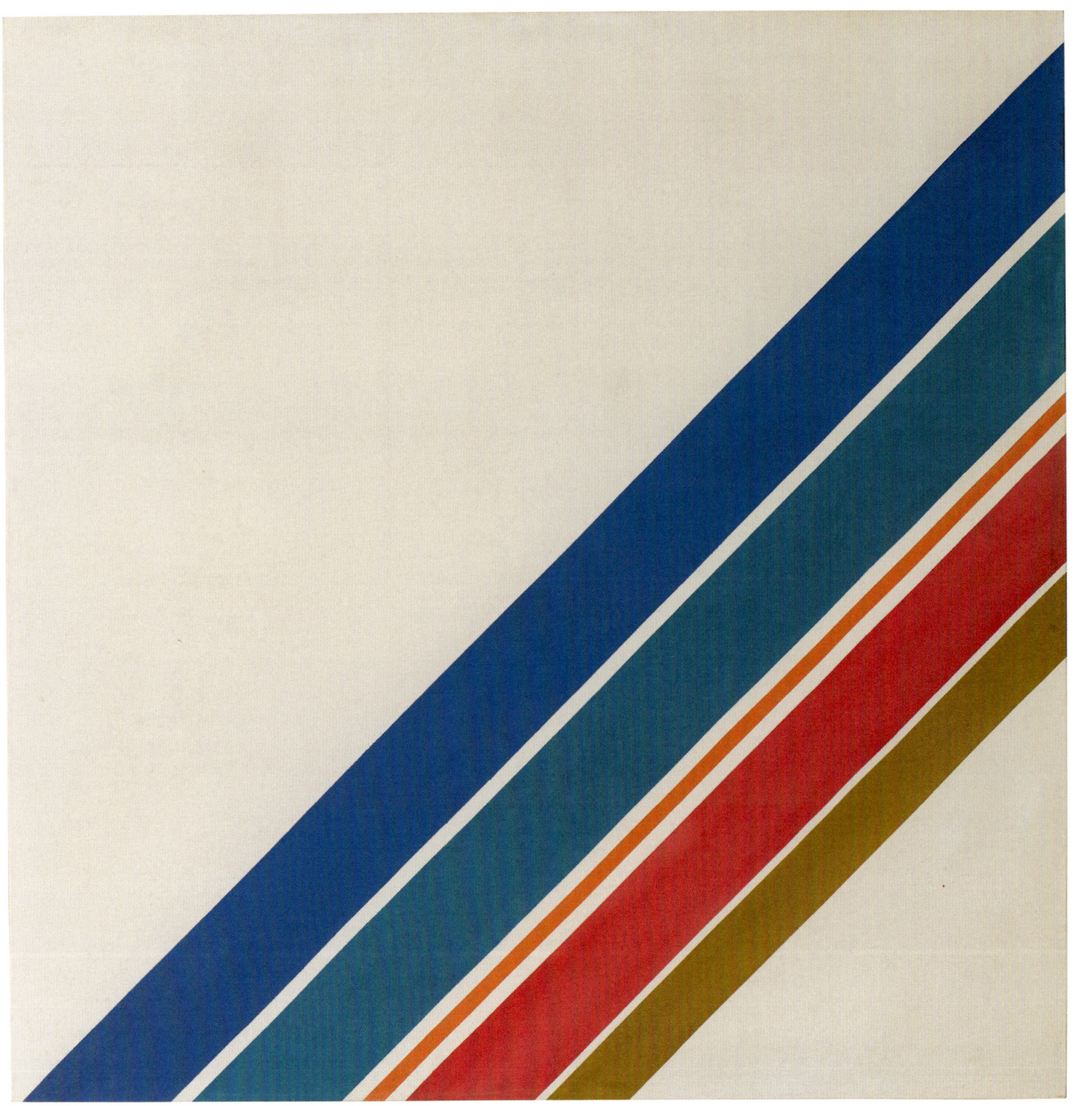

Helles, 1965

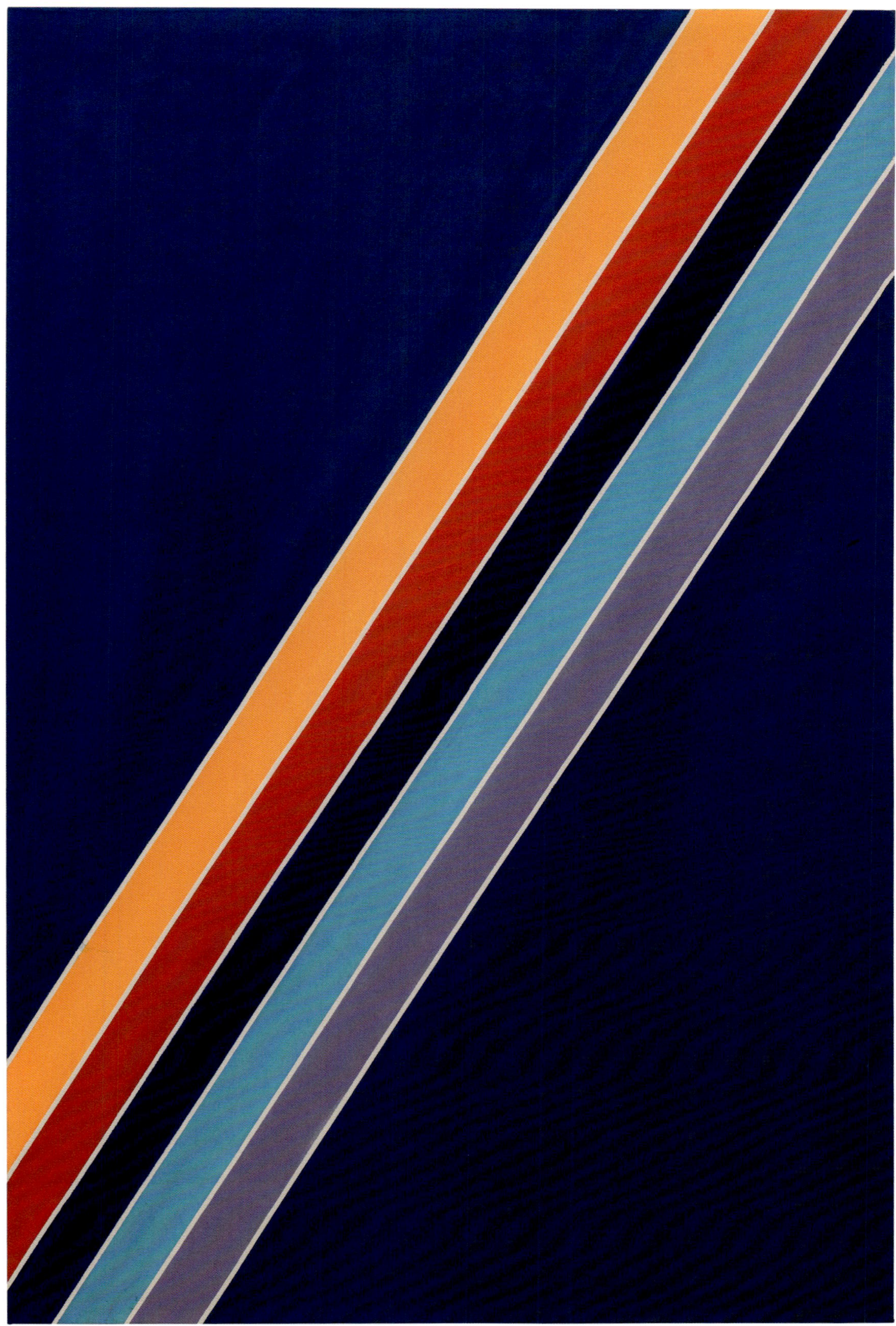

Blue Let, 1965

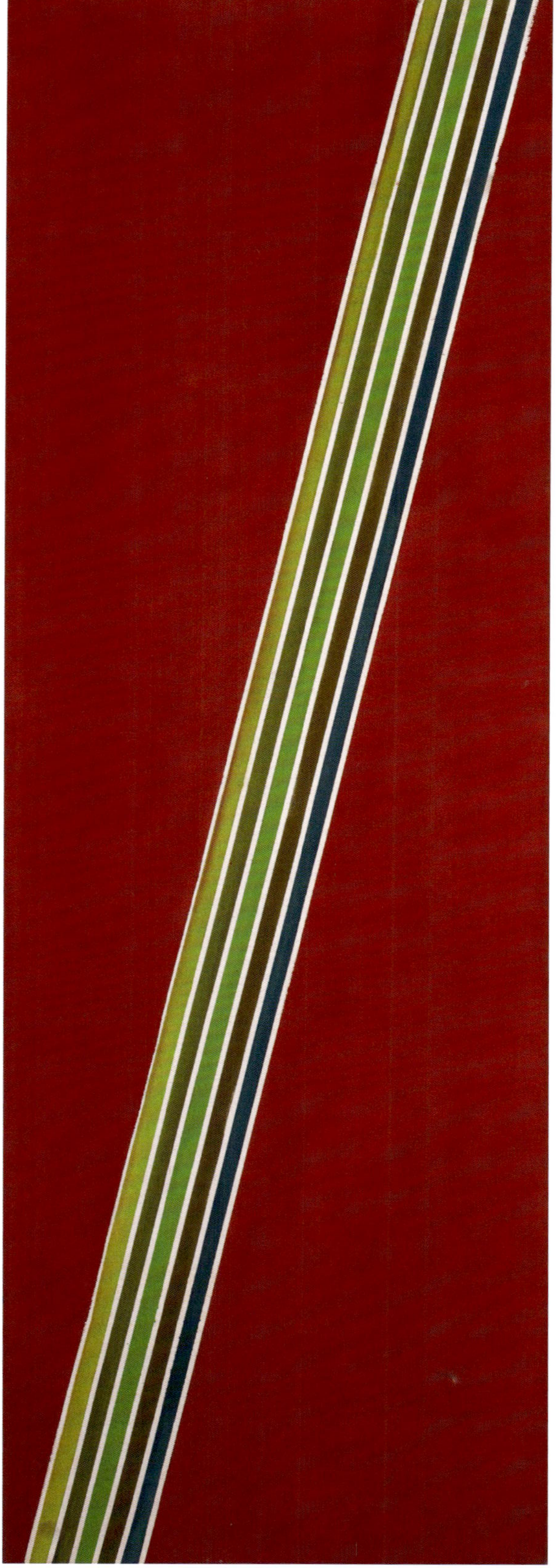

Long Green, 1965

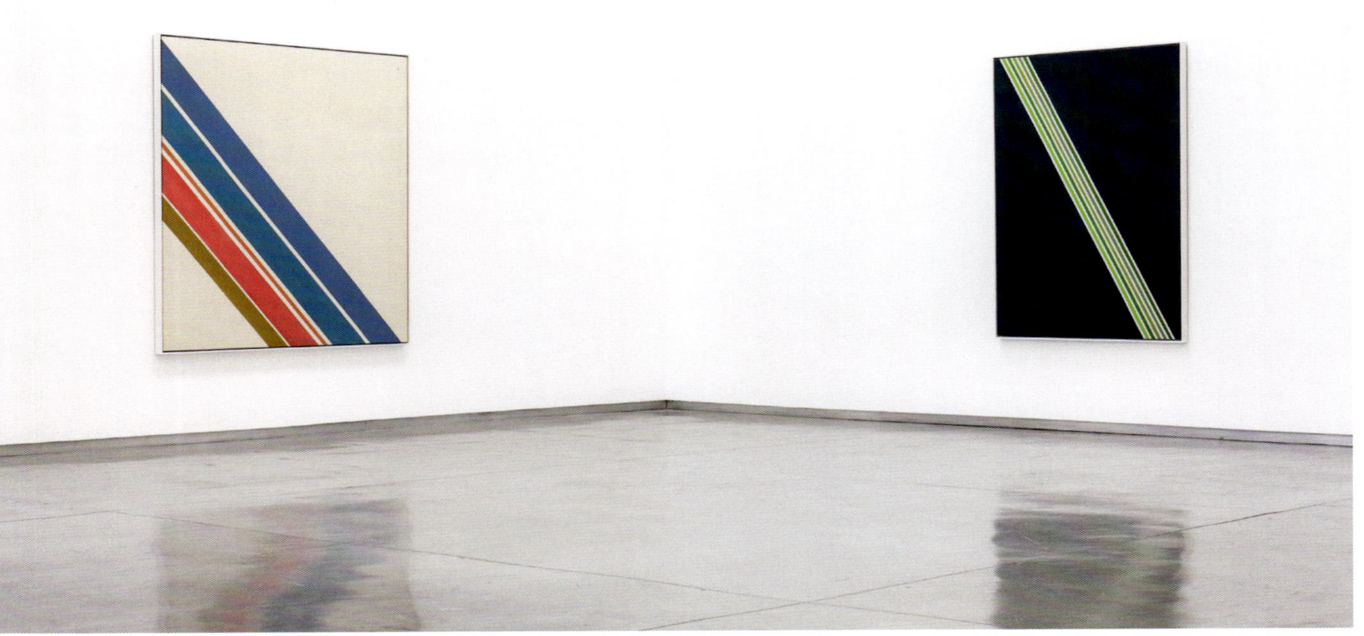

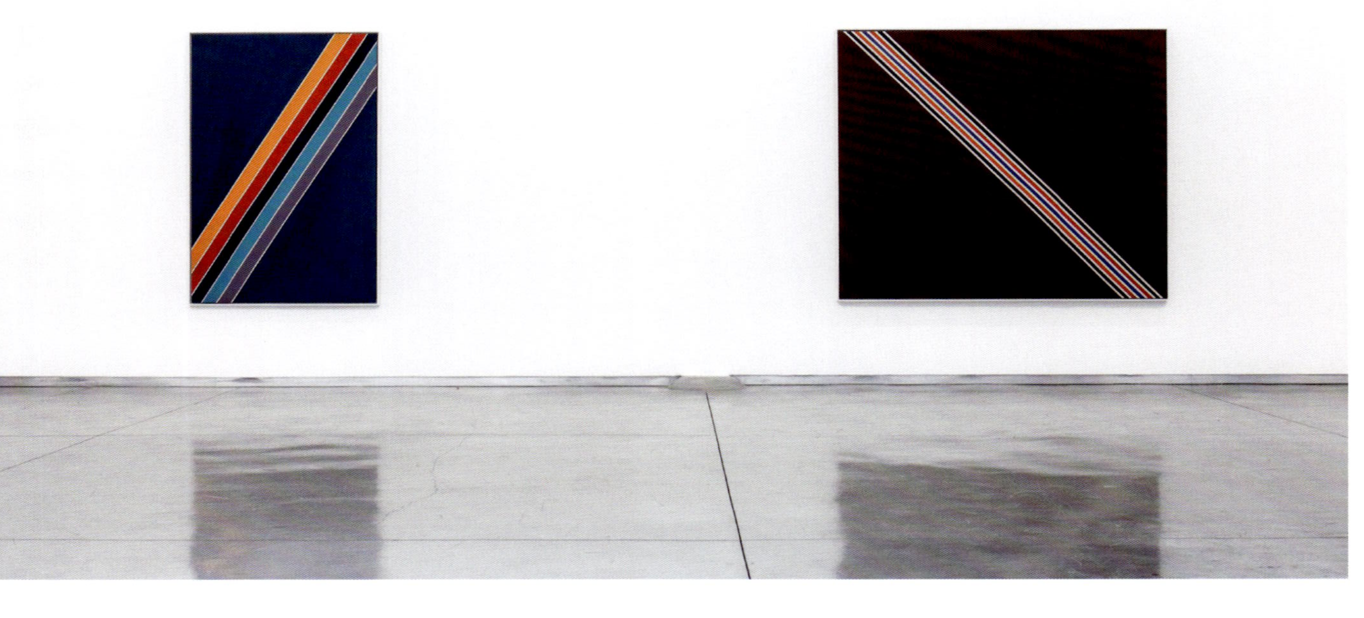

Installation views of 'Hard Edge Paintings 1963–1966', David Kordansky Gallery, Los Angeles, 2013

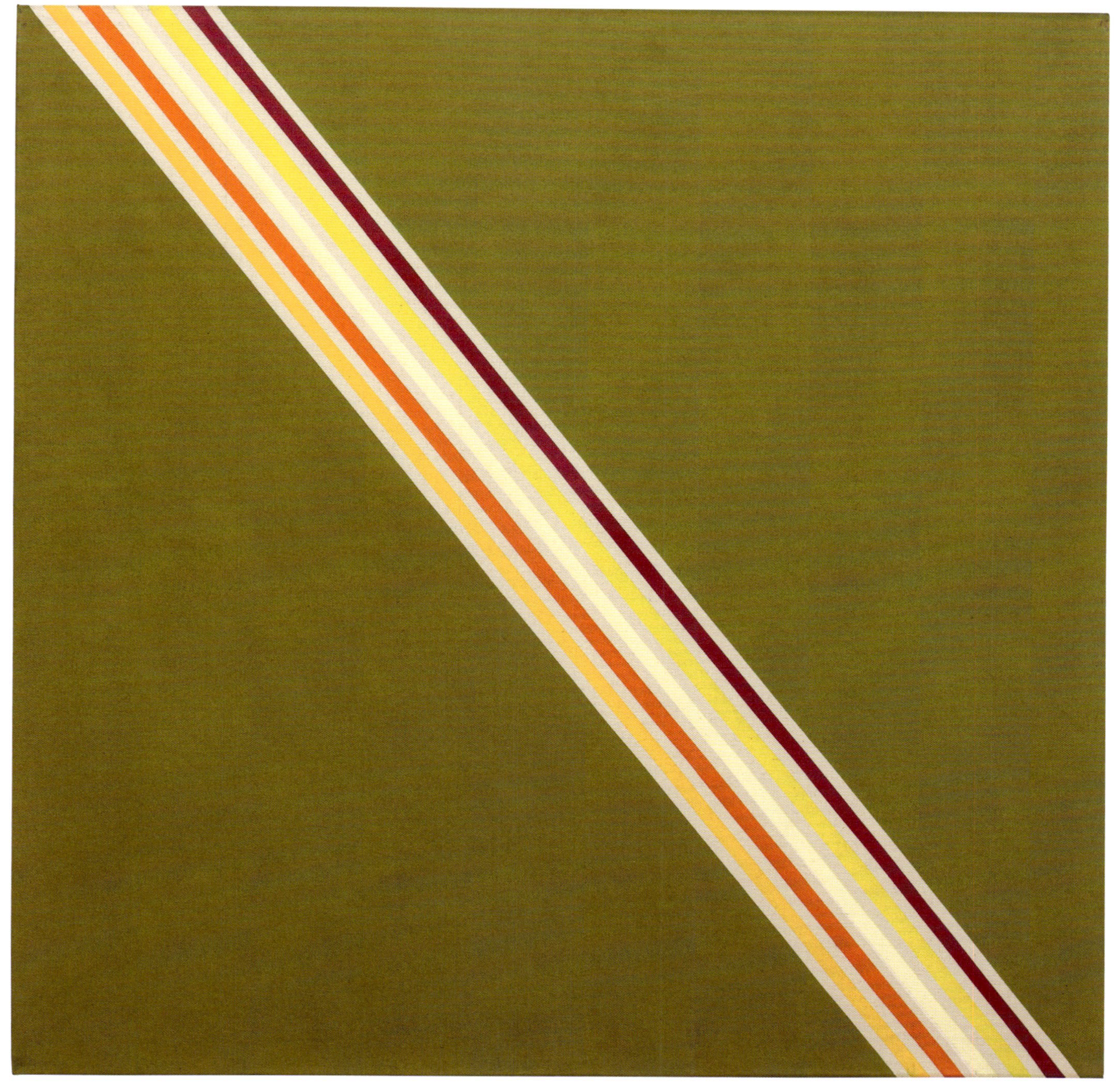

Dual Rod, 1965

Snakebite, 1968

Following pages: *Rouge*, 1968

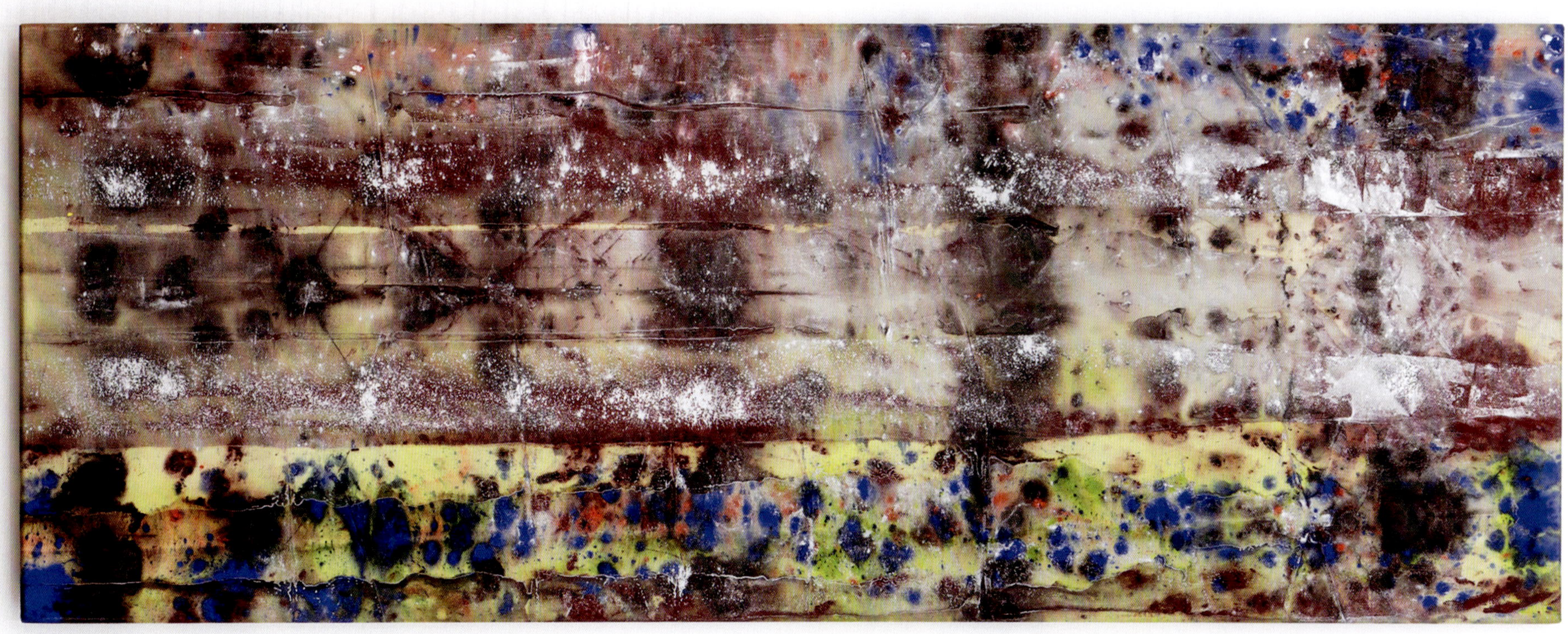

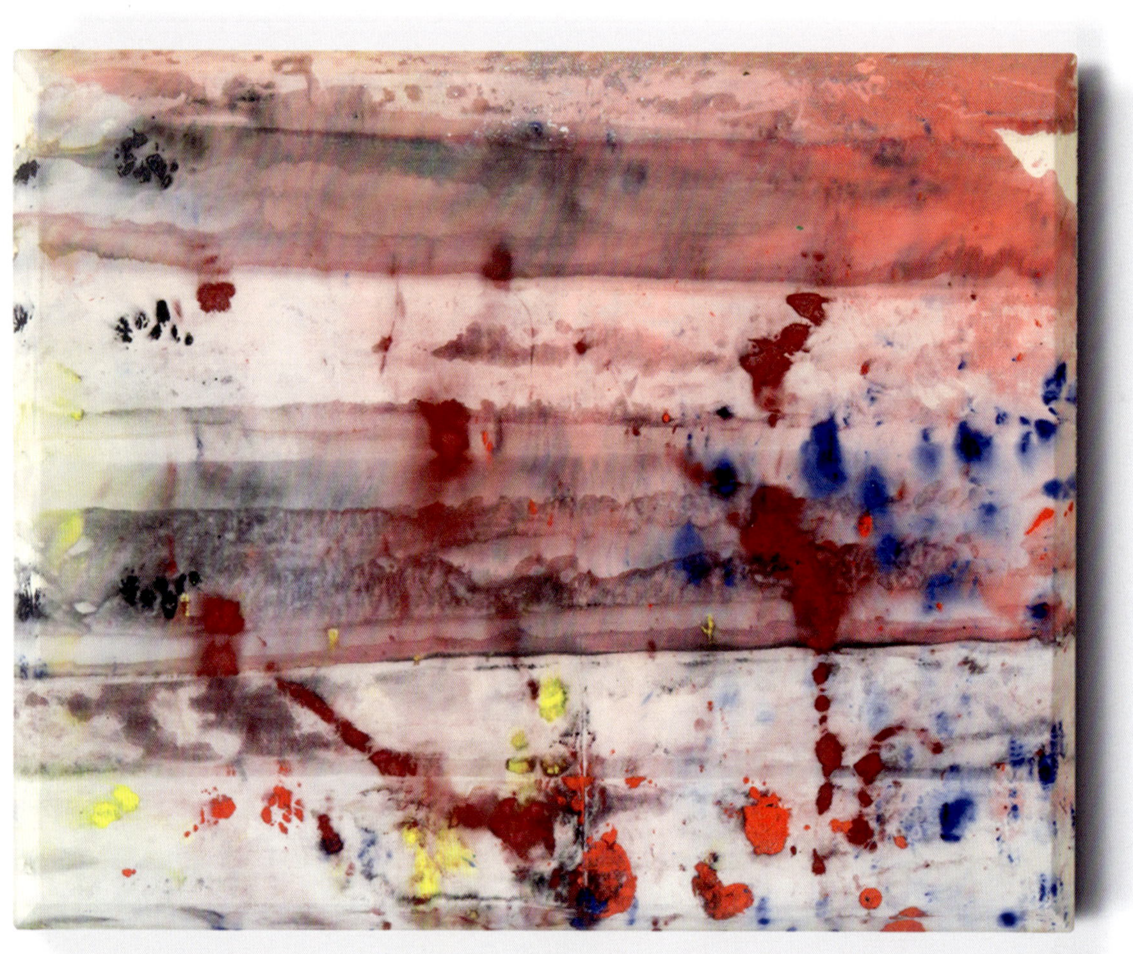

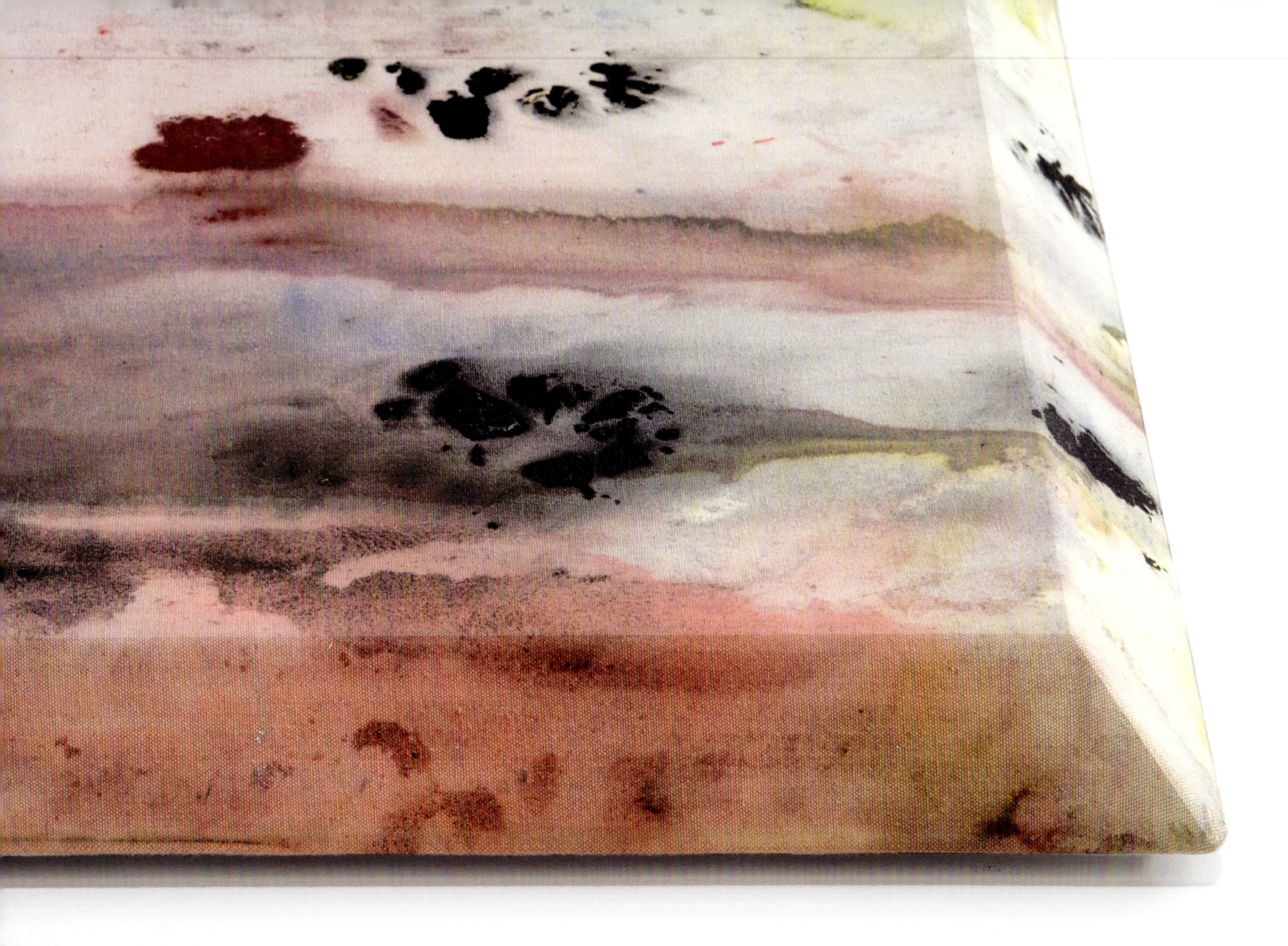

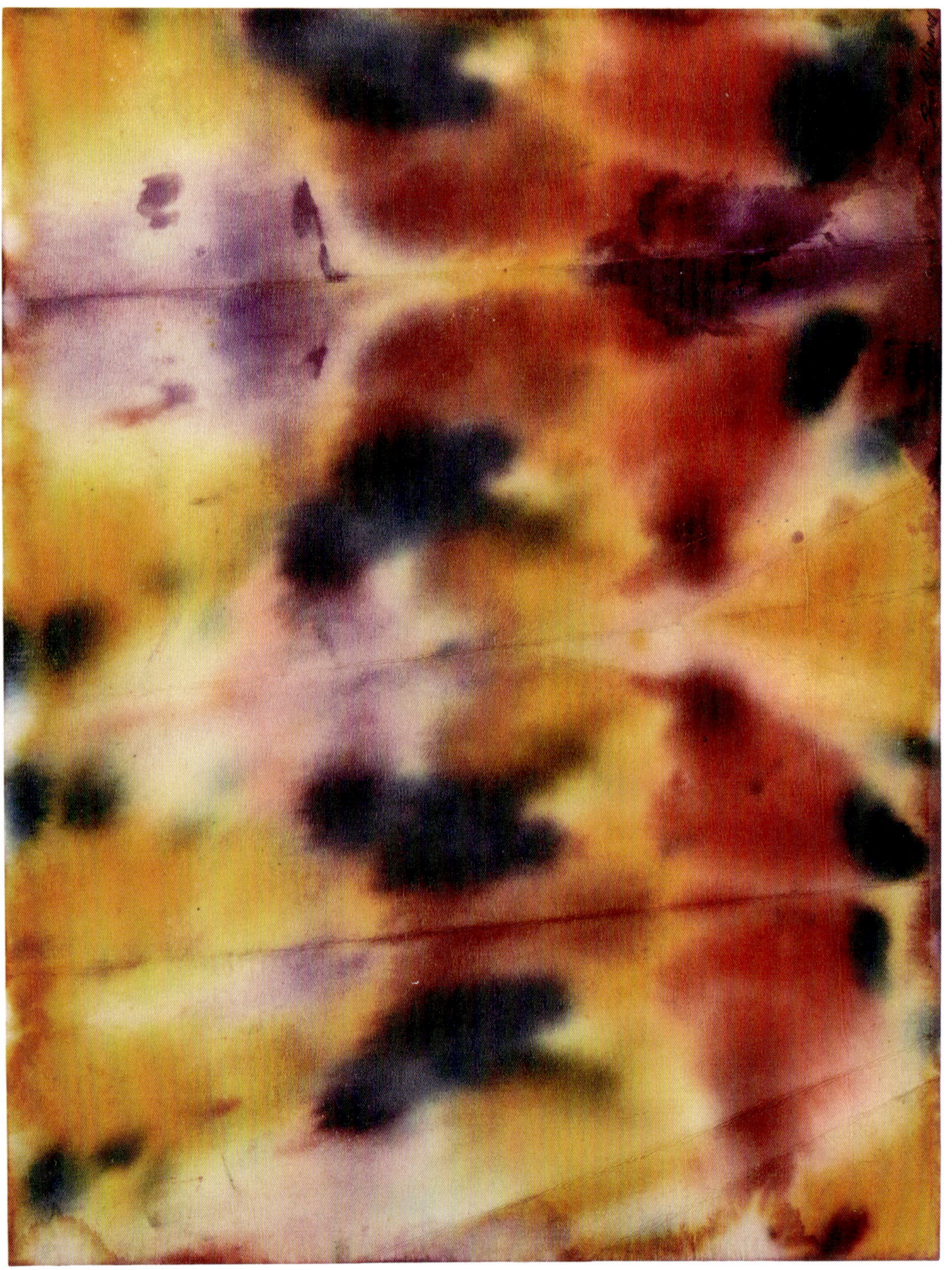

Untitled, 1967

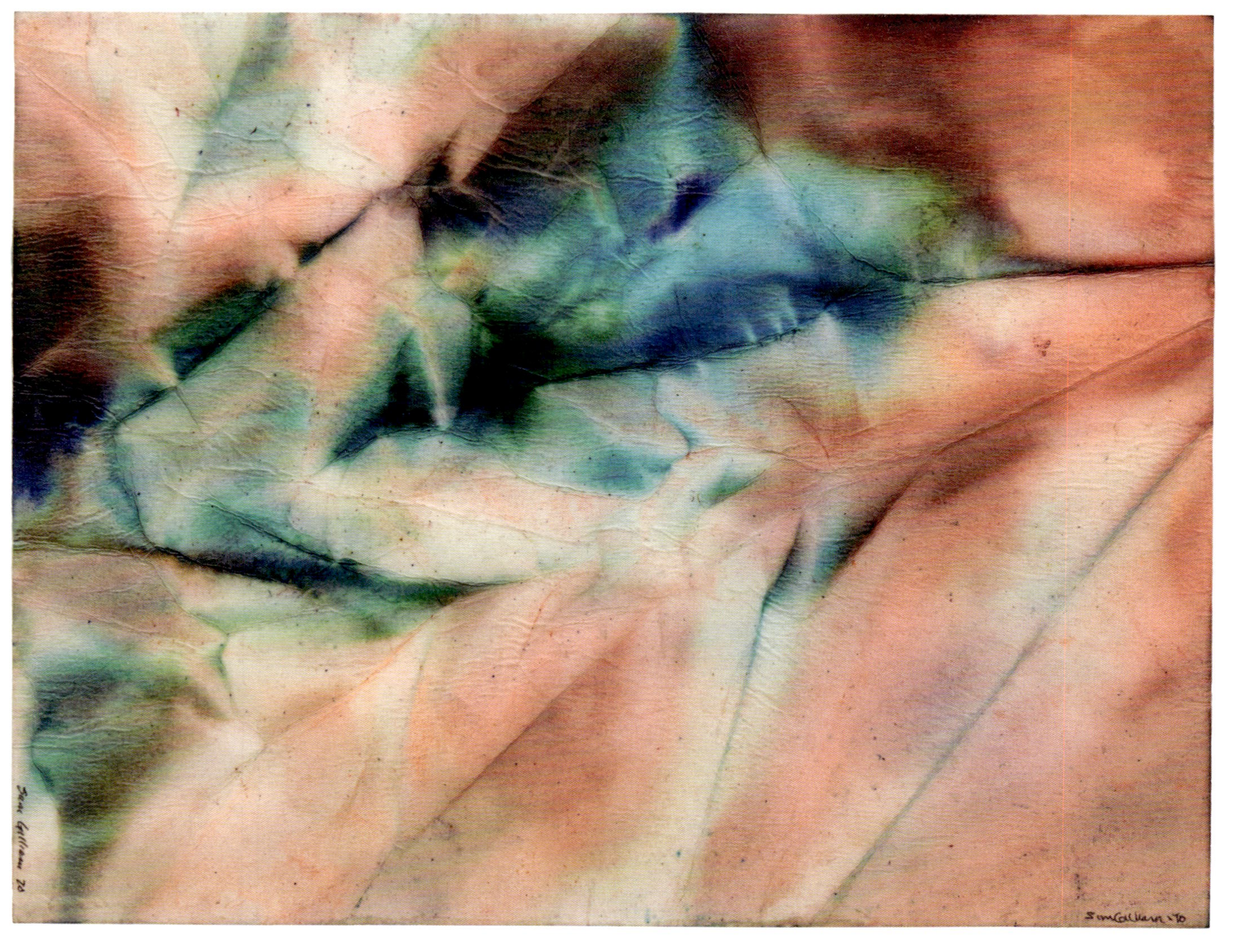

Untitled, 1970

Following pages: Installation views of 'The Music of Color. Sam Gilliam 1967–1973', Kunstmuseum Basel, 2018

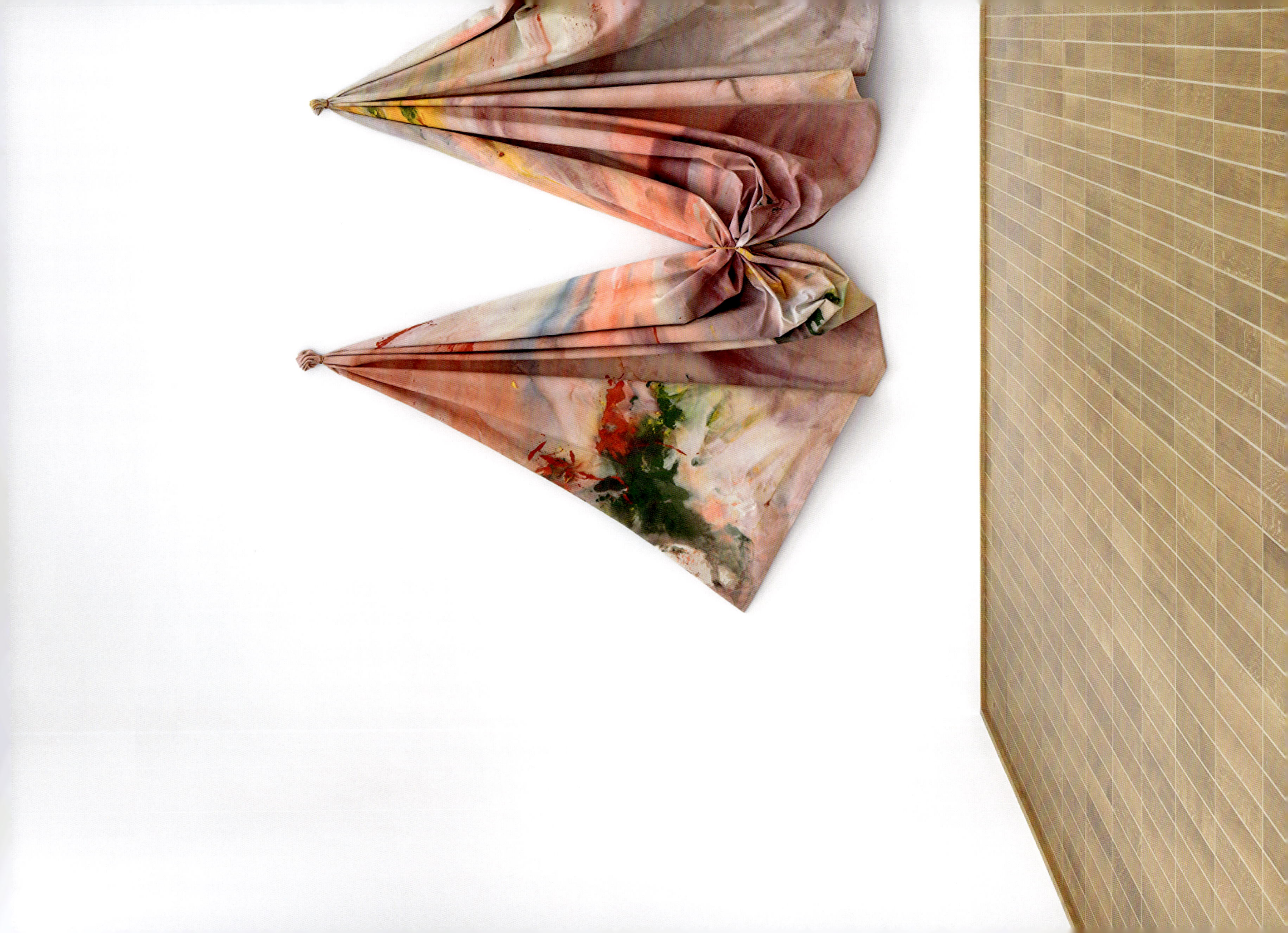

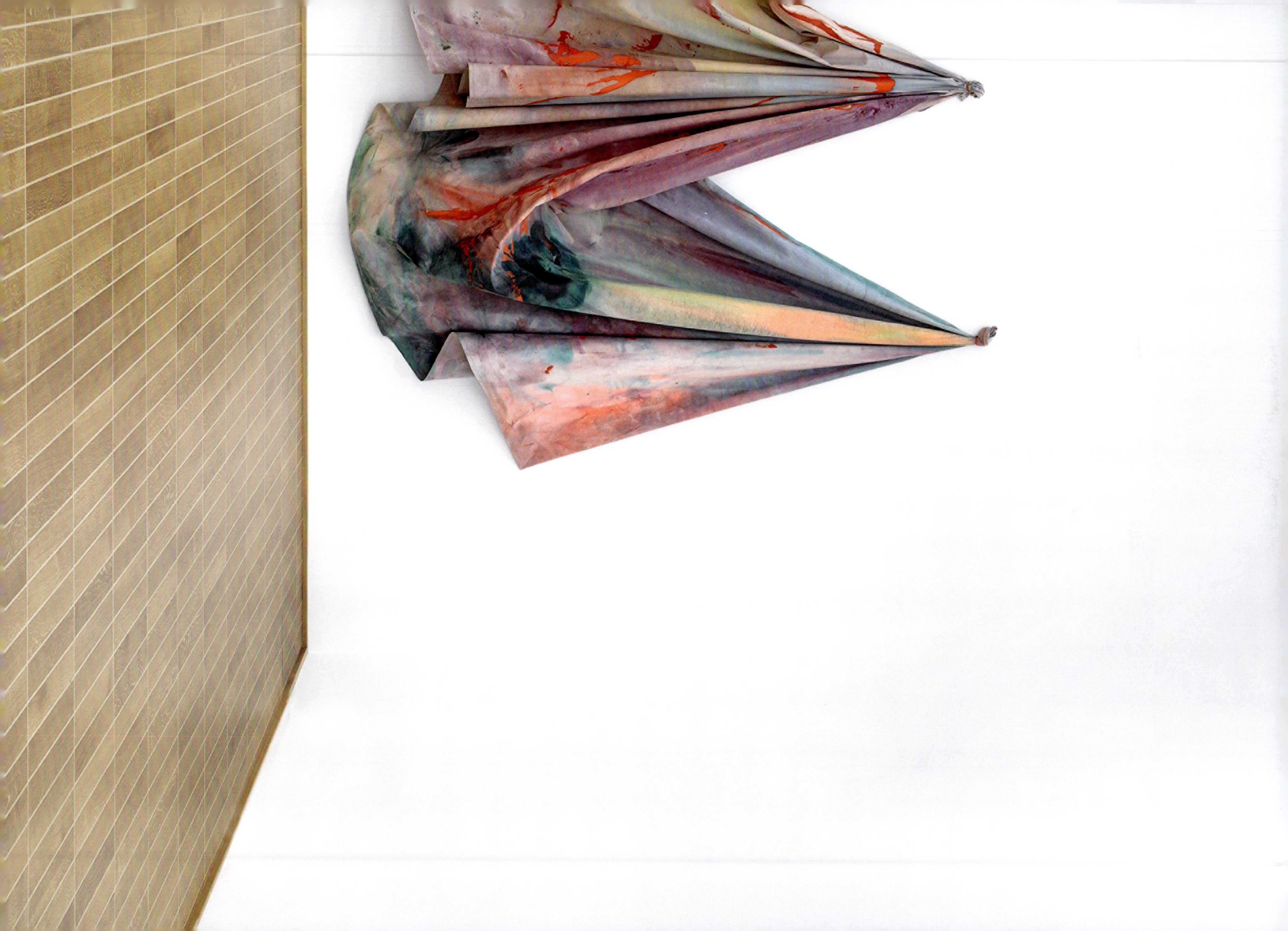

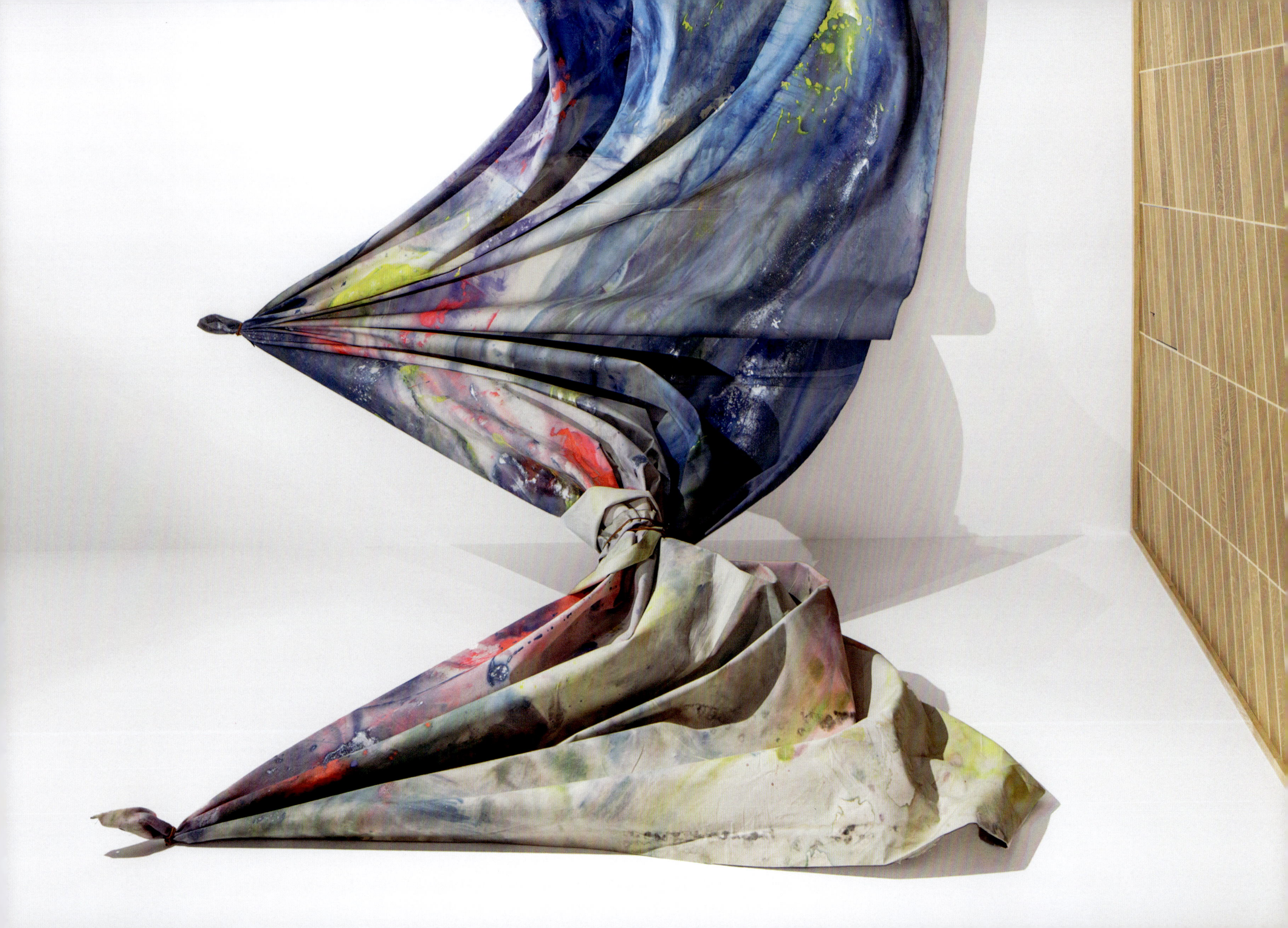

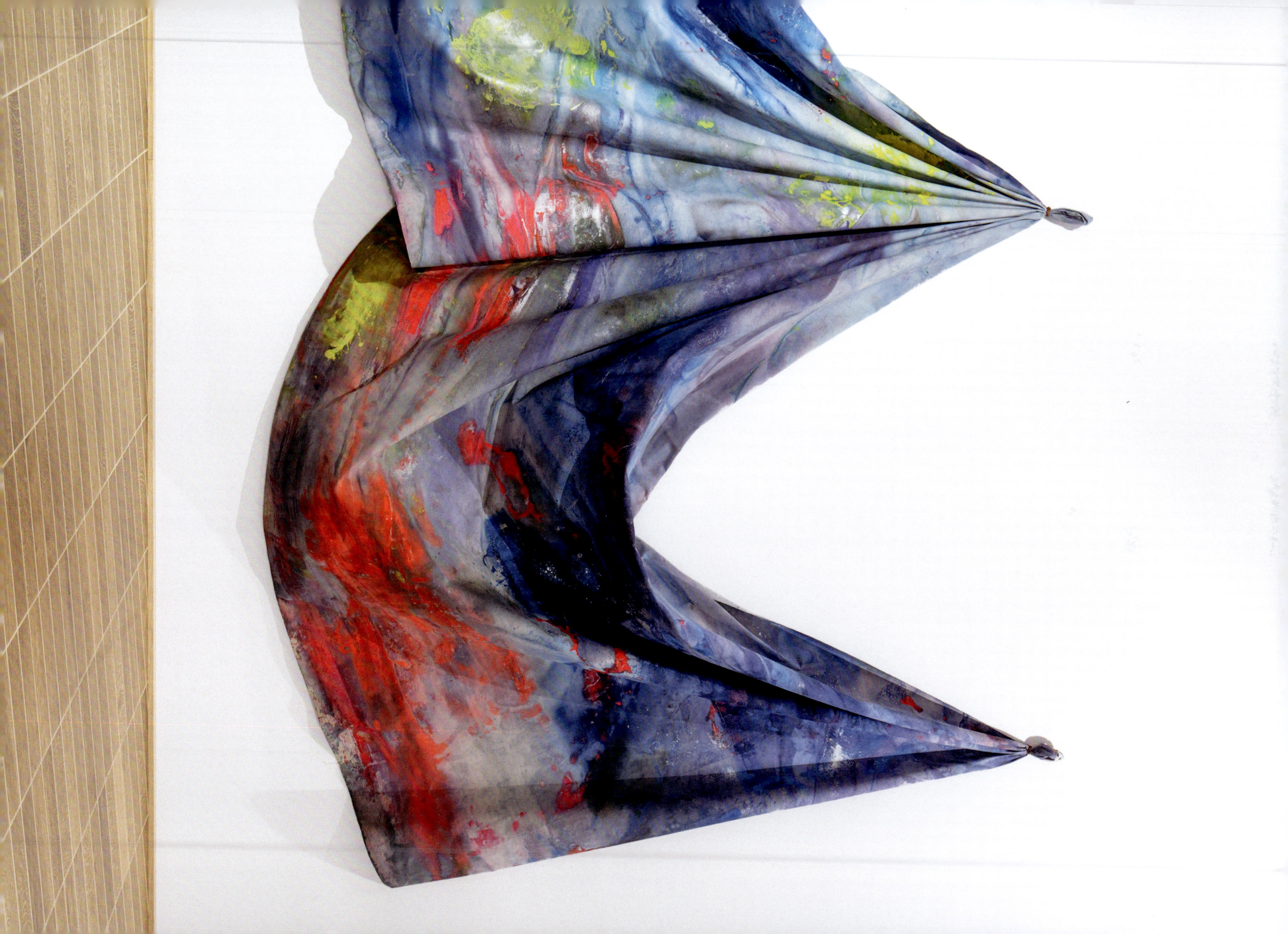

Previous pages and right: *Niagra*, 1968

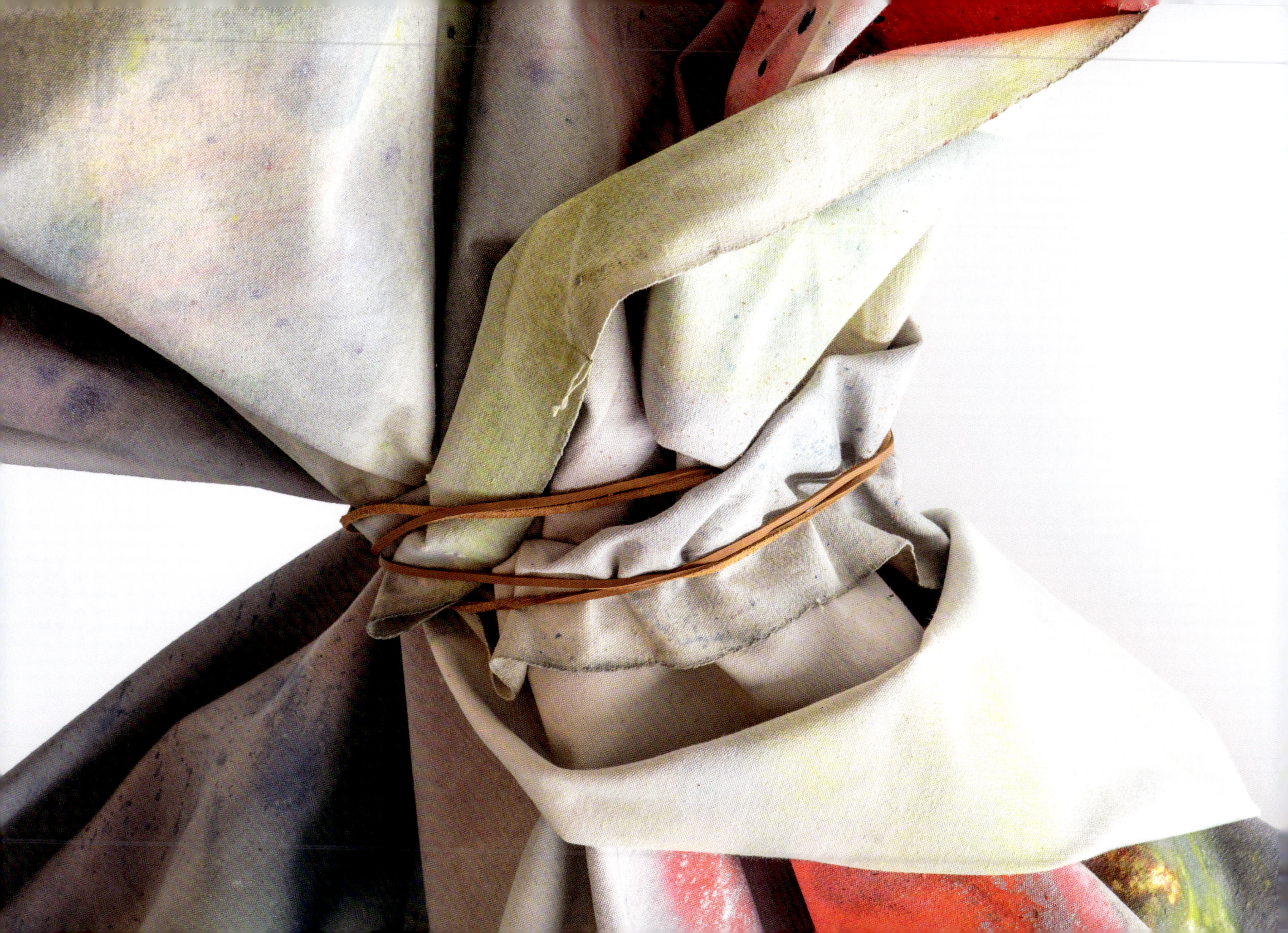

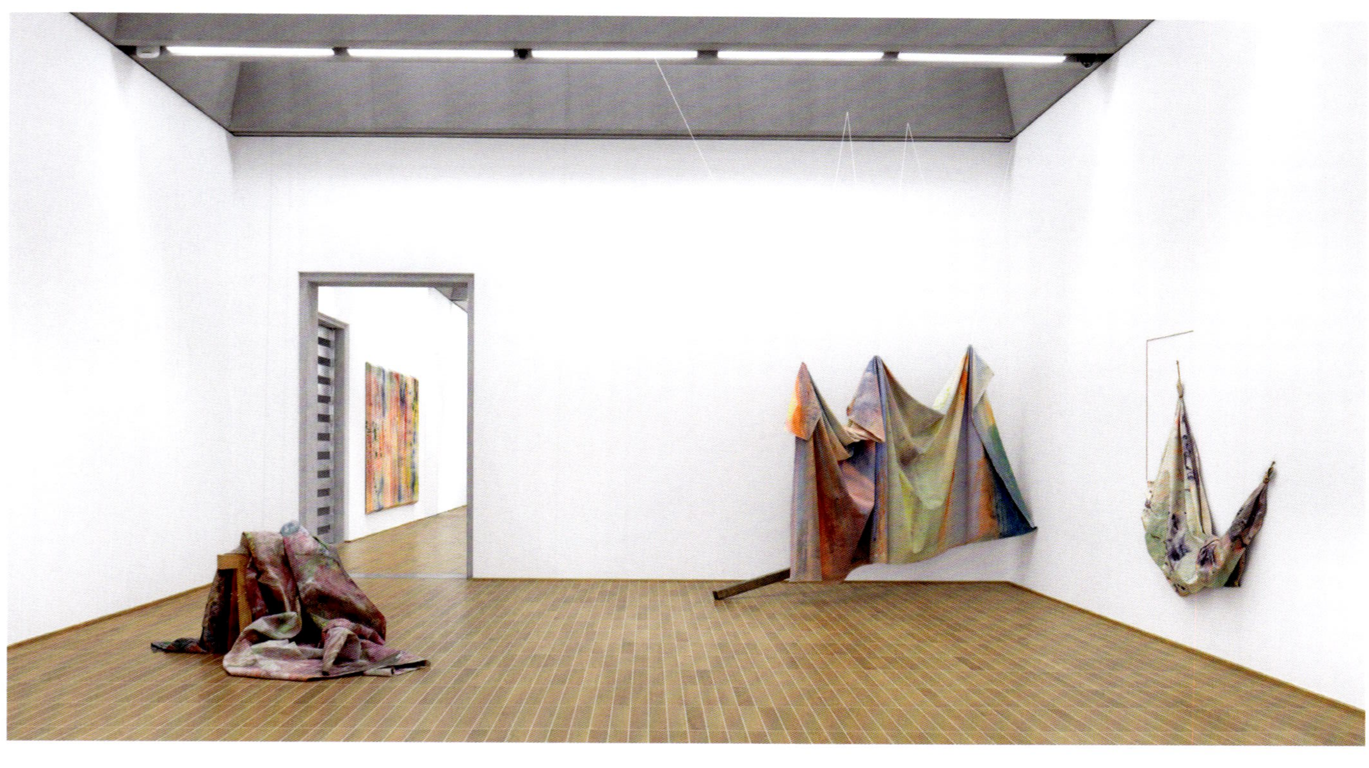

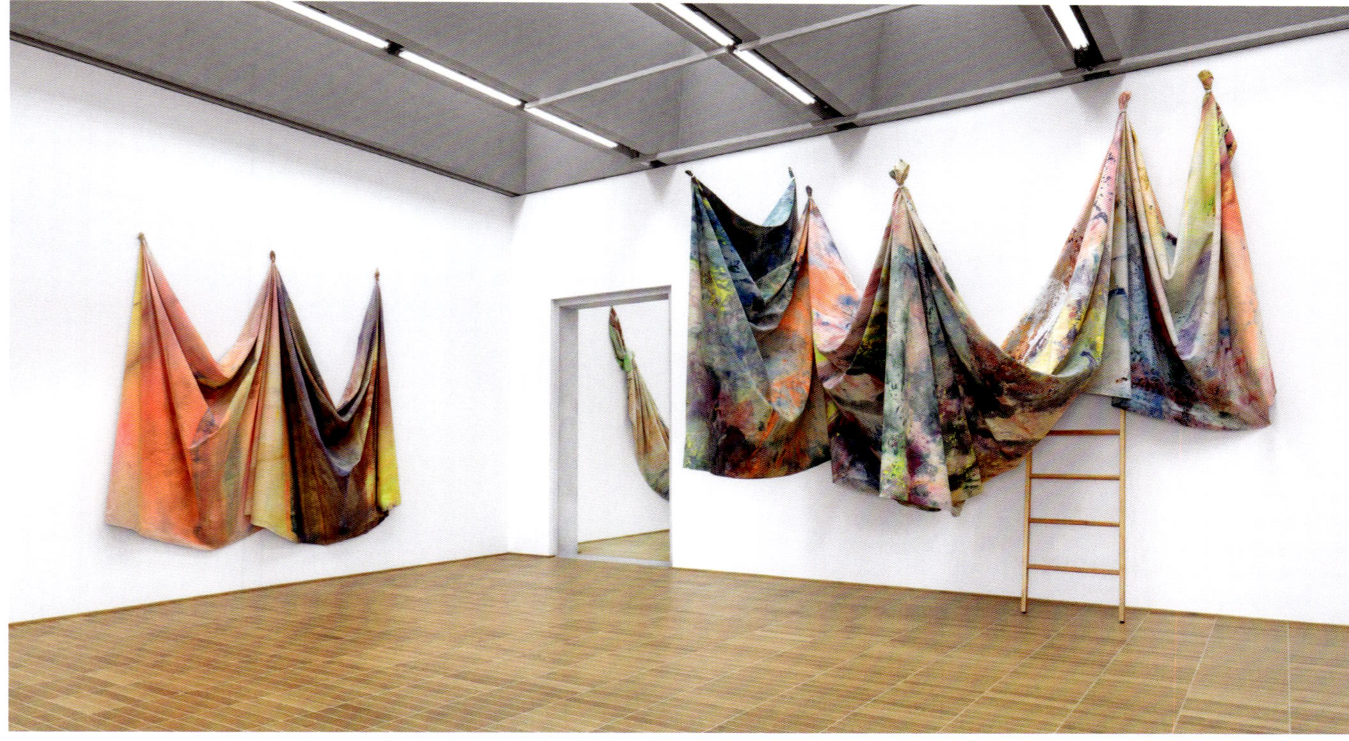

Installation views of 'The Music of Color. Sam Gilliam 1967–1973', Kunstmuseum Basel, 2018

Following pages: *Light Depth*, 1969

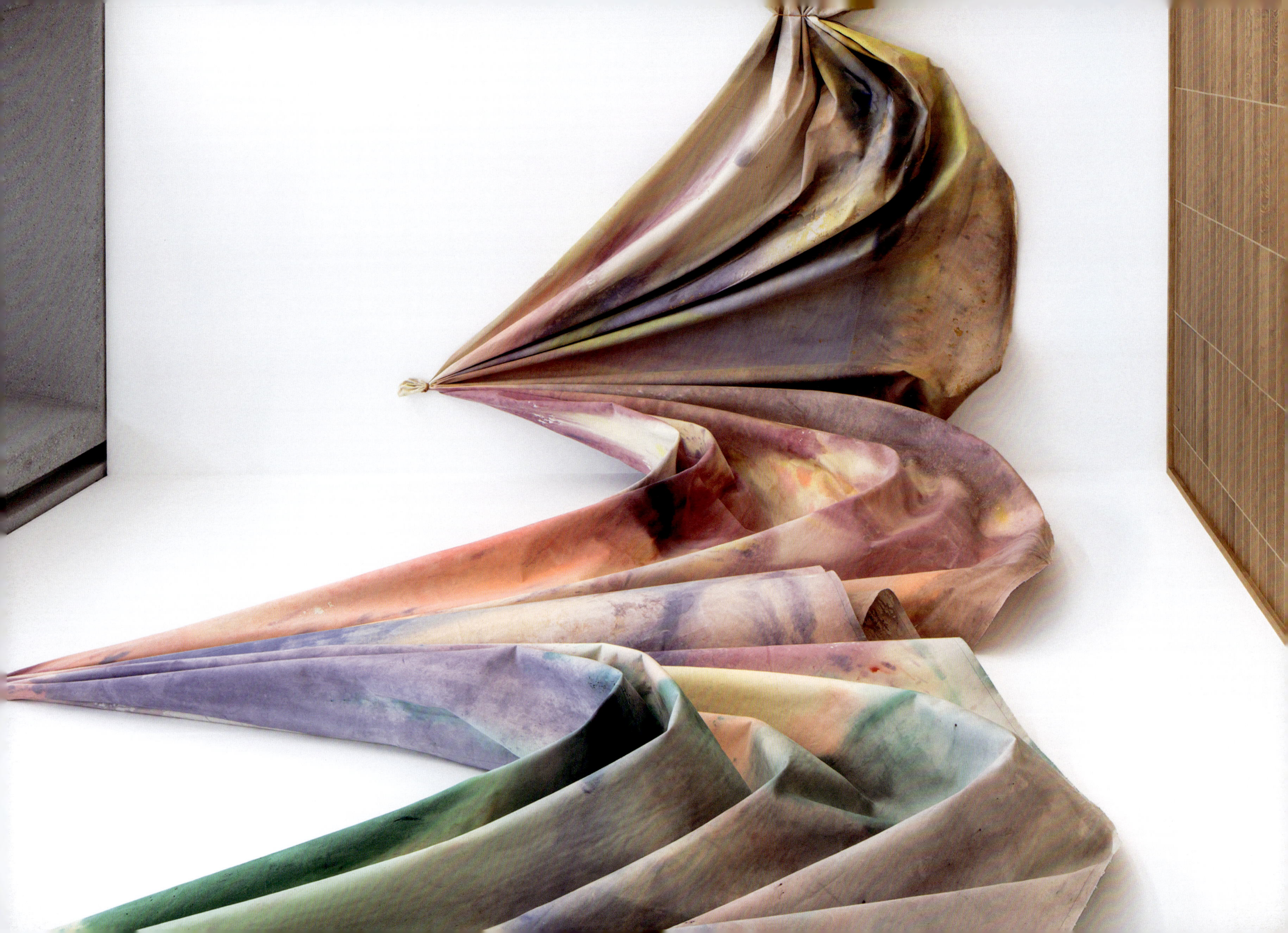

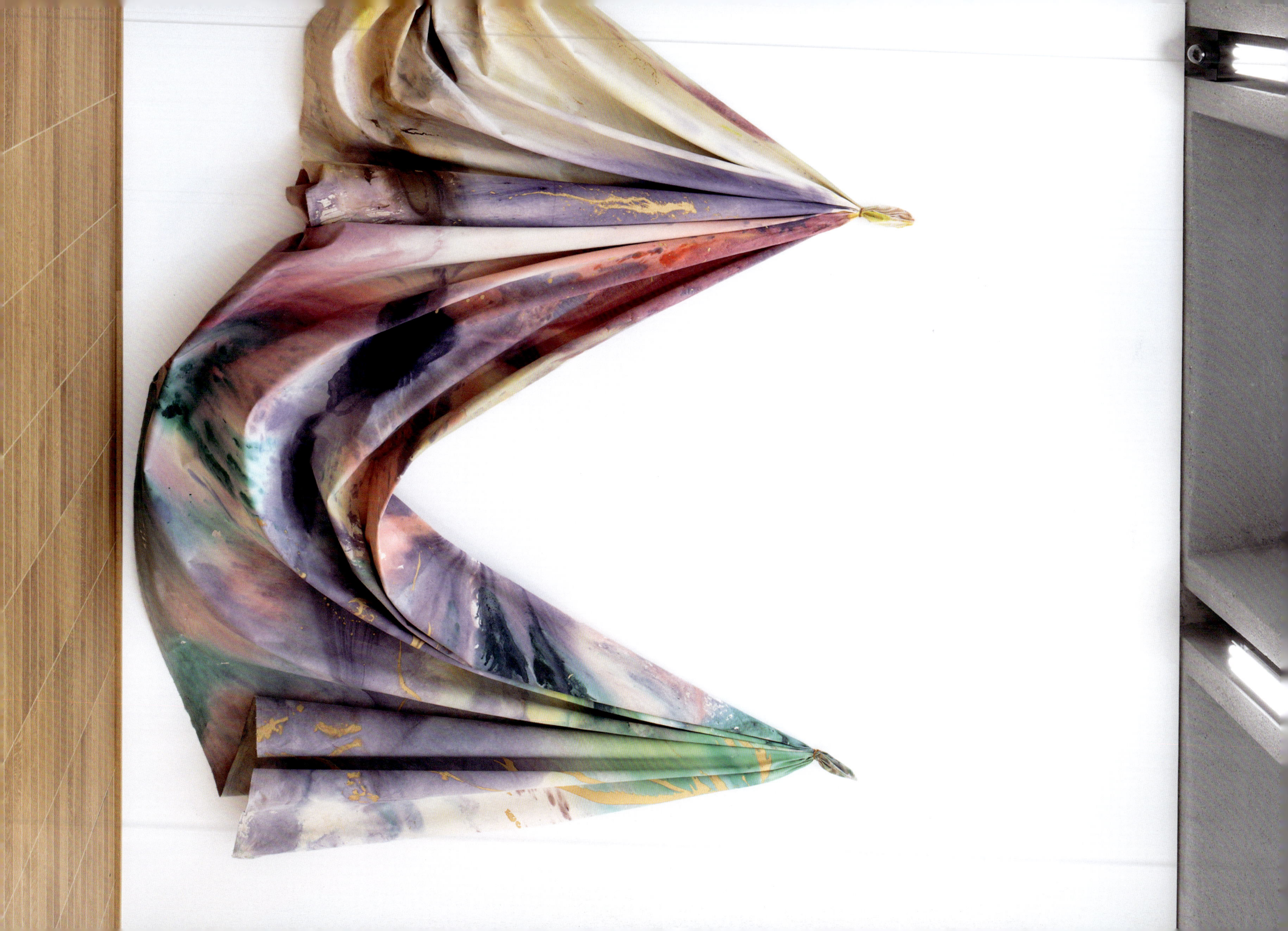

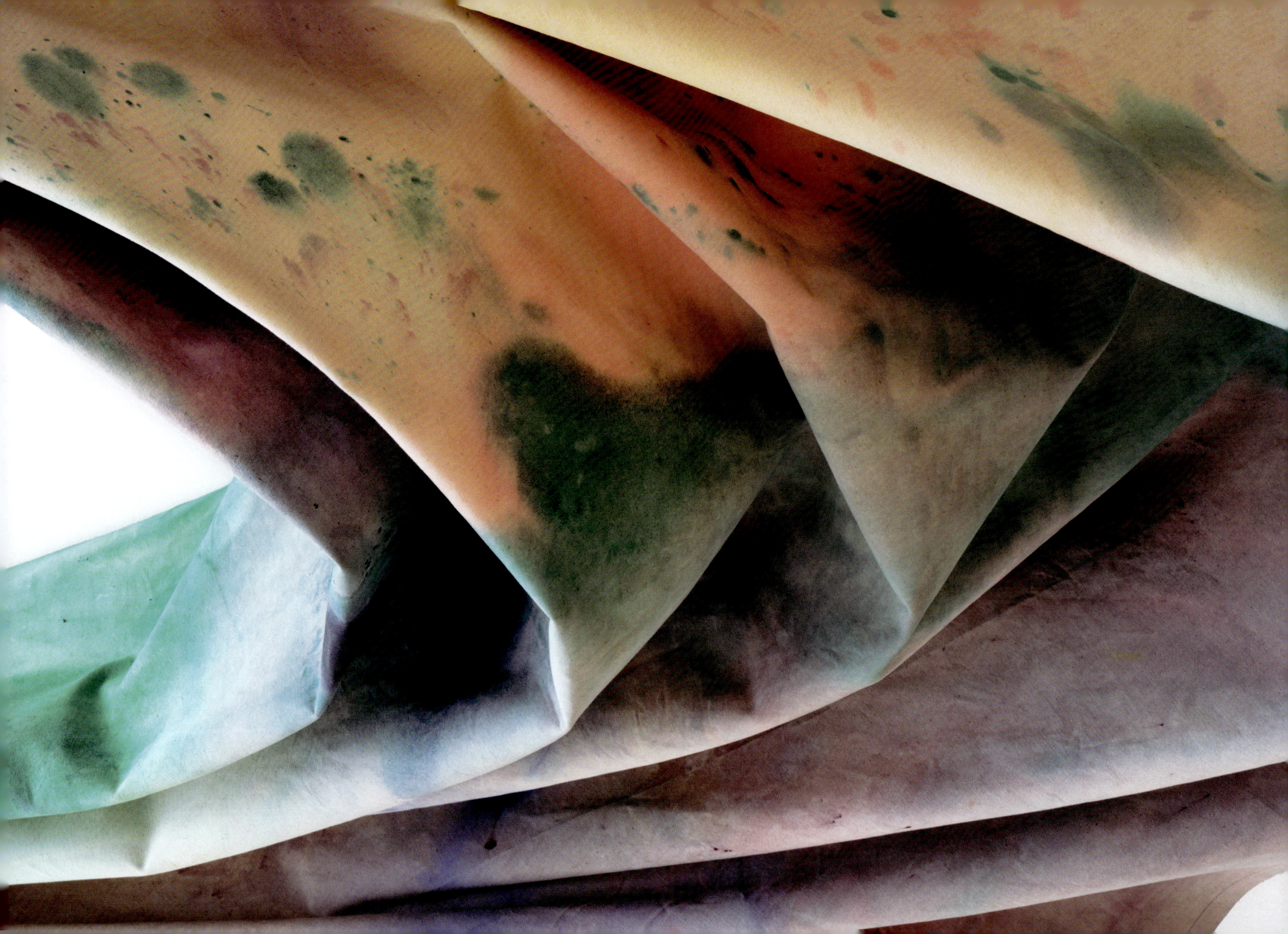

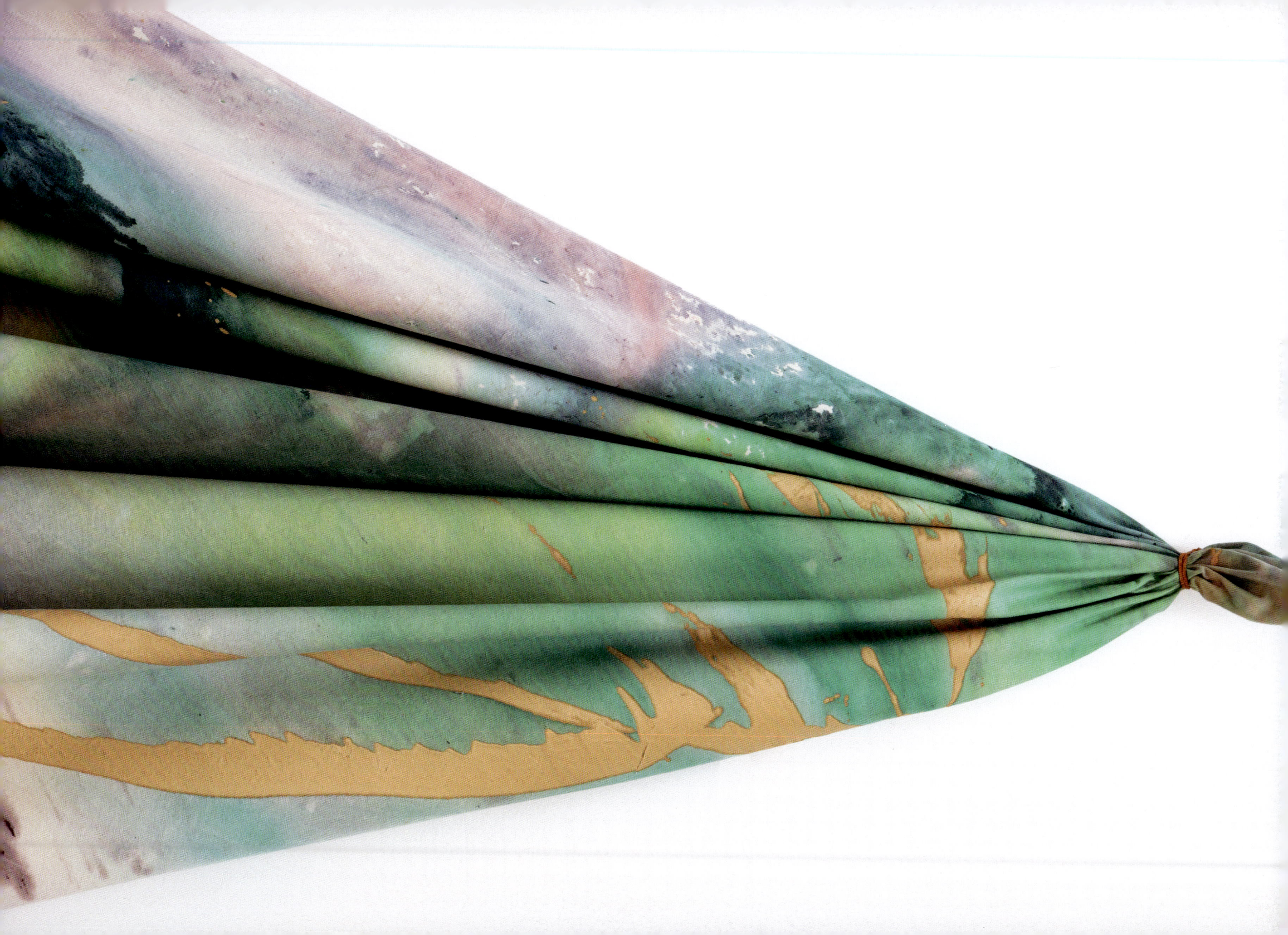

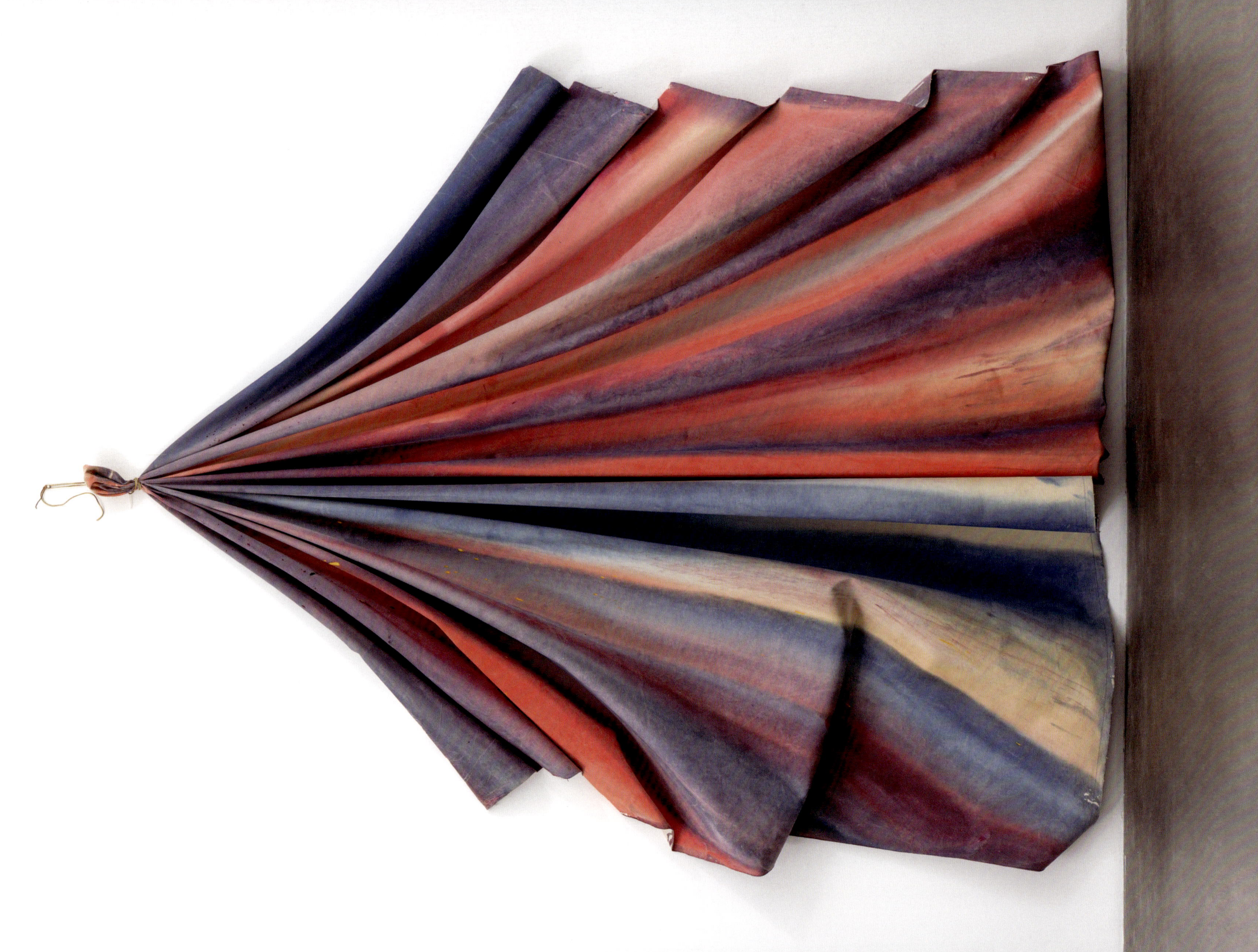

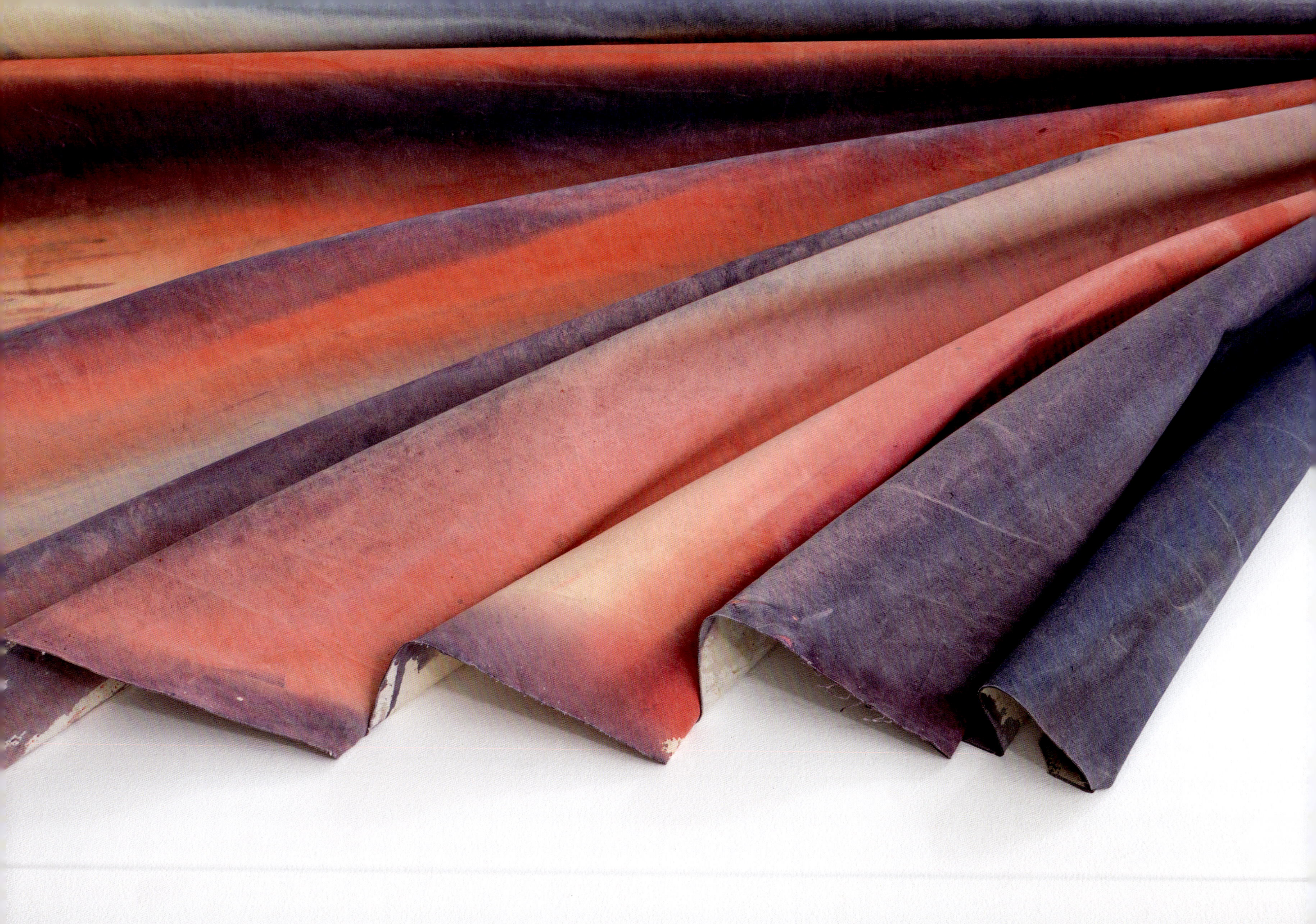

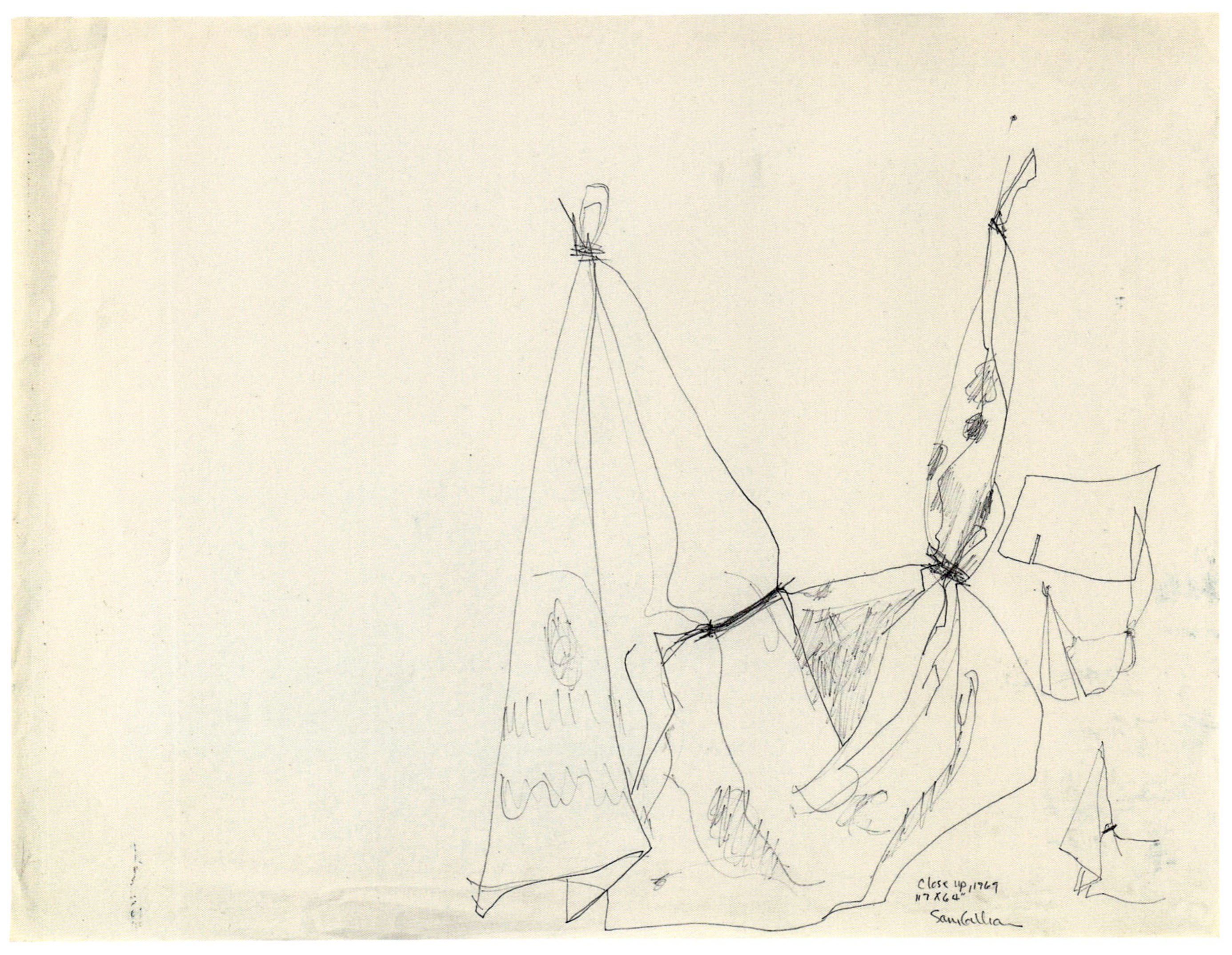

Previous pages: *One On*, 1970

Close-Up, 1969

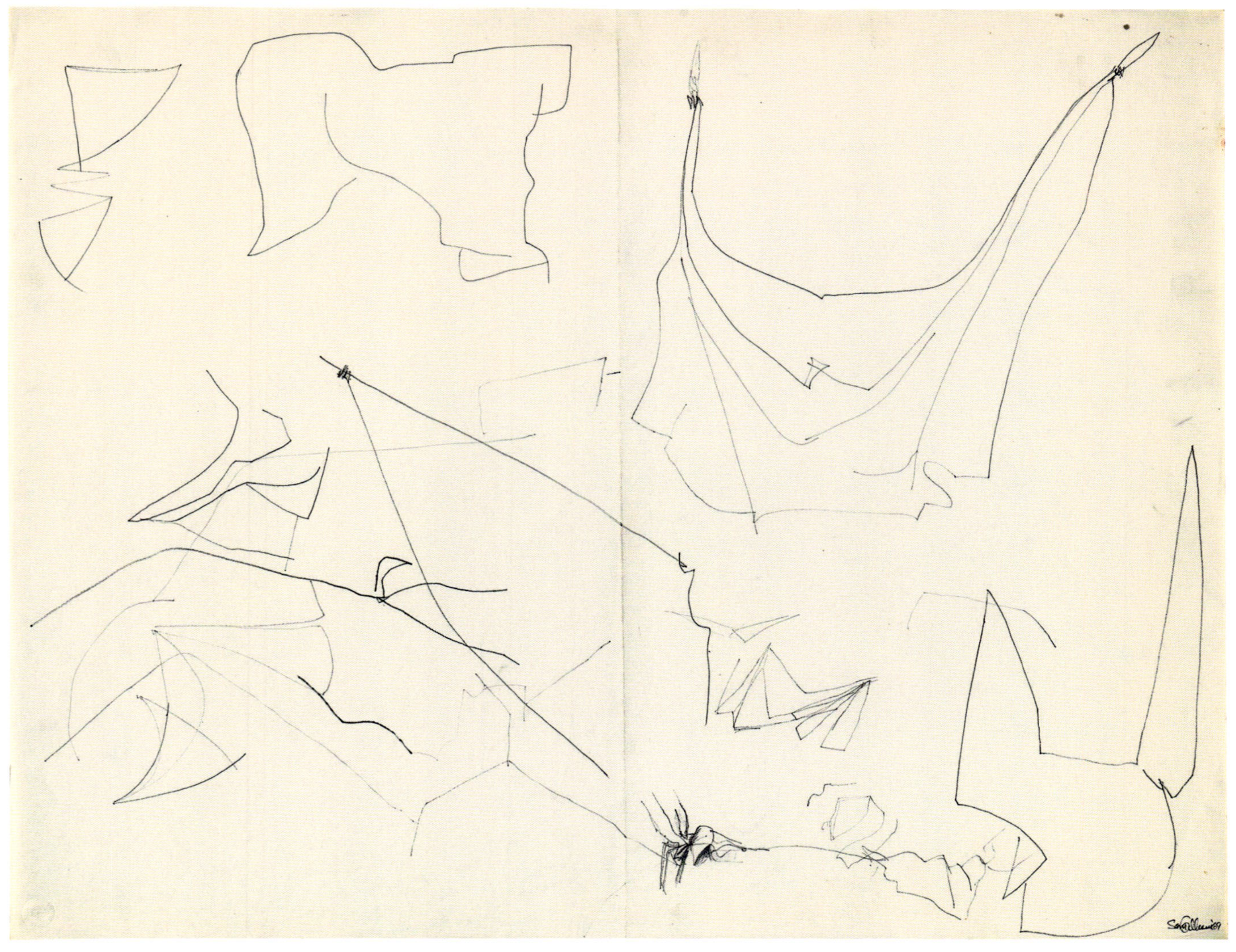

Untitled, 1969

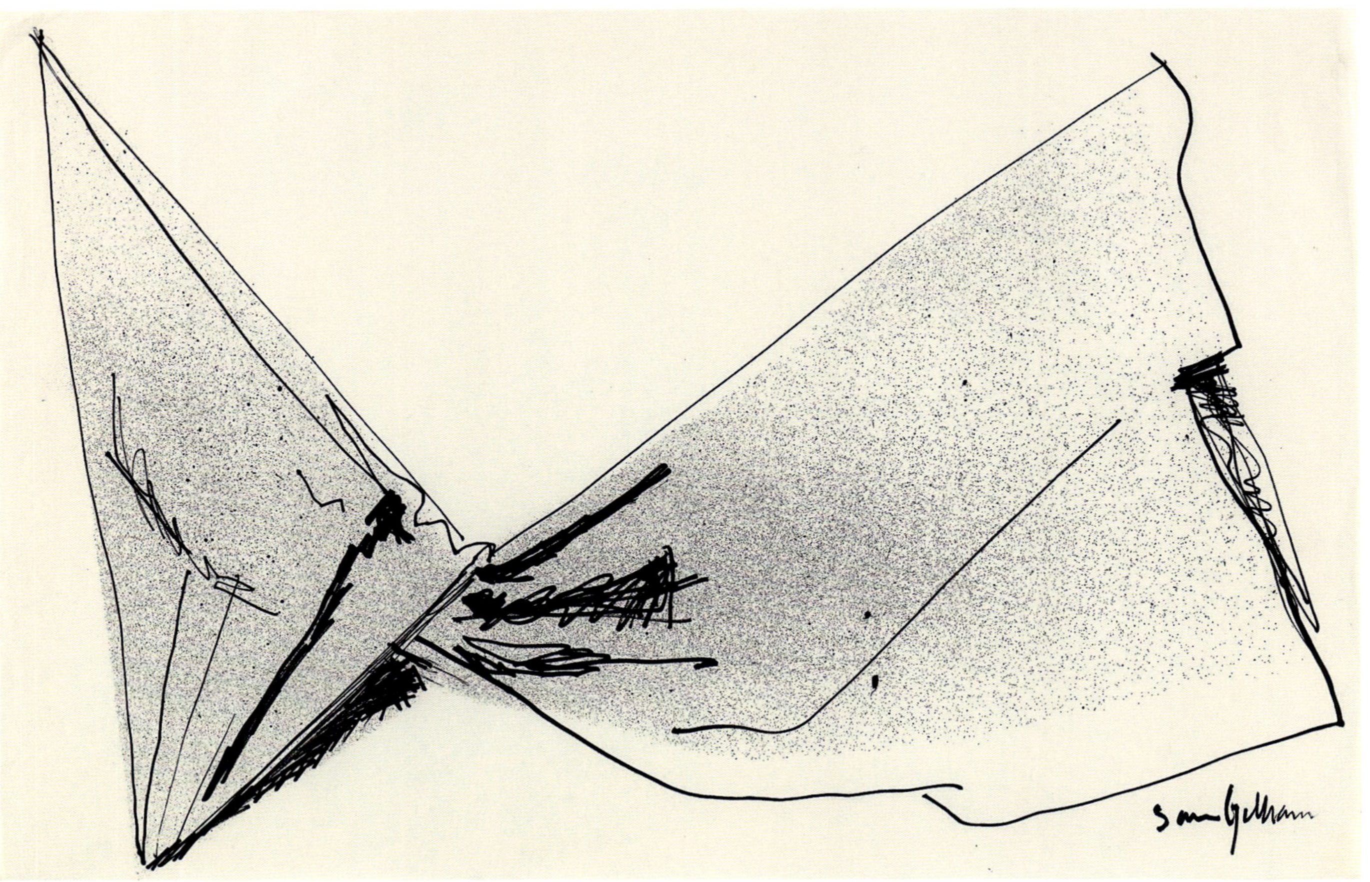

Untitled, 1969

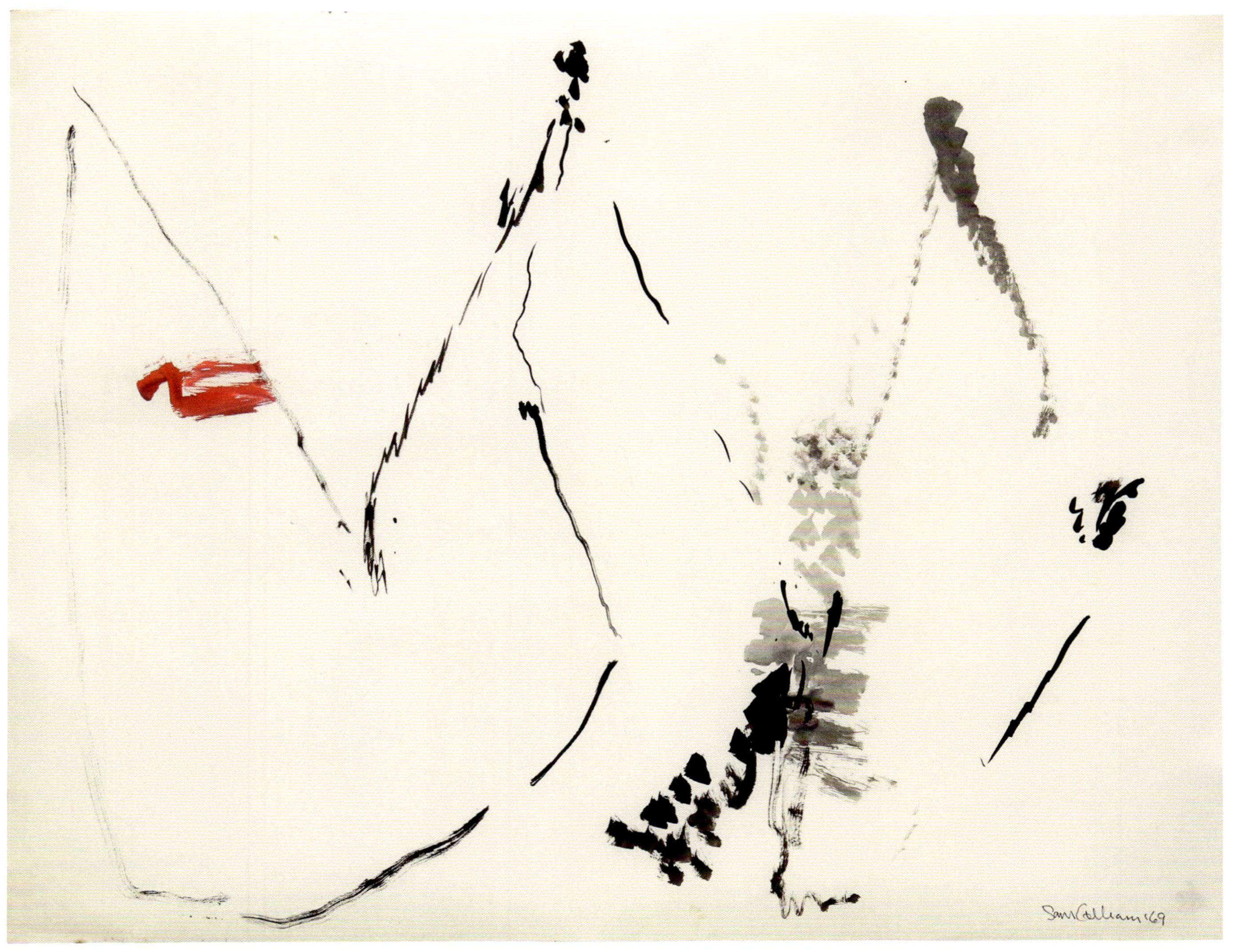

Untitled, 1969

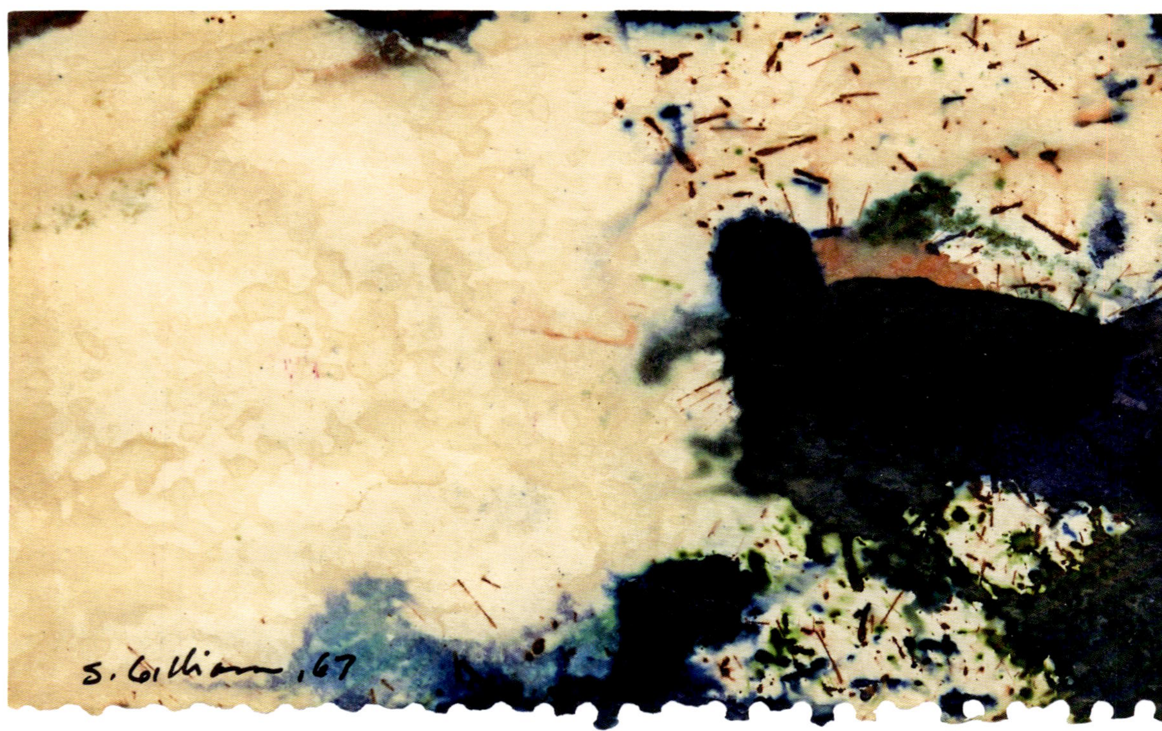

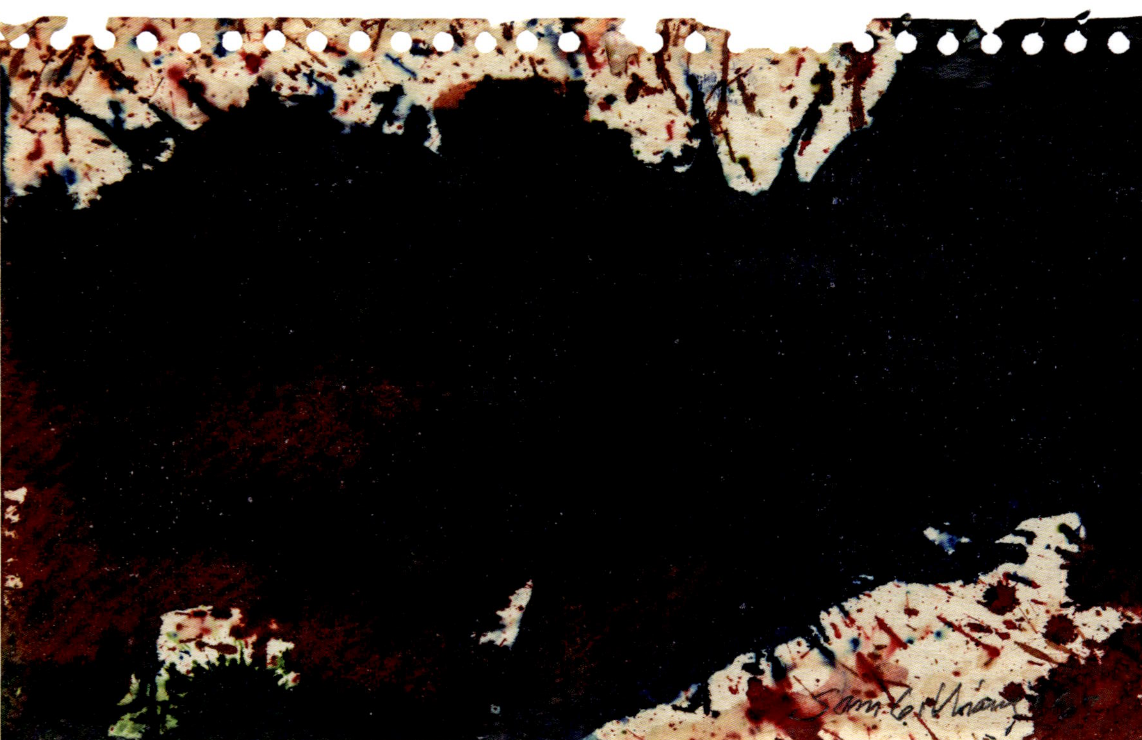

Top and bottom: *Untitled* (from 'Rock Creek' series), 1967

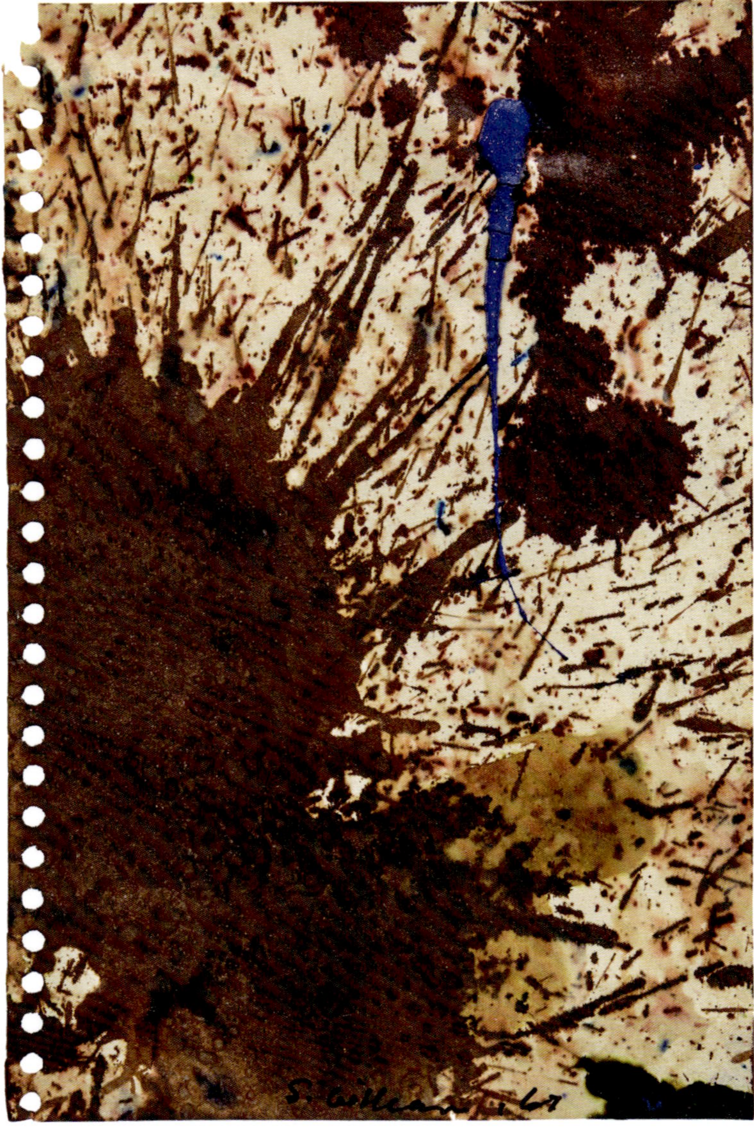

Above and right: *Untitled* (from 'Rock Creek' series), 1967

Leaf, 1970

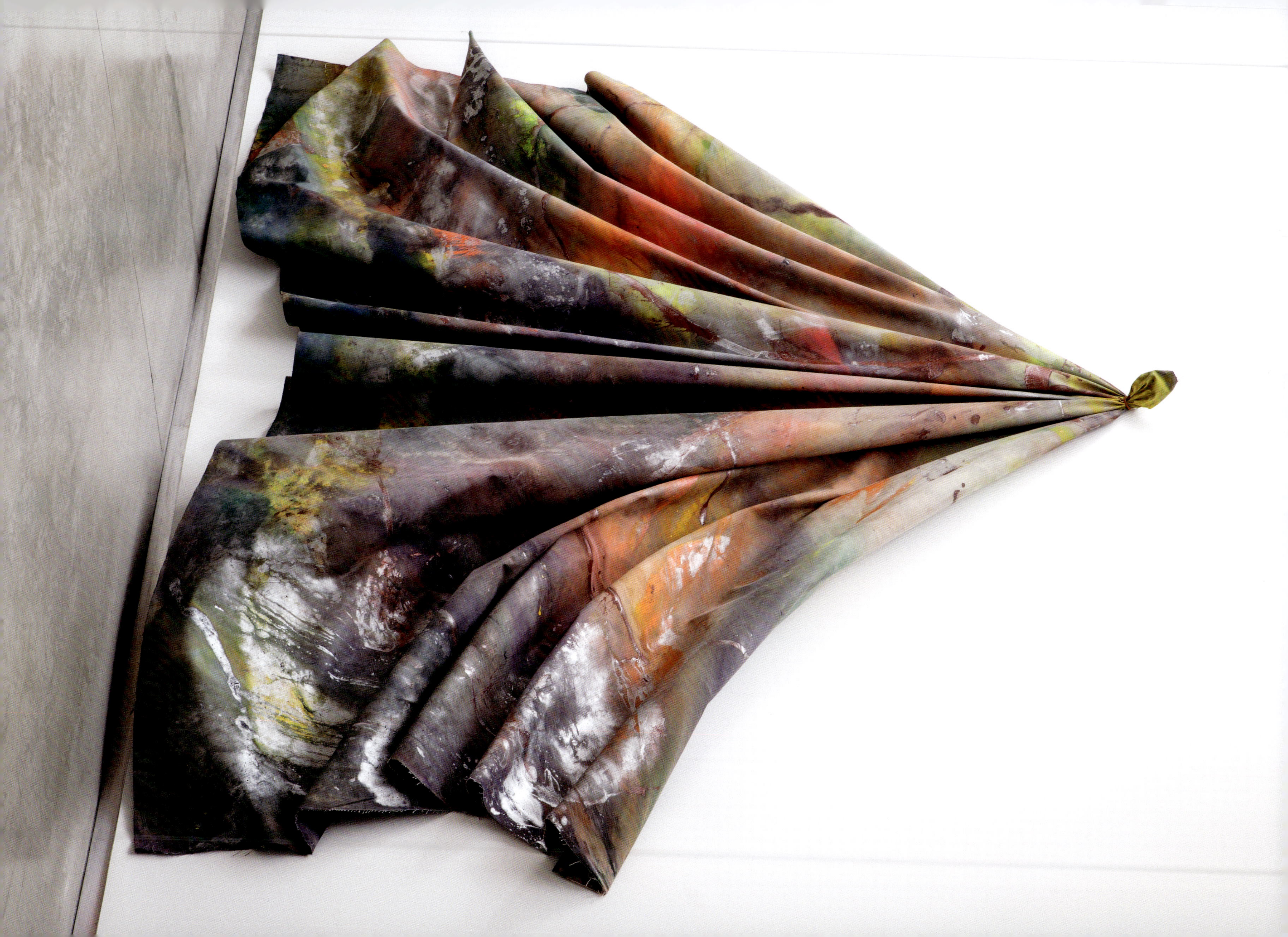

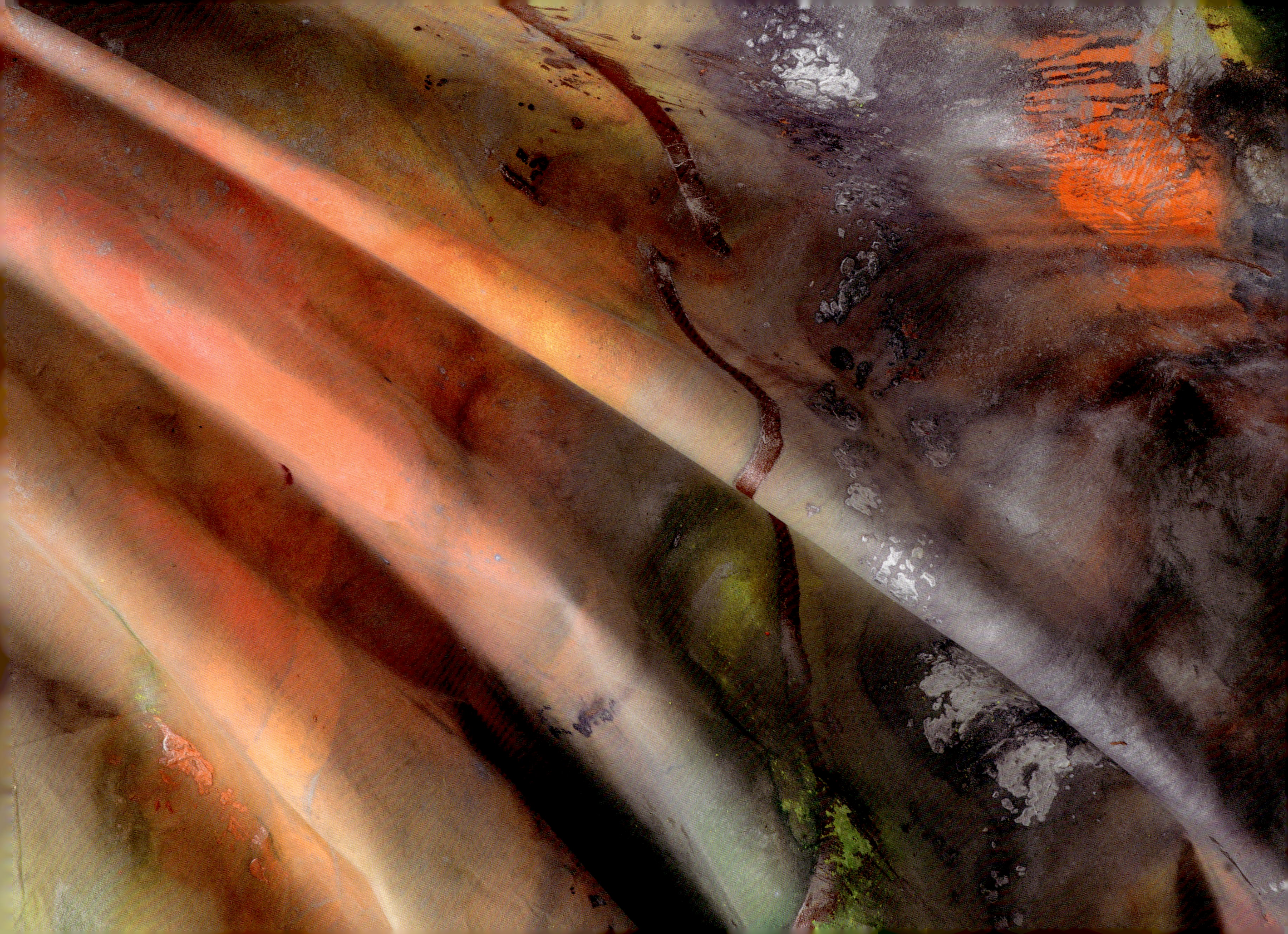

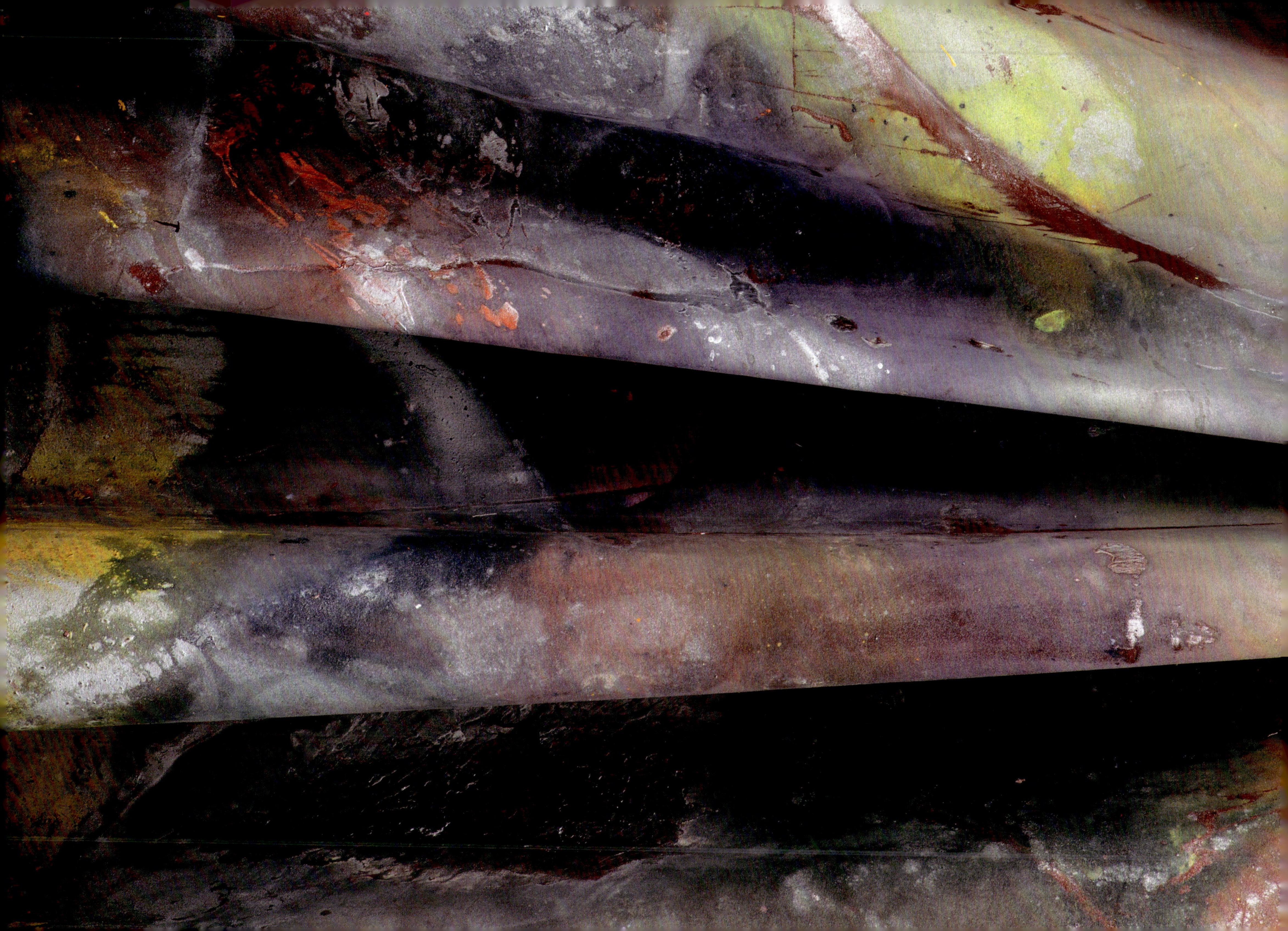

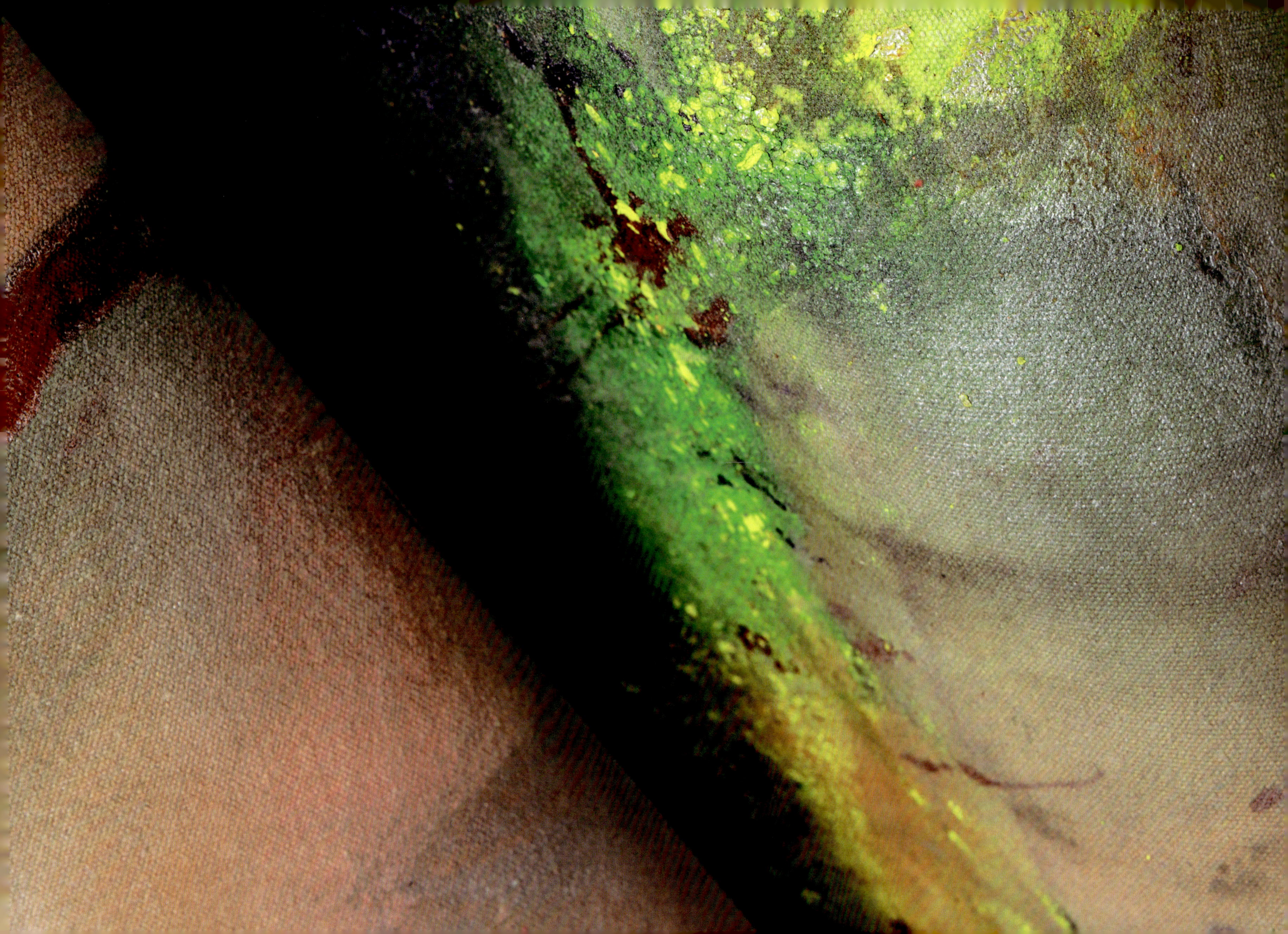

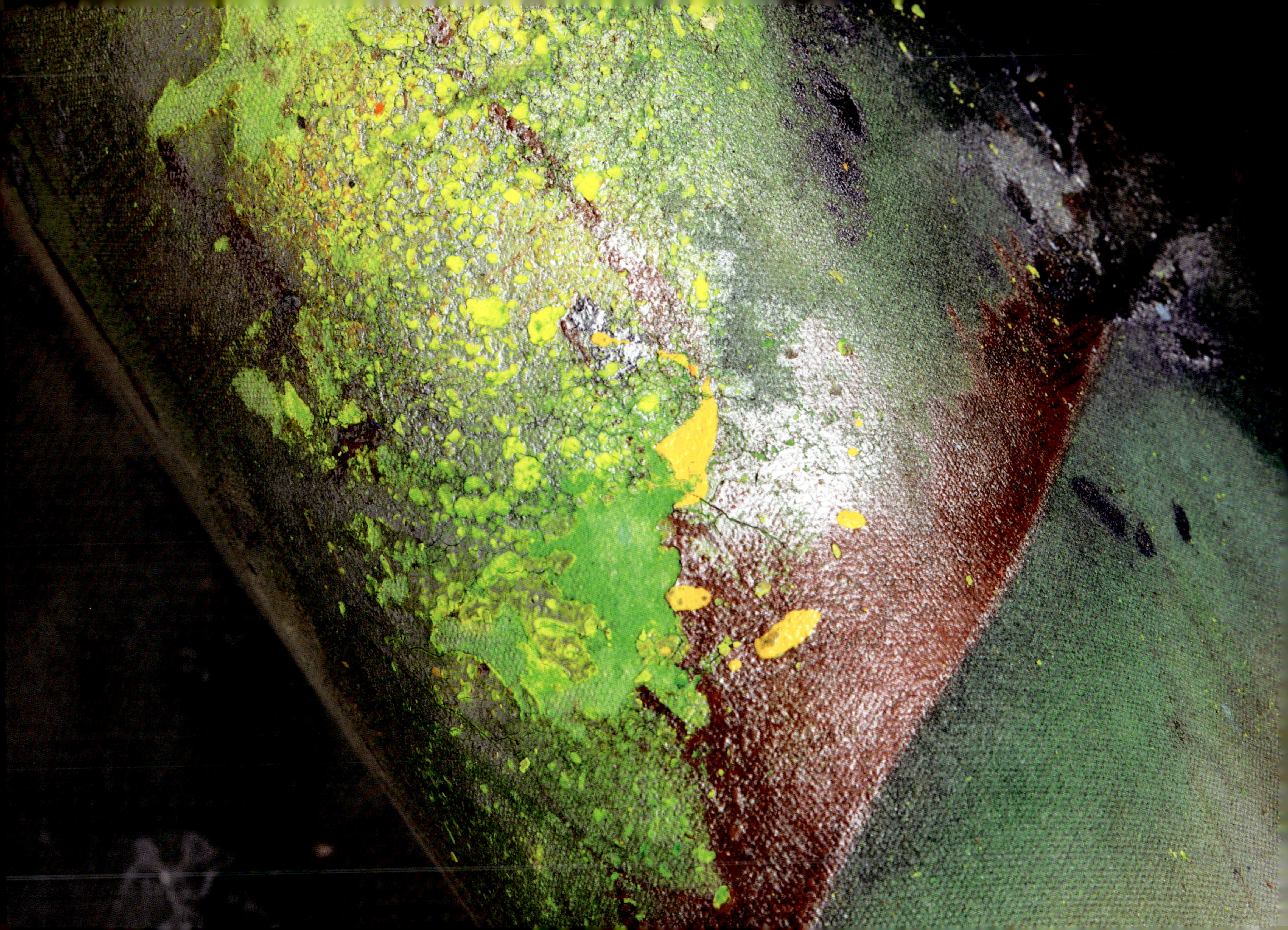

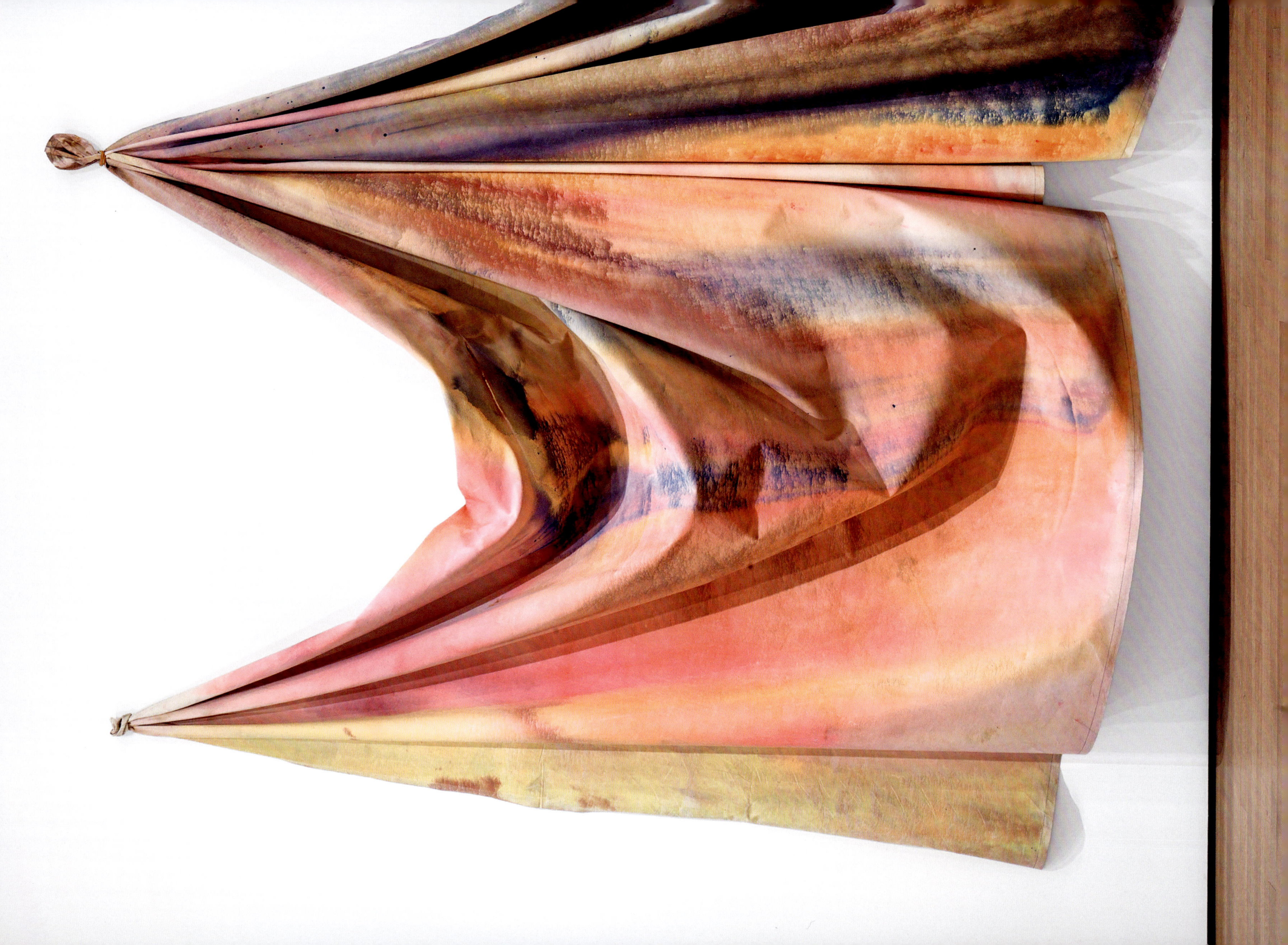

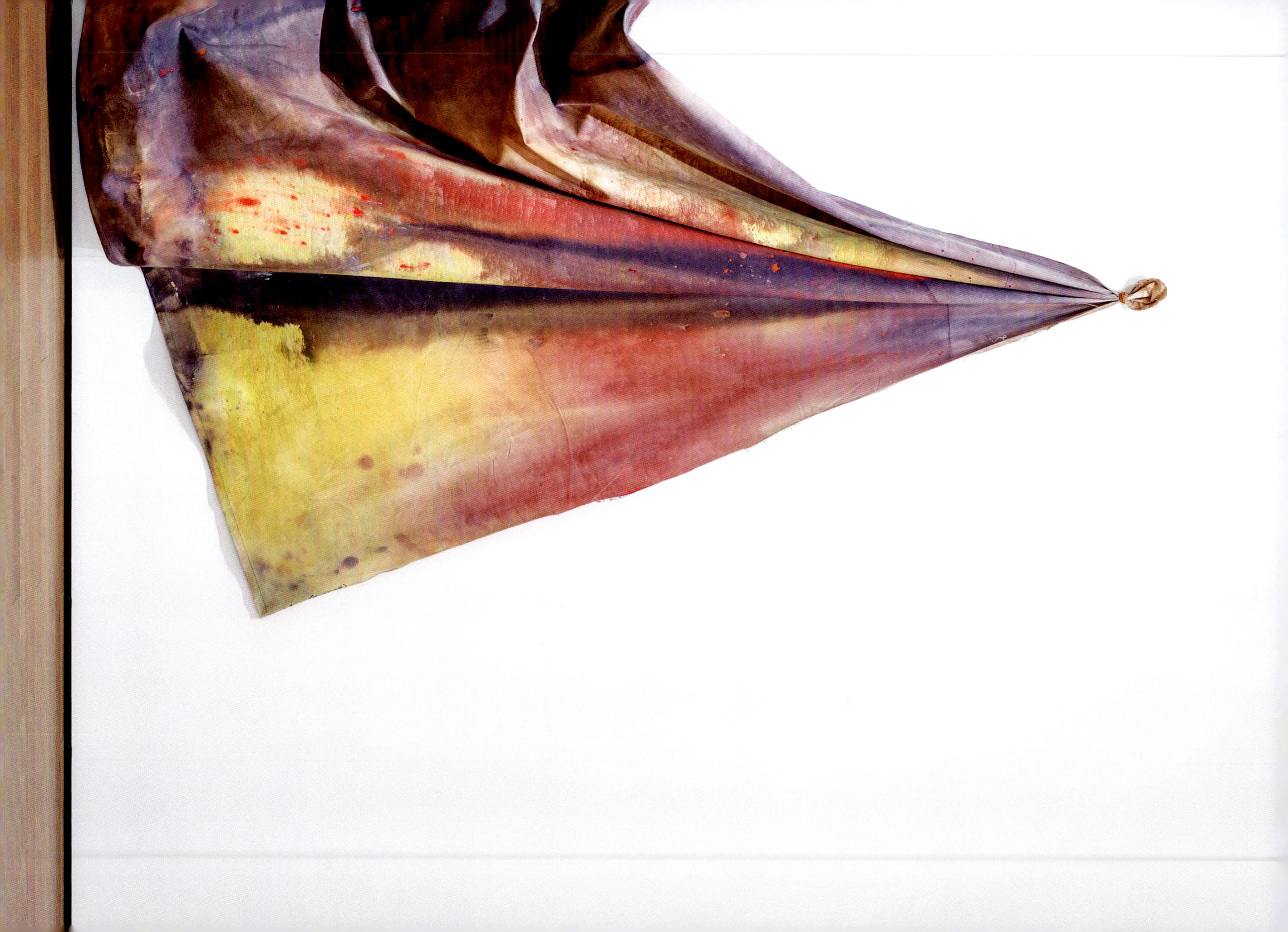

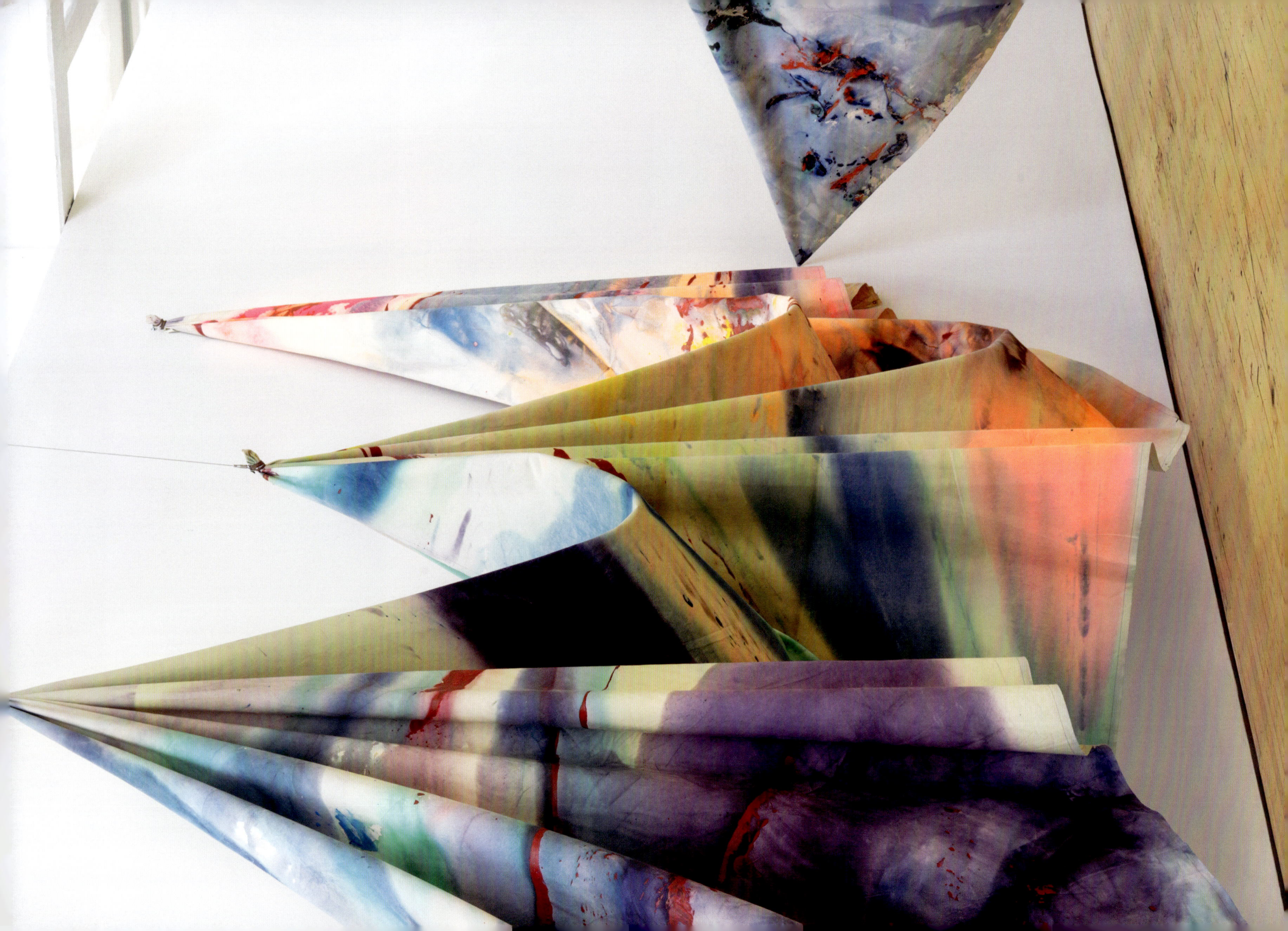

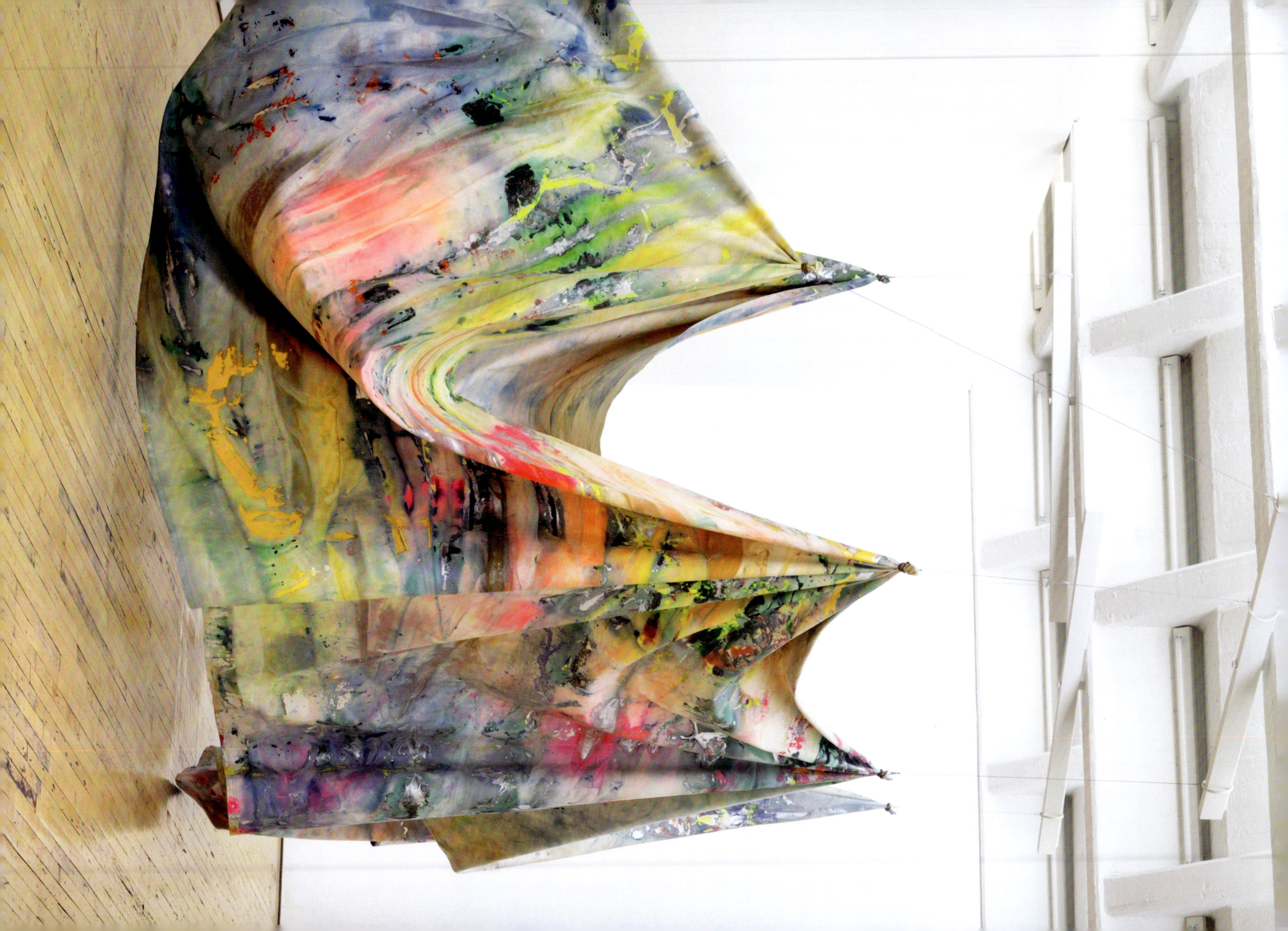

Pages 98–99: *10/27/69*, 1969

Previous pages: *Double Merge*, 1968

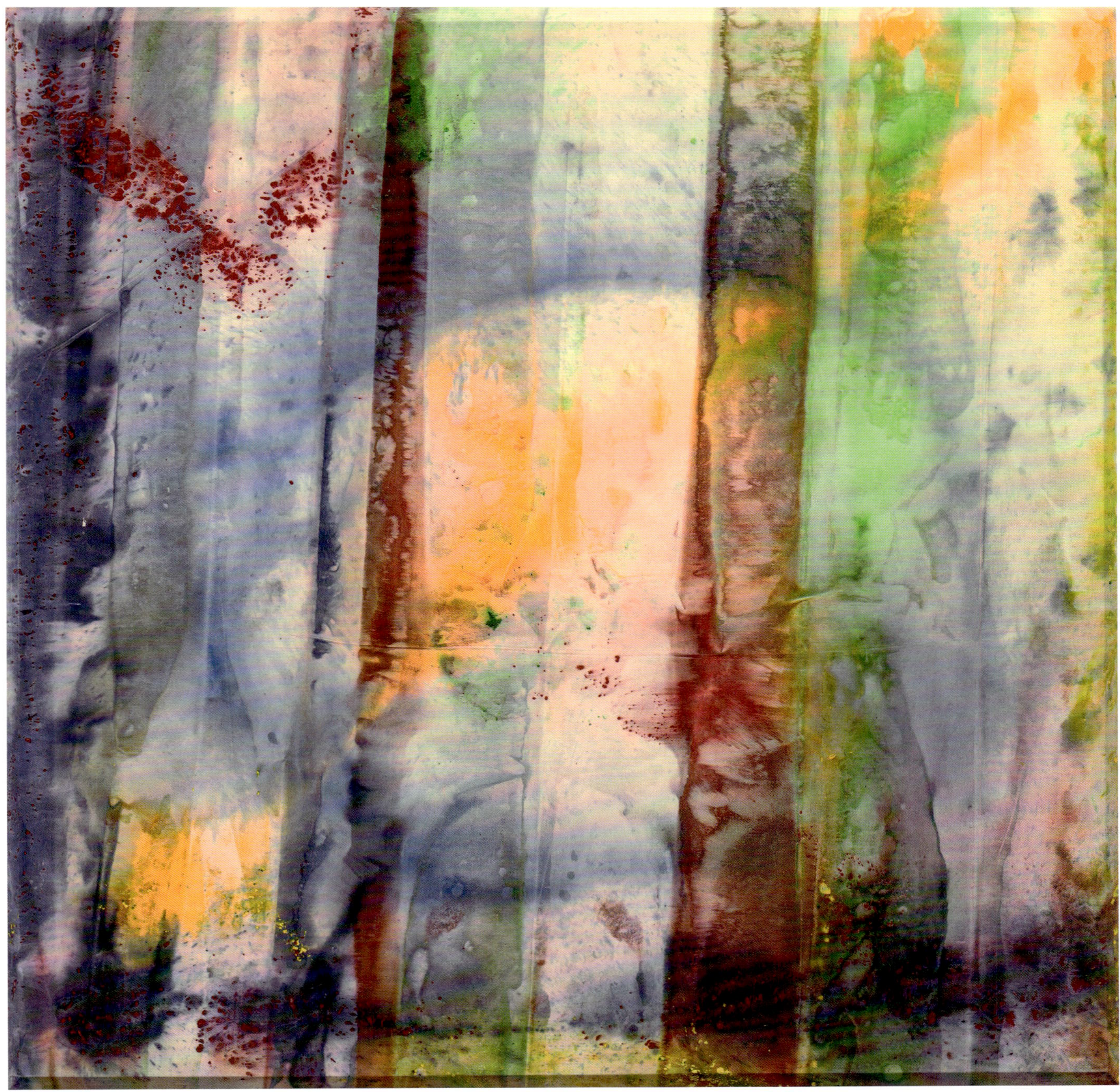

Change, 1970

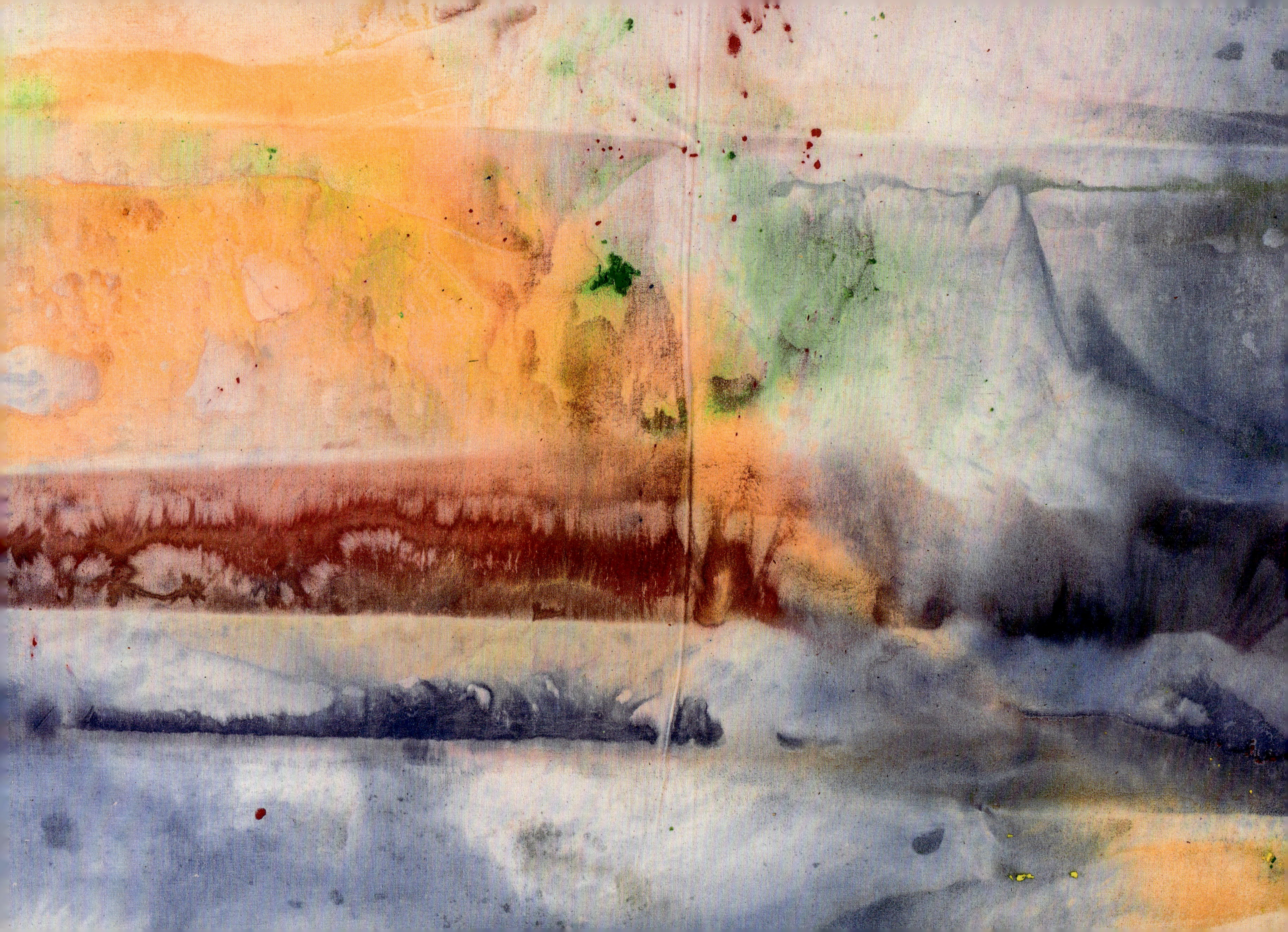

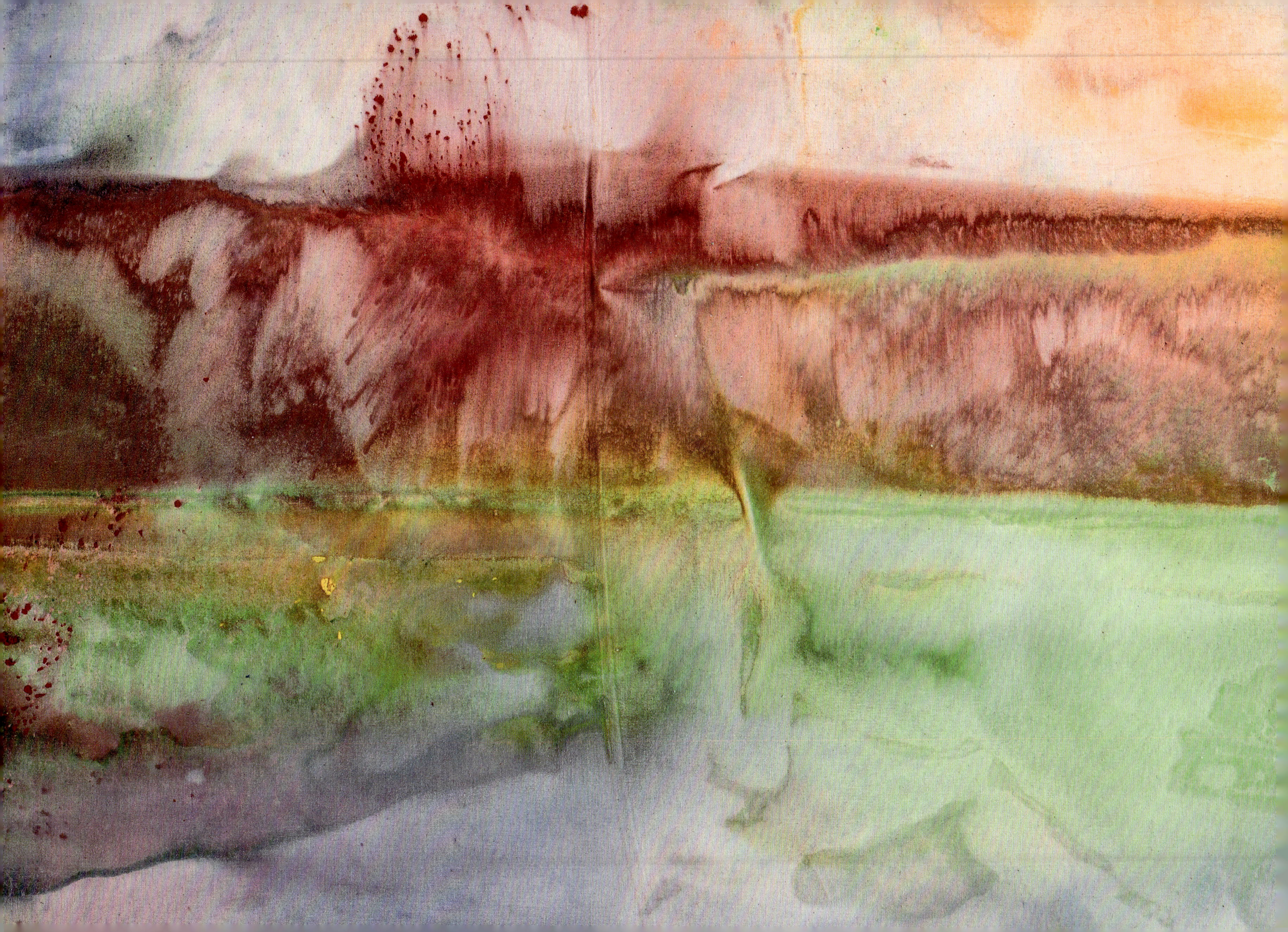

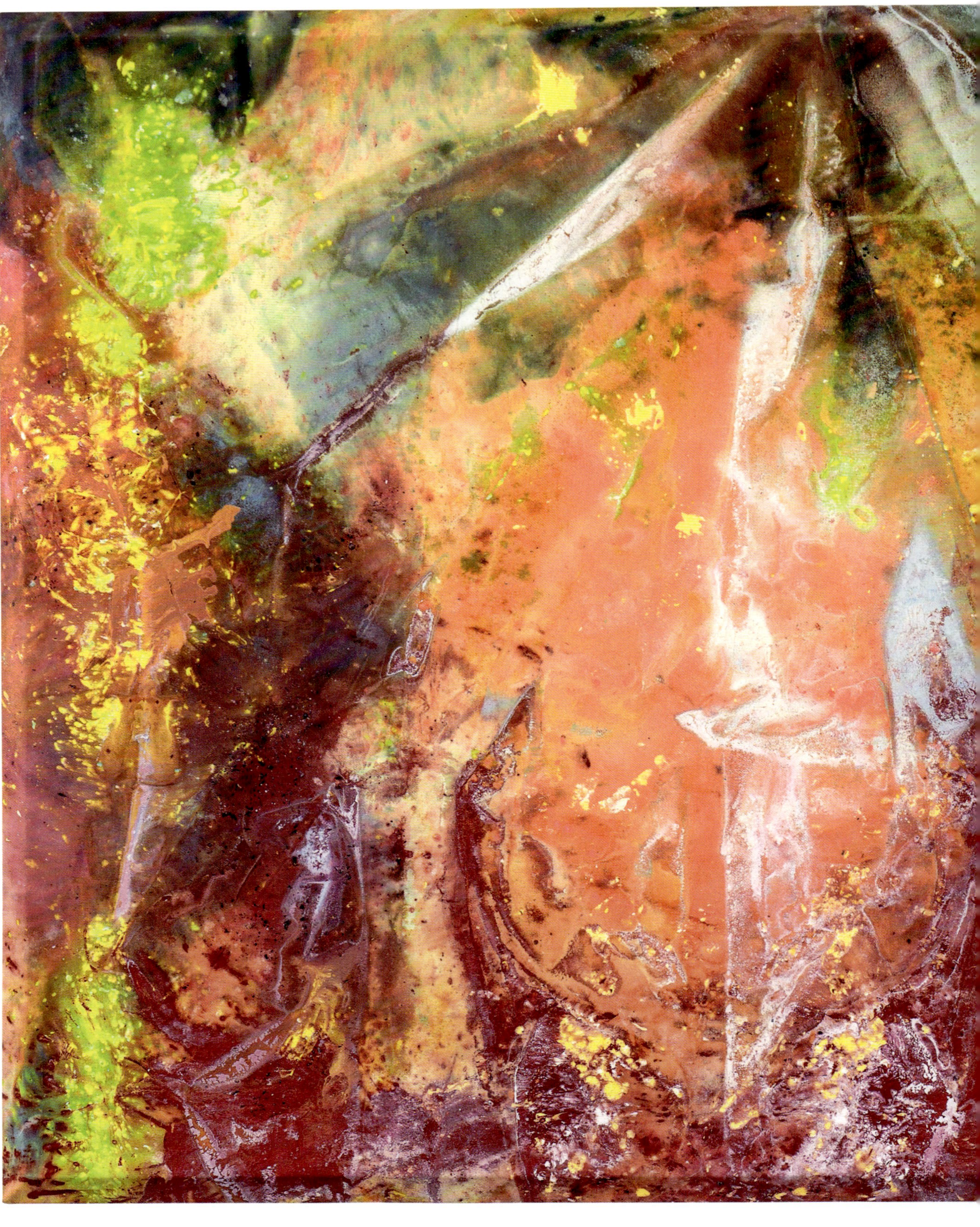

Spread, 1973

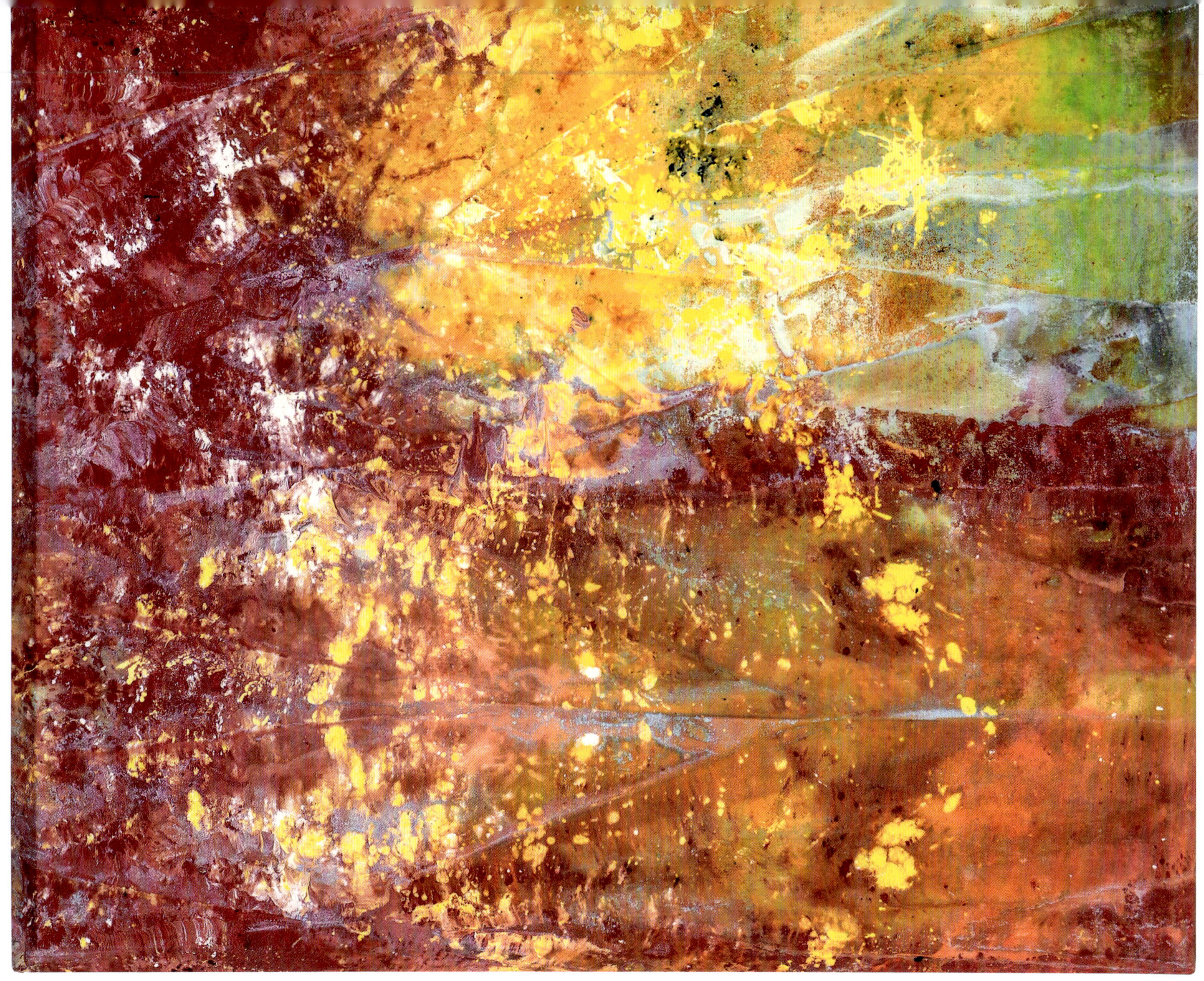

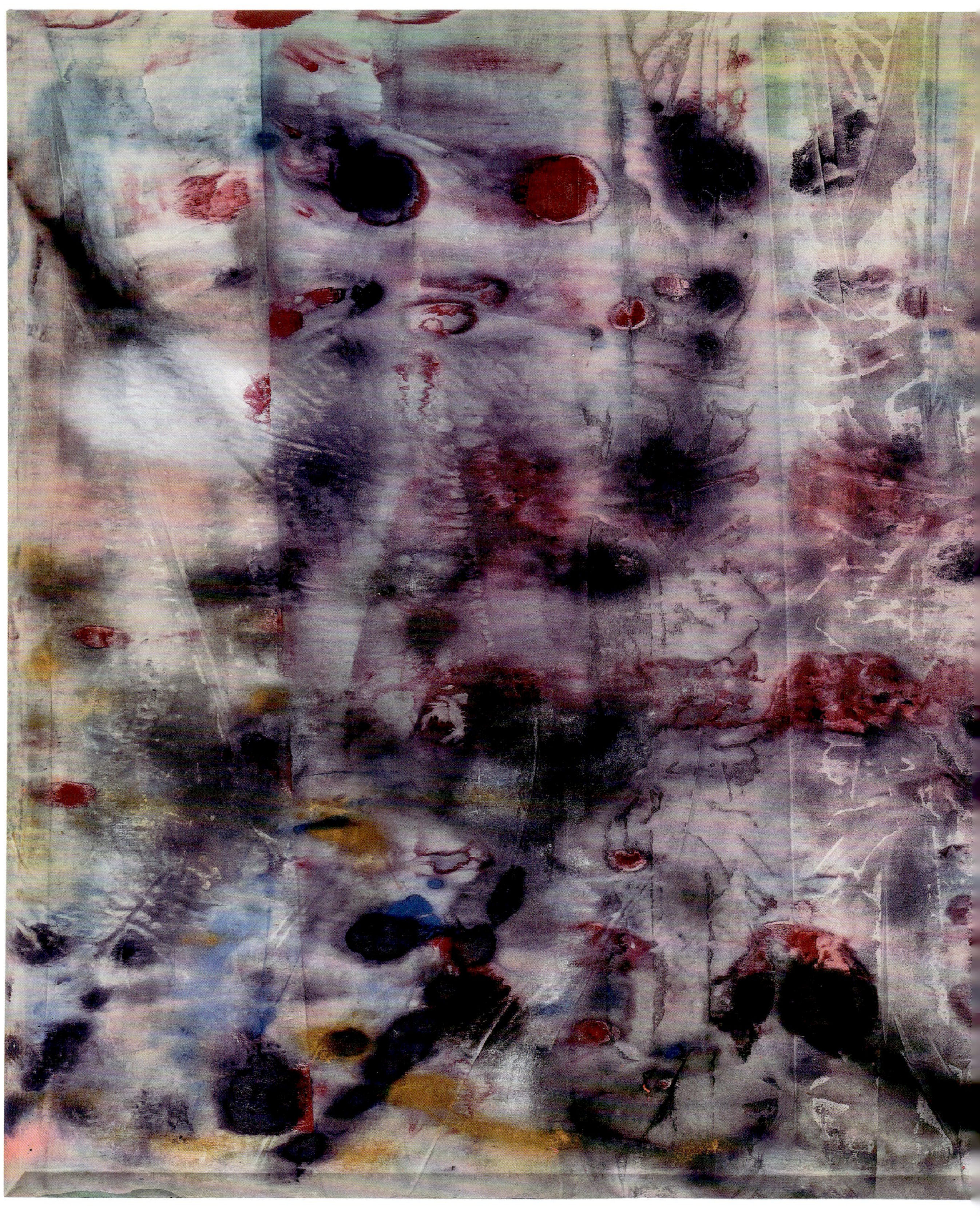

April 4, 1969

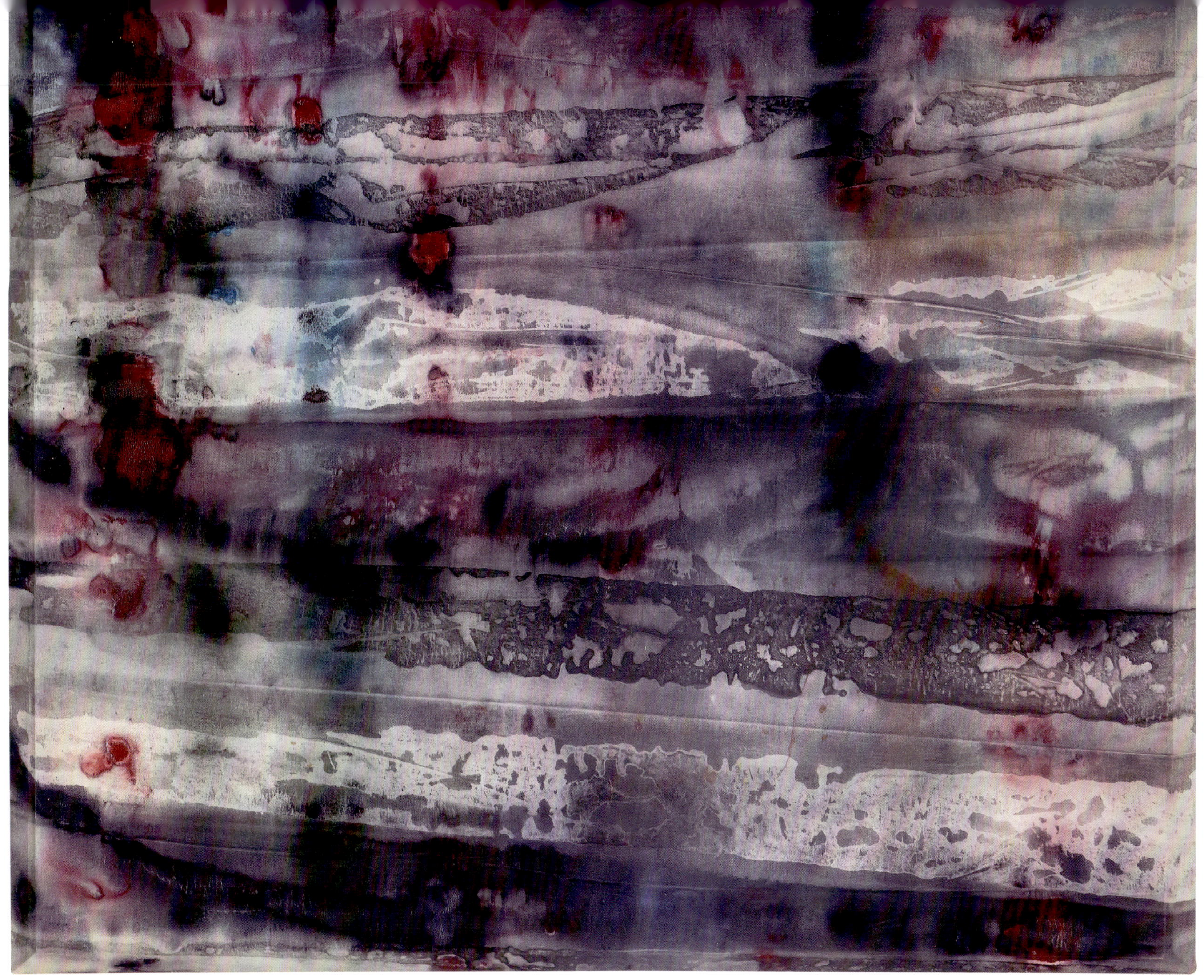

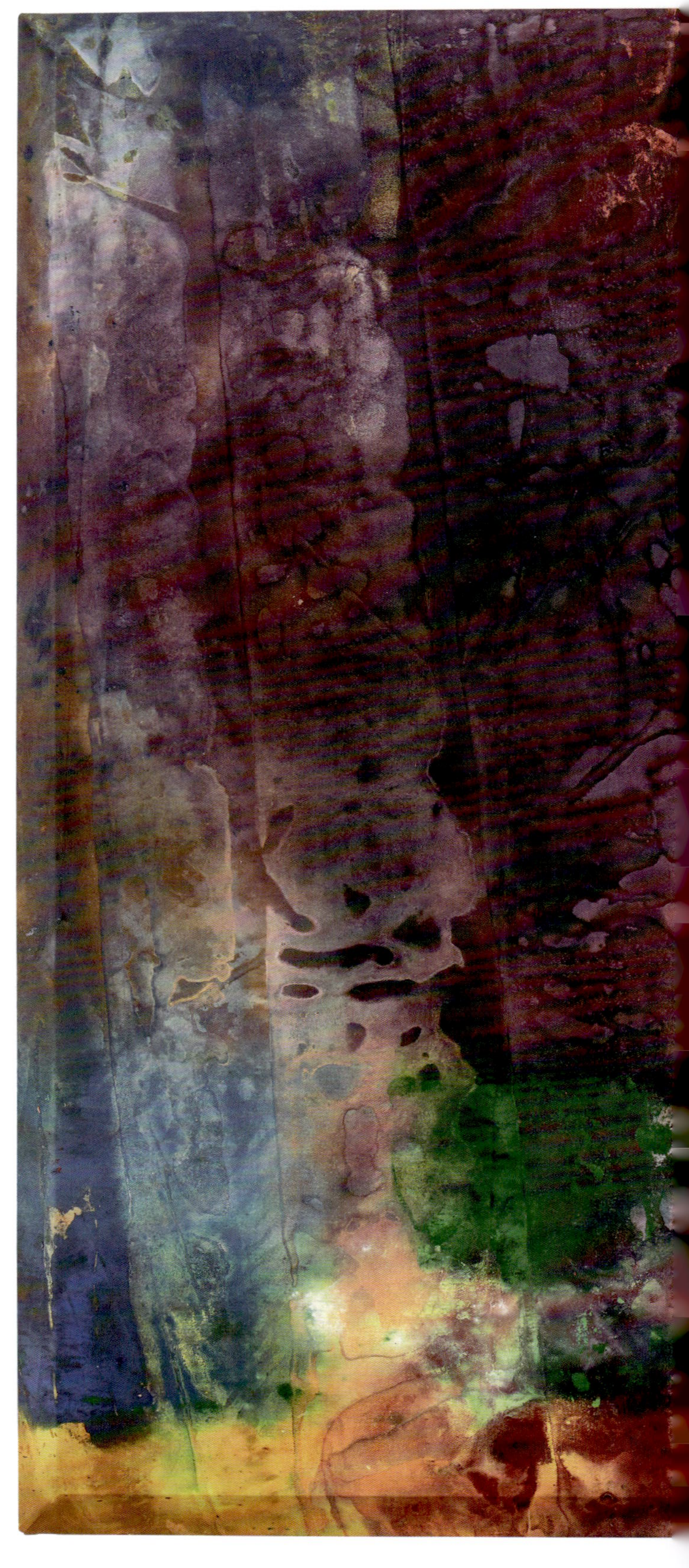

Rose Rising, 1968

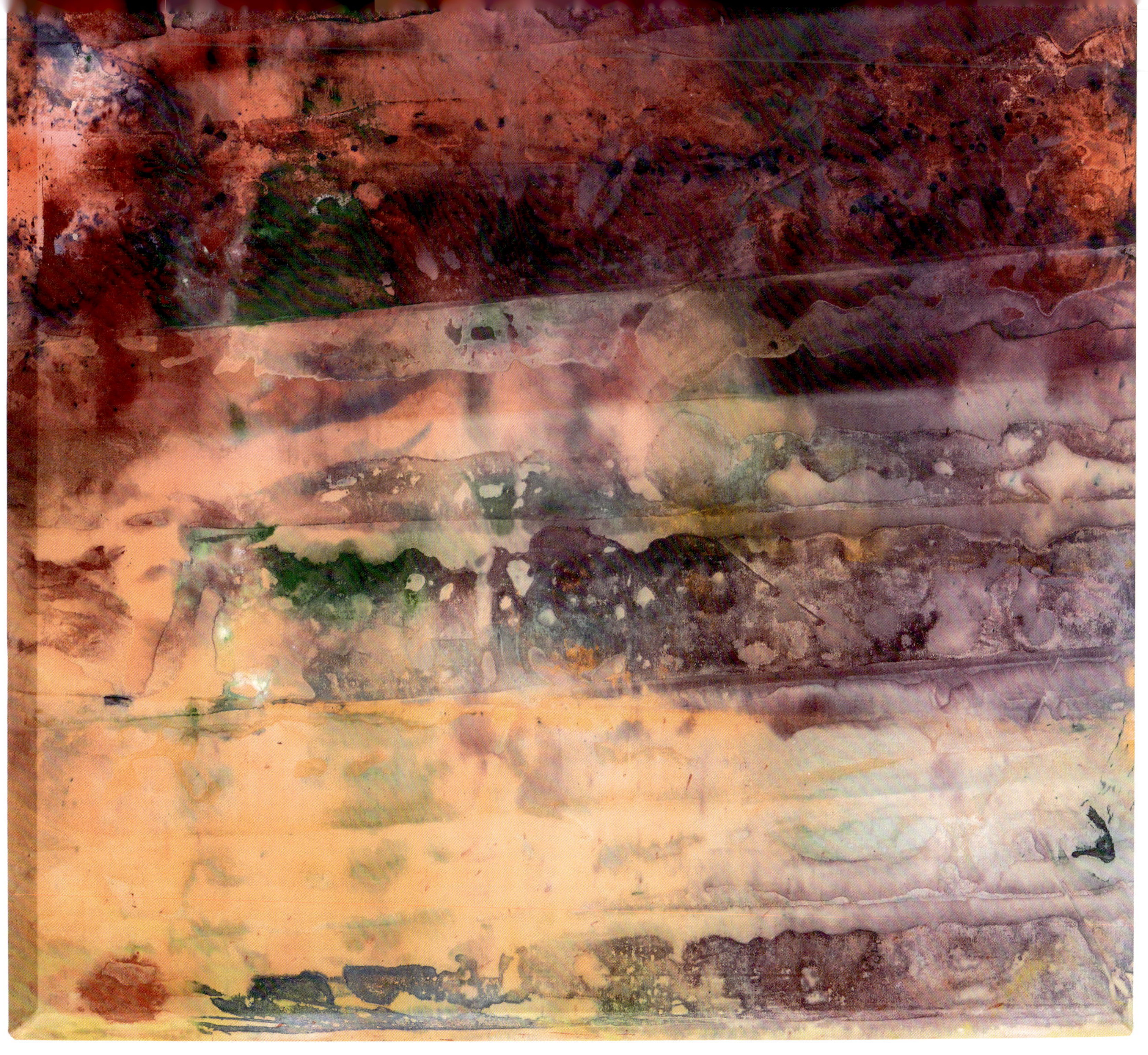

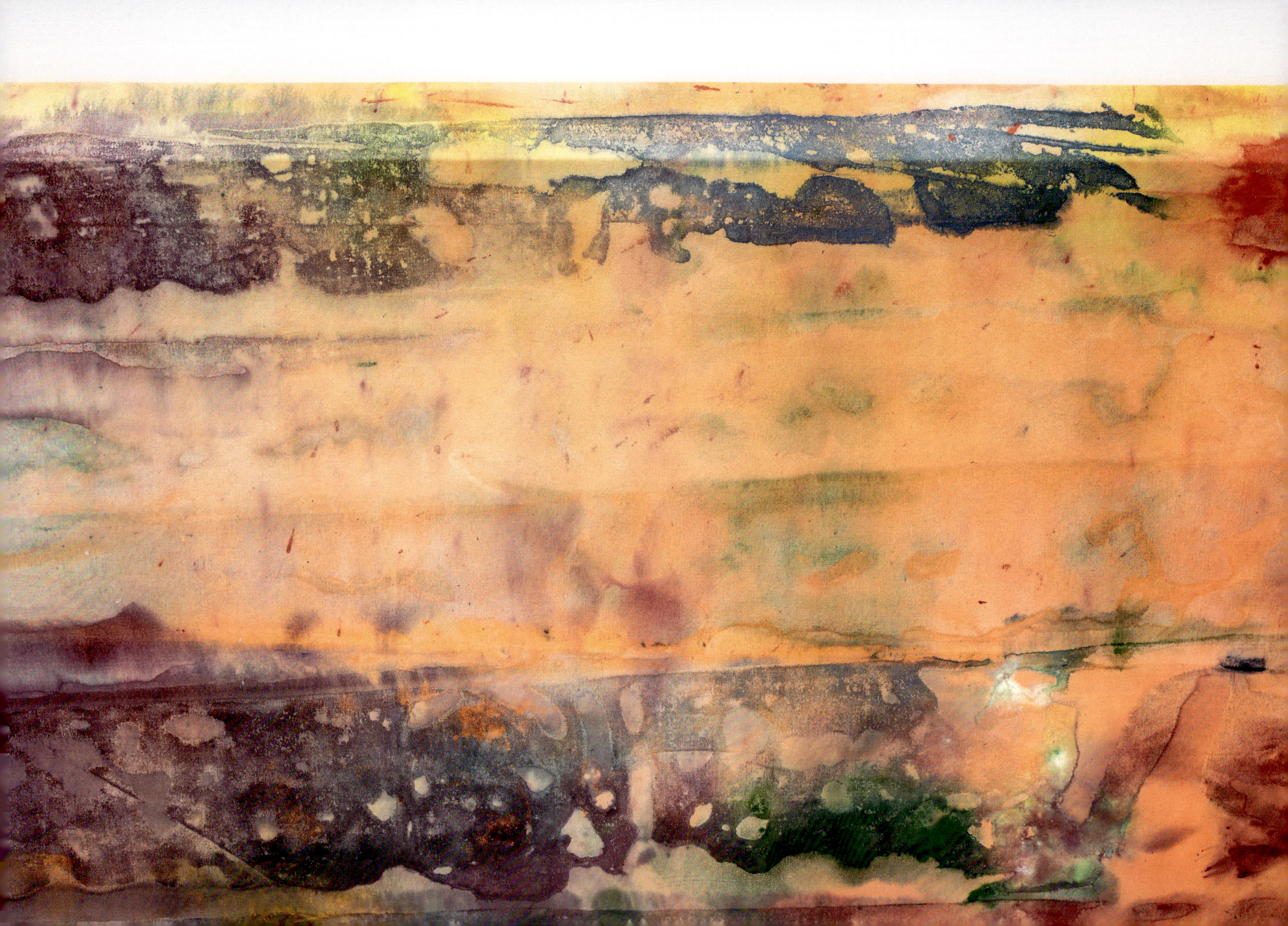

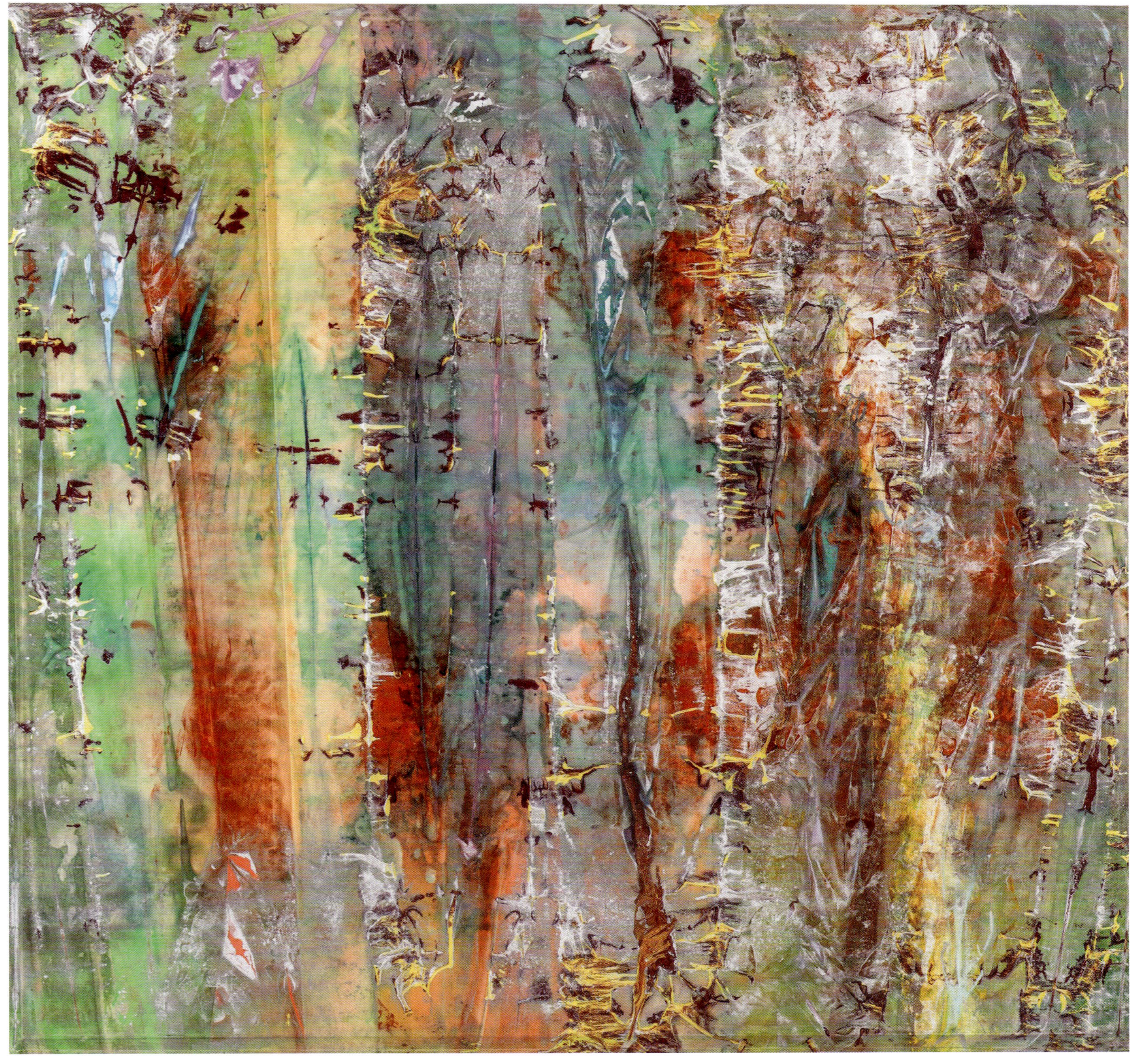

Whirlirama, 1970

Following pages: *Out*, 1969

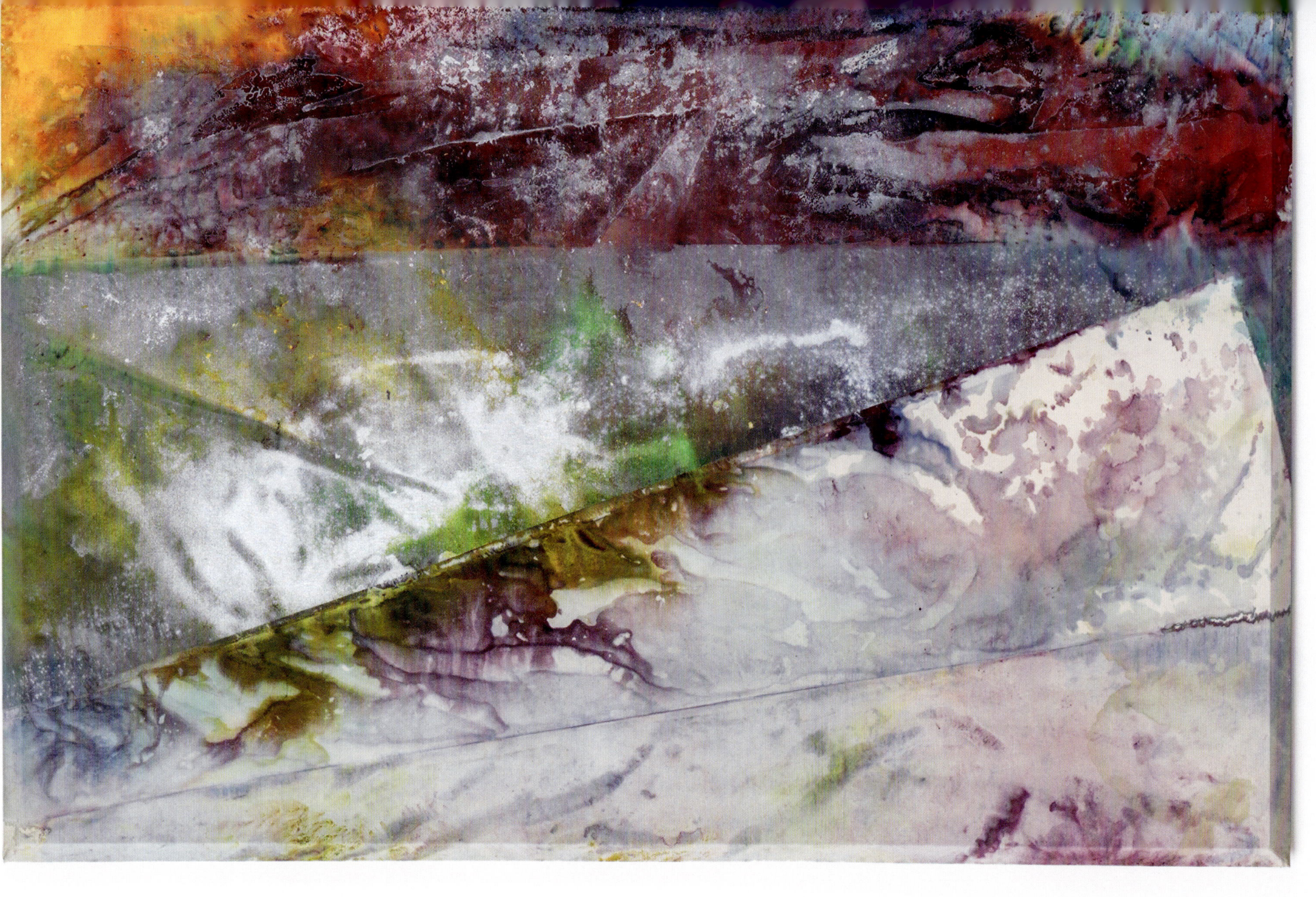

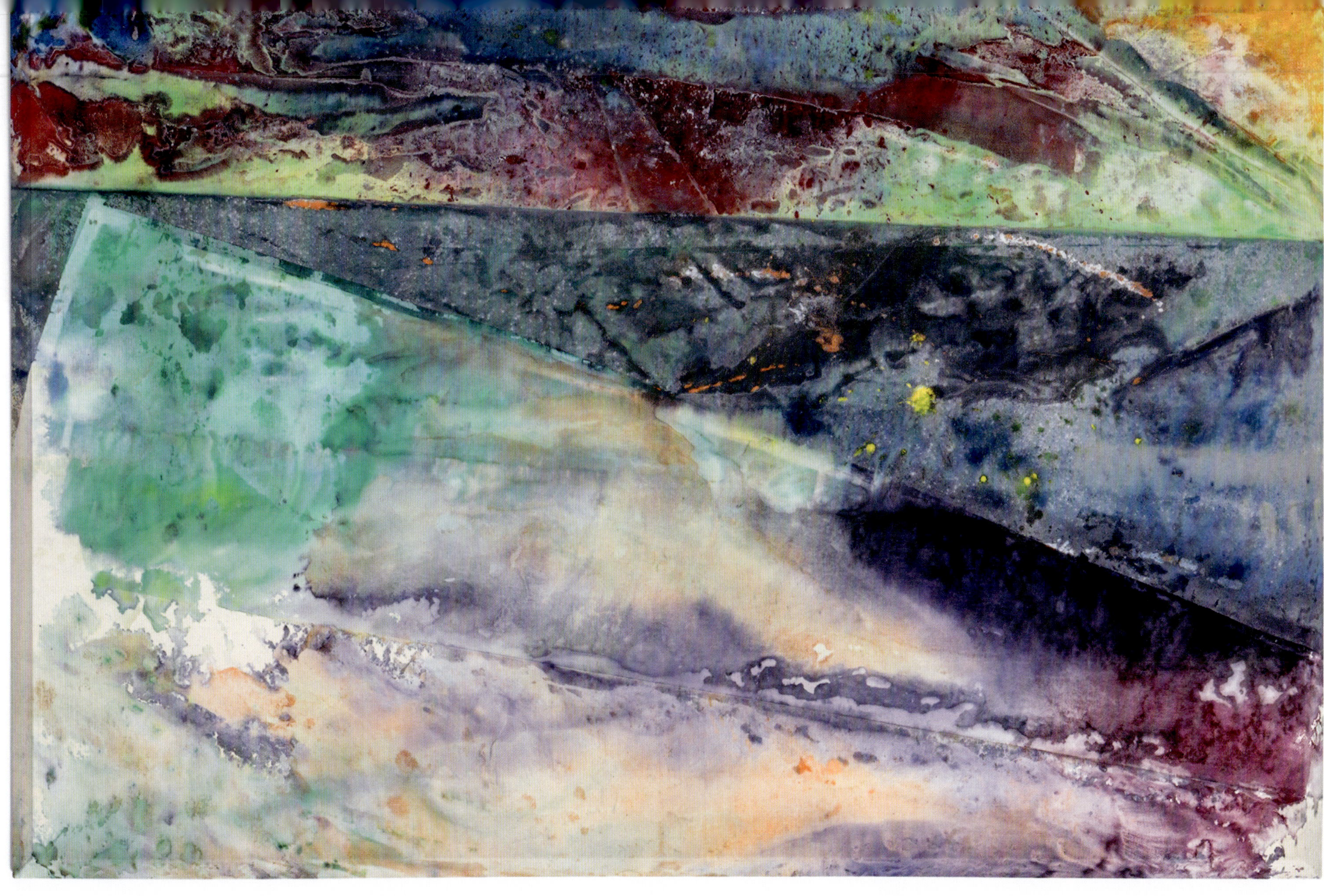

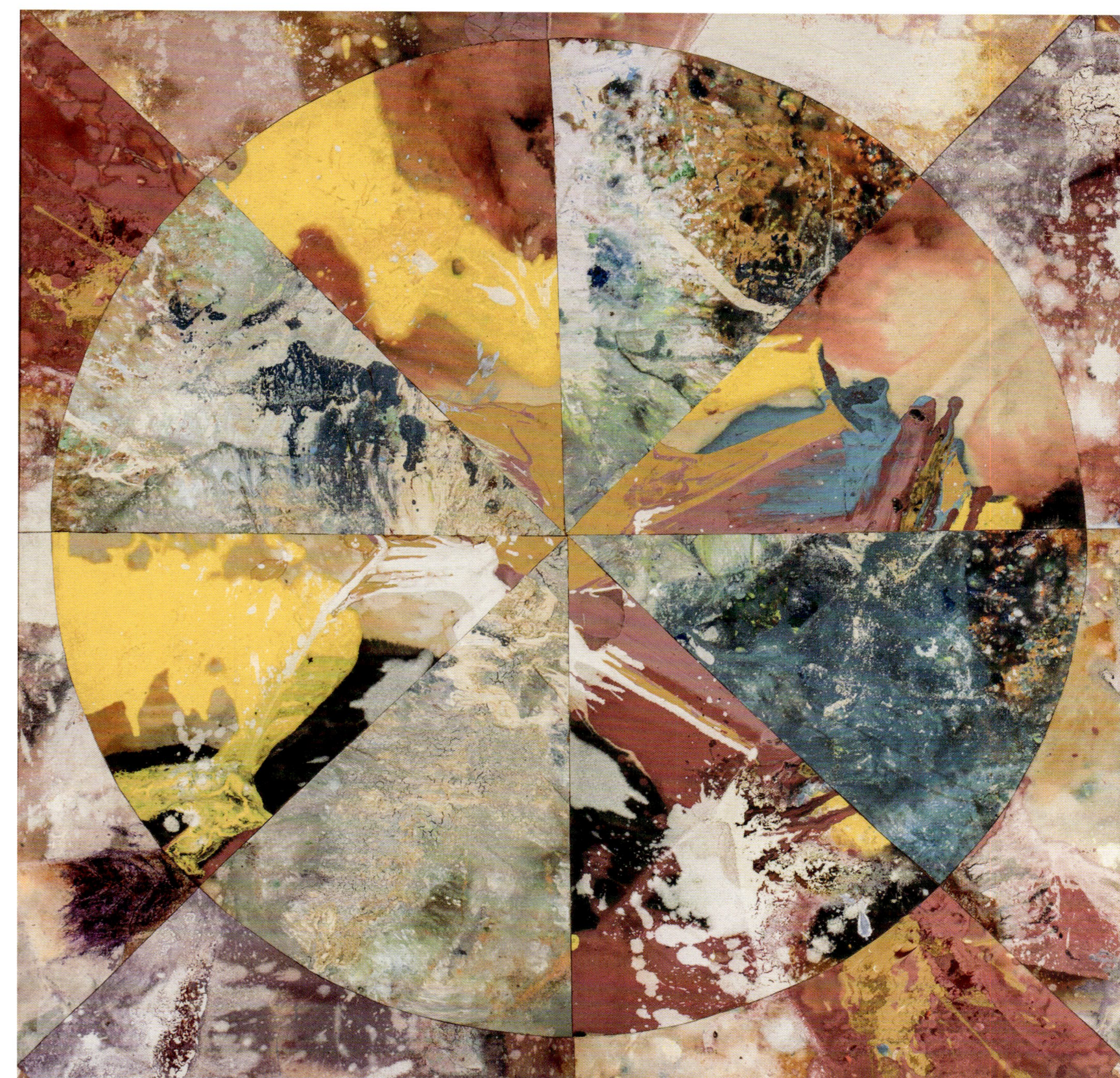

For Day One, 1974–75

Crystal, 1973

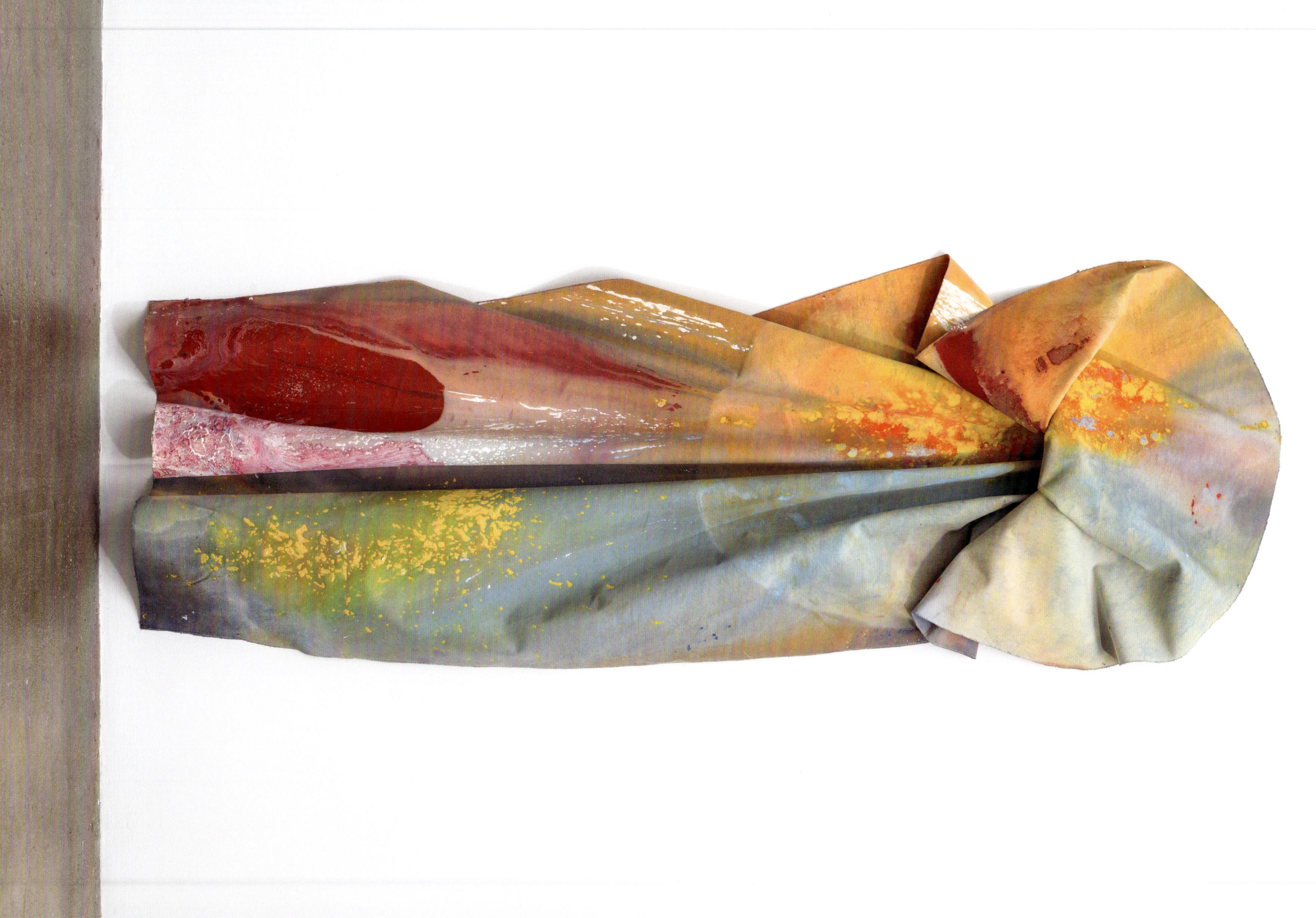

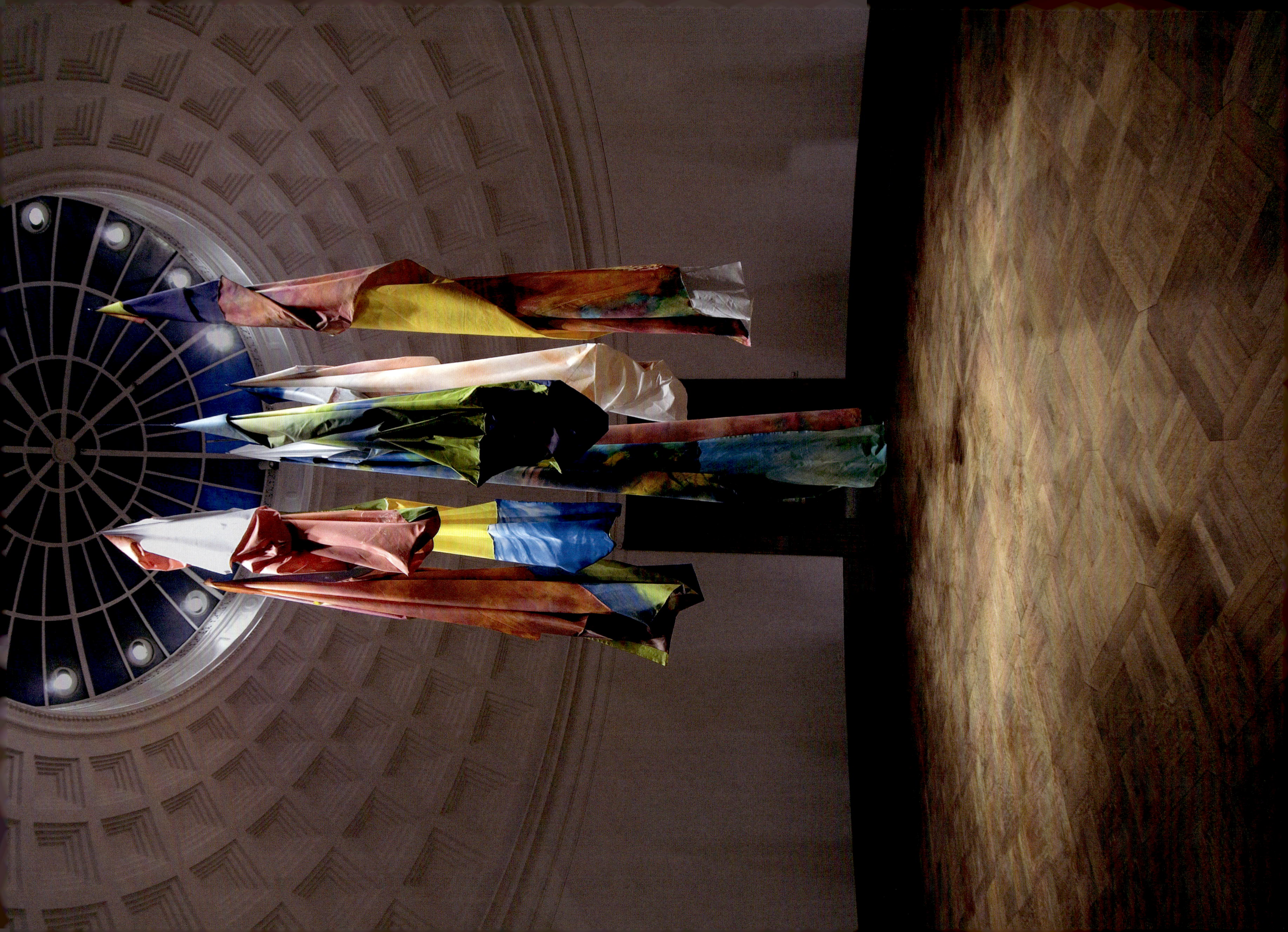

Installation view of exhibition 'Sam Gilliam: A Retrospective', Corcoran Gallery of Art, Washington, D.C.

Following pages: *"A" and the Carpenter I*, 1973

Pages 126–127: *Softly Still*, 1973

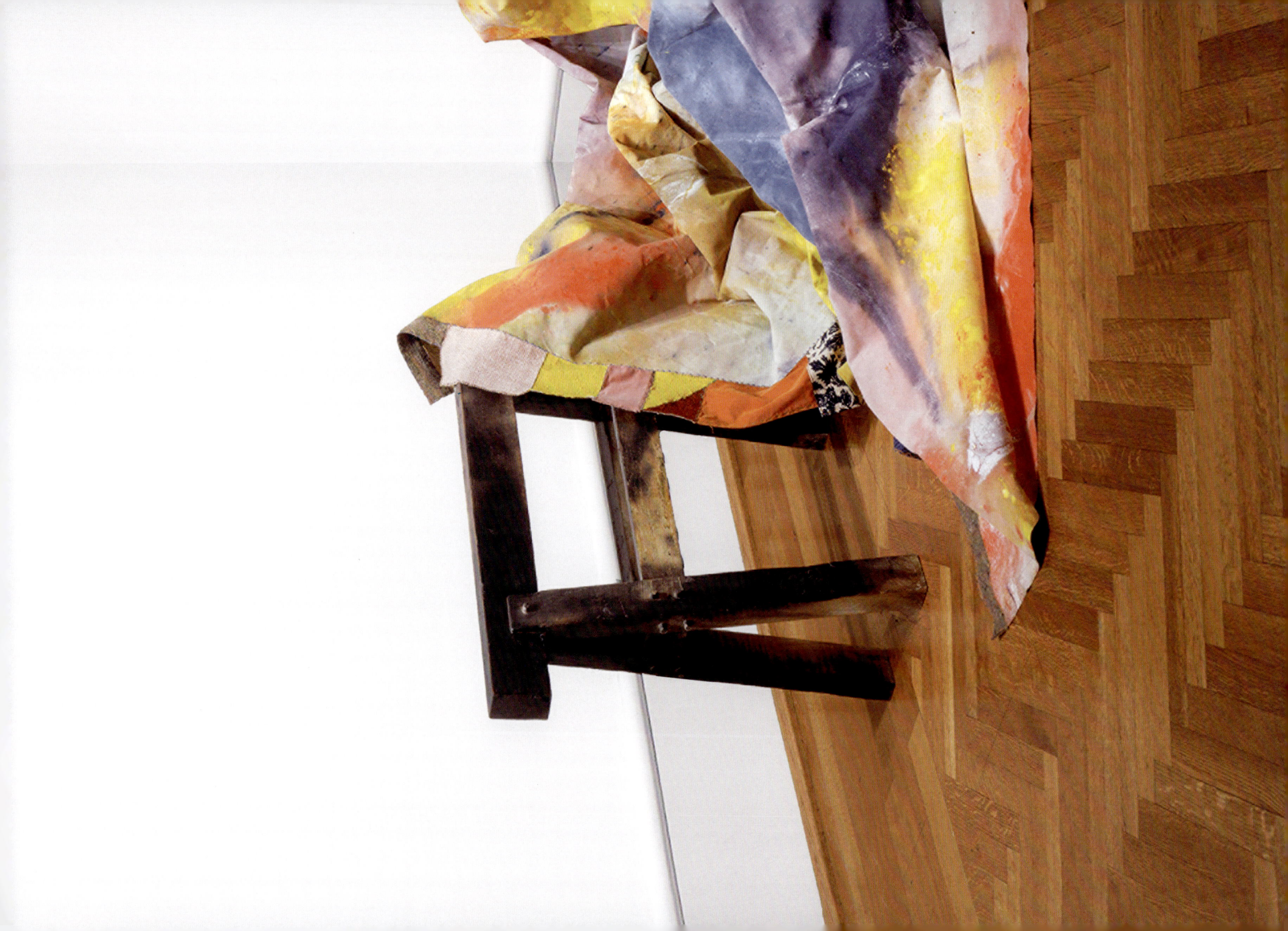

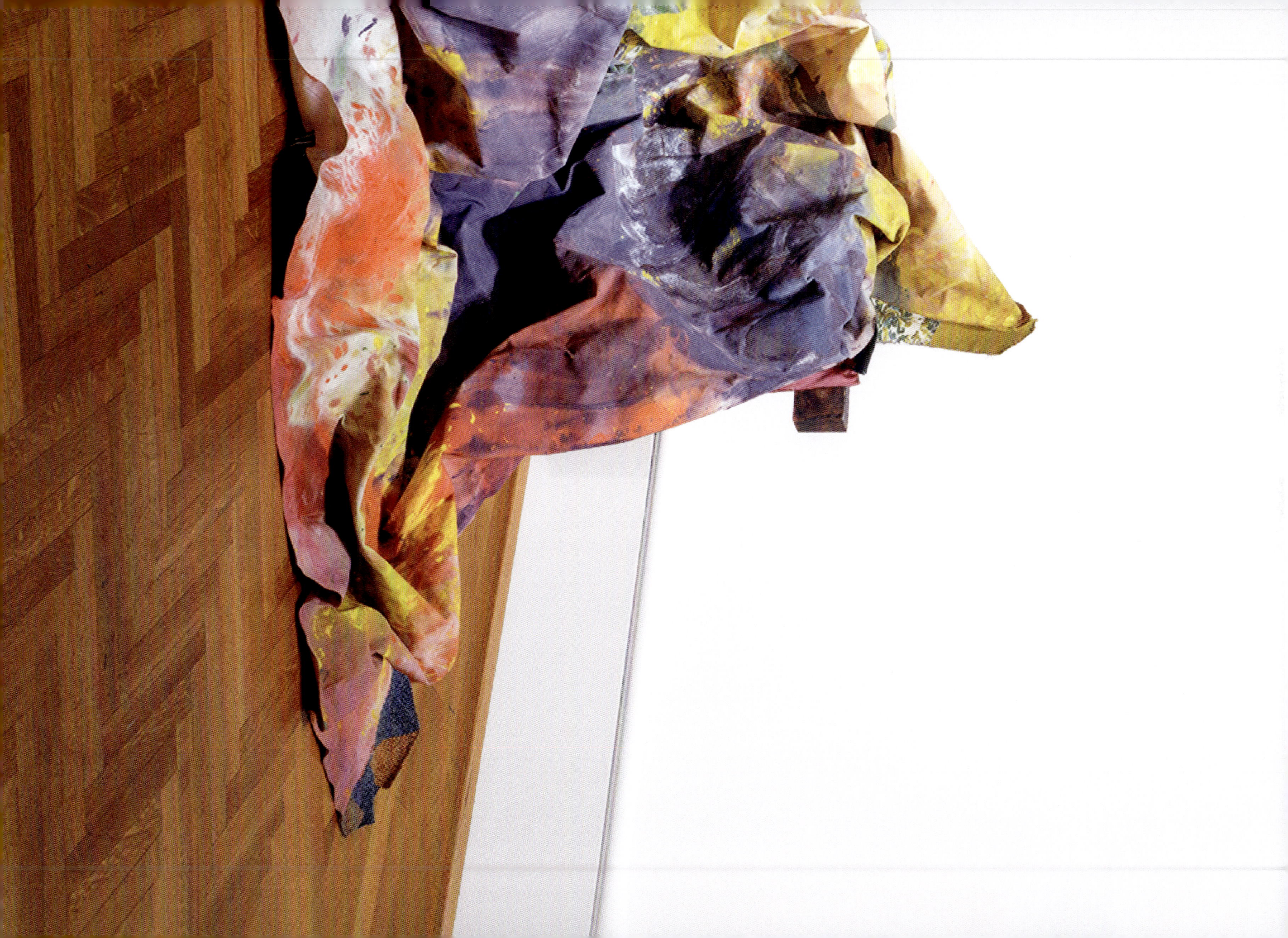

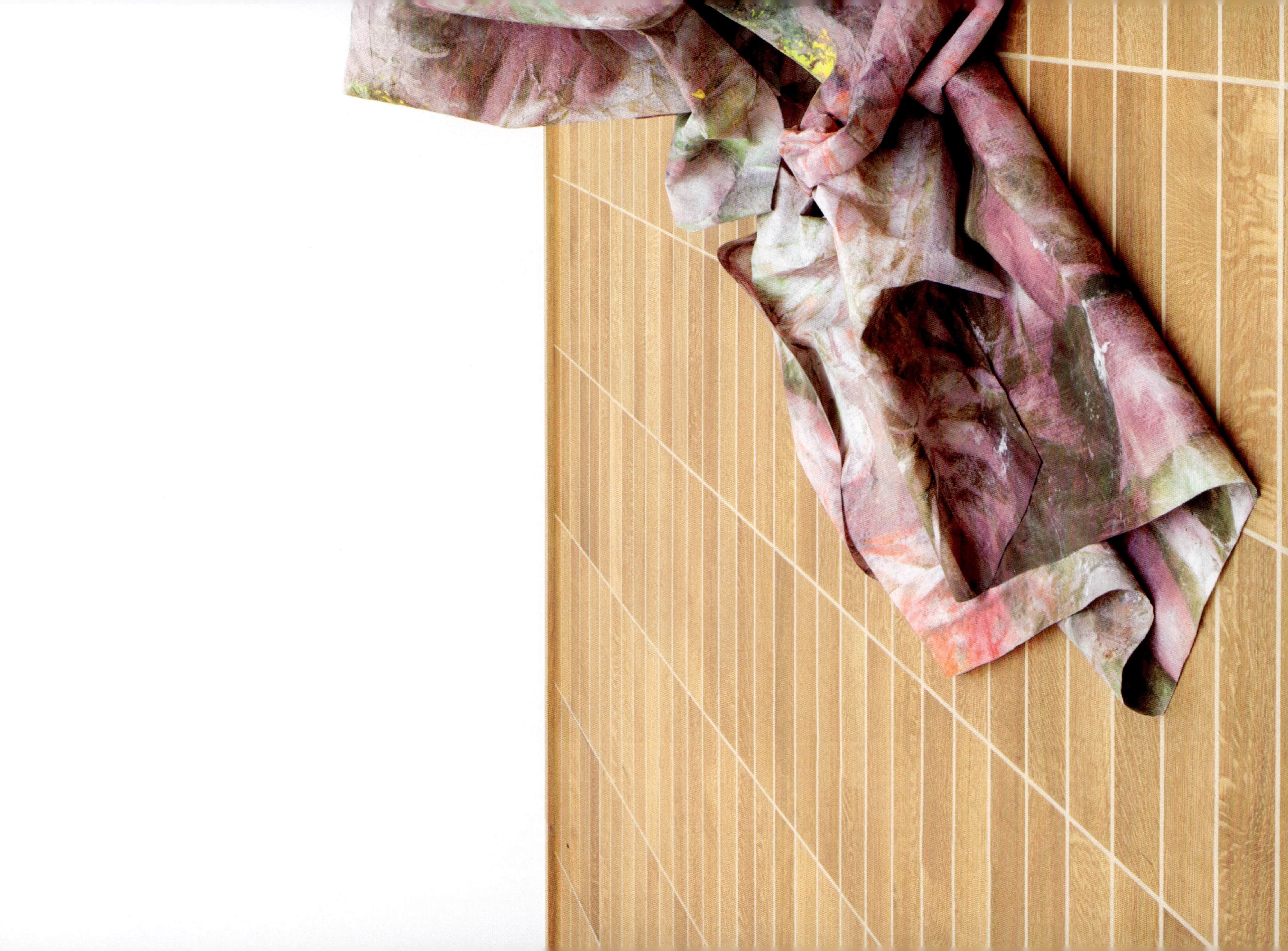

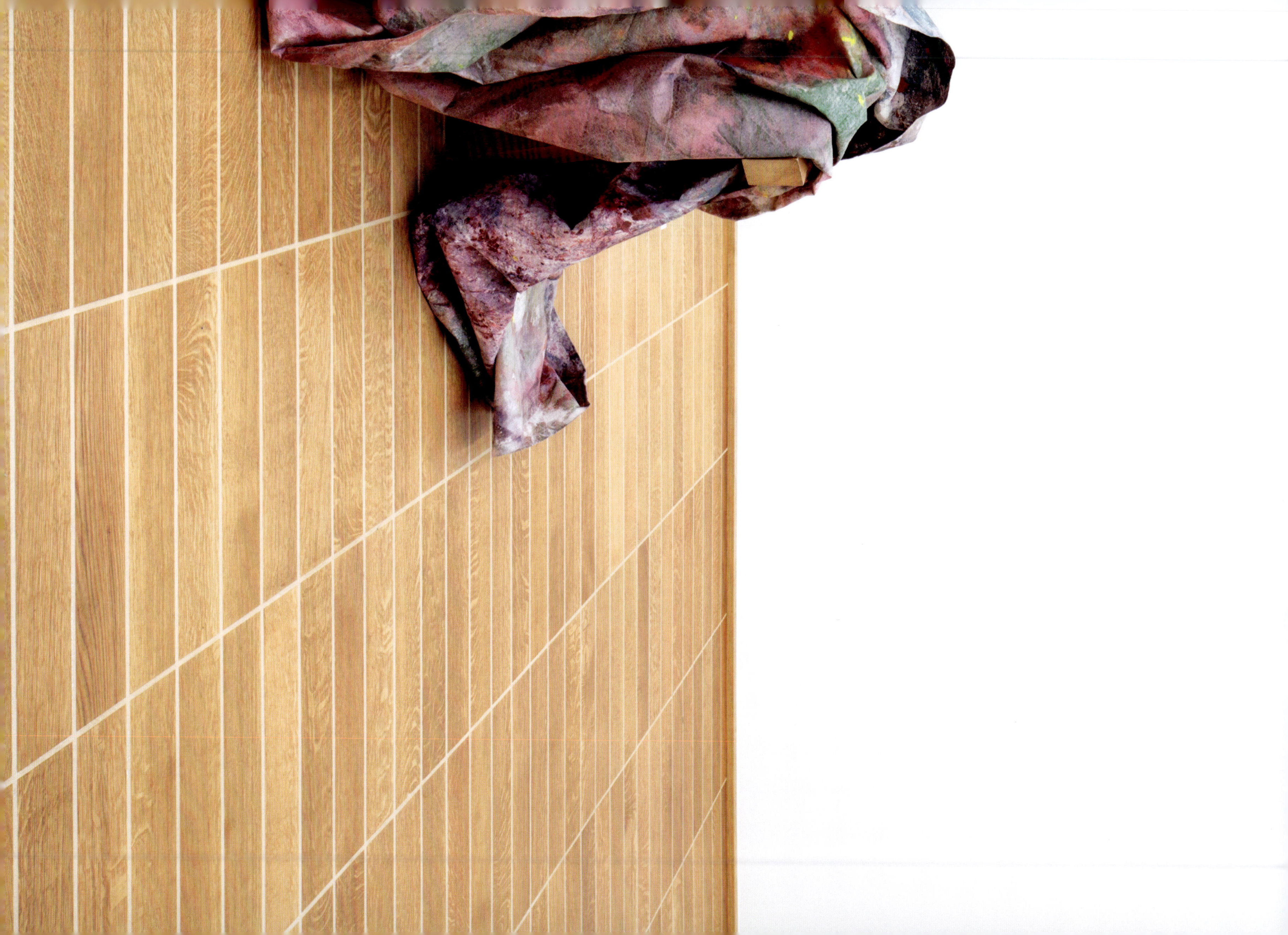

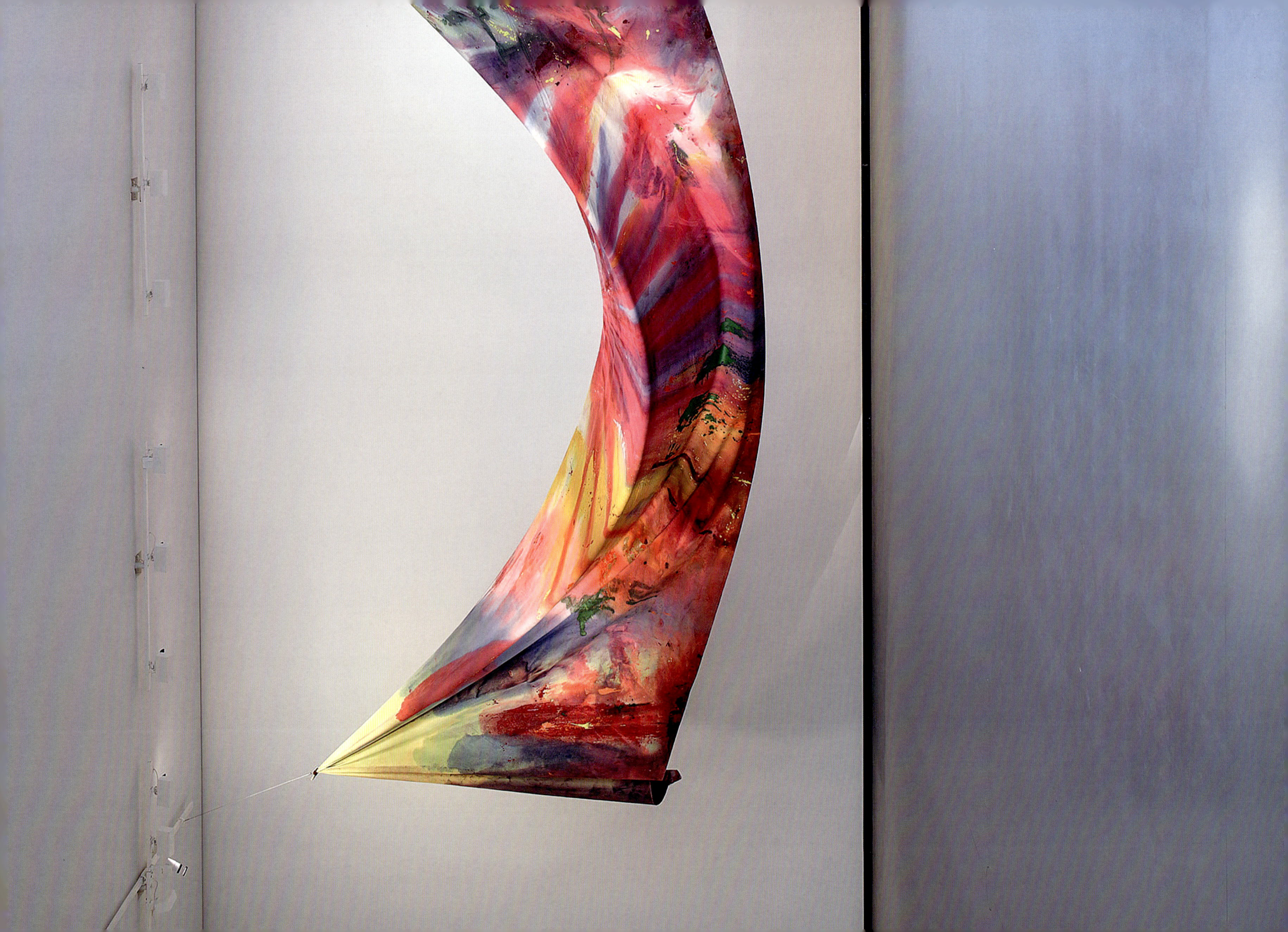

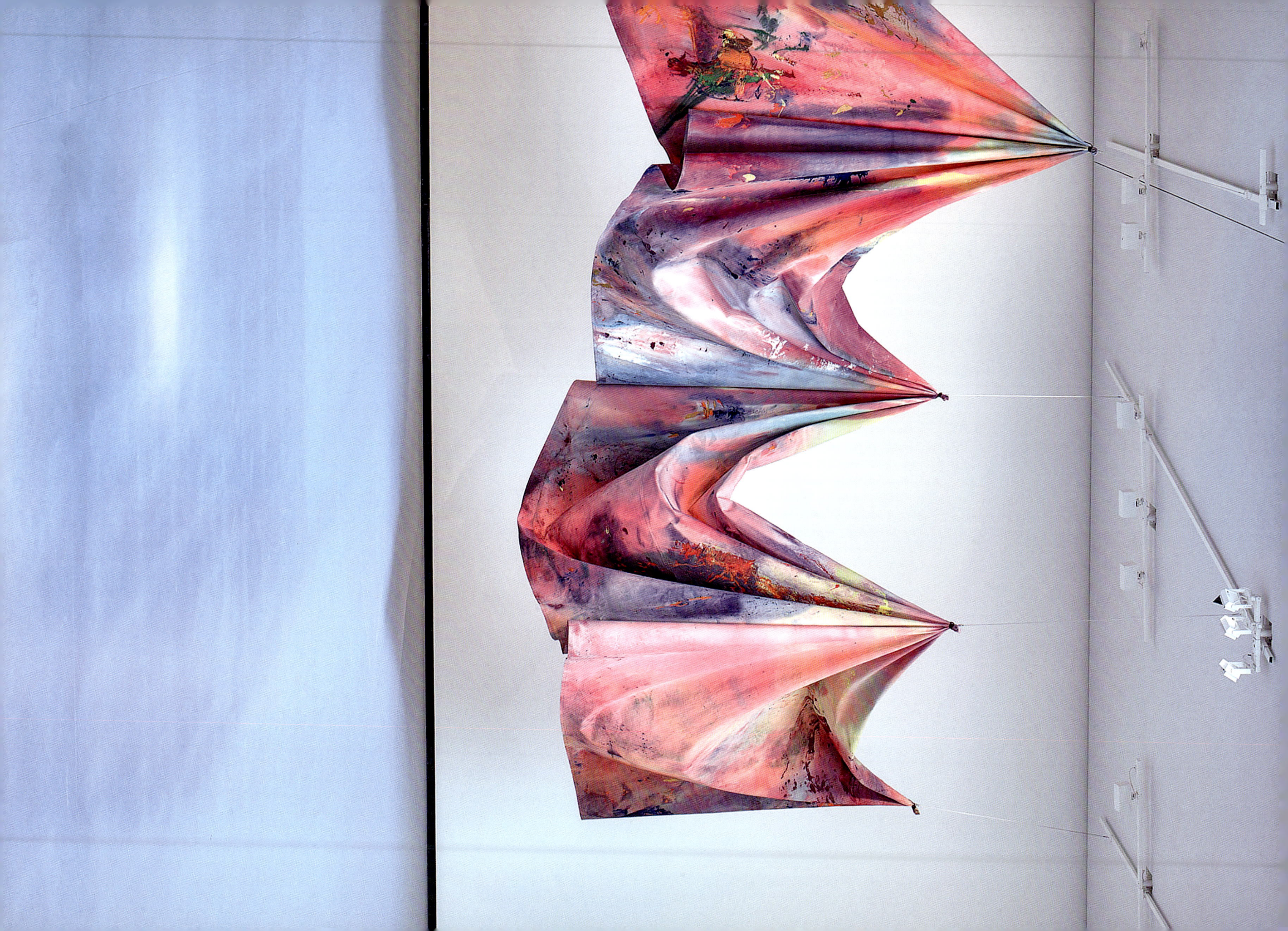

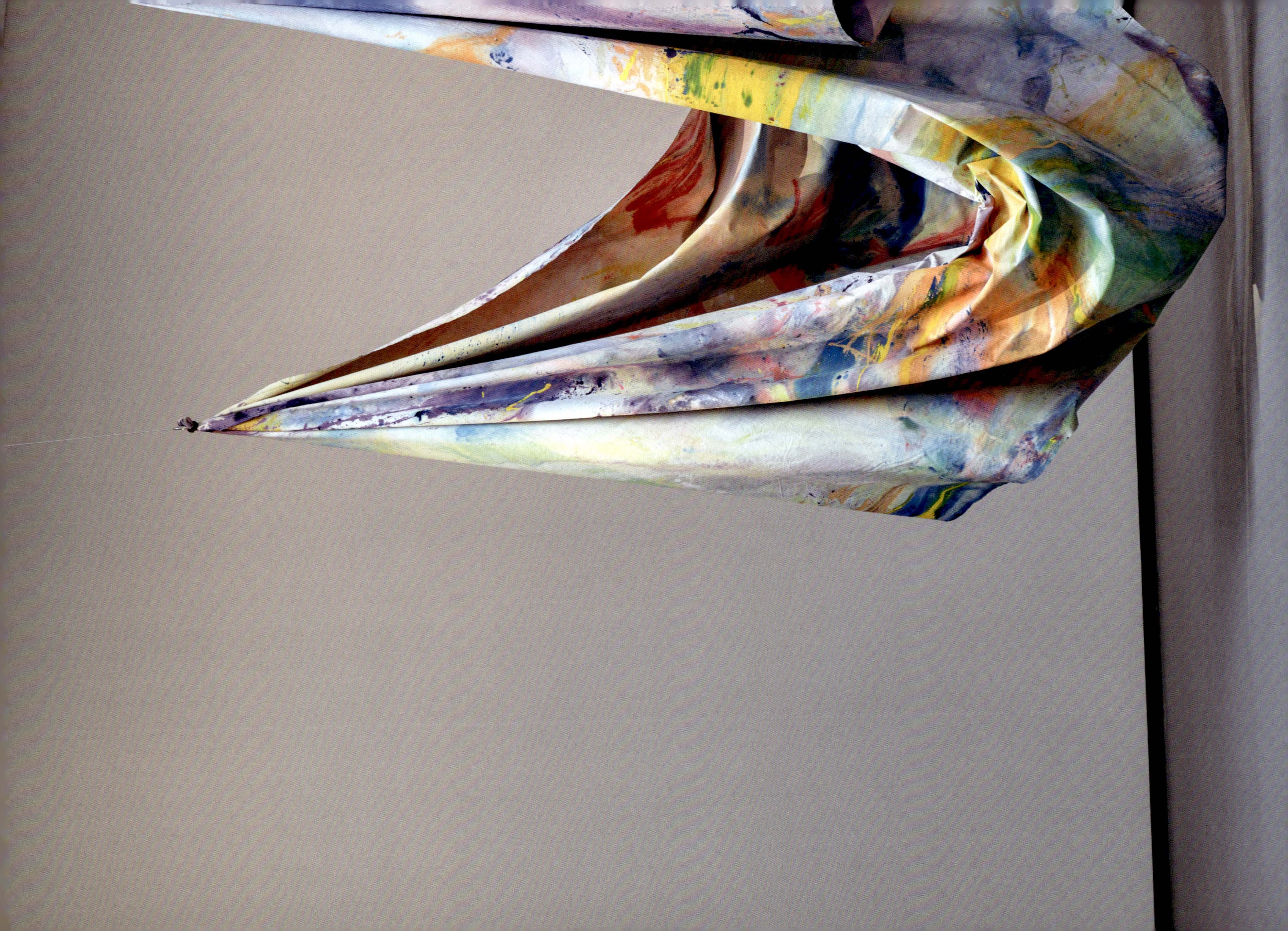

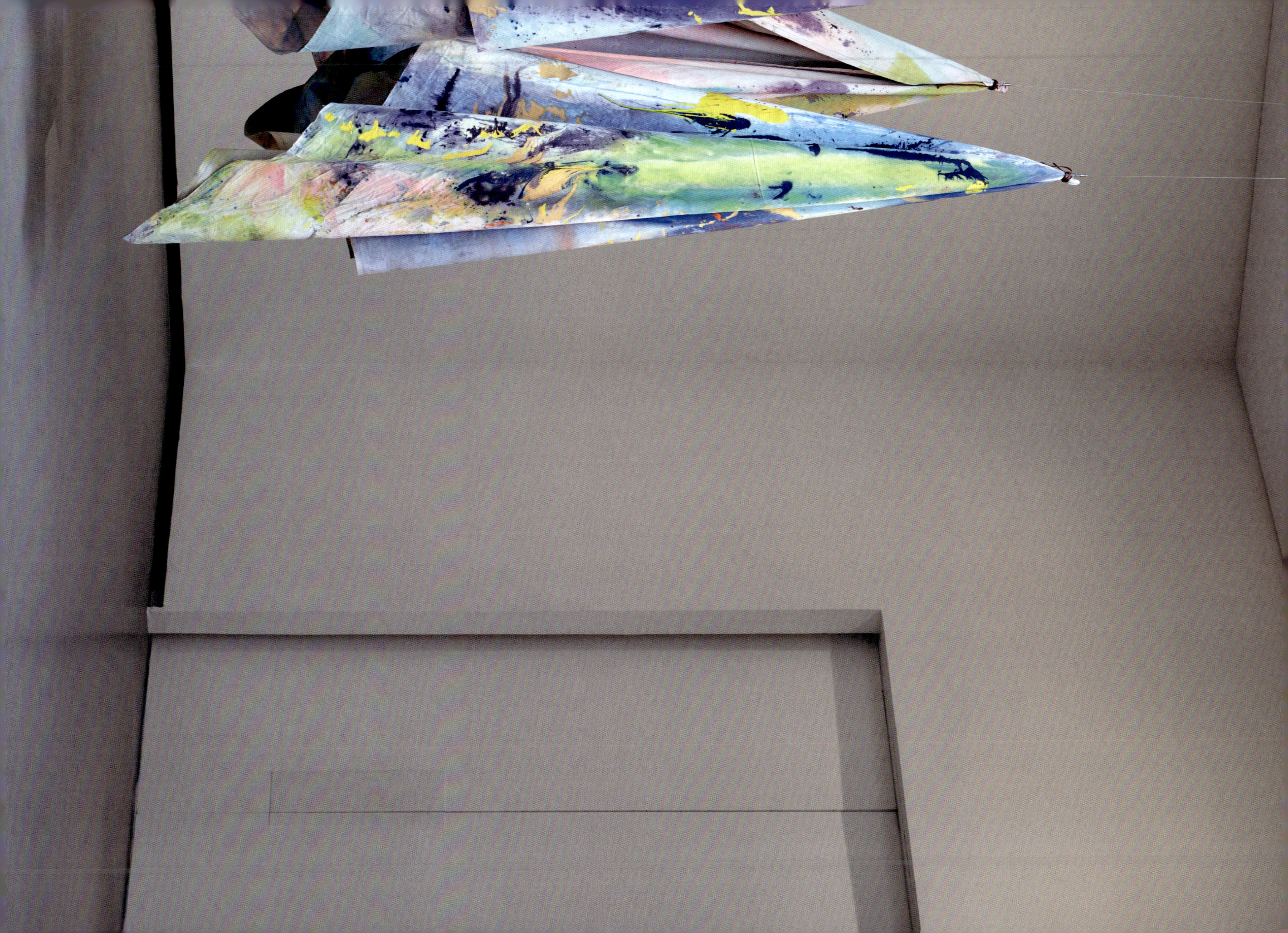

Right: *Rondo*, 1971

Pages 128–129: *Carousel Merge*, 1971

Pages 130–131: *Carousel*, 1970

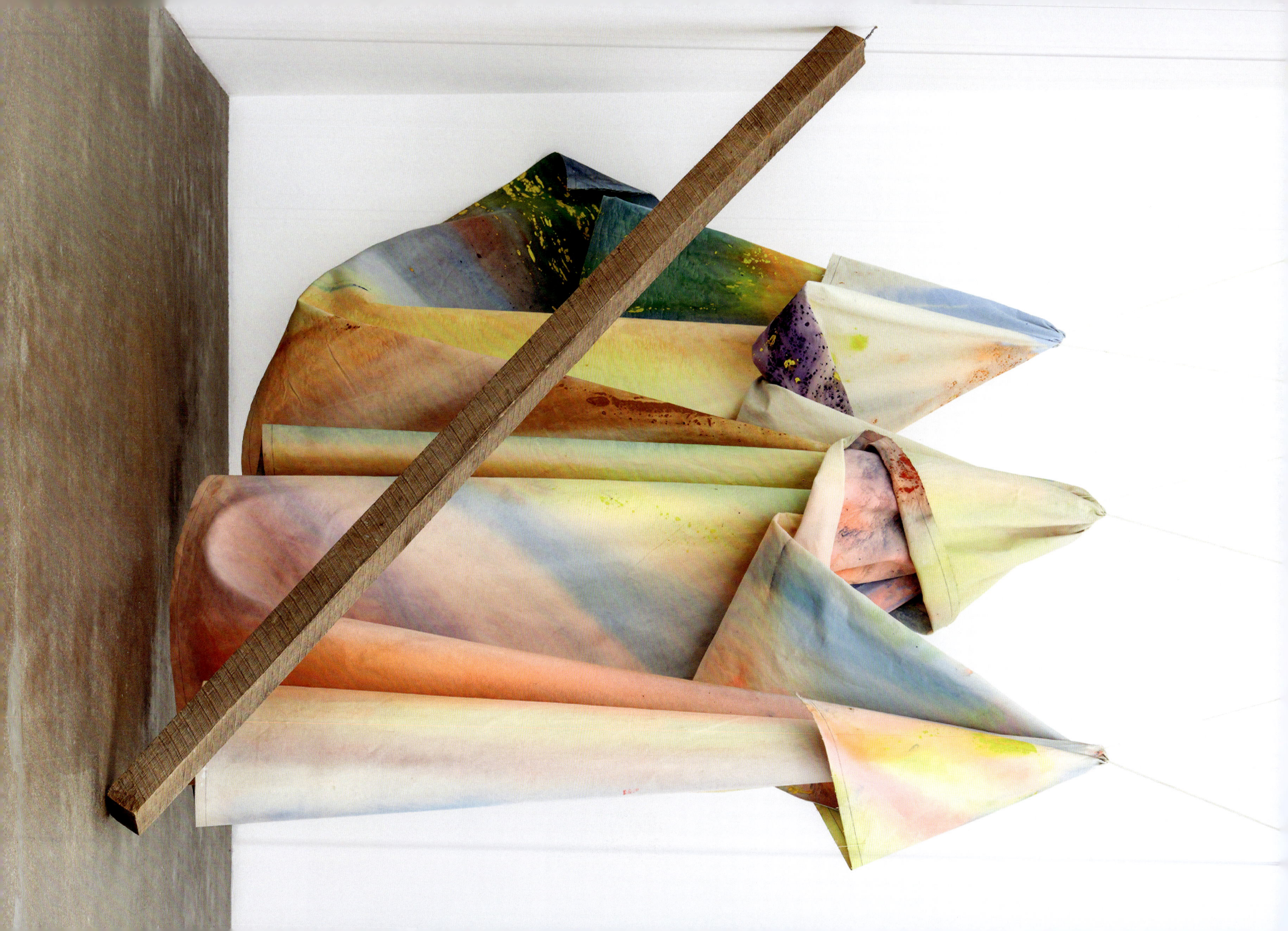

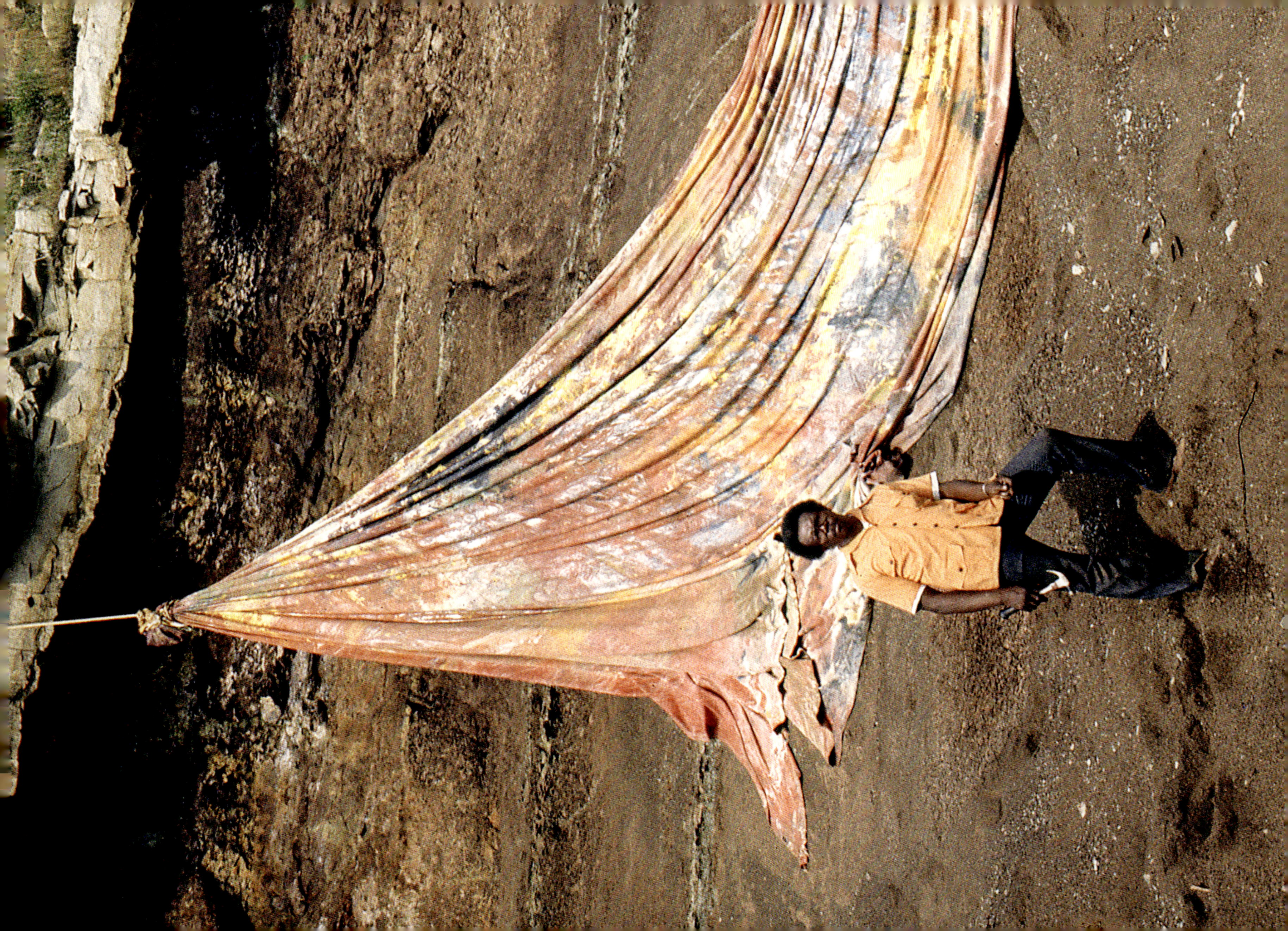

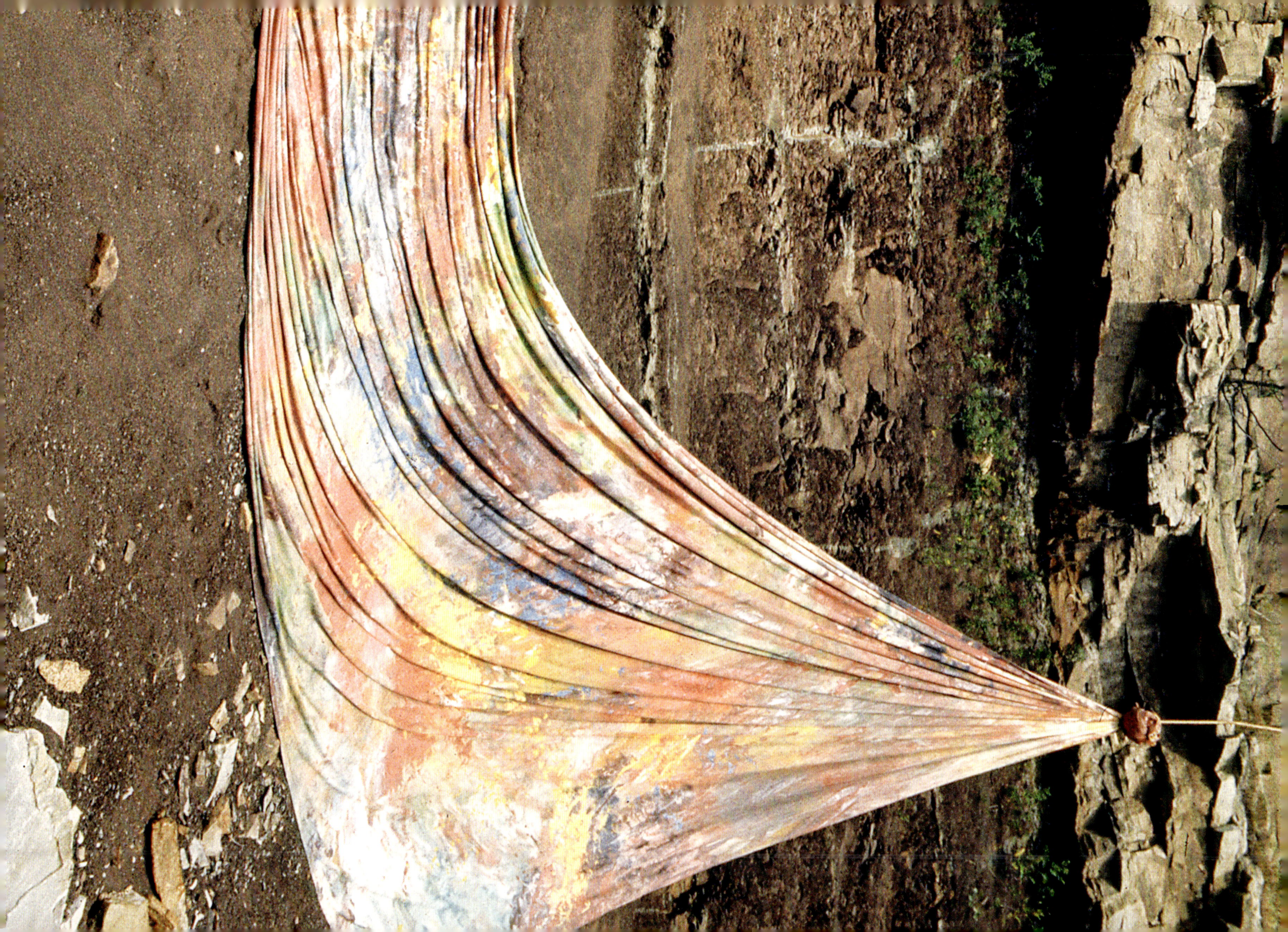

Previous pages: Gilliam with his installation *Custom Road Slide* at Artpark, Lewiston, New York, 1977

Of Fireflies and Ferris Wheels: Monastery Parallel, 1997

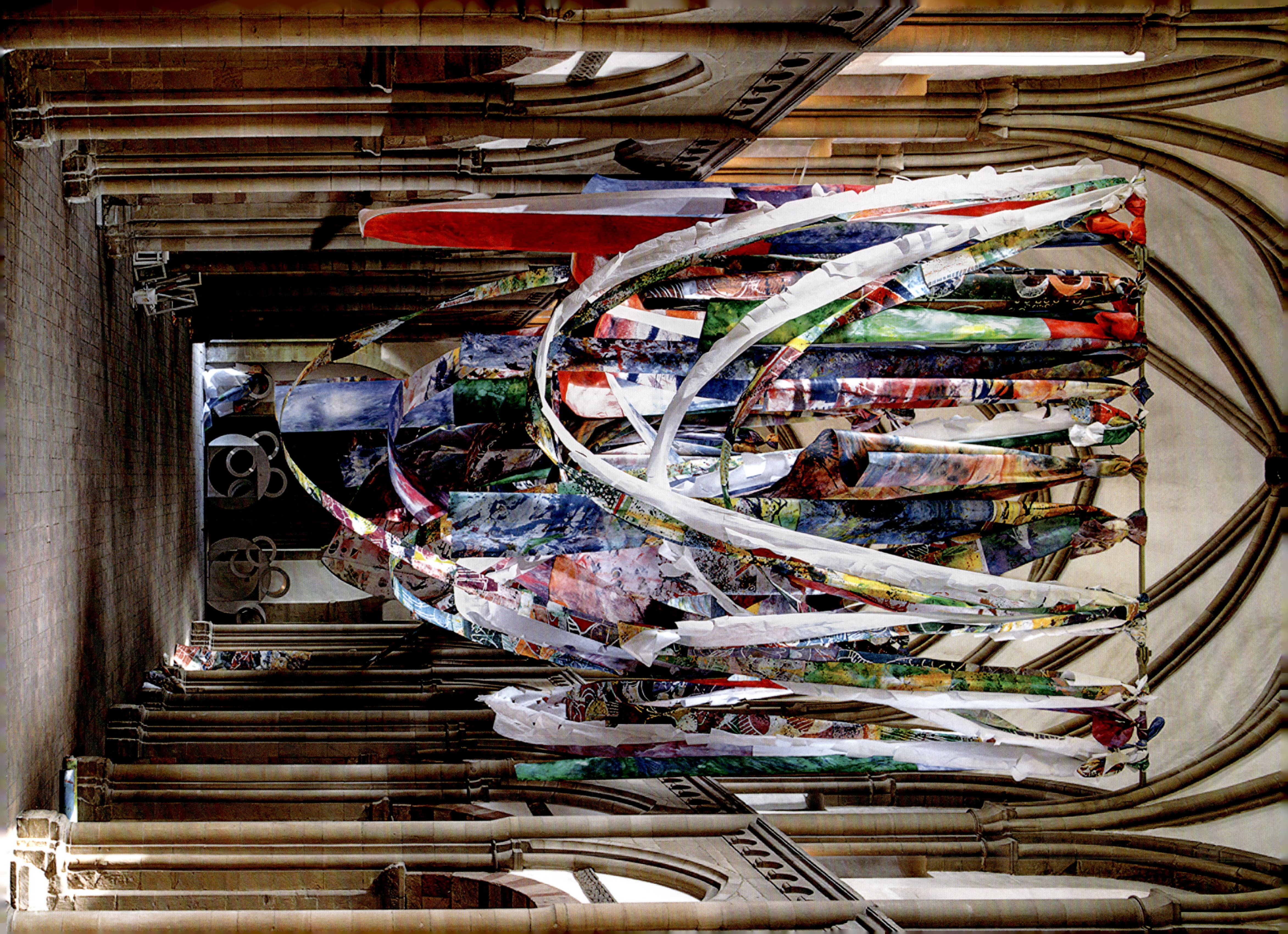

—THE WORK
YOU HAVE
DONE IS MUCH
LIKE A

**KNAPSACK
OF YOUR
ANTICIPATED
BELONGINGS.**

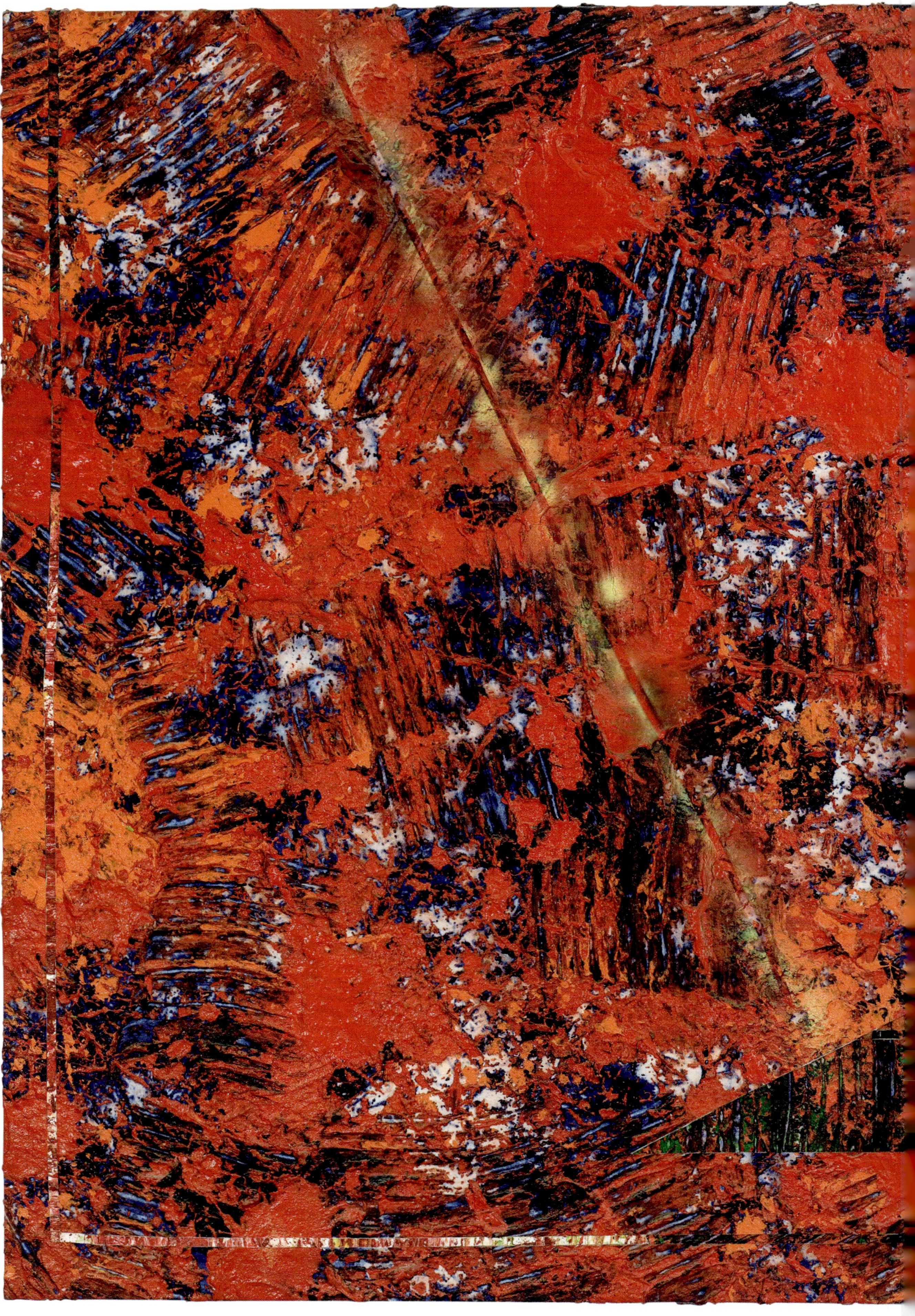

Cartouche, 1981

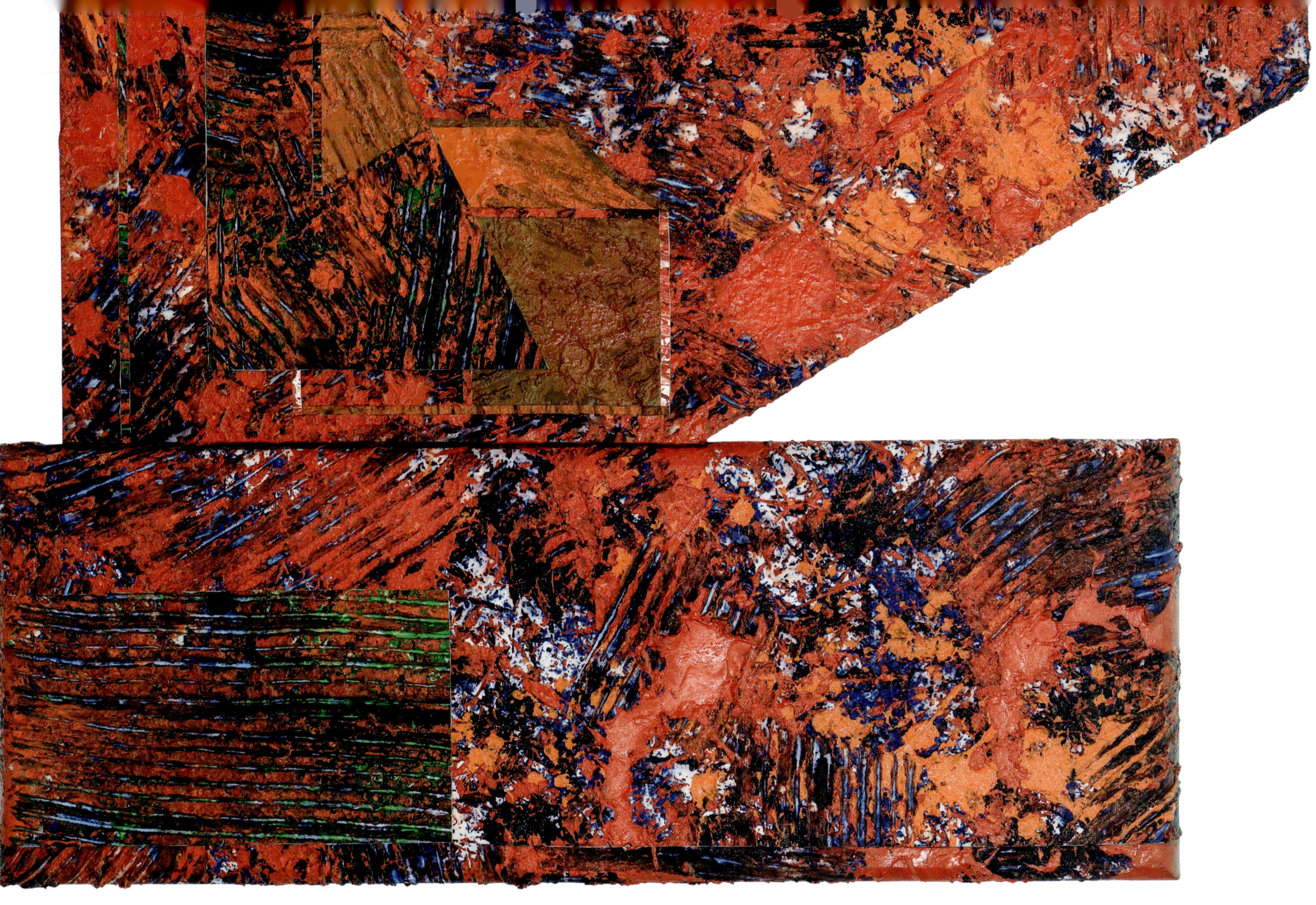

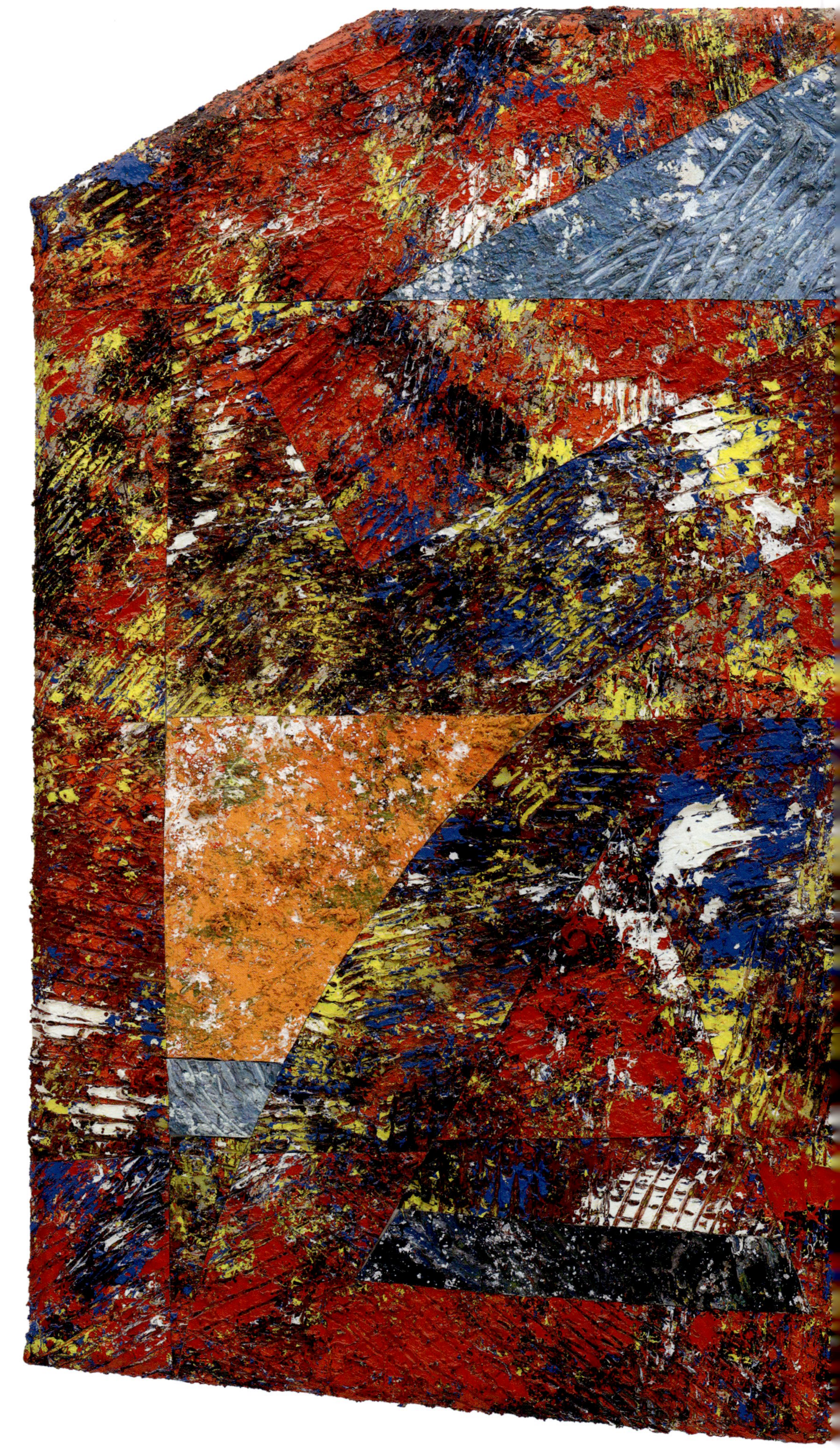

Robbin' Peter, 1980

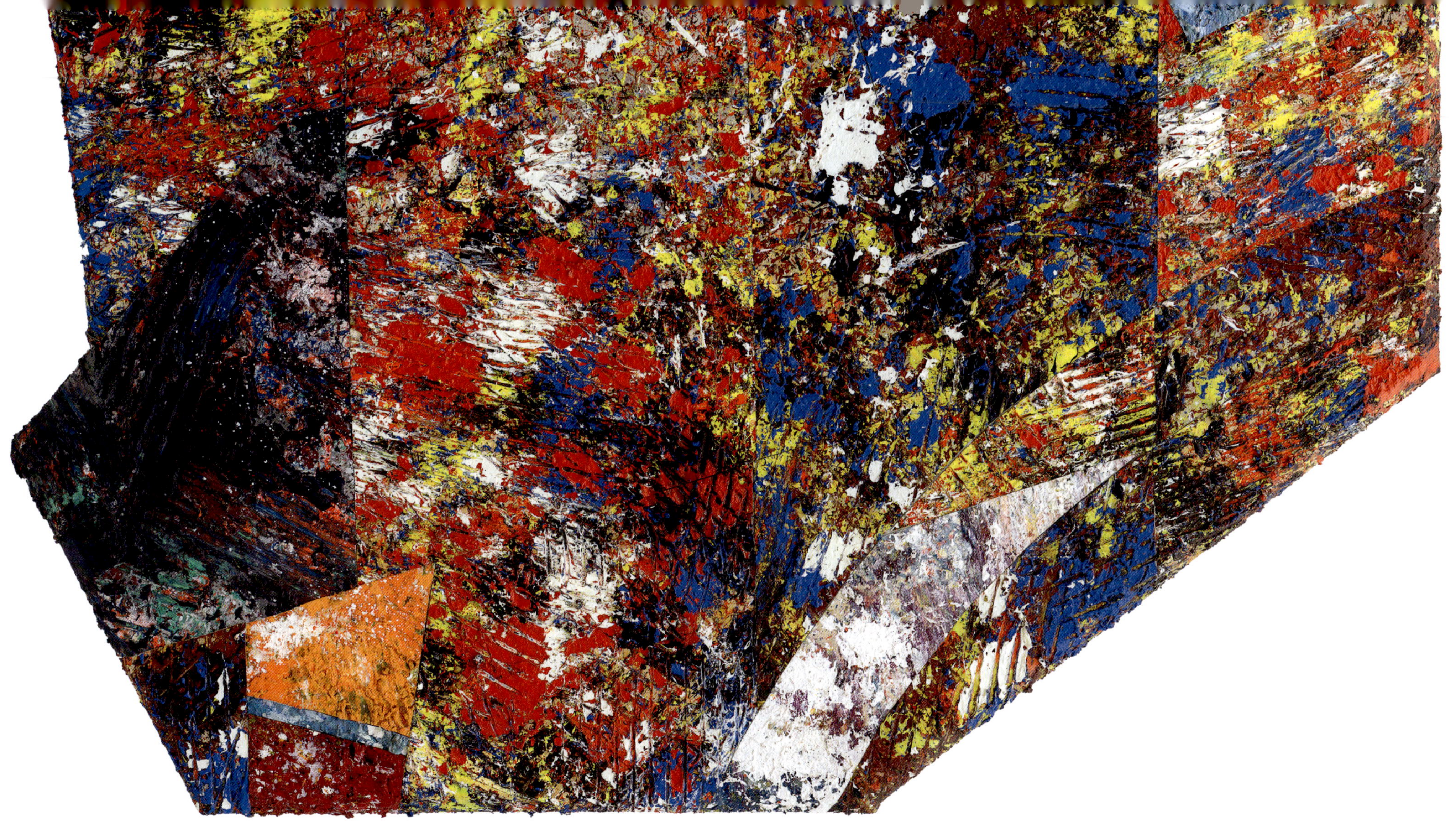

The Arc Maker I & II, 1981

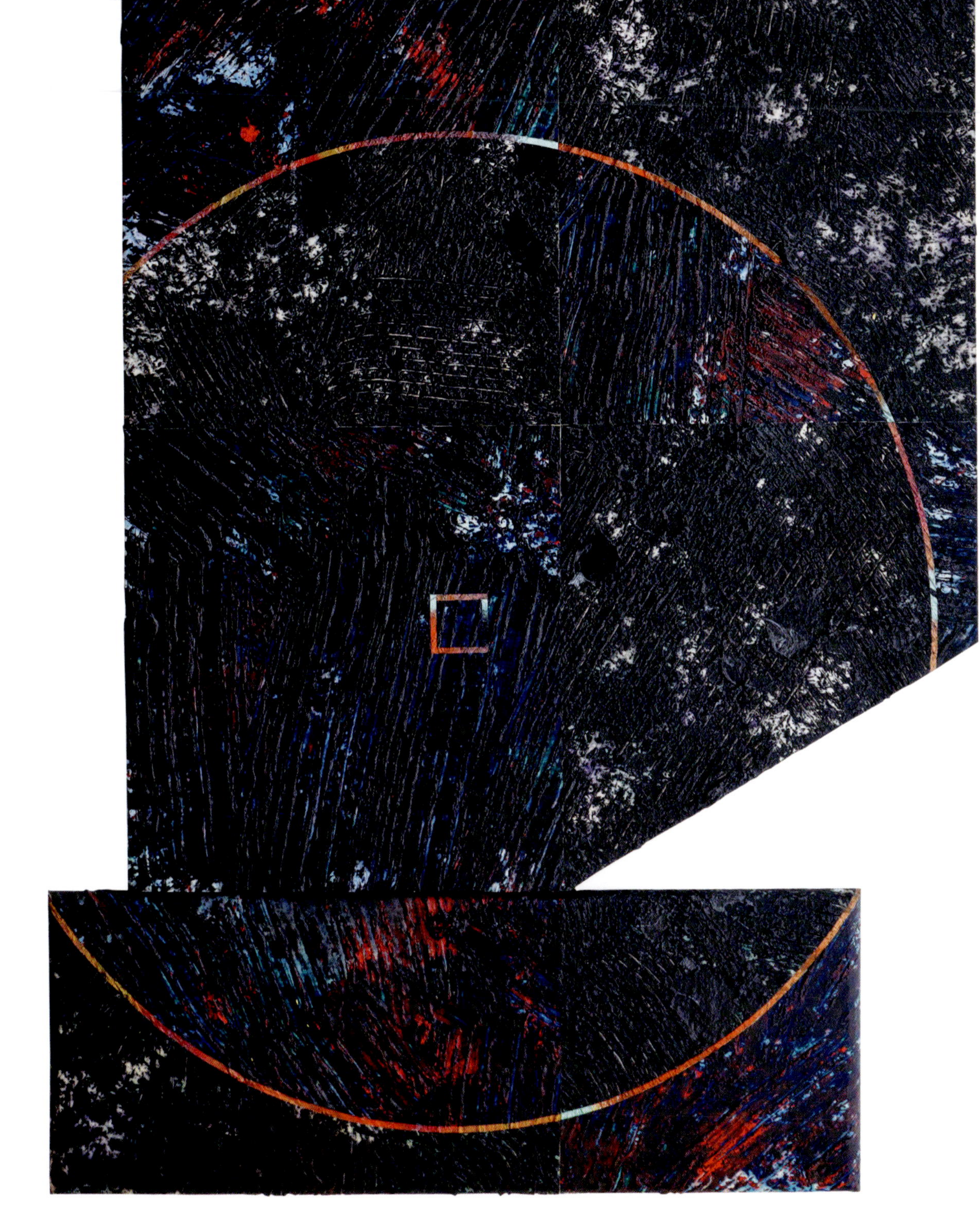

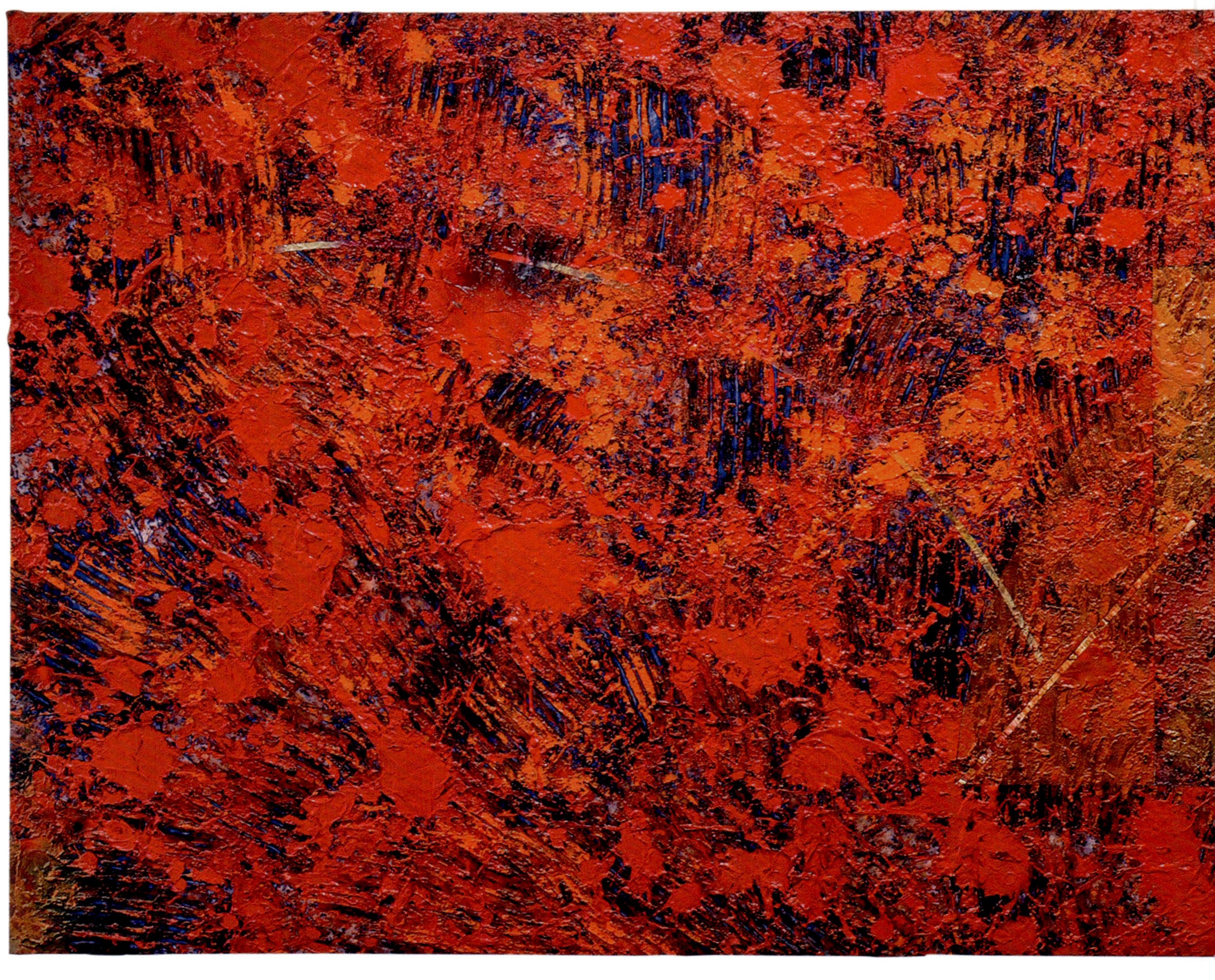

Lion's Rock Arc, 1981

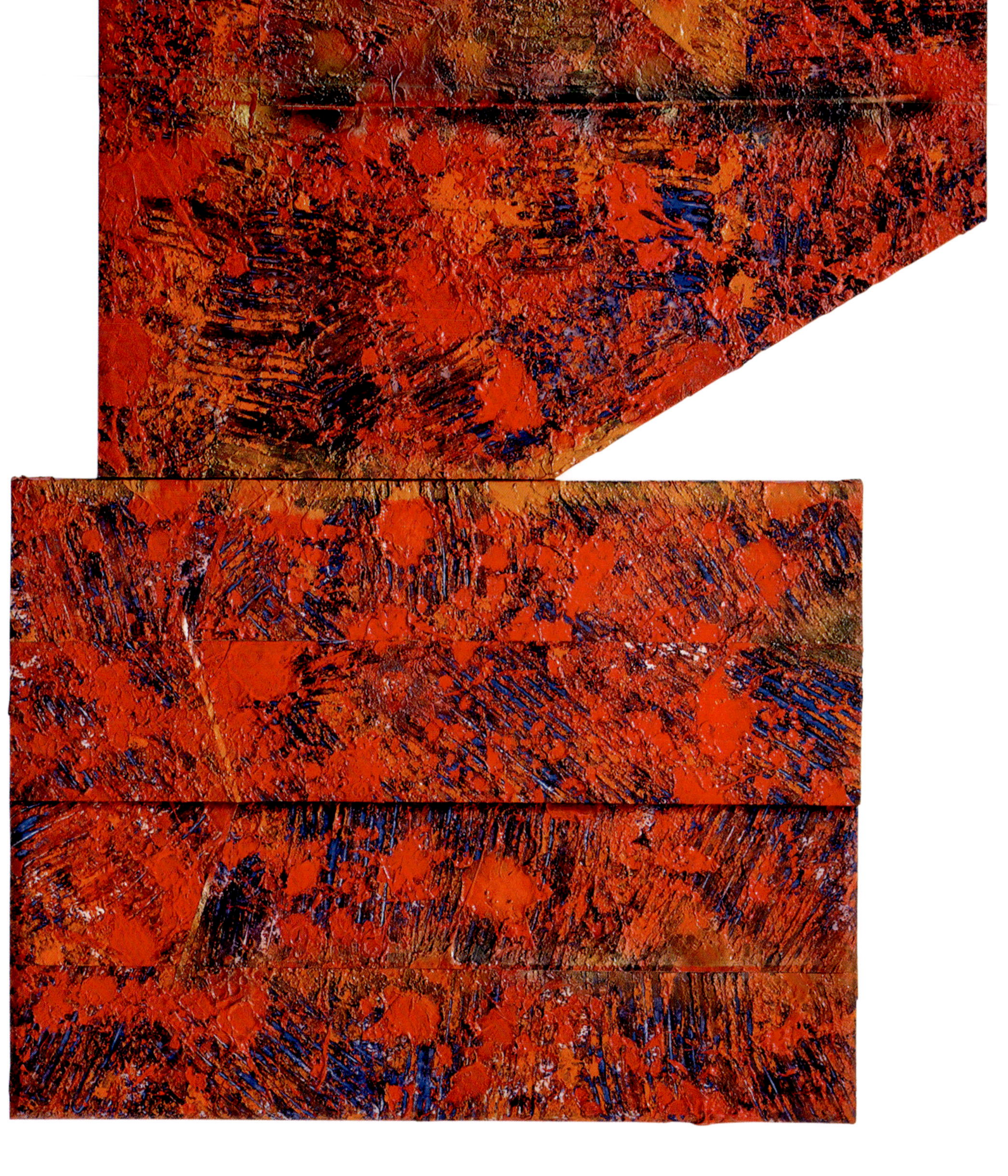

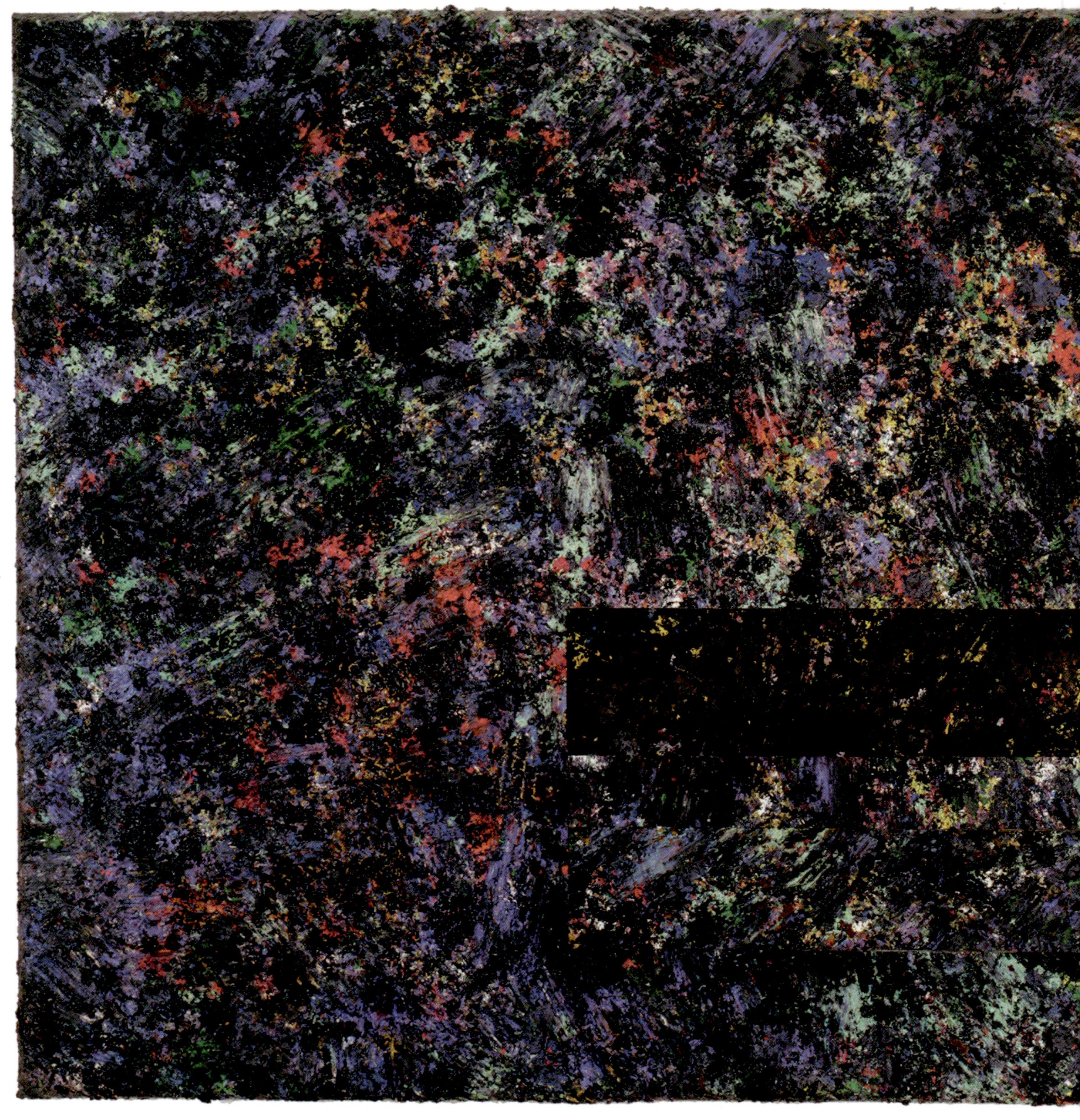

Rail, 1977

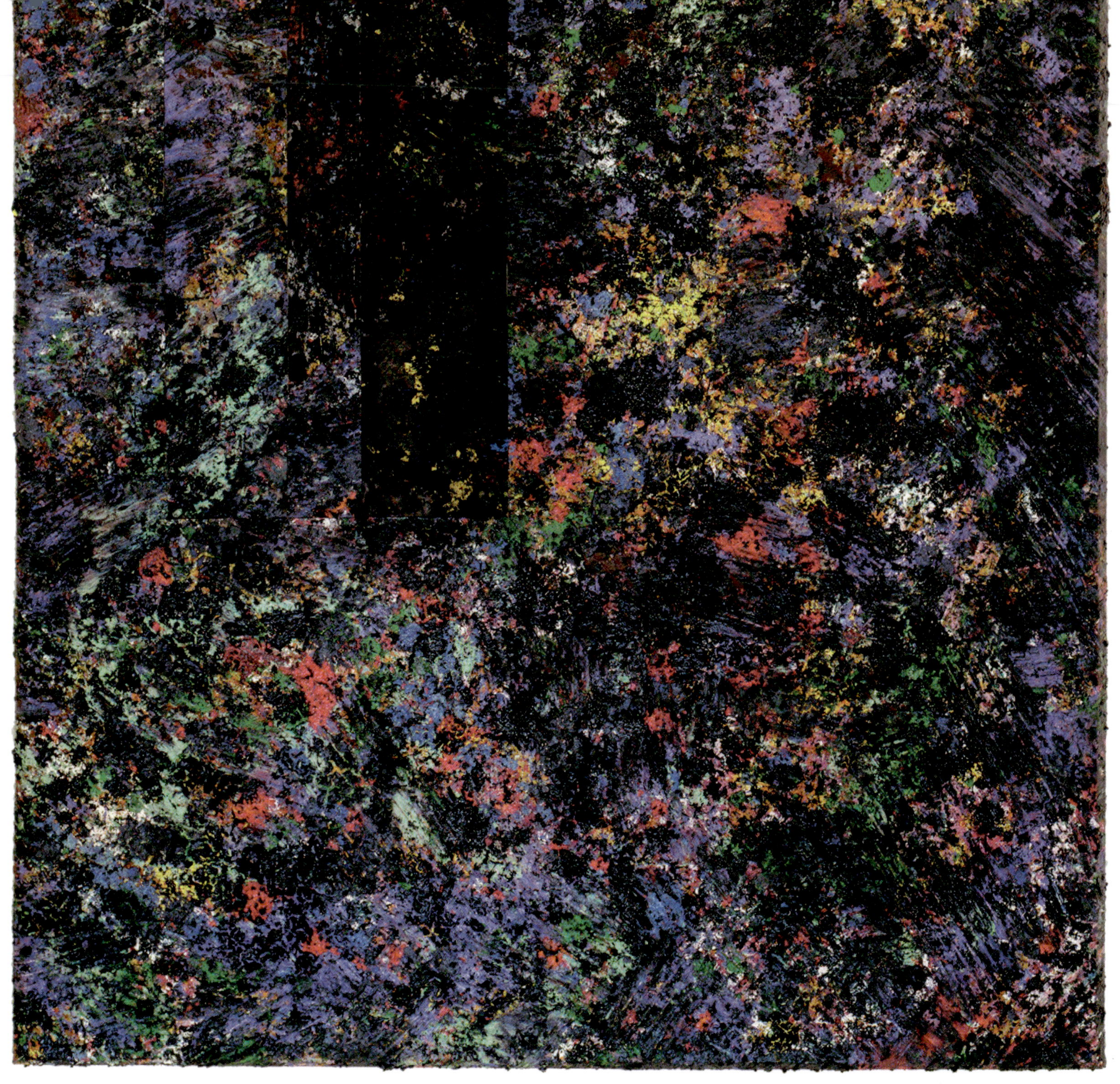

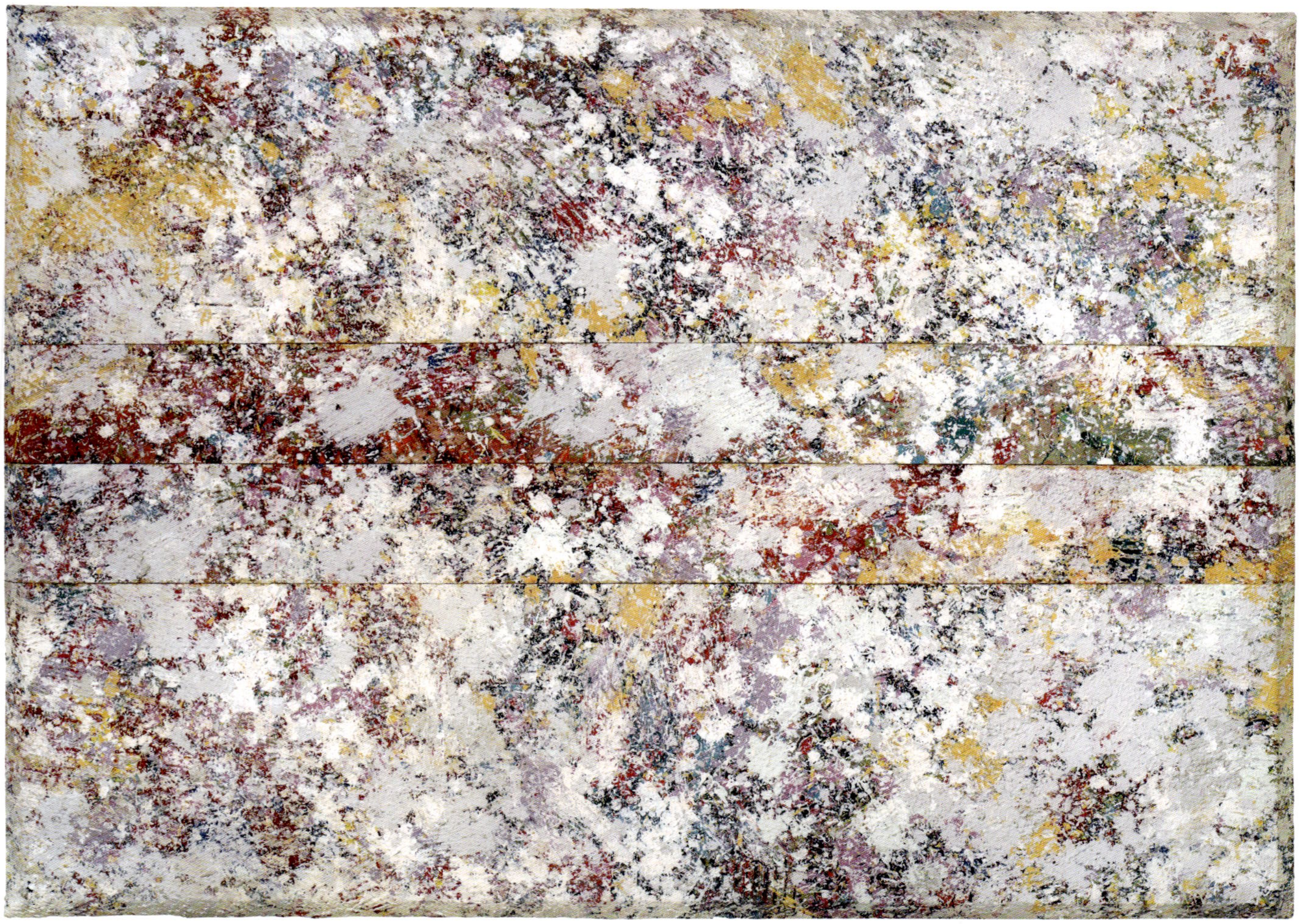

For Brass, 1976

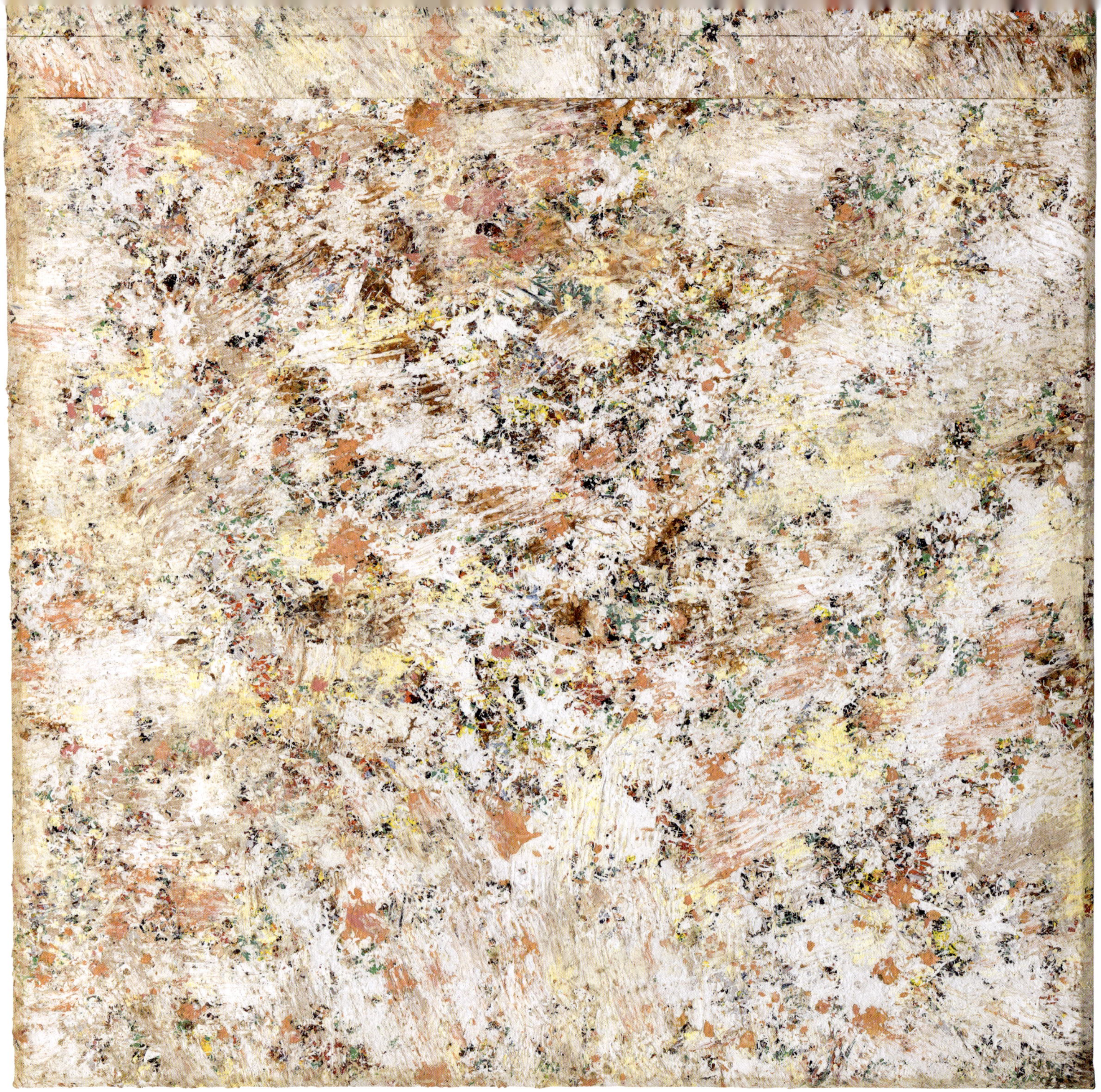

Double River, 1976

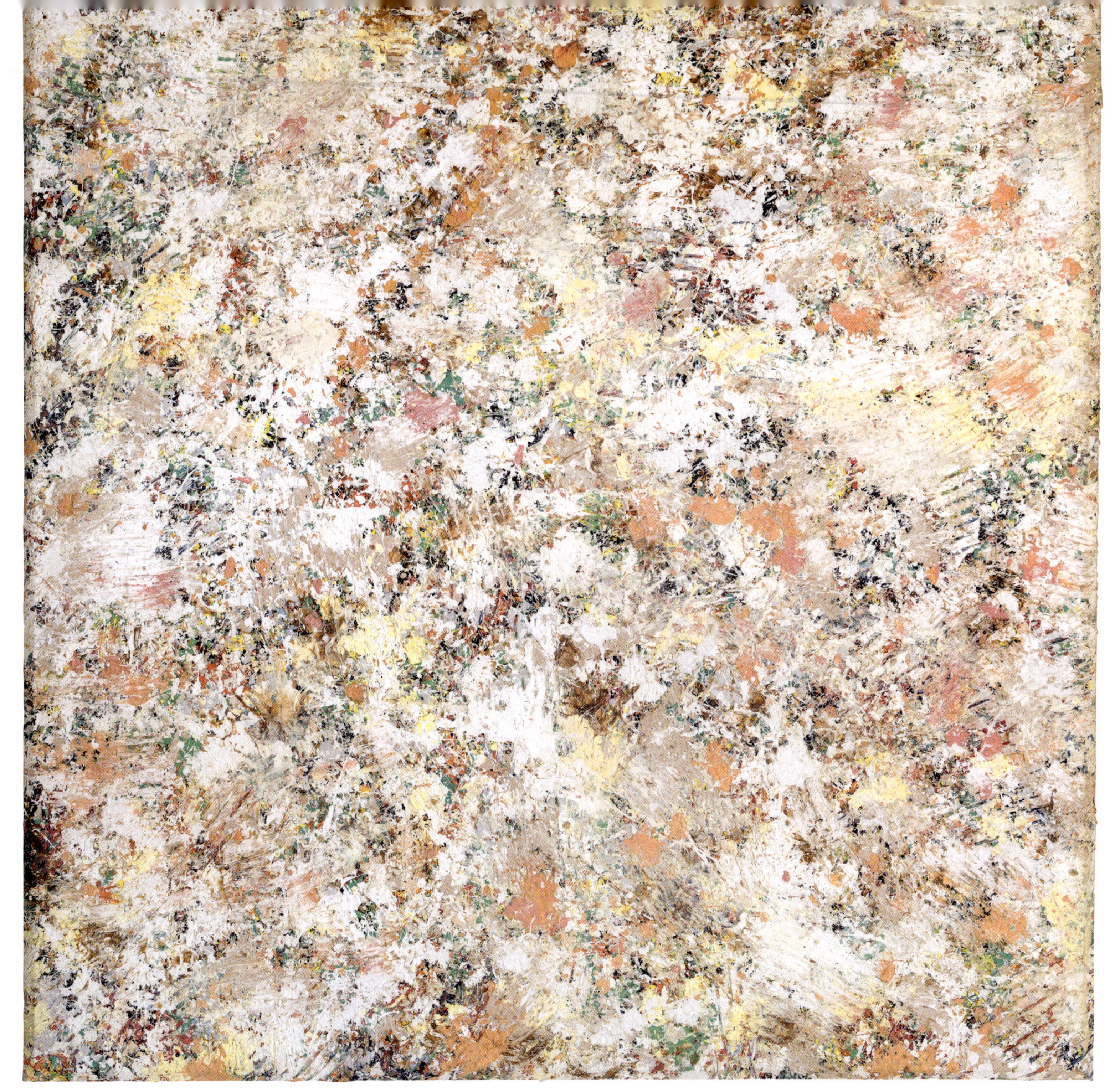

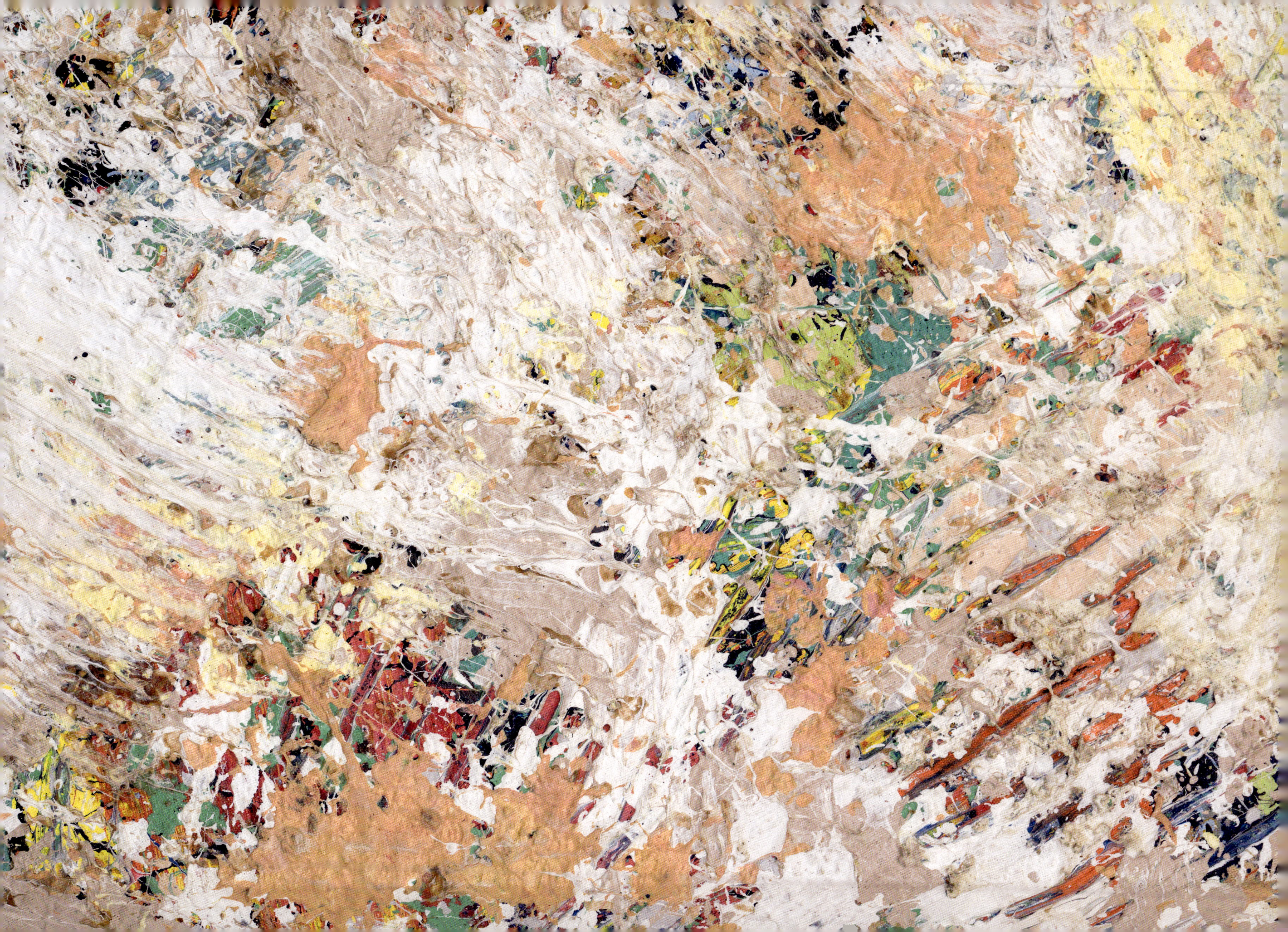

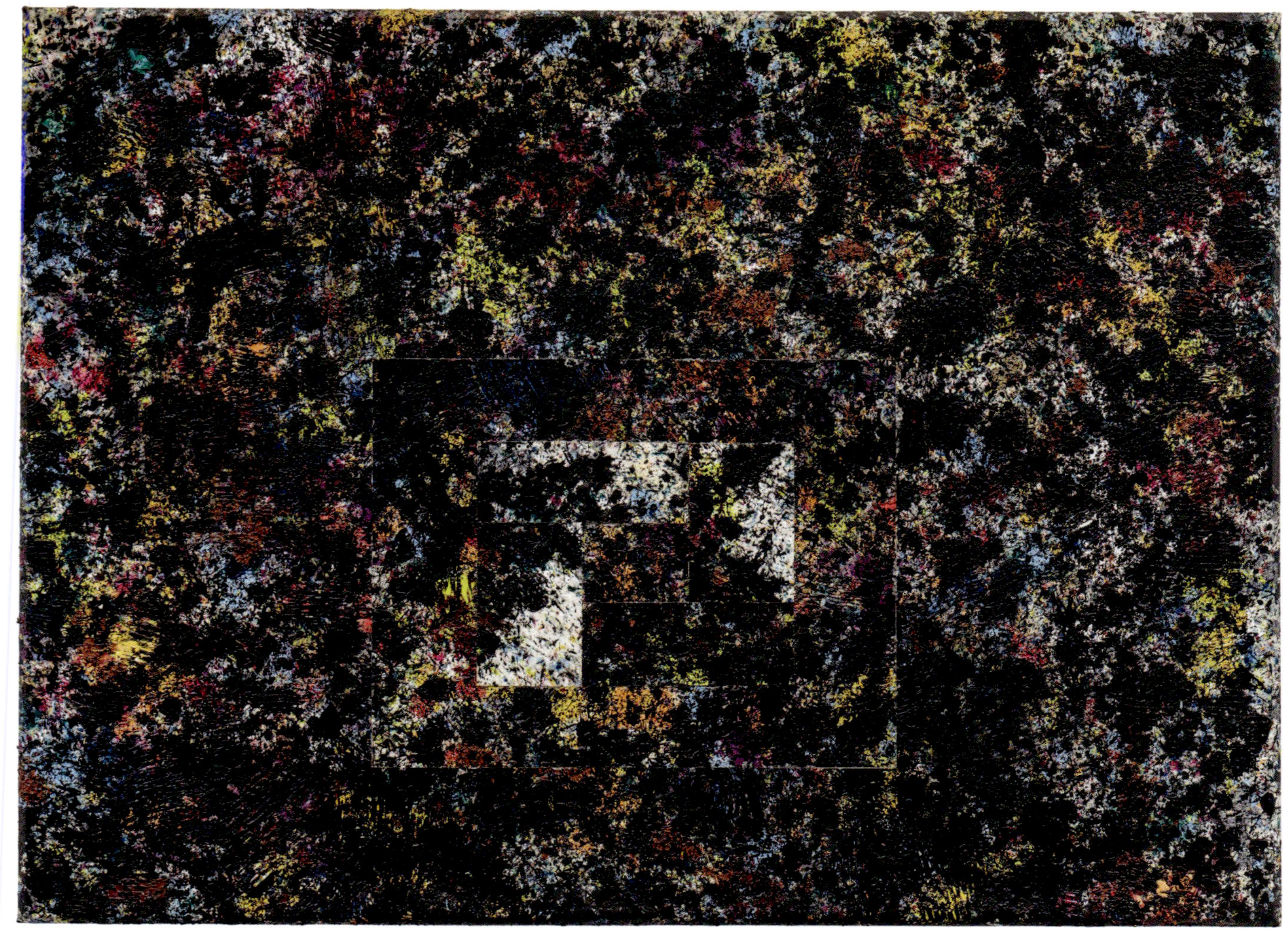

Abacus Sliding, 1977

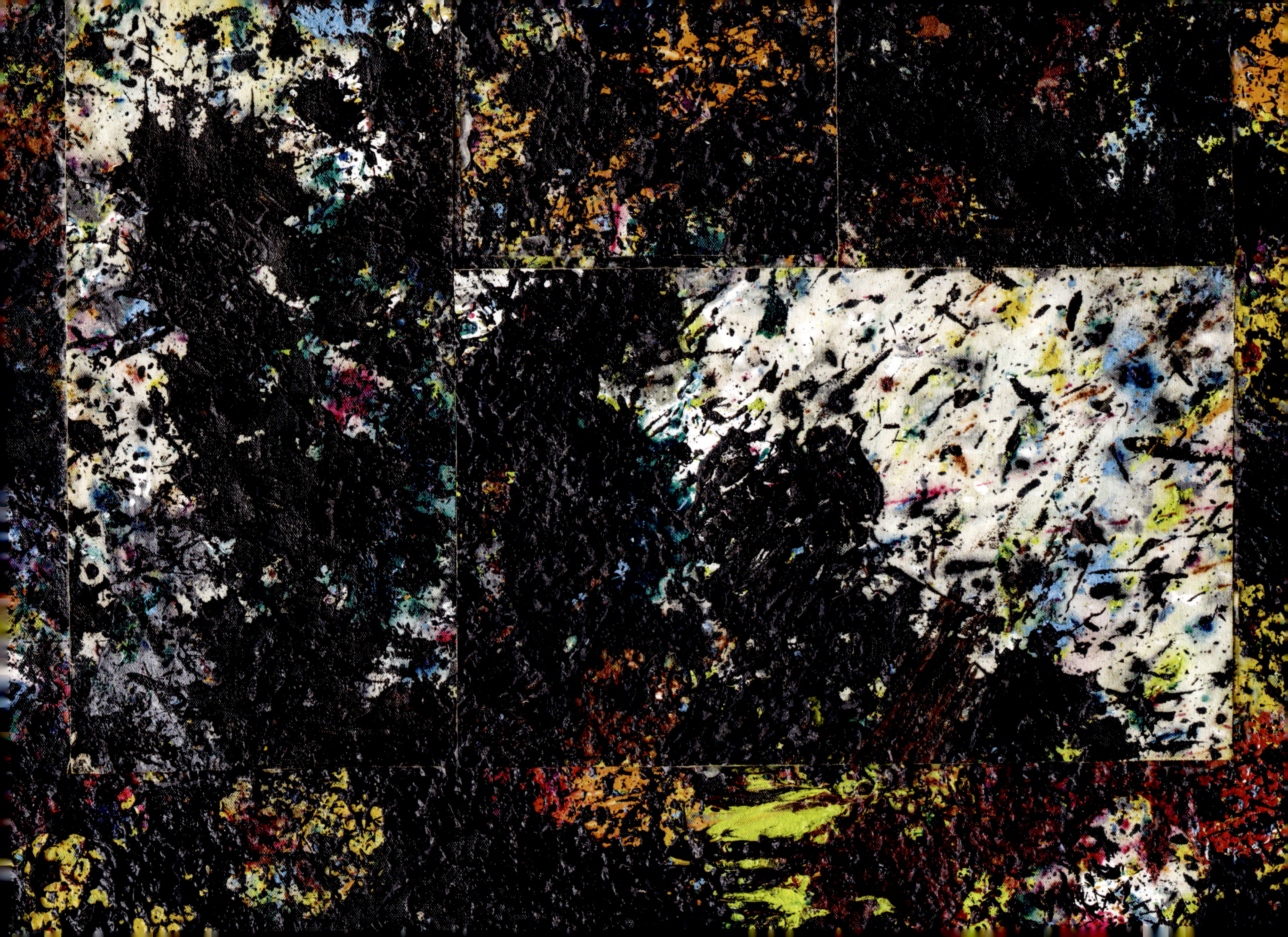

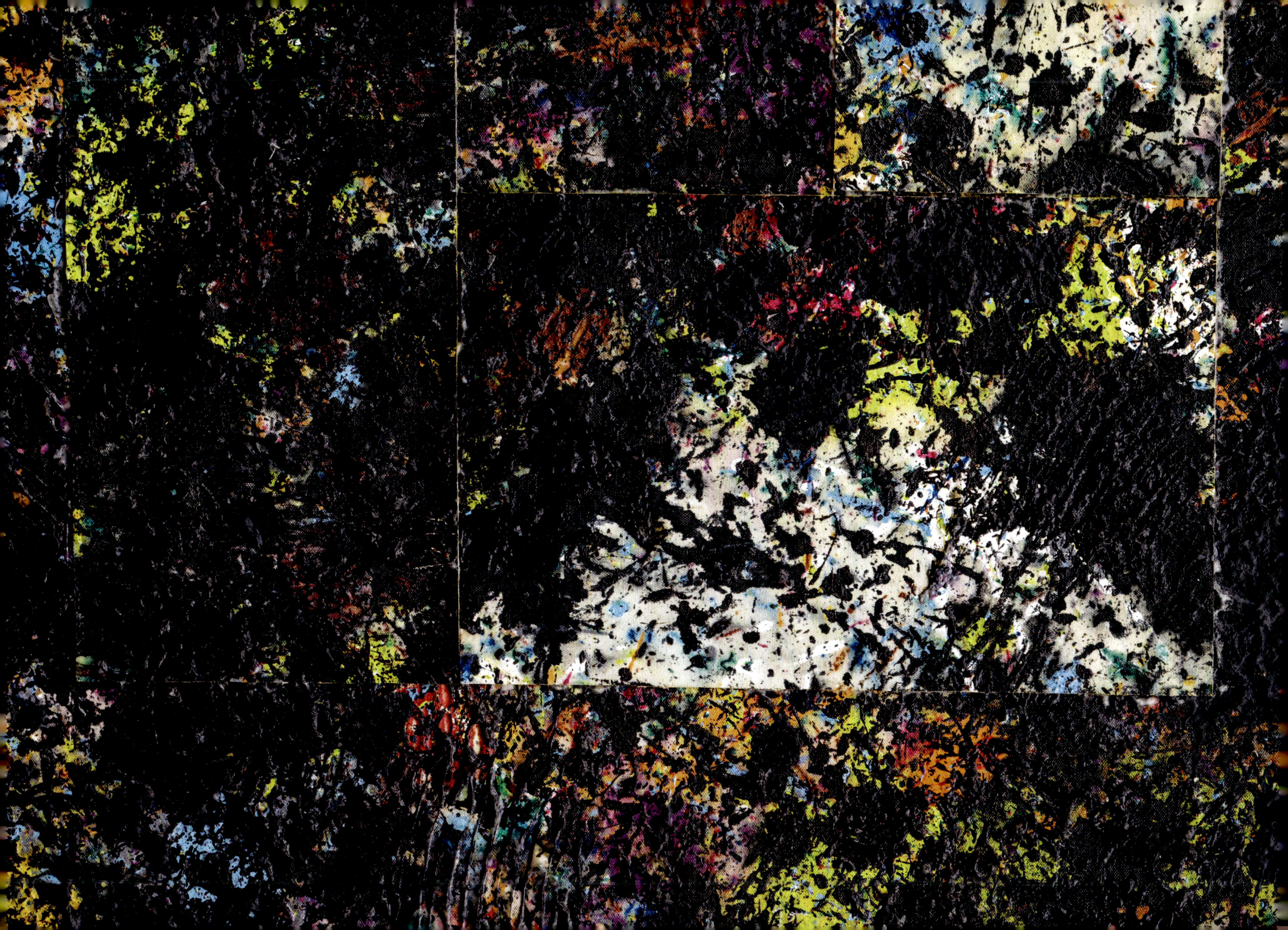

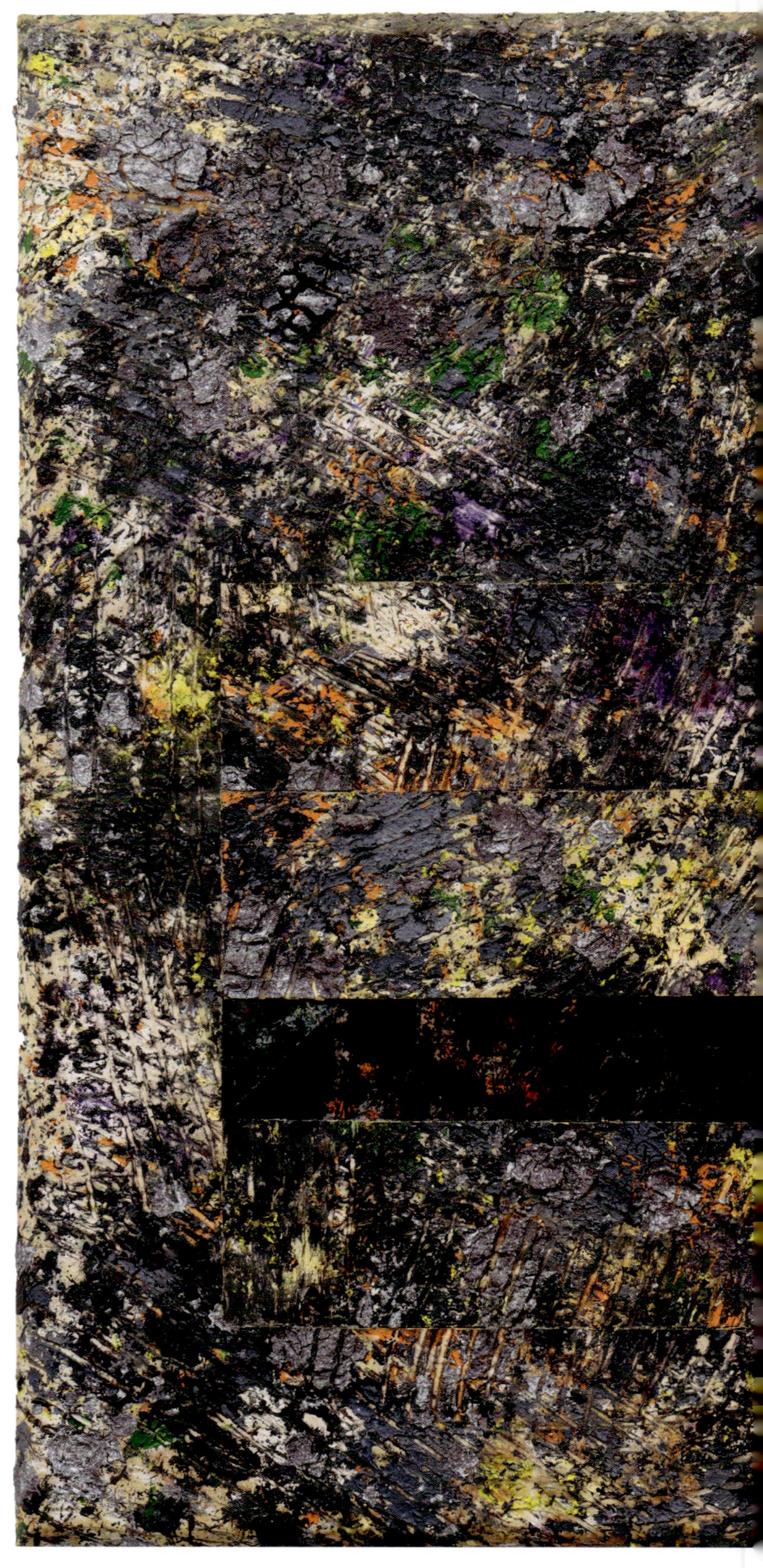

Earth Element, 1977

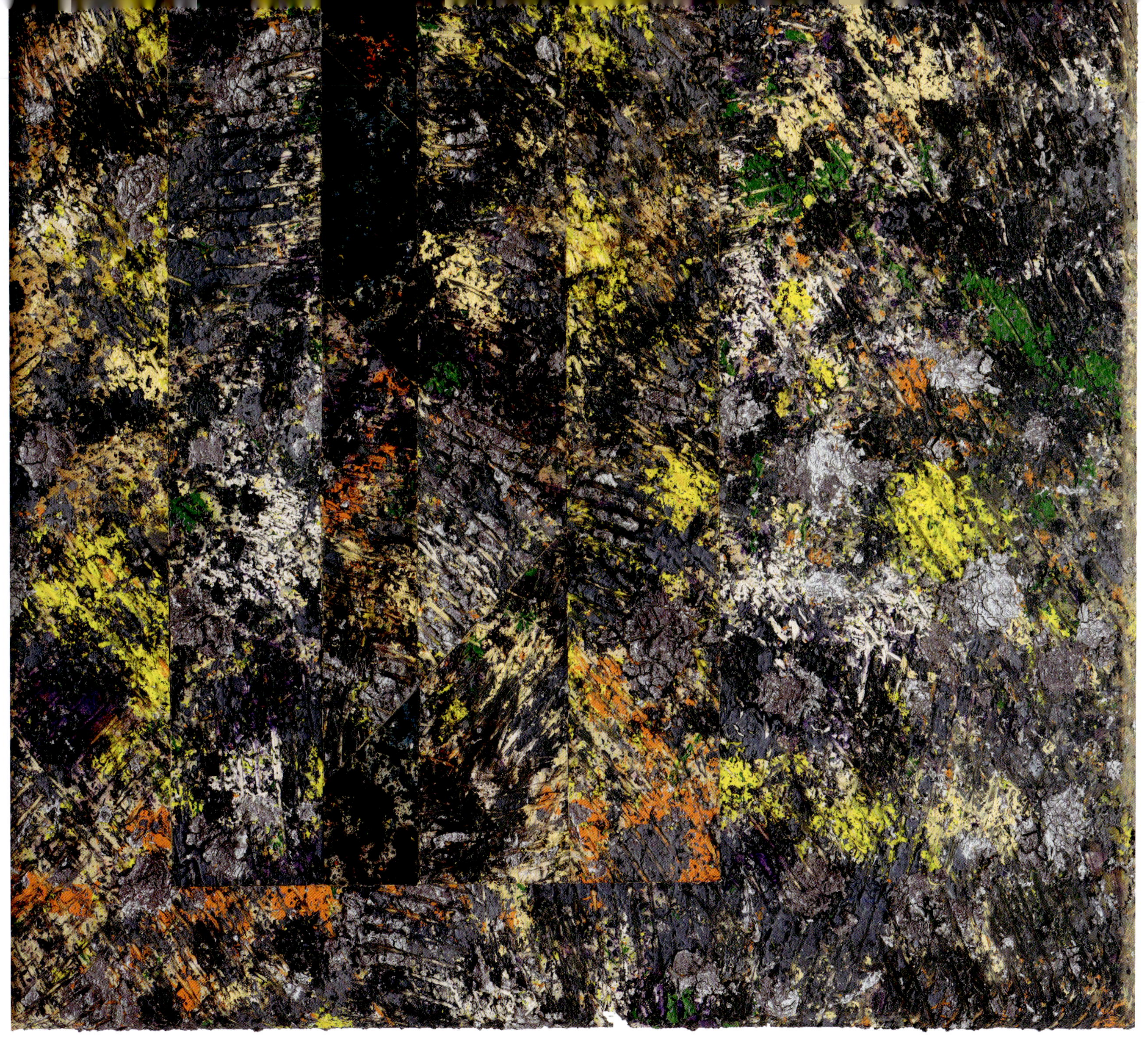

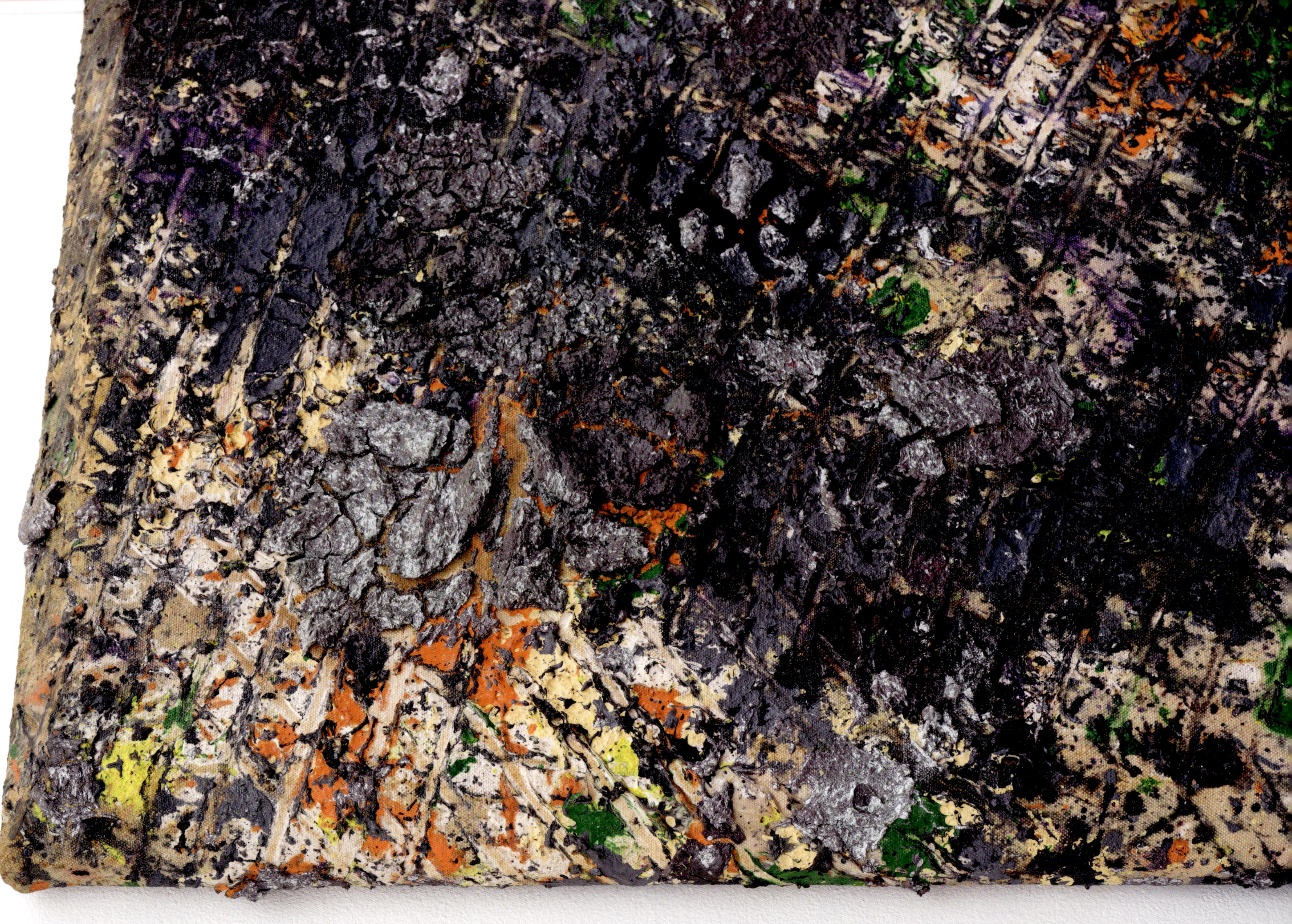

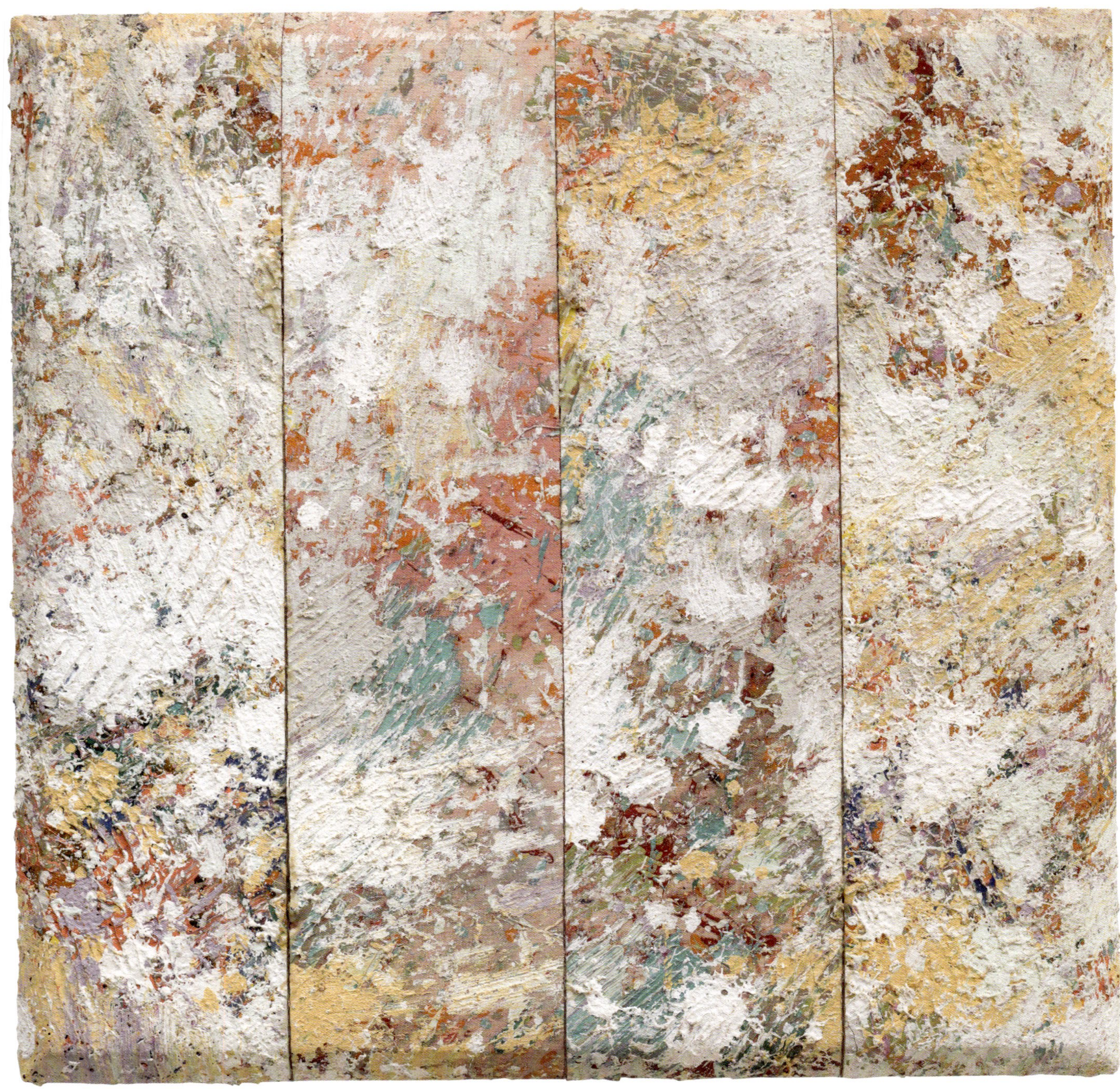

Untitled, 1975

—THE WORK
THAT YOU HAVE
DONE IS ALSO
A CRYSTAL AND
WHEN HELD UP
TO THE SUN WILL
RADIATE THE

ASPIRATIONS OF THE WHOLE OF SOCIETY WHOM IT IS YOUR INTENTION TO SERVE.

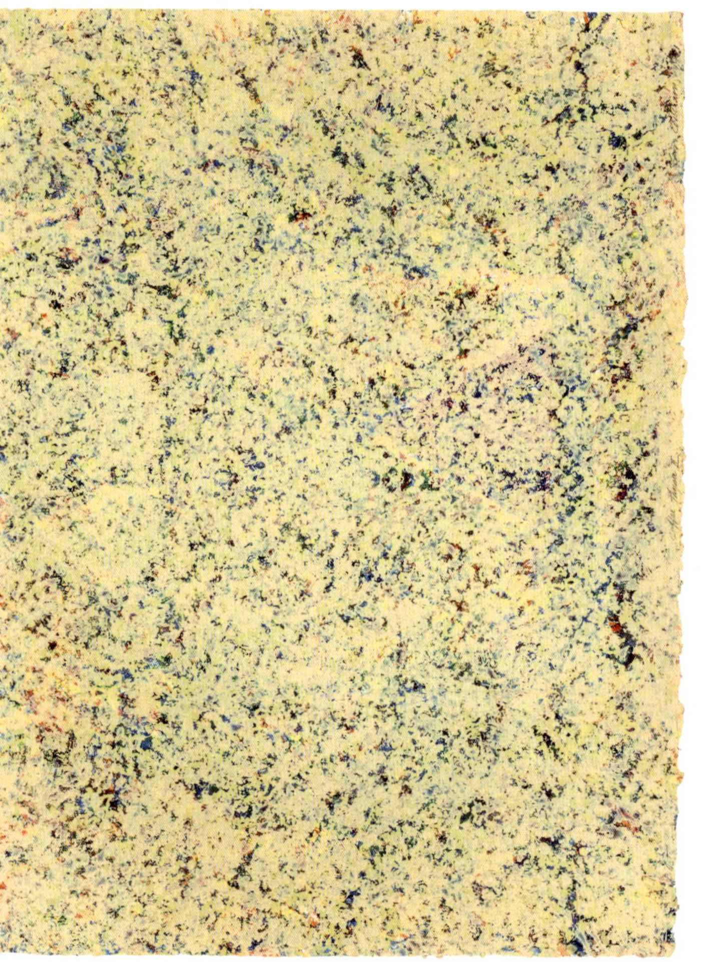

Top: *Coffee Thyme I*, 1979
Bottom: *Coffee Thyme II*, 1982

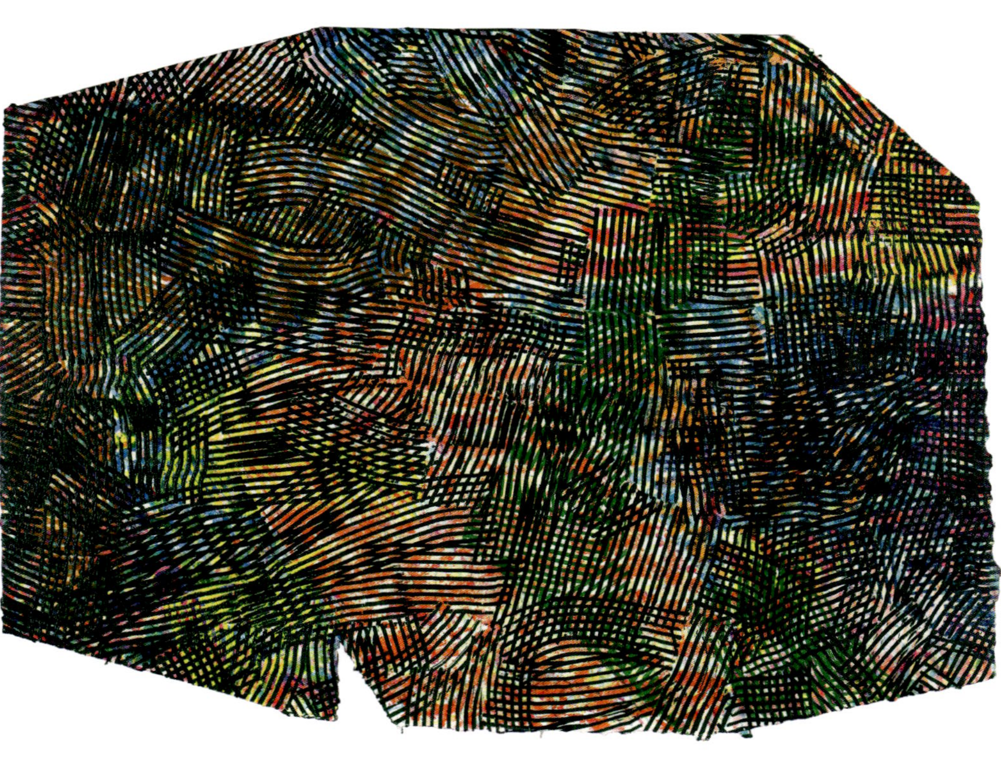

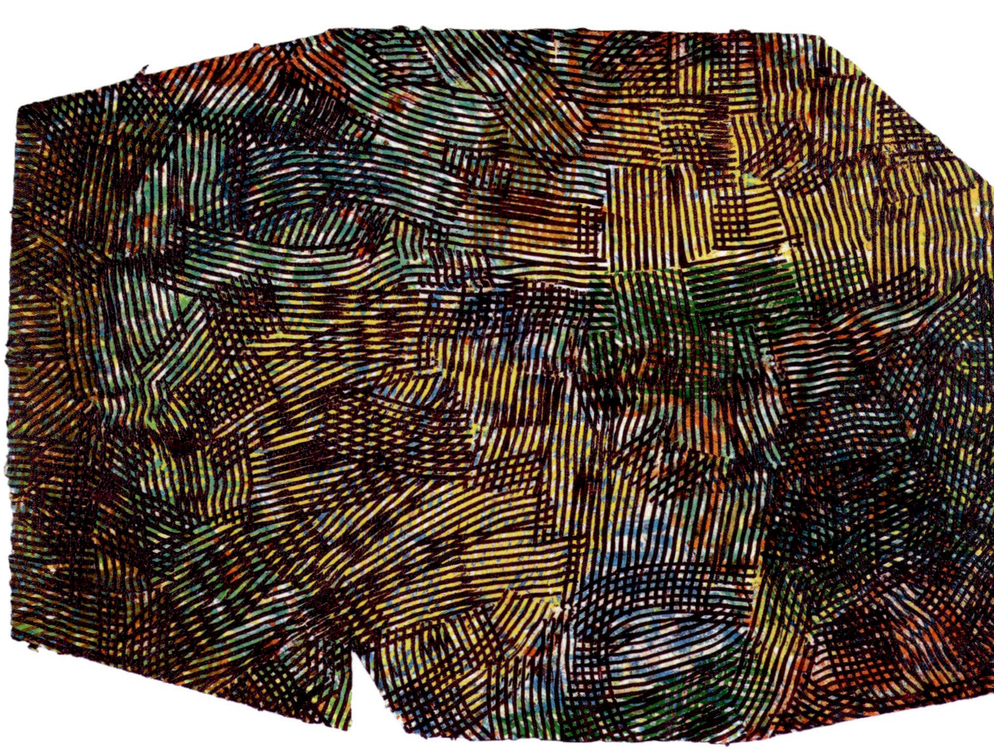

Top: *Lattice II*, 1982
Bottom: *Lattice IV*, 1982

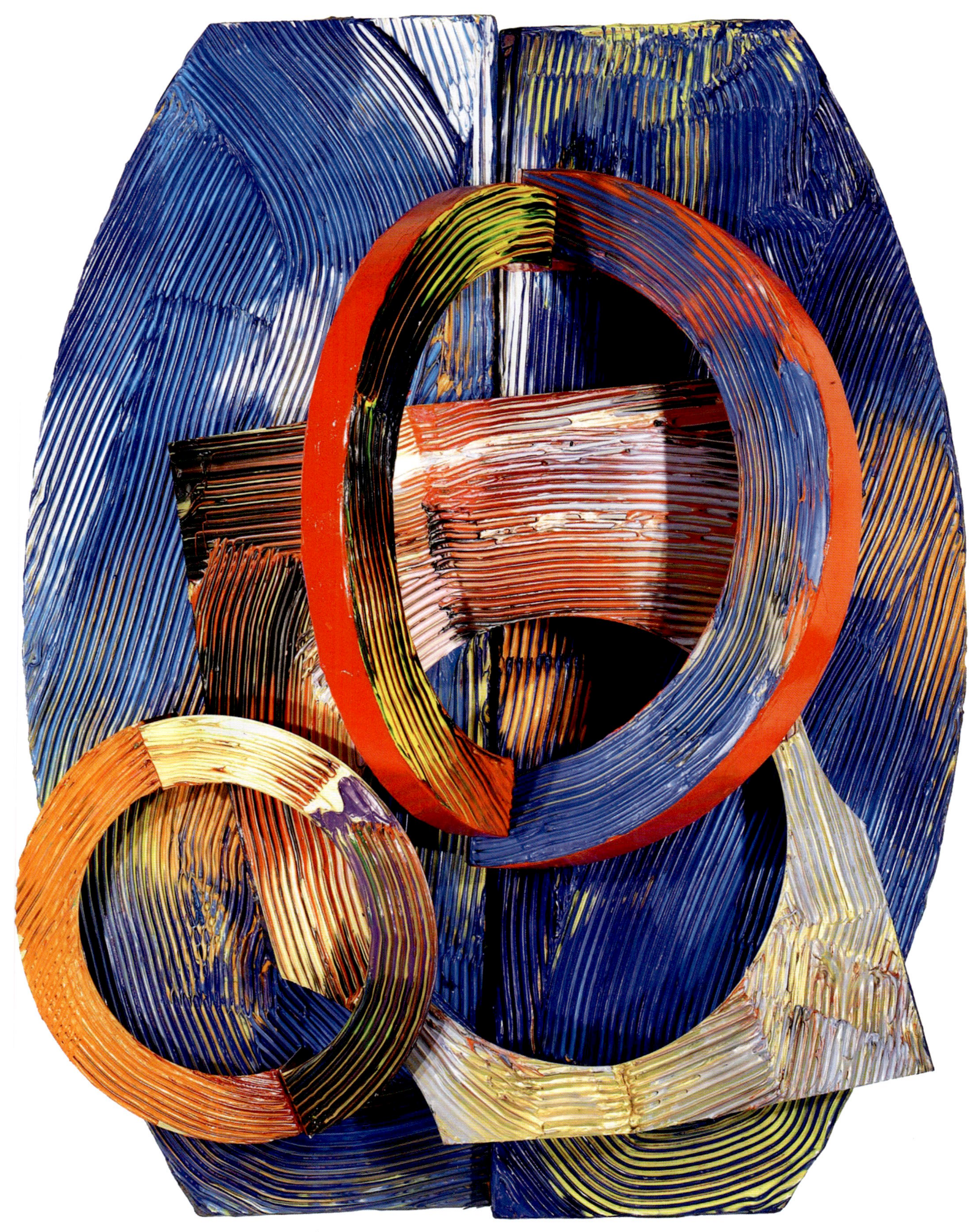

The Petition, 1990

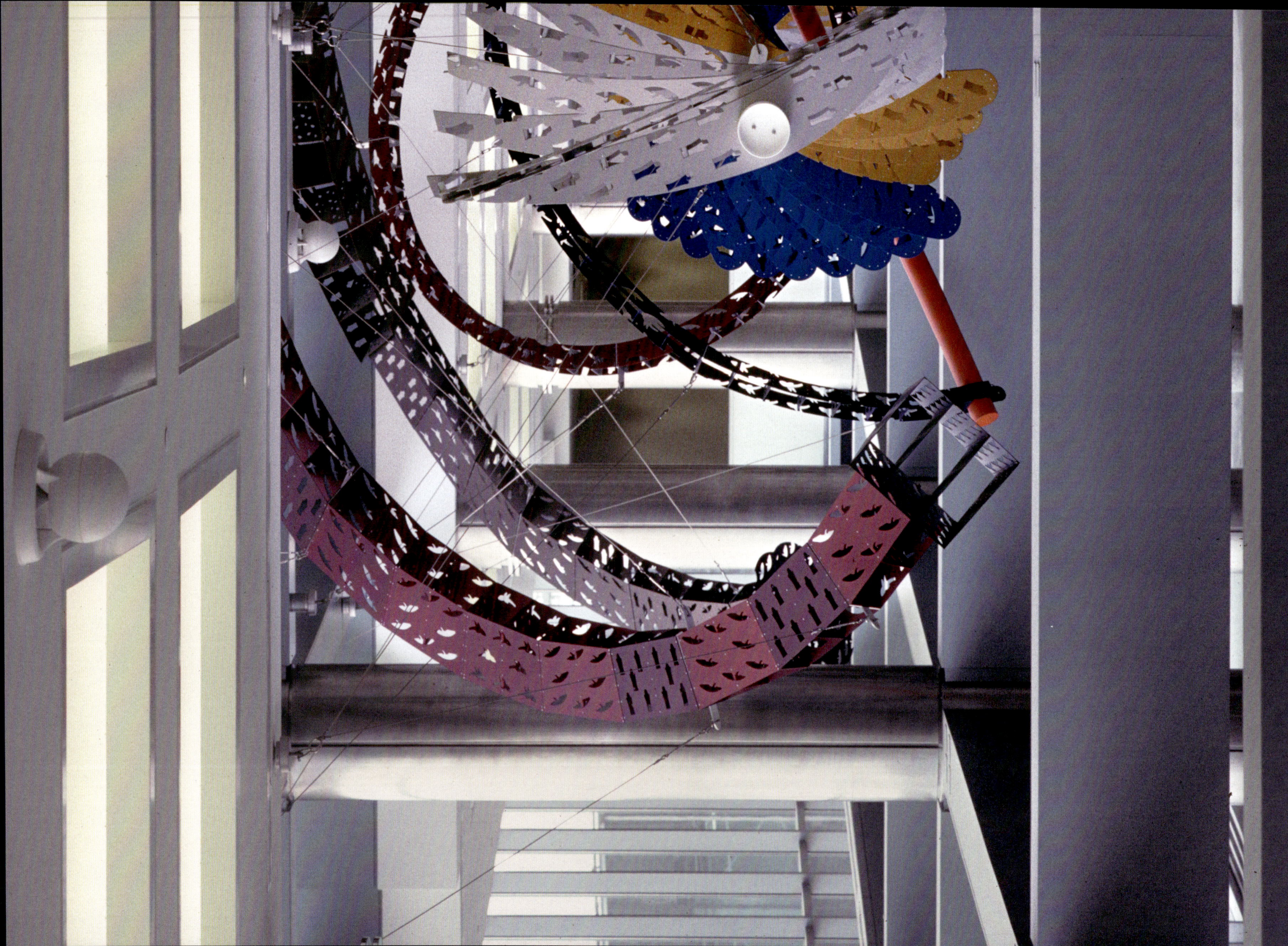

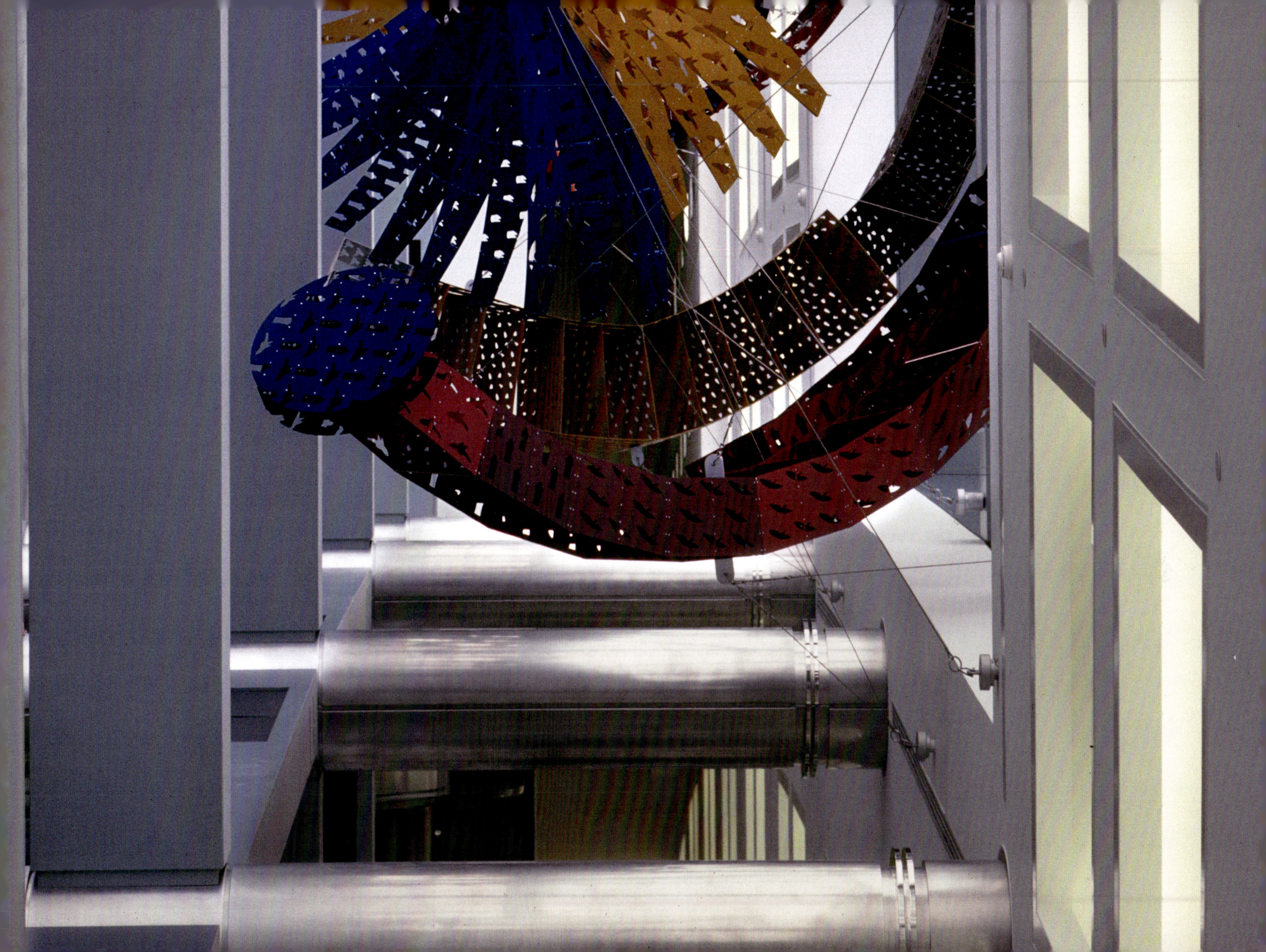

Previous pages: *Dihedral*, 1996

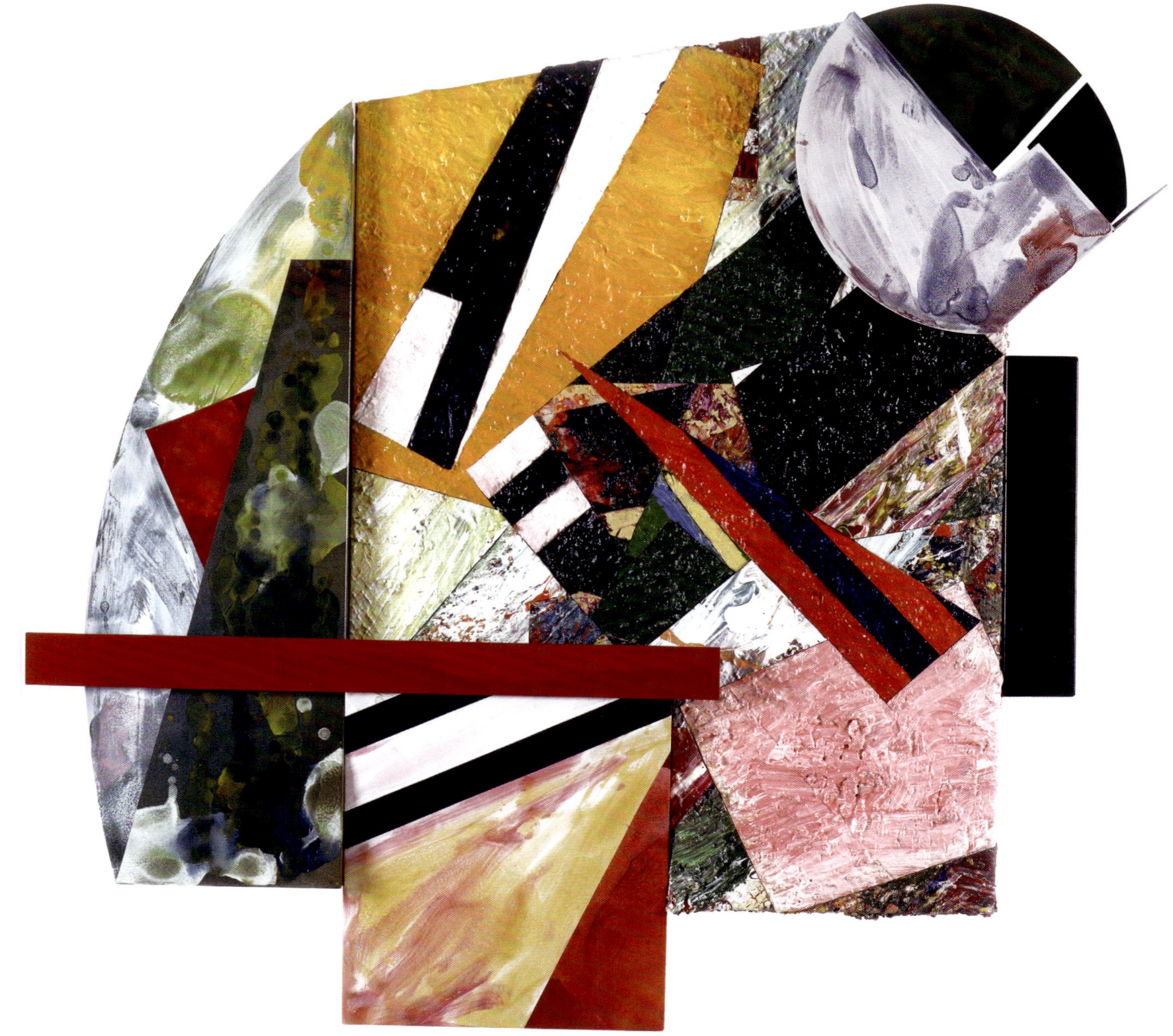

The Saint of Moritz Outside Mondrian, 1984

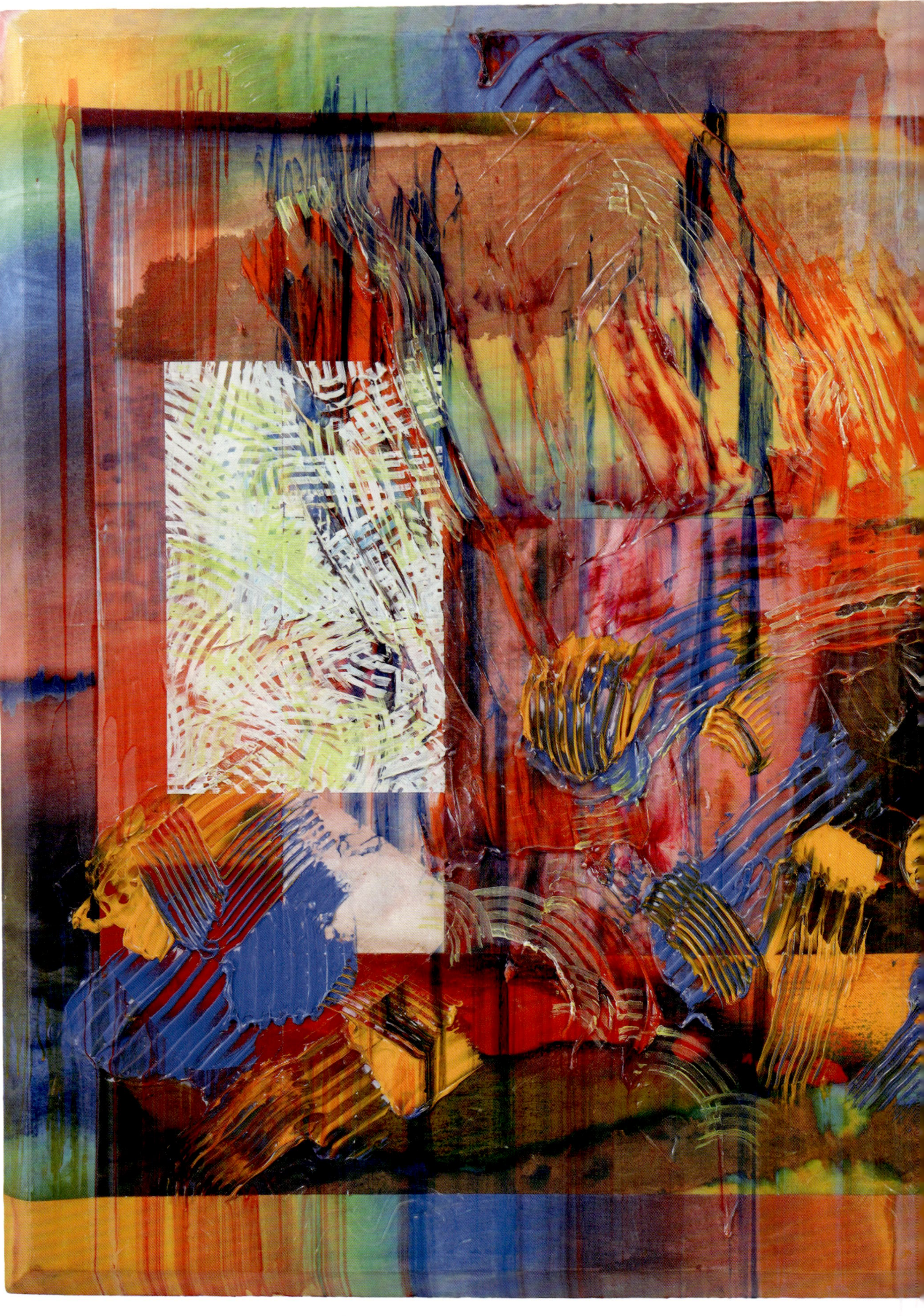

More Than Water (Assisi) Subtle Jungle, 1997

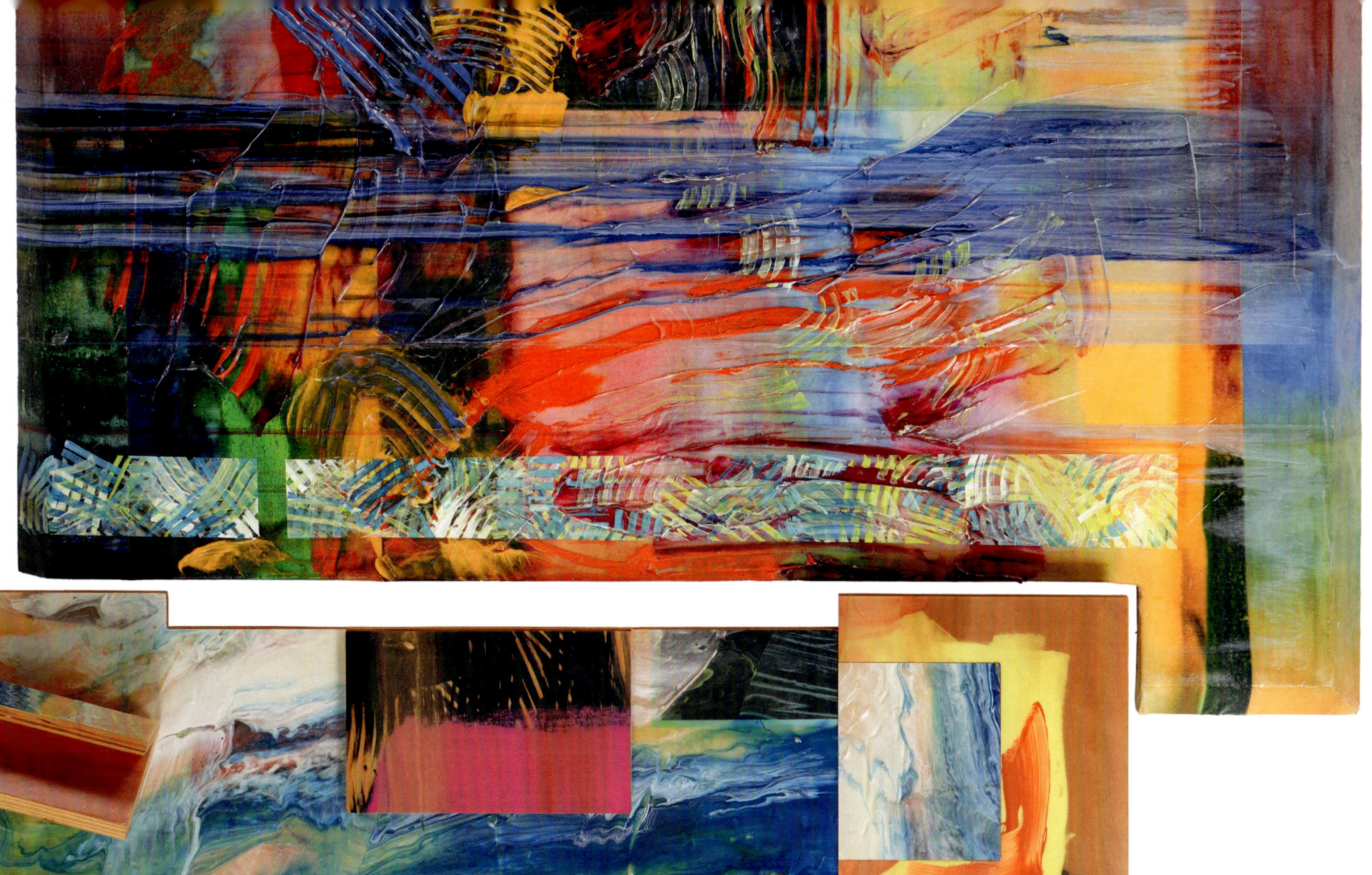

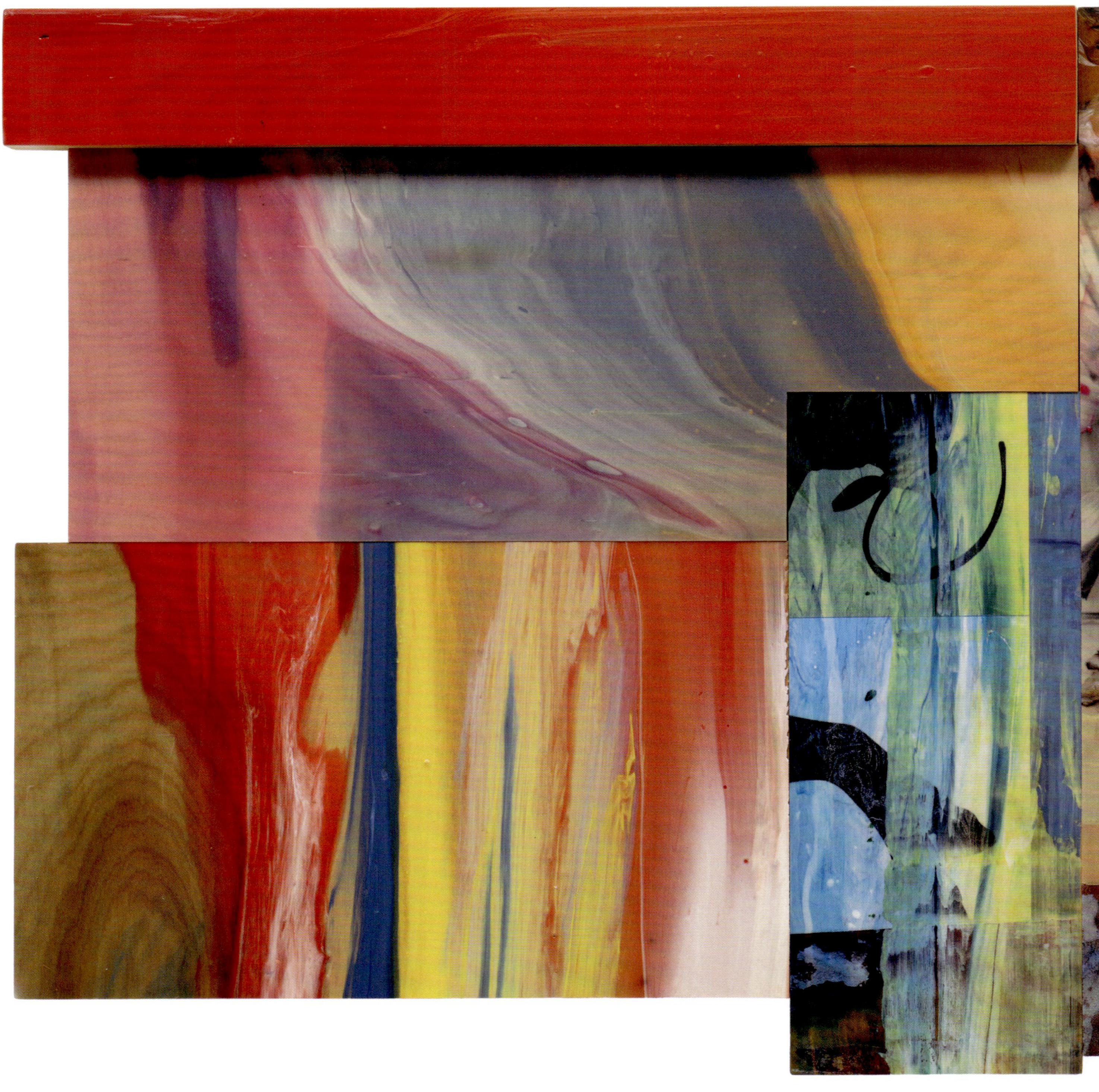

Red Line, 1999

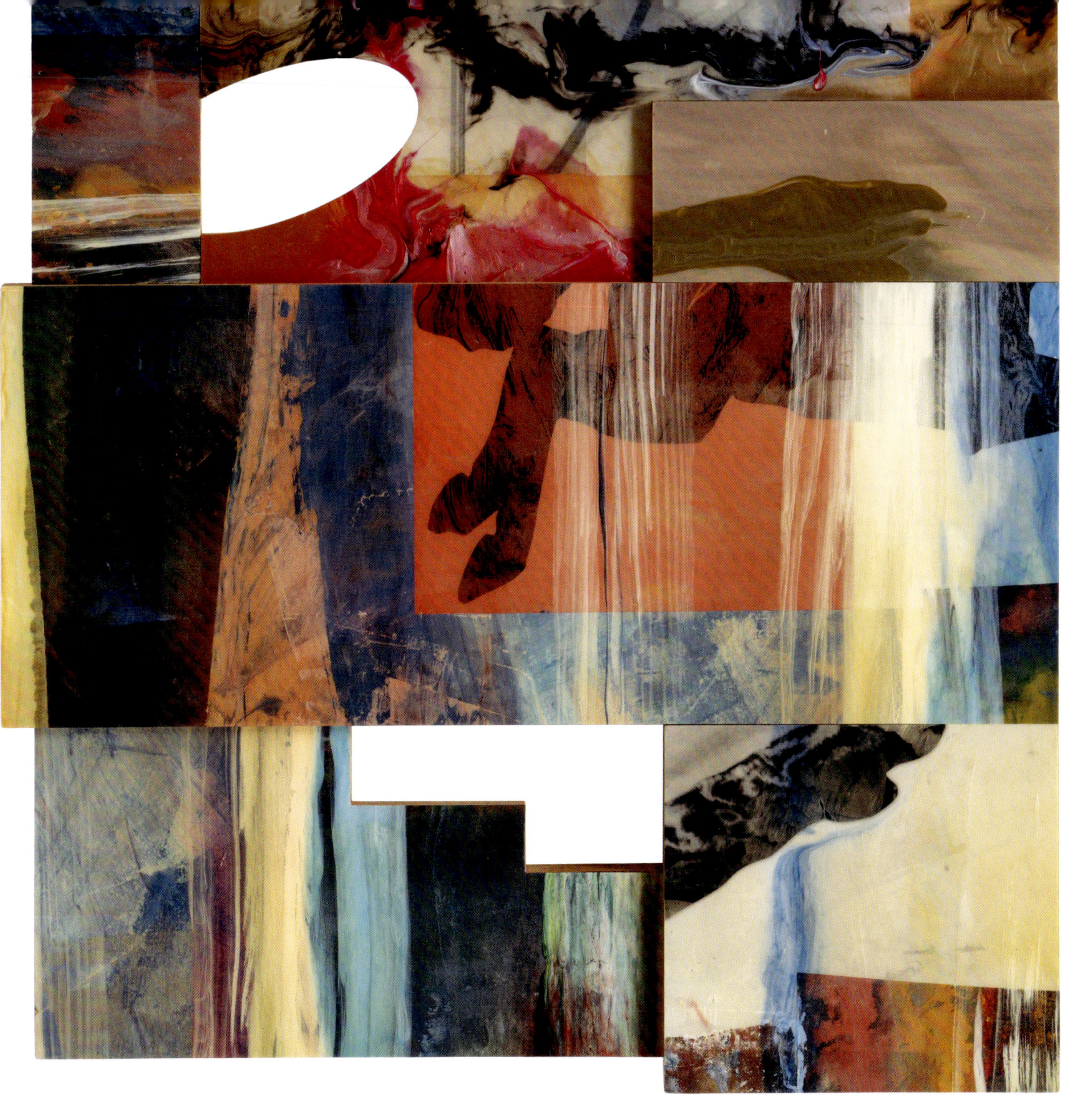

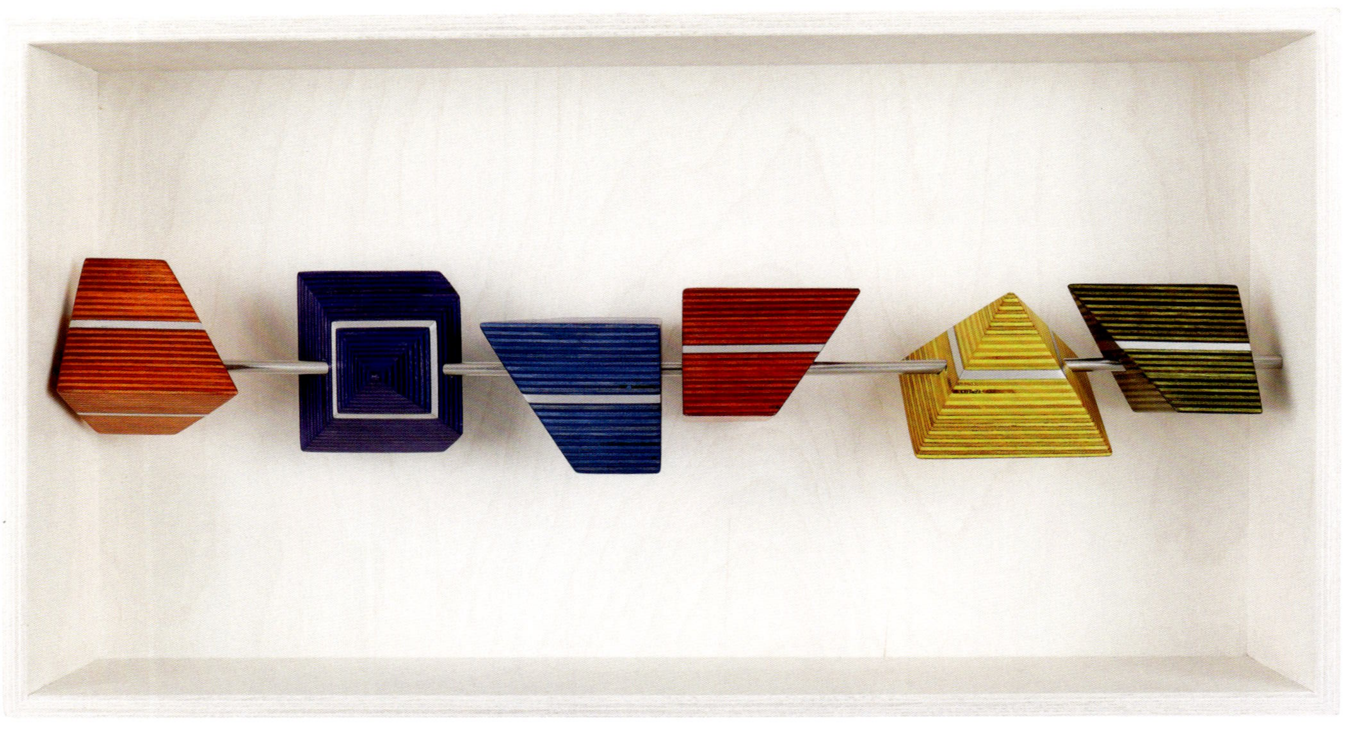

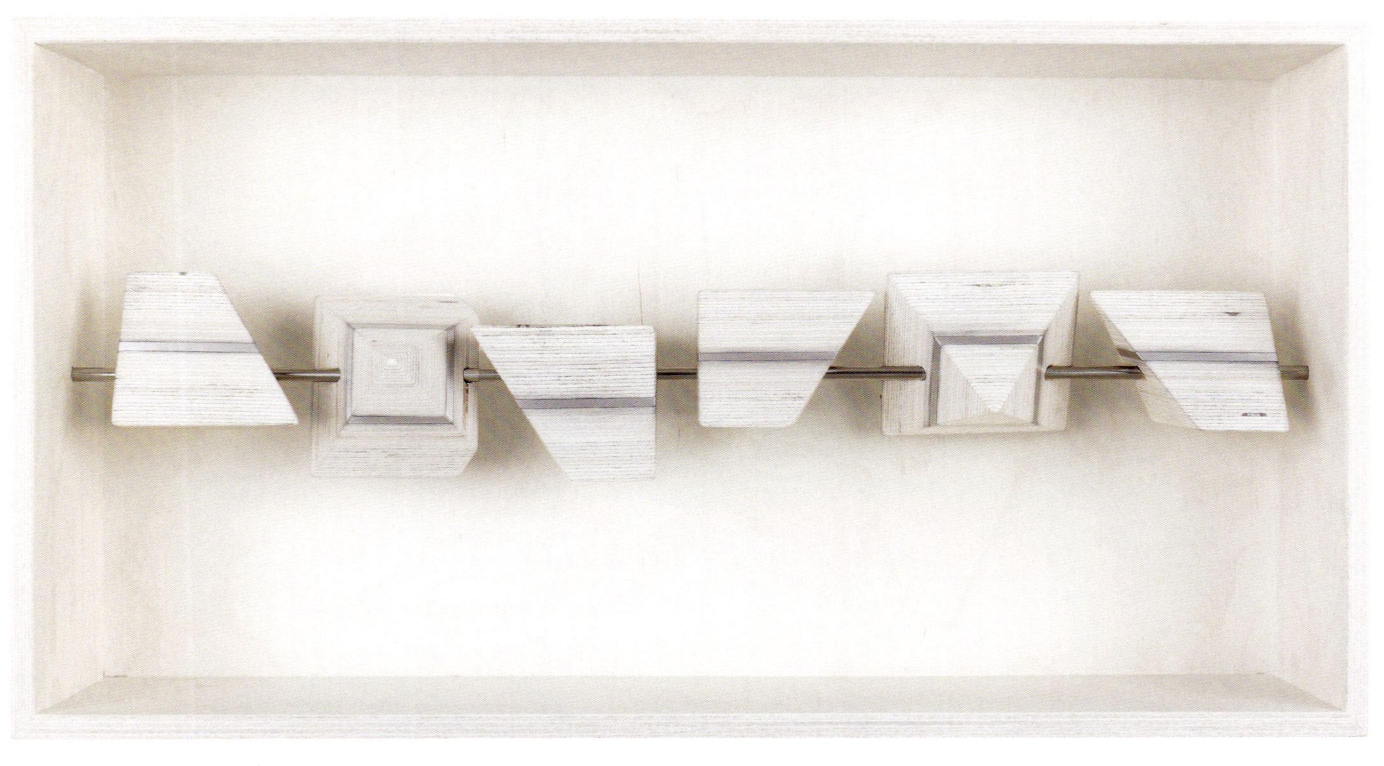

Top: *Color Abacus*, 2020
Bottom: *White Abacus*, 2020

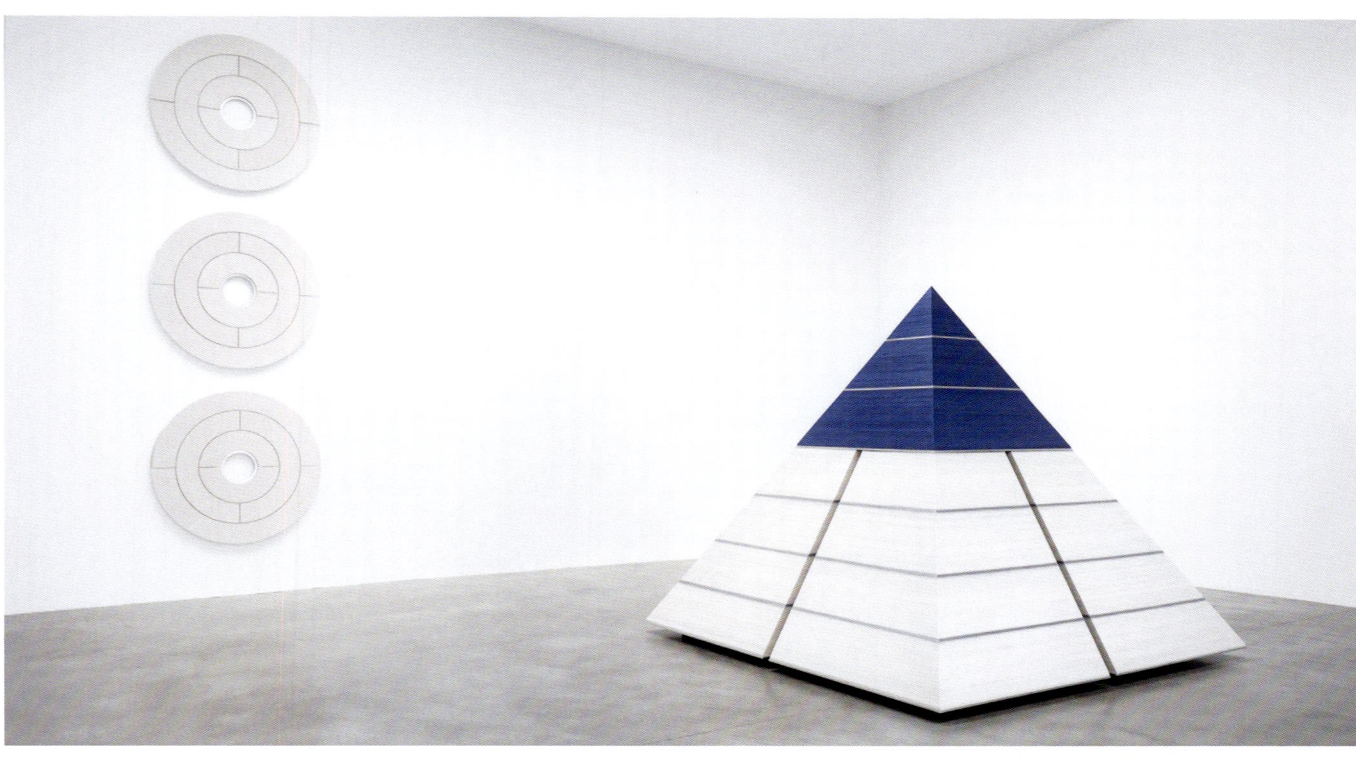

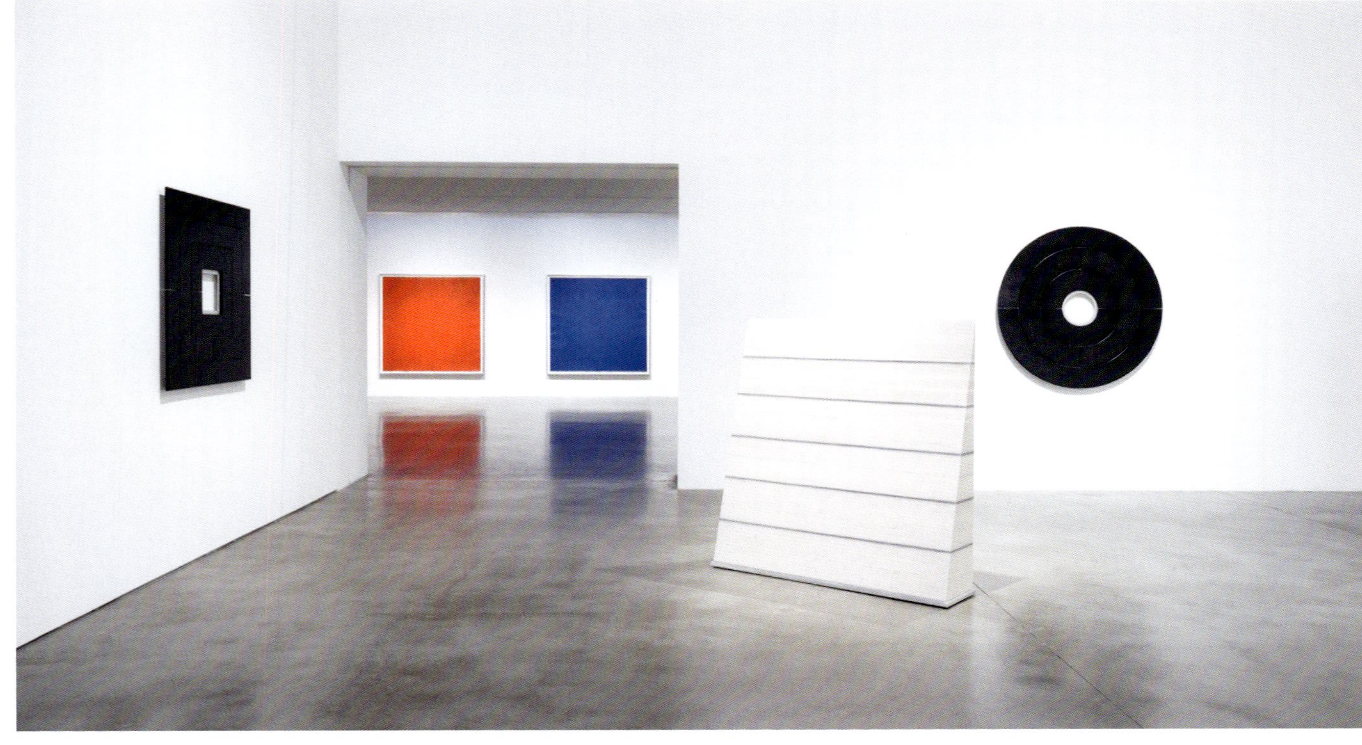

Installation views of 'Sam Gilliam: Existed Existing', Pace Gallery, New York, 2020

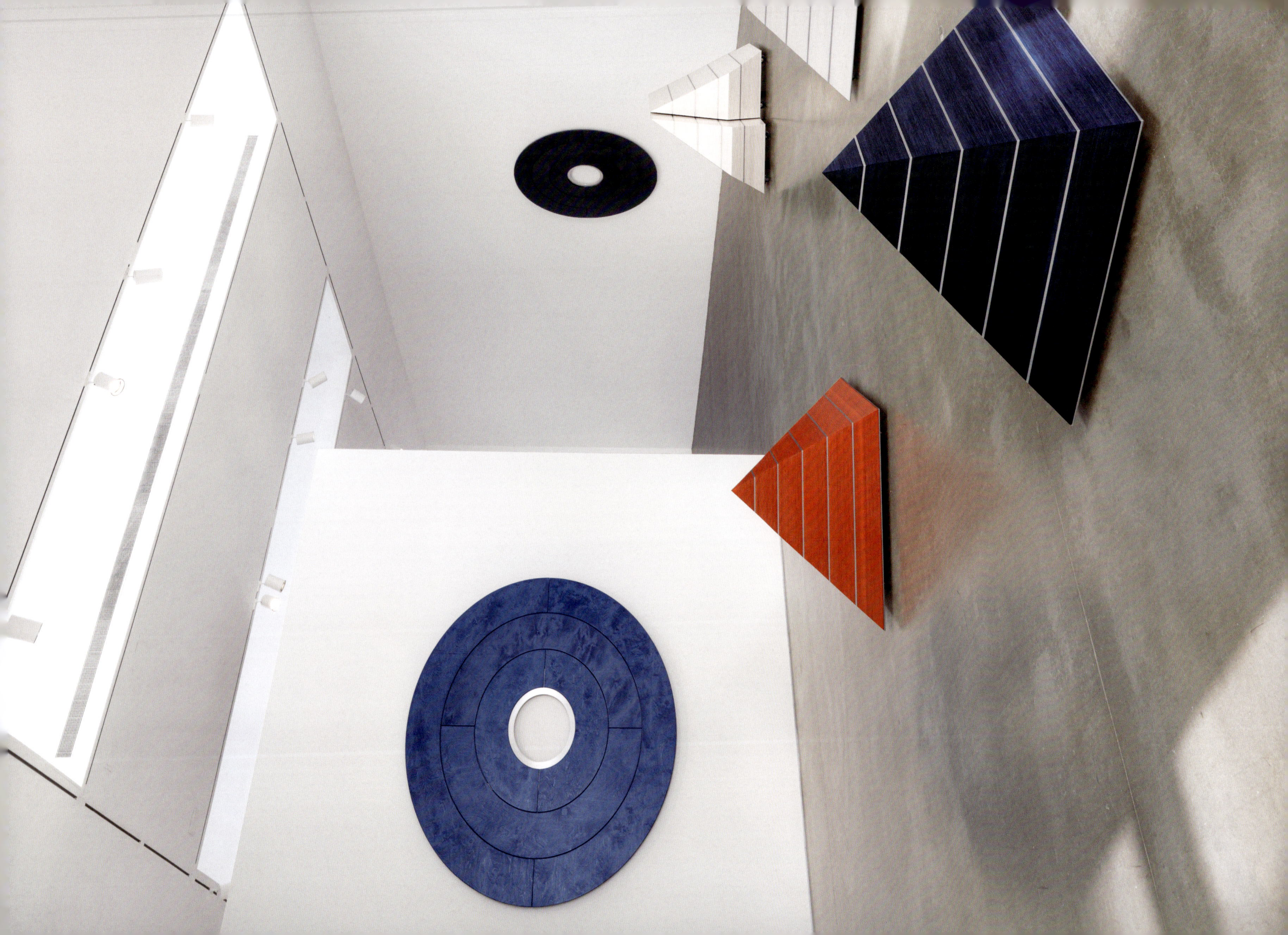

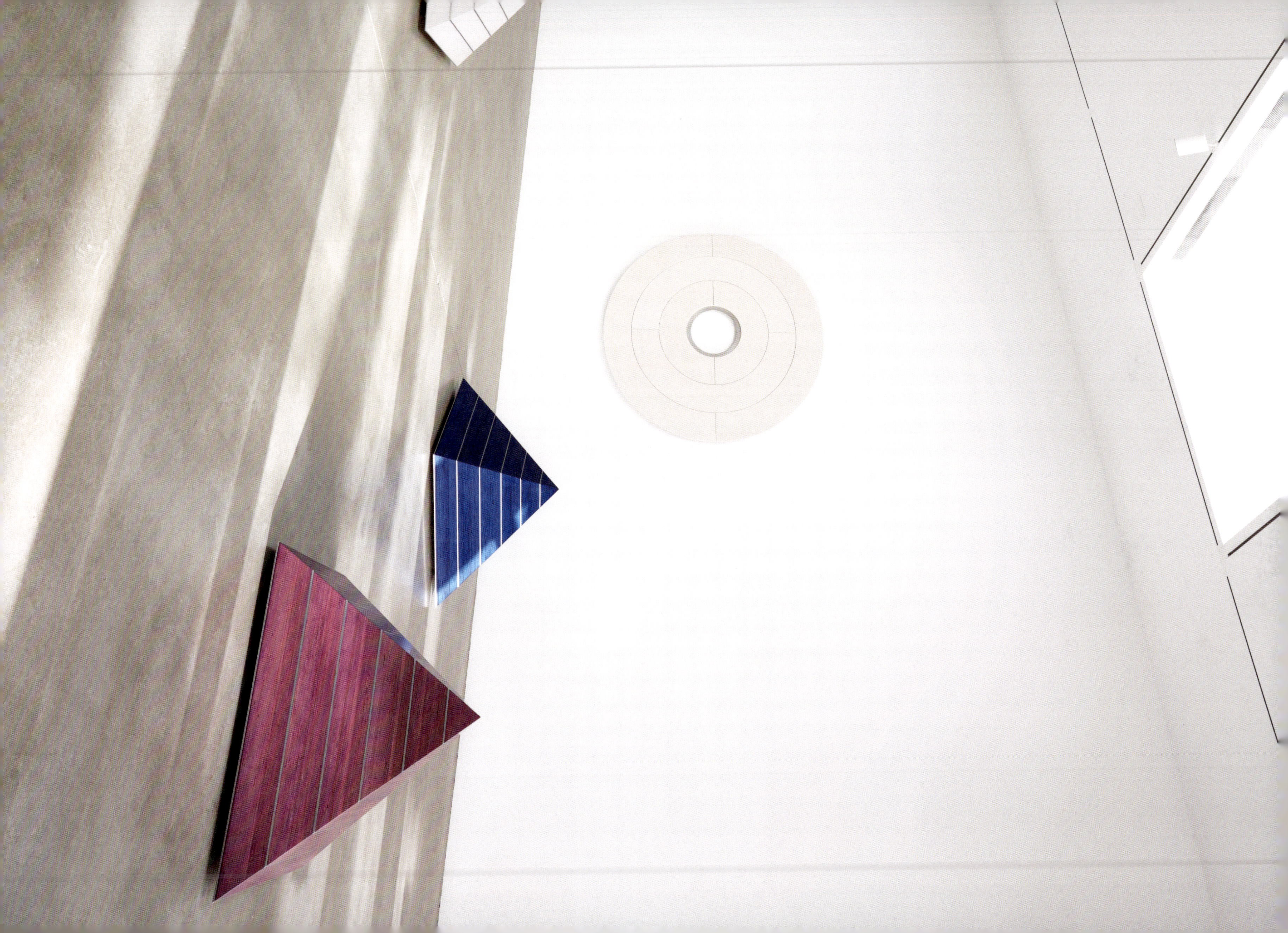

Blue 96" Disc, 2020

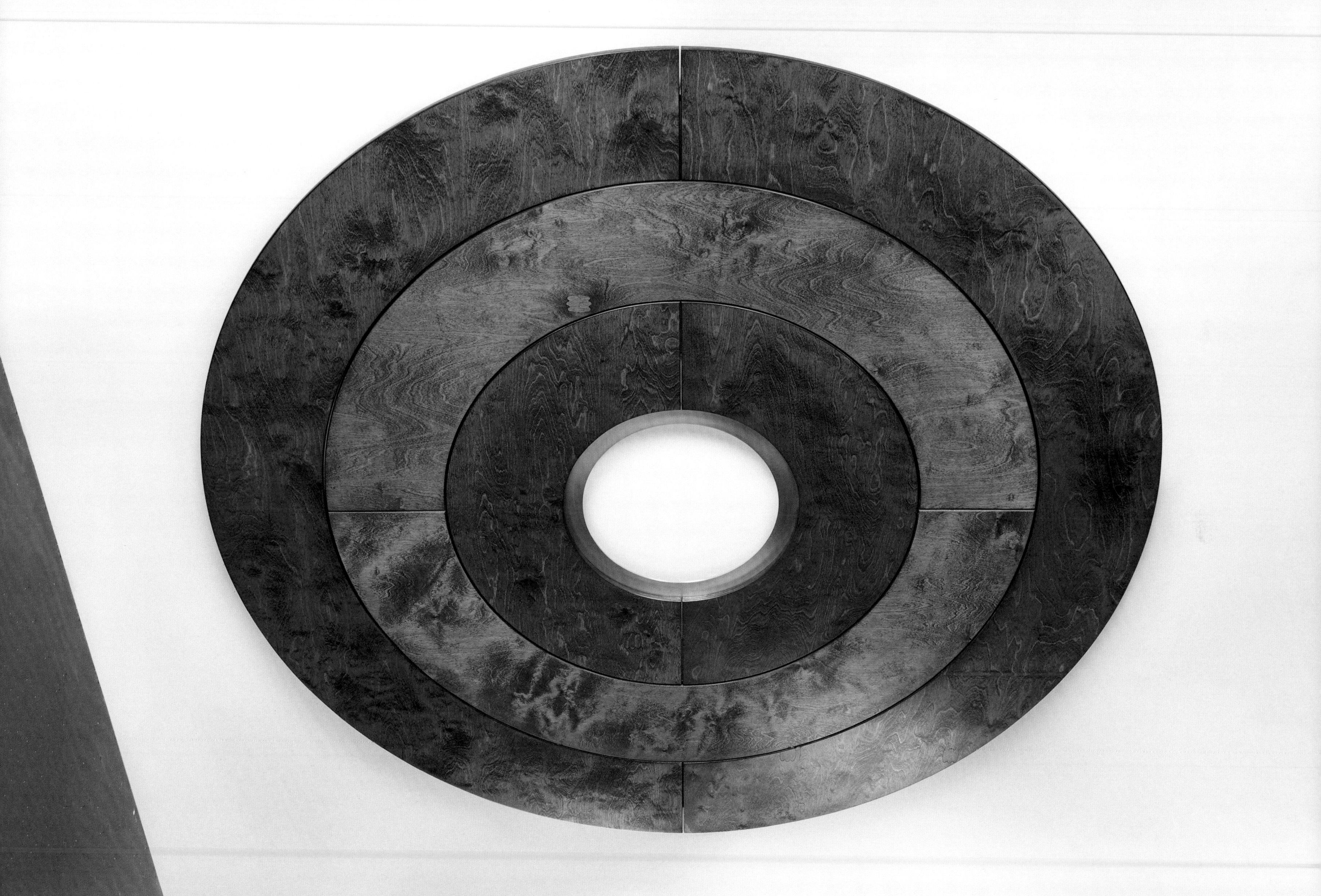

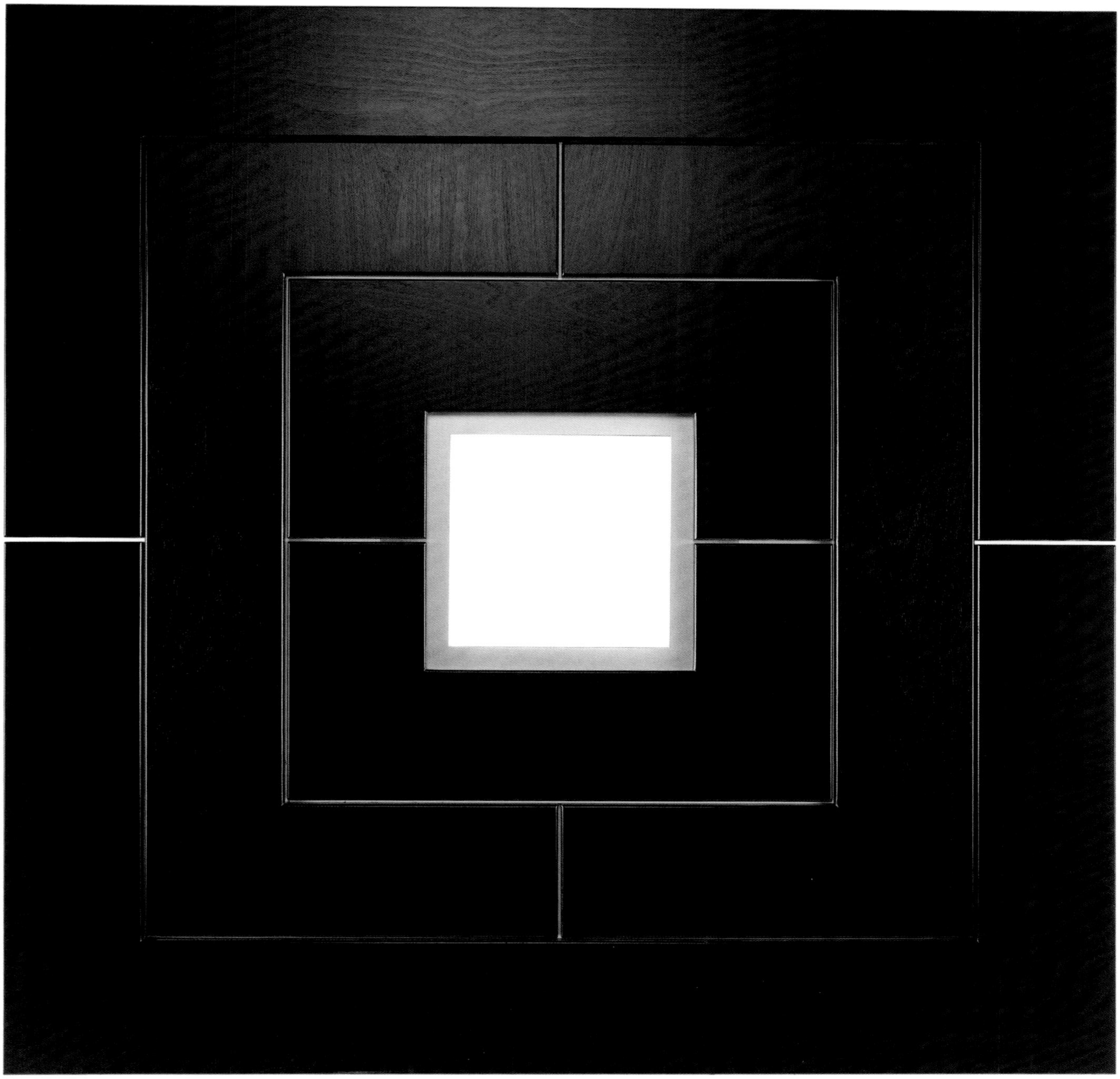

Black 48" Square, 2020

Washi Paper – Green, 2020

Washi Paper – Blue, 2020

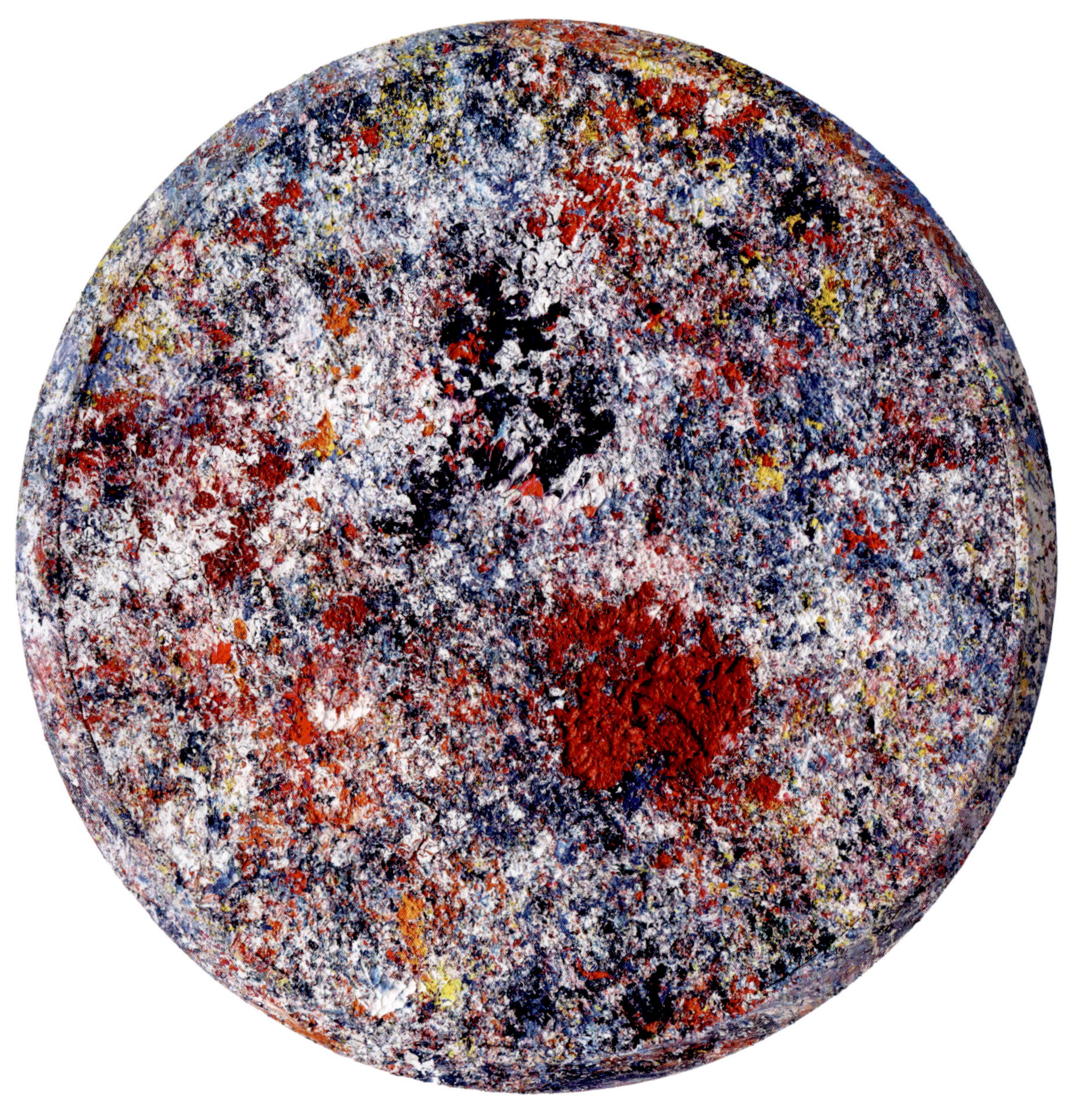

Something is Going On!, 2021

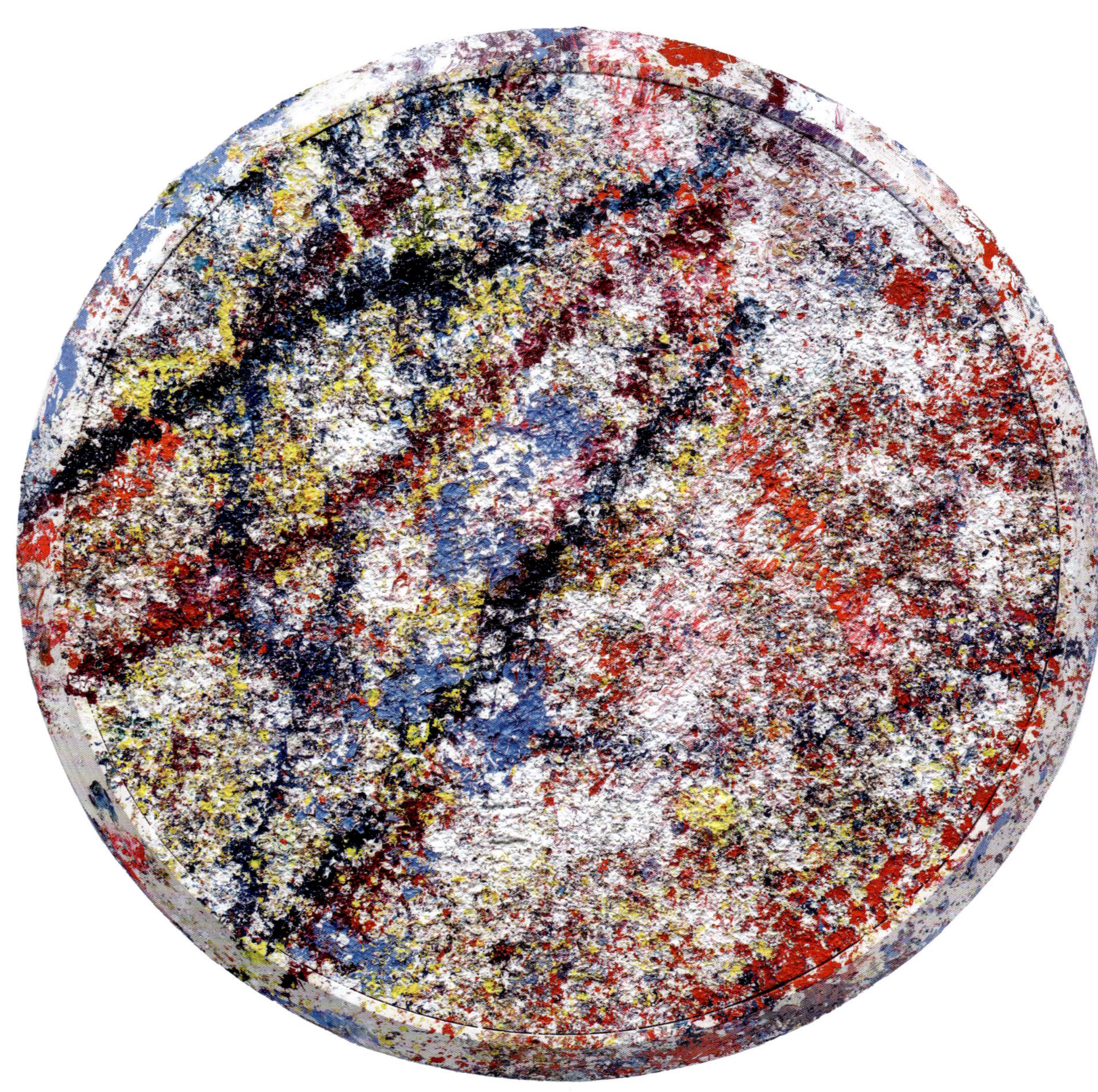

Lucky, 2021

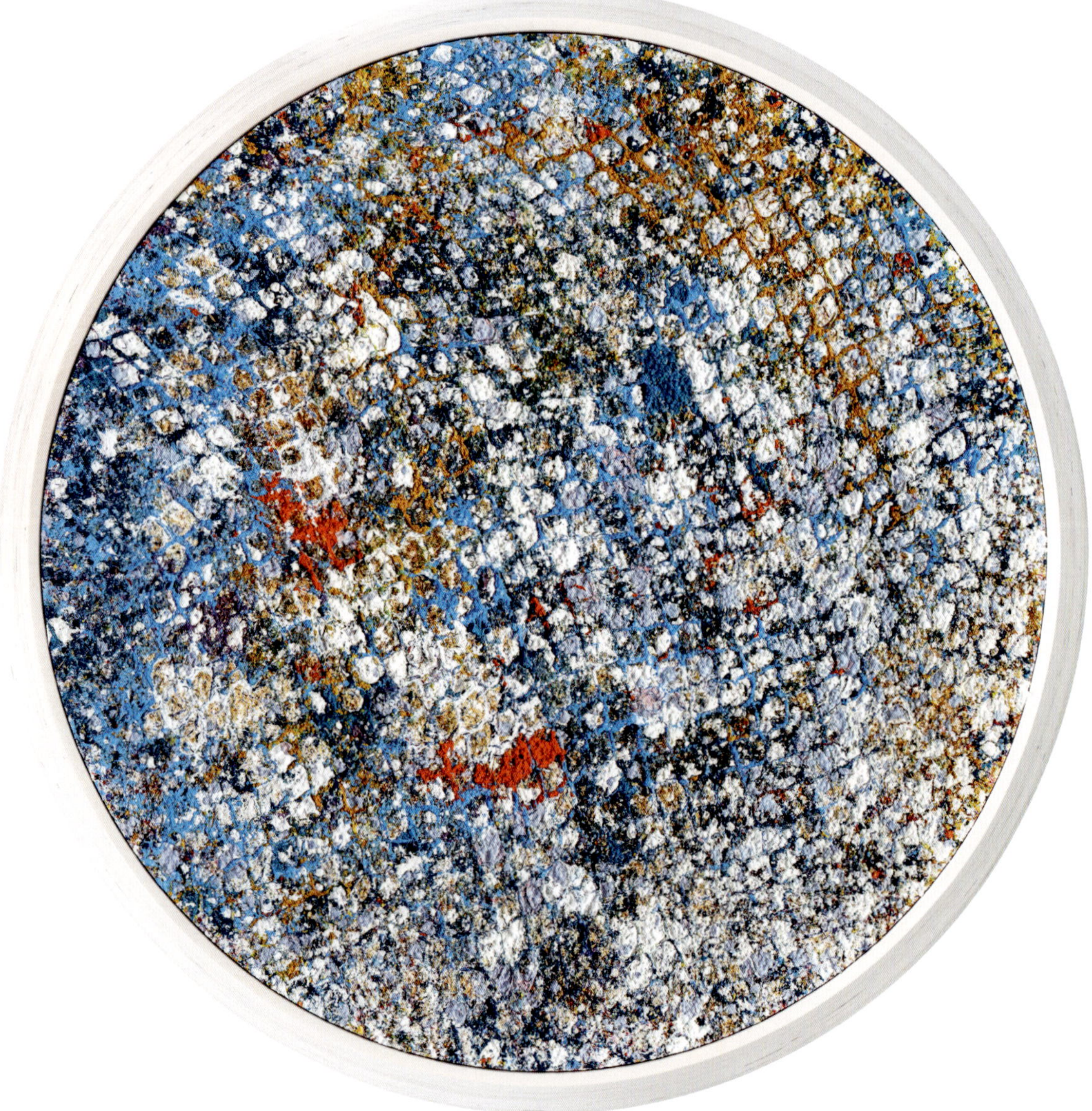

You Blue Moon, 2021

exciting, 2021

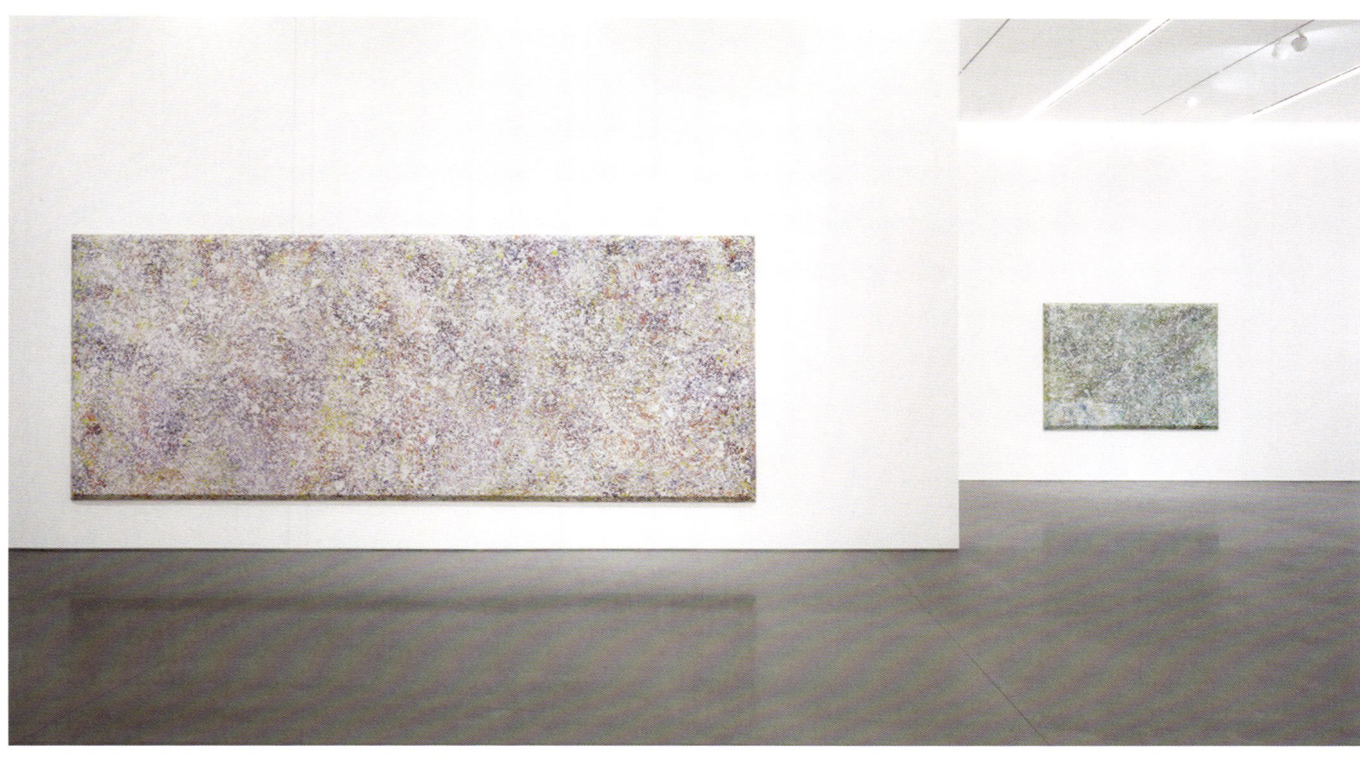

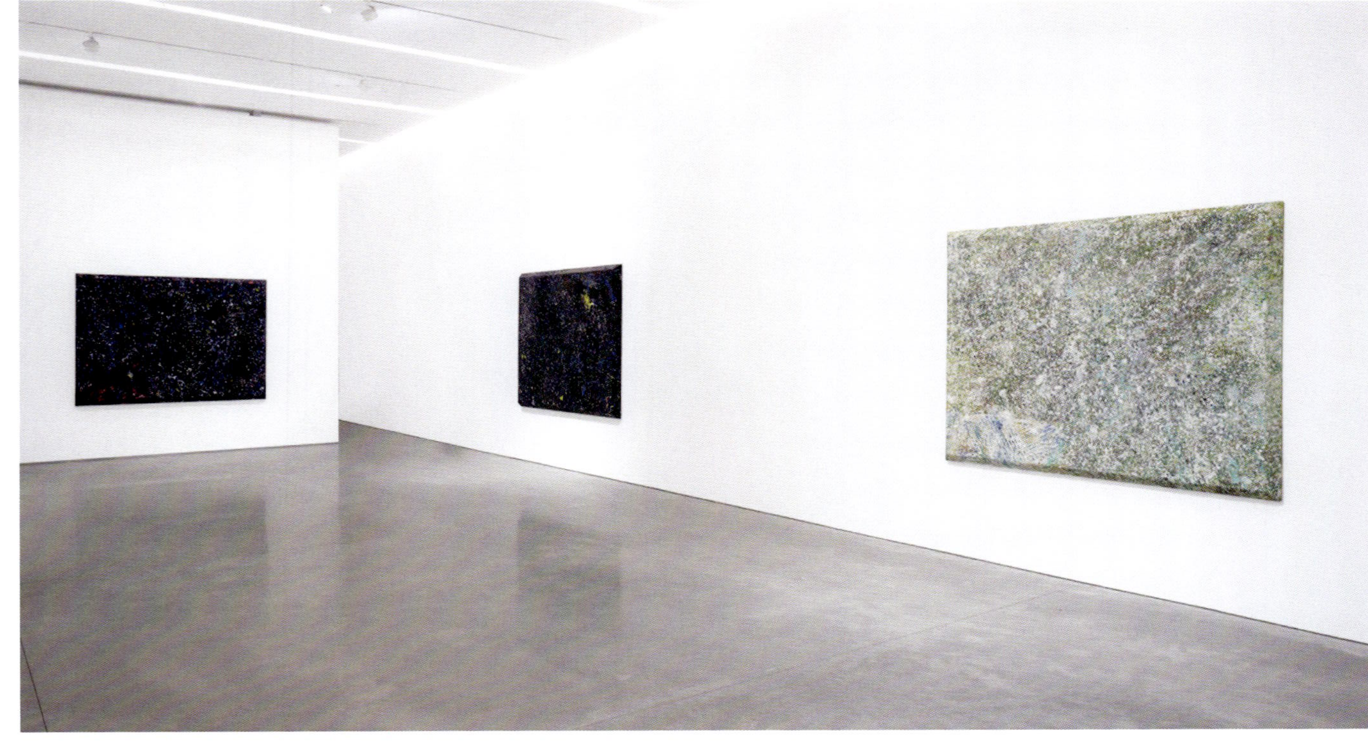

Installation views of 'Sam Gilliam: Existed Existing', Pace Gallery, New York, 2020

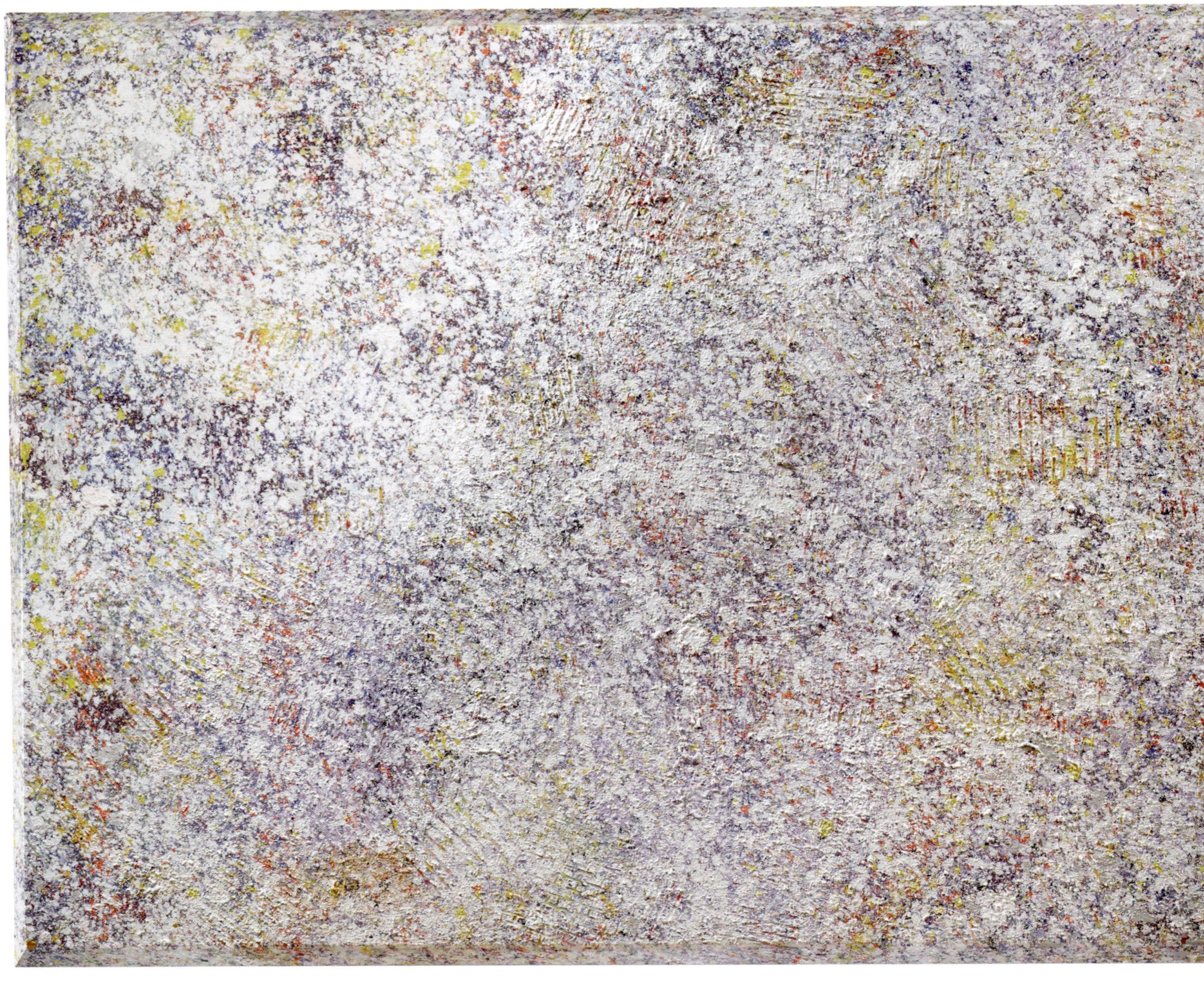

October 18, 2020

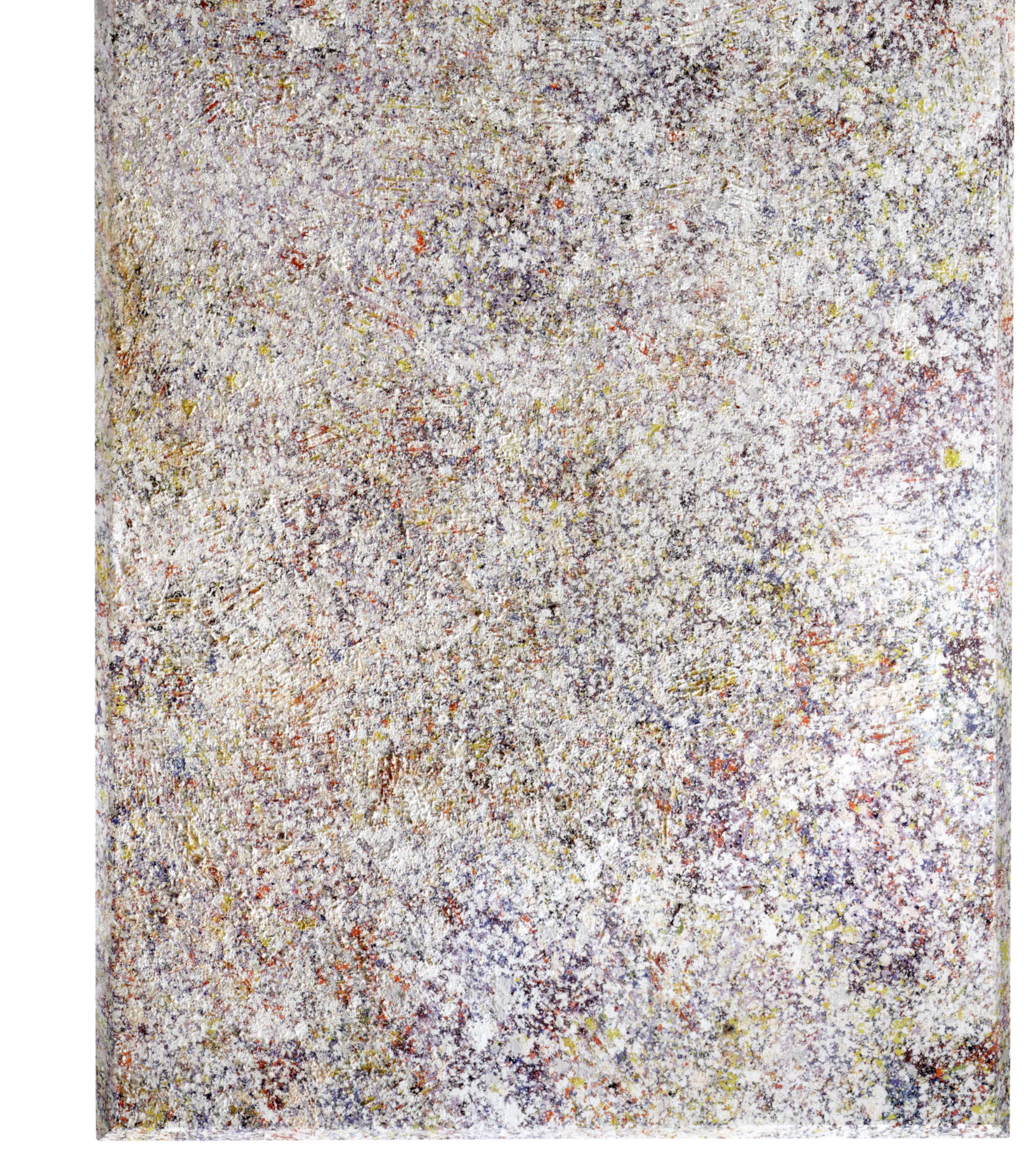

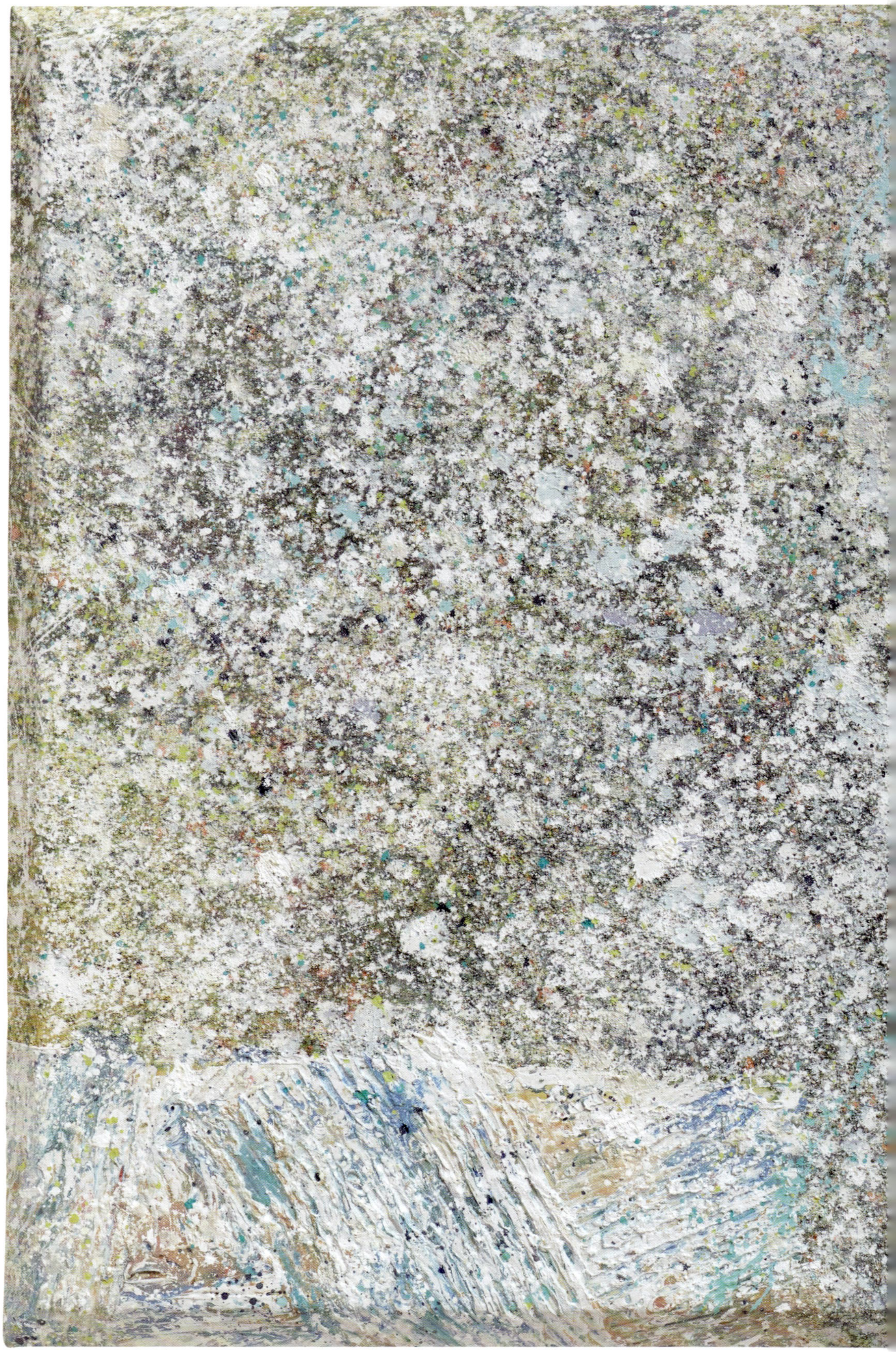

A New Generation, 2020

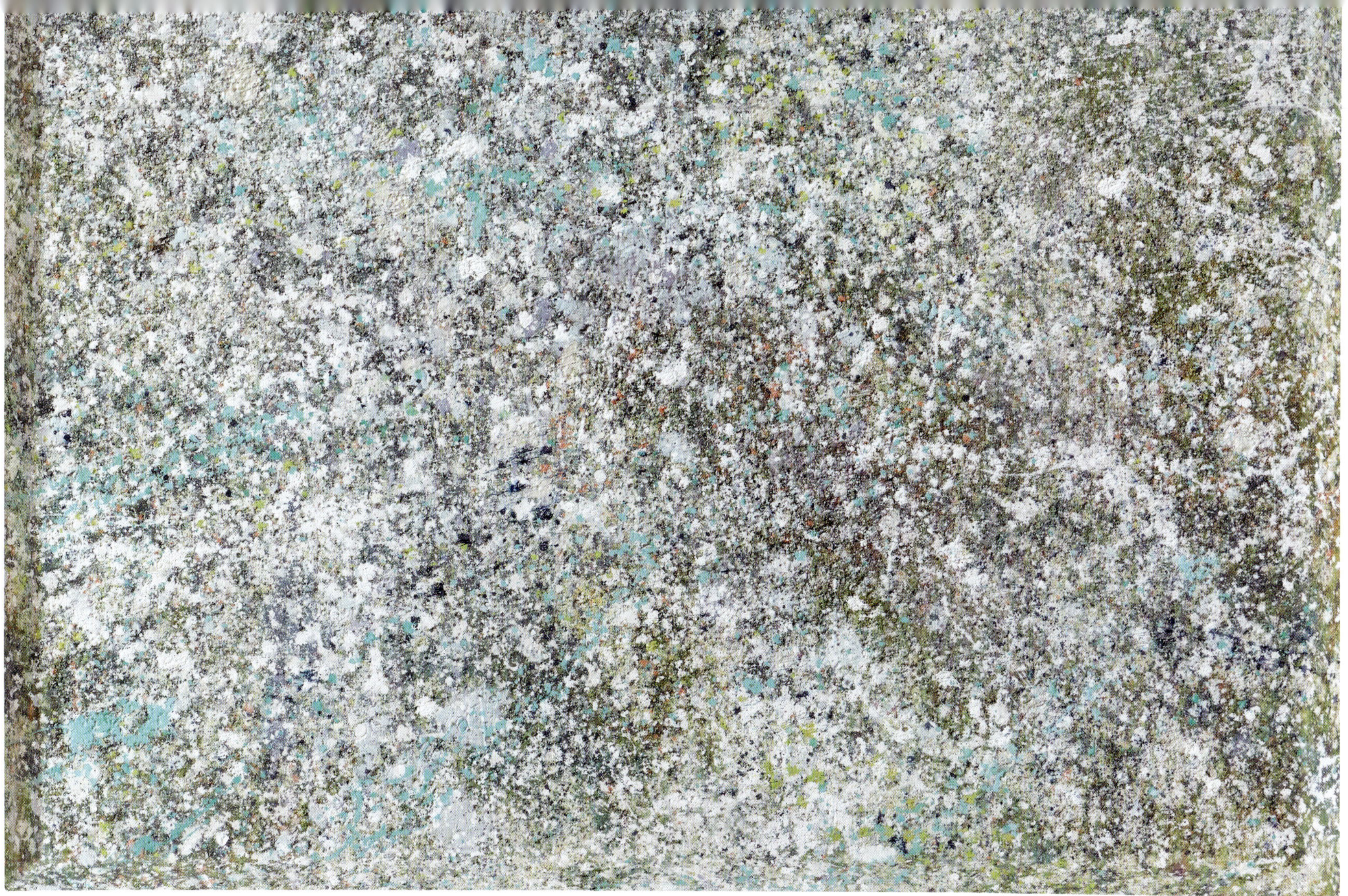

Waiting for "Dutchman", 2020

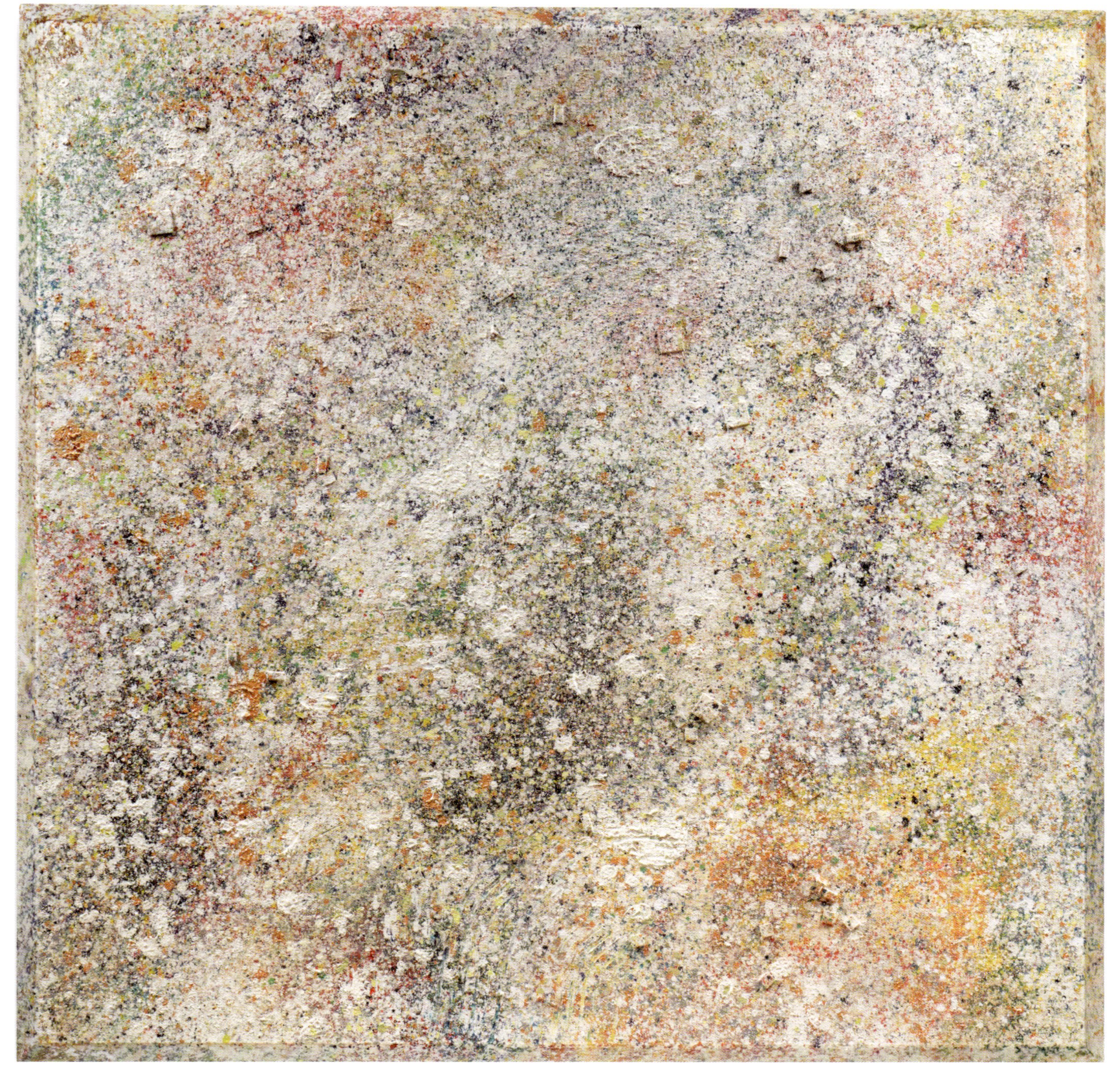

The Mississippi "Shake Rag", 2020

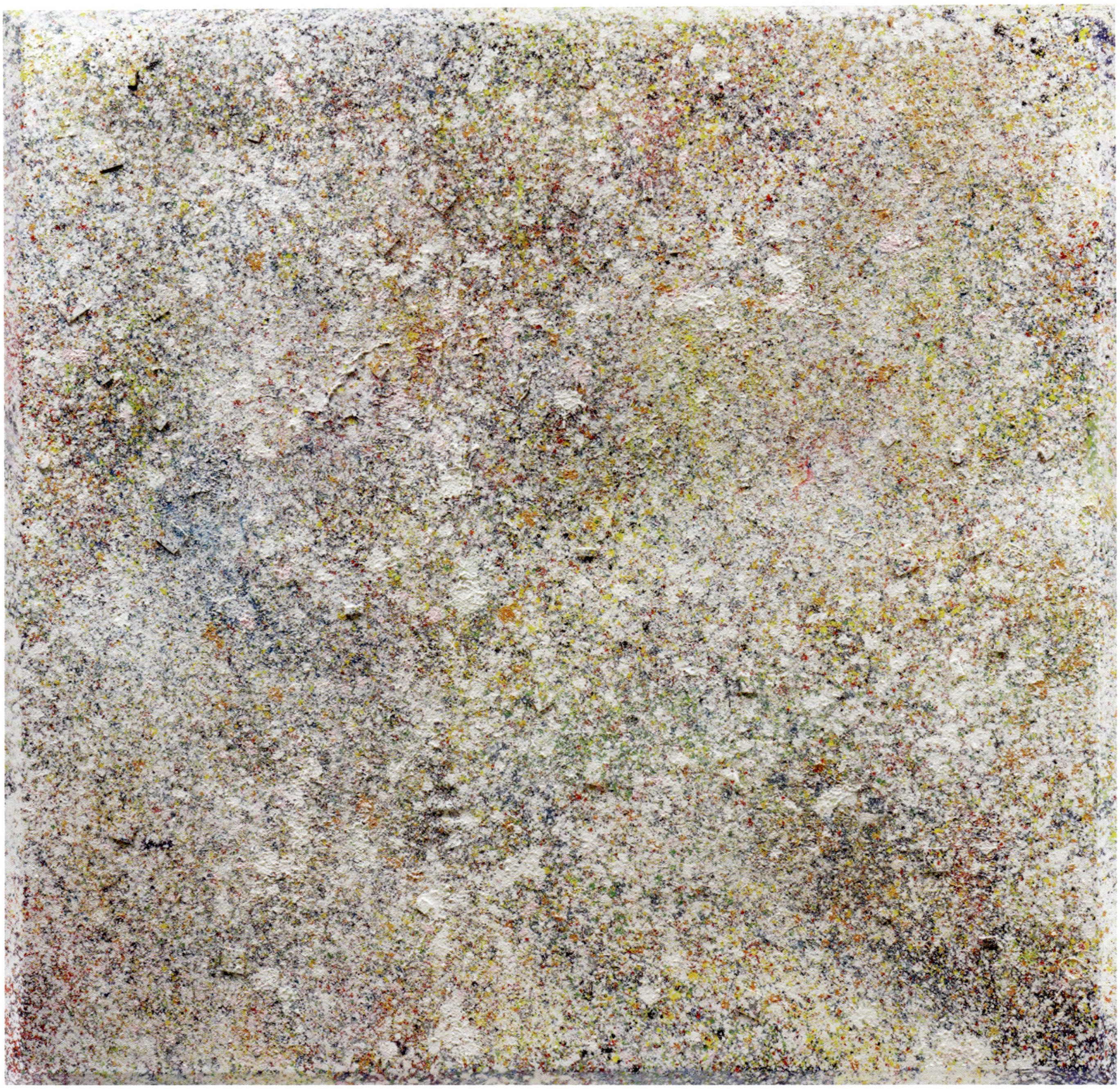

Nikki Giovanni, 2020

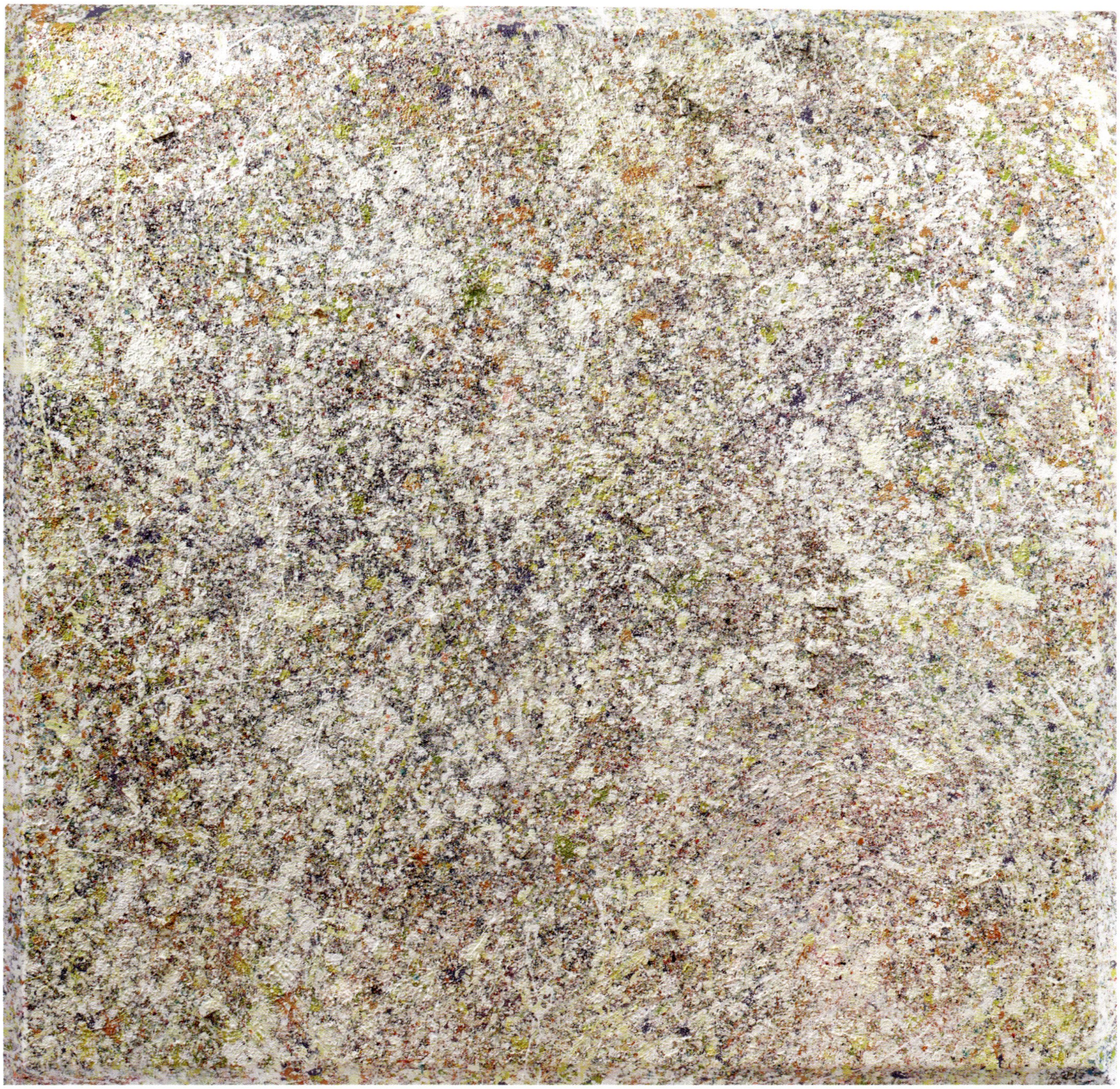

Any Minute Now, 2020

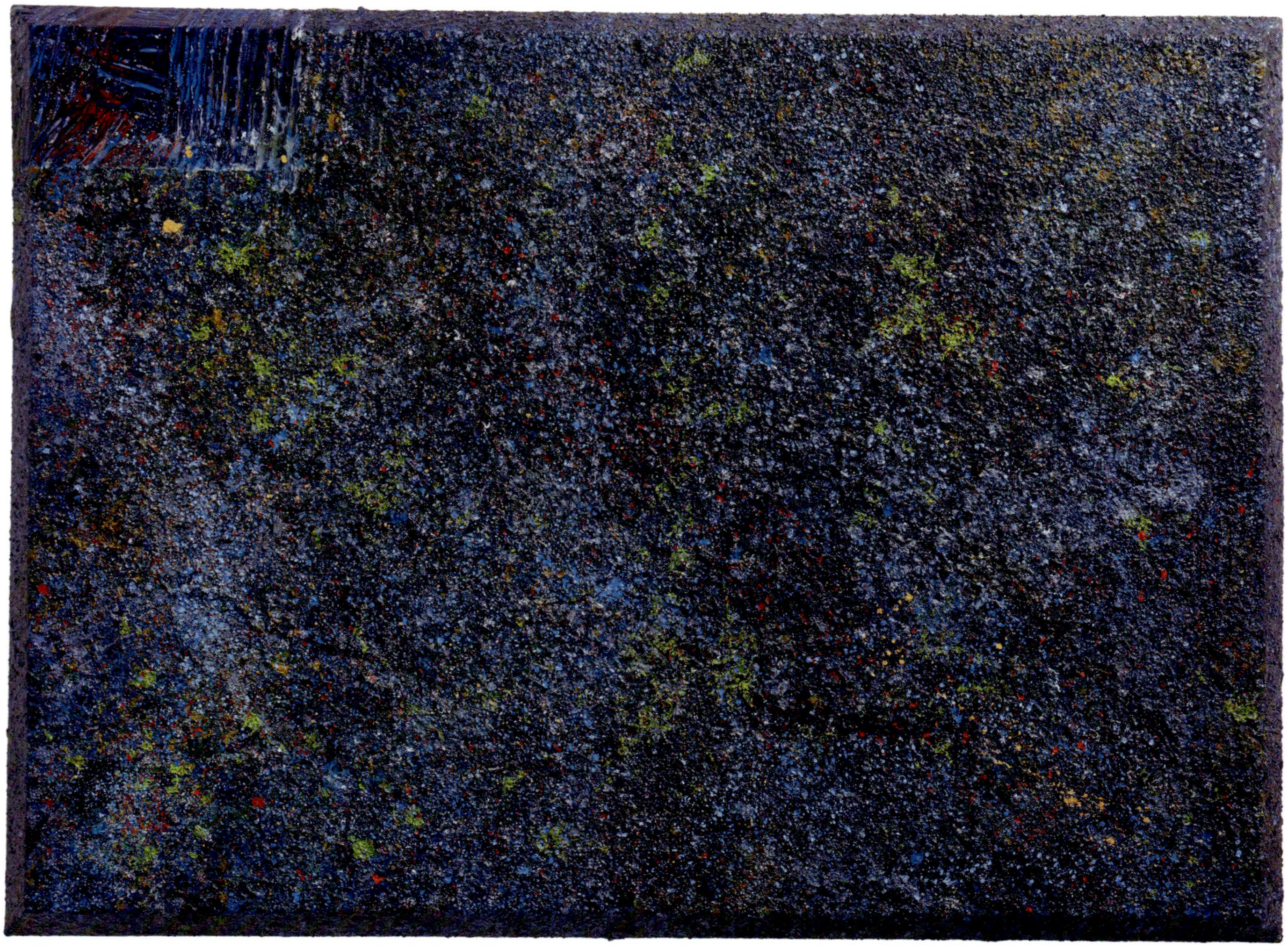

Heroines, Beyoncé, Serena and Althea, 2020

Purple Orpheus, 2020

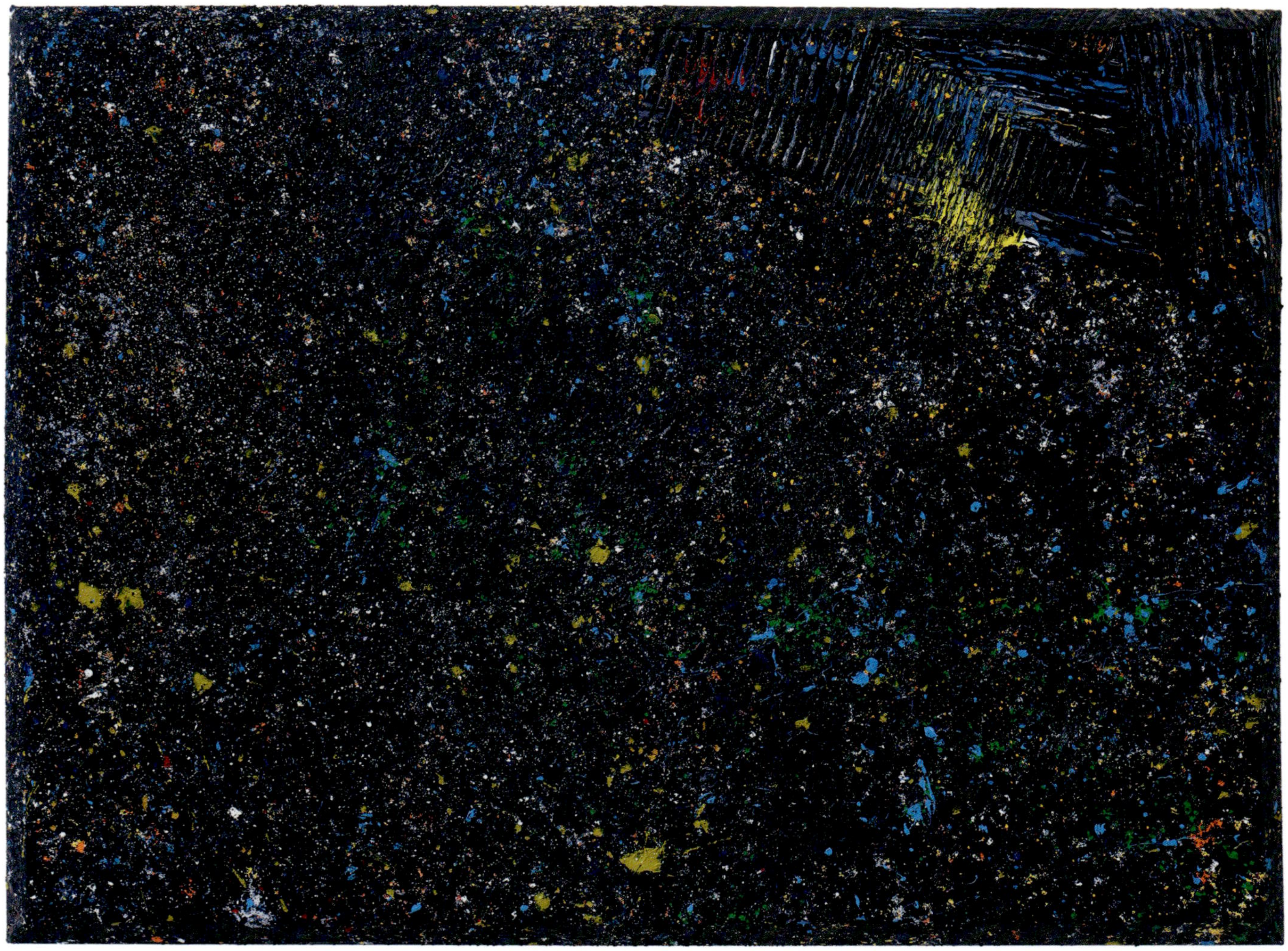

For John Lewis, 2020

—I KNOW
THAT THE
NATURE OF

MAN AS DEFINED BY ART, IS IN ME.

Wizard XX, 2014

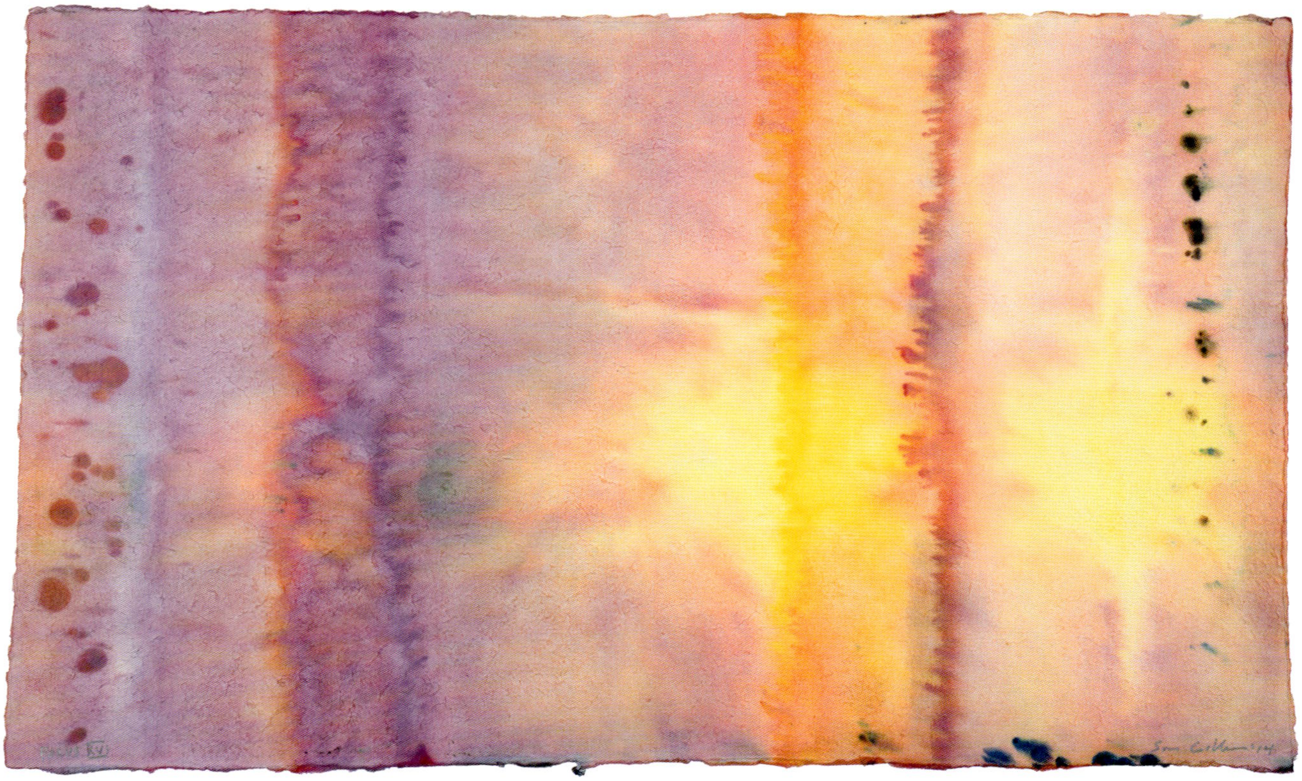

Focus XVI, 2014

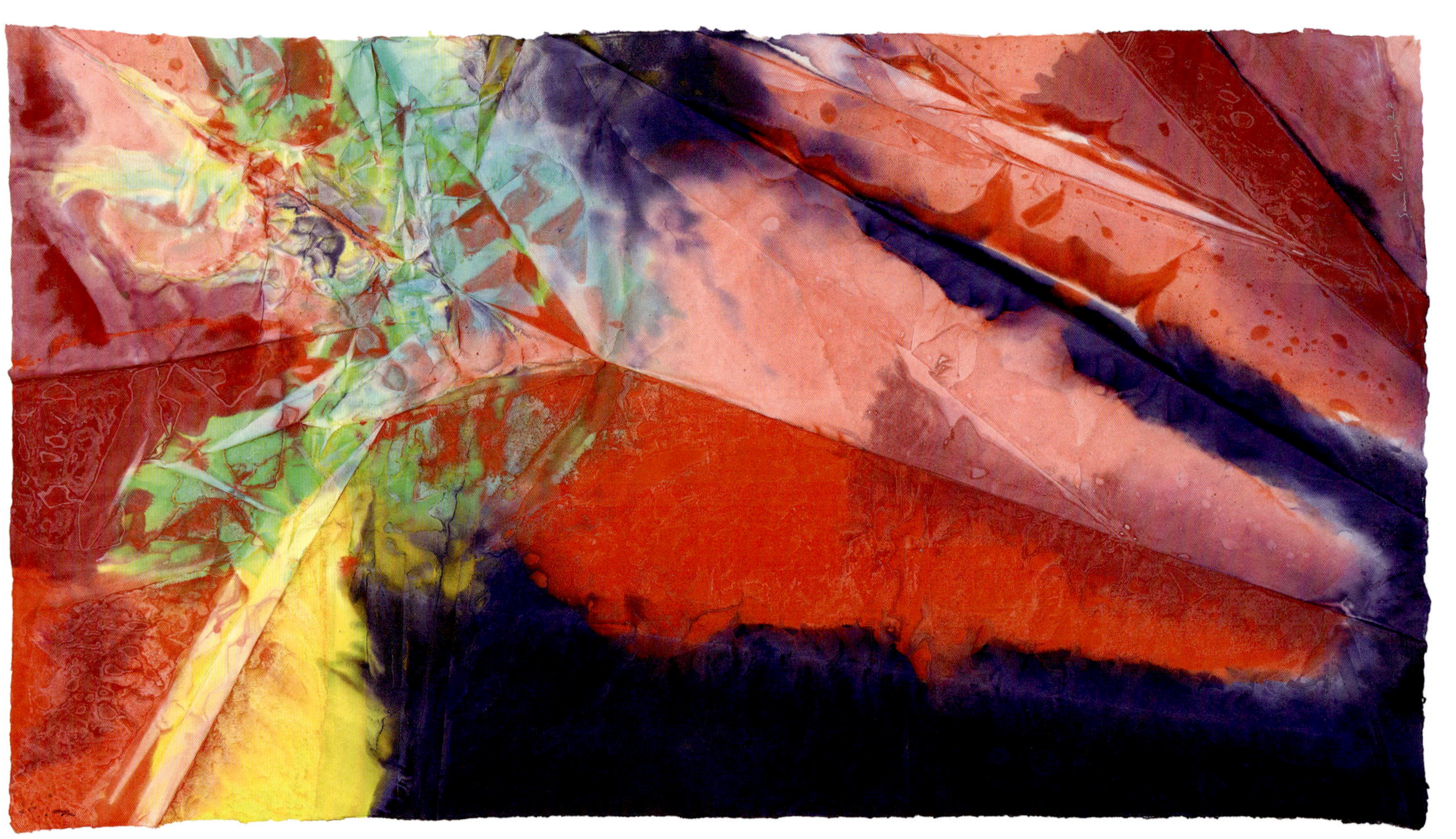

Untitled, 2022

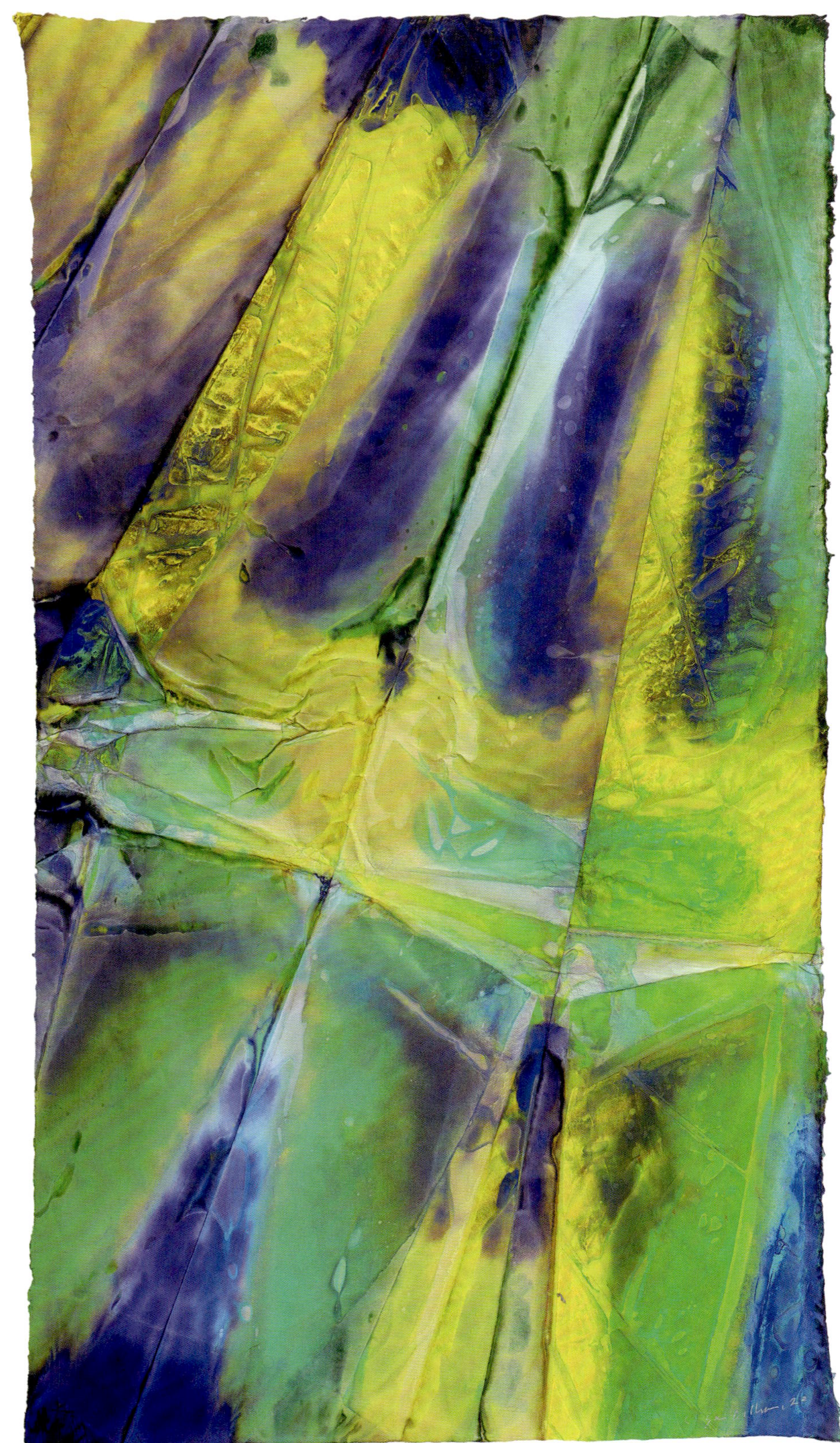

Untitled, 2022

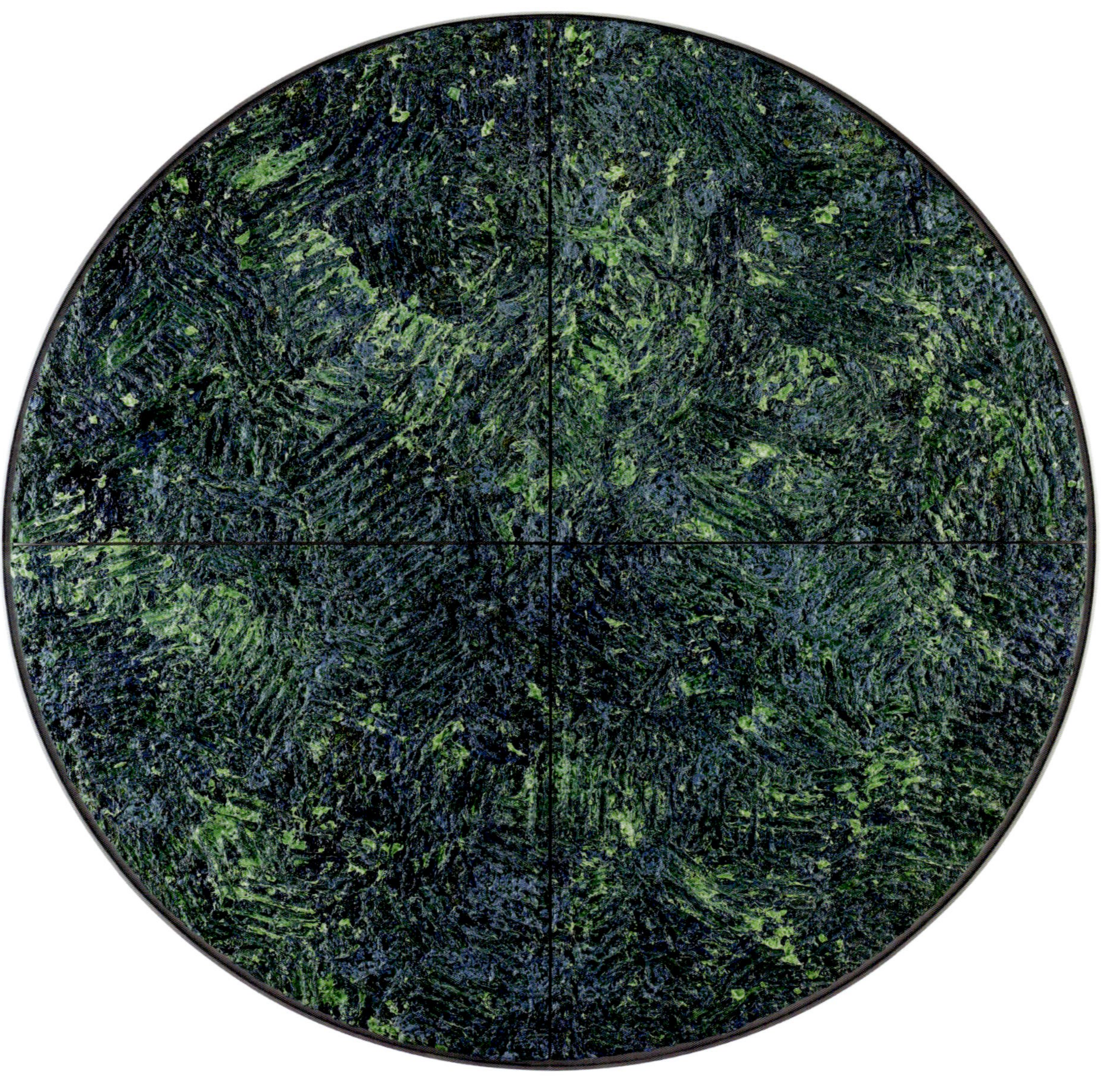

Untitled, 2022

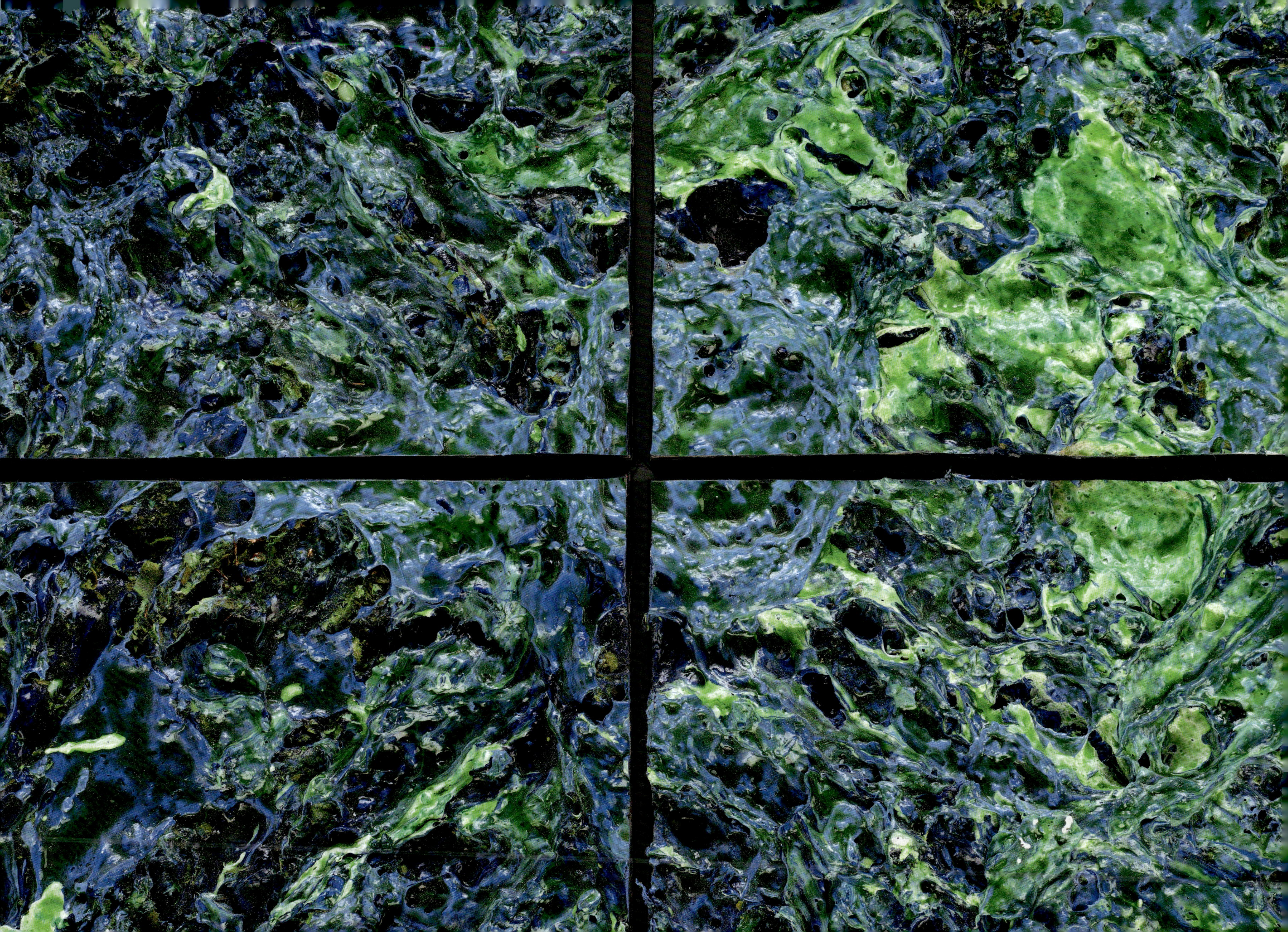

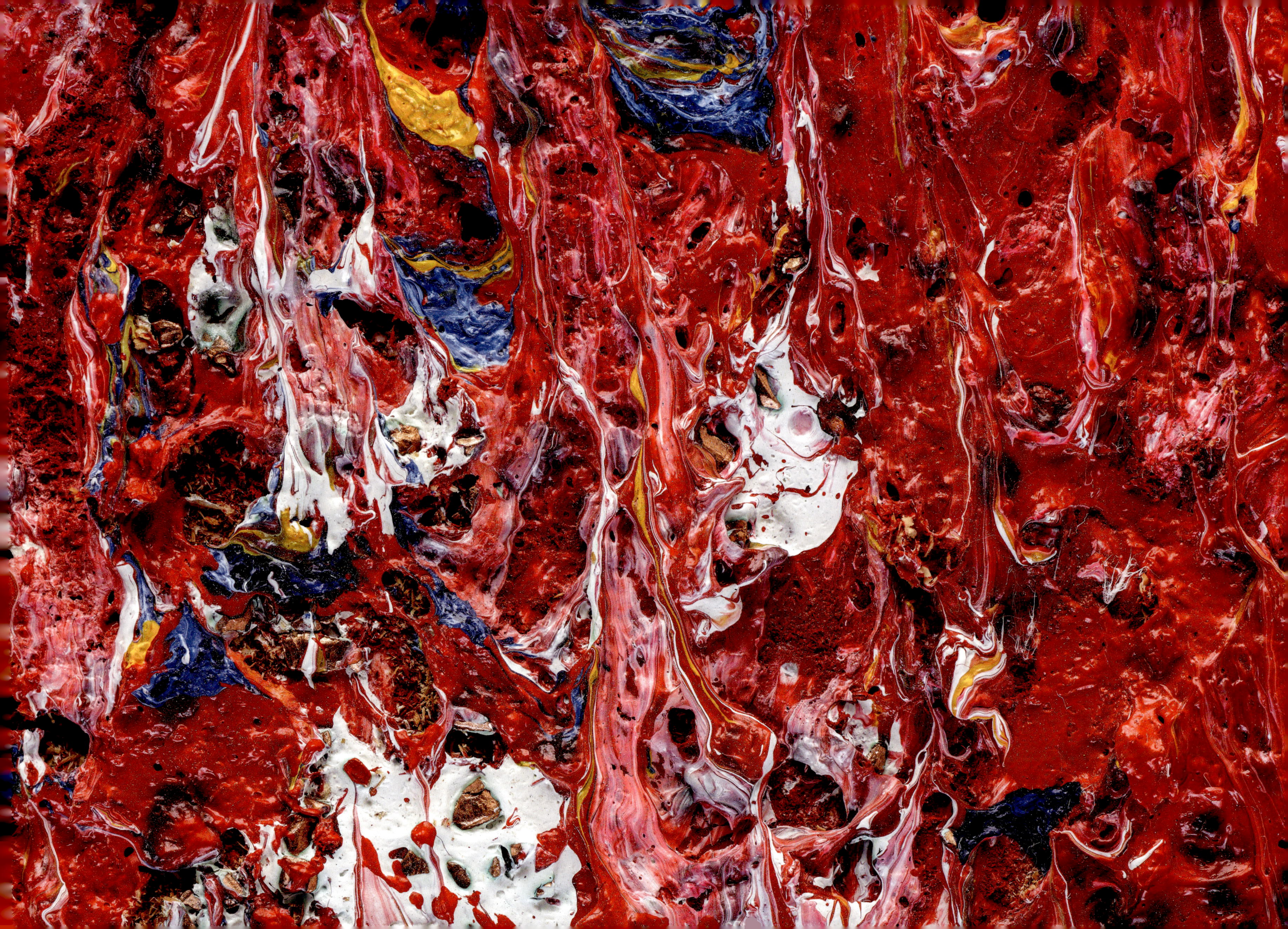

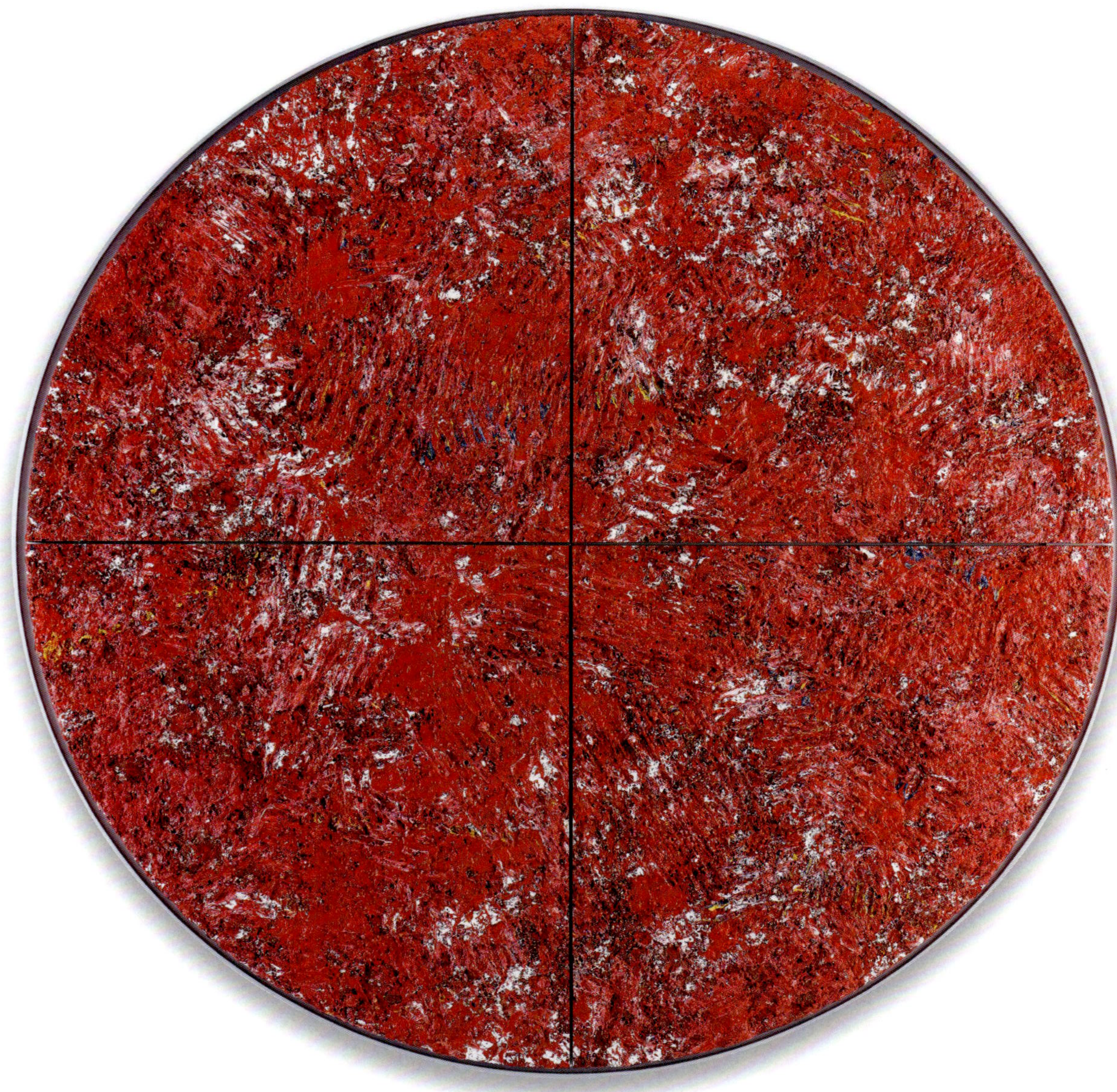

Untitled, 2022

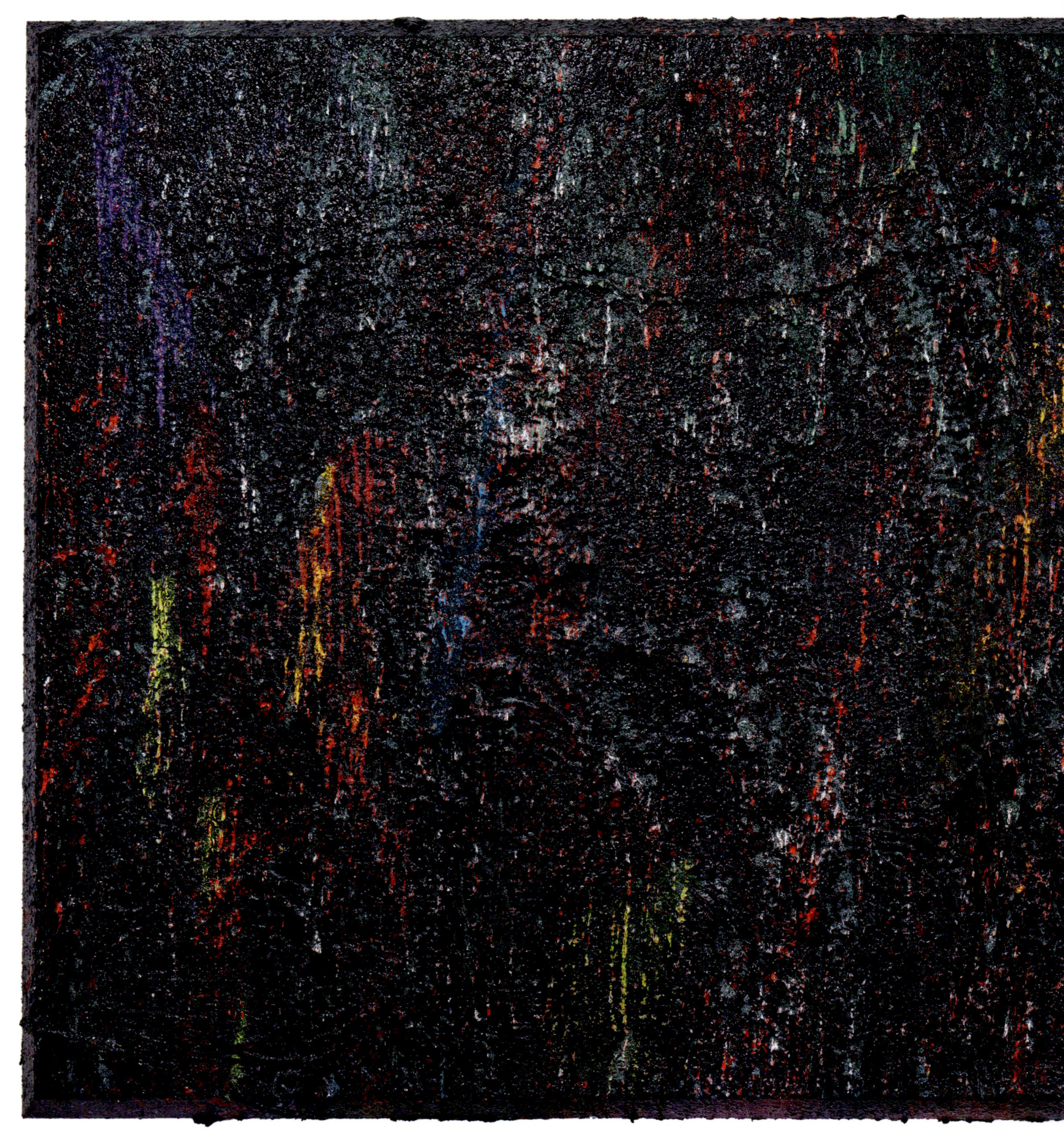

What!, 2021

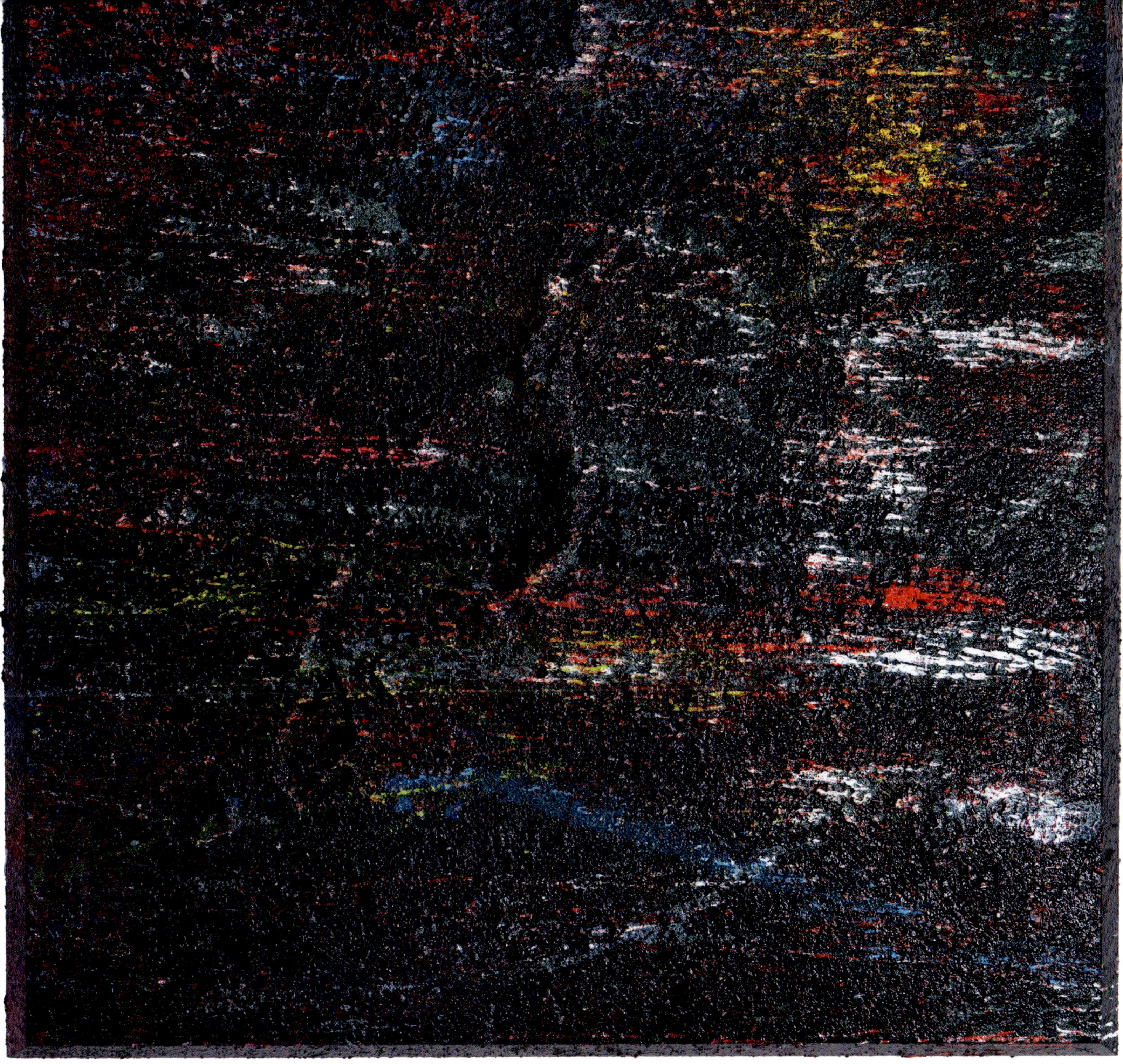

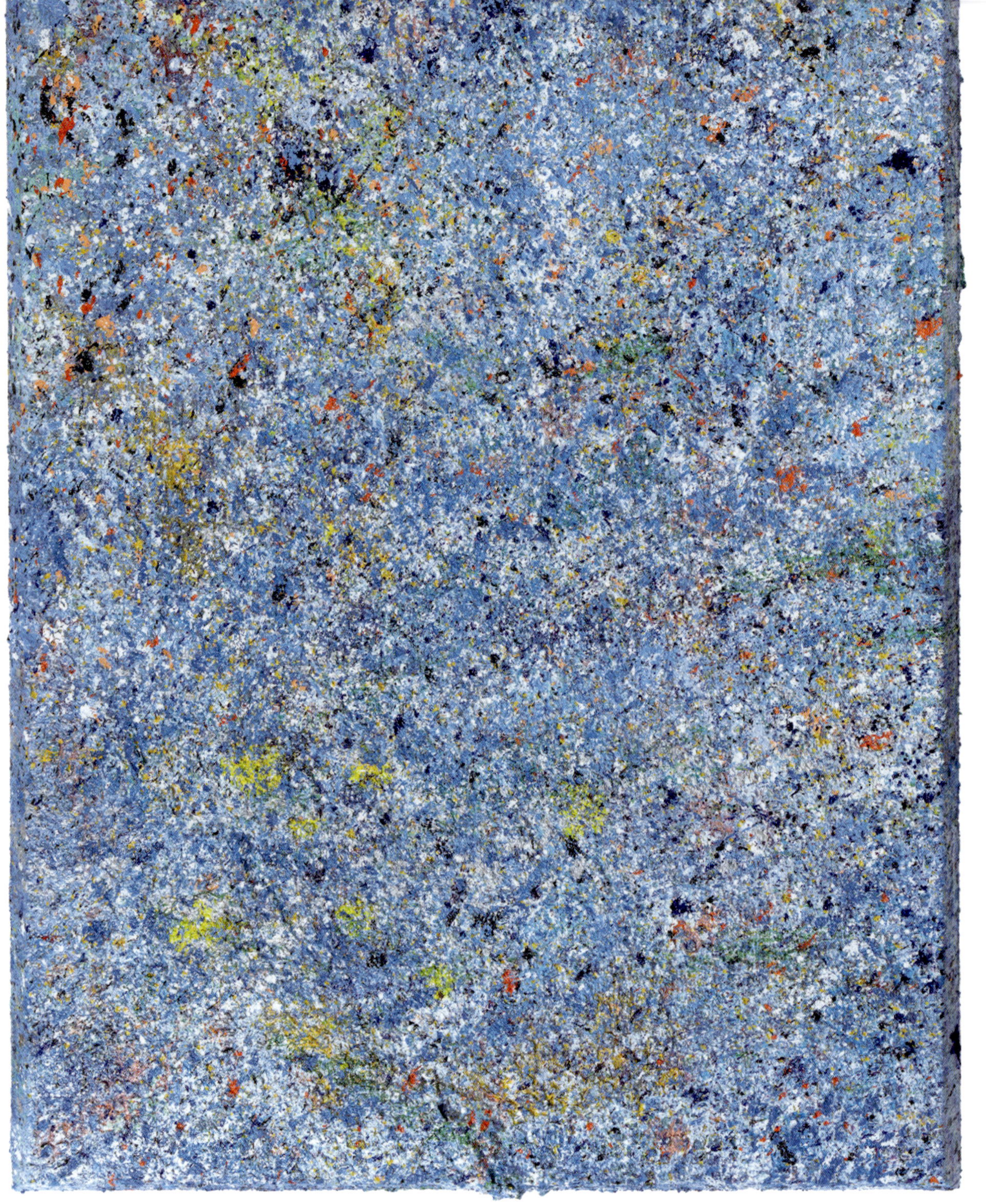

A Lovely Blue And!, 2021

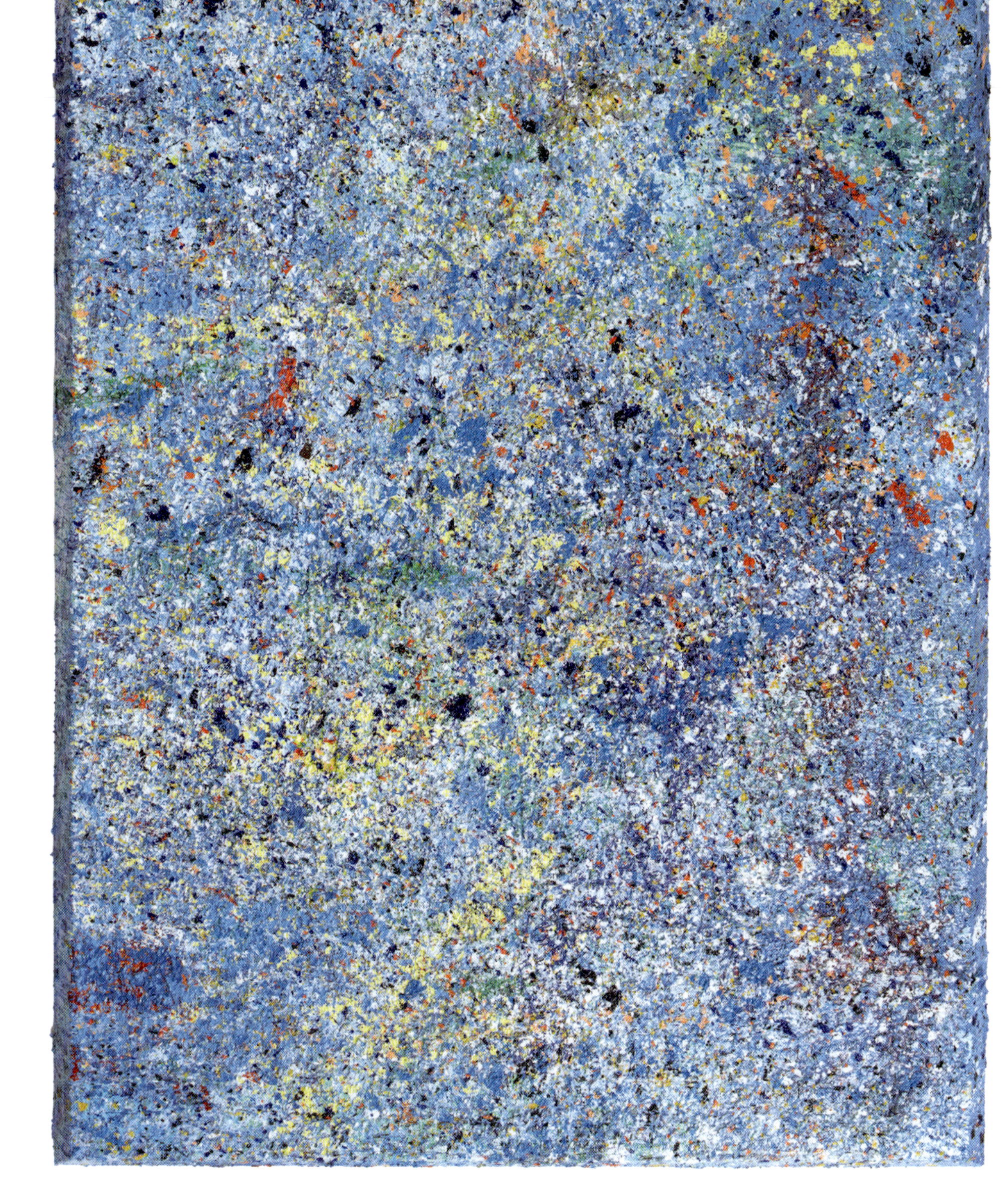

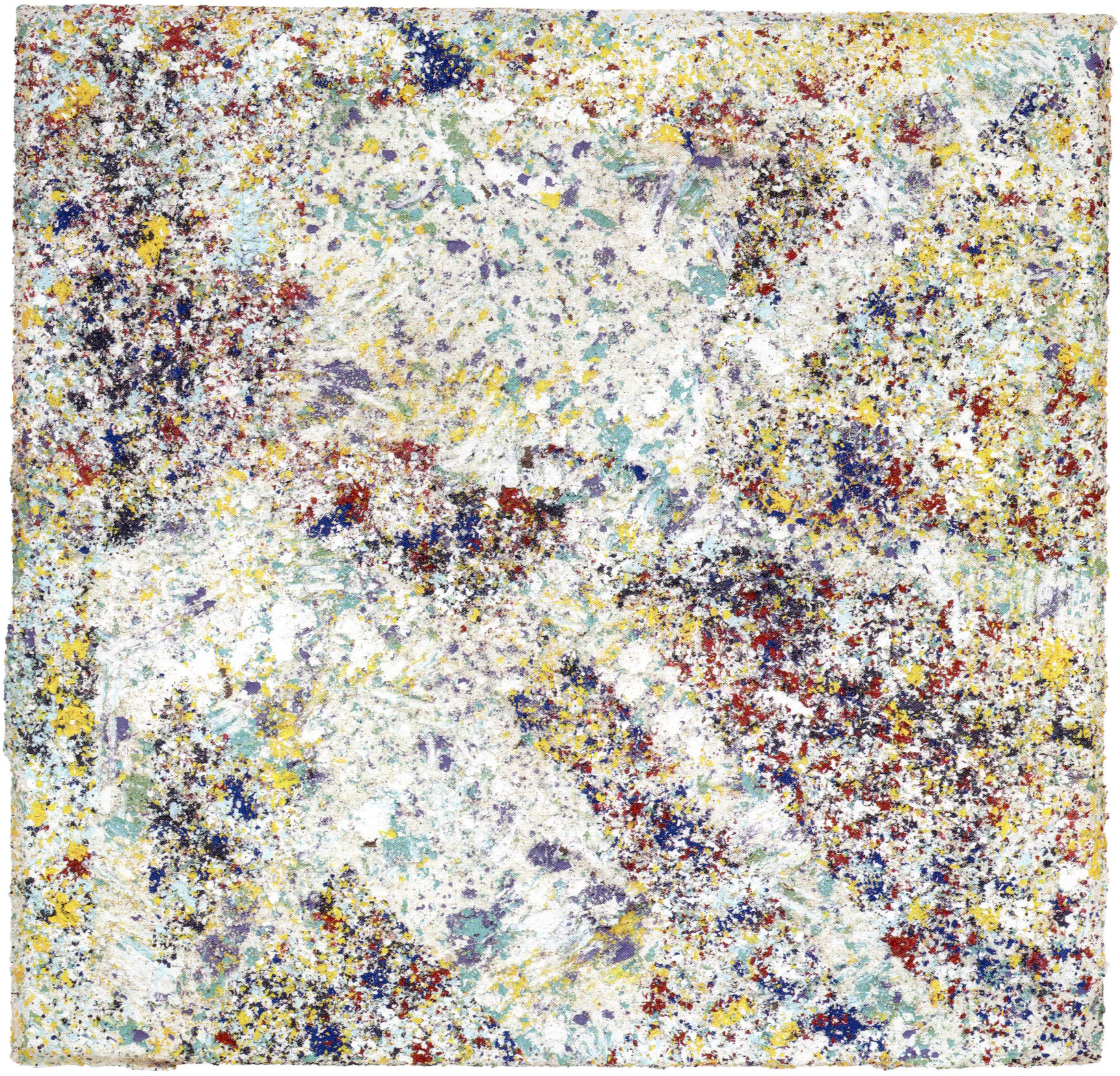

Lilly, 2022

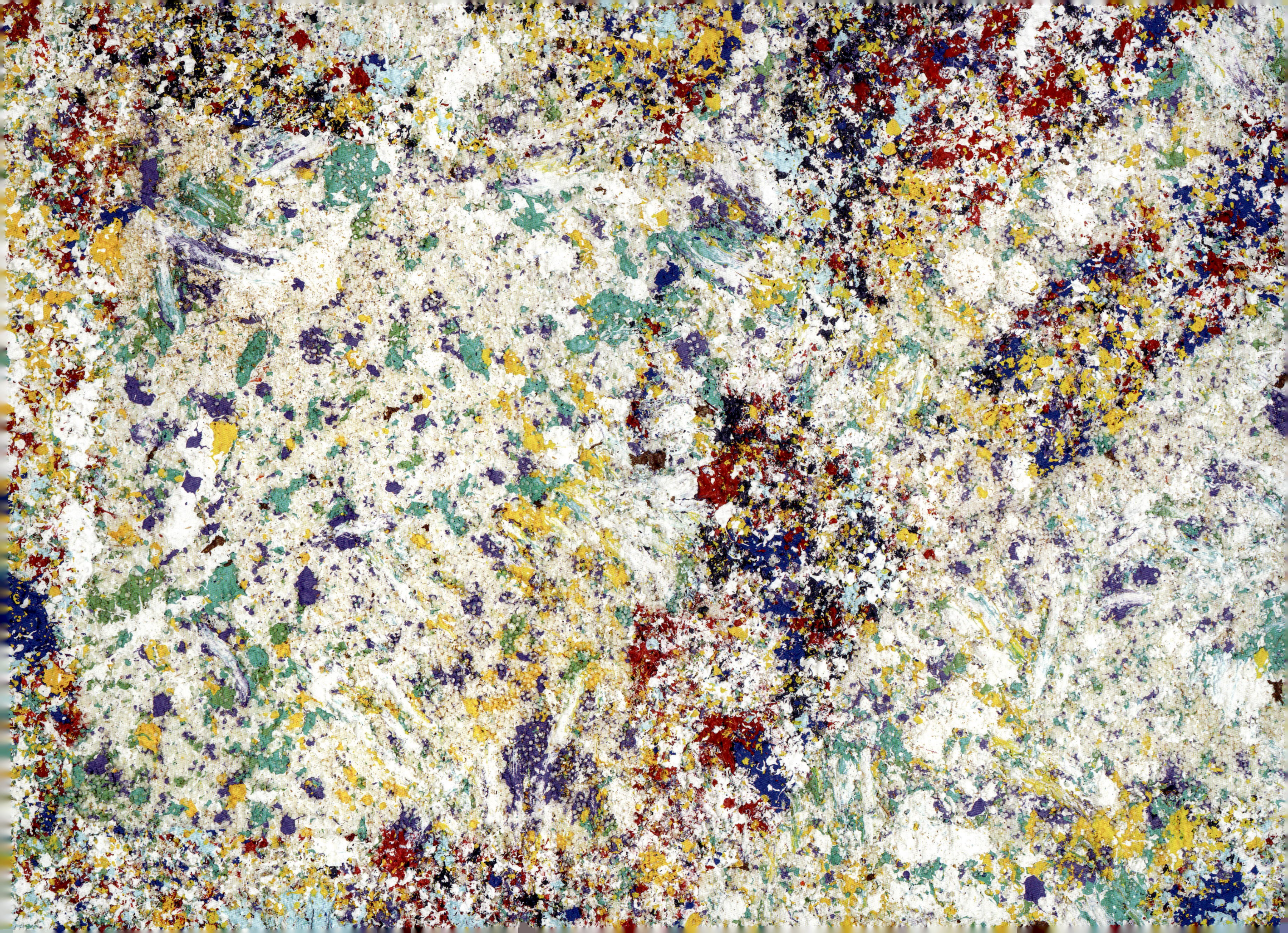

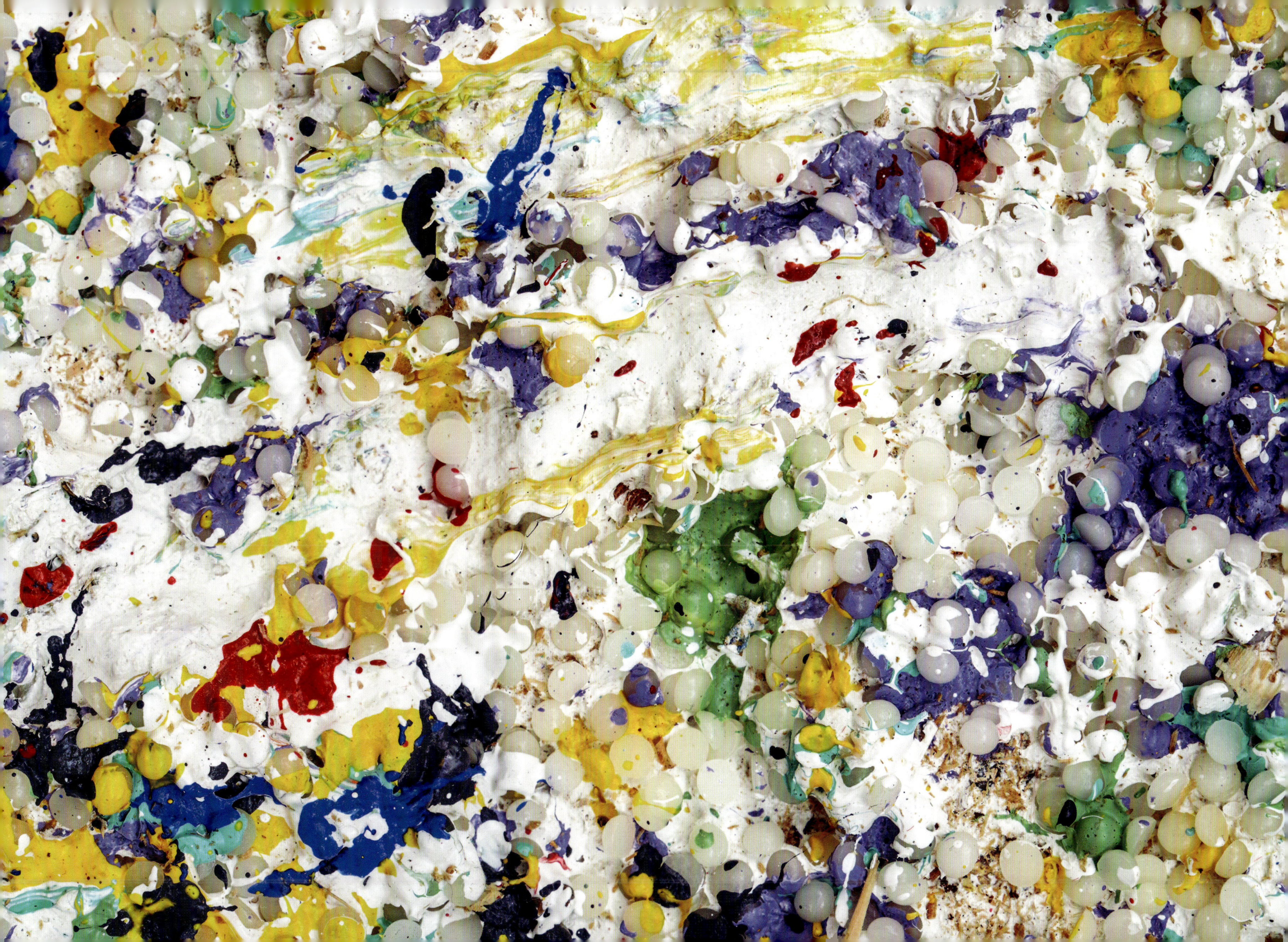

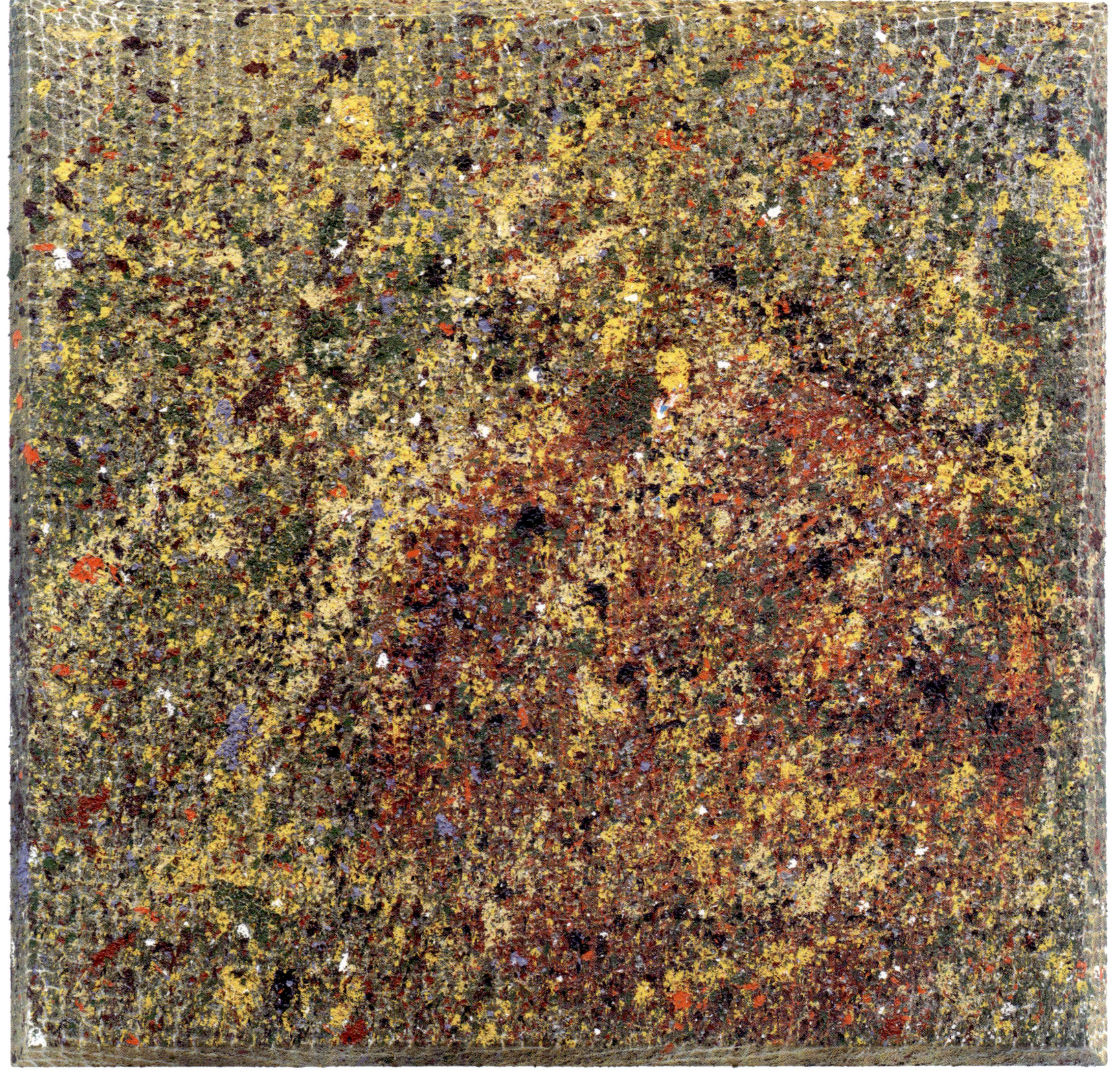

Gold Mine, 2021

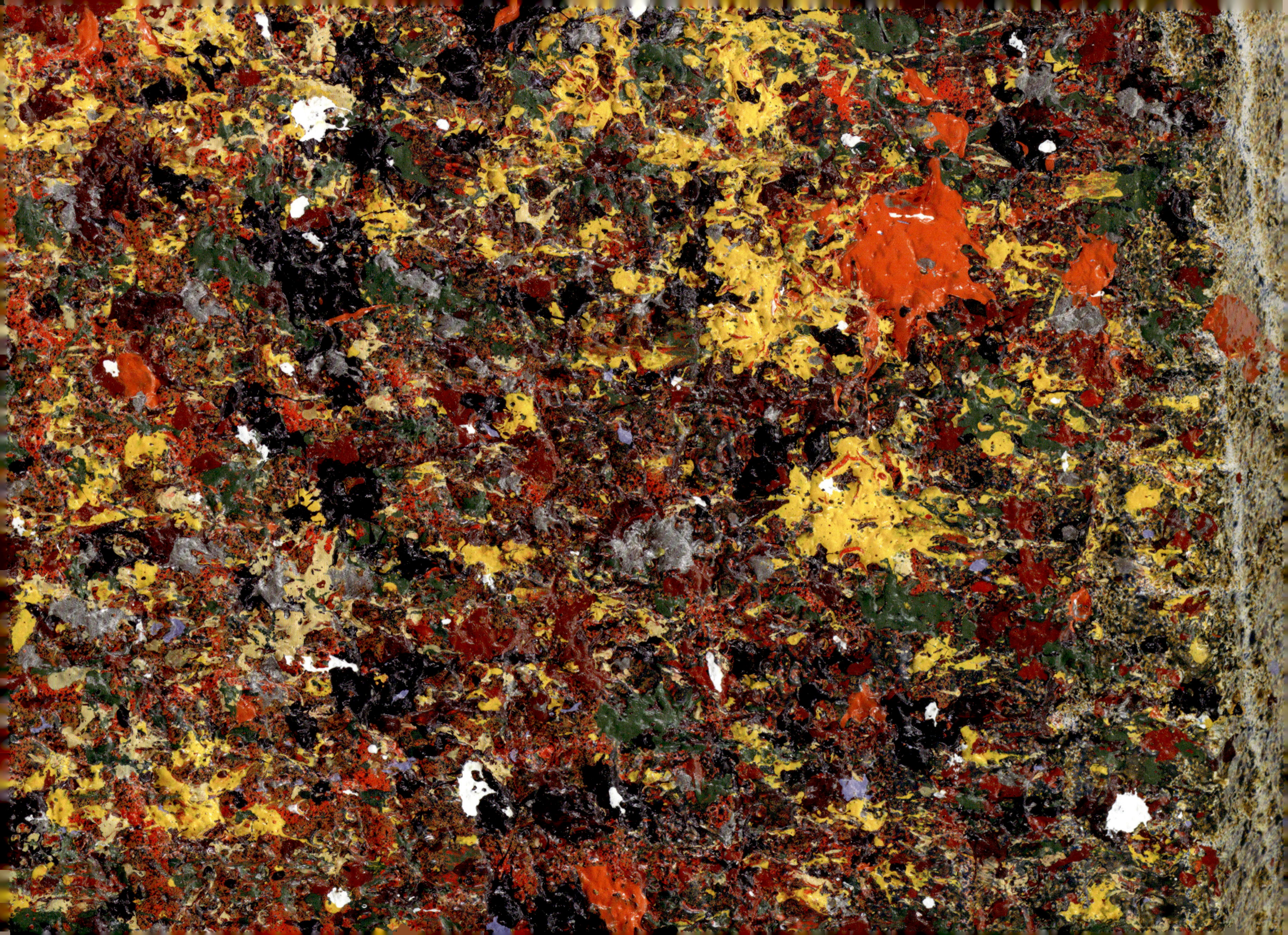

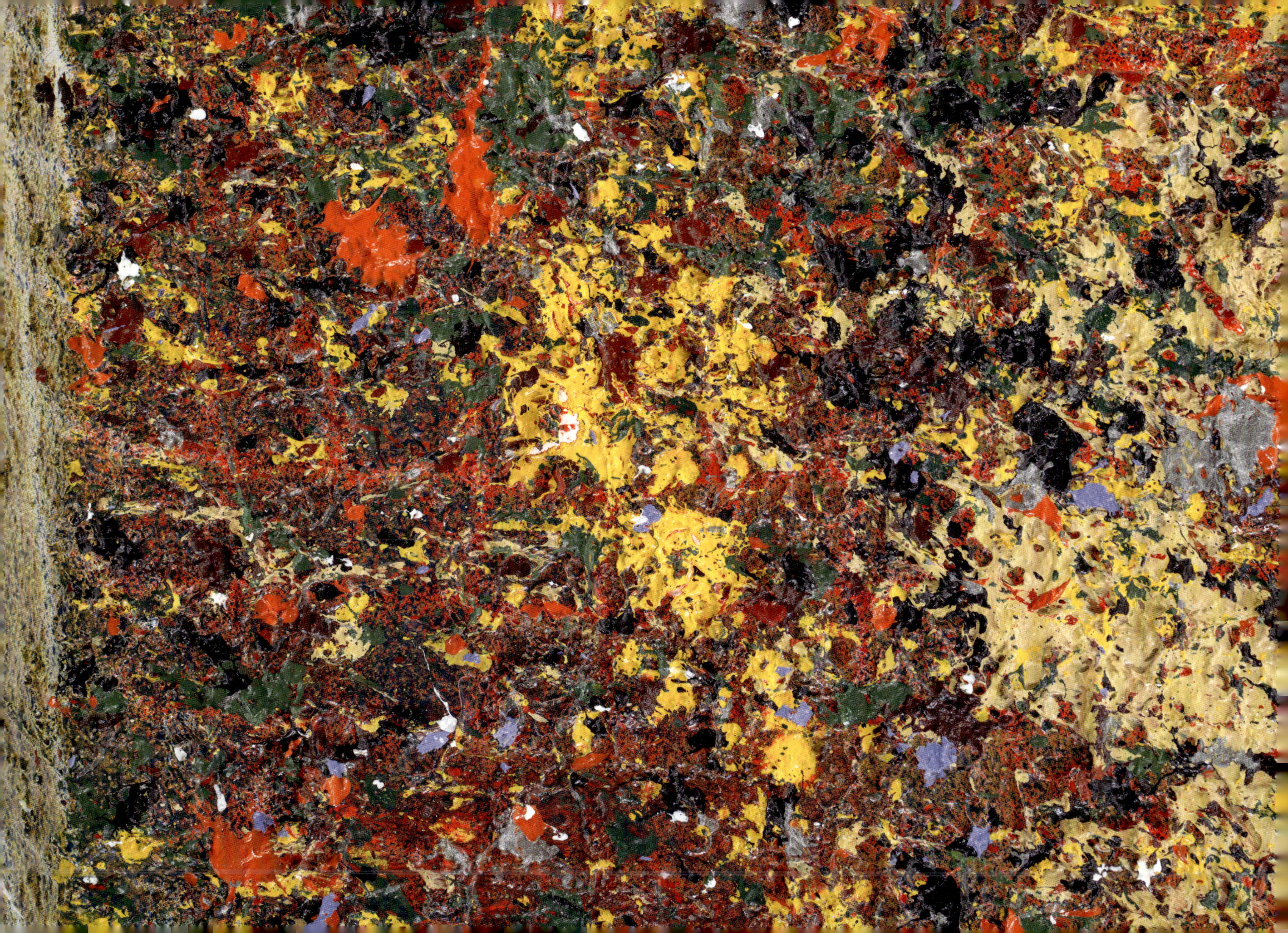

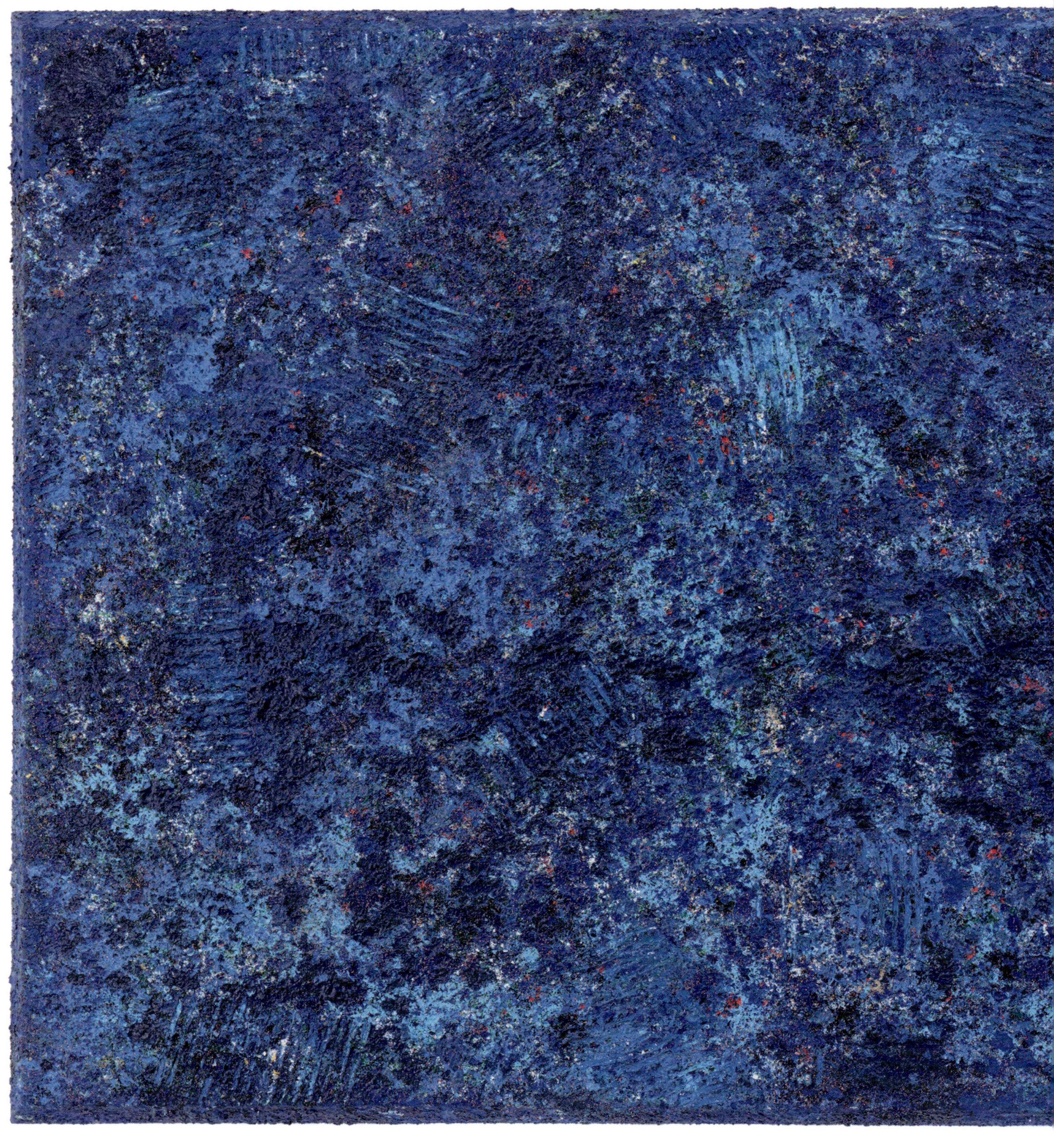

Nina's Buffalo, 2022

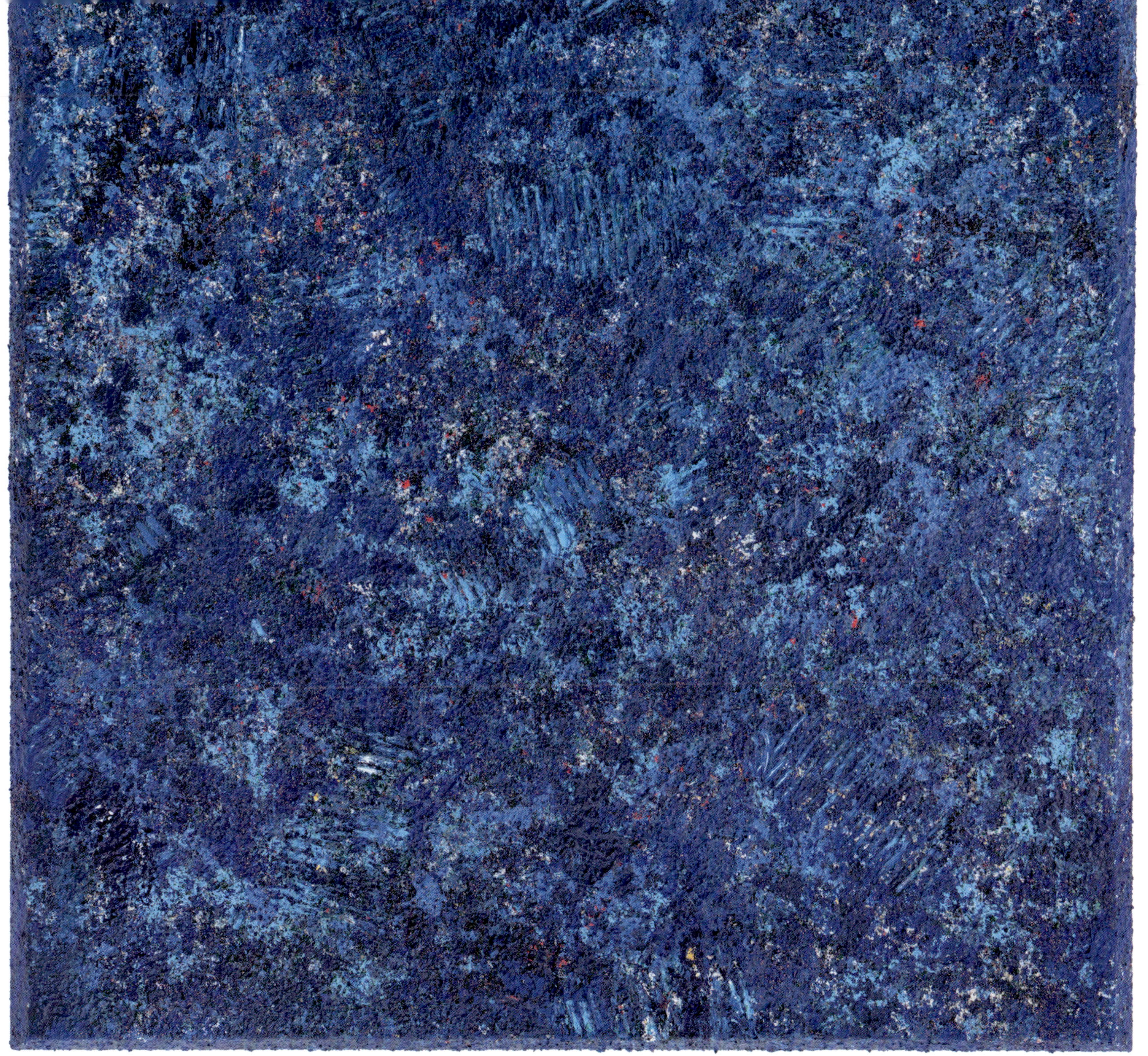

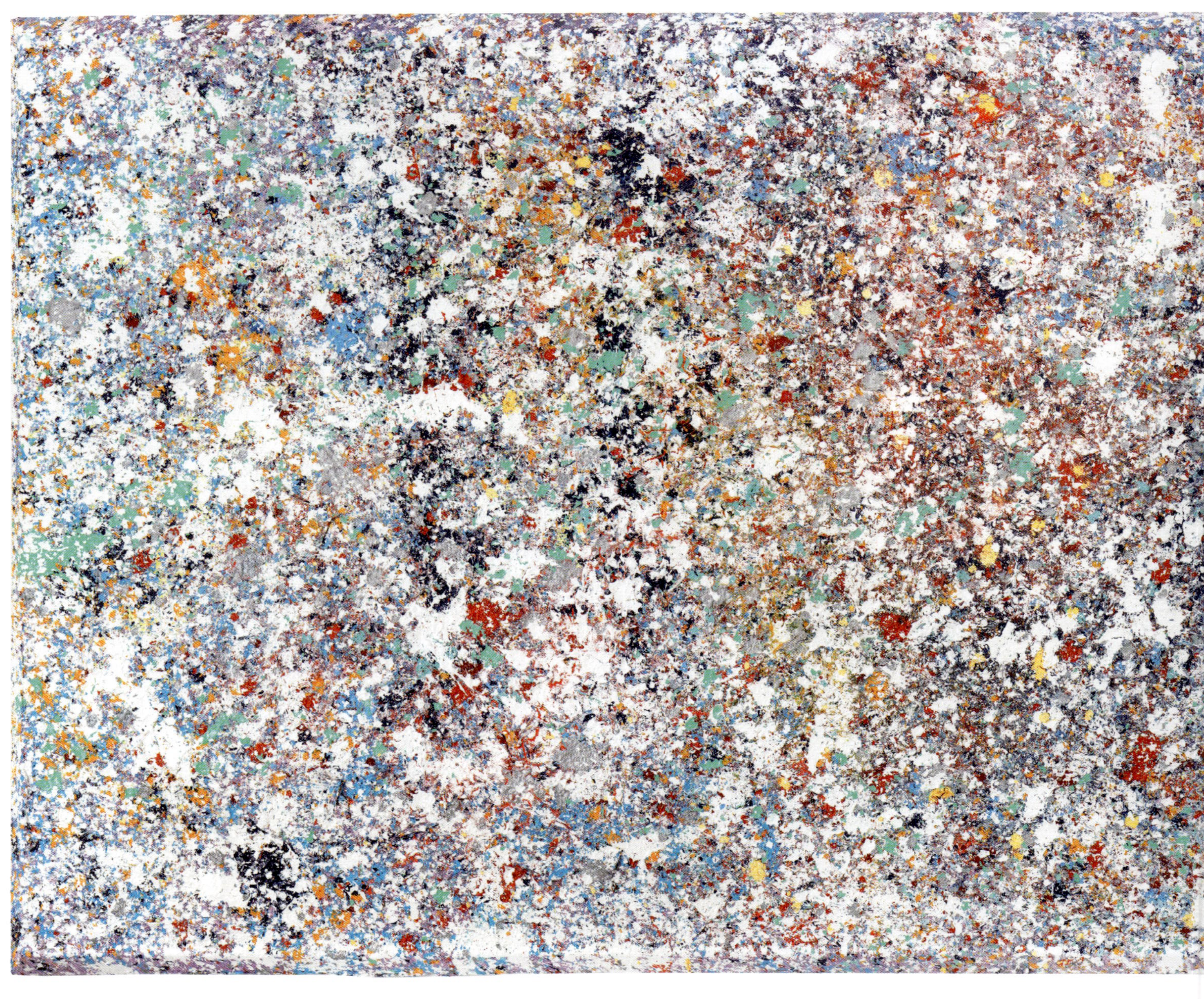

For "The Friend", 2021

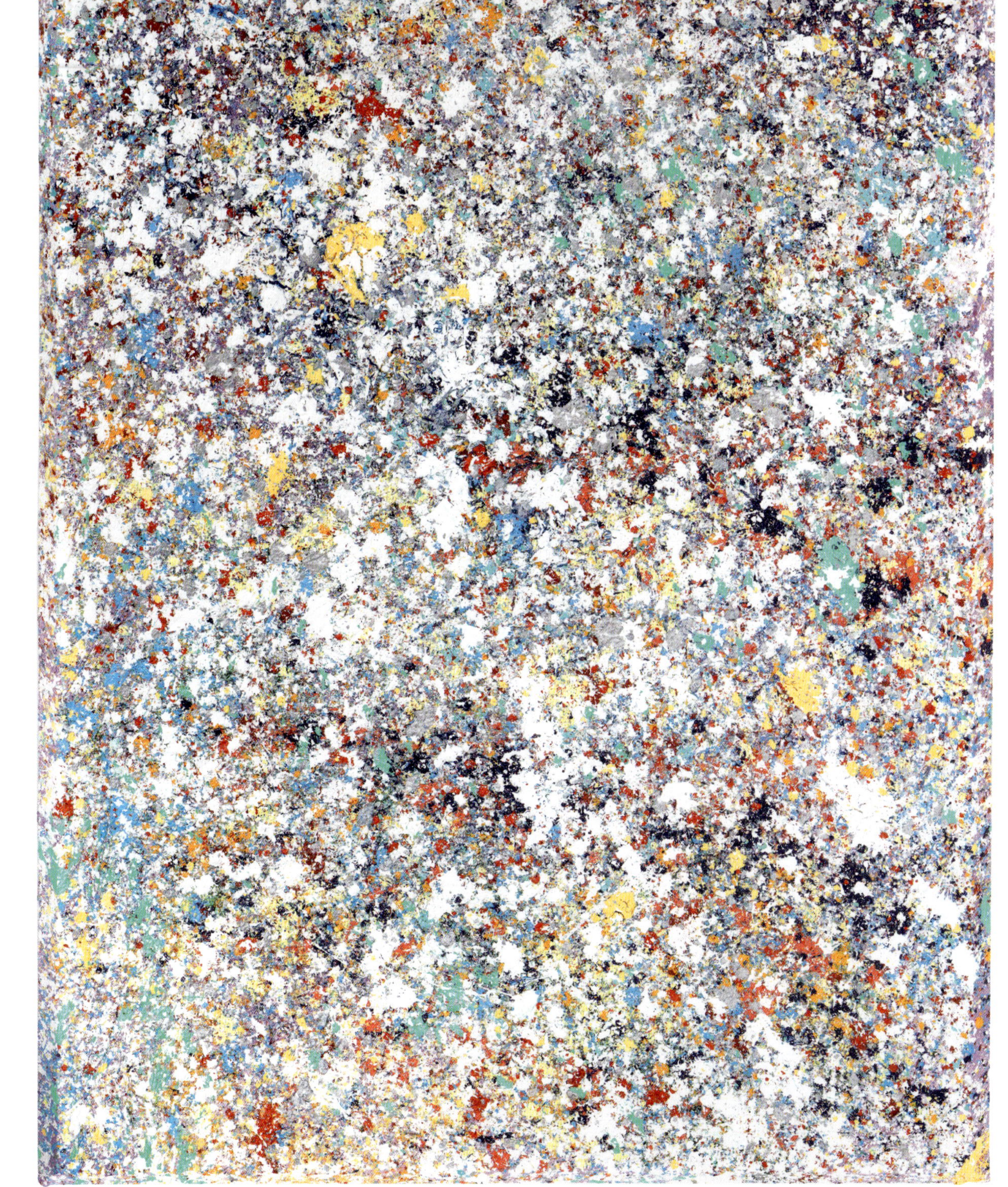

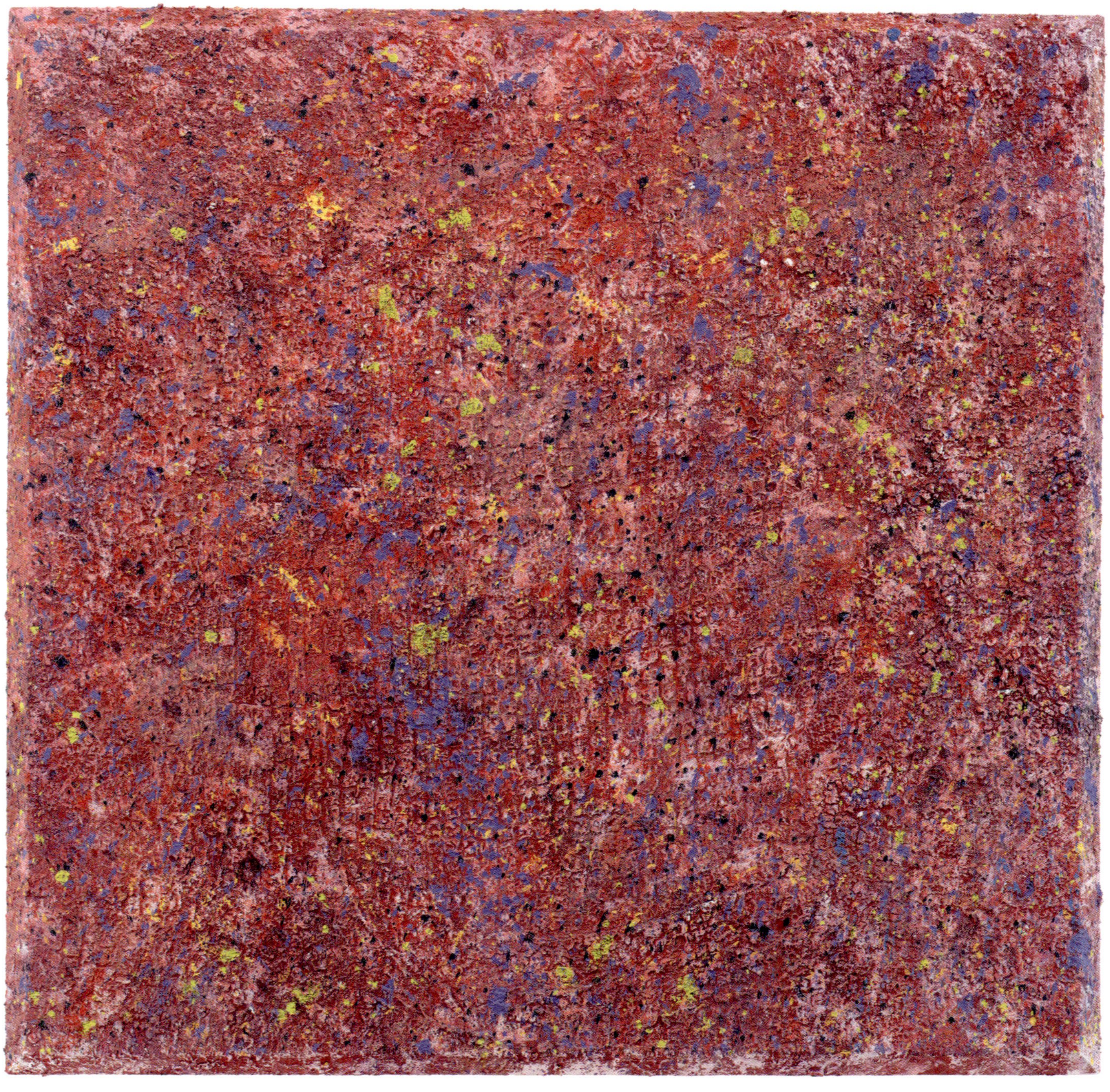

Oak, Net and This!, 2021

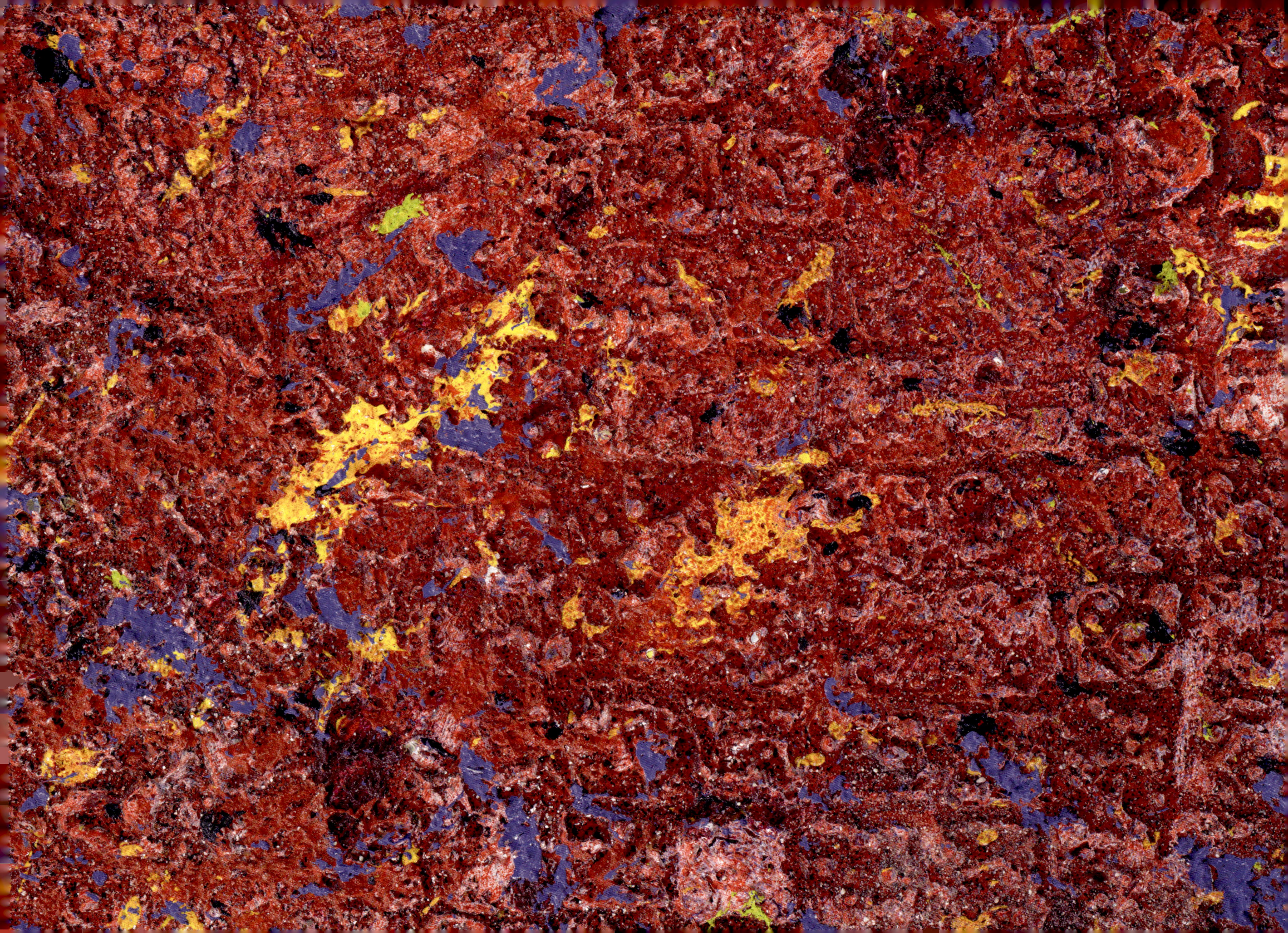

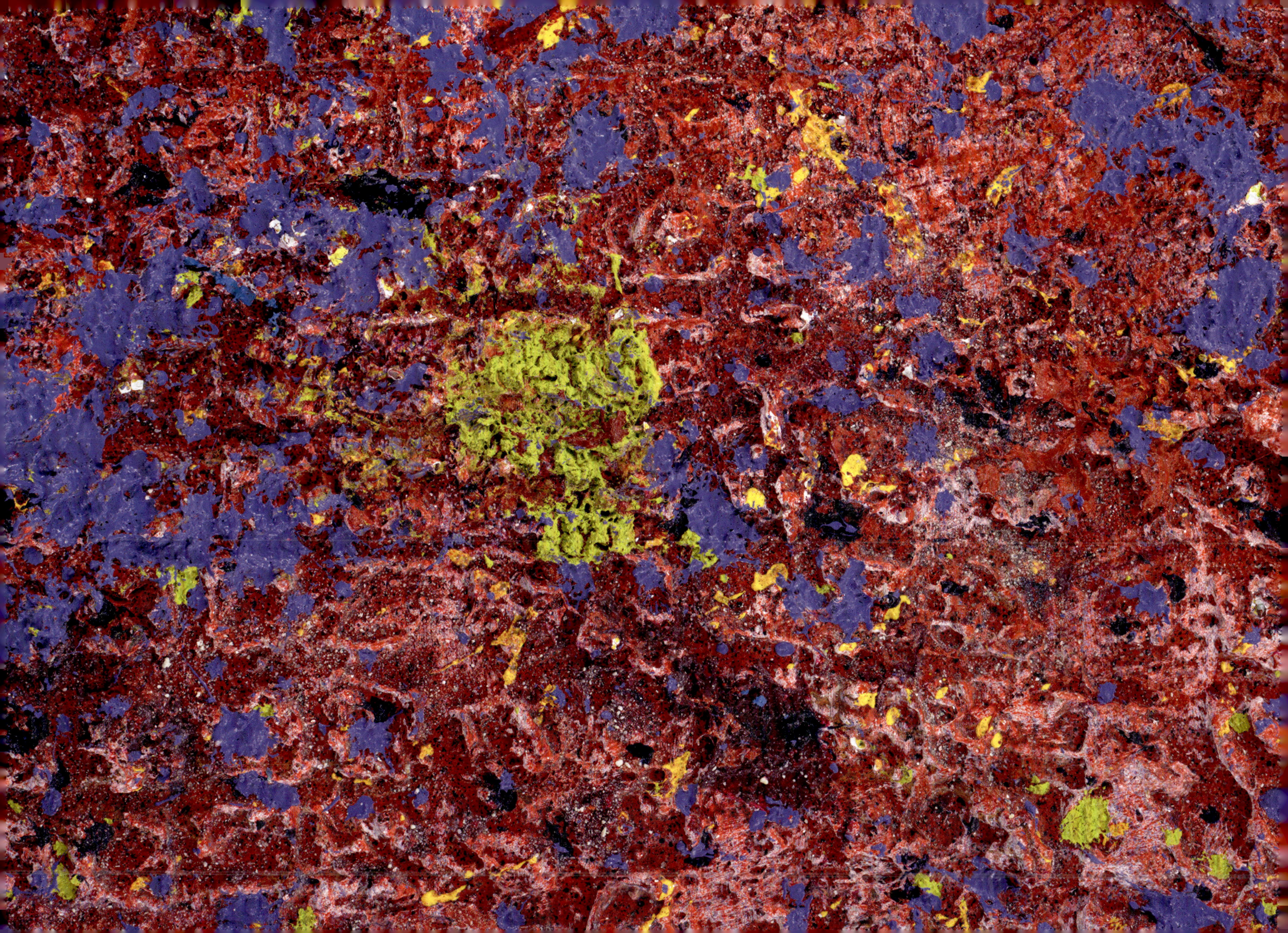

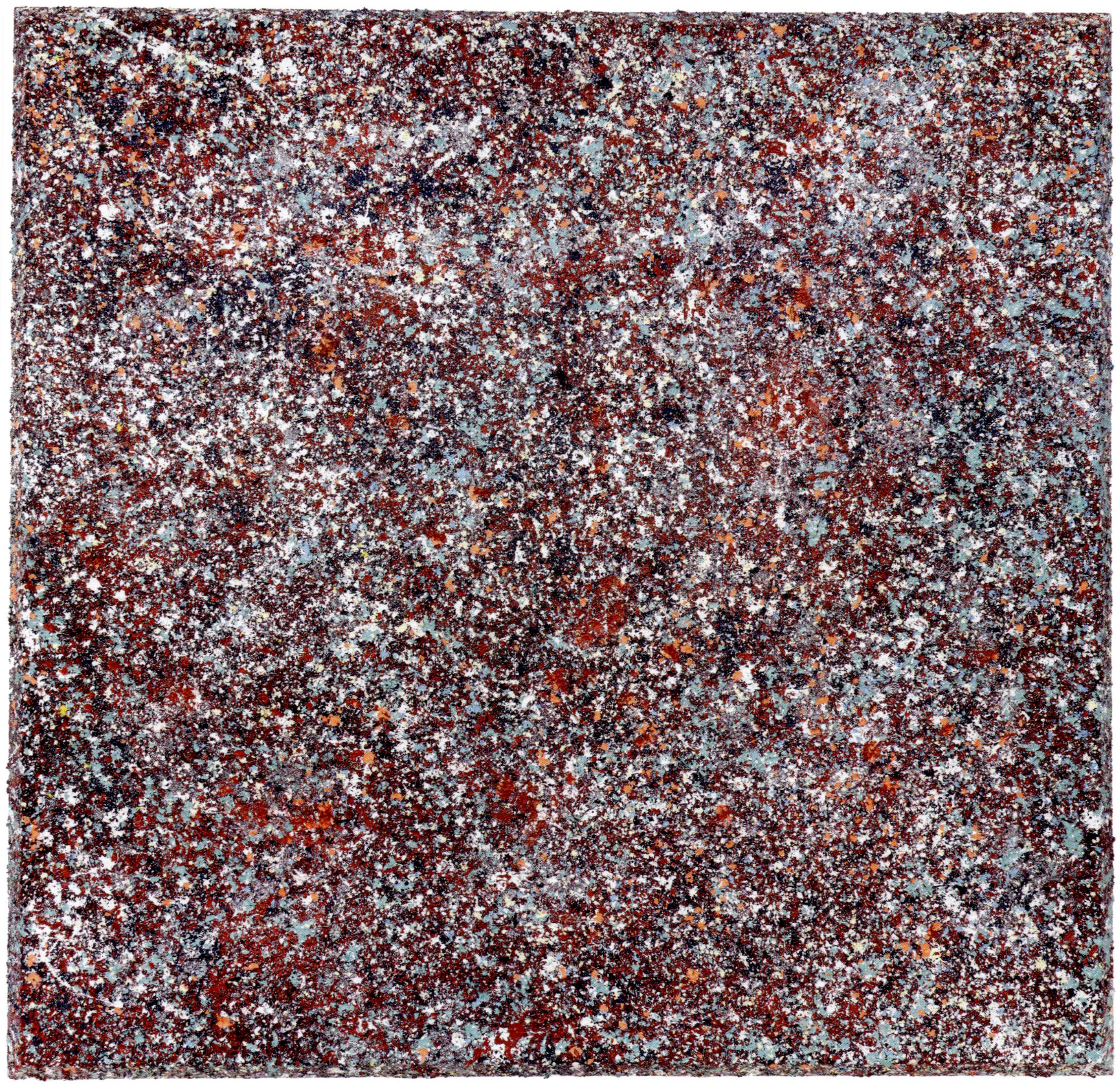

Up Sally, 2022

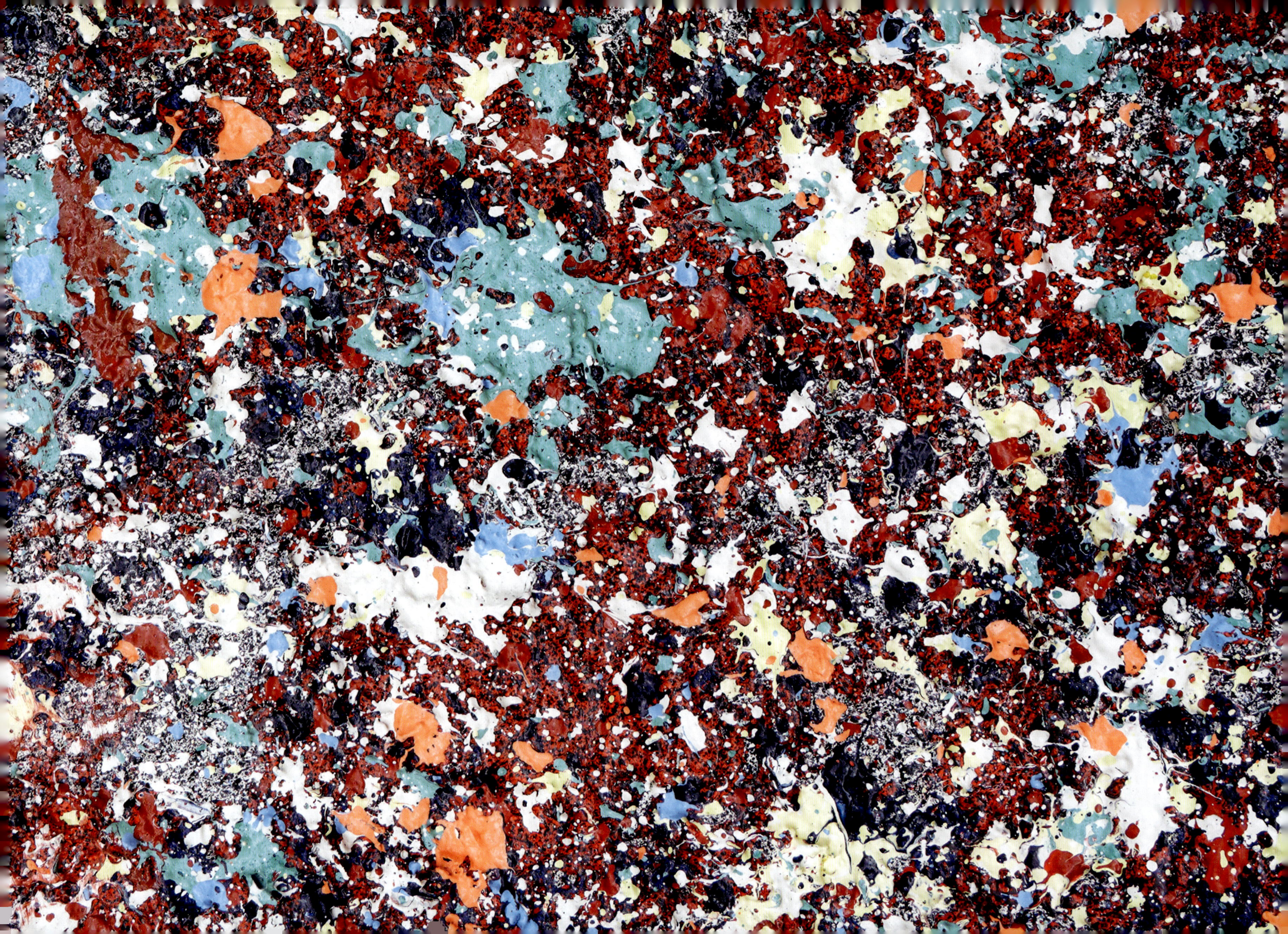

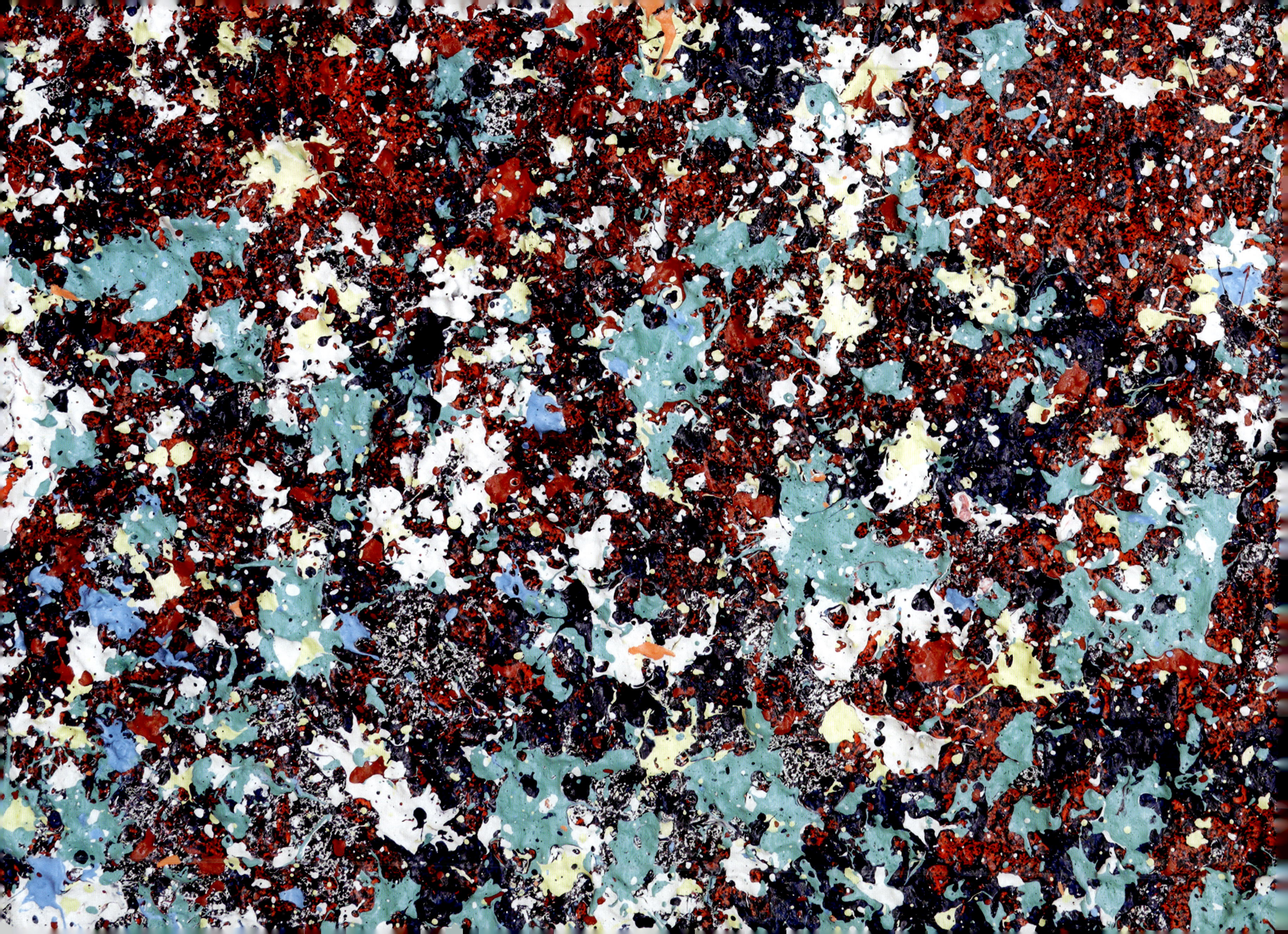

Spring This Time, 2021

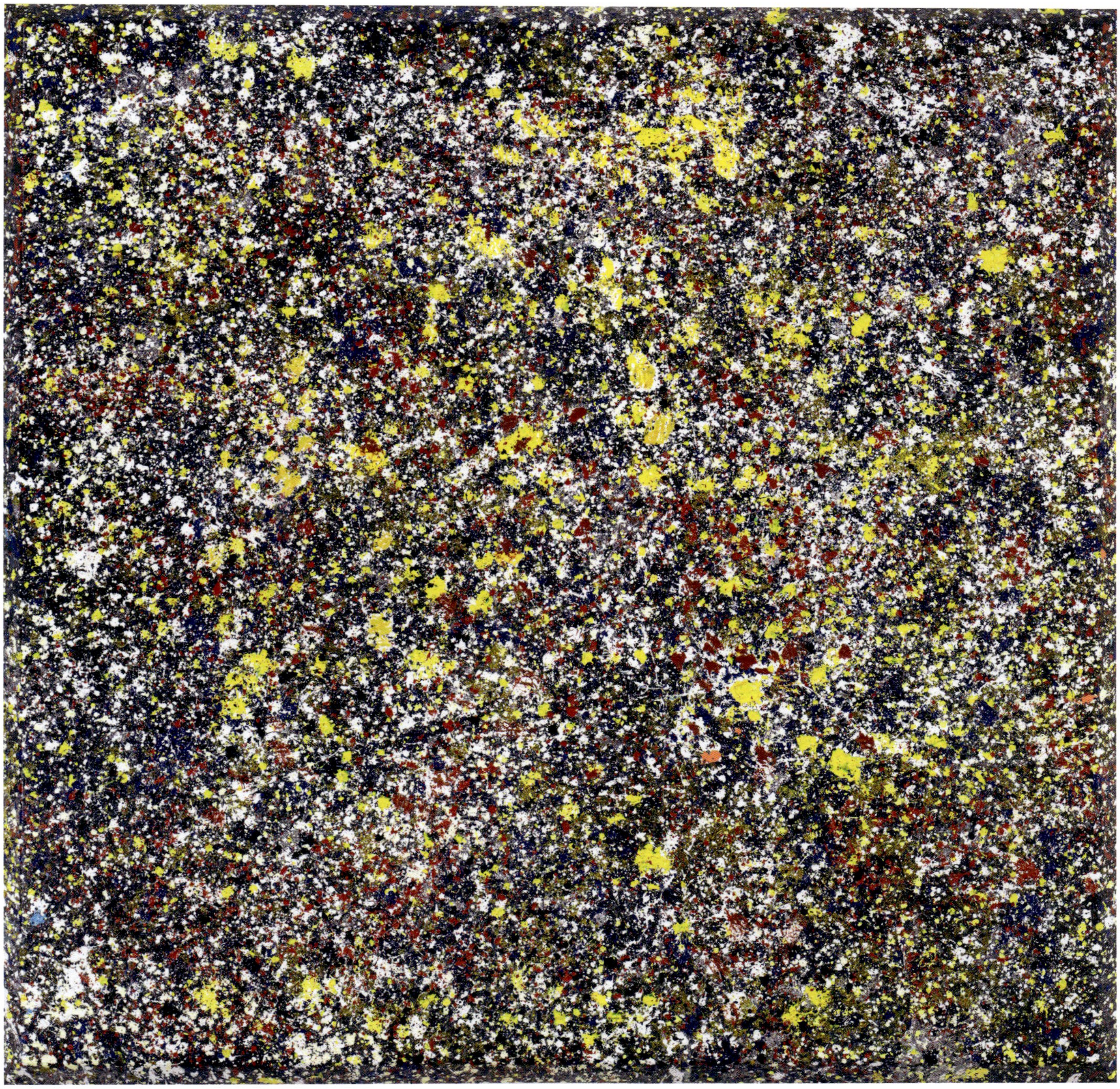

Beyoncé, 2022

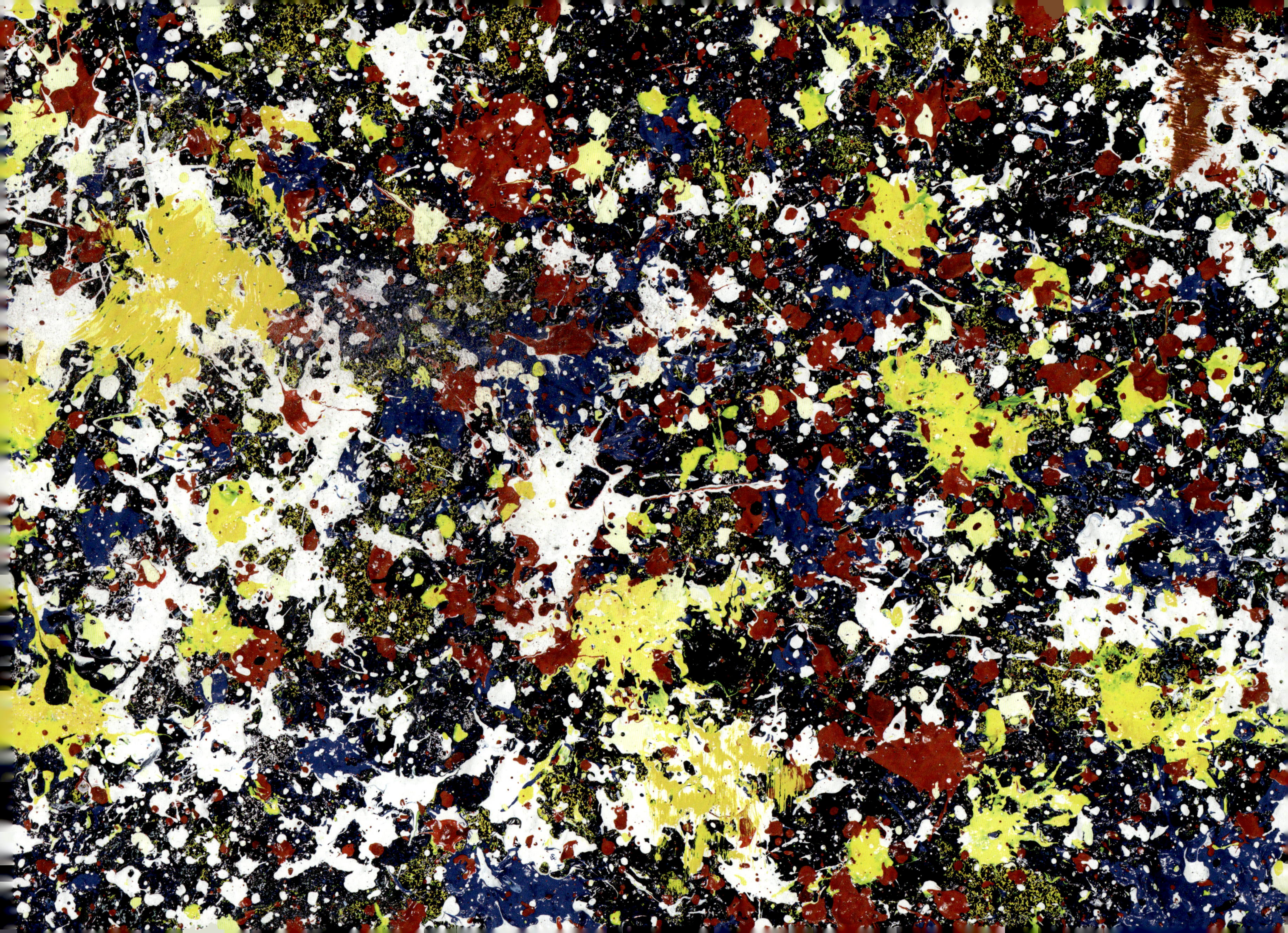

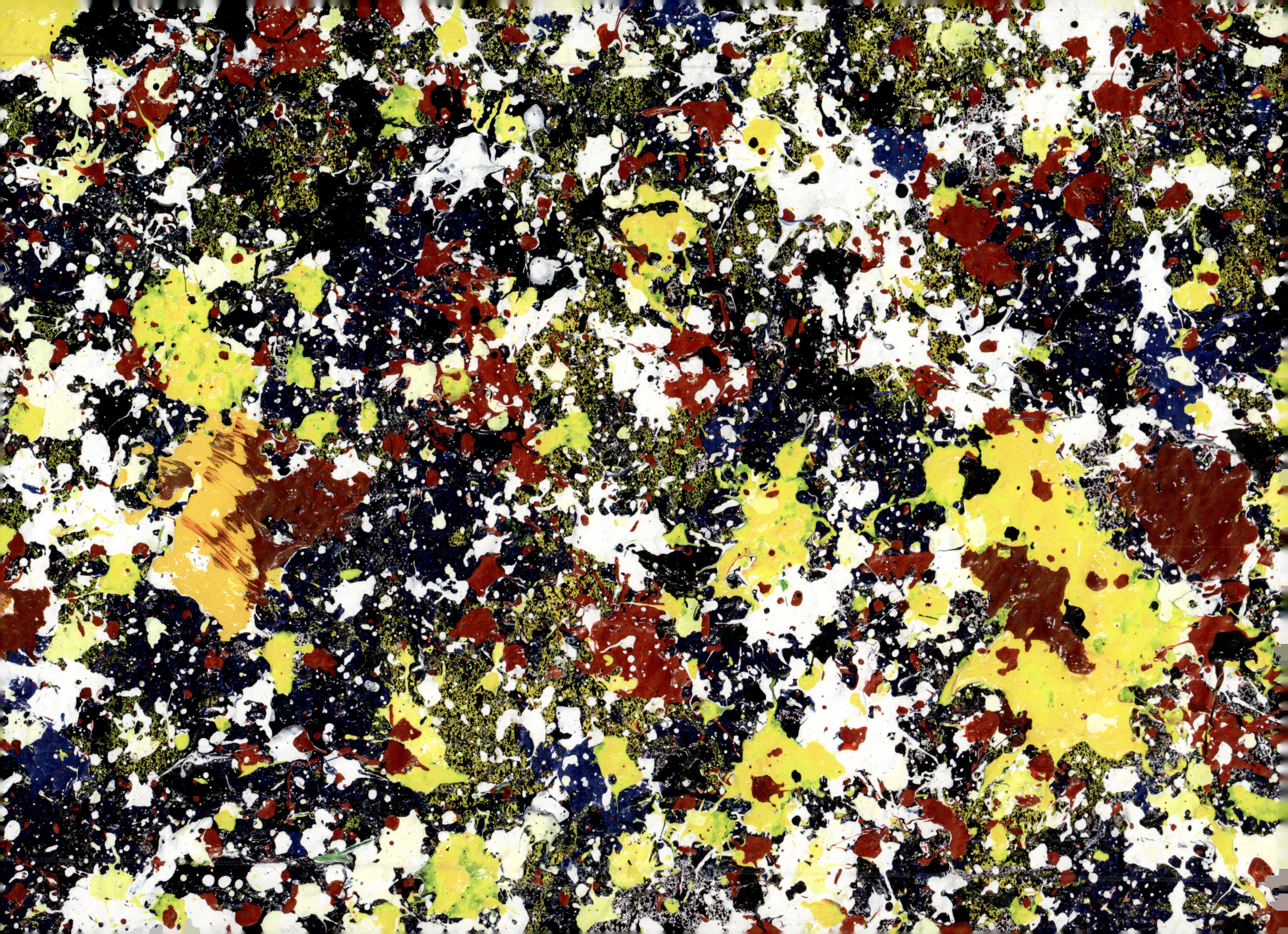

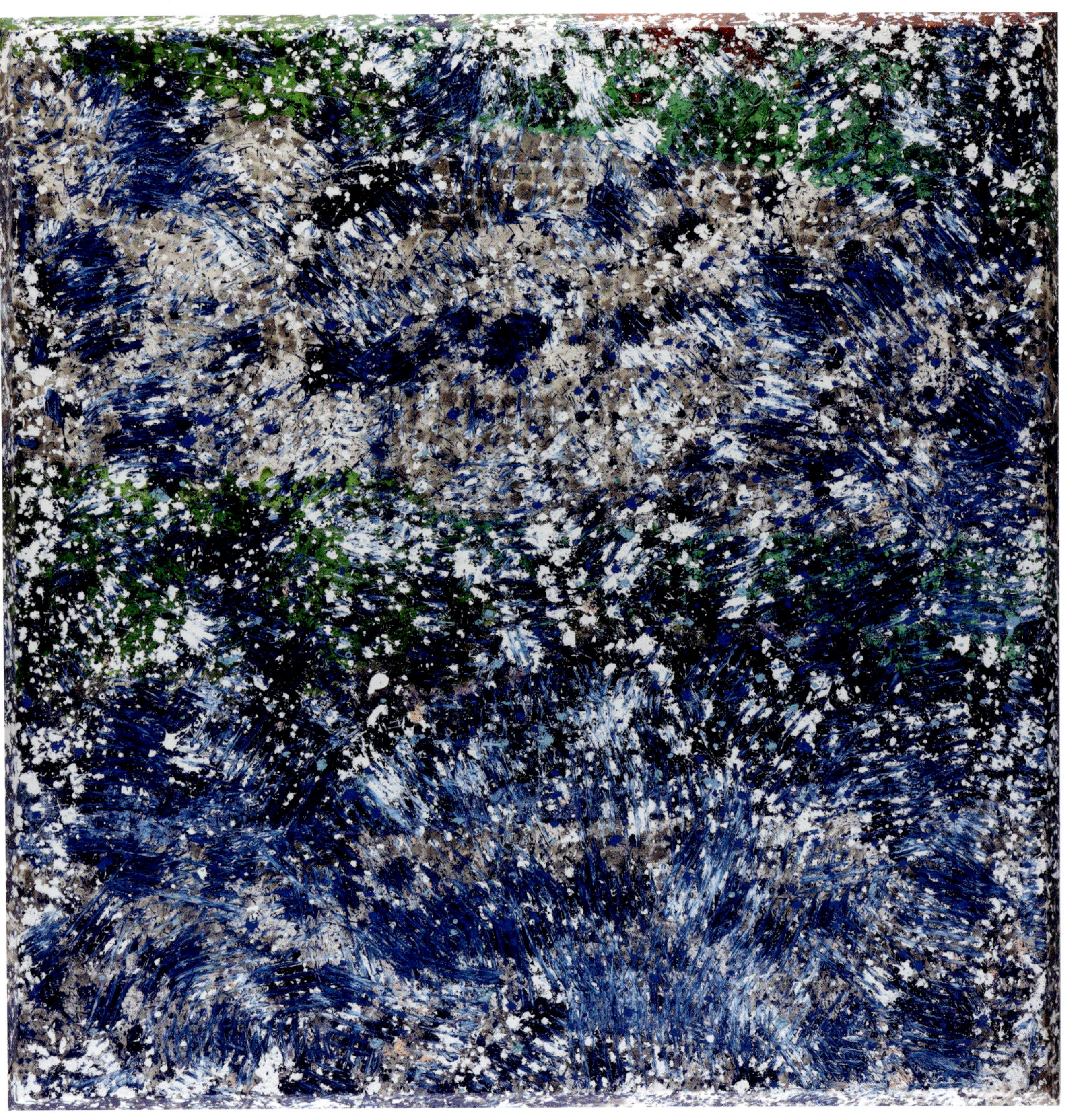

The Business, 2022

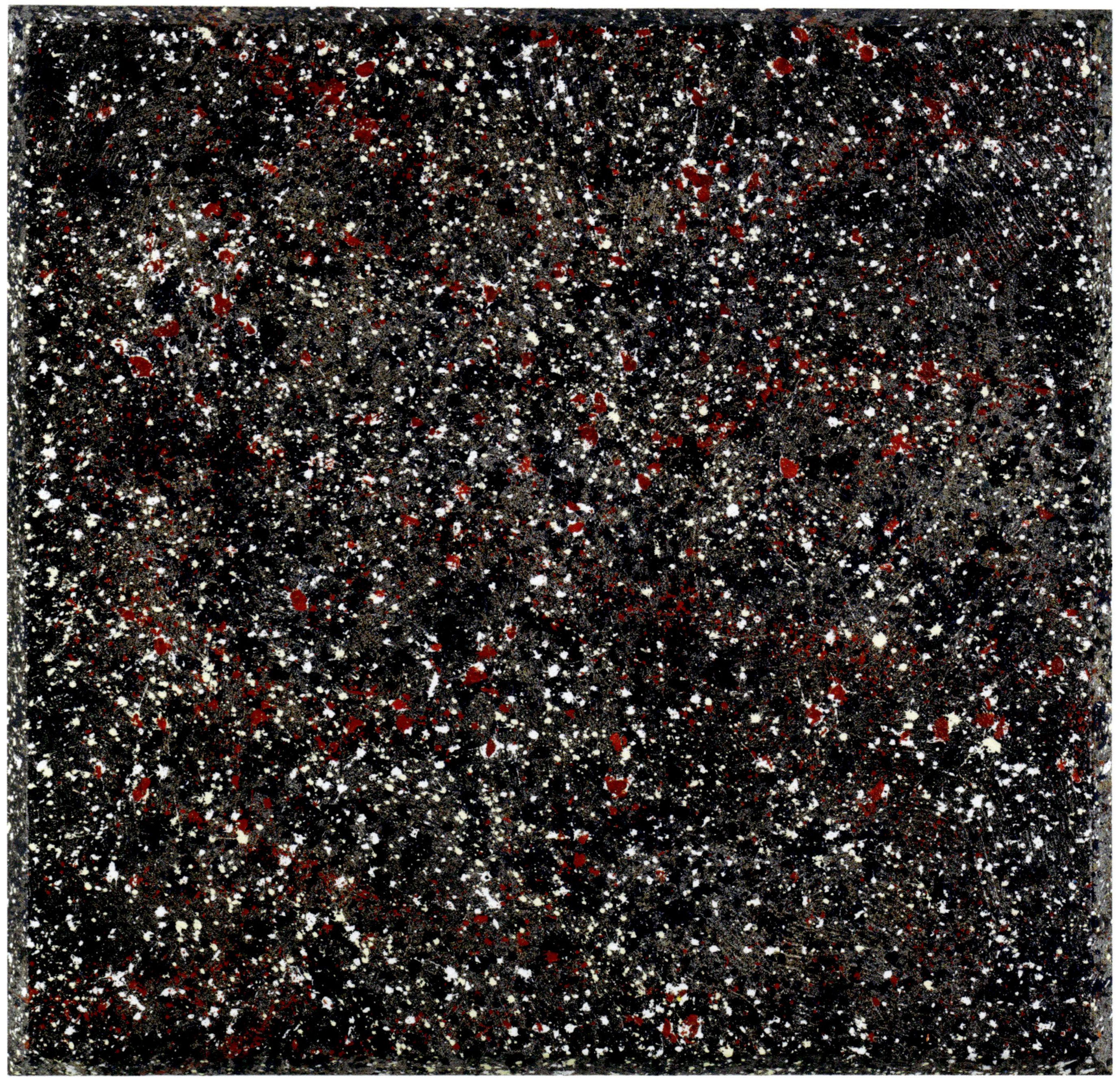

Arne, 2022

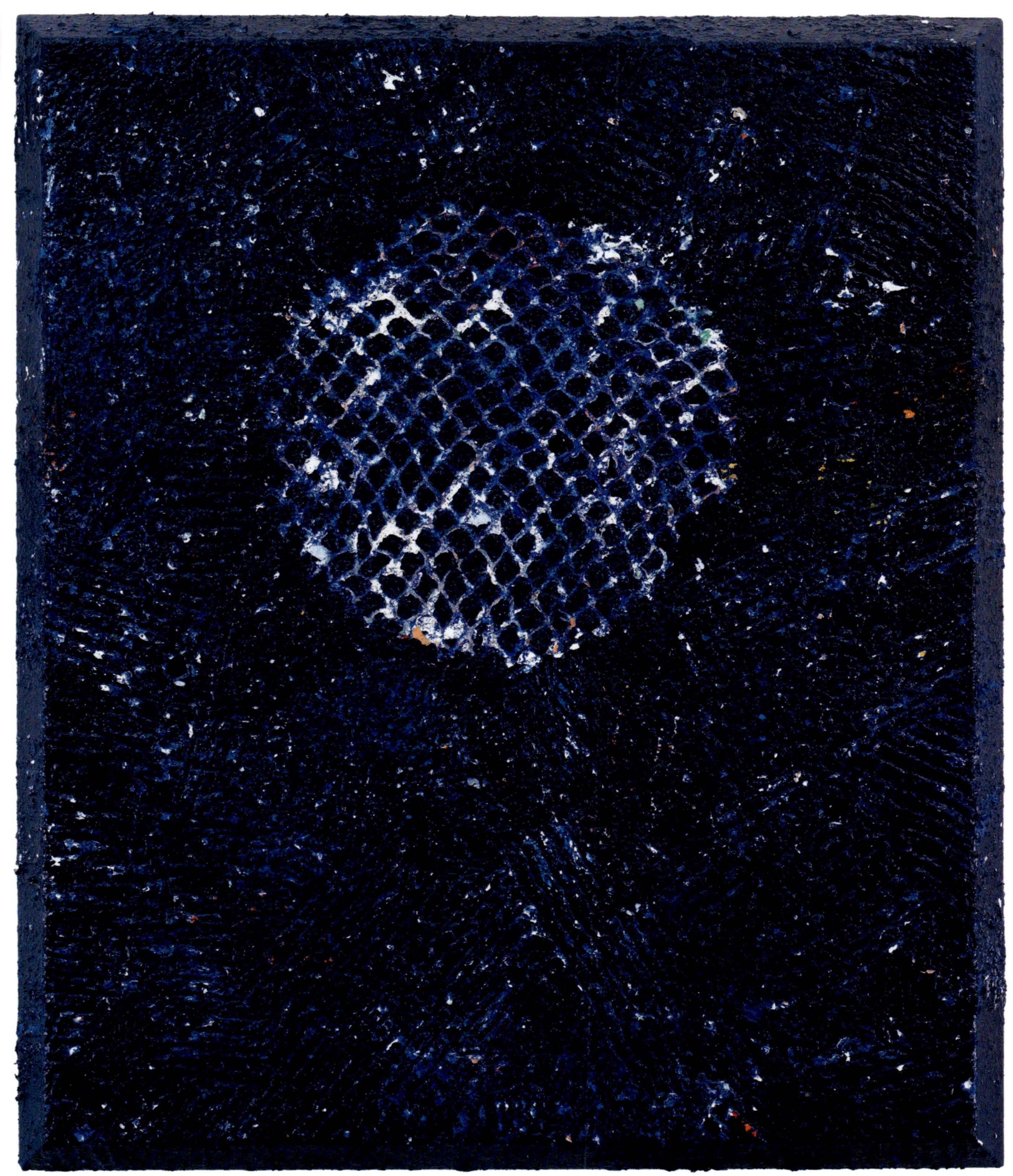

Irish, County Mayo, 2022

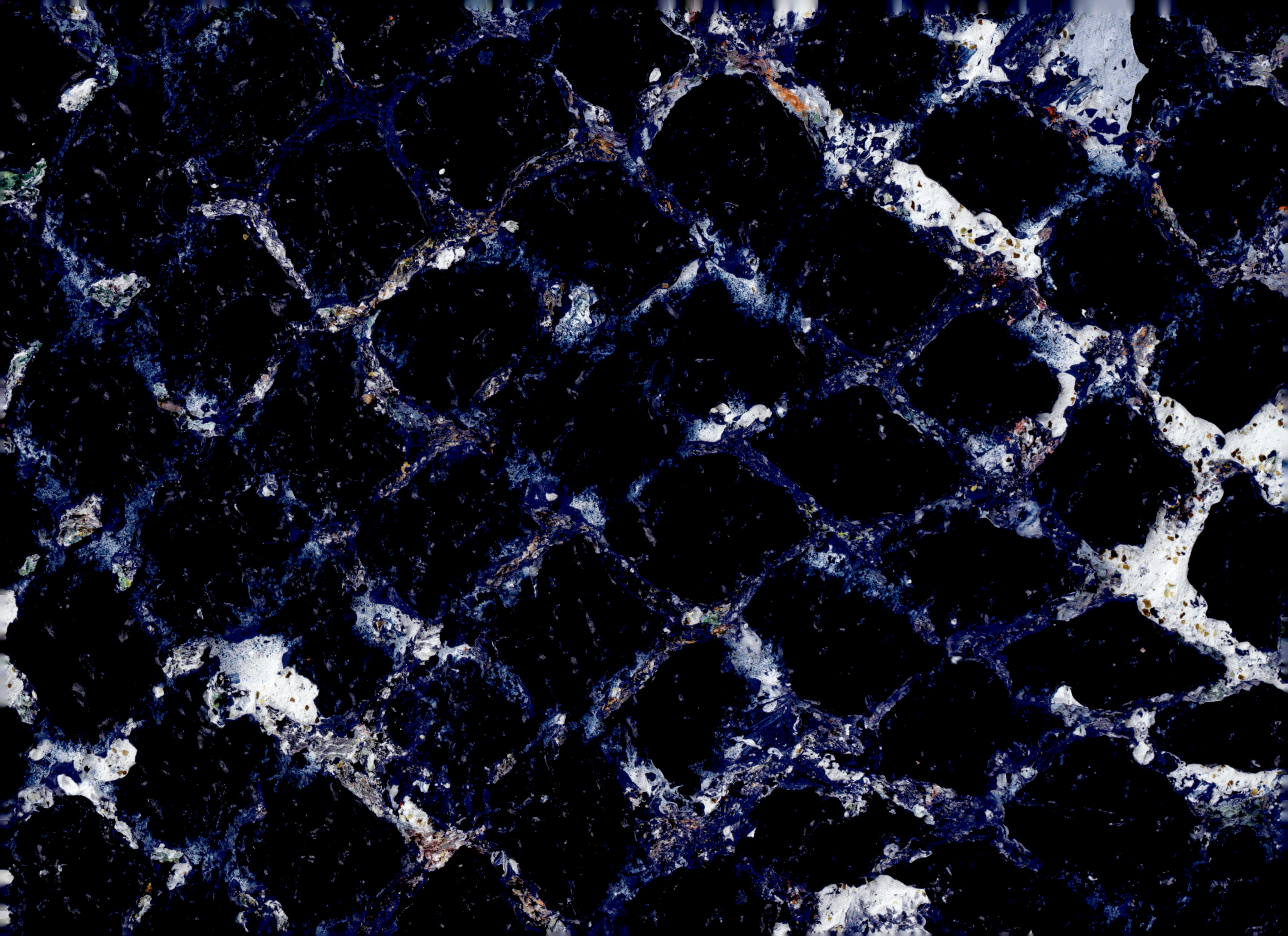

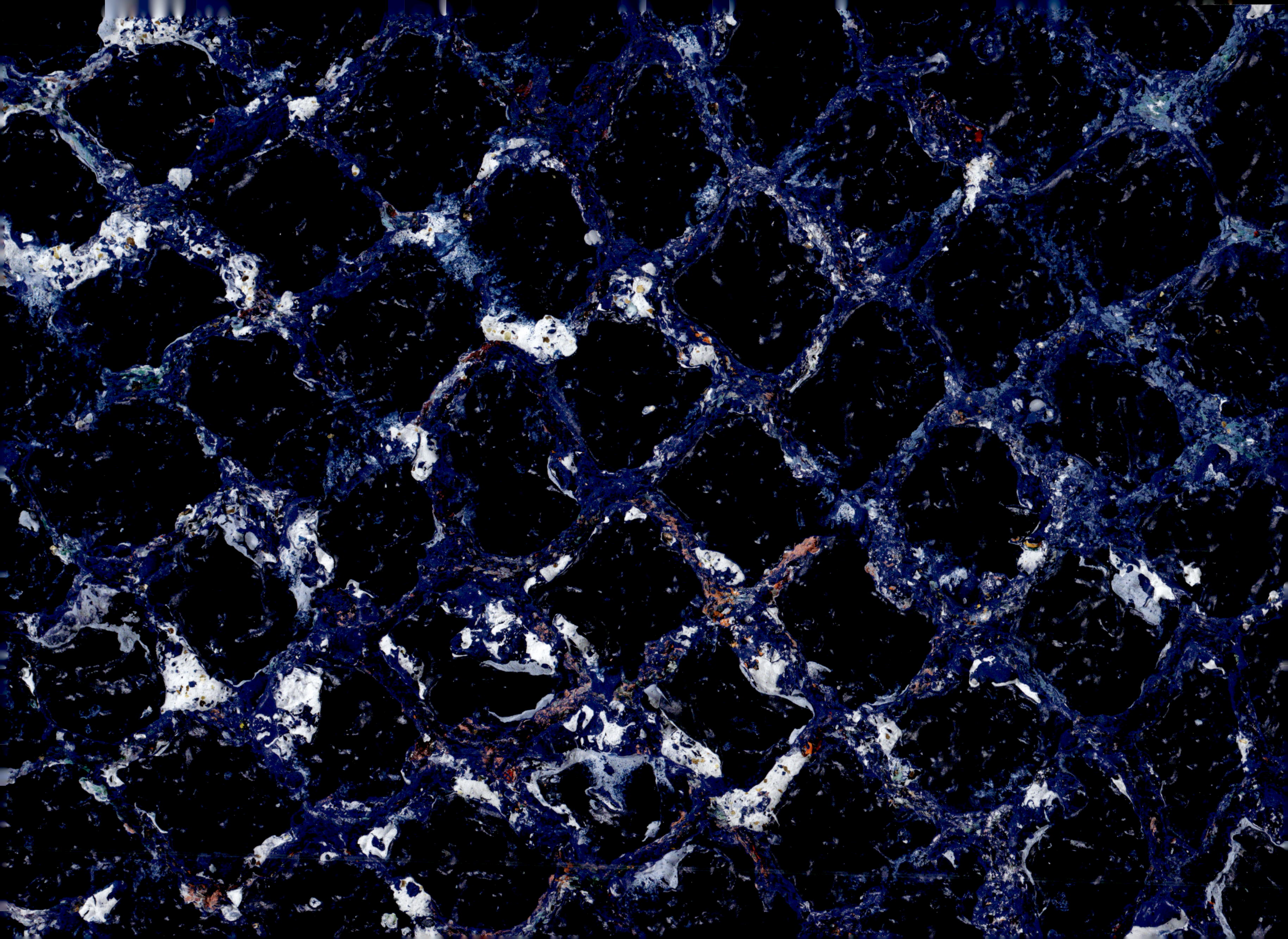

—IN SECONDS
NOT IN
SECONDS
NOT IN
BUT THROUGH
THROUGH

EXPANSES
COLLIDINGS
KNOWINGS
FORGETTINGS
FINDINGS
KNOWINGS.

SAM GILLIAM: A DANCE OF ENDURANCE CHRONOLOGY 1933–2022

Andria Hickey

This chronology of Sam Gilliam's life and work draws on the extensive research provided in a chronology compiled by Jonathan Binstock and Tatum Webb Read in 2005 and included in the catalogue accompanying the exhibition 'Sam Gilliam: A Retrospective' at the Corcoran Gallery of Art, Washington, D.C., as well as important updates included in the chronology compiled by the curatorial team at Kunstmuseum Basel for the catalogue accompanying 'The Music of Color. Sam Gilliam 1967–1973', on view in Basel, Switzerland, in 2018.

This timeline also relies on first-hand accounts and is indebted to the interviews and conversations that Gilliam recorded in his lifetime, specifically the Smithsonian's 1984 Oral History interview between Gilliam and Kenneth Young and the 1989 Oral History interview between Ben Forgey and Gilliam, both for the Archives of American Art, as well as Binstock's ongoing conversations with Gilliam, published in 'The Music of Color', and Gilliam's interview with Hans Ulrich Obrist published in the *Sam Gilliam: Existed Existing* exhibition catalogue in 2020. Digital archives and object files in various museums throughout the United States also provided important insight into Gilliam's exhibition history, public engagements and acquisitions. Additionally, this chronology draws on personal interviews conducted with Gilliam's friends and colleagues, who generously contributed to this process, among them Arne Glimcher, Melvin Edwards, Rashid Johnson, David Kordansky, Thaddeus Mosley and William T. Williams. The stewards of Gilliam's archive and estate, Annie Gawlak, studio manager Jenn DePalma and studio assistant Olivia Armacost Bliven, along with Pace Gallery and David Kordansky Gallery, provided invaluable guidance and support, in particular Arne Glimcher and Jon Mason, Director of Research and Archives, as well as David Kordansky Gallery's Senior Director Kurt Mueller and archivist Ashley Park.

All exhibition dates have been added where possible, but in some instances it has been impossible to find complete details.

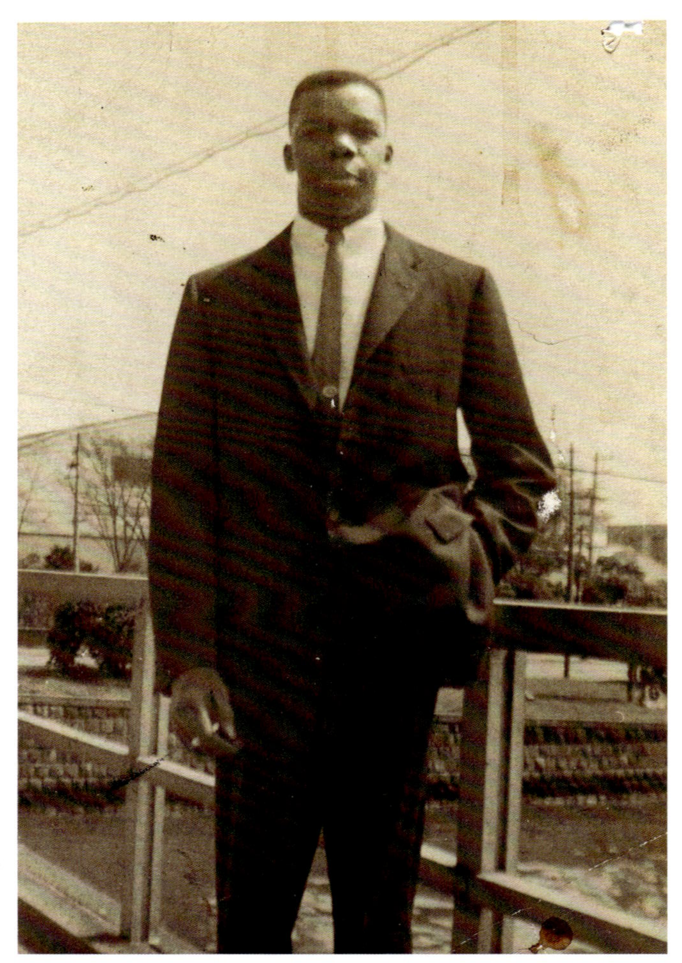

Sam Gilliam, 1950s

1933

Sam Gilliam is born on Thanksgiving Day in Tupelo, Mississippi. He is the seventh of eight children of Sam and Estery Gilliam. Sam Sr. is a carpenter, while Estery is the primary caregiver for the large family.

My dad ... he did everything: he was a farmer, a baseball pitcher, a deacon, a janitor. He was born in Mississippi, in the Delta, which is a very rich source of music – Mississippi John Hurt, Muddy Waters, all those great singers and guitarists. They made work songs.

The memory of my father became more meaningful when I became much older. I tend to think that he was a great guy. He was beautiful. Wonderful. Very strong. He said I asked too many questions. He is who I became. I always thought that being one of the youngest in the family, that I saw more, I saw it from a different position.[1]

– Sam Gilliam

1942

The Gilliam family moves to Louisville, Kentucky, when Sam is seven years old. He attends segregated schools until college. At Virginia Avenue Elementary School his creativity and artistic interests are encouraged and supported by both his teachers and parents. Sam attends a junior high school with a special art program, but in tenth grade he transitions to Central High School, which is without a dedicated art program. Nonetheless, Gilliam will continually reflect on the support he received from his teachers for his interest in art throughout his time in school.

1951

Gilliam graduates from high school and begins studies at the University of Louisville. It is one of the first southern universities to be desegregated – in 1950 and 1951. Gilliam is a member of the second admitted class of Black undergraduate students.

I was lucky to go to a great school, the University of Louisville. I was part of the second Black class. I decided I wanted to be an artist, and I was determined. There was an art center off campus. The head of the art center was a Yale graduate, a portrait painter, Eugene Leake, who then became president of Maryland Institute College of Art in Baltimore.

My first professor was a design professor [Edgar Pillet], who also taught painting. He was from Paris, and he loved music. Louisville was where Count Basie was born and it was home to the Kentucky Derby. It was an amazing time. Paul Robeson came to speak, and there were very few Black students at the time. He said he wouldn't speak without Black students, so they bussed in students from the Black college nearby.[2]

– Sam Gilliam

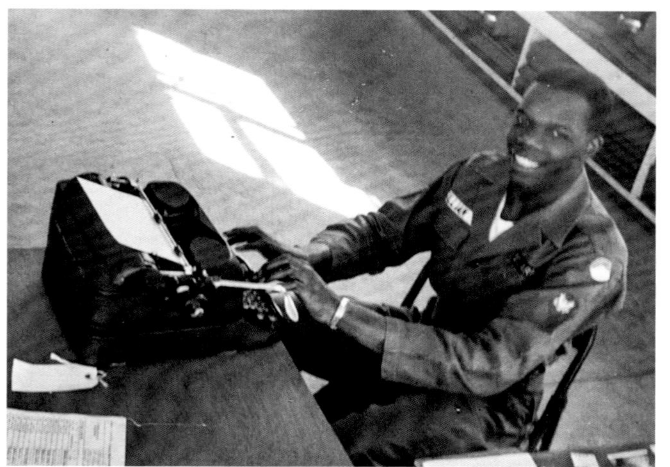

Gilliam, Unit Clerk, U.S. Army, Yokohama, February 1958

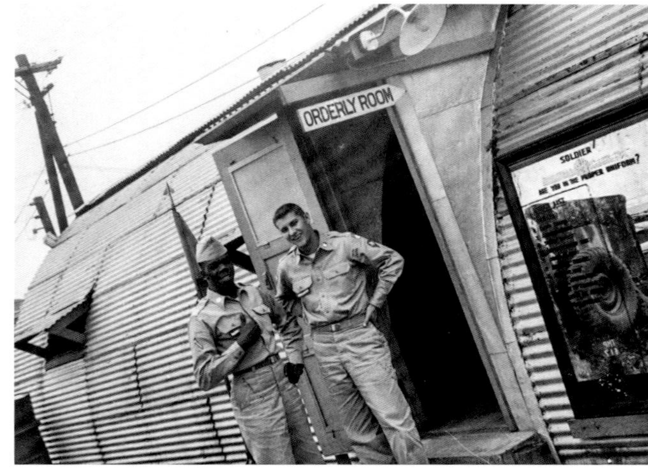

Gilliam, U.S. Army barracks, Yokohama, 1957

1954

Gilliam begins a relationship with Dorothy Butler, a Louisville native who is studying at Lincoln University in Jefferson City, Missouri.

1955

Gilliam graduates from the University of Louisville, Kentucky, with a BA in Creative Arts. His first solo exhibition as a student takes place at the University of Kentucky's Frame House Gallery, where he presents a selection of paintings of single abstracted figures walking in the landscape, which he refers to as images of Dorothy Butler walking.

1956–1958

Gilliam is drafted into the Reserve Officers Training Corps (ROTC) of the US Army. He is stationed for basic training in Texas and later stationed as a company clerk at a base in Yokohama, Japan. In Japan he discovers new printmaking techniques, Kabuki theatre and sees exhibitions by Yves Klein in Tokyo and Picasso in Yokohama. Upon completing his tour in Japan, Gilliam realizes he is not interested in being a soldier and leaves the army to complete his graduate studies in art.

I was in the ROTC, and I did basic training in Texas. We were stationed with Airborne troops and drilled by Airborne sergeants. After that I was quite lucky to be stationed in Japan. Japan was just marvelous. There were galleries and art stores, and a woodcut studio near the base. There was one person in our unit who did nothing but go to Kabuki theater. From what I had seen of the art world, I wasn't sure if I still wanted to be an artist, but I knew I didn't want to be a soldier. So, I grew up. I went back to school to do my thesis.[3]

I first encountered Yves Klein while stationed with the army in Japan. There was a Klein exhibition in Tokyo. The Gutai group was being born, and I was in the army, and I thought nothing about whether I would be an artist or not. In fact, I probably thought that I would never be an artist. But Klein had an effect on me, and I thought about making art beyond the interiors that it is usually presented in, about making art more in the outside world.[4]

– Sam Gilliam

1958–1961

Gilliam attends the MFA graduate program at the Hite Art Institute of the University of Louisville, Kentucky. He teaches public school by day and pursues his studies at night. During this time, he works with professors who influence his approach to art-making. In particular, Ulfert Wilke, a German expressionist painter, takes a special interest in Gilliam's talent and encourages him to go

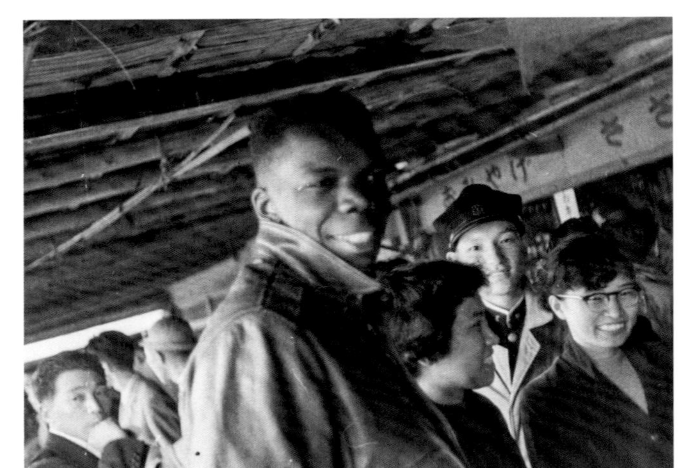

Gilliam with the Japanese/American English Speaking Society, January 1957

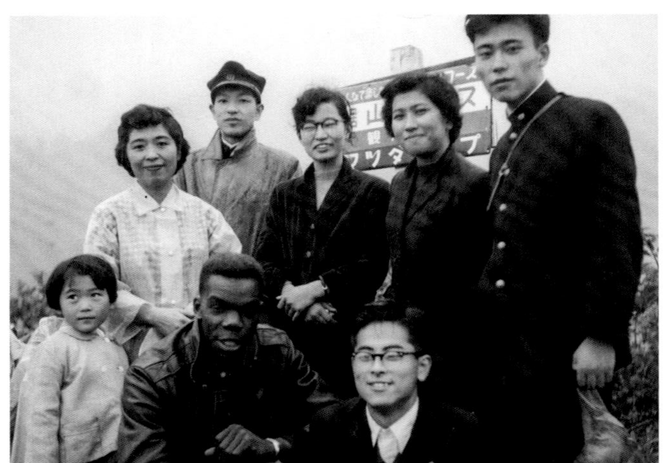

Gilliam hiking with the Japanese/American English Speaking Society, January 1957

to Europe, offering him a scholarship to study in Munich, which does not materialize, but encourages Gilliam to keep painting. Another German professor visiting from the Bavarian Academy of Art, Charles Crodel, is also deeply influential and remains in Gilliam's mind throughout his career because of his encouragement to persevere in creating one's own unique and steadfast vision and approach to art-making. Gilliam will later reference the importance of Cordel's guidance and inspiration in a Commencement speech in 1986.

Gilliam is active in the local artists' community and cofounds Gallery Enterprises Collective (1957–71), which includes artists Kenneth Young and Bob Thompson. Gilliam is also president of the university's youth council and a regular participant in National Association for the Advancement of Colored People (NAACP) programs at the University of Louisville.

The professors from Europe were actually more involved in Black culture than the American professors. They were mostly Germans. Our visiting professor, Ulfert Wilke, had an interest in African sculpture. I figured the only way I was going to be an artist was to be his studio assistant.

I worked as a fellowship student in the university library and the art library. I showed all the slides to the art history classes. I worked in the art library and got the books that professors needed to prepare for their lectures. There was nothing that kept me from reading them. So, I had two occupations'.

One of the good things about the University of Louisville was that most of the professors had come from Europe, and in particular Germany, as émigrés fleeing from Nazi Germany and World War II. For example, Edgard Pillet, who was a Parisian designer, painter, sculptor, printmaker, and a tapestry designer, among other things, and Charles Crodel, a printmaker and very important stained glass window designer from the Bavarian State Academy of Fine Arts in Munich. I in fact did my thesis with Crodel, who even though he was known for his stained-glass window design, conceptually believed more in drawing in regard to constructing planes and then building volumes. His method of teaching figure drawing was first, for example, to draw a silhouette and then determine the volume by layers of cross strokes, and that was within the tradition of drawing that I learned. I soon realized that a painter like Tintoretto did the same; creating flat back planes before moving.[5]

– Sam Gilliam

Gilliam continues to date Butler, who is enrolled in the Graduate School of Journalism at Columbia University in New York, following her time as a reporter for the Black weekly, *The Memphis Tri-State Defender*, where she covered the integration of Little Rock Central High school by the Little Rock Nine. They continue an on-again, off-again, long-distance relationship while Butler pursues her education and work opportunities in journalism.

Gilliam graduates in 1961 with an MFA in Painting.

He works on the Great Northern Railroad between Minneapolis and Seattle as a waiter during the summer of 1961.

1962

Gilliam and Butler are married on September 1. Together they move to Washington, D.C. after Butler is offered a position as reporter on the City Desk at the *Washington Post*, becoming the first Black female reporter at the newspaper.

Gilliam begins teaching at McKinley Technical High School, an art-focused public school where he will teach until 1967.

I came to Washington because Dorothy and I had decided to get married. [Before that] if I was in the Army here, she was in school someplace else. And finally when I was in school in Louisville she was in school in Columbia, in New York City. Then she started working for the [Washington] *Post. That was close enough for me to really commute in to see her. So before we got married I decided to come here.*

One of the things that I actually tried to do was to teach at Howard. It was at that time that I met Doctor [James A.] *Porter. He felt that I was too – what he said was – that I was too "passionate" a painter to be worried about teaching. But if I was going to teach, I should try to teach in high school. So I did that.*[6]

– Sam Gilliam

1963

Gilliam establishes his first Washington, D.C. studio on 17th and Q Street and presents his work with the D.C. gallery, Adams-Morgan Gallery. His first exhibition includes watercolours and a single large-scale painting.

The exhibition is an occasion for him to meet Washington Color School painter Tom Downing, who becomes an important influence and mentor throughout Gilliam's early career. He also meets fellow Color School painters Howard Mehring and Paul Reed. Downing introduces Gilliam to Rockne Krebs; Krebs will become an important friend, collaborator and studio mate of Gilliam for several decades.

At this time, Gilliam also meets Washington-based senior painter Alma Thomas, who shows at Barnett-Aden Gallery along with other senior Black artists Romare Bearden, Charles White and Elizabeth Catlett; the gallery is the first successful Black-owned private art gallery in the United States and is a stalwart amongst the artist community in D.C.

On 28 August, Gilliam and Butler participate in the historic March on Washington for Jobs and Freedom, together with over 250,000 people, advocating for the civil and economic rights of African Americans. At the march, final speaker Dr. Martin Luther King, Jr., delivers his historic speech, 'I Have a Dream'.

The Gilliam's first daughter, Stephanie Jessica, is born.

Solo Exhibitions:
'Recent Paintings by Sam Gilliam', Adams-Morgan Gallery, Washington, D.C., through 8 March.

Rockne, Sam and I agreed to meet at their studios on 14th & U. I would photograph the 2 of them "for the art history books". It unfolded differently than I imagined. [...] *Sam Gilliam asked him to come downstairs from his studio to beat me in ping pong. I won. Rockne won the second game by one point.*[7]

– Carol Harrison

My serve is so good, even you would be surprised. I am fond of this waiting/expecting photo – I feel comfortable with chair legs to see/ in order to see trees...[8]

– Sam Gilliam, a note to Carol Harrison

I approached this person, as a Southerner is prone to do, and said, "How do you like my show?" And he didn't say anything. He said, "Well, I'd really tell you. I didn't come in because of the one in the window. I came in for the little watercolors." I said, "Well, how do you feel about them?" He said, "Man, you're scared." And I said, "What do you mean, that I'm scared?" He said, "In those big paintings, you're real scared. In these little ones, you pretty hot." This was Tom. It was in this sense that I decided to take Tom's advice. He said, "If you really want to see some painting, why don't you come to my studio?" I recall that I'd seen Thomas Downing's name in an article in the paper. So I chose to go by this studio. And I walked into his studio and there was this huge painting of nothing but dots. And he said, "Now that's painting!" (laughing) And I can recall that my wife was with me. And we didn't say anything. But at the bottom of the steps, on the way out, I said, "If he calls that painting, he's crazy." And in that sense it was the beginning of one of many instant shocks for me and I relate to this experience as being that of shock because I learned to pay attention to that kind of experience and realized that the more I tried to do figurative painting – little watercolors and things like this – I began to wonder, "What is it that this person gets out of painting those dots?" And it worried me so that I called him and invited him out for a drink so we could discuss it. And he said, "You are an o-o-o-ld man to be so young." He said, "These dots are the same thing that Monk is doing."[9]

– Sam Gilliam on meeting Tom Downing

There was a sense of being associated with a very radical group within Washington. Because abstract painting wasn't that accepted, there was the feeling that your understanding of it was personal and that it had a necessary significance for your personal survival. Your understanding of it made you part of the rest of the community. For the first time I felt like an artist ought to feel. Not only did I create an image, but my personality took hold. It became very important to become known as one of the youngest members of the Washington Color Field school.[10]

– Sam Gilliam

1964

Group Exhibitions:
'Nine Contemporary Painters, USA', Pan American Union, Washington, D.C., 21 May–10 June.

1965

Gilliam begins to exhibit his work with Jefferson Place Gallery. The gallery will represent the artist until 1973.

The Gilliam's second daughter, Melissa Lynne, is born.

Butler leaves her position at the *Washington Post* to work as a freelance journalist so that she can devote more time to raising the family's young daughters.

Solo Exhibitions:
'Sam Gilliam', Jefferson Place Gallery, Washington, D.C., 7–26 June 1965.

Group Exhibitions:
Institute of Contemporary Art, Washington, D.C., curated by Alice Denny.

1966

Gilliam participates in significant group exhibitions that are nationally and internationally recognized, in particular, 'The Negro in American Art' at University of California, Los Angeles and 'The First World Festival of Negro Arts', in Dakar.

He meets curator and museum director Walter Hopps, who has recently moved to D.C. to work at the progressive think tank, the Institute of Policy Studies. Hopps will become a confidante and supporter of Gilliam's work throughout Hopps's lifetime, providing Gilliam with important exhibition opportunities, advice and avenues for financial support.

Gilliam's exhibition at Jefferson Place Gallery is his first presentation of his stained canvases.

Solo Exhibitions:
'Sam Gilliam', Jefferson Place Gallery, Washington, D.C., 28 November–16 December.

Group Exhibitions:
'The First World Festival of Negro Arts', Dakar, 1–24 April.

Time leaves memoirs playing

" The five prints make a landscape"

Memories are embracing

" The purple areas are known"

Kisses are fulfilling

" They are the trees of our winters"

An embrace is warming

" Blue and red are the paths of fantasies"

Love is everlasting

"The yellow buoys mark the way to the purple dreams"

sam gilliam, jr.

1752 lamont street nw · washington, d.c. 20010

Poem by Gilliam, c. 1965

‘The Negro in American Art’, Dickson Art Center at UCLA, 11 September–16 October.
‘Artists in Washington’, Institute of Contemporary Arts, Washington, D.C..

When I arrived [in Washington, D.C.], *I discovered that the city had far more interesting and diverse artists living and working there than I had imagined. On P Street, for instance, in a section where most of the contemporary galleries came to be, I discovered Sam Gilliam's paintings at the Jefferson Place Gallery. They were lyrical abstract stained and painted works unlike any I had ever seen. As the artists and I came to know one another, I discovered that we both loved the work of John Coltrane, the great jazz tenor saxophone player. I later learned that the melodic structure that Coltrane often used, which he called 'sheets of sound' was a significant influence for Gilliam's work.*[11]

– Walter Hopps

1967

Gilliam's focus turns almost exclusively to a process of staining and folding unstretched canvas, which will become a hallmark of his work. Paint is poured on a wet canvas, which is then folded; additional paint is applied to the folded canvas, which is then, once dry, stretched onto a wooden support.

Marjorie Phillips, wife of Duncan Phillips and Director of the Phillips Collection, sees *Red Petals* (1966) in Gilliam's exhibition at Jefferson Place Gallery. She purchases the painting for the Phillips Collection and decides to host a solo exhibition of Gilliam's work.

Gilliam receives his first Individual Artist Grant from the National Endowment for the Arts, allowing him to leave full-time teaching at McKinley Technical High School to concentrate on art-making.

Gilliam begins teaching at the Maryland Institute College of Art, Baltimore. He will teach there until 1982.

The Gilliam's third child, Leah Franklin, is born.

Gilliam meets artist Kenneth Noland at a party in New York City with Tom Downing and Dorothy Butler. Shortly afterwards, he visits Noland's studio in South Shaftsbury, Vermont.

Solo Exhibitions:
‘Paintings by Sam Gilliam’, The Phillips Collection, Washington, D.C., 7 October–14 November.
‘Sam Gilliam’, Jefferson Place Gallery, Washington, D.C., 28 November–16 December.

Group Exhibitions:
‘Art for Embassies’, Washington Gallery of Modern Art, Washington, D.C.

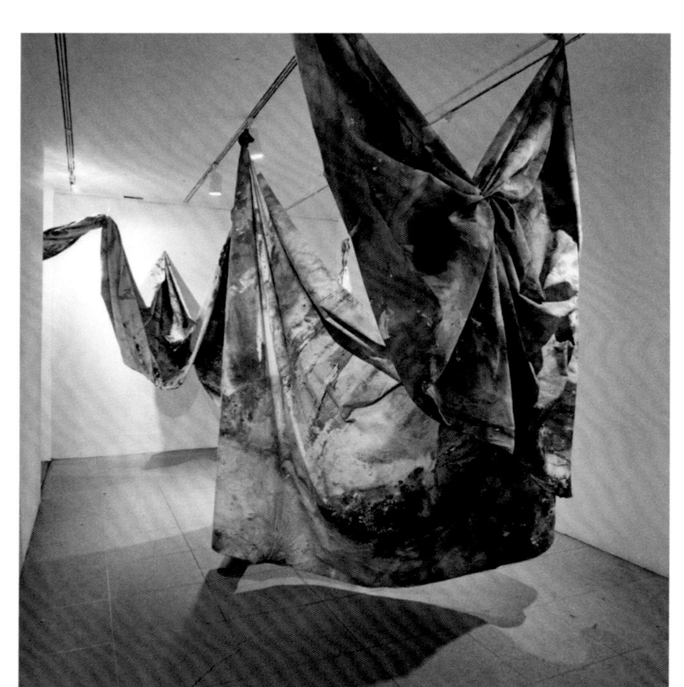

Installation view of ‘Projects: Sam Gilliam’, Museum of Modern Art, New York, 1971

Once when I was invited to a party where Noland was going to appear, and he did show up, I hung out in the corner and tried to "out-cool" him. I mean, I wouldn't speak to him. So my wife said, "You know you like the man's work. You're always in New York in a phone booth crying and saying you can't stay here because you don't have enough money. Why don't you go up and meet him?" [affecting growling kind of voice] "I don't want to meet him!" I said. So Dorothy approached him and said, "My husband is one of your greatest fans. He's too shy to come over and say, 'Hello, Mr. Noland.' Will you come over [he breaks up, laughing] and say hello to him?" And he came over, and much in the sense of people who are people, he said, "I've heard about you." And he mentioned that Cornelia, his previous wife, had sent him a copy of the article, and that I should come up and visit him some time. Immediately I said, "When?" [he laughs] So we drove from here to South Shaftsbury and spent the weekend with him.[12]

– Gilliam on meeting Kenneth Noland

1968

Gilliam receives a significant grant from the Washington Gallery of Modern Art, now under the direction of Walter Hopps, who initiates a programme to support artists through long-term fellowships, known as the Washington Gallery of Modern Art Workshop Program. Gilliam receives a $50,000 grant to fund the studio's operations at 1737 Johnson Avenue, NW, as well as a yearly $5,000 stipend, and begins to explore new ways of working on a larger scale.

Gilliam exhibits a 30-foot-long bevelled-edge painting as part of his solo exhibition at Byron Gallery in New York.

He is asked to donate a painting to 'In Honor of Dr. Martin Luther King, Jr.', a benefit exhibition for the Southern Christian Leadership Conference at the Museum of Modern Art in New York, where Gilliam's work, *Away* (1969) is notably priced third highest in the auction, after Tony Smith and Barnett Newman.[13]

Gilliam travels to Paris and Nice, France.

Solo Exhibitions:
'Sam Gilliam', Byron Gallery, New York, 11 May–28 July.

Group Exhibitions:
'In Honor of Dr. Martin Luther King, Jr.', Museum of Modern Art, New York, 31 October–3 November.
'Invisible Americans: Black Artists of the 30s', Studio Museum in Harlem, New York.
'Thirty Contemporary Black Artists', Minneapolis Institute of Art, Minneapolis.
'Art in Washington', Washington Gallery of Modern Art, Washington, D.C.

Sam Gilliam arrived in Washington in 1962 after completing graduate work in painting at the University of Louisville. Like Krebs and McGowin at the time of their arrivals, Gilliam knew virtually nothing of the artistic scene that already existed in the nation's Capital. During his first two years in Washington he continued to pursue the painterly abstracted figurative art that was the direct consequence of his art school training under Ulfert Wilke and Charles Crodel. [...] The drawings and, particularly, the watercolors Gilliam produced while still in art school and during his first years in Washington reveal certain qualities that relate directly to the work of the last five years. The fluid, clear colors, surface soaking, composition involving the edge and a certain abrupt yet flowing sense of draftsmanship lend great authority to these drawings and watercolors which contain echoes of Helen Frankenthaler of the early 50's and hints of what Pollock might have looked like had he worked directly from nature as a mature artist.[14]

– Walter Hopps, 1970

1969

Gilliam's exhibition at Jefferson Place Gallery features the artist's first large-scale Drape paintings, including *Carousel Form II* (1969).

Gilliam also works on a series of red and black paintings. One is significantly titled *April 4* – the date of Dr. Martin Luther King, Jr.'s assassination. The paintings are made a year after Gilliam is witness to the looting, fires and civil unrest along 14th Street in Washington, D.C., from his studio on Johnson Avenue, following the news of King's death.

Gilliam is awarded the Art Institute of Chicago's Norman W. Harris prize.

Gilliam is invited to participate in 'X to the Fourth Power', a group exhibition curated by fellow Black abstract artist William T. Williams at the Studio Museum in Harlem, New York, which also includes the work of Melvin Edwards. As artists working in abstraction at a time when the Black art community is rejecting the tropes of post-war abstraction in favour of figurative and representational works, the trio begin to organize their own exhibitions – first at Black galleries, colleges and universities – Morgan State, Howard and Fisk universities and later, on the invitation of other mainstream institutions such as the Wadsworth Atheneum. They will go on to exhibit together five times between 1969 and 1976 and again in 2022 in one of the last exhibitions in which Gilliam will participate before his death.

Walter Hopps invites Gilliam, Rockne Krebs and Ed McGowin to present new site-specific commissions at the Corcoran Gallery of Art, where he is now director. Hopps encourages the artists to expand their work for the show in both scale and ambition. Gilliam includes a monumental Drape painting, *Light Depth* (1969), responding directly to the museum's architecture.

Solo Exhibitions:
'Sam Gilliam: New Paintings', Jefferson Place Gallery, Washington, D.C., 1–19 April.

Group Exhibitions:
'Other Ideas', Detroit Institute of Art, 10 September–19 October.
'The Washington Painters', Ringling Museum, Sarasota, Florida, 1–28 December.
'1969 Annual Exhibition of Contemporary American Painting', Whitney Museum of American Art, New York, 16 December 1969–1 February 1970.
'Gilliam, Krebs, McGowin', Corcoran Gallery of Art, Washington, D.C.
'X to the Fourth Power', Studio Museum in Harlem, New York.

When Walter Hopps made that show with Rockne, Ed, and me, he had two things in mind: teaching us how to survive by following our own instincts and to see things broadly. We had been around a very full tradition with the Washington Color painters, but why necessarily follow it? You can't see it if you keep doing ... you must take a chance and work differently.[15]

Exhibiting with Mel Edwards and Bill Williams was extremely important for me ... After ['X to the Fourth Power'] *we got together and just talked. We could talk about things like tennis and football, but always we ended up talking about art. Then we arrived at a point where we had to start talking about showing, and we showed together. We started worrying about the real things that an artist ought to worry about, such as the quality of the exhibition, the quality of the catalogue and various things like that. And the experience made us very, very close. And this spiritual closeness got us objectively closer to seeing more work of each other ... we would show each other more work than the normal person would dare to reveal ... It meant we could count on each other.*[16]

A single work can and frequently does contain many different, non-hierarchic events or climaxes that together cover a variety of the qualities above. Some of Gilliam's finest, toughest and most beautiful paintings are, in fact, those in which a delicate balance is sustained between seemingly disparate characteristics. The sense of controlled chaos that his work communicates is another example of Gilliam's ability to create and maintain a high level of tension between opposing forces.[17]

– Walter Hopps

1970

Gilliam presents his work in Europe for the first time, at Galerie Darthea Speyer, who will represent the artist in Paris for over three decades, until 2007. His work is also included in several exhibitions surveying the Washington Color School at institutions throughout the US and Canada, in which he is identified as part of a second generation of artists influenced by the work of Morris Louis, Helen Frankenthaler and Kenneth Noland, among others. In several of these exhibitions, including the influential 'Ten Washington Artists', he is the only Black artists to be invited.

Gilliam is an artist-in-residence at Oberlin College in March. He later gifts the Allen Memorial Art Museum a significant Drape painting, *Softly Still* (1973).

Gilliam serves on a six-person jury for the National Council on the Arts fellowship awards for twenty young painters and sculptors of 'exceptional talent', together with William Seitz, director of the Rose Art Museum at Brandeis University; James Speyer, curator of contemporary art at the Art Institute of Chicago; James Melchert, artist and teacher at the University of California at Berkeley; Vanderen Coke, a historian of art and photography at the University of New Mexico; James Camp, an art historian at the University of South Florida.

Solo Exhibitions:
'Sam Gilliam: Recent Paintings and Watercolors', Jefferson Place Gallery, Washington, D.C., 11 December 1970–2 January 1971.
'Sam Gilliam', Galerie Darthea Speyer, Paris.

Group Exhibitions:
'69th American Exhibition', Art Institute of Chicago, 17 January–22 February.
'Ten Washington Artists', Edmonton Art Gallery, Alberta, Canada, 5 February–8 March.
'Dimensions of Black', La Jolla Museum of Art, San Diego, 15 February–29 March.
'Washington: Twenty Years', Baltimore Museum of Art, Maryland, 12 May–21 June.
'Two Generations of Color Painting', Institute of Contemporary Art at University of Pennsylvania, Philadelphia, 1 October–6 November.
'Paperworks', Museum of Modern Art, New York, 24 November 1970–10 January 1971.

1971

Gilliam presents his first major solo exhibition at a New York institution at The Museum of Modern Art as part of its 'Projects' series.

Gilliam's work is also included in notable group exhibitions defining shifts in contemporary art, including, 'Works for New Spaces', the Walker Art Center's inaugural exhibition in its new building in Minneapolis, Minnesota. Gilliam's contribution is *Carousel Merge* (1971), a 75-foot-long Drape painting hung from the ceiling in the public space between the museum's galleries.

Gilliam is also included in *DE-LUXE*, a groundbreaking exhibition presented in a dilapidated movie theatre in

Houston's Fifth Ward. Curated by artist Peter Bradley, the exhibition brings together 18 artists, including Anthony Caro, Ed Clark, Virginia Jaramillo, Al Loving, Kenneth Noland and Jules Olitski among others. The exhibition is regarded as one of the first racially integrated exhibitions.

Gilliam, together with Richard Hunt, Daniel LaRue Johnson and Roy DeCarava, among others, withdraws from 'Contemporary Black Artists in America', an exhibition of 75 Black artists at the Whitney Museum of American Art in New York, in solidarity with the Black Emergency Cultural Coalition, a group of Black artists co-led by Benny Andrews. The Coalition initiated the project in 1969 following long consultations with the museum on the lack of representation of Black artists in the museum's exhibition programme and collection. However, the Coalition is ultimately critical of the exhibition being organized by a white curator, the museum's lack of consultation with Black art experts in the selection of artists and the timing of the exhibition.

Gilliam co-authors an Op-Ed in *Artforum* on the subject with John Dowell, Melvin Edwards, Richard, Daniel Johnson, Joe Overstreet and William T. Williams.

Gilliam receives a Guggenheim Foundation Award.

Gilliam travels to Rome, Beirut, India, Greece and Kassel, Germany. This same year he also travels to other parts of Germany, Poland, Yugoslavia and Venice.

As African Americans and artists involved personally and publicly as citizens and creative people, we feel that the quality of such a survey to a large extent depends on the intentions and integrity of the institution and its delegated curators.

We say that the Whitney Museum has anti-curated its survey which results in misrepresenting and discrediting the complex and varied culture and visual history of the African American. The museum thus acts as a falsifier of history and minimizes the value of our works and therefore ourselves. This exhibition has been organized and developed in the worst form of tokenism without any regard for our real qualities.[18]

– John Dowell, Sam Gilliam, Daniel Johnson, Joe Overstreet, Melvin Edwards, Richard Hunt and William T. Williams

Solo Exhibitions:
'Sam Gilliam: Watercolors and Multiples', Jefferson Place Gallery, Washington, D.C., 13 July–8 August.
'Projects: Sam Gilliam', The Museum of Modern Art, New York, 9 November–8 December.

Group Exhibitions:
'2nd Indian Triennale', Lalit Kala Akademi, New Delhi, India, 23 January–23 March.
'Works for New Spaces', Walker Art Center, Minneapolis, 18 May–25 July.

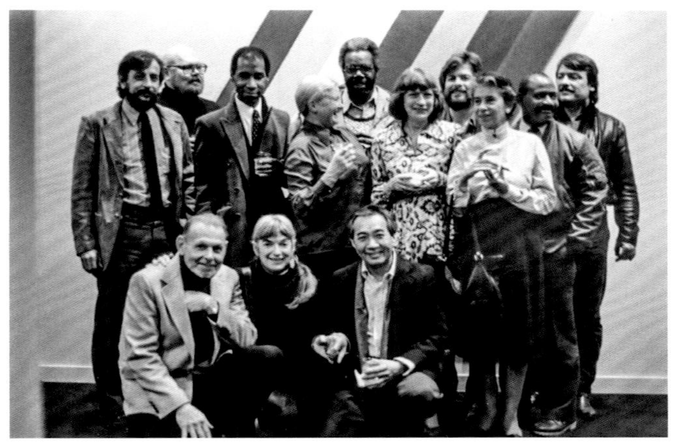

Back row, from left: Ed Zerne, Sam Gilliam, Eric Rudd, Rockne Krebs. Middle row: John Wise, Carroll Sockwell, V.V. Rankin, Nesta Dorrance, Alice Denney, Franklin White. Front row: Ben Abramowitz, Hilda Thorpe, David Moy

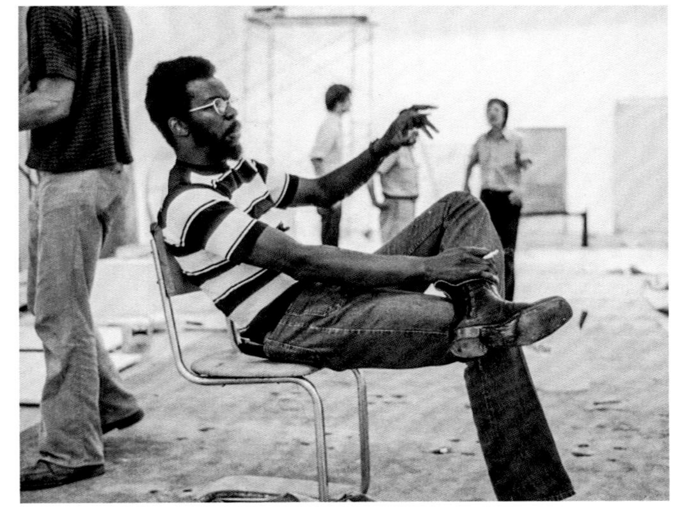

Gilliam during installation of The De Luxe show, Houston, 1971

'Directions 3: Eight Artists', Milwaukee Art Center, 19 June–8 August.
'Kid Stuff', Albright-Knox Art Gallery, Buffalo, New York, 25 July–6 September.
'De Luxe Show', The De Luxe Theater, Houston, 22 August–29 September.
'Washington Art', Columbia Museum of Art, South Carolina, 3 November–3 December.
'Washington Art', Madison Art Center, Wisconsin.

1972

Gilliam's work is included in the 36th Venice Biennale at the US Pavilion, curated by Walter Hopps. Six artists are represented along with Gilliam: Ron Davis, Richard Estes, James Nutt, Keith Sonnier and Diane Arbus.

Dorothy Gilliam returns to a full-time position at the *Washington Post* as Style section assistant editor.

Solo Exhibitions:
'Sam Gilliam', Jefferson Place Gallery, Washington, D.C., 27 November–16 December.

Group Exhibitions:
36th Venice Biennale, US Pavilion, 11 June–1 October.
'Interconnections: An Exhibit of Painting and Sculpture by Three Major Black Artists', Wabash Transit Gallery at School of the Art Institute of Chicago, 1–30 November.
'Color Forum', University of Texas, Austin.

In 1972, I was in Venice to install my work Baroque Cascade, *which measured ten by seventy-five feet when undraped. I was there alongside Ron Davis, Diane Arbus, Keith Sonnier, Jim Nutt, Richard Estes, and Walter Hopps. I went over early to assist with the installation. I was particularly excited to show my work because of my desire to connect painting and architecture.*[19]

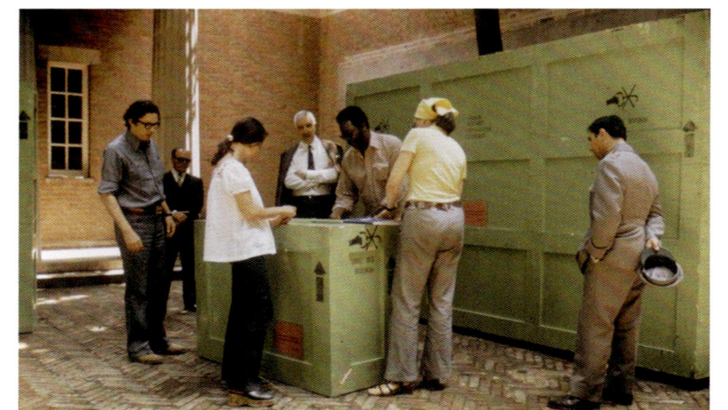

Gilliam with Walter Hopps (far left) unpacking crates during the installation of the 36th Venice Biennale, 1972

1973

Gilliam continues to explore large-scale works that expand painting beyond the frame of the canvas. He contributes a newly commissioned large-scale Drape painting to 'Works in Spaces', at the San Francisco Museum of Modern Art, titled *Autumn Surf* (1973), which is made with 150 yards of polypropylene and suspended and draped over long redwood beams.

Gilliam is awarded a National Endowment for the Arts grant for his studio workshop activities, which he also receives in 1974 and 1975.

Gilliam is a visiting artist at the University of Wisconsin and begins to create prints with fellow faculty member, William Weege, founder and master printer of Jones Road Print Shop and Stable, in Barneveld, Wisconsin.

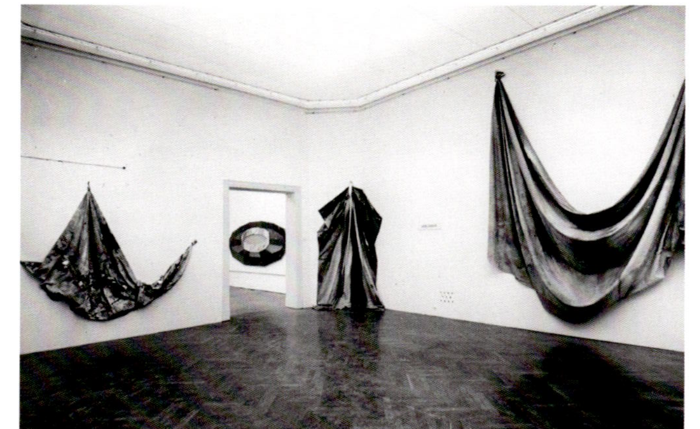

Installation view of Gilliam's presentation at the United States pavilion at the 36th Venice Biennale, 1972

Solo Exhibitions:
'Sam Gilliam', Jefferson Place Gallery, Washington, D.C., 27 November–31 December.
'Sam Gilliam', Galerie Darthea Speyer, Paris.
'Sam Gilliam', Fendrick Gallery, Washington, D.C., November.
'Sam Gilliam', University of California, Irvine, April.
'Sam Gilliam', Greenberg Gallery, St. Louis, March.
'Sam Gilliam', Howard University Gallery of Art, Washington, D.C., March.
Maison de la Culture, Rennes, France

Group Exhibitions:
'Works For Spaces', San Francisco Museum of Modern Art, 9 February–8 April.

1974

Gilliam presents his work for the second time with Melvin Edwards and William T. Williams (following the 1969 show 'X to the Fourth Power', Studio Museum in Harlem, New York), at the Wadsworth Atheneum Museum of Art, Hartford, Connecticut.

Solo Exhibitions:
'Sam Gilliam', Carl Solway Gallery, Cincinnati, September.
'Sam Gilliam: Paintings, Watercolors, Prints', Linda Farris Gallery, Seattle, August.
'Sam Gilliam', Phoenix Gallery, San Francisco.

Group Exhibitions:
'Gilliam/Edwards/Williams: Extensions', Wadsworth Atheneum Museum of Art, Hartford, Connecticut, 6 February–17 March.
'Expo '74', Spokane, Washington, 4 May–3 November.
'Printed, Cut, Folded and Torn', Museum of Modern Art, New York, 10 May–11 August.
'Art Now', The Kennedy Center, Washington, D.C.
'Tokyo Print International', Tokyo, Japan.
'Black Artists', University of California, Fresno.

Sam was a very fine painter who was curious and experimental. Thinking about the surfaces art was made on didn't start with Sam – but he took a step most people didn't understand was possible. Sam took the step. He got seen the right way by some people who were paying attention to that kind of thing, and they immediately blessed it.

Often fellow artists are pretty quick to recognize the implications of style and possible significance. One of the earliest things I did involved suspended elements of steel and chains. When Sam and I showed together at the Studio Museum in Harlem [in a landmark 1969 show], I was doing the first of the barbed wire pieces of mine, some of which were wall-attached, some of which were suspended. And we almost took it for granted that we were both taking steps.[20]

– Melvin Edwards

1975

Gilliam exhibits his first outdoor installation of large-scale Drape paintings, *Seahorses*, presented on the façade of the Philadelphia Museum of Art as part of the summer Philadelphia Festival, organized by the Greater Philadelphia Cultural Alliance. The paintings are installed the following summer at the Brooklyn Museum.

Gilliam makes *Three Panels for Mr. Robeson* (1975), named in honour of the Civil Rights activist, actor and singer Paul Robeson, who is also the subject of Dorothy Gilliam's 1976 biography, *Paul Roberson: All American*. The three-panel painting is considered a masterwork of Gilliam's suspended canvases. The piece is first presented in the Corcoran Gallery of Art's 34th Biennial of Contemporary American Painting.

Gilliam becomes an early board member of the Washington Project of the Arts, along with William Christenberry, Tom Green, E. Ethelbert Miller, Robert Rauschenberg, Renée Stout and Maida Withers.

Gilliam is the inaugural artist-in residence at the Brandywine Workshop in Philadelphia. He will become a longstanding supporter of the workshop and will return several times to make prints.

Gilliam receives a Distinguished Alumni Award from the College of Arts and Sciences, University of Louisville.

Solo Exhibitions:
'Seahorses by Sam Gilliam', Philadelphia Museum of Art, 26 April–25 May.
'Sam Gilliam: Paintings 1970–1975', Fendrick Gallery, Washington, D.C., 15 October–8 November.
'Sam Gilliam', Linda Ferris Gallery, Seattle.

Group Exhibitions:
34th Biennial of Contemporary American Painting, Corcoran Gallery of Art, Washington, D.C., 22 February–6 April.

1976

Solo Exhibitions:
'Sam Gilliam: Paintings and Works on Paper', J.B. Speed Art Museum, Louisville, Kentucky, 12 January–8 February.
'Sam Gilliam', Galerie Darthea Speyer, Paris, 13 May–18 June.
'Sam Gilliam: An Exhibition of Paintings', Rutgers University Art Gallery, New Brunswick, New Jersey, 14 November–19 December.
'Sam Gilliam', Fendrick Gallery, Washington, D.C., November.
'Sam Gilliam', Nina Freudenheim Gallery, Buffalo, New York, May.

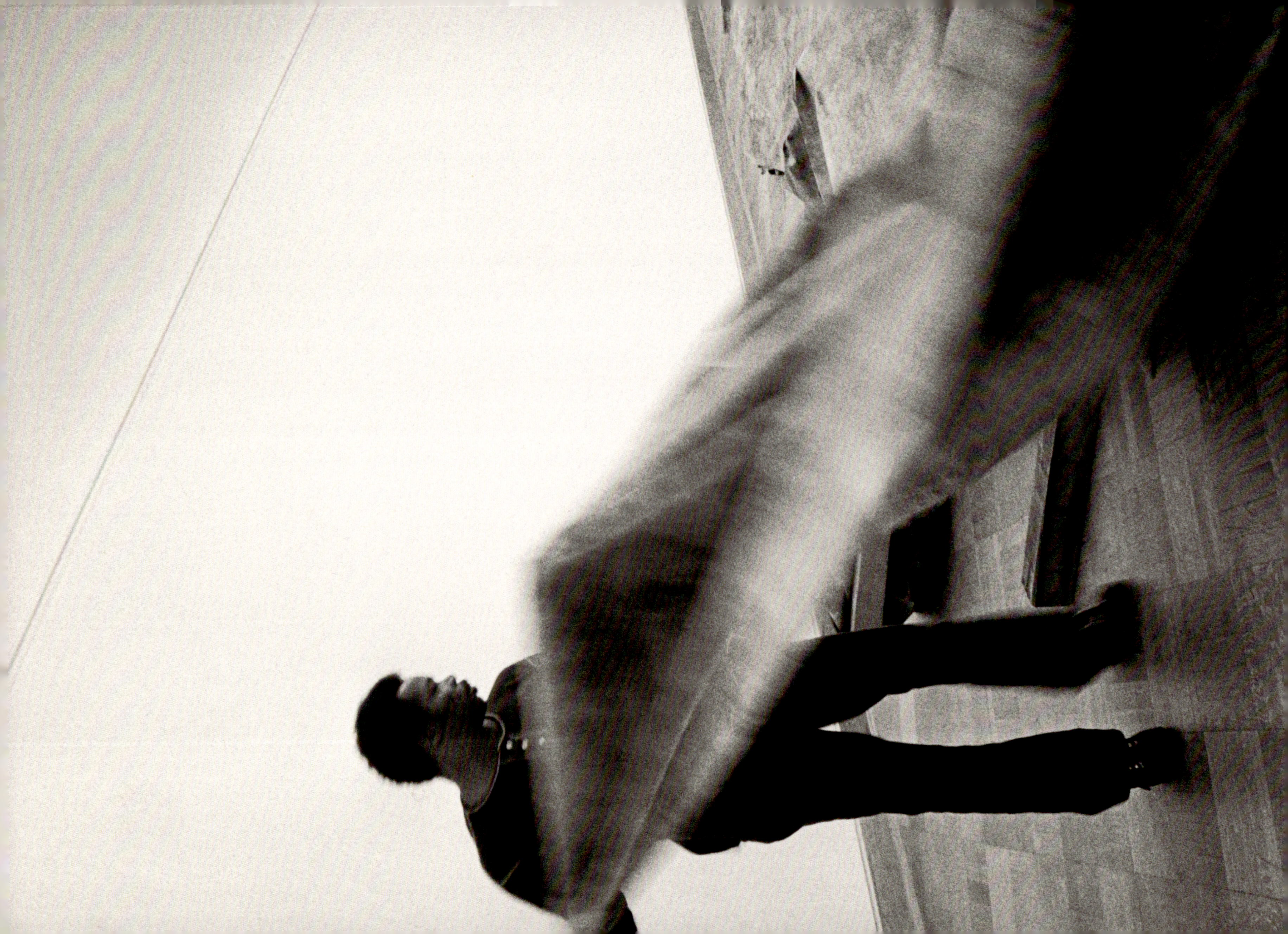

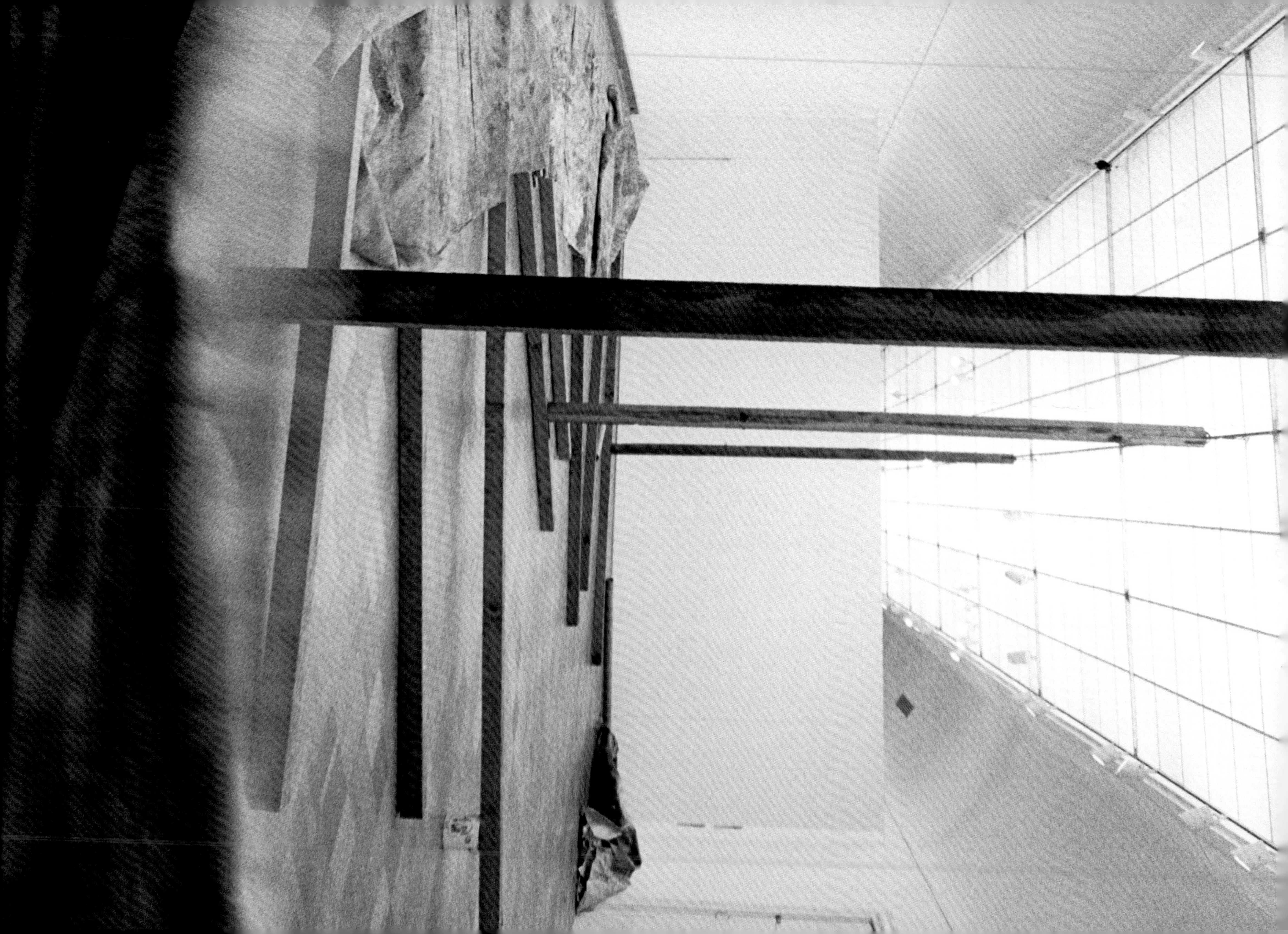

Group Exhibitions:
'72nd American Exhibition', Art Institute of Chicago, 13 March–9 May 1976.
'Handmade Paper Prints and Unique Works', Museum of Modern Art, New York, 28 June–12 September 1976.
'Resonance: Williams, Edwards, Gilliam', Murphy Fine Arts Center, Morgan State University, Baltimore, 25 October–19 November.
'National Print Exhibition, 20th Biennial: 30 Years of American Printmaking', Brooklyn Museum, New York, 20 November 1976–30 January 1977.
14th Festival Internationale de la Peinture, Cagnes-sur-Mer, France.

1977

Gilliam creates *Custom Road Slide* (1977) a series of fourteen ephemeral outdoor 'constructions' of fabric, wood, shale and pigment, placed along 400 yards of roadway lining the Niagara Gorge.

Gilliam creates inventive print works using new techniques, *Philly* and *Philadelphia Soft*, at the Fabric Workshop. They are 7' 10" and 8' 5", exceeding the usual dimensions of prints, and are displayed suspended from the ceiling, similarly to Gilliam's Drape paintings.

Solo Exhibitions:
'New Paintings by Sam Gilliam', Dart Gallery, Chicago, 23 April–21 May.
'Sam Gilliam', Oliver Dowling Gallery, Dublin, October–12 November.
'Sam Gilliam', Artpark, Lewiston, New York, July–August.
'Sam Gilliam', Pennsylvania State University, University Park, March.

Group Exhibitions:
'12th International Biennial of Graphic Art', Modern Gallery, Ljubljana, Yugoslavia, 13 May–31 August.
'New in the Seventies', University of Texas, Austin.
'Le Peinture et le Tissu', Museum of Modern Art, Lyon.

1978

Gilliam's survey exhibition, 'Indoor & Outdoor Paintings 1967–1978', at the University Gallery, University of Massachusetts, Amherst, is accompanied by the artist's first major exhibition monograph, featuring texts by Hugh Marlais Davies and Jay Martin Kloner. The show features four outdoor paintings, including *Circular Place Reflection* (1978), commissioned by the University Gallery and installed on its exterior wall.

Solo Exhibitions:
'Sam Gilliam', Carl Solway Gallery, New York, January–February.
'Sam Gilliam', University of Kentucky, Lexington,

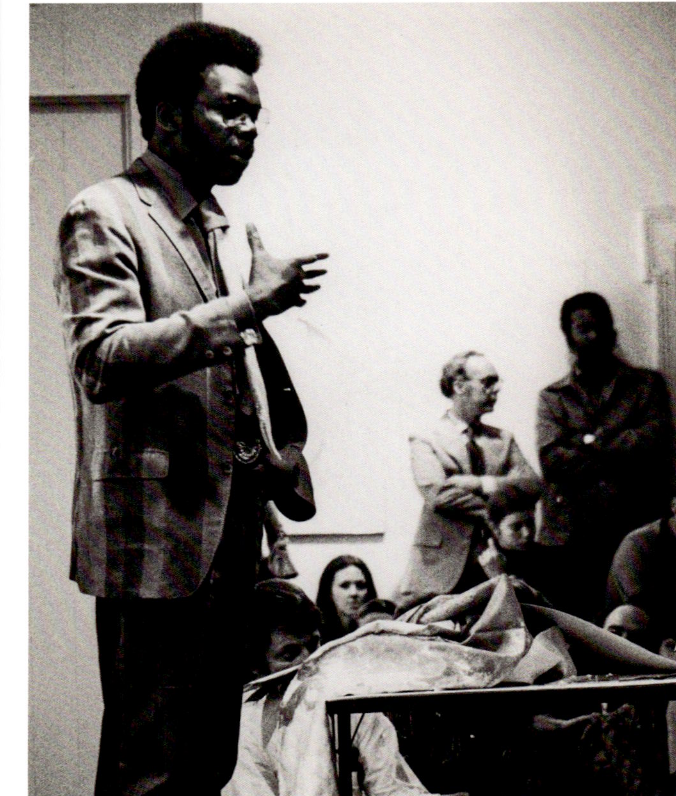

Gilliam during a lecture, late 1970s

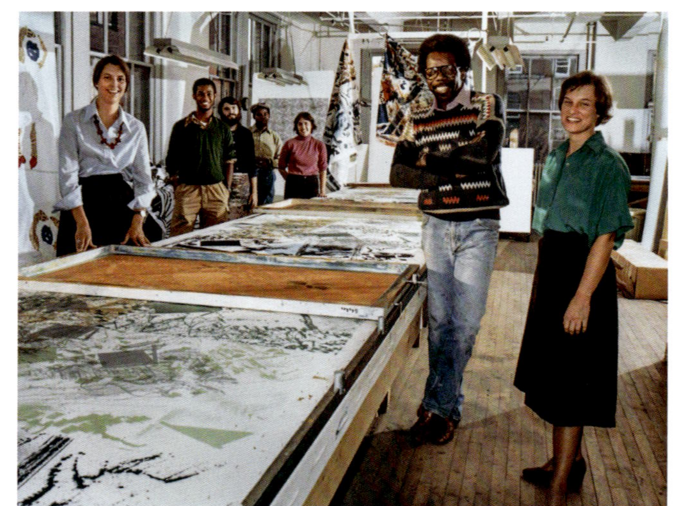

Gilliam printmaking at The Fabric Workshop and Museum, Anne d'Harnoncourt, Homer Jackson, Tim VanCampen, Will Stokes, Jr., Lucile Michels, and Marion Boulton 'Kippy' Stroud, 1977, Philadelphia

February–March.
'Sam Gilliam', Fendrick Gallery, Washington, D.C., February–March.
'Sam Gilliam', Anderson Gallery, Virginia Commonwealth University, Richmond, February–March.
'Sam Gilliam', Arnold Gallery, Atlanta, March–April.
'Sam Gilliam: Indoor & Outdoor Paintings 1967–1978', University Gallery, University of Massachusetts, Amherst, 16 September–5 November.
'Sam Gilliam', Galerie Darthea Speyer, Paris, 8 November–15 December.

Group Exhibitions:
'American Artists' Work in Private French Collections', Museum of Modern Art, Lyon.
'Foulkes/Gilliam', Galerie Darthea Speyer, Paris.
'American Black Artists', Dade County Library, Miami.
'Paper', The Dayton Art Institute, Ohio.

1979

The US General Services Administration (GSA) commissions *Triple Variants*, an artwork comprised of a large unstretched canvas, an aluminium beam and two large stones, installed on the 23rd-floor lobby of Richard B. Russell Federal Building and US Courthouse in Atlanta.

Gilliam is an artist in residence at Vermillion Editions Ltd, in Minneapolis, Minnesota, where he completes a series of monoprints, *Coffee Thyme*, with master printer Steve Anderson. He will return several times to work with the print studio in Minneapolis.

Solo Exhibitions:
'Sam Gilliam', Hamilton Gallery, New York, 10–31 March.
'Sam Gilliam', Dart Gallery, Chicago.
'Sam Gilliam', Middendorf/Lane Gallery, Washington, D.C.
'Sam Gilliam', Montgomery Community College, Rockville, Maryland.
'Sam Gilliam', Florence Duhl Gallery, New York.

Group Exhibitions:
'Art of the Eighties', The Grey Gallery at New York University, New York.
'Color and Structure', Hamilton Gallery, New York.

1980

Gilliam receives an Honorary Doctorate of Humane Letters from his alma mater, the University of Louisville. He is also named Visiting Distinguished Louis D. Beaumont Professor of Art, School of Fine Arts, Washington University in St Louis.

The GSA commissions another work for its collection, *Box Cars Grand*, which is installed in the lobby of the federal building in Detroit.

Gilliam's work is included in the influential exhibition, 'Afro-American Abstraction', curated by April Kingsley and organized by P.S. 1 Contemporary Art Center, which travels to nine institutions throughout the US. Featuring works by nineteen artists, including Ellsworth Ausby, Barbara Chase-Riboud, Edward Clark, Houston Conwill, Melvin Edwards, Sam Gilliam, David Hammons, Maren Hassinger, Richard Hunt, Jamillah Jennings, James Little, Alvin Loving, Tyrone Mitchell, Senga Nengudi, Howardena Pindell, Martin Puryear, Charles Searles, Jack Whitten and William T. Williams, the exhibition offers a counter-argument to Greenbergian formalism through an exploration of the relationship between African art and culture and abstract art created by Black artists in the United States.

Solo Exhibitions:
'Sam Gilliam', Simon Lowinsky Gallery, San Francisco, 15 January–16 February.
'Sam Gilliam', University of Wisconsin, Stevens Point, 15 February–8 March.
'Sam Gilliam', Middendorf/Lane Gallery, Washington, D.C., 18 October–8 November.
'Sam Gilliam', Dart Gallery, Chicago.

Group Exhibitions:
'Six Black Americans', New Jersey State Museum, Trenton, 28 January–30 March 1980.
'Afro-American Abstraction', P.S. 1 Contemporary Art Center, Long Island City, New York, 17 February–6 April 1980. Travelled to: Everson Museum of Art, Syracuse, New York, 6 February–29 March 1981; Los Angeles Municipal Art Gallery, 1 July–30 August 1982; Oakland Museum of California, 13 November 1982–2 January 1983; Brooks Memorial Art Gallery, Memphis, 2 February–20 March 1983; The Art Center, South Bend, Indiana, 4 September–16 October 1983; Toledo Museum of Art, Ohio, 22 January–26 February 1984; Bellevue Art Museum, Washington, 25 March–6 May 1984; Laguna Gloria Art Museum, Austin, 1 June–15 July 1984; Mississippi Museum of Art, Jackson, 14 September–4 November 1984.
'Fabric into Art', State University of New York, College at Old Westbury, NY.
'Planar Painting: Constructs 1975–1980', Alternative Museum, New York, 18 October–15 November.
'Alternatives by Black Artists', Washington Project for the Arts, Washington, D.C.
'Fabrications', Lowe Art Museum, Miami.
'Aspects of the 70s: Spiral', Museum of the Center of Afro-American Artists, Inc., Boston.
'Arts on the Line: Art for Public Transit Space', Hayden Gallery, Massachusetts Institute of Technology, Cambridge.

1981

Solo Exhibitions:
'Sam Gilliam', Gallery of Art, Washington University, St. Louis, 21 October–15 November.

'Sam Gilliam "New Work"', Nina Freudenheim Gallery, Buffalo, New York, 21 November–12 December.
'Sam Gilliam', Dart Gallery, Chicago.
'Sam Gilliam', Nexus, Atlanta.
'Sam Gilliam', Hamilton Gallery, New York.

Group Exhibitions:
'Installations: Stephen Antonakos, Sam Gilliam, Rockne Krebs', Middendorf/Lane Gallery, Washington, D.C.
'Sam Gilliam and Auste', Hamilton Gallery, New York.

1982

Gilliam is commissioned by the Boston Mass Transit Authority to create *Sculpture with a "D"* (1982) for the Davis Square Subway station in Sommerville, Massachusetts.

He becomes involved in lobbying for the rights of artists in D.C. and co-founds the Washington Coalition of Artists together with Lindsey Makepeace, Rockne Krebs, Lizette Brennan and Sheila Ishan.

Gilliam has his second solo institutional exhibition in New York at the Studio Museum in Harlem, curated by the museum's Director, Mary Schmidt Campbell.

He begins teaching painting at the University of Maryland, College Park, where he will be a member of the faculty until 1985.

Gilliam receives the Mayor's Art Award for the District of Columbia.

Gilliam and wife Dorothy separate.

Solo Exhibitions:
Birke Art Gallery, Marshall University, Huntington, West Virginia, 21 January–19 February.
'Red & Black to "D": Paintings by Sam Gilliam', Studio Museum in Harlem, New York, 16 November 1982–7 February 1983.
Richard Barry Gallery, Minneapolis.
Robert Kidd Gallery, Birmingham, Michigan.
Dart Gallery, Chicago.

Group Exhibitions:
'Painterly Abstraction', Fort Wayne Museum of Art, Indiana, 5 February–14 March.
'American Abstraction Now', Institute of Contemporary Art at Virginia Museum of Fine Art, Richmond, 1 September–3 October.
'10 + 10 + 10', Corcoran Gallery of Art, Washington, D.C.

1983

Gilliam meets Annie Gawlak, a curator and art consultant in Washington, D.C., with whom he begins a relationship

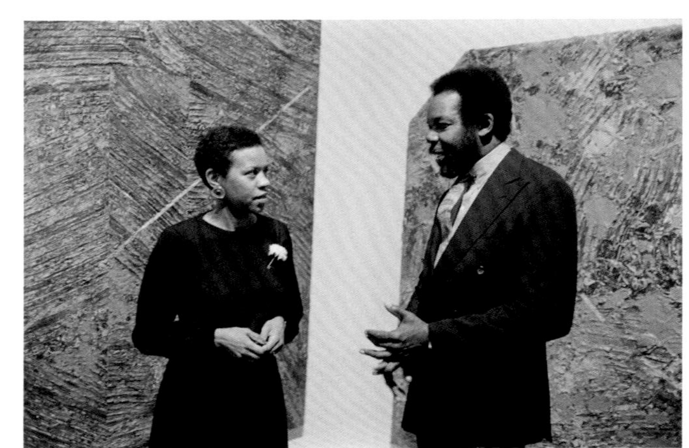

Gilliam and Mary Schmidt Campbell during the exhibition 'Red and Black to "D"', The Studio Museum in Harlem, New York, New York, 1982

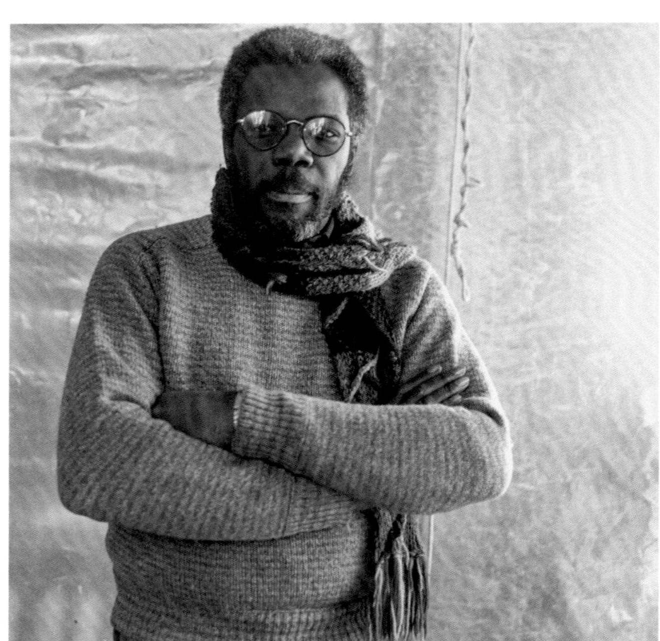

Gilliam in his studio,Washington, D.C., 1980s

in 1986. Gawlak opens G. Fine Art in 2001, which becomes an important and influential contemporary art gallery focused on supporting younger artists in Washington, D.C. Gilliam will occasionally exhibit his work at G. Fine Art throughout its tenure. Gawlak and Gilliam work closely together on exhibitions, sometimes writing together on the conceptual themes of Gilliam's painting.

Solo Exhibitions:
'Modern Painters at the Corcoran: Sam Gilliam', Corcoran Gallery of Art, Washington, D.C., 24 March–2 May.
'Sam Gilliam', Galerie Darthea Speyer, Paris.
'Sam Gilliam', McIntosh-Drysdale Gallery, Houston.
'Sam Gilliam', Middendorf/Lane Gallery, Washington, D.C.

Group Exhibitions:
'Dimensional Aspects of Painting', Klein Gallery, Chicago.

My work consists of solids and veils: the union of solids, or metal forms, seen as volumes against a raked and grooved paint surface. It is constructed painting, in that it crosses the void between object and viewer, to be part of the space in front of the picture pane. It represents an act of pure passage. The surface is no longer the final plane of the work. It is instead the beginning of an advance into the theatre of life.[21]

–Sam Gilliam with Annie Gawlak

1984

Gilliam receives the Distinguished Award for Pioneering in the Arts from American Black Artists, Inc.

Solo Exhibitions:
'Sam Gilliam: Recent Paintings', Herter Art Gallery, University of Massachusetts, Amherst.
Middendorf Gallery, Washington, D.C.

Group Exhibitions:
'Black History Month', University of Virginia, Charlottesville.
'Painting in the South', Virginia Museum of Fine Arts, Richmond, Virginia.
'Black Artists – Harlem Renaissance', Bucknell University Center Gallery, Lewisburg, Pennsylvania.

1985

Gilliam begins teaching at Carnegie Mellon University, Pittsburgh, where he will teach until 1989. He spends significant time in Pittsburgh but does not relocate. He becomes close to many local artists and jazz musicians, among them sculptor Thaddeus Mosley, with whom he will enjoy a lifelong friendship.

Solo Exhibitions:
'Sam Gilliam', Monique Knowlton Gallery, New York.

Group Exhibitions:
'Artistic Collaboration', The Water Tower Art Association, Louisville, Kentucky.

I first met Sam about 1972 when he did a show at a little gallery not far from the Carnegie. The gallery was called The King Pitcher Gallery. They had an after party at the hostess' home, and that's where I first met Sam and Dorothy Gilliam. We hit it off right away; we were both talking about the circumstances of us being the only Afro-Americans at this party, and we kept in touch. I told him I had gotten his Art in America cover magazine about two years ago. I'd been following his work and he wanted to see what I was doing and we became fast friends. And then after he started teaching graduate painting at CMU, he would come in on Wednesday and leave Friday morning.

At that time there were a lot of clubs and a lot of good music playing and we'd go to hear anyone who was playing in town, and we'd also have dinner. Sometimes I'd cook at my house and then after his marriage dissolved, I started going down to D.C., since I was single. And I'd go by and we'd go out and particularly when he had a show up, I'd go down and see the show. I saw most of the shows that he was doing then.

We talked a great deal about art and about people, friends of his like Jack Whitten?, who was slightly discouraged because he wasn't getting any attention back in those days. And Sam told him, "You just keep painting. You're doing great and just keep piling them up. People will notice it for sure." Anyhow, because he always encouraged me and I encouraged him, I remember one time when he was preparing for a show in San Francisco or somewhere, and I said, "Wow, it really looks great." He says, "Can't you see how worried I am? It doesn't look great to me." And so we were sort of laughing, and that pretty much was us, encouraging each other and being in touch. When people were down on Sam because he wasn't doing the type of painting a lot of people thought he should be doing, back in the Black painter's movement, I would say, "Well, you just got to do what you want to do because that's what I'm doing. I don't care what anybody thinks." And so that pretty much sums up our basic friendship and encouragement and so forth.

I always thought that Sam was one of the finest painters in the country. He never really got the dues, but that didn't matter. I think the students and other people recognized his talent and his individuality and also his persistence because when Sam was out there as an abstract painter, there weren't many Afro-American painters in the 1970s who were known for abstraction. And so he was one of the people that were holding forth on his own ideas and had the courage and integrity to just be Sam Gilliam, which I admired him for. [22]

– Thaddeus Mosley, 2023

Thad is the most beautiful artist you'll want to see. He used to be a postman and then a jazz musician and critic. He is

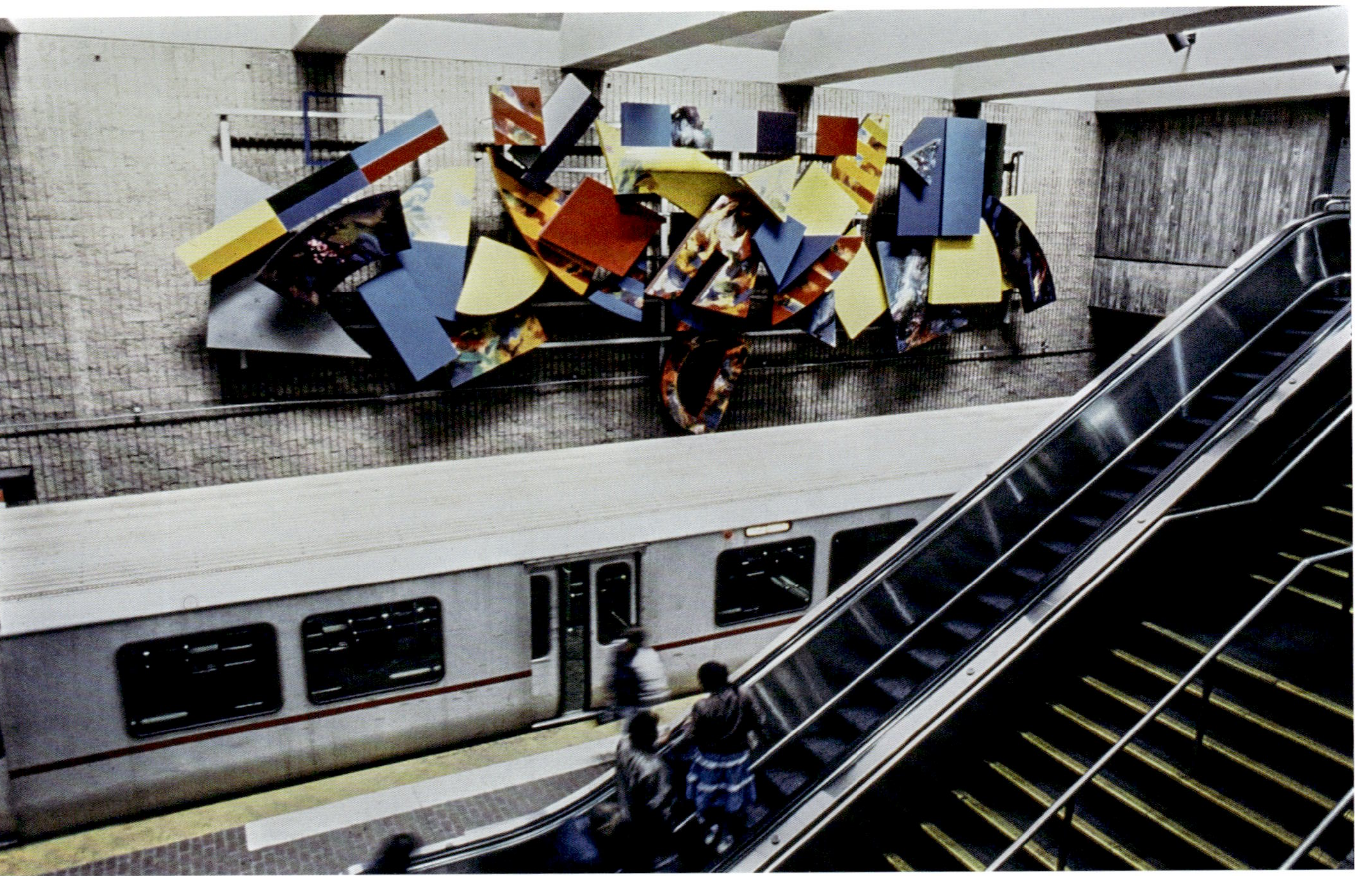

Sculpture with a "D", Davis MBTA Subway Station, Somerville, Massachusetts, 1983

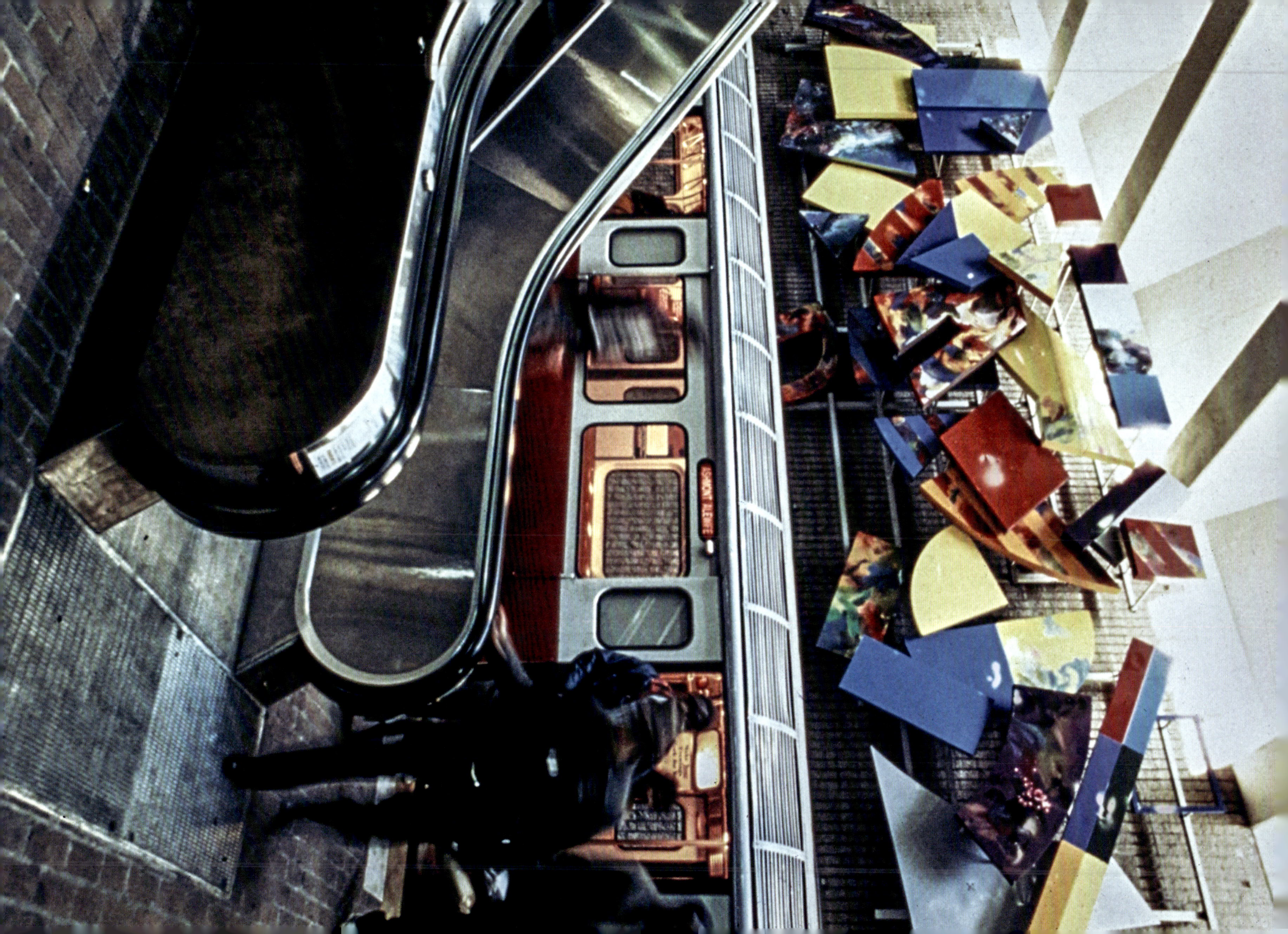

actually the soul of Pittsburgh ... I knew Thad before I came to Pittsburgh – he invited me to the city. He just knew everybody. When I taught at Carnegie Mellon, Thad and I spent more time together. I taught there for five years, mainly because they were being penalized for not allowing Black people to be a part of the university, so they had to hire a teacher who would also be paid a commensurate salary. If I ever got locked out, which I did sometimes at university, I'd go spend the night with Thad. I wrote an essay that got him into his first gallery. That was the beautiful thing about Pittsburgh when the steel mills died: there was the Mattress Factory, there was a celebration of Warhol, there was the Carnegie and the Carnegie International, and then there was Thad. We talk all the time. Thad is the future.[23]

– Sam Gilliam

1986

Gilliam is invited to present a solo exhibition at Carnegie-Mellon University Art Gallery, in Pittsburgh, where he is also a faculty member. He requests that other artists be invited to participate in the exhibition, resulting in the group show, 'Abstraction/Abstraction', which includes Emily Cheng, Sharon Gold, Jonathan Lasker, Kathleen Montgomery, Michael Mulhern, David Reed and Stephen Westfall.

In May, Gilliam gives the Commencement speech at the Memphis School of Art, 'The Transformation of Nature through Nature'. The speech is republished multiple times. Gilliam receives the President's Award from the Maryland College of Art and Design, Silver Spring, as well as the Order of Merit Award from the Alumni Association at the University of Louisville and an Honorary Doctorate from the Atlanta College of Art.

Solo Exhibitions:
'Sam Gilliam', Davis/McClain Gallery, Houston.

Group Exhibition:
'Abstraction/Abstraction', Carnegie-Mellon University Art Gallery, Pittsburgh, 22 March–27 April.

It is said at this time in 1986 there is a lull in art, that the thing that was sought in Post WWII years by many immigrants coming here has been lost. It is said that even the sense of this land as honored by the Hudson River School is lost from American art. What has come to replace this great inheritance is known as rampant commercialism and production. It is suggested that there is not a transcendence between the public and the art, that only a special group counts. It sounds like Sodom and Gomorrah reigns in this mythical land with the gigantic volcano. Many of us have come to recognize the absence of the Centaur, the lowering of the light. But do we recognize more specifically, the possibility of losing the nature of humanity in this way? Do we realize that there is a need for the artist to act as an artist? Where does this come from?

I guess the most immediate answer is contained in something I have already expressed earlier in this speech. That is of the professor who even though on the run, made drawings, who even though imprisoned kept art alive in his head and who upon release went around the world to make sure that the world was still there, who created the mighty Centaur as a symbol of himself, as an artist to remind himself that the artist was still there.

[...] *Thus I want to say to you, as the artist, you are nature. I must say that you as the artist must always make new work. You as the artist must keep the Centaur present. You as the artist must keep the fire blazing.*[24]

– Sam Gilliam

1987

Curator David Driskell invites Gilliam to present a solo exhibition at the inaugural exhibitions of the Anacostia Community Museum, in Washington, D.C. Always interested in supporting the broader artist community, Gilliam requests that Driskell expand the exhibition and they work together to invite fellow artists Martha Jackson-Jarvis, Keith Morrison and William T. Williams to participate.

Gilliam continues to work with printmaker and photographer Bill Weege, now at Tandem Press, in Madison, Wisconsin. Gilliam and Weege collaborate over many years, with Gilliam visiting the printshop every summer with his daughters. Together they experiment with innovative techniques and Gilliam produces large-scale prints.

Solo Exhibitions:
'Sam Gilliam: Paintings 1985–1986', Carl Solway Gallery, Cincinnati, 20 February–28 March.

Group Exhibitions:
'Contemporary Visual Expressions', Anacostia Community Museum, Washington, D.C., 27 May–31 July.

So Gilliam is in many ways a blues man. He is a farmer of the untilled "bottoms" of rich sonorous soil refined and polished to visual perfection. His art sings the blues that were blue before Picasso knew that African art contained a blues formula, or even before the Cubist and modernist experimenters bothered to examine the shrines of Gilliam's African ancestors, and once having been informed then "invented" assemblages and installations. So I caution the viewer; "do not go gently into that good night" of Gilliam's artistic statement hoping to find only a second-generation Washington Color Painter or an abstractionist preoccupied with Euclidean geometry and expressionist and neo-plastic patterns. There is in the words of the untutored bluesman "more to be seen there than what meets the eye" in Gilliam's art. Here one sees the raw account of

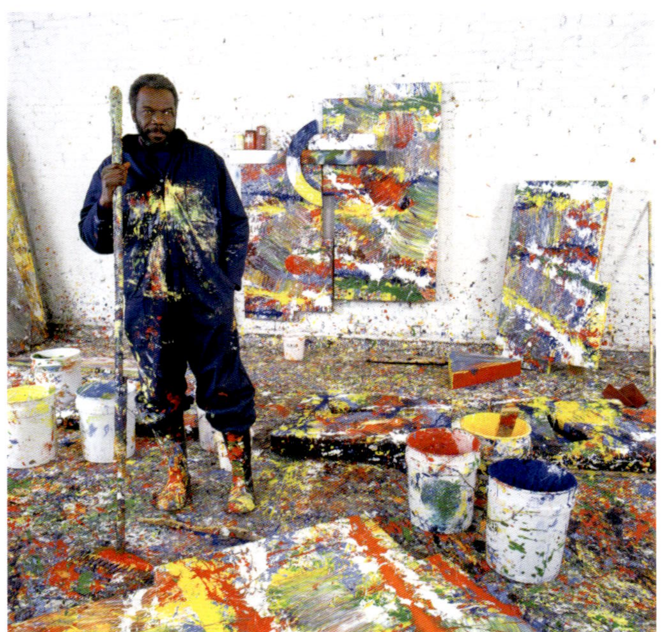

Gilliam in his U Street studio, Washington, D.C., 1990

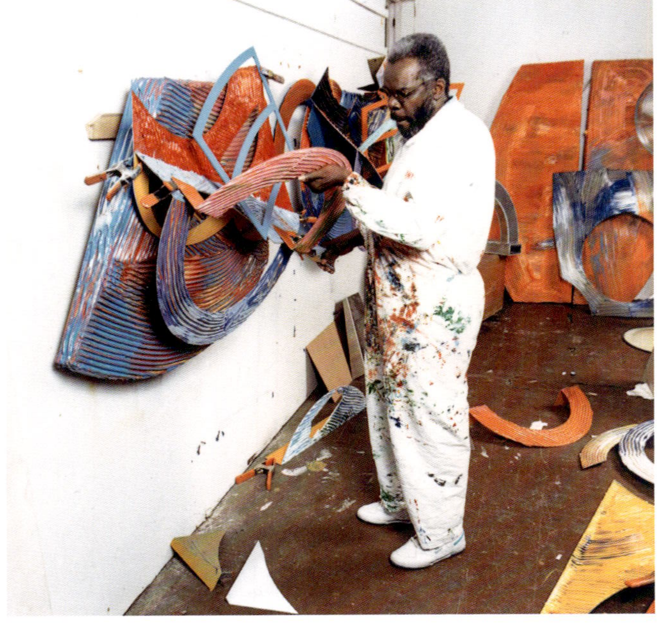

Gilliam in his U Street studio, Washington, D.C., late 1980s

impromptu inventiveness associated with change and the physical reaction one makes of it to the visual world.[25]
– David Driskell

1989

Gilliam receives a National Endowment for the Arts Individual Grant and retires from full-time teaching.

Solo Exhibitions:
'Sam Gilliam: Recent Paintings', Barbara Fendrick Gallery, New York, 15 November–16 December.

Group Exhibitions:
'The Blues Aesthetic: Black Culture and Modernism', Washington Project for the Arts, Washington, D.C., 14 September–9 December 1989. Travelled to: California Afro-American Museum, Los Angeles, opened on 14 January 1990; Duke University Museum of Art, Durham, North Carolina, 1990.

1990

Gilliam receives an honorary Doctorate of Humane Letters at Northwestern University, Evanston, Illinois.

Solo Exhibitions:
'Sam Gilliam: Small Drape Paintings 1970–1973', Middendorf Gallery, Washington, D.C., 24 February–24 March.
'Sam Gilliam: 1969–1975', Klein Art Works, Chicago, 10 June–29 July.

1991

The Metropolitan Transportation Authority Arts for Transit commissions a new work by Gilliam for the Jamaica Center train station in Queens, NY. *Jamaica Center Station Riders, Blue* is a large aluminium sculpture of geometric shapes painted in primary colours and mounted high outside on a wall above one of the entrances.

Working closely with master printer Bill Weege at Tandem Press, Gilliam creates a new large-scale print. *Of Fireflies and Ferris Wheels* (c. 1990) is printed on pelon fabric and spans 100 yards; it is first exhibited in Seoul and later in Helsinki.

Solo Exhibitions:
'Sam Gilliam: Paintings 1970–1973', Barbara Fendrick Gallery, New York, 19 April–25 May.
'Sam Gilliam'', American Craft Museum, New York.
'Sam Gilliam', Galerie Darthea Speyer, Paris.
'Sam Gilliam', Walker Hill Arts Center, Seoul.

Group Exhibitions:
'Abstraction: The 90s', Andre Emmerich Gallery, New York.

1992

Gilliam receives an Honorary Doctor of Arts & Letters from the University of Louisville, Louisville, Kentucky.

Solo Exhibitions:
'Sam Gilliam: Of Fire and Ferris Wheels', Arts America Program, United States Information Agency, Helsinki, 1992.

1993

Gilliam receives an Honorary Doctorate of Fine Arts from the Corcoran Gallery and School of Art.

1994

Solo Exhibitions:
'Sam Gilliam: Golden Element Inside Gold', Whitney Museum of American Art at Philip Morris, New York, 20 January–1 July.
'Sam Gilliam: Bikers Move Like Swallows', Baumgartner Galleries, Washington, D.C., through 26 November.

1995

Group Exhibitions:
'44th Biennial Exhibition of Contemporary American Painting', Corcoran Gallery of Art, Washington, D.C., 16 December 1995–19 February 1996.
'Richard Artschwager, Sam Gilliam, Jim Hyde', Baumgartner Gallery, Washington, D.C.

1996

Gilliam's commission for the La Guardia Airport in Queen's New York is unveiled. *Dihedral* is comprised of polychromed aluminium suspended on aircraft cables, and measures some 80 feet long and 30 feet high: the shape suggests the form of a bird or an airplane's cockpit.

He receives an honorary Doctorate of Fine Arts from the American University, Washington, D.C.

Solo Exhibitions:
'Sam Gilliam: Construction', J.B. Speed Memorial Museum, Louisville, Kentucky, 1996.
'Sam Gilliam: A Still on the Potomac', Baumgartner Galleries, Washington, D.C., 1996.

1997

Gilliam receives an Honorary Doctorate at the University of Wisconsin-Madison.

Solo Exhibitions:
'Sam Gilliam', Klein Gallery, Chicago, opened 22 February 1997.
'Sam Gilliam: Of Fireflies and Ferris Wheels: Monastery Parallel', Kunstmuseum Kloster Unser Lieben Frauen, Magdeburg, Germany, 3 May–22 June.
'Sam Gilliam: The Three Musketeers', Baumgartner Galleries, Washington, D.C.

Group Exhibitions:
'Seeing Jazz', International Gallery of the Smithsonian Institution, Washington, D.C., 30 October 1997–19 January 1998.

1998

Gilliam's solo exhibition at the Kreeger Museum in Washington, D.C. features a series of newly commissioned paintings and is the artist's first solo museum show in Washington since his exhibition at the Corcoran Gallery of Art in 1983.

Commissioned by the Art in Architecture Program for the Fine Arts Collection of US General Services Administration, *Color of Medals* (1998), is installed at the Philadelphia Veterans Administration. The work features multiple hinged panels in addition to shapes and colours inspired by iconography drawn from historical military medals.

Gilliam receives an Honorary Doctorate from the University of Tampa, Florida.

Solo Exhibitions:
'Sam Gilliam in 3-D', Kreeger Museum, Washington, D.C., 16 October 1998–2 January 1999.
'Sam Gilliam', Klein Gallery.

1999

Solo Exhibitions:
'Sam Gilliam: New Paintings and Sculpture', Klein Gallery, Chicago, 27 March–24 April.
'Sam Gilliam: Works '99', Marsha Mateyka Gallery, Washington, D.C., 15 October–27 November.

2000

Solo Exhibitions:
'Sam Gilliam', Georgetown Gallery, Georgetown, Kentucky.

Group Exhibitions:
'The Chemistry of Color: African American Artists is Philadelphia, 1970–1990', Pennsylvania Academy of Fine Arts, Philadelphia, 5 February–9 May.
'Abstract Notions: Selections for the Permanent Collection',

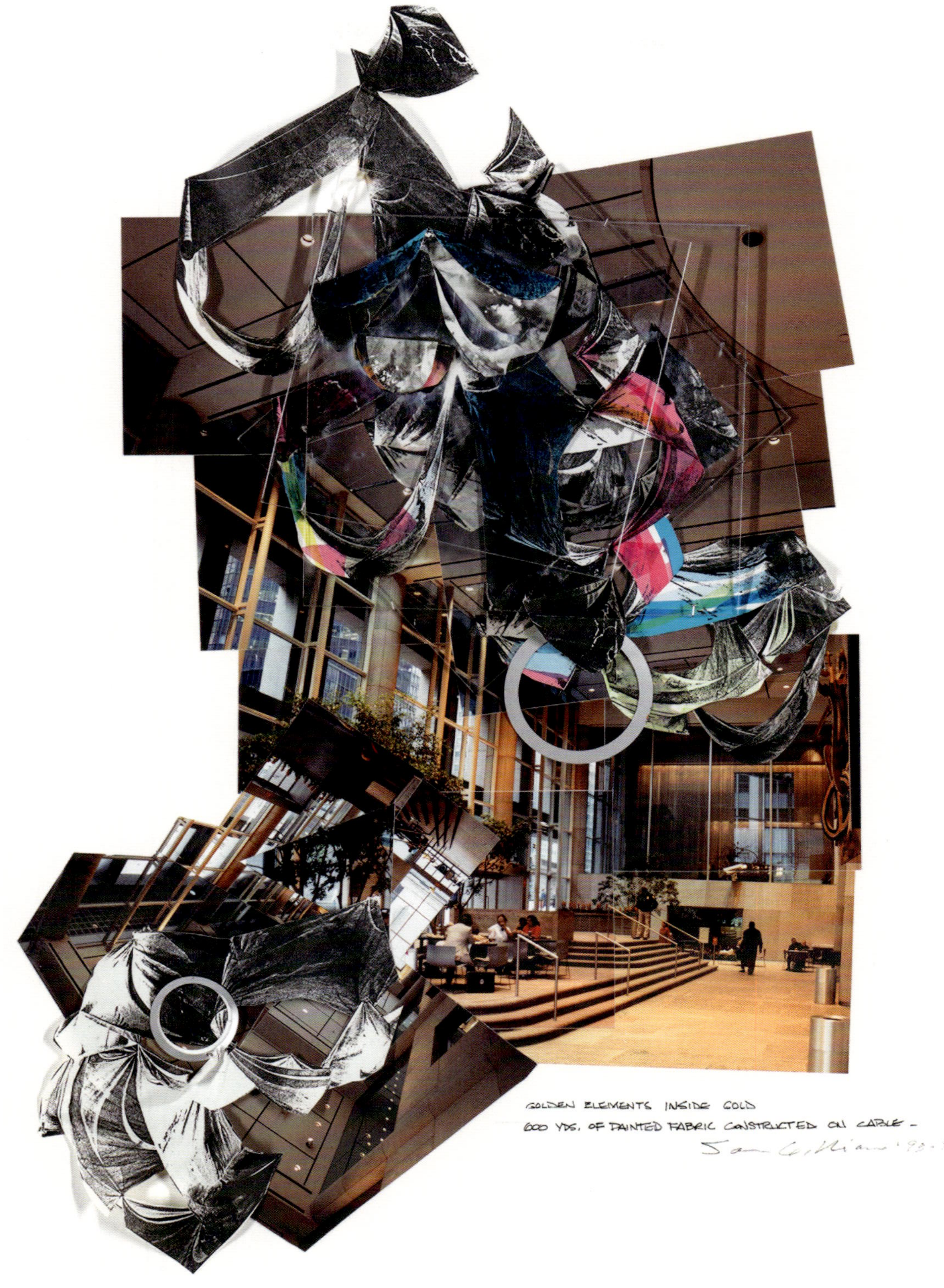

Maquette for Golden Elements Inside Gold, 600 Yds. of Painted Fabric Constructed on Cable, 1993–94

University of Massachusetts, Amherst, Massachusetts, 16 September–28 October.

2001

Gilliam is inducted into the National Academy Of Design.

Solo Exhibitions:
'Sam Gilliam', Imago Galleries, Palm Desert, California.
'Sam Gilliam: From Shiraz', Marsha Mateyka Gallery, Washington, D.C.

2002

Gilliam collaborates with the Washington Ballet's artistic director Septime Webre to create a complex suspended scenography for the company's production, *Journey Home*, which is performed at the Kennedy Center and later tours.

Solo Exhibitions:
'Sam Gilliam: New Paintings: Slats', Marsha Mateyka Gallery, Washington, D.C., 5 April–25 May 2002.

2004

Solo Exhibitions:
'Sam Gilliam', Sande Webster Gallery, Philadelphia, through 30 April.
'Sam Gilliam: New Work: 3', Marsha Mateyka Gallery, Washington, D.C., 3 April–22 May.
'Sam Gilliam: Folded & Hinged', Louisiana Art & Science Museum, Baton Rouge, 28 February–18 April. Travelled to: Lauren Rogers Museum of Art, Laurel, Mississippi, 15 May–3 July.

2005

A major US touring retrospective exhibition is organized by the Corcoran Gallery of Art, curated by Jonathan Binstock, its Curator of Contemporary Art. The exhibition is accompanied by a significant scholarly catalogue and reintroduces audiences to the breadth of Gilliam's practice over five decades.

Solo Exhibitions:
'Sam Gilliam: A Retrospective', Corcoran Gallery of Art, Washington, D.C., 15 October 2005–24 January 2006. Travelled to: Speed Art Museum, Louisville, 6 June–3 September 2006; Telfair Museum of Art, Savannah, 11 October–31 December 2006; Contemporary Arts Museum, Houston, 27 January–6 May 2007.
'Sam Gilliam: Sunlight', Marsha Mateyka Gallery, Washington, D.C., 8 October–26 November 2006.
'Sam Gilliam: Fixed Between Painting and Sculpture', Angie Newman Johnson Gallery, Episcopal High School, Alexandria, Virginia.

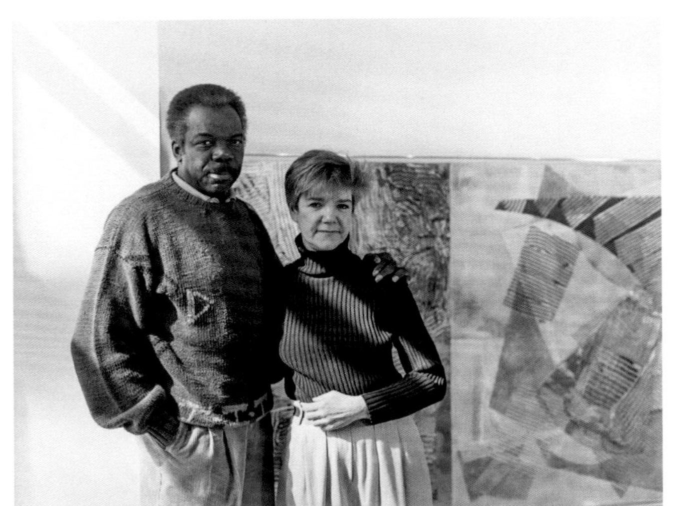

Gilliam and Annie Gawlak, U Street studio, Washington, D.C., mid 1990s

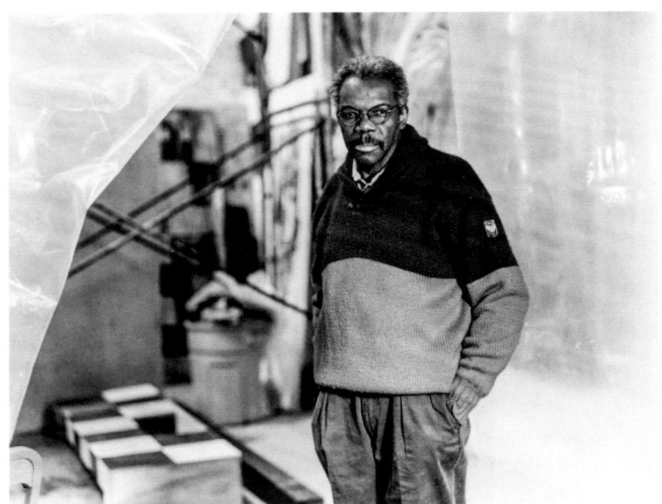

Gilliam in his studio, Washington, D.C., mid 2000s

Group Exhibitions:
'The Shape of Color', Art Gallery of Ontario, Toronto, 1 June–7 August.
'Resurfaced', Boston University Art Gallery, 9 September –30 October.

2006

Gilliam is named University of Louisville Alumnus of the Year.

Group Exhibitions:
'Sam Gilliam: Prints from the Artist's Collection', Luther W. Brady Art Gallery, George Washington University, Washington, D.C., 8 February–31 March 2006; Second Street Gallery, Charlottesville, Virginia, November 2006.
'Generations: African-American Art in the VMFA Collection', Virginia Museum of Fine Arts, Virginia Beach, Virginia, 19 January–12 March 2006.

2007

Gilliam receives Mississippi Governor's Award for Excellence in the Visual Arts.

The Art in Architecture Program of the Fine Arts Collection of the US General Services Administration (GSA) commissions Gilliam to create a new work for the Census Bureau Headquarters. *Census* (2007), is painted on sheets of birch plywood, cut into individual pieces and joined with piano hinges. It is the fourth and final commission Gilliam will produce for the GSA.

Solo Exhibitions:
'Sam Gilliam', Scarfone/Hartley Gallery, University of Tampa, 16–29 March.
'Sam Gilliam: White Papers and Paintings', Sande Webster Gallery, Philadelphia, 1–31 May.
'Sam Gilliam: New Work', Marsha Mateyka Gallery, Washington, D.C., 19 May–28 July.
'Sam Gilliam', Imago Galleries, Desert Springs, California.
'Sam Gilliam', Galerie Darthea Speyer, Paris.

Group Exhibitions:
'5 X 5: Five Artists choose Five Artists to Watch', Ann Loeb Bronfman Gallery at Washington District of Columbia Jewish Community Center, Washington, D.C., 15 February–13 May.

2008

Solo Exhibitions:
'Sam Gilliam: I Adapt to Eatonville', Zora Neale Hurston Museum of Fine Arts, Eatonville, Florida, 15 May–24 August.

Group Exhibitions:
'Three American Masters: Gene Davis, Sam Gilliam, Nathan Oliveira', Marsha Mateyka Gallery, Washington, D.C., 5 September–11 October.

2009

Gilliam receives the Key of Life Award from the NAACP.

Solo Exhibitions:
'Sam Gilliam: New Paintings', Marsha Mateyka Gallery, Washington, D.C., 9 May–3 July.

2010

Group Exhibitions:
'Colorscape: Abstract Painting, 1960–1979', Santa Barbara Museum of Art, California, 20 March–15 August.
'New Visions: Contemporary Masterworks from The Bank of America Collection', Mint Museum, Charlotte, North Carolina, 1 October 2010–17 April 2011.

2011

Gilliam's new public art commission, *From a Model to a Rainbow*, is installed in Washington, D.C.'s Metro underpass at 4th and Cedar Street, near Takoma Station, as part of D.C. Metro's Art-in-Transit Program.

Solo Exhibitions:
'Sam Gilliam: New Paintings', Marsha Mateyka Gallery, Washington, D.C., 22 January–12 March.
'Sam Gilliam: Flour Mill', The Phillips Collection, Washington, D.C., 29 January–24 April.
'Sam Gilliam: Close to Trees', Katzen Arts Center, American University, Washington, D.C., 2 April–14 August.
'Sam Gilliam: Paintings', Marsha Mateyka Gallery, Washington, D.C., 17 September–29 October.

2012

Rashid Johnson, an artist two generations younger than Gilliam, is a long-standing admirer of Gilliam's work and includes the artist in a group show he curates at South London Gallery.

Sam was like a giant. This is an artist who had exhibited in the most important venues in the world, whose work had been written about and discussed in some of the most critical of circles, whose ideas has been explored and examined and interrogated by artists and critics for the duration of the time he was making it. I think sometimes the art world is shortsighted in that it doesn't necessarily really understand its own canonical agency. Sam Gilliam has always been a giant of abstract painting. He's one of

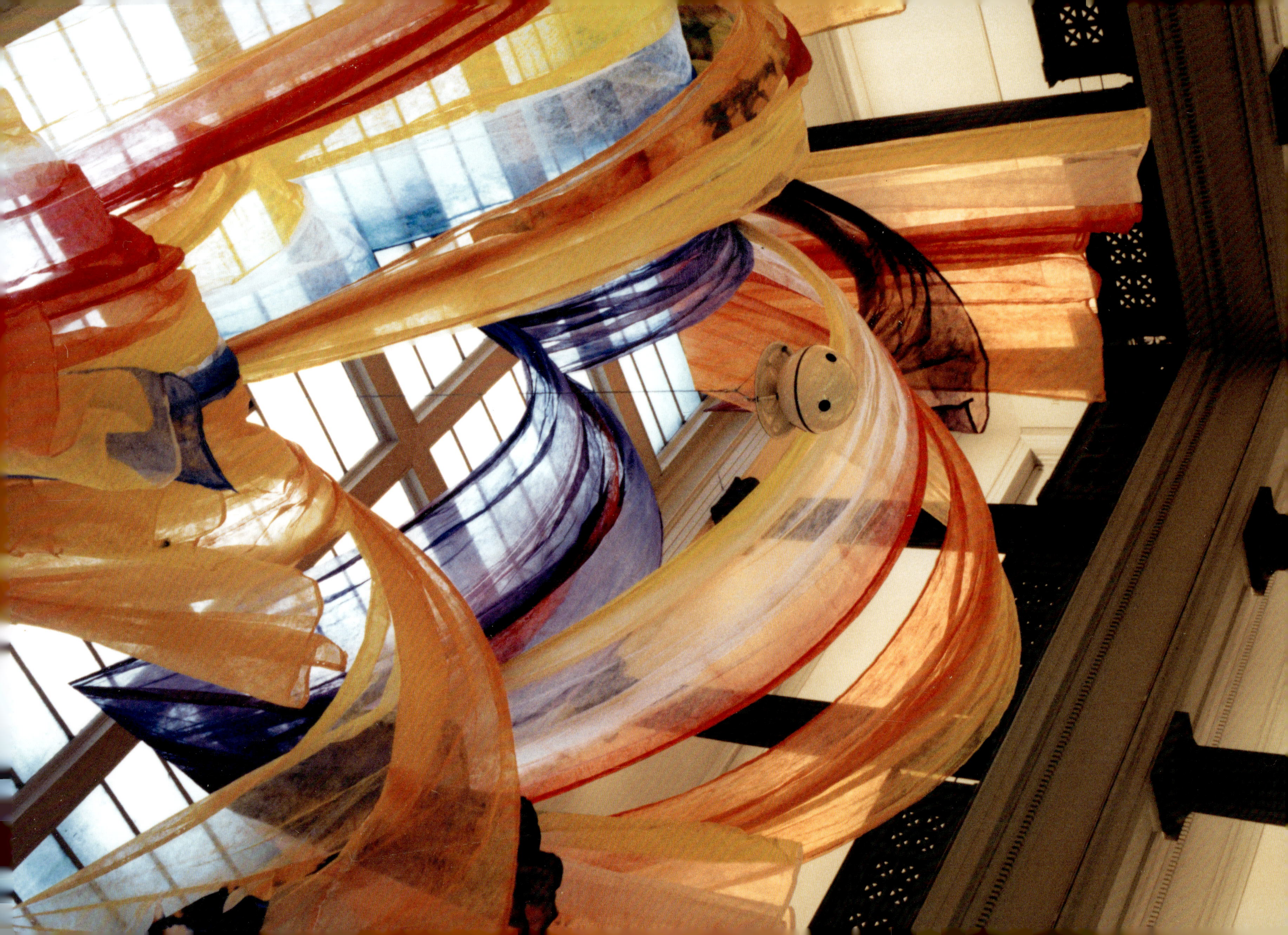

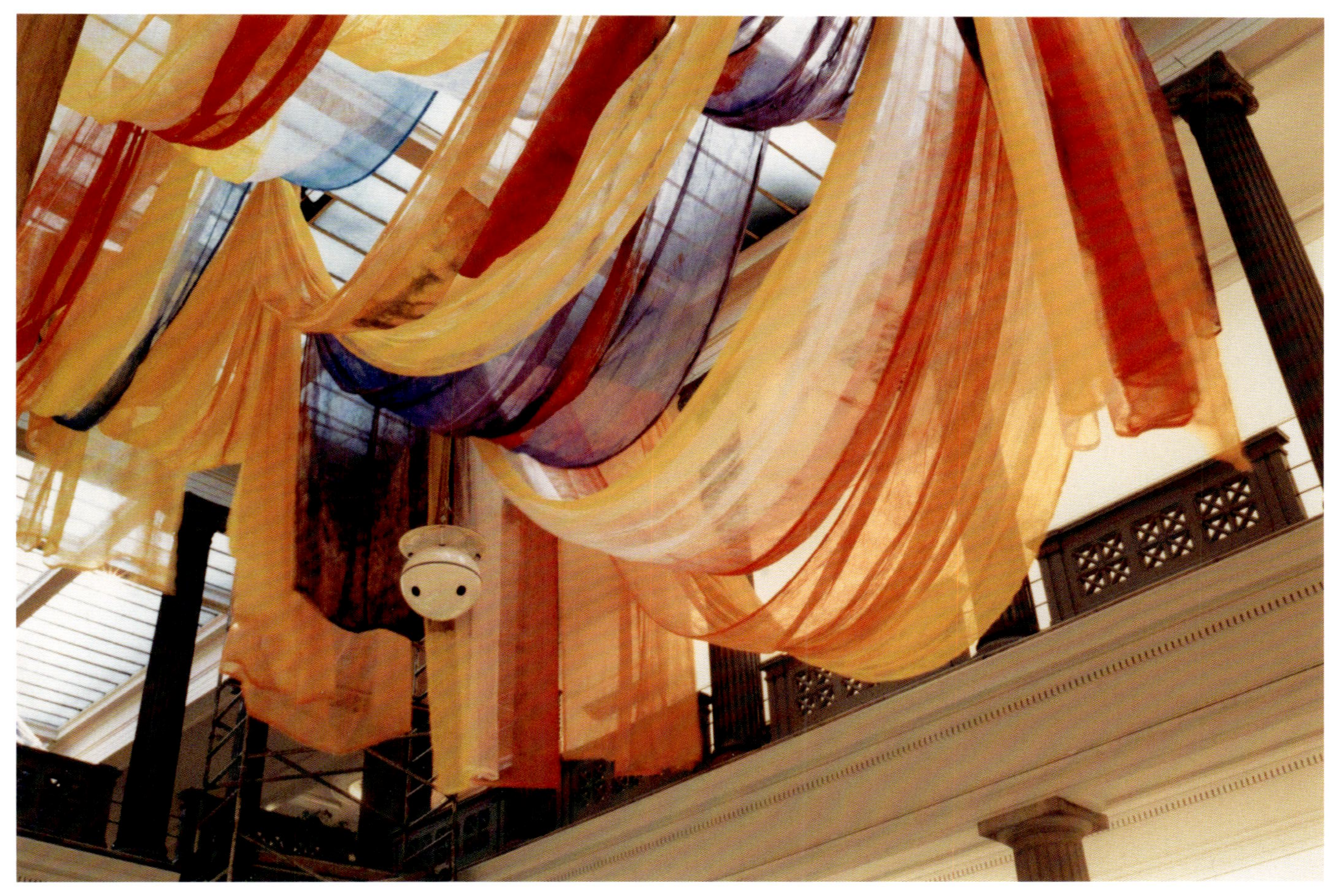

Bikers Move Like Swallows II, Corcoran Gallery of Art, Washington, D.C., 1995–96

the most innovative artists to ever create a picture. And I think that from the time he started making paintings until it ended, he was an enormous influence to a lot of people, and it's not a recent phenomenon by any stretch of imagination. My interest in Sam Gilliam came from the fact that Sam Gilliam was already an enormous artist in my eyes. It wasn't the opportunity to introduce him, it was the opportunity to collaborate with him that I was interested in.[26]

– Rashid Johnson, 2023

Johnson shares this admiration with his Los Angeles gallerist, David Kordansky and the two visit Gilliam's studio and are deeply moved by the artist's expansive, decades-long painting practice and his continued prolific production.

Gilliam joins David Kordansky Gallery, where his first solo exhibition is curated by Johnson. His work is also featured by Kordansky at Frieze Masters, London, with an in-depth presentation of his early works. The presentation receives great critical acclaim internationally and Gilliam begins to experience an elevation in his career which results in a significant increase in exhibition invitations, institutional acquisitions, scholarly criticism and rising auction records.

I found myself discussing Sam's work with Rashid Johnson over late-night drinks, a conversation that lasted well into the early morning hours. At the time, Rashid was not represented by my gallery, but it was through our shared love and respect for Sam's practice that a bridge was formed between us. Sam was a bridge in a myriad of other ways too. He conjured the daring spirit and divine power of John Coltrane, McCoy Tyner, Charles Mingus, Thelonious Monk, Miles Davis, and Pharoah Sanders – the jazz heavyweights of exploration and improvisation. Sam was an architect of color whose vision propelled him into cosmic realms where experimentation and the moral compass provided by brave beauty were the only constants.

In 2012, Rashid, Mike Homer, and I decided to find Sam and propose an exhibition of his work. At that first visit to Sam's Washington, D.C. studio – the first of many over the years – he responded to our proposal with what we thought was laughter, but soon realized were tears of joy. He quipped, "What took you so long?" and then we all cried together. For me, it was the beginning of an incredible adventure and collaboration rooted in love, art, and friendship.[27]

– David Kordansky, 2022

Group Exhibitions:
'The Spirit Level', Gladstone Gallery, New York, 24 March –21 April, curated by Ugo Rondinone.
'African American Art: Harlem Renaissance, Civil Rights Era, and Beyond', Smithsonian American Art Museum, Washington, D.C., 27 April–3 September 2012. Travelled to: Muscarelle Museum of Art at The College of William and Mary, Virginia, 28 September 2012–6 January 2013; Mennello Museum of American Art, Orlando, Florida, 1 February–28 April 2013; Peabody Essex Museum, Salem, Massachusetts, 1 June–2 September 2013; Hunter Museum of American Art, Chattanooga, Tennessee, 14 February–25 May 2014; and Crocker Art Museum, Sacramento, 29 June–21 September 2014.
'Constant Artist', Katzen Arts Center at American University, Washington, D.C., 9 June–12 August.
'Washington Color and Light', Corcoran Gallery of Art, Washington, D.C., 24 June–14 August.
'The 100th Annual Exhibition of Contemporary Art: The Vision Endures', Maier Museum of Art at Randolph College, Lynchburg, Virginia, 6 July–12 August.
'African American Art Since 1950: Perspectives from the David C. Driskill Center', the David C. Driskill Center at the University of Maryland, 20 September–14 December 2012. Travelled to: Taft Museum of Art, Cincinnati, 15 February–28 April 2013; The Harvey B. Gantt Center for African-American Arts, Charlotte, North Carolina, 16 January–15 June 2014; Figge Art Museum, Davenport, Iowa, 15 September 2014–4 January 2015; Polk Museum of Art, Lakeland, Florida, 21 March–29 June 2015; Susquehanna Art Museum, Harrisburg, Pennsylvania, 7 October 2016–22 January 2017.
'Drip, Drape, Draft', South London Gallery, London, 28 September–25 November, curated by Rashid Johnson.
'A Bigger Splash: Painting after Performance', Tate Modern, London, 14 November 2012–1 April 2013.

2013

Solo Exhibitions:
'Sam Gilliam: Hard Edge Paintings 1963–1966', David Kordansky Gallery, Los Angeles, 28 March–11 May, curated by Rashid Johnson.

Group Exhibitions:
'The Force of Color', Madison Museum of Contemporary Art, Wisconsin, 19 January–28 April.
'Assembly Required: Selections from the Permanent Collection', Studio Museum in Harlem, New York, 28 March–30 June.
'Black in the Abstract, Part 1: Epistrophy', Contemporary Arts Museum Houston, 31 October 2013–5 January 2014.

2014

Group Exhibitions:
'Black in the Abstract, Part 2: Hard Edges/Soft Curves', Contemporary Arts Museum Houston, 25 January 2014–23 March.
'Witness: Art and Civil Rights in the Sixties', Brooklyn Museum, New York, 7 March–13 July 2014. Travelled to: Hood Museum of Art at Dartmouth College, Hanover, New Hampshire, 30 August–14 December 2014; Blanton Museum of Art at the University of Texas, Austin, 15 February–10 May 2015.
'K@20', The Kreeger Museum, Washington, D.C., 20 February–31 July.
'Make it New: Abstract Painting from the National Gallery

of Art, 1950–1975', The Clark Art Institute, Williamstown, Massachusetts, 2 August–13 October.
'Sense of Place II: Selections from the Permanent Collection', Ogden Museum of Southern Art, New Orleans.

2015

Gilliam receives the inaugural Medal of Arts Lifetime Achievement Award by the US State Department for his long-time contributions to Art in Embassies and cultural diplomacy.

Group Exhibitions:
'Represent: 200 Years of African American Art', Philadelphia Museum of Art, 10 January–5 April.
'New Acquisitions', Rose Art Museum at Brandeis University, Waltham, Massachusetts, 11 February–7 June.
'Pretty Raw: After and Around Helen Frankenthaler', Rose Art Museum at Brandeis University, Waltham, Massachusetts, 11 February–7 June.
'Great Impressions IV: An Exhibition of Contemporary Prints', Dean Jensen Gallery, Milwaukee, on view through 14 June.
'Art in the Making: A New Adaptation', Luther W. Brady Art Gallery at George Washington University, Washington, D.C., on view through 17 July.
'Affecting Presence and the Pursuit of Delicious Experiences', The Menil Collection at Houston Museum District, 17 July–8 November.
'You Have to See This: Abstract Art from the Permanent Collection', Palmer Museum of Art at Pennsylvania State University, University Park, 1 September–6 December.
'Surface Tension', The FLAG Art Foundation, New York, 17 September–12 December.
'Surface Matters', Edward H. Linde Gallery at Museum of Fine Arts Boston, 31 October 2015–10 April 2016.
'Black: Color, Material, Concept', Studio Museum in Harlem, New York, 12 November 2015–6 March 2016.
'On Paper: Howard Hodgkin, Sam Gilliam, Gene Davis, Sheila Rotner, Andrea Way, Athena Tacha, Agnes Denes, Kathleen Kucka', Marsha Mateyka Gallery, Washington, D.C., 12 December 2015–23 January 2016.

2016

Gilliam is commissioned to produce a new work for the grand opening of the Smithsonian's National Museum of African American History. The large-scale painting, *Yet Do I Marvel (Countee Cullen)* (2016) references Harlem Renaissance poet Countee Cullen's poem on the resilient nature of creativity.

YET DO I MARVEL
Countee Cullen

I doubt not God is good, well-meaning, kind,
And did He stoop to quibble could tell why
The little buried mole continues blind,
Why flesh that mirrors Him must some day die,

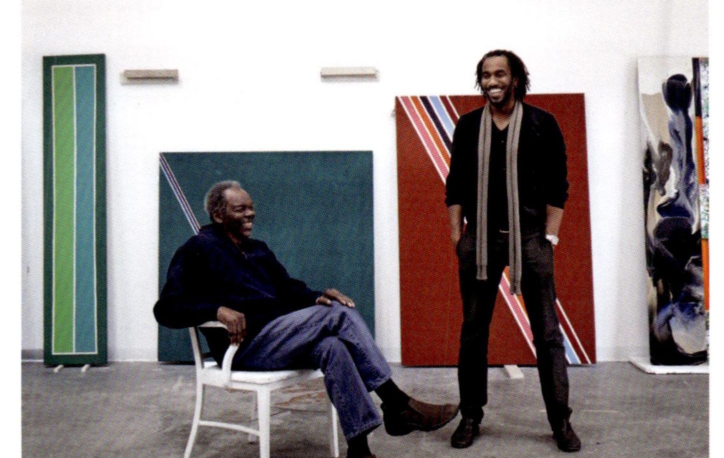
Gilliam with Rashid Johnson in front of Gilliam's early hard-edged abstractions, Washington, D.C., 2013

Make plain the reason tortured Tantalus
Is baited by the fickle fruit, declare
If merely brute caprice dooms Sisyphus
To struggle up a never-ending stair.
Inscrutable His ways are, and immune
To catechism by a mind too strewn
With petty cares to slightly understand
What awful brain compels His awful hand.
Yet do I marvel at this curious thing:
To make a poet black, and bid him sing![28]

Solo Exhibitions:
'Sam Gilliam: Green April', David Kordansky Gallery, Los Angeles, 4 June–16 July.

Group Exhibitions:
'Not New Now: Marrakech Biennale 6', Morocco, 24 February–8 May.
'Landmark: A Decade of Collecting at the Jepson Center', Telfair Museums, Savannah, Georgia, 11 March–14 August.
'A Celebration of the Speed Collection', Speed Art Museum, Louisville, Kentucky, opened on 12 March.
'Passages in Modern Art: 1946–1996', Dallas Museum of Art, 13 March 2016–18 June 2017.
'Close Readings: American Abstract Art from the Vanderbilt University Fine Arts Gallery', Vanderbilt University, Nashville, Tennessee, 17 March–26 May.
'Approaching American Abstraction: The Fisher Collection', San Francisco Museum of Modern Art, 14 May 2016–1 January 2017.
'Big & Bold: Selections from the Collection', Columbia Museum of Art, South Carolina, 27 May–23 October.
'Modern Heroics: 75 Years of African-American Expressionism', Newark Museum, New Jersey, 18 June 2016–8 January 2017.
'Artworks by African Americans from the Collection', Smithsonian American Art Museum, Washington, D.C., 31 August 2016–28 February 2017.
'Three American Painters: David Diao, Sam Gilliam, Sal Sirugo', Zimmerli Art Museum at Rutgers University and The State University of New Jersey, New Brunswick, 2 September 2016–30 July 2018.
'Complex Uncertainties: Artists in Postwar America', Jepson Center at Telfair Museums, Savannah, Georgia, 30 September 2016–8 May 2022.
'Circa 1970', Studio Museum in Harlem, New York, 17 November 2016–2 April 2017.
'Dimensions of Black', Jacobs Building at the Museum of Contemporary Art San Diego downtown, 16 December 2016–30 April 2017.
'Visual Art and the American Experience', National Museum of African American History and Culture, Washington, D.C.

2017

Mnuchin Gallery in New York presents an exhibition of early paintings by Gilliam.

Solo Exhibitions:
'Sam Gilliam', Seattle Art Museum, 6 May–19 November.
'Sam Gilliam: 1967–1973', Mnuchin Gallery, New York, 2 November–16 December.

Group Exhibitions:
'Revelations: Masterworks by African American Artists', McNay Art Museum, San Antonio, Texas, 10 January–7 May.
'AfroFantastic: Black Imagination and Agency in the American Experience', Cornell Fine Arts Museum at Rollins College, Orlando, Florida, 14 January–14 May.
'The Evolution of Mark-Making', Museum of Contemporary Art Jacksonville, Florida, 28 January–14 May.
'Investigating Identity: Race, Gender, and Sexuality in Contemporary Art', Maier Museum of Art at Randolph College, Lynchburg, Virginia, 3 February–9 April.
'Colour Is', Waddington Custot, London, 1 March–28 April.
'Approaching Abstraction: African American Art from the Permanent Collection', La Salle University Art Museum, Philadelphia, 15 March 2016–15 June 2017.
'Washington Color School: 50 Years Later', Bethesda Fine Art, Washington, D.C., on view through 15 December.
'Please Fasten Your Seat Belt as We Are Experiencing Some Turbulence', Leo Xu Projects, Shanghai, 18 March–30 April.
'Viva Arte Viva: 57th Venice Biennale', 13 May–26 November 2017.
'Spirit of Collaboration: Sam Gilliam and Lou Stovall', Griots' Art Gallery, Center for Haitian Arts, Miami, 10 June–30 September.
'Color People', Rental Gallery, East Hampton, New York, 1–25 July.
'Soul of a Nation: Art in the Age of Black Power', Tate Modern, London, 12 July–22 October 2017. Travelled to: Crystal Bridges Museum of American Art, Bentonville, Arkansas, 3 February–23 April 2018; Brooklyn Museum, New York, 14 September 2018–3 February 2019; The Broad, Los Angeles, 23 March–1 September 1 2019; de Young Museum, San Francisco, 9 November 2019–8 March 2020; and The Museum of Fine Arts, Boston, 2020.
'Art Into Life! Collector Wolfgang Hahn and the 60s', Museum Ludwig, Cologne, Germany, 24 June–24 September.
'Simple Passion, Complex Vision: The Darryl Atwell Collection', Harvey B. Gantt Center for African-American Arts + Culture, Charlotte, North Carolina, 22 July 2017–22 January 2018.
'Start at Home: Art from the Frank W. Hale, Jr. Black Cultural Center Collection', Hagerty Hall, Hopkins Hall Gallery, Thompson Library at The Ohio State University, Hale Black Cultural Center, King Arts Complex and Urban Art Space, Columbus, Ohio, 24 August–4 November.
'Art of Rebellion: Black Art of the Civil Rights Movement', Detroit Institute of Arts, Michigan, 23 July–22 October.
'Apparitions', Joan Hisaoka Healing Arts Gallery at Smith Center for Healing and The Arts, Washington, D.C., 8 September–27 October.

'Disorderly Conduct: American Painting and Sculpture, 1960–1990', Nasher Museum of Art at Duke University, Durham, North Carolina, 21 September 2017–28 February 2018.
'Solidary and Solitary', Ogden Museum of Southern Art, New Orleans, 30 September 2017–21 January 2018. Travelled to: The Nasher Museum of Art at Duke University, Durham, North Carolina, 22 February 2018–15 July 2018; Snite Museum of Art at the University of Notre Dame, South Bend, Indiana, 18 August–15 December 2018; David and Alfred Smart Museum of Art at the University of Chicago, 29 January–19 May 2019; Baltimore Museum of Art, March–July 2019; Berkeley Art Museum and Pacific Film Archive at the University of California, August 2019–January 2020; and Pérez Art Museum Miami, 2020.
'Impulse!' Pace Gallery, London, 3 November–22 December.
'BIG', Madison Museum of Contemporary Art, Wisconsin, 4 November 2017–6 May 2018.
'Picturing Mississippi, 1817–2017: Land of Plenty, Pain, and Promise', Mississippi Museum of Art, Jackson, 9 December 2017–8 July 2018.

2018

Gilliam's major European retrospective 'The Music of Color. Sam Gilliam 1967–1973', opens at Kunstmuseum Basel in June, coinciding with the international art fair, Art Basel. The exhibition is seen as a significant breakthrough for the artist, (re)introducing the breadth of his practice in painting and sculpture over more than six decades to international audiences.

Gilliam marries longtime partner Annie Gawlak.

He receives the Archives of American Art Medal, New York, New York.

Solo Exhibitions:
'The Music of Color. Sam Gilliam 1967–1973', Kunstmuseum Basel, 9 June–30 September.

Group Exhibitions:
'Experiments in Form: Sam Gilliam, Alan Shields, Frank Stella', The Block Museum of Art at Northwestern University, Evanston, Illinois, 13 January–24 June.
'The Conscientious Objector', The Schindler House at the MAK Center for Art and Architecture, West Hollywood, 3 February–6 April.
'The New Art: A Milestone Collection Fifty Years Later', The Oklahoma City Museum of Art, 15 February–13 May.
'Sam Gilliam in Dialogue: Race + Representation', Williams College Museum of Art, Williamstown, Massachusetts, 15 February–22 April.
'Hopes Springing High: Gifts of Art by African American Artists', Crocker Art Museum, Sacramento, 18 February–15 July.
'Indulge, Art Movement', Los Angeles, 1 March–28 April.
'Reclamation! Pan-African Works from the Beth Rudin DeWoody Collection', Taubman Museum of Art, Roanoke, Virginia, 3 March–9 September.
'Problem Solving: Highlights from the Experimental Printmaking Institute', Mechanical Hall Gallery at the University of Delaware, Newark, 5 March–11 May.
'Expanding Narratives: The Figure and the Ground', Smart Museum of Art at the University of Chicago, 24 April–16 December.
'Sam Gilliam in Dialogue: Form', Williams College Museum of Art, Williamstown, Massachusetts, 26 April–3 June.
'Collecting Contemporaries: Recent Acquisitions from The Koch And Wolf Collections', Indianapolis Museum of Art, Newfields, 4 May–16 December.
'Inherent Structure', Wexner Center for the Arts, Columbus, Ohio, 19 May–12 August.
'Sam Gilliam in Dialogue: The Topographies of Color', Williams College Museum of Art, Williamstown, Massachusetts, 7 June–3 September.
'Summer 2018', Mnuchin Gallery, New York, 18 June–31 August.
'Painting: Now and Forever, Part III', Matthew Marks Gallery, New York, 28 June–17 August.
'One Shot: Featuring Works by Color Field Artists', UTA Artist Space, Beverly Hills, 12 July–18 August.
'Public Artworks of Rockne Krebs and Sam Gilliam, Built and Unbuilt', The Washington Studio School, Washington, D.C., 19 July–3 August 2018.
'Alma Thomas: The Light of the Whole Universe', Smith College Museum of Art, Northampton, Massachusetts, 27 July 2018–1 December 2019.
'Remember to React: 60 Years of Collecting', NSU Art Museum Fort Lauderdale, Florida, 9 September 2018–30 October 2019.
'Second Look, Twice: Selections from the Collections of Jordan D. Schnitzer and His Family Foundation', Museum of the African Diaspora, San Francisco, 19 September–16 December.
'The Fabricators', Akron Art Museum, Ohio, 22 September 2018–3 March 2019.
'Abstraction, Color, and Politics in the Early 1970s', University of Michigan Museum of Art, Ann Arbor, Michigan, 22 September 2018–19 May 2019.
'American Abstract', Charles Riva Collection, Brussels, 28 September 2018–23 February 2019.
'Pattern, Decoration and Crime', Musée d'Art Moderne et Contemporain, Geneva, 10 October 2018–2 March 2019.
'The Gift of Art: Permanent Collection Exhibition in Celebration of Its 35th Anniversary', Pérez Art Museum Miami, opened on 25 October.

2019

Gilliam joins Pace Gallery, marking the first time he is represented by a New York gallery. Owner Arne Glimcher is of the same generation and he and Gilliam swiftly form a deep friendship – they speak daily and visit often.

From 2018–2022, Gilliam is prolific in his production of new work. He continues to experiment, creating a new series of sculptures composed of laminated birch plywood, dyed and stacked alongside new series of large-scale bevelled-edge paintings and monochromatic watercolour paintings on washi paper.

Despite physical challenges, Gilliam pursues larger scale works that require physical endurance and strength. He is supported by studio assistants whom he trains to help maneuver mark-making materials in tandem with the movements of his own arms and hands.

Solo Exhibitions:
'Sam Gilliam. Starting: Works on Paper 1967–1970', David Kordansky Gallery, Los Angeles, 16 March–27 April.
'Sam Gilliam: New Works on Paper', Flag Art Foundation, New York, 6 June–16 August.
'Sam Gilliam', Dia:Beacon, New York, opened 10 August.

Group Exhibitions:
'Black Refractions: Highlights from the Studio Museum in Harlem', Museum of the African Diaspora, San Francisco, 16 January–14 April 2019. Travelled to: Gibbes Museum of Charleston, South Carolina, 24 May–18 August 2019; Kalamazoo Institute of Arts, Michigan, 13 September–8 December 2019; Smith College Museum of Art, Northampton, Massachusetts, 17 January–12 April 2020; Frye Art Museum, Seattle, 9 May–2 August 2020; Utah Museum of Fine Arts, Salt Lake City, 28 August–13 December.
'Mapping Black Identities', Minneapolis Institute of Art, 21 February 2019–15 March 2020.
'Spilling Over: Painting Color in the 1960s', Whitney Museum of American Art, New York, 29 March–18 August.
'Count of Three', Alexander Gray Associates, New York, 18 April–24 May.
'Postwar Abstraction: Variations', Oklahoma City Museum of Art, 19 April 2019–31 December 2020.
'A Time for Action: Washington Artists Circa 1989', Luther W. Brady Art Gallery at George Washington University, Washington, D.C., 13 June–5 October.
'REACH Opening Festival', John F. Kennedy Center for the Performing Arts, Washington, D.C., 7–22 September.
'Generations: A History of Black Abstract Art', The Baltimore Museum of Art, 29 September 2019–19 January 2020.
'With Pleasure: Pattern and Decoration in American Art 1972–1985', Museum of Contemporary Art, Los Angeles, 27 October 2019–11 May 2020. Travelled to: Hessel Museum of Art, Center for Curatorial Studies at Bard College, Annandale-on-Hudson, New York, 27 June 2020–11 December 2020.

The same year as Sam's Venice show [1972], I met him for the first time at an opening for another mutual friend, the artist Kenneth Noland, at the André Emmerich Gallery in New York. I was younger than Sam, still in my early thirties, and I was immediately impressed by the fierce

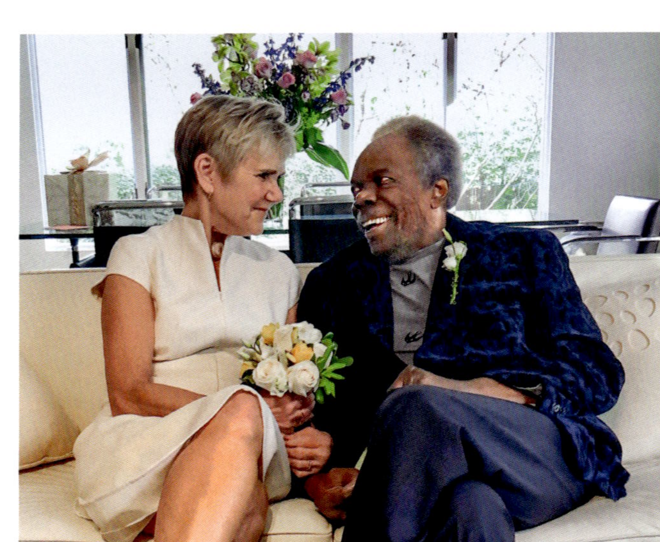
Gawlak and Gilliam on their wedding day, Washington, D.C., 2018

intelligence and magnetic presence of this tall, handsome individual. Even then, as a relatively young artist, he wore his independence and self-confidence on his sleeve. He was a D.C. figure – already recognized as an important member of the Washington Color School together with Noland – and fiercely proud of his association with his chosen city, where he would live and work for more than six decades.

We were from the same generation and shared the same fundamental understanding of the power and possibilities of abstraction. In recent years, I've cherished the experience of visiting Sam in his studio, often experiencing goosebumps when I walk in and encounter a fresh group of paintings. I've rarely had such an experience in an artist's studio. It reminded me of visiting Rothko in my twenties. I think Sam's recent works may be some of the greatest abstract paintings ever made. His experiments with color and surface are right up there with the achievements of Rothko and Pollock.[29]

– Arne Glimcher

2020

Gilliam's first solo exhibition at Pace Gallery in New York takes over the ground-floor galleries of both Chelsea spaces and features multiple new bodies of work, from stained wooden sculptures and wall works to new watercolour monochromes. Here Gilliam presents a suite of large scale bevelled-edge paintings that mark the start of a new series and prolific final chapter. Despite opening during the COVID-19 pandemic, it is widely attended and receives many positive reviews.

Solo Exhibitions:
'Sam Gilliam: Existed Existing', Pace Gallery, 540 West 25th Street and 510 West 25th Street, New York, 6 November–19 December.
'Sam Gilliam: Watercolors', Pace Gallery, Palm Beach, Florida, 11 December 2020–3 January 2021.

Group Exhibitions:
'Presence: African American Artists from the Museum's Collection', The Honolulu Museum of Art, Hawaii, 7 March–31 May.
'Allied with Power: African and African Diaspora Art from the Jorge M. Pérez Collection', Pérez Art Museum Miami, Autumn 2020–Summer 2021.
'Bloom of Joy', Pace Gallery, 12/F, H Queen's, 80 Queen's Road Central, Hong Kong, 4 September–15 October.

2021

Solo Exhibitions:
'Sam Gilliam: Watercolors', Pace Gallery, Geneva, 21 January–19 March.
'Sam Gilliam: Selections', The Ringling Museum of Art Searing Galleries, Sarasota, Florida, 21 February–15 August.

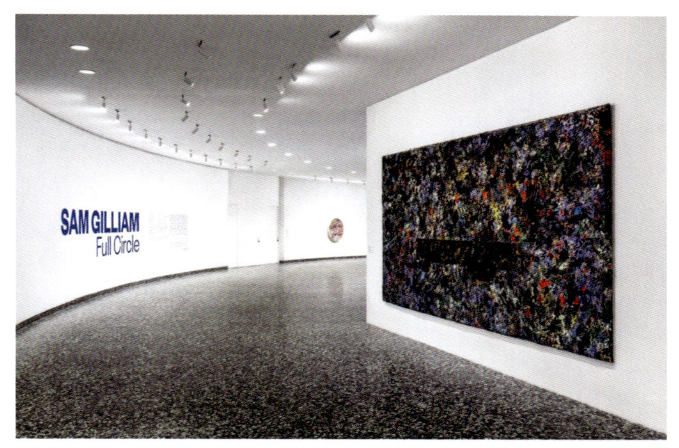

Installation view of 'Sam Gilliam: Full Circle', Hirshhorn Museum and Sculpture Garden, Washington, D.C., 2022

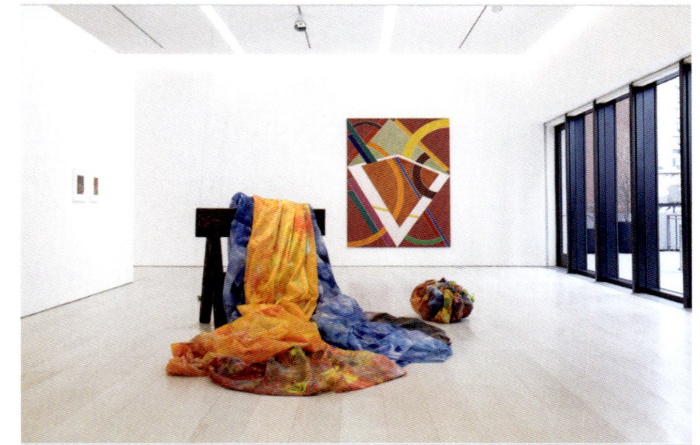

Installation view of 'Melvin Edwards, Sam Gilliam, and William T. Williams: Epistrophy', Pace Gallery, New York, 2022

'Sam Gilliam', Pace Gallery, Seoul, 27 May–10 July.
'Sam Gilliam', Pace Gallery, Hong Kong, 22 July–2 September.

Group Exhibitions:
'Artists and the Rothko Chapel: 50 Years of Inspiration', The Moody Center for the Arts, Rice University, Houston, 23 February–15 May.
'Modal Painting: Sam Gilliam, Frank Bowling, Reginald Sylvester II, John Hoyland & John Golding', Maximillian William, London, March–April.
'Off the Wall', Mnuchin Gallery, New York, 24 April–12 June.
'Hiding in Plain Sight', Pace Gallery, New York, 14 July–21 August.
'Convergent Evolutions: The Conscious of Body Work', Pace Gallery, New York, 10 September–23 October.

2022

Gilliam is elected to the American Academy of Arts and Sciences.

Gilliam opens his first major museum survey exhibition in the United States since 2017, at the Hirshhorn Museum and Sculpture Garden in Washington, D.C. on 25 May. He presents his newest body of work, a series of tondos, acrylic on circular wood panels with laminated bevelled-edge frames, alongside the historic black painting *Rail*, 1977.

The group exhibition, 'Melvin Edwards, Sam Gilliam, and William T. Williams: Epistrophy' at Pace Gallery in April marks the final exhibition of the trio in their lifetimes.

The State Department acquires a major late painting and installs it in the lobby of their Washington, D.C. offices.

Gilliam passes away at his home on 25 June, from renal failure. He is 88 and survived by his wife Annie Gawlak; three daughters from his first marriage, Stephanie Gilliam, Melissa Gilliam and Leah Franklin; three sisters; and three grandchildren.

Solo Exhibitions:
'Sam Gilliam: Full Circle', Hirshhorn Museum and Sculpture Garden, Washington, D.C., 25 May–11 September.
'Sam Gilliam: Late Paintings', Pace Gallery, London, 11 October–12 November.
'White and Black Paintings, 1975–1977', David Kordansky Gallery, Los Angeles, 5 November–17 December.

Group Exhibitions:
'Melvin Edwards, Sam Gilliam, and William T. Williams: Epistrophy', Pace Gallery, New York, 1–30 April.
'Fugues in Color', Fondation Louis Vuitton, Paris, 4 May–29 August.

2023

Solo Exhibitions:
'Asking, The Hyde Collection', Glens Falls, New York, 28 January–23 April.
'Recollect: Sam Gilliam', Madison Museum of Contemporary Art, Wisconsin, 10 August–3 March 2024
'Sam Gilliam' Atlanta Contemporary, Atlanta, Georgia, 24 August–23 December.
'The Last Five Years', Pace Gallery, New York, 15 September–28 October.
'Make it Wonderful', Pace Prints, New York, 15 October–18 November.

Group Exhibitions:
'Texas Collects: Curtis E. Ransom Collection', curated by Joan Davidow, SITE131, Dallas, 28 January–25 March.
'Ways of Seeing: The Paul R. Jones Collection of American Art at The University of Alabama', Flint Institute of Arts, Michigan, 29 January–23 April.
'Processing Abstraction', The Fralin Museum of Art at the University of Virginia, Charlottesville, Virginia, 4 February–31 December.
'Calling on the Past: Selections from the Collection', Smart Museum of Art, The University of Chicago, 21 March–4 February 2024.
'Love by Looking: Selections from the Alitash Kebede Collection of African American Art', Elizabeth Myers Mitchell Art Museum, Annapolis, Maryland, 9 April–5 June
'American Watercolors, 1880–1990: Into the Light', Harvard Art Museums, Cambridge, Massachusetts, 20 May–13 August.
'Highlights of the Collection', The Cafesjian Art Trust, Shoreview, Minnesota, 1 June–14 October.
'Among Friends: The Generosity of Judy and Ken Dayton', Walker Art Center, Minneapolis, 10 June–19 May 2024.
'Ecstatic: Selections from the Hammer Contemporary Collection', Hammer Museum, Los Angeles, 10 June–27 August.
'Innovation In American Art / 1970 to 1975 / A Fifty Year Perspective', Phillips, New York, opened 29 June.
'20', David Kordansky Gallery, Los Angeles, 8 July–19 August.
'Jump, Twist, Flow...', Hemphill Artworks, Washington, D.C., 14 July–19 August.
'Silver Linings: Celebrating the Spelman Art Collection', Frances Lehman Loeb Art Center, Vassar College, Poughkeepsie, New York, 29 September–28 January 2024
'Reunion', Connersmith, Washington, D.C., 11 October–9 December.
'All Stars: American Artists from The Phillips Collection', Denver Art Museum, 12 November–3 March 2024
'Glory of the World: Color Field Painting (1950s to 1983)', NSU Art Museum Fort Lauderdale, Florida, 21 November–25 August 2024.
'Not Your Mother's Wrapping Paper: Works on Paper', Addison/Ripley Fine Art, Washington, D.C., 9 December–13 January 2024.
'American Voices and Visions: Modern and Contemporary

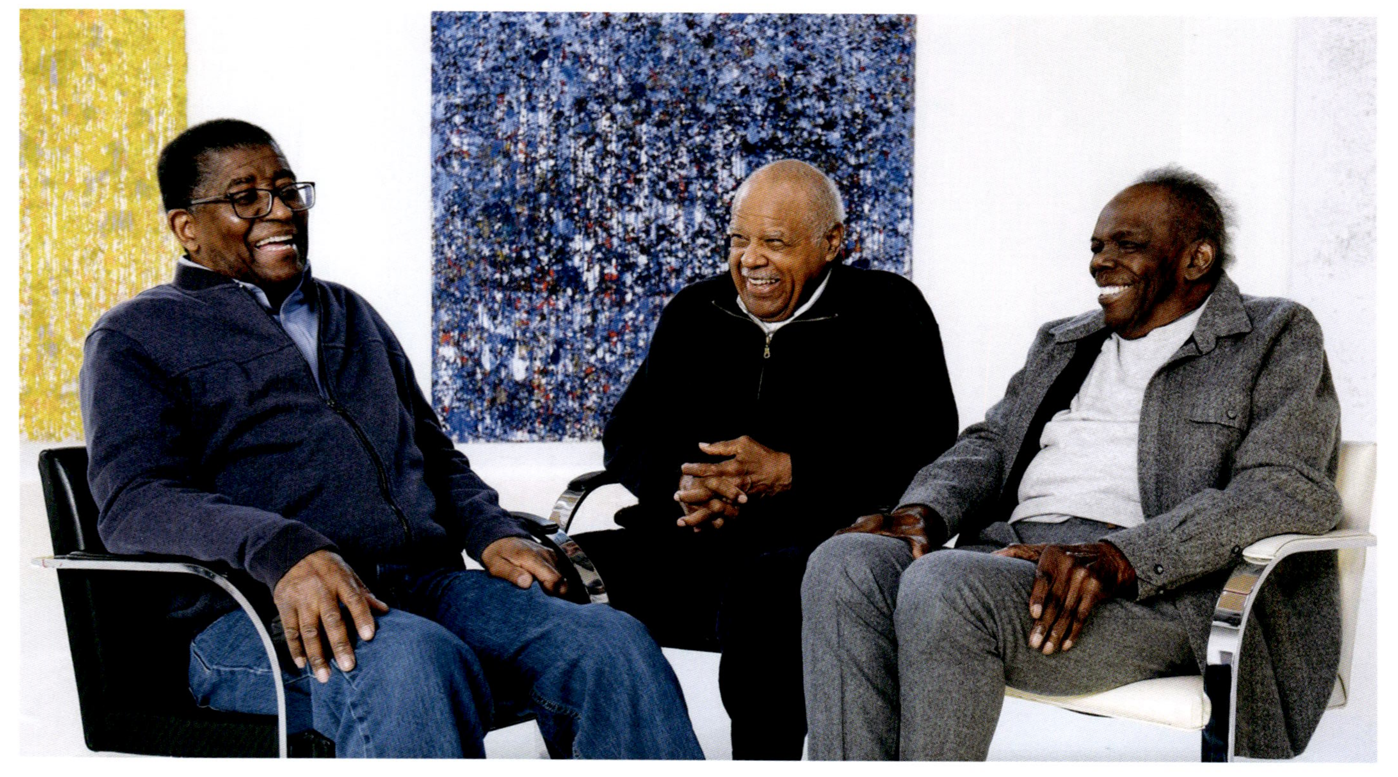

Gilliam, Melvin Edwards and William T. Williams, 14th Street studio, Washington, D.C., 2022

Art', The Smithsonian American Art Museum, Washington, D.C., ongoing.

2024

Solo Exhibitions:
'The Last Five Years', David Kordansky Gallery, Los Angeles, 14 April–14 July.

Group Exhibitions:
'Greatness Revealed: The Art of African Americans from the Butler Collection', The Butler Institute of American Art, Youngstown, Ohio, 4 February–17 March.
'Memories & Inspiration: The Kerry and C. Betty Davis Collection of African American Art', Oklahoma State University Museum of Art, Stillwater, 20 February–11 May.
'Silver Linings: Celebrating the Spelman Art Collection', Boise Art Museum, Boise, Idaho; University of Michigan Museum of Art, Ann Arbor, Michigan, 24 February–21 July
'A Bold and Beautiful Vision: A Century of Black Arts Education in Washington, D.C., 1900–2000', Anacostia Community Museum, Washington, D.C., 23 March–2 March 2025.
'Day for Night: New American Realism', organized by the Aishti Foundation, Palazzo Barberini, Rome, 14 April–14 July.
'The Portal: An Art Experience by Jewel', Crystal Bridges Museum of American Art, Bentonville, Arizona, 4 May–28 July.

ENDNOTES

1 Sam Gilliam quoted in Hans Ulrich Obrist, 'A Conversation with Sam Gilliam', 1 December 2019, https://www.pacegallery.com/journal/hans-ulrich-obrist-conversation-with-sam-gilliam/ (accessed 28 May 2024).

2 Gilliam quoted in Obrist, 'A Conversation with Sam Gilliam', 1 December 2019.

3 Gilliam quoted in Jennifer Samet, 'Beer With a Painter', *Hyperallergic*, 19 March 2016, https://hyperallergic.com/284543/beer-with-a-painter-sam-gilliam/ (accessed 28 May 2024).

4 Gilliam quoted in Andrianna Campbell, 'Sam Gilliam', *Artforum*, 11 July 2017, https://www.artforum.com/interviews/sam-gilliam-discusses-his-work-showing-in-the-venice-biennale-and-the-nea-69537 (accessed 28 May 2024).

5 Gilliam quoted in Tom McGlynn, 'Sam Gilliam with Tom McGlynn', *The Brooklyn Rail*, September 2019, https://brooklynrail.org/2019/09/art/sam (accessed 28 May 2024).

6 Gilliam quoted in Ben Forgey, 'Oral History Interview with Sam Gilliam, 1989 Nov. 4–11', Archives of American Art, Smithsonian Institution, https://www.aaa.si.edu/collections/interviews/oral-history-interview-sam-gilliam-11472 (accessed 28 May 2024).

7 Carol Harrison, quoted in 'Sam Gilliam, Carol Harrison, Rockne Krebs and ping pong', Rockne Krebs official website, https://www.rocknekrebsart.com/commentary-on-the-art-of-rockne-krebs/archives/07-2014 (accessed 28 May 2024).

8 Carol Harrison, quoted in 'Sam Gilliam, Carol Harrison, Rockne Krebs and ping pong'. (accessed 28 May 2024).

9 Gilliam quoted in Kenneth Young, 'Oral History Interview with Sam Gilliam, 1984 September 18, 1984', Archives of American Art, Smithsonian Institution, https://www.aaa.si.edu/collections/interviews/oral-history-interview-sam-gilliam-11449 (accessed 28 May 2024).

10 Gilliam quoted in Jonathan P. Binstock, *Sam Gilliam: A Retrospective*, (California: University of California Press, 2005), p. 19.

11 Walter Hopps quoted in Binstock, *Sam Gilliam: A Retrospective*, p. 7

12 Gilliam quoted in Young, AAA Oral History Interview, 1984.

13 Press release and checklist for 'In Honor of Dr. Martin Luther King, Jr.', 31 October–3 November, 1968, at the Museum of Modern Art, New York. https://www.artnews.com

14 Hopps, Walter, and Osnos, Nina Felshin. 'Three Washington Artists: Gilliam Krebs McGowin', *Art International*, 20 May, 1970, pp. 32–42

15 Gilliam quoted in Jack Rasmussen, 'Close to Trees' (exh. cat), American University Museum, Katzen Arts Center, 2 April –14 August 2011.

16 Gilliam quoted in Binstock, 2005, p. 83.

17 Hopps and Osnos, 'Three Washington Artists: Gilliam Krebs McGowin', pp. 32–42.

18 John Dowell, Sam Gilliam, Daniel Johnson, Joe Overstreet, Melvin Edwards, Richard Hunt, William T. Williams, 'Politics', *Artforum*, May 1971, https://www.artforum.com/print/197105/politics-73609 (accessed 28 May 2024).

19 Gilliam quoted in *Artforum*, 11 July 2017.

20 https://www.nytimes.com/2022/06/28/arts/design/sam-gilliam-melvin-edwards-rashid-johnson-appraisal.html.

21 Sam Gilliam, with Annie Gawlak, 'Solids and Veils', *Art Journal*, Spring 1991, 50:1, pp 10–11.

22 Conversation with the author.

23 Gilliam quoted in Obrist, 'A Conversation with Sam Gilliam', 1 December 2019.

24 Gilliam, 'The Transformation of Nature Through Nature', in Kristen Stiles and Peter Selz, eds, *Theories and Documents of Contemporary Art: A Sourcebook of Artists' Writings* (Berkeley: University of California Press, 1996, revised and expanded in 2012), pp. 727–729. See also pp. 56–57 of this volume.

25 David C. Driskell, 'Sam Gilliam', *Contemporary Visual Expressions: The Art of Sam Gilliam, Martha Jackson-Jarvis, Keith Morrison, William T. Williams*, (Washington, D.C.: Smithsonian Institution Press, 1987), pp. 22–28.

26 Conversation with the author.

27 David Kordansky, 'In Memoriam: Sam Gilliam', 27 June 2022, https://www.davidkordanskygallery.com/artist/in-memoriam-sam-gilliam (accessed 28 May 2024).

28 Countee Cullen, 'Yet Do I Marvel' from *Color*. Copyright 1925 by Harper & Brothers, New York. Renewed 1953 by Ida M. Cullen. Published in *My Soul's High Song: The Collected Writings of Countee Cullen* (New York: Anchor Books, 1991), p 103.

29 Arne Glimcher, 'Arne Glimcher Recounts His Friendship with Sam Gilliam', https://www.pacegallery.com/journal/arne-glimcher-recounts-his-friendship-sam-gilliam/

LIST OF WORKS

All dimensions, unless otherwise noted, listed, h x w x d.

p. 6 –
Gilliam in his U Street studio, Washington, D.C., 1990

p. 10–11 –
Nina's Buffalo, 2022
Acrylic on canvas with bevelled-edge stretcher, 96 x 180 x 4 in. (243.8 x 457.2 x 10.2 cm), private collection, Washington, D.C.

p. 12 –
Sam Gilliam at his 14th Street studio in Washington, D.C., 2018

p. 17 (top) –
Stems, 1965
Acrylic on canvas, 69 x 50 x 1 ½ in. (175.3 x 127 x 3.8 cm)

p. 17 (bottom) –
Shoot Six, 1965
Acrylic on canvas, 56 x 56 ⅛ in. (142.2 x 142.6 cm), Corcoran Collection (Gift of Walter Hopps in memory of Bradley Pischel)

p. 18 (top) –
Theme of Five I, 1965
Acrylic on canvas, 70 x 83 x 1 ½ in. (177.8 x 210.8 x 3.8 cm), private collection, Washington, D.C.

p. 18 (bottom) –
Red Petals, 1967
Acrylic on canvas with bevelled-edge stretcher, 88 x 93 in. (223.5 x 236.2 cm), The Phillips Collection, acquired 1967

p. 19 –
Green Slice, 1967
Watercolour on Japanese paper, 38 x 23 in. (96.5 x 58.4 cm), Collection SFMOMA, gift of John Hale Stutesman

p. 20–21 –
Green April, 1969
Acrylic on canvas with bevelled-edge stretcher, 98 x 271 x 3 ⅞ in. (248.9 x 688.3 x 9.8 cm), Kunstmuseum Basel, gift from the Foundation for the Kunstmuseum Basel, 2018

p. 22 –
Restore, 1968
Magna, acrylic and aluminum powder on canvas with bevelled-edge stretcher, 108 ⅞ x 152 ¾ in. (276.5 x 388 cm) Collection of the Speed Art Museum, Louisville, Kentucky. Gift of the artist and purchased with funds from the Alice Speed Stoll Accessions Trust, 2010

p. 24–25 –
Niagra, 1968
Acrylic on canvas, 120 x 528 in. (304.8 x 1,341 cm), private collection, Washington, D.C.

p. 26–27 –
Light Depth, 1969
Acrylic on canvas, installation size varies: 120 x 900 in. (304.8 x 228.6 cm), Corcoran Collection, Washington, D.C.

p. 28 –
Swing Sketch, 1968
Acrylic on canvas with leather cord, dimensions variable, overall: 73 ¾ x 89 ¾ x 9 in. (187.3 x 228 x 22.9 cm), Sami and Hala Mnaymneh

p. 29 –
Dakar I, 1969
Acrylic on canvas, 113 x 59 in. (287 x 149.9 x 35.6 cm), Philadelphia Museum of Art, purchased with the Katharine Levin Farrell Fund and the Joseph E. Temple Fund, 2007

p. 32 (top) –
Simmering, 1970
Acrylic on canvas, 85 x 52 in. (215.9 x 132.1 cm), Philadelphia Museum of Art, purchased with the Katharine Levin Farrell Fund and the Joseph E. Temple Fund, 2007

p. 32 (bottom) –
Composed (formerly Dark As I Am), 1968–74
Acrylic clothing, backpack, painter's tools, wooden closet pole on wood door, 87 x 47 x 3 ½ in. (221 x 119.4 x 8.9 cm), Private Collection, Washington, D.C.

p. 34–35 –
Toward a Red, 1975
Acrylic on canvas with bevelled-edge stretcher, collage elements, 32 ½ x 48 in. (82.6 x 121.9 cm)

p. 36–37 –
Leah's Renoir, 1979
Acrylic on canvas with bevelled-edge stretcher, collage elements, 80 x 195 in. (203.2 x 495.3 cm), Metropolitan Museum of Art, New York

p. 40–41 –
Seahorses, 1975
Acrylic on canvas, installation dimensions variable
Courtesy of the Philadelphia Museum of Art

p. 42 (top) –
Yet Do I Marvel (Countee Cullen), 2016
Acrylic on birch, 96 x 258 x 4 ½ in. (243.8 x 655.3 x 11.4 cm), Collection of the Smithsonian National Museum of African American History and Culture

p. 42 (bottom) –
Homage to the Square, 2016–17
Acrylic on wood, four parts, each: 60 x 60 x 3 ⅜ in. (152.4 x 152.4 x 8.6 cm)
overall: 122 x 122 x 3 ⅜ in. (309.9 x 309.9 x 8.6 cm), private collection, Washington, D.C.

p. 45 –
Master Builder Piece, 1981
Acrylic on canvas, in two pieces, (A): 75 x 81 in. (190.5 x 205.7 cm) (B): 75 x 25 in. (190.5 x 63.5 cm), The Studio Museum in Harlem; gift of Dr. Morton Jay Roberts, M.D.

p. 50–51 –
"A" and the Carpenter II, 2022
Acrylic on polypropylene, wood, and leather string, 127 x 195 in. (322.6 x 495.3 cm), private collection, Washington, D.C.

p. 58 –
Helles, 1965
Acrylic on canvas, 71 ¾ x 71 5⁄16 x 1 ½ in. (182.2 x 181.1 x 3.8 cm)

p. 59 –
Blue Let, 1965
Acrylic on canvas, 71 ⅜ x 47 ⅛ x ¾ in. (181.3 x 119.7 x 1.9 cm), private collection,
Washington, D.C.

p. 61 –
Long Green, 1965
Acrylic on canvas, 72 ¼ x 24 x ⅞ in. (183.5 x 61 x 2.2 cm), Anacostia Community Museum Collection, Gift from the Trustees of the Corcoran Gallery of Art (Walter Hopps in memory of Bradley Pischel)

p. 62 –
Installation views of 'Hard Edge Paintings 1963–1966', David Kordansky Gallery, Los Angeles, 2013

p.63 –
Dual Rod, 1965
Acrylic on canvas, 47 ⅞ x 47 9⁄16 x 1 ½ in. (121.6 x 120.8 x 3.8 cm)

p. 65 –
Snakebite, 1968
Acrylic on canvas with bevelled-edge stretcher, 114 x 43 x 2 ¼ in. (289.6 x 109.2 x 5.7 cm), private collection, London

p. 66–67 –
Rouge, 1968
Acrylic on canvas with bevelled-edge stretcher, 25 x 52 x 1 ½ in. (65.1 x 132.7 x 4.8 cm)

p. 68 –
Untitled, 1967
Watercolour on paper, 18 ¼ x 23 ¾ in. (46.4 x 60.3 cm)

p. 69 –
Untitled, 1970
Watercolour on paper, 13 ¾ x 17 ½ in. (34.9 x 44.5 cm)

p. 70 –
Relative, 1969
Acrylic on canvas, 120 x 528 in. (304.8 x 1,341.1 cm), National Gallery of Art, Washington, D.C., Anonymous Gift

p. 72–75 –
Niagra, 1968
Acrylic on canvas, 120 x 528 in. (304.8. x 1.341.1 cm), private collection, Washington, D.C.

p. 77 –
Installation views of 'The Music of Color. Sam Gilliam 1967–1973', Kunstmuseum Basel, 2018

p. 78–81 –
Light Depth, 1969
Acrylic on canvas, installation size varies: 120 x 900 in. (304.8 x 2,286 cm), Corcoran Collection, Washington, D.C.

p. 82–83 –
One On, 1970
Acrylic on canvas, dimensions variable, approximately 123 x 93 x 13 in. (312.4 x 236.2 x 33 cm), Emanuel Family Collection

p. 84 –
Close Up, 1969
Ink on paper, 23 x 29 in. (58.4 x 73.7 cm), private collection, Washington, D.C.

p. 85 –
Untitled, 1969
Ink on paper, 23 x 29 in. (58.4 x 73.7 cm), private collection, Washington, D.C.

p. 86 –
Untitled, 1969
Ink on paper, 20 x 30 in. (50.8 x 76.2 cm), private collection, Washington, D.C.

p. 87 –
Untitled, 1969
Ink on paper, 23 x 29 in. (58.4 x 73.7 cm)

p. 89 (top) –
Untitled (from 'Rock Creek' series), 1967
Watercolour on paper, 5 ⅜ x 8 ½ in. (13.7 x 21.6 cm)

p. 89 (bottom) –
Untitled (from 'Rock Creek' series), 1967
Watercolour on paper, 5 ½ x 8 ½ in. (14 x 21.6 cm)

p. 90 –
Untitled (from 'Rock Creek' series), 1967
Watercolour on paper, 8 ½ x 5 ½ in. (21.6 x 14 cm)

p. 91 –
Untitled (from 'Rock Creek' series), 1967
Watercolour on paper, 8 ½ x 5 ⅜ in. (21.6 x 13.7 cm)

p. 93–97 –
Leaf, 1970
Acrylic on canvas, installation dimensions variable, approximate: 130 x 160 x 16 in. (330.2 x 406.4 x 40.6 cm), Dallas Museum of Art

p. 98–99 –
10/27/69, 1969
Acrylic on canvas, installation dimensions variable, approximate: 140 x 185 x 16 in. (355.6 x 469.9 x 40.6 cm), Collection of The Museum of Modern Art, New York

p. 100–101 –
Double Merge, 1968
Acrylic on canvas, left panel: 120 x 796 in. (304.8 x 2,021.8 cm), right panel: 120 x 852 in. (304.8 x 2,164.1 cm), purchased jointly by Dia Art Foundation, and the Museum of Fine Arts, Houston, with funds from the Caroline Wiess Law Accessions Endowment Fund

p.103–105 –
Change, 1970
Acrylic on canvas with bevelled-edge stretcher, 112 ⅛ x 112 ⅛ x 1 ⅞ in. (284.8 x 284.8 x 4.8 cm), Louisiana Museum of Modern Art, Humlebæk, Denmark

p. 106–107 –
Spread, 1973
Acrylic on canvas with bevelled-edge stretcher, 69 x 113 ½ x 1 ¾ in. (175.3 x 288.3 x 4.4 cm), collection Glenn and Amanda Fuhrman NY, courtesy the FLAG Art Foundation

p. 108–109 –
April 4, 1969
Acrylic on canvas with bevelled-edge stretcher, 110 x 179 ¾ in. (279.4 x 456.6 cm), Smithsonian American Art Museum, Museum purchase, 1973

p. 110–112 –
Rose Rising, 1968
Acrylic on canvas with bevelled-edge stretcher, 97 x 132 x 3 ⅞ in. (246.4 x 335.3 x 9.8 cm)

p. 115 –
Whirlirama, 1970
Acrylic on canvas with bevelled-edge stretcher, 111 ¼ x 116 ½ in. (282.6 x 293.4 cm), The Metropolitan Museum of Art, New York, purchase, Arthur Hoppock Hearn Fund and Pamela Joyner Gift, 2014

p. 116–117 –
Out, 1969
Acrylic on canvas with bevelled-edge stretcher, 113 ½ x 152 ½ x 2 in. (288.3 x 387.4 x 5.1 cm)

p. 119 –
For Day One, 1974–75
Acrylic, oil dye pigments on collaged, flat-mounted canvas, 48 ½ x 48 ½ x 1 ¼ in. (123.2 x 123.2 x 3.2 cm), Speed Art Museum, Louisville, Gift of Henry V. Heuser Jr. and museum purchase 1976

p. 121 –
Crystal, 1973
Acrylic on canvas
Installation, dimensions variable
92 ¾ x 29 ¾ x 7 ½ in. (235.6 x 75.6 x 19.1 cm), private collection, Washington, D.C.

p. 122 –
Installation view of exhibition 'Sam Gilliam: A Retrospective', Corcoran Gallery of Art, Washington, D.C., 2005–2006

p. 124–125 –
"A" and the Carpenter I, 1973
Acrylic on canvas draped over wooden sawhorses. Install (floor) 96 x 132 in. (243.8 x 335.2 cm), size varies with installation. Art Institute of Chicago, Twentieth-Century Purchase Fund, 1973.681

p. 126–127 –
Softly Still, 1973
Acrylic, latex and dyes on polypropylene, ponderosa pine sawhorse. Painting: 182 x 119 in. (462.3 x 302.3 cm) sawhorse: 30 ¼ x 36 x 13 in. (76.8 x 91.4 x 33 cm), Allen Memorial Art Museum, Oberlin College, Ohio, gift of the artist

p. 128–129 –
Carousel Merge, 1971
Acrylic and powdered aluminum on canvas, 120 x 900 in. (304.8 x 2,286 cm), Walker Art Center, Minneapolis

p. 130–131 –
Carousel, 1970
Acrylic and powdered aluminum on canvas, 120 x 803 in. (304.8 x 2,042 cm), Madison Museum of Contemporary Art, Wisconsin

p. 133 –
Rondo, 1971
Acrylic on canvas with oak beam, 103 x 144 x 78 in. (261.6 x 365.8 x 198.1 cm), Kunstmuseum Basel, acquired with the support of the Arnold Rüdlinger-Fonds, Freiwillige Akademische Gesellschaft Basel 2017

p. 134–135 –
Custom Road Slide at Artpark, Lewiston, New York, 1977

p. 137 –
Installation view of exhibition 'Of Fireflies and Ferris Wheels: Monastery Parallel', Kunstmuseum Kloster Unser Lieben Frauen, Magdeburg, Germany

p. 140–141 –
Cartouche, 1981
Acrylic on canvas, 81 x 106 ¾ x 2 ¼ in. (205.7 x 271.2 x 5.7 cm), Museum of Contemporary Art Chicago, Gift of Scott and Willa Lang

p. 142–143 –
Robbin' Peter, 1980
Acrylic on canvas, 80 x 90 in. (203.2 x 228.6 cm), The Doris and Donald Fisher Collection at the San Francisco Museum of Modern Art

p. 144–145 –
The Arc Maker I & II, 1981
Acrylic on canvas with collage, 75 x 213 x 1 ½ in. (152.4 x 541 x 3.8 cm), Detroit Institute of Arts, Gift of the Friends of African Art, 1983

p. 146–147 –
Lion's Rock Arc, 1981
Acrylic on canvas with collage, 72 ½ x 190 ½ in. (184.2 x 483.9 cm), Studio Museum in Harlem; gift of Morton J. Roberts, M.D.

p. 148–149 –
Rail, 1977
Acrylic and canvas on canvas with bevelled-edge stretcher, 90 ¾ x 180 ¾ in. (230.5 x 459.1 cm), Hirshhorn Museum and Sculpture Garden, Smithsonian Institution, Washington, D.C., Museum purchase, 1978

p. 151 –
For Brass, 1976
Acrylic on canvas with bevelled-edge stretcher, 62 ⅜ x 84 ⅜ in. (158.4 x 214.3 cm), Collection of the Hirshhorn Museum and Sculpture Garden, Smithsonian Institution, Washington, D.C., Gift of Dr. and Mrs. Bernard R. Shochet, 1997

p. 152–155 –
Double River, 1976
Acrylic on canvas with bevelled-edge stretcher, collage elements, 90 ½ x 181 x 3 in. (229.9 x 459.7 x 7.6 cm), private collection, Wisconsin

p. 157–159 –
Abacus Sliding, 1977
Acrylic on canvas with bevelled-edge stretcher, 90 ¼ x 120 ½ x 1 ¾ in. (229.2 x 306.1 x 4.4 cm), Collection of the Denver Art Museum: Funds from the National Endowment for the Arts and the United Bank of Denver, 1978

p. 160–162 –
Earth Element, 1977
Oil on canvas with bevelled-edge stretcher, 60 x 84 ½ x 2 ⅜ in. (152.4 x 214.6 x 6 cm), private collection, New York

p. 165 –
Untitled, 1975
Acrylic on canvas with bevelled-edge stretcher, 32 ¾ x 32 ¾ x 2 in. (83.2 x 83.2 x 5.1 cm), private collection, California

p. 168 (top) –
Coffee Thyme I, 1979
Colour intaglio with lithography, rubber stamp and debossing on paper, 30 ¾ x 40 ¾ in. (78 x 103.5 cm), Art Institute of Chicago, Gift of Dr. Glen D. Nelson, 1998

p. 168 (bottom) –
Coffee Thyme II, 1982
Colour intaglio with lithography, rubber stamp and debossing on paper, 31 ¹⁄₁₆ x 40 ⅞ in. (78.8 x 103.8 cm), Art Institute of Chicago, Gift of Dr. Glen D. Nelson, 1998

p. 169 (top) –
Lattice II, 1982
Colour intaglio with lithography on paper, 32 ⅛ x 44 ⁵⁄₁₆ in. (81.5 x 112.5 cm), Art Institute of Chicago, Gift of Dr. Glen D. Nelson, 1998

p. 169 (bottom) –
Lattice IV, 1982
Colour lithograph and etching, 32 x 44 ½ in. (81.28 x 113.3 cm), Minneapolis Institute of Art, Vermillion Archival Collection, Gift of The Northern Star Foundation and The Fiduciary Fund, 1986

p. 171 –
The Petition, 1990
Mixed media, 96 x 60 x 32 in. (243.8 x 152.4 x 81.3 cm), Smithsonian American Art Museum, Gift of the James F. Dicke Family, 2006

p. 172–173 –
Dihedral, 1996
Polychromed aluminum and steel, Laguardia Airport, Queens, NY

p. 175 –
The Saint of Moritz Outside Mondrian, 1984
Acrylic on canvas and metal, 59 x 63 ½ x 5 in. (149.9 x 161.3 x 12.7 cm), The Menil Collection, Houston, Texas

p. 176–177 –
More Than Water (Assisi) Subtle Jungle, 1997
Two elements: acrylic and polypropylene on canvas with bevelled-edge stretcher; collage and acrylic on panel construction, 73 ½ x 98 ½ x 9 in. (186.7 x 250.2 x 22.9 cm)

p. 178–179 –
Red Line, 1999
Acrylic on birch, 24 ¾ x 51 x 3 in. (62.9 x 129.5 x 7.6 cm)

p. 180 (top) –
Color Abacus, 2020
Wood, aluminum, die-stain, lacquer, 12 x 22 x 5 in. (30.4 x 55.8 x 12.7 cm), variant 1 of 4, private collection, Washington, D.C.

p. 180 (bottom) –
White Abacus, 2020
Wood, aluminium, die-stain, lacquer, 12 x 22 x 5 in. (30.4 x 55.8 x 12.7 cm), variant 1 of 4, private collection, Washington, D.C.

p. 183–185 –
Installation views of 'Sam Gilliam: Existed Existing', Pace Gallery, New York, 2020

p. 187 –
Blue 96" Disc, 2020
Wood, aluminum, die-stain, lacquer, 96 x 96 x 2 ¼ in. (243.8 x 243.8 x 5.7 cm), private collection, Washington, D.C.

p. 189 –
Black 48" Square, 2020
Wood, aluminum, die-stain, lacquer, 48 x 48 x 2 ¼ in. (121.9 x 121.9 x 5.7 cm), private collection, Washington, D.C.

p. 190 –
Washi Paper – Green, 2020
Acrylic on washi, 79 x 79 in. (201 x 201 cm), private collection, Washington, D.C.

p. 191 –
Washi Paper – Blue, 2020
Acrylic on washi, 79 x 79 in. (201 x 201 cm), private collection, Washington, D.C.

p. 192 –
Something is Going On!, 2021
Acrylic and mixed media on panel in bevelled frame, 60 x 60 x 4 in. (121.9 x 121.9 x 10.2 cm)

p. 193 –
Lucky, 2021
Acrylic with tin, copper, encaustic, sawdust, and aluminium on wood ply panel in bevelled-edge frame, 60 x 60 x 4 in. (152.4 x 152.4 x 10.2 cm)

p. 194 –
You Blue Moon, 2021
Acrylic and mixed media on panel in bevelled frame, 60 x 60 x 4 in. (152.4 x 152.4 x 10.2 cm), courtesy of Jeffrey Pechter.

p. 195 –
exciting, 2021
Acrylic and mixed media on panel in bevelled frame, 48 x 48 x 4 in. (121.9 x 121.9 x 10.2 cm)

p. 197 –
Installation views of 'Sam Gilliam: Existed Existing', Pace Gallery, New York, 2020

p. 198–199 –
October 18, 2020
Acrylic on canvas with bevelled-edge stretcher, 96 x 240 x 3 ¾ in. (20.3 x 50.8 x 9.5 cm)

p. 200–201 –
A New Generation, 2020
Acrylic on canvas with bevelled-edge stretcher, 72 x 96 x 3 ¾ in. (182.8 x 243.8 x 9.5 cm)

p. 202 –
Waiting for "Dutchman", 2020
Acrylic on canvas with bevelled-edge stretcher, 96 x 96 x 4 ¾ in. (243.8 x 243.8 x 12.1 cm)

p. 203 –
The Mississippi "Shake Rag", 2020
Acrylic on canvas with bevelled-edge stretcher, 96 x 96 x 4 ¾ in. (243.8 x 243.8 x 12.1 cm)

p. 204 –
Nikki Giovanni, 2020
Acrylic on canvas with bevelled-edge stretcher, 96 x 96 x 4 ¾ in. (243.8 x 243.8 x 12.1 cm)

p. 205 –
Any Minute Now, 2020
Acrylic on canvas with bevelled-edge stretcher, 96 x 96 x 4 ¾ in. (243.8 x 243.8 x 12.1 cm)

p. 207 –
Heroines, Beyoncé, Serena and Althea, 2020
Acrylic on canvas with bevelled-edge stretcher, 72 x 96 x 3 ¾ in. (182.8 x 243.8 x 9.5 cm)

p. 208 –
Purple Orpheus, 2020
Acrylic on canvas with bevelled-edge stretcher, 72 x 96 x 3 ¾ in. (182.8 x 243.8 x 9.5 cm)

p. 209 –
For John Lewis, 2020
Acrylic on canvas with bevelled-edge stretcher, 72 x 96 x 3 ¾ in. (182.8 x 243.8 x 9.5 cm)

p. 212 –
Wizard XX, 2014
Watercolour on handmade paper, 27 ¾ x 45 ⅞ in. (70.5 x 116.5 cm)

p. 213 –
Focus XVI, 2014
Watercolour on handmade paper, 28 x 45 ⅞ in. (71.1 x 116.5 cm), private collection, Washington, D.C.

p. 214 –
Untitled, 2022
Watercolour on washi paper, 77 ¾ x 42 ⅛ in. (197.5 x 107 cm)

p. 215 –
Untitled, 2022
Watercolour on washi paper, 78 x 43 ¼ in. (198.1 x 109.9 cm), private collection,Washington, D.C.

p. 216–217 –
Untitled, 2022
Acrylic and mixed media on wood panel in aluminium frame, 68 x 68 in. (172.7 x 172.7 cm), private collection, Washington, D.C.

p. 218–219 –
Untitled, 2022
Acrylic and mixed media on wood panel in aluminium frame, 68 x 68 in. (172.7 x 172.7 cm)

p. 220–221 –
What!, 2021
Acrylic with polypropylene on canvas with bevelled-edge stretcher, 96 x 180 x 4 in. (243.8 x 157.2 x 10.2 cm), private collection, Washington, D.C.

p. 222–223 –
A Lovely Blue And!, 2021
Acrylic and sawdust on canvas with bevelled-edge stretcher, 96 x 240 x 4 in. (243.8 x 609.6 x 10.2 cm)

p. 225–227 –
Lilly, 2022
Acrylic with sawdust, encaustic, and polypropylene on canvas with bevelled-edge stretcher, 72 x 72 x 6 in. (182.9 x 182.9 x 15.2 cm)

p. 229–231 –
Gold Mine, 2021
Acrylic on canvas with bevelled-edge stretcher, 96 x 96 x 4 in. (243.8 x 243.8 x 10.2 cm)

p. 232–233 –
Nina's Buffalo, 2022
Acrylic on canvas with bevelled-edge stretcher, 96 x 180 x 4 in. (243.8 x 457.2 x 10.2 cm)

p. 234–235 –
For "The Friend", 2021
Acrylic on canvas with bevelled-edge stretcher, 96 x 240 x 4 in. (243.8 x 609.6 x 10.2 cm)

p. 237–239 –
Oak, Net and This!, 2021
Acrylic with sawdust, flocking, and sand on canvas with bevelled-edge stretcher, 96 x 96 x 4 in. (243.8 x 243.8 x 10.2 cm)

p. 241–243 –
Up Sally, 2022
Acrylic with sawdust, flocking, and sand on canvas with bevelled-edge stretcher, 96 x 96 x 4 in. (243.8 x 243.8 x 10.2 cm), private collection, Washington, D.C.

p. 244–245 –
Spring This Time, 2021
Acrylic on canvas with bevelled-edge stretcher, 96 x 180 x 4 in. (243.8 x 457.2 x 10.2 cm), private collection, Washington, D.C.

p. 247–249 –
Beyoncé, 2022
Acrylic on canvas with bevelled-edge stretcher, 96 x 96 x 4 in. (243.8 x 243.8 x 10.2 cm)

p. 250 –
The Business, 2022
Acrylic on canvas with bevelled-edge stretcher, 96 x 96 x 4 in. (243.8 x 243.8 x 10.2 cm), private collection, Washington, D.C.

p. 251 –
Arne, 2022
Acrylic on canvas with bevelled-edge stretcher, 96 x 96 x 4 in. (243.8 x 243.8 x 10.2 cm), private collection, Washington, D.C.

p. 253–255 –
Irish, County Mayo, 2022
Acrylic with copper chop on canvas with bevelled-edge stretcher, 72 x 60 x 4 in. (182.9 x 152.4 x 10.2 cm), private collection, Washington, D.C.

p. 258 –
Sam Gilliam, 1950s

p. 259 (top) –
Gilliam, Unit Clerk, U.S. Army, Yokohama, February 1958

p. 259 (bottom) –
Gilliam, U.S. Army barracks, Yokohama, 1957

p. 260 (top) –
Gilliam with the Japanese/American English Speaking Society, January 1957

p. 260 (bottom) –
Gilliam hiking with the Japanese/American English Speaking Society, January 1957

p. 263 –
Poem by Gilliam, c. 1965

p. 264 –
Installation view of exhibition 'Projects: Sam Gilliam', MoMA, New York, 1971

p. 267 (top) –
Back: Ed Zerne, Sam Gilliam, Eric Rudd, Rockne Krebs. Middle: John Wise, Carroll Sockwell, V. V. Rankin, Nesta Dorrance, Alice Denney, Franklin White. Front: Ben Abramowitz, Hilda Thorpe, David Moy, 1971

p. 267 (bottom) –
Gilliam during installation of The De Luxe show, Houston, Texas, 1971

p. 268 (top) –
Gilliam with Walter Hopps (far left) unpacking crates during the installation of the 36th Venice Biennale, Italy, 1972

p. 268 (bottom) –
Installation view of Gilliam's presentation at the United States pavilion at the 36th Venice Biennale, Italy, 1972

p. 270–271 –
Gilliam installing *Autumn Surf*, San Francisco Museum of Modern Art, 1973

p.272 (top) –
Gilliam during a lecture, late 1970s

p. 272 (bottom) –
Gilliam printmaking at The Fabric Workshop and Museum, Anne d'Harnoncourt, Homer Jackson, Tim VanCampen, Will Stokes, Jr., Lucile Michels, and Marion Boulton 'Kippy' Stroud, 1977, Philadelphia, Pennsylvania

p. 274 (top) –
Gilliam and Mary Schmidt Campbell during the exhibition 'Red and Black to "D"', The Studio Museum in Harlem, New York, New York, 1982

p. 274 (bottom) –
Gilliam in the studio,Washington, D.C., 1980s

p. 276–277 –
Sculpture with a "D", Davis MBTA Subway Station, Somerville, Massachusetts, 1983

p. 279 (top) –
Gilliam in his U Street studio, Washington, D.C., 1990

p. 279 (bottom) –
Gilliam in his U Street studio, Washington, D.C., late 1980s

p. 281 –
Maquette for *Golden Elements Inside Gold, 600 Yds. of Painted Fabric Constructed on Cable*, 1993–1994

p. 282 (top) –
Gilliam and Annie Gawlak, U Street studio, Washington, D.C., mid 1990s

p. 282 (bottom) –
Gilliam in his studio, Washington, D.C., mid 2000s

p. 284 –
Bikers Move Like Swallows II, Corcoran Gallery of Art, Washington, D.C., 1995–96

p. 285 –
Bikers Move Like Swallows II, Corcoran Gallery of Art, Washington, D.C., 1995–96

p. 288 –
Gilliam with Rashid Johnson in front of Gilliam's early hard-edged abstractions, 2013

p. 290 –
Gawlak and Gilliam on their wedding day, Washington, D.C., 2018

p. 291 (top) –
Installation view of 'Sam Gilliam: Full Circle' at the Hirshhorn Museum and Sculpture Garden, Washington, D.C., 2022

p. 291 (bottom) –
Installation view of 'Melvin Edwards, Sam Gilliam, and William T. Williams: Epistrophy', Pace Gallery, New York, 2022

p. 293 –
Gilliam, Melvin Edwards and William T. Williams, 14th Street studio, Washington, D.C., 2022

AUTHOR BIOGRAPHIES

Ishmael Reed is an Oakland-based poet, novelist, essayist, playwright, cartoonist, songwriter, public media commentator, lecturer, publisher and musician. He is the author of more than thirty books, including the critically acclaimed novels *Yellow Back Radio Broke-Down* (1969), *Mumbo Jumbo* (1972), *The Last Days of Louisiana Red* (1974), *Flight to Canada* (1976) and *Japanese by Spring* (1993). Reed is a recipient of the Anisfield-Wolf Lifetime Achievement Award, an inductee to the American Academy of Arts and Sciences as well as a MacArthur Fellow and a Lila Wallace-Reader's Digest Awardee. His book of poetry *Conjure* (1972) made him one of a handful of authors nominated for the National Book Award and Pulitzer Prize in the same year.

Mary Schmidt Campbell is an art historian, former curator, museum director and academic administrator who was 10th President of Spelman College in Atlanta, from 2015 to 2022. Campbell began her career in New York as Executive Director of the Studio Museum in Harlem (1977–87), where she organized landmark exhibitions such as 'Harlem Renaissance: Art of Black America' and 'Tradition and Conflict: Images of a Turbulent Decade 1963–1973'. She has written monographs on a number of artists including Romare Bearden, Houston Conwill, Jack Whitten, Melvin Edwards, Betye Saar and Barkley L. Hendricks. Campbell served two mayors as New York City's Commissioner of Cultural Affairs (1987–1991), after which she entered academia as Dean of the Tisch School of the Arts at New York University (1991–2014). In 2008, then President Barack Obama appointed her Vice-Chair of the President's Committee on the Arts and Humanities. Her award-winning biography of Bearden, *An American Odyssey: The Life and Work of Romare Bearden,* was published in 2018. She serves on the boards of the Getty Trust, Juilliard, The Public Theater, Doris Duke Foundation, Unity Technologies and is a member of the UBS Americas Advisory Council.

Andria Hickey is Head of Programmes at Fogo Island Arts and Shorefast in Newfoundland and Labrador, Canada. Prior to this, she oversaw the visual art program at The Shed, a multidisciplinary cultural center dedicated to new art forms in New York, and was a global Senior Director and Curator at Pace Gallery, where she established a new curatorial team and initiated the live arts program Pace Live.

Quotes by Sam Gilliam are from *The Constant Artist*, The Katzen at American University Museum College of Arts and Sciences, Washington, D.C., 2012 (pp. 54–55); 'The Transformation of Nature through Nature', a Commencement speech given at the Memphis School of Art, May 1986. (pp. 138–139, 166–167 and 210–211, see also pp. 56–57 of this volume); Leslie Judd Ahlander (ed.), *Art in Washington: 1969 Calendar and Diary* (pp. 256–257).

CREDITS AND ACKNOWLEDGEMENTS

Photographers: Anthony Barboza (pp. 6, 279 [top]); Mark Blower (pp. 108–109); Ron Blunt (p. 291); Christopher Burke Studio (pp. 10–11, 222–223, 229, 232–239, 244–249, 251–255); Kathy Carver (pp. 148–149, 151); John Condax (p. 272 [bottom]); Gabriella Demczuk (p. 12); Phoebe d'Heurle (pp. 176–177); Phoebe d'Heurle and Christine Ann Jones (pp. 183–185, 197, 198–199); Marc Domage (p. 128–31); Katherine du Tiel (pp. 142–143); Flying Studio (pp. 214, 215); Max Frietch (pp. 172–173); Stephen Frietch (pp. 58, 66–67); Melissa Goodwin (pp. 180 [bottom], 187, 190, 216–219, 220–221, 225–227, 250); Melissa Goodwin and Robin Lehr Caspare (pp. 180 [top], 189); John Gossage (pp. 40–41); Kris Graves (pp. 178–179); Mark Gulezian (pp. 32, 45, 84–87, 146–147, 279 [bottom], front endpapers 1 and 2, back endpaper 1); Carol Harrison (p. 267 [top], 274 [bottom], 282); Hickey & Robertson (p. 267 [bottom]); Paul Hoffman (pp. 270–271); Kyle Knodell (pp. 50–51, 144–145, 193, 194); Aleksey Kondratyev (front endpaper 3, back endpapers 2 and 3); Johansen Krause (pp. 40–41, 190–191); Hans-Wulf Kunze (p. 137); Bill Jacobson Studio (pp. 100–101); Walter Larrimore (p. 42); Jeff McLane (pp. 157–165, 212, 213); Jonathan Nesteruk (pp. 192, 195, 200–209, 241–243); Frederick Nielsen (pp. 17 [top], 18 [top], 42, 62, 65, 82–83, 93–97, 103–105, 106–107, 115, 116–117, 121, 152–155); Ed Owen (p. 17 [bottom], 18 [bottom]); Cymie R. Payne (pp. 276–277); Matthew Placek (p. 288); Daniel Spehr and Kathrin Schulthess (pp. 24–25, 26–27, 28, 29, 70–71, 72–73, 75, 77, 78–81, 126–127); Jared Soares (p. 293); Frank Stewart (p. 274 [top]); Lee Thompson (pp. 20–21, 68, 69, 89, 91, 110–112, 133); Brandon Webster (pp. 59, 63); Wilbur Wright (pp. 259, 260).

We would also like to thank the following institutions: Allen Memorial Art Museum, Oberlin College, Ohio; Anacostia Community Museum, Washington, D.C.; Art Institute of Chicago; Artpark Lewinston, New York; Denver Art Museum; Dia Art Foundation, New York; Fondazione La Biennale di Venezia, Venice; Fondation Louis Vuitton, Paris; Hirshhorn Museum and Sculpture Garden, Washington, D.C.; Kunstmuseum Basel; Kunstmuseum Kloster Unser Lieben Frauen, Magdeburg; The Menil Collection, Houston; The Metropolitan Museum of Art, New York; Museum of Contemporary Art, Chicago; The Museum of Modern Art, New York; National Museum of African American History and Culture, Washington, D.C.; The Philadelphia Museum of Art, Library and Archives; Phillips Collection, Washington, D.C.; San Francisco Museum of Modern Art; Smithsonian American Art Museum, Washington, D.C.; Smithsonian Institution Archives, Washington, D.C.; Speed Art Museum, Louisville, Kentucky; The Studio Museum in Harlem, New York; Tate, London; Walker Art Center, Minneapolis; Whitney Museum of American Art, New York; The Amistad Research Center, Tulane University, New Orleans; Michael Rosenfeld Gallery, New York; Artists Rights Society (ARS), New York; Getty Images, Seattle; The New York Times/Redux, New York; Quicksilver, Washington, D.C., Scala/Art Resource, Florence.

Phaidon Press Limited
2 Cooperage Yard
London E15 2QR

Phaidon Press Inc.
111 Broadway
New York, NY 10006

phaidon.com

ISBN 978 1 83866 393 3

A CIP catalogue record for this book is available from the British Library and the Library of Congress.

Commissioning Editor: Michele Robecchi
Project Editor: Charlotte Flint
Production Controller: Andie Trainer
Design & Layout: Henrik Nygren Design, Stockholm

Publisher's Acknowledgements: We would like to thank Annie Gawlak, Jenn DePalma and Olivia Armacost Bliven at the Sam Gilliam Foundation, Washington, D.C.; David Kordansky, Maia Asshaq, Amanda Ball, Patricia Blanton, Teresa Eggers and Parker Matthews at David Kordansky Gallery, Los Angeles; Arne Glimcher, Kathleen McDonnell, Oliver Shultz and Ian Densford at Pace Gallery, New York; Henrik Nygren, Keun Kim Roland and Ludvig Östman at Henrik Nygren Design, Stockholm; Clive Burroughs, Victoria Clarke, Julia Hasting, João Mota, Tracey Smith, Hans Stofregen, Elaine Ward and Jonathan Whale at Phaidon Press, London; Melvin Edwards, Juli Folk, Ronald Gerber, Halley K. Harrisburg, Rashid Johnson, Stuart Krimko, Melissa Larner, Violeta Mitrova, Thaddeus Mosley, Kurt Mueller, Chris Vacchio, William T. Williams.

Printed in China

Cover: *Gold Mine*, 2021
Acrylic on canvas with bevelled-edge stretcher, 96 x 96 x 4 in. (243.8 x 243.8 x 10.2 cm)

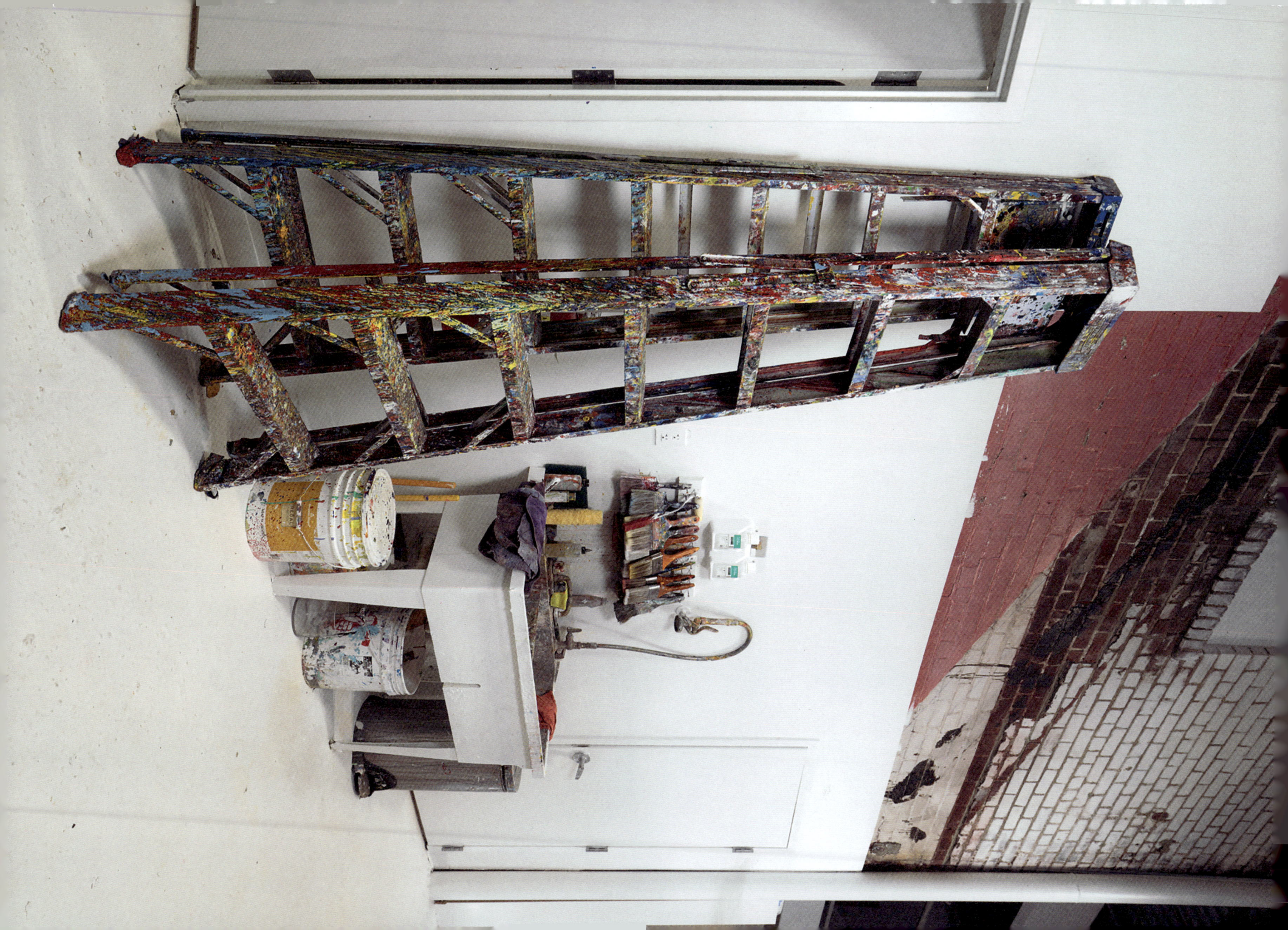

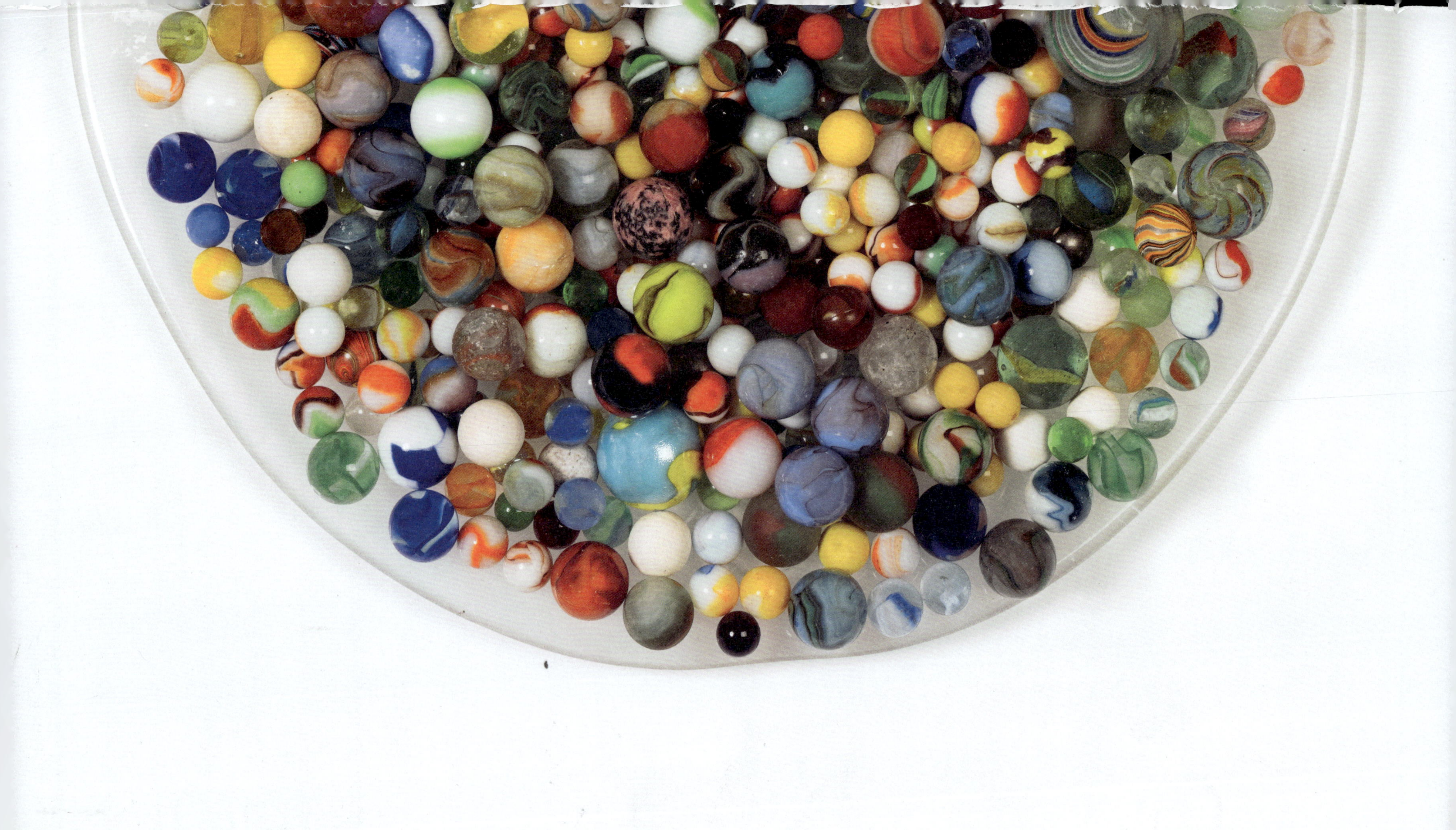